LONG LOAN

LONG LOAN

LONG LOAN
Items must be returned by the last date
stamped below or immediately if recalled.
To renew telephone 01792 295178.

U.W.S.
-5 DEC 2004

RETURN BY
2 0 JAN 2005

U.W.S.

RETURN BY

1 JUL 2005
U.W.S.

BENTHYCIAD HIR
Dylid dychwelyd eitemau cyn y dyddiad a
stampiwyd olaf isod, neu ar unwaith os
gofynnir amdanynt yn ôl.
I adnewyddu ffôn 01792 295178.

e.commerce economics

David VanHoose
Baylor University

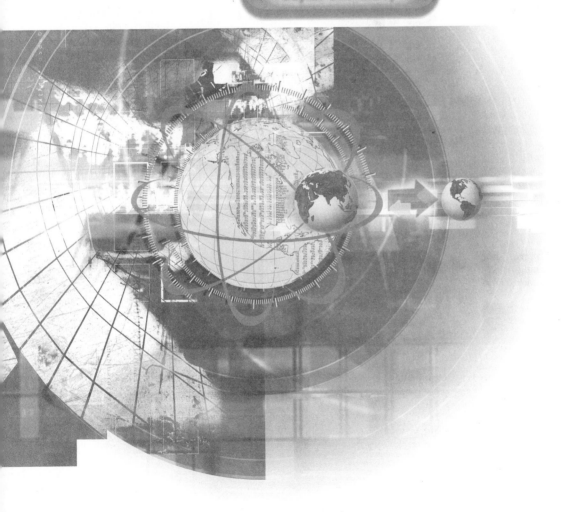

THOMSON LEARNING

Australia · Canada · Mexico · Singapore · Spain · United Kingdom · United States

SOUTH-WESTERN ™

THOMSON LEARNING

E-Commerce Economics

David D. VanHoose

Vice President/Editor-in-Chief:
Jack W. Calhoun

Vice President/Team Director:
Michael P. Roche

Publisher of Economics:
Michael B. Mercier

Acquisitions Editor:
Michael W. Worls

Developmental Editor:
Jan Lamar

Marketing Manager:
Lisa L. Lysne

Production Editor:
Daniel C. Plofchan

Media Developmental Editor:
Peggy Buskey

Media Production Editor:
Pamela Wallace

Manufacturing Coordinator:
Sandee Milewski

Compositor:
Shepherd, Inc.

Printer:
QuebecorWorld–Taunton, MA

Design Project Manager:
Rik Moore

Internal Designer:
John W. Robb,
JWR Design Interaction

Cover Designer:
John W. Robb,
JWR Design Interaction

Cover Photo Source:
PhotoDisc, Inc.

LIBRARY OF CONGRESS
CATALOGING-IN-PUBLICATION
DATA
VanHoose, David D.
    E-commerce economics / David D.
    VanHoose.—1st ed. p. cm
    Includes bibliographical references
    and index.
    ISBN 0-324-12880-0 (alk. paper)
    1. Electronic commerce. I. Title.

HF5548.32.V36 2002
381'.1—dc21

2001049472

Contents

Chapter 2

Applying Basic Economic Principles to Electronic Commerce

Preface

 ## To the Instructor

Electronic commerce is one of the most interesting current topics in economics, and this text has been written to provide a foundation for covering this important subject within college and university economics curricula. My objective in writing *E-Commerce Economics* has been to provide the student reader with a sophisticated, yet accessible, understanding of the subject matter while simultaneously providing the instructor with a well-organized presentation of the full range of appropriate topics. I have attempted to achieve this two-part objective in several ways:

- Full coverage is given to the implications of electronic commerce within the various areas of the discipline, ranging from industrial organization and public economics to monetary economics and international economics.
- The book provides balanced examinations of how basic economic principles continue to apply to the electronic marketplace and how features of certain products sold in this marketplace have required rethinking some of those principles.
- Current-interest features underscoring the real-world relevance of the study of e-commerce economics appear in each chapter.
- Frequent margin references to Internet resources are included, along with end-of-chapter *Online Application* questions.
- The 85 graphs for this textbook are designed to enhance learning. All lines and curves are drawn in a consistent manner, and full explanations appear underneath or alongside each graph or set of graphs.
- An electronic *Study Guide* and *Instructor's Manual,* plus a test bank, are available for use with the text, and are downloadable at the book's Web site: http://vanhoose.swcollege.com.

Complete Coverage of the Economics of Electronic Commerce

All of the essential elements of e-commerce economics are covered in this textbook. These include:

- The extent to which basic principles of perfect competition and monopoly can be applied to analysis of e-commerce issues
- The economics of virtual products and network industries
- Strategic pricing and price discrimination in electronic commerce
- Imperfect consumer information about prices and quality and the role of e-commerce intermediaries
- The economics of Web advertising
- Intellectual property and the Internet
- Web-based financial market trading and online banking
- Digital cash and electronic payments
- Regulatory and antitrust issues in the electronic marketplace
- The Internet, taxes, and the public sector
- Monetary policy with electronic money
- Macroeconomic implications of electronic commerce

Uses for This Text

Electronic commerce is an emerging area of study within economics, business, and public policy curricula, and it is an appropriate subject of study in a variety of contexts. *E-Commerce Economics* has been written for use in any of the following environments:

1) **An e-commerce economics course**—*E-Commerce Economics* can be used as the primary text for a stand-alone economics course. The text is readily accessible to a student who has completed principles of economics. Although an instructor can choose chapters to emphasize in light of specific course goals, the fourteen chapters of the text provide a complete foundation for a one-semester economics course.

2) **A general business or public policy course in electronic commerce**—Many business and public policy schools have developed integrated e-commerce curricula, and an increasing number offer major fields or certifications in electronic commerce. *E-Commerce Economics* can be used as a core text within a general survey course in electronic commerce. Instructors teaching students who have little or no background in economics can allocate extra time to the material in Chapters 2 and 3, which together provide students with a sufficient foundation in economics to apply throughout the remainder of the text.

3) **Other courses in economics**—Electronic commerce is one of the more fascinating current subjects for discussion in courses in principles of economics, intermediate economic theory, industrial organization, and money and banking. Increasingly, e-commerce issues also are finding their way into the subject matter of courses in public economics, international trade, and international finance. With very few exceptions, however, texts in these various areas contain at most only a few pages here and there examining e-commerce topics. By way of contrast, the economics of electronic commerce is the sole focus of this book. Instructors can weave selected chapters of *E-Commerce Economics* into their courses to reinforce student understanding of essential course concepts by relating them to cutting-edge issues in electronic commerce that are of considerable interest to today's students.

 # Features that Teach and Reinforce

The study of e-commerce provides abundant opportunities to apply fundamental economic concepts.

APPLYING ECONOMICS TO THE ELECTRONIC MARKETPLACE

To motivate student learning, *E-Commerce Economics* includes more than seventy real-world examples within three categories of features that are incorporated and referred to throughout the text: *globalization online, policymaking online*, and *management online*.

Globalization Online
Because electronic commerce is a global issue, international applications receive considerable coverage in *E-Commerce Economics*. In addition to addressing international topics directly at various points throughout the text, features such as the following provide international applications of concepts in e-commerce economics:

- In France, Has U.S.-Style E-Commerce Mass Marketing Met Its Match?
- Should Developing Nations Agree to Protect Intellectual Property Rights in the Electronic Marketplace?
- Shrinking the World Marketplace via Multicurrency Payment Processing
- Stored-Value and Debit Cards May Be the Ticket to E-Commerce in Russia
- In Japan, Corner Shops Become Web Banks—and E-Commerce Package Pick-Up Centers
- Should U.S. Internet Sellers Have to Collect European Taxes?
- The Current U.S. Advantage in Electronic Commerce—Comparative or Absolute?
- Dodging Regulations by Making a Mouse Click Reverberate around the Globe

Policymaking Online

Electronic commerce raises a host of public policy issues, and these and a number of other features explore many of those issues:

- How *Not* to Gain Certification of Internet-Snooping Technology
- Patent Pending—Does the U.S. Patent and Trademark Office Know What It's Doing?
- Should Just Anyone Be Able to Broker Internet Currency Trades?
- Helping Consumers Distinguish Cyberdocs from Cyberquacks
- Internet Privacy and the Federal Government—"As We Say, Not As We Do!"
- Using the Internet to Cut the Bureaucratic Costs of Trade in Singapore and Elsewhere
- That Price Is Too Low!—German Booksellers Try to Short-Circuit Belgian E-Commerce Competition
- Will the Fed Lose Its Ability to Affect Aggregate Demand in a Digital Economy?

Management Online

Business applications of electronic commerce provide perhaps the greatest motivation for student learning of economic concepts. For this reason, *E-Commerce Economics* includes many features focusing on management issues that arise in the electronic marketplace, including the following:

- How an Employment Crunch Helped Make Trucking an E-Commerce Success Story
- Are Web Booksellers Destined to Be the Publishers of E-Books?
- Reducing the Pricing Power of the Press
- PayPal Pays Up
- What the Powerpuff Girls and Scooby Doo Have in Common Online
- Is Internet Psychotherapy the Wave of the Future?
- Turning the Art of Persuasion into a Science
- Renting E-Textbooks—The Future of Copyright Protection in Electronic Publishing?
- Selling Distressed Debt at "Vulture Sites"
- Making Islamic Financial Services Available on the Internet
- Will Trading Services on the Internet Bolster the U.S. Trade Balance?

CRITICAL THINKING EXERCISES

Critical thinking is an important aspect of every college student's education. This text makes sure that students are introduced to critical-thinking activities by ending each feature with critical-thinking questions called "For Critical Analysis." The suggested answers to these critical-thinking questions are included in the *Instructor's Manual*.

Web Applications

In addition to the electronic supplements available at the book's Web site (http://vanhoose.swcollege.com), the text provides two other features that direct both students and instructors to helpful Internet resources.

MARGIN URLs

Throughout the text, there is a recurring feature called "On the Web." This feature directs readers to relevant URLs pertaining to the subject discussed in that section.

CHAPTER-ENDING ONLINE APPLICATIONS

At the end of every chapter is an extensive Internet exercise, which takes the student to a particular URL and then asks the student to engage in an application. Because URLs change from time to time, each *Online Application* provides navigation instructions as well as specific URLs.

 # Key Pedagogy

Learning cannot occur in a vacuum. Students using this text will encounter an ample number of pedagogical devices that will help them master the material.

FUNDAMENTAL ISSUES AND ANSWERS WITHIN THE TEXT OF EACH CHAPTER

Each chapter of *E-Commerce Economics* opens with four to six fundamental issues. Within the text itself, the fundamental issues are repeated with the appropriate answers. Students will find these questions and answers invaluable when reviewing the readings and studying for quizzes and examinations.

EMPHASIZING VOCABULARY

Vocabulary can be a stumbling block in e-commerce economics, so key vocabulary terms are **boldfaced** within the text. Definitions appear immediately in the margin beside the first appearance of a key term, and all vocabulary terms are further defined in the end-of-text glossary.

CHAPTER SUMMARY

The chapter summary uses a numbered point-by-point formatting style that corresponds to the chapter-opening fundamental issues, further reinforcing the full circular nature of the learning process for each chapter.

QUESTIONS AND PROBLEMS

Each chapter ends with several questions and problems. Suggested answers are provided in the *Instructor's Manual.*

SELECTED REFERENCES AND FURTHER READING

Appropriate references for materials in the chapter are given in this section.

 # Electronic Supplements

E-Commerce Economics is supported by an array of supplementary materials, all of which are downloadable from the book's Web site (http://vanhoose.swcollege. com).

STUDY GUIDE

The *Study Guide* is designed to facilitate active learning by students. It provides outline summaries of chapter contents, along with lists of the key terms for students to identify and to define in their own words as they read the text. To assist students in testing their understanding of the material, sections from the *Study Guide* have been incorporated into the Interactive Study Center on the book's Web site, including true–false and multiple-choice questions.

INSTRUCTOR'S MANUAL

The *Instructor's Manual* is designed to simplify the teaching tasks that instructors face. It offers an overview of key concepts and objectives of each chapter, an outline built on chapter headings in the text, proposed answers to critical-thinking questions, and answers to end-of-chapter questions.

TEST BANK

One of the most challenging aspects of teaching is evaluation of student performance. To assist instructors in this endeavor, a *Test Bank* is available to all adopters of *E-Commerce Economics.*

▶ Acknowledgments

This first edition of *E-Commerce Economics* benefited from an extremely active and conscientious group of reviewers. They were tough and demanding, but the rewrites of the manuscript improved accordingly. To the following reviewers, I express my sincere appreciation for the critical nature of your comments, which helped make this a better text.

REVIEWER LIST

Robert Becker
Indiana University

Jen Chi Cheng
Wichita State University

Eric Drabkin
Hawaii Pacific University

Larry Malone
Harwick College

Neil Niman
University of New Hampshire

Michael Shields
Central Michigan University

William J. Trainor, Jr.
Virginia State University

A textbook project is never completed solely by the author. I want to thank Mike Worls, the economics editor, for his hard work on this project and for his direction at various steps. As usual, I owe a considerable debt to Jan Lamar, the developmental editor, who has patiently provided invaluable feedback and guidance. Dan Plofchan, the production editor, put together an excellent design and never let me fall behind schedule. Cheryl Ferguson, the copyeditor, did a fine job of making the book read more smoothly.

I look forward to revising this text as the electronic marketplace evolves during the years to come. Therefore, I welcome comments and criticism from both students and teachers.

D.D.V.

E-Commerce
Economics

David D. VanHoose
Baylor University

Unit One

Electronic Commerce —
Markets and Prices

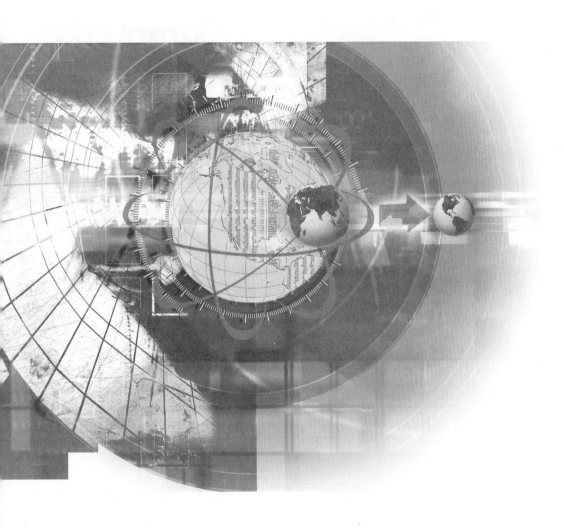

Foundations of Electronic Commerce

\<E-Commerce Today\>

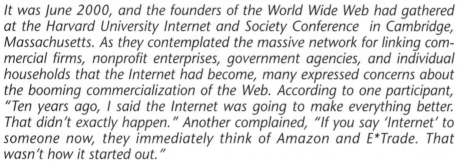

Maybe We Should Change It to 'Commercial Wide Web'

It was June 2000, and the founders of the World Wide Web had gathered at the Harvard University Internet and Society Conference in Cambridge, Massachusetts. As they contemplated the massive network for linking commercial firms, nonprofit enterprises, government agencies, and individual households that the Internet had become, many expressed concerns about the booming commercialization of the Web. According to one participant, "Ten years ago, I said the Internet was going to make everything better. That didn't exactly happen." Another complained, "If you say 'Internet' to someone now, they immediately think of Amazon and E*Trade. That wasn't how it started out."

Indeed, times had changed since the Web's founders had dreamed of developing a tool for uniting communities for the purpose of developing solutions to social ills. When the Yahoo.com search engine appeared on the Web in 1994, it did not have a single link to Internet shopping sites. In 2000, as the Web founders looked back on their handiwork, Yahoo was promoting itself as "a global Internet communications, commerce, and media company that offers a comprehensive branded network of services to more than 145 million individuals each month worldwide." To a number of those who were involved in developing the World Wide Web, the problematic word in Yahoo's self-description was company. They had envisioned the Internet as a place to freely exchange ideas and information, not as a commercial enterprise.

By early 2001, however, a number of Web-based commercial enterprises—including previously high-flying Auctions.com, Beautyjungle.com, eToys.com, IcanBuy.com, Mortgage.com, and Streamline.com—had closed down their operations. Amazon.com and E*Trade.com had embarked on rounds of employee layoffs. Yahoo was missing revenue projections and had begun cutting back as well. Media pundits opined that the dot-com boom had turned into a "dot-bomb" bust. More generally, it appeared possible that critics of the commercialization of the Web might get their wish for a reduction in Internet commercialization.

Nevertheless, today data flows on the Internet continue to double every three to four months. Every few weeks, entrepreneurs open new commercial Web sites offering services as diverse as ticket ordering via Web-connected wireless devices, online foreign-exchange trading, and Internet-based backup computer data storage. In addition, manufacturers and retailers continue to press forward in their efforts to sell goods on the Web. Hence, even as a number of commercial sites failed, others emerged in search of market niches where profit opportunities might exist.

What transformed the World Wide Web into a business hub as well as a repository for new ideas to address the world's problems? What are the implications of this transformation for the U.S. and world economies? How can we apply basic economic reasoning to evaluate factors that account for dot-com booms and dot-bomb busts? In this chapter, you will begin to contemplate these and other important questions.

Objectives of This Book, and How They Relate to You

The objective of this text is to help you develop the skills required to evaluate current and future economic issues associated with electronic commerce, or *e-commerce*. To achieve this goal, you must learn how to apply basic economic reasoning to practical problems that consumers and businesses face in the, **electronic marketplace,** which is a virtual location for prospective sellers and buyers to effectively gather through network-communications links made possible by computer-assisted information technologies. In addition, you must develop a fundamental understanding of the key features of this virtual marketplace.

Electronic Marketplace
A virtual location for prospective sellers and buyers to electronically meet through network-communications links.

APPLYING BASIC ECONOMIC CONCEPTS TO A NEW TYPE OF MARKETPLACE

As part of your study of electronic commerce, you will also find yourself learning more than you might expect about "old-fashioned" bricks-and-mortar markets. Many of the firms competing for online business have long possessed—and still maintain—a significant offline presence. A number of these same companies also face at least a few government regulations relating to their offline activities, and going online does not necessarily allow them to escape these regulations. Increasingly, even businesses that sell their wares only through cyberspace face governmental restrictions. It is often said that Internet-based transactions know no borders, so firms all over the world are beginning to view the entire world as a potential market for their products. Trying to compete in global markets, however, requires understanding basic concepts relating to international trade and finance. Finally, every few years Internet sellers confront proposals for applying existing sales taxes to sales generated as a result of mouse clicks—sales that in most areas are not currently taxed.

The economics of electronic commerce draws on several areas of study within the discipline of economics. Understanding different modes of competition and the many issues relating to business pricing, marketing, and product-innovation strategies requires drawing from the field of economics known as *industrial organization*. This field of economics also provides a basic framework for trying to determine how government regulations are likely to affect interactions among consumers and firms in the electronic marketplace. These are the "bread-and-butter" issues of e-commerce economics, so you will find yourself learning new ways to apply essential principles of industrial organization.

Another field of economics that is important in the study of electronic commerce is the broad area of *money, banking, and financial markets.* Today, many businesses raise funds on the Internet, and a significant portion of individual and institutional investors purchase stocks and bonds online. Nearly every U.S. financial institution either has a Web site or is in the process of developing one. A number of financial institutions already give their customers online access to many traditional banking services. In various locales, electronic payments already are commonplace, and the technology now exists to store and transmit "cash payments" digitally using microprocessors built into personal computers, computer servers, or even plastic cards.

Issues regarding taxes, trade and tariffs, and the broader implications of electronic commerce for the national and global economy relate to the traditional fields of *public sector economics, international economics,* and *macroeconomics,* respectively. Consequently, the study of e-commerce economics entails new learning about these fields as well.

LEARNING ABOUT E-COMMERCE ECONOMICS IN BITS AND BYTES

Today, consumers, businesses, and governments face issues relating to all the above fields simultaneously. Nevertheless, it is possible to learn about the economics of electronic commerce without trying to apply concepts from these diverse areas all at once.

This chapter provides a general overview of electronic commerce and discusses the key economic issues that accompany the ebbs and flows of the electronic marketplace. Chapter 2 begins an examination of the industrial organization of electronic commerce by applying basic concepts of perfect competition and monopoly to the electronic marketplace. Chapter 3 explains how oligopoly and monopolistic competition approaches may prove more useful to understanding how firms— particularly those that sell virtual products in network industries—may compete in the electronic marketplace. Chapter 4 then evaluates methods that Internet sellers can use to price their products and to organize their operations. The focus of Chapter 5 is on the crucial role that information plays in shaping business–customer interactions in the electronic marketplace. Chapter 6 examines how Internet sellers use advertising to provide information and to shape consumer perceptions of their online products. Then Chapter 7 describes the process by which new products emerge in the electronic marketplace and considers how patents, copyrights, and intellectual property protection influence this process.

Our investigation of the financial and monetary aspects of e-commerce economics begins with Chapter 8, which overviews the significant changes in financial market trading that have been brought about by electronic trading mechanisms.

Chapter 9 then discusses how banks and other financial institutions have seized on the Internet as a means of delivering a number of traditional banking services, and Chapter 10 explains how money can take the form of computer algorithms and how payments can be transmitted as electronic impulses.

Many governments and regulatory agencies have adopted a "hands-off" attitude toward electronic commerce, but in recent years these institutions have become more predisposed to intervening in the electronic marketplace using laws originally tailored to the activities of traditional bricks-and-mortar businesses. Chapter 11 identifies specific regulatory issues that have arisen—or are likely to arise—in the electronic marketplace. Chapter 12 contemplates the broader role of the public sector in electronic commerce, including both the potential for e-commerce taxes and the possibility of government expenditures to promote access to the electronic marketplace.

The economic implications of electronic commerce are much broader than the markets for specific goods and services produced, marketed, and sold by various Internet sellers. The focus of Chapter 13 is on how electronic commerce is already reshaping and ultimately may transform the international trading environment. Chapter 14 considers how developments in electronic payments are likely to affect monetary policy and evaluates the potential effects of electronic commerce on the overall performance of the national and global economy.

WHY STUDY E-COMMERCE ECONOMICS?

Many students flock to enroll in classes in which e-commerce is prominently featured in course titles. Students have read or heard about—or perhaps even know people who have earned big profits from—Internet-based businesses. They hope to acquire skills they will need to go to jobs with such firms, or perhaps even to launch their own companies. Some students may have concerns about privacy and security of electronic commerce. These students also might be worried about people who are being left behind by the e-commerce revolution, and they might even wonder if some forms of government regulation might not be warranted. Other students are simply looking for a way to apply what they have learned in previous economics courses to a subject of practical interest. Still others are simply curious about whether all the "media hype" about electronic commerce is really justified by the facts.

This book is designed to address this potentially diverse set of student interests. Students who hope to someday earn a livelihood in the electronic marketplace will not be able to use this book to learn how to post a Web site or establish hot links among Web pages, but they *will* be able to apply what they learn in this text to help determine how to position an Internet-based business within the electronic marketplace. They also will learn about fundamental issues that arise in operating the business, such as how to gauge the competitive environment, what products to offer and how to market them, and how to price those products. This text will provide the conceptual tools that socially conscious students require to evaluate the proper scope of public policies relating to electronic commerce. For students interested in learning about how to apply what they learned in economics principles, electronic commerce is one of the most interesting, and certainly one of the most current, areas of real-world application of economics. Finally, the text is designed to help all students "get up to speed" on electronic commerce and the host of economic issues it poses for consumers, businesses, and governments. Although some aspects of electronic commerce may indeed be "over-hyped" by the media, the electronic marketplace is not going to go away, nor are the various issues that have arisen from its development and continuing growth.

What Is Electronic Commerce?

We have already referred to *electronic commerce* several times. Almost everyone has a notion of what this term means. It conjures up various images, however, depending on the perspective of the person who uses or hears it. Clearly, it is important to be precise about what we mean whenever we refer to electronic commerce.

DISTINGUISHING E-COMMERCE FROM E-BUSINESS

Someone employed by a telecommunications company would naturally tend to think of e-commerce as the delivery of information-related products or services via computer connections to customers facilitated by telephone lines, fiber-optic cable, or wireless communications devices. To the owner of an Internet start-up engaged in matching prospective home buyers with realtors and mortgage companies, the term undoubtedly refers, at least in part, to the mechanism by which the company attracts customers and seeks to provide them, at a competitive price, with low-cost services. To a consumer who searches through Web sites to locate and order the best deal on a new laptop computer equipped with all the latest bells and whistles, electronic commerce is a means for gathering information and purchasing a product online.

In fact, all these perspectives are correct. **Electronic commerce** refers to any process that entails exchanging ownership of or rights to use goods and services via electronically linked devices that communicate interactively within networks. In most instances, the electronically linked devices that people use to engage in electronic commerce are computers, but in some instances they might be items that most of us usually regard as computer components, such as microprocessors. In addition, the most important type of interactive communications network for electronic commerce is the Internet.

Note that this definition of electronic commerce excludes certain types of electronic transactions that some people might have in mind when they think of

Electronic Commerce (e-commerce)
Using a computer-mediated electronic network such as the Internet as a mechanism for transferring ownership of or rights to use goods and services.

e-commerce. To many people, using computer networks such as the Internet to provide customer service, to develop plans with business partners, or to process transactions among units within the same business organization ought to be regarded as "e-commerce." For instance, an individual who manages an auto parts store might well think of an electronic system linking the store to other franchise stores as a facility for inventory distribution and management throughout the company. Someone who has just spent several hours surfing the Internet to gather information about different versions of a product to buy at a retail department store tomorrow also might think that electronic commerce has transpired.

Electronic Business (e-business)

Any internal decision-making or implementation processes that organizations such as commercial firms, nonprofit organizations, or government agencies conduct using computer-mediated electronic networks.

Nevertheless, in neither of these situations did the individuals actually engage in a transaction that transferred ownership or the right to use a good, service, or asset. They did, however, conduct **electronic business** (or **e-business**), which is a catchall term for the use of computer-mediated networks by commercial firms and nonprofit organizations. E-business processes include the use of electronic networks to coordinate decision making and implementation of an organization's production, marketing, and management functions. For example, many organizations establish their own internal electronic-communications networks, called *intranets*. A company, for instance, may use an intranet to enable its business units, such as marketing, human resources, or production departments, to implement paperless transmittals within the organization. A number of noncommercial organizations, including social and religious groups and government agencies, now use the Internet or intranets to provide services to their constituencies.

Thus, it is important to distinguish e-commerce from e-business:

E-business refers to the use of electronic networks *within* an organization. E-commerce refers to exchanges of goods and services in a market transaction *between* parties.

This book addresses the implications of exchanges of goods and services that individuals, firms, and governments initiate in cyberspace. Although e-business issues will arise from time to time in this book, its focus is on the economics of *electronic commerce*.

THE ELECTRONIC MARKETPLACE

Market

An arrangement that people have for trading goods and services.

It is also important to be specific about what we mean when we use the term electronic marketplace. In general, **markets** are arrangements that people have for exchanging with one another. Thus, economists commonly speak of the market for desktop personal computers, the market for labor services, the stock market, or the market for any other particular good, service, or asset. It is rare for all exchanges to take place at any single location. For instance, the market for desktop personal computers is a global market. Additionally, even though there are organized stock exchanges in cities such as New York, Tokyo, or London, buyers and sellers who trade on these exchanges are located all over the world.

Nevertheless, long ago people who lived in societies with much less mobility and no telecommunications systems commonly exchanged goods at specific locations, which came to be known as *marketplaces*. Buyers and sellers would meet in a city square or other agreed-upon location. Within this marketplace, sellers could display their wares, prospective buyers could evaluate them, and a buyer and seller would try to agree upon a price.

To a limited extent, marketplaces still exist in many towns and cities around the world. There are still street markets for fresh fish in port cities, farmers' markets in agricultural areas, and marketplaces for used goods and antiques. Since the development of sophisticated systems of boat, train, bus, and auto transit in the late nineteenth and early twentieth centuries, however, prospective buyers have tended to shop for a good, service, or asset by traveling around among fixed retail locations established by sellers. With the advent of telecommunications, buyers have been able to cut down on their travel time by "phoning around" for product and pricing information. The process by which sellers market their products, buyers evaluate them, and prices are determined has been dramatically decentralized.

Electronic networks, however, now allow people to create a "virtual" marketplace. For example, a seller can post photos of goods, descriptions of services, or information about assets on a Web site that can be visited by anyone with access to the Internet. A prospective buyer can evaluate the item and, if the buyer agrees to the price—or, in some cases, can convince the seller to agree to a price following an e-mail negotiation process—an exchange can then be arranged. Hence, electronic networks permit the establishment of electronic marketplaces. Even though both sellers and buyers remain geographically separated, in an electronic marketplace they are directly linked within a communications network. In principle, this permits them to engage in the same kinds of marketplace activities as people who meet in physical marketplaces.

CLASSIFYING E-COMMERCE TRANSACTIONS

There are three primary ways in which people "gather" to engage in electronic commerce within an electronic marketplace:

- Business-to-consumer e-commerce
- Business-to-business e-commerce
- Consumer-to-consumer e-commerce

These forms of e-commerce are defined by the nature of the parties that conduct transactions and by the types of transactions that they undertake.

The Business-to-Consumer Electronic Marketplace

If you have purchased a book online from an Internet bookseller such as Amazon.com or Barnesandnoble.com, then you have engaged in a **business-to-consumer (B2C) e-commerce** transaction, in which a business, a nonprofit organization, or a government agency sells a product to an individual consumer online.

Business-to-Consumer (B2C) E-Commerce
Exchanges of goods and services that are transacted via computer networks and involve sales by businesses to individual consumers.

Note that this definition of B2C e-commerce includes online sales to consumers by both commercial and noncommercial enterprises. Several of the reports by government agencies and international organizations that appear among the end-of-chapter references are available for free download at the agencies' and organizations' Web sites. Many of these sites also contain pages at which you can arrange to purchase bound versions of the reports. At some sites, you can view report summaries, but if you wish to read the entire report you must purchase it, either by calling an 800 number to place an order or by engaging in an e-commerce transaction online.

The bulk of B2C transactions, however, involve online market transactions between commercial enterprises and consumers. If you have ordered an interactive magazine subscription online, purchased a computer accessory, paid to download music onto your computer's hard drive, or perhaps even bought groceries or a pizza on the Internet, then you have engaged in a B2C transaction.

The Business-to-Business Electronic Marketplace

Business-to-Business (B2B) E-Commerce
Online purchases and sales that involve business firms on both sides of the transactions.

As you will learn in later chapters, a form of electronic commerce that is largely invisible to consumers is **business-to-business (B2B) e-commerce.** B2B is a rapidly growing sector of e-commerce that consists of online buying and selling in which both parties to the transactions are commercial firms, nonprofit organizations, or government agencies. When an employee of Ford Motor Company points and clicks to finalize an order from an auto parts supplier, a B2B e-commerce transaction takes place. Likewise, a B2B exchange occurs when a church secretary transmits an online order for office equipment, a college cafeteria requests a delivery of supplies via a Web site, or an official at the Internal Revenue Service downloads new word-processing software.

The Consumer-to-Consumer Electronic Marketplace

Did you ever come across items in your closet that you no longer use, but you hate to throw them away because they might have value to someone else? Perhaps you have sold such items in a garage sale or a yard sale. Another way to try to earn revenues from items you no longer want is to sell them on the Internet. You can post classified advertisements on many sites, such as Yahoo.com. Alternatively, you may attempt to auction the item. Several Internet-based companies, such as eBay.com, allow people to put items up for auction.

Consumer-to-Consumer (C2C) E-Commerce
The sale of an item by one individual to another individual, sometimes with the assistance of an e-commerce intermediary.

Of course, your merchandise might not be as small as a few old baseball gloves stored in a back corner of your closet. You might have something bigger in mind that you wish to try to sell, such as a used automobile or a house. Irrespective of the item, when you use an electronic network such as the Internet to sell the item to another individual, you engage in **consumer-to-consumer (C2C) e-commerce.** C2C e-commerce has grown considerably in recent years, and this form of electronic commerce has done much to expand the role of *e-commerce intermediaries,* or third parties that help coordinate exchanges between a buyer and seller in an e-commerce transaction.

FUNDAMENTAL ISSUES ▼

1.
2.
3.
4.

1. What is electronic commerce?

Electronic commerce is the process of transferring ownership of or rights to use goods and services through a computer-mediated electronic network. Electronic commerce may accompany, but is distinguished from, e-business processes through which firms use electronic networks to coordinate decision making and implementation of business functions such as production, marketing, and management functions. The main types of electronic commerce are business-to-consumer, business-to-business, and consumer-to-consumer transactions. These take place in electronic marketplaces, which are cyberspace locations where prospective sellers and buyers can effectively transact exchanges via interactions on electronic networks.

How It Works—The Infrastructure of E-Commerce

In 1958, in an article published in *American Mathematical Monthly,* a Princeton mathematician named John Tukey wrote, "Today, the 'software' comprising the carefully planned interpretive routines, compilers, and other aspects of automative programming are at least as important to the modern electronic calculator as its 'hardware' of tubes, transistors, wires, tapes, and the like." Tukey thus introduced two words that we now commonly encounter: *hardware* and *software.*

About ten years later, the roots of the Internet emerged within the Advanced Research Projects Administration, a division of the U.S. Defense Department. This agency developed a computer network, called ARPAnet, to link universities and research groups of defense contractors. As part of this effort, the *Transmission Control Protocol/Internet Protocol (TCP/IP)* was developed as a common communications language for computer interactions and transmissions within networks. The TCP portion of the protocol ensures that two computing devices can share information, while the IP portion permits the devices to keep track of transmitted information by dividing a communication into packets of data that are labeled with the addresses of the sending and receiving devices.

During the 1980s, the National Science Foundation used the TCP/IP protocol as a basis for creating a broader network, the NSFNET, to assist universities and government agencies in connecting to supercomputer centers in various locales. Quickly, computer scientists began to develop software applications that enabled researchers to communicate using what came to be known as electronic mail, or e-mail, and to transfer computer files. Other academic, government, and then commercial networks began to connect to this broader network, and within a few years there was a large network composed of thousands of networks, all linked via the TCP/IP protocol, which we now call the Internet. By the early 1990s, most federal funding for operating the Internet was discontinued, and much of the responsibility for operating the Internet shifted to the private sector.

THE BASIC COMPONENTS OF THE INTERNET

At some time—especially if you are on a modem connection to an older, slower phone line—you may have noticed that when you enter a Web address such as http://www.barnesandnoble.com (also http://www.bn.com), a message appears for a few seconds that indicates a site number to which your browser is connecting. This is a currently standard IP address written as four sets of numbers separated by periods. This numerical address, which is assigned by the Internet Network Information Center, is "mapped" to the Web address that you have typed into the browser. It is used to transmit your site access request via devices called *routers,* which break the information in your request into the data packets that make their way to the host computer for the Web site you want to access, such as a computer operated by Barnes & Noble, the bookseller. The routers send these packets by the most efficient available pathways using the most recent maps of the Internet's various interconnected network. The packets then converge at the computer for which your request was intended, which then processes your request for a return flow of data to your computer.

Domain Names

Domain Name

An electronic network address recognizable by browser programs, which includes a top-level domain such as "com" and a subdomain indicating the specific location of the host, such as "Lands' End."

A name for a Web site that you type into your browser to reference the host computer of the site, such as http://www.landsend.com, is called a **domain name.** The "com" on the right-hand side of the domain name refers to the *top-level domain,* which in this case is a commercial enterprise. There are two types of top-level domains. The list of *generic* top-level domains includes educational institutions (edu), nonprofit organizations (org), and U.S. governmental institutions (gov); it was recently expanded to include a television category (tv). Panel *(a)* of Figure 1-1 displays recent estimates of the distribution of generic top-level domains. There are also top-level *country code* domains, such as uk (United Kingdom), de (Germany), and so on. The estimated distribution of these domains is displayed in panel *(b)* of Figure 1-1.

The middle portion of the Internet address, "landsend," is the *subdomain* that indicates the part of the top-level domain that this site occupies, namely Lands' End, the direct retailer. The left-hand portion of the domain name, "www," is a convention for indicating that the specific computer is located on the World Wide Web.

For some years, this system of domain names was administered solely by the Internet Assigned Numbers Authority (http://www.iana.org). Recently, however, private domain-registration names have emerged. Anyone can apply, directly or indirectly through a registration company, for a domain name from the Internet

Figure 1-1:
Distributions of Top-Level Domains.

▼

Panel (a) shows that about 86 percent of the generic top-level Internet domains are either "com" or "net." Most of those domains are owned by individuals or firms located in the United States, so the "us" share of the distribution of country top-level domains displayed in panel (b) tends to understate the extent to which the United States currently dominates ownership of domain names.

Source: Internet Domain Survey, Internet Software Consortium http://www.isc.org/ds, January 2001. Used with permission.

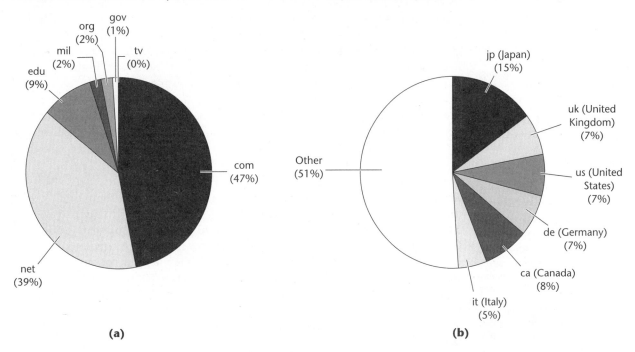

(a)   (b)

Corporation for Assigned Names and Numbers (ICANN; http://www.icann.org). The domain names "edu," "gov," "mil" (U.S. military), and "int" (organizations established by international treaties) are reserved only for qualifying organizations. In 2000 ICANN added "pro" (professionals), "museum," "aero" (airlines), "coop" (business cooperatives), "name" (personal Web sites), "info," and "biz" (business).

An unsurprising difficulty that has emerged in recent years is that some organizations have similar names or abbreviated names, but each can have only a single domain name. There are also only so many generic terms for activities to which a company or organization may wish to lay claim via its domain name, such as business services (for instance, "business.com"), lending services (for example, "loans.com"), and the like. Hence, there is a scarcity of desirable domain names. So-called *cyber-squatters*—individuals or groups who profit from establishing web addresses with the single goal of selling them to someone else—have profited from this scarcity, as evidenced by the high prices that domain names can command on the secondary market. A few years ago, "business.com" sold for $7.5 million, and "loans.com" sold for just over $3 million.

Connecting Computers

When you type in a domain name, it is converted to its associated numerical address by a *domain name server,* which determines the destination point for your request to access the Web site at that address. The superstructure that supports this process is operated by **network service providers,** such as MCI and Sprint, whose systems handle high volumes of data flow at high speeds. Local and regional **Internet service providers (ISPs)** use devices called *servers* to connect to network service providers. They serve as the point of connection to the overarching Internet system for individual households and businesses.

The message containing the domain name requesting access to the associated site thus begins at your computer and traverses through your ISP's server to a point of access to a network service provider. Then the routers of network service providers direct it to its final destination.

Communications Tools

At the first step in this process, however, you must be able to communicate with the ISP's server. The address scheme for use with a browser to connect to sites using domain names is known as a **Universal Resource Locator (URL).** The URL—the complete "Internet address" address—for Lands' End, *http://www.landsend.com,* indicates that the method of accessing this site via your computer is "http," which stands for **HyperText Transfer Protocol (HTTP),** which is the means by which individual computers communicate with servers of ISPs. The most common version of HTTP is said to be *stateless,* because after your browser opens a connection to a site and downloads the associated document, access to the site immediately terminates.

Continuing a series of applications across Web pages at the same site certainly is a common event when someone engages in Internet shopping. Finding ways for prospective buyers to remain "linked" to a seller's site within a given session, or perhaps into future sessions, requires overcoming the statelessness of HTTP. That is, the programmers for the site that the prospective consumer visits must create a mechanism for maintaining "state"—recognition of a specific consumer's browser connection so that quick navigation among pages can take place.

THE PROCESS OF SELLING ON THE WEB

Clearly, on the seller's side of an Internet connection, a Web site must already be constructed and in place on a server. There are now a number of ways to construct Web sites. The bigger challenge is to develop a site that will attract visitors, that will keep their attention long enough to interest them in investigating the

---

Network Service Providers

Companies operating systems that support electronic networks by handling large volumes of data flow at high speeds.

Internet Service Providers (ISPs)

Companies that provide individuals and businesses with access to the Internet via server devices linked to network services providers.

Universal Resource Locator (URL)

The address scheme that a browser program uses to connect to sites using domain names.

HyperText Transfer Protocol (HTTP)

A stateless communications procedure by which individual computers communicate with server devices operated by Internet service providers.

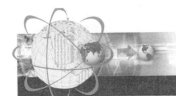

MANAGEMENT *Online*

Allocating Scarce Space on the Screen

Tens of millions of people visit the Internet each day. Nevertheless, nearly half of them visit fewer than three Internet sites per week. Companies that want to sell their products on the Web know this. They also know that when an individual opens her Web browser, her home page is typically the home page of her Internet service provider, the browser's home page, or a search engine such as Yahoo.com. For this reason, many companies try to attract your attention to their Web sites by advertising on these sites.

Consequently, every time you access the Net, you see advertising—banners, buttons, keywords, co-branded ads, or other promotions or Web links. Some of the biggest advertisers on the Web are International Business Machines, Microsoft, Toyota, General Motors, Disney, and American Express. Web-based companies such as E*Trade.com and Amazon.com also are major Web advertisers. Some estimates indicate that, all told, these and other companies will spend more than $20 billion on the Web by 2005.

The owner of any Web page that carries an ad faces an opportunity cost, because space on a computer screen is scarce. When a search engine such as Yahoo devotes any space to promoting its own products or services, there is less space available to sell to, say, Visa or Amazon. Yet if the screen becomes too cluttered, some users will switch to a competing search engine. Yahoo and others who sell space on their Web pages take these trade-offs into account when designing how pages will appear on a computer screen. Increasingly, the design of a Web page is a crucial business decision.

For Critical Analysis:
Which parts of a Web page do you think is "prime real estate" for advertisements? Why?

company's products, and that is easy to use for searching among, evaluating, and hopefully ordering those products. (A key constraint is the size of a computer screen; see *Management Online: Allocating Scarce Space on the Screen.*)

Conducting a Transaction
Any business transaction transferring ownership of or the right to use a good or service entails six essential stages:

1) **Customer product discovery and review**—A prospective buyer must first learn about the availability of a seller's product and must have the opportunity to review the features of the product.
2) **Price determination**—The prospective buyer has to determine the seller's asking price for the product. There must also be an established procedure for price negotiations to take place between the buyer and the seller.

3) **Payment**—The two parties to the transaction have to agree on a method of payment and a means by which a payment will be transferred from the buyer to the seller.

4) **Delivery of the product**—The terms by which the seller will deliver the good or service have to be established, and the seller must have a mechanism in place to ensure that it honors its delivery commitment.

5) **Resolution of any disputes**—If miscommunications have occurred in any previous steps of the transaction, some means of resolving these miscommunications must be in place before the transaction can be finalized.

6) **Final settlement**—The transaction is finalized once the seller delivers the product and the buyer transmits payment.

As you will learn in the following chapters, each step is likely to proceed differently in e-commerce transactions as compared with traditional exchanges. The pricing process, for instance, is likely to be much different for e-commerce firms. Payment methods also may differ. Electronic commerce also may offer advantages for dispute resolution. The most noticeable difference, however, is at the first stage, when a prospective buyer attempts to shop for a product via communication with an Internet seller's Web pages.

Web Servers

Web Server

A software program residing on an Internet seller's server that controls access to the seller's Web site, enables the seller to easily update the site as needed, compiles logs of transactions with those who visit the site, and operates external programs that assist the buyer in engaging in transactions with the seller.

An Internet seller uses a software program called a **Web server** to communicate with the HTTP requests received from the browsers of potential customers. This program resides on the physical server device used by the seller to connect to the Internet (or intranets, in many B2B applications). There are a number of Web servers that sellers can use, but all perform the following essential functions:

1) **Controlling access**—The Web server must establish what directories or files a visitor to a site can access, thereby determining how the visitor can navigate through Web pages at the site.

2) **Updating Web site**—Businesses often change prices, add new brands or products, and so on. They use Web servers, together with databases and software to change page links or other aspects of site operation as circumstances warrant.

3) **Compiling transaction logs**—For a typical Internet seller, a key function of a Web server is to transfer customer transaction data to databases. This allows the seller to analyze data about the characteristics of potential customers, such as how many pages they visited at the site, and which specific pages.

4) **Operating external programs**—As part of its marketing effort, an Internet seller may wish to give a potential customer additional information about its product, perhaps in the form of a word-processing file. The Web server

accesses additional programs that enable the visitor to the seller's site to initiate downloads of such materials.

Cookies

One type of external file commonly downloaded from sellers' Web servers is known as a **cookie.** This is a small text file recorded in the hard drive of the computer of the visitor to the seller's site. The seller's Web server can read information stored on the cookie to "remember" users across the pages of a site. If the visitor does not delete the cookie from the computer's hard drive, the seller's Web server can read the cookie during a later connection session and recognize the potential customer as a return visitor to the site.

Thus, cookies are a way to maintain "state or continuous connection" within a session in which a potential buyer to the seller's Web site. For instance, suppose that a visitor to the seller's site places an item in a "shopping cart" on the seller's Web server but wishes to return to search the seller's catalog at another Web page at the site. The seller's Web server uses the cookie to maintain a "connection" between the shopper's initial order and any additional items added following a further search of the catalog—up to the final step at which the shopper verifies payment and completes the purchase.

As you will learn about in greater detail in Chapter 11, cookies have become controversial. Certainly, cookies help to simplify an individual's shopping experience—for instance, in some e-commerce applications having a cookie on your computer's hard drive, and being immediately recognized by a seller's site can save considerable time you would otherwise have to spend "logging on" to the site. Nevertheless, some people object to having data or programs automatically downloaded onto their computers without their permission. Cookies record considerable information about the shopper, such as the address of the user's ISP. It is also feasible to match these data with the shopper's e-mail address, and even the shopper's physical address, using information from the shopper's purchase forms accessed via the attached cookie. Consequently, a number of privacy concerns have emerged in recent years.

Cookie
A small text file that an Internet seller's Web server may download onto the hard drive of the computer of the visitor to the seller's site; this text file can store information about Web transactions by the visitor that the Web server can use to recognize the visitor as the visitor navigates the seller's Web pages or when the visitor reestablishes connection with the site at a later date.

Beyond the Seller's Web Site: A Flesh-and-Blood Business

An Internet seller needs more than an attractive and easy-to-use Web site. What is also required is a business model consistent with maximizing the rate of return on the owners' interest in the company. Many Internet sellers have created sites that have received positive reviews from marketing analysts, yet have failed to follow through on customer service, product quality, and simply delivering the product.

Consider the true story of a college professor who read that big booksellers keep their costs down by getting bulk discounts on relatively small numbers of books. With the help of several outside investors, he decided to start his own

Internet bookselling company, and his wife and children helped him track book orders, unpack boxes of books as they arrived, and repackage books to fill customer orders. Orders began to stream in, and the future of his company looked bright. Soon the media put together stories about how even an individual family could easily form and operate Web-based start-up companies. Following this publicity bonanza, orders began to pour in, and suddenly fulfilling those orders became a logistical nightmare. The professor's house rapidly filled with boxes, and it became impossible to keep up with new orders. Yet the scale of the family business was not large enough to support moving the company's operations to a larger facility. Eventually the professor, his family, and the outside investors had to cut their losses and shut down the business.

Even the big Internet bookseller Amazon confronted a similar situation in late 1999. Amazon was in the middle of launching an expansion into toy sales when Christmas season arrived. The marketing effort for the company's new toy business was such a success that it found itself struggling to fill orders. On some days, Amazon executives joined other workers at loading docks to load and unload boxes from truck trailers. Worse, stocks of toys advertised in the company's online catalog were depleted, and it had to cancel orders. Parents who had felt self-satisfied that their Internet adventure had secured the hot toys for their kids instead found themselves joining the mad pre-Christmas shopping rush at bricks-and-mortar retail outlets.

Beyond the Firm: Market and Legal Constraints

An Internet seller typically is not the only seller of its particular goods or services. Often there are also other companies trying to generate sales offline or online. Consequently, an Internet seller faces constraints determined by the behavior of its rivals. How stringent these constraints may be depends on the characteristics of the market for its products, such as the number of rivals, the similarities and differences among their products, and ease of entry by potential new rivals.

Internet sellers also confront nearly all the same legal restraints that traditional bricks-and-mortar companies face, including consumer protection statutes, antitrust laws, and the like. Although many products sold online currently are not subjected to sales taxes, Web-based companies are beginning to face increased government scrutiny rules (e.g., privacy rules) aimed solely at them.

Thus, Internet sellers must deal with standard business problems relating to organizing production, marketing, sales, bookkeeping, delivery, and so on; the competitive situation dictated by characteristics of the markets for their products; and fundamental government rules applying to both offline and online sellers. In addition, they must contend with issues specific to cyberspace operations, including how to organize their Internet marketing and sales processes and how to address cyberspace interventions by the government.

FUNDAMENTAL ISSUES ▼

1.

2.

3.

4.

2. How does electronic commerce work?

Currently, the focus of most e-commerce activity is the Internet, which is a network of networks originally established as a cooperative arrangement among the U.S. government, universities, and private research facilities but now largely operated within the private sector. A prospective buyer uses a browser program on a device such as a personal computer to type in a Universal Resource Locator (URL) that communicates a specific Web site address to a server device operated by the buyer's Internet service provider. This device is connected to a network service provider, whose system includes routers that transmit the request to access the Web site to the server of the Internet seller that operates the site. The seller uses a Web server program to automatically govern the prospective buyer's navigation through the site, to compile information about the buyer's visit, to keep the site updated for each use by this and other prospective buyers, and to operate external programs that the buyer can access. An Internet seller faces basic business operational problems and market and legal constraints that are generally analogous to, but sometimes distinct from, those faced by traditional firms.

 ## Who Is Online, and Where Are They?

A fundamental factor determining the scope for future growth of electronic commerce is the number of people with access to computer-mediated networks and, in particular, the Internet.

INTERNET ACCESS IN THE UNITED STATES

The U.S. government presided over the birth of the Internet, and the United States is one of the wealthiest of the world's nations. It should come as no surprise, therefore, that many U.S. residents now have Internet access—or that the United States is at the center of e-commerce activities.

A Nation Goes Online

As Figure 1-2 on page 20 indicates, today about 120 million U.S. residents have access to the Internet. Nearly all of these people go online using personal computers

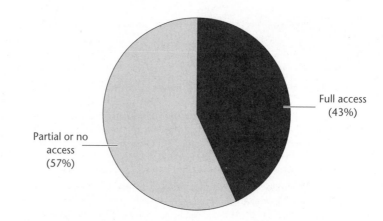

Figure 1-2:
Percentage of U.S. Population with Internet Access.

About 43 percent of the U.S. population has ready access to the Internet. The remainder has partial access at schools or libraries or no access at all.

Source: U.S. Department of Commerce, Bureau of the Census and author estimates.

with wired connections to servers—telephone modems, cable modems, and direct service lines (DSLs). A small but rapidly increasing number connect to the Internet via wireless technologies, including satellite and microwave services and cell phones.

Roughly half of these people access the Internet from their homes using ISP services. The remaining Internet users rely on online connections available to them at work or school. A recent survey indicated that about one in five U.S. adults now spends at least 5 or more hours online each week. One in ten are online more than 10 hours per week.

Are There Digital Divides?

Surveys also reveal that some groups within the United States have more access to the Internet than others. This propensity for some groups to have greater Internet access than others has come to be known as a **digital divide.** Because there are a number of ways to categorize people, there are several possible digital divides that might conceivably exist.

Digital Divide
The observed propensity for some groups of people to have greater Internet access than others; the most important source of digital divides is income differences across groups.

Most recent studies indicate that income is a key criterion determining whether a U.S. resident has Internet access. A recent report by the Commerce Department, for instance, found that the highest-income U.S. residents were twenty times more likely to be online than people at the lowest-income threshold. Thus, there is evidence of an income-based digital divide in the United States. The expense of purchasing hardware and software is daunting for lower-income individuals, as are the monthly fees to ISPs. By way of contrast, such expenses constitute much smaller portions of total expenditures by higher-income people.

At one time, there were widespread concerns about the possible existence of racial and ethnic digital divides. Although these concerns still exist, recent research indicates that because race and ethnicity are often correlated with income, perceived racial and ethnic digital divides in Internet access probably reflect the income-based division separating Internet users from nonusers. Indeed, as a

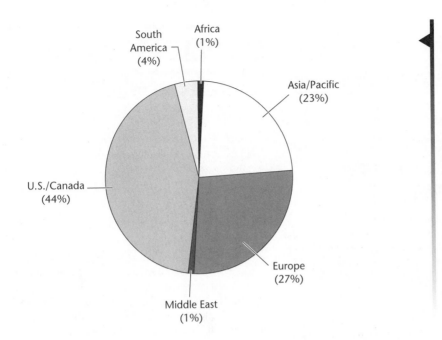

South America (4%)

Africa (1%)

Asia/Pacific (23%)

U.S./Canada (44%)

Europe (27%)

Middle East (1%)

Figure 1-3: The Distribution of the World's Online Population.

The vast majority of people with Internet access reside in the developed nations in North America, Europe, and Asia.

Source: Organization for Economic Cooperation and Development.

percentage, white residents actually trail African Americans and Hispanic Americans in online access. Nevertheless, African Americans are less likely than whites to own a computer or to have Internet access directly from their homes. Furthermore, while African Americans and Hispanic Americans make up nearly 20 percent of the U.S. work force, they hold less than 5 percent of the jobs in high-paying occupations in information technologies. So certain types of race- and ethnicity-based "divides" clearly do exist.

GLOBALIZATION OF INTERNET ACCESS

A more dramatic type of digital divide is apparent in Figure 1-3, which displays the distribution of the world's online population. Currently 44 percent of people with access to the Internet reside in the United States and Canada. Those two wealthy North American countries and Europe together contain just under three-fourths of the world's online population, and developed portions of Asia contain most of the rest. (The Internet predominance of the United States has some residents of non–English-speaking countries worried about the future of their languages, though perhaps unnecessarily; see on page 22 the *Globalization Online: Will the Internet Be the Death of Languages Other than English?*) Most people in less-developed regions of the world—those with less wealth and lower incomes—have little or no access to basic telecommunications services, let alone to the Internet.

GLOBALIZATION *Online*

Will the Internet Be the Death of Languages Other than English?

A language is an example of a *nonexclusive resource,* which means that everyone who uses a language owns it and cannot be excluded from using it. In some instances, of course, we may use language for communicating only with ourselves, such as when we save notes in a computer file to access for reference at a later date. Most often, however, we use language to communicate with others.

The Internet is now one of the world's key modes of communication. Nevertheless, the bulk of Internet hosts and users are in located the United States, where English is the predominant language. Estimates are that about 80 percent of the *stock* of all information stored on the world's computers is in English. The English language is used in roughly the same percentage of the *flow* of information transmissions over the

Internet—e-mail messages, file transfers, and the like. Undoubtedly, this increases the incentive for the world's non–English speakers to learn English. According to Berlitz International, the world's largest language school, the study of English accounts for about 70 percent of the 5 million language lessons it provides each year. Even though Spanish is the fastest-growing spoken language on the Internet, it is used by far fewer of the world's people than English.

According to a number of language experts, English has become so ingrained within the global communications network that its dominance is unassailable by any other language. This has led some to worry that English ultimately may "replace" other languages, thereby damaging traditional cultural identities. According to a former president of France, this makes the Internet "a major risk for humanity."

Nevertheless, there are some solid arguments favoring the view that widespread use of the Internet actually will *reduce* the chances that languages other than English will fall

continued

Overall Internet connectivity is proceeding rapidly, as evidenced by the dramatic global increase in the number of Internet hosts, depicted in Figure 1-4. Media pundits marvel at the significant expansion of Internet access among the U.S. population, which continues at an annual pace exceeding 15 percent. Nevertheless, annual growth rates of the online populations of Europe and South America slightly exceed 100 percent. In Africa, the online population growth rate is about 150 percent. The Asia/Pacific region of the world has the fastest growth of online access, which is 155 percent. Currently, more than 500 million people worldwide have regular access to the Internet.

Recent estimates indicate that 85 percent of people who have access to the Internet have purchased at least one item online. Budding entrepreneurs who are not daunted by the technology of Internet selling have consequently developed an interest in electronic commerce. The potential market for electronic commerce is large, and it is growing.

into disuse. Before the Internet, media that relied solely on one-way transmissions, such as television and radio, pushed languages into head-on competition. For example, European broadcasters often found that the time it took to transmit a recent Hollywood action movie dubbed in Ukranian on a given bandwidth could more effectively—in terms of increasing the odds of reaching target advertising audiences—be devoted to transmitting of the original English version that more people were able to understand. On the Internet, however, Web sites and e-mail transmissions in various languages do not directly compete. Promoters of a Ukranian folk art festival can post Web advertisements for the festival in English and German, but they can also post them in Ukranian.

Applying economic analysis to competition among languages indicates that the key factor determining which ones are most likely to survive is gains in specialization. People will continue to use their native tongue when they want to communicate with others with shared knowledge of that language, whether the communication is a discussion on a street corner, on the editorial page of a local newspaper, or in an Internet chat room. They will tend to choose to use a non-native tongue, such as English, for formal communications with others around the globe who have a shared knowledge of that language.

Some who study languages believe it is possible that widespread use of English on the Internet actually could induce a greater assault on English than on other languages if a "techie" version of English begins to develop alongside traditional English—such as "LOL" for "laughing out loud" or "GL" for "good luck." Someday even English speakers may have to know two languages: the version of English they read and speak at home and the offshoot of English that they use in their Web-based communications.

For Critical Analysis:

What factors are likely to determine whether English remains the predominate language on the Internet?

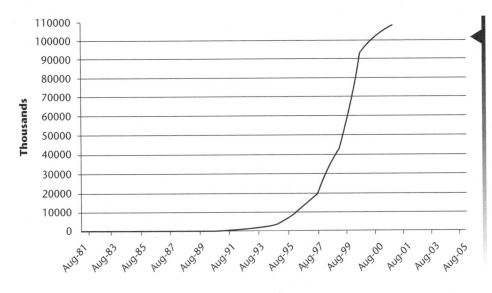

**Figure 1-4:
The Number of Internet Hosts Worldwide.**

Growth in the number of Internet hosts has only recently shown signs of leveling off somewhat.

Source: Internet Domain Survey, Internet Software Consortium http://www.isc.org/ds, January 2001. Used with permission.

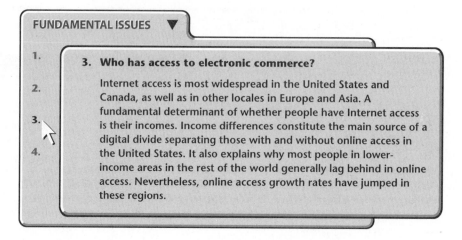

FUNDAMENTAL ISSUES ▼

1.

2.

3.

4.

3. Who has access to electronic commerce?

Internet access is most widespread in the United States and Canada, as well as in other locales in Europe and Asia. A fundamental determinant of whether people have Internet access is their incomes. Income differences constitute the main source of a digital divide separating those with and without online access in the United States. It also explains why most people in lower-income areas in the rest of the world generally lag behind in online access. Nevertheless, online access growth rates have jumped in these regions.

Just How Important Is Electronic Commerce?

What are the latest trends in e-commerce retail sales? To find out, go to http://www.census.gov, and next to "Business" click on "E-Stats."

The U.S. Department of Commerce did not begin estimating B2C sales until early 2000. Its recent quarterly dollar estimates of all e-commerce sales, excluding sales by travel agencies, ticket agencies, and financial brokers, are reported in Figure 1-5. As you can see, the Commerce Department estimates that B2C sales now account for at least $20 billion per year.

Nevertheless, only recently have B2C sales even exceeded a meager 1 percent of total retail sales in the United States. This fact has caused some to question whether electronic commerce has been over-hyped by media pundits, economists, and e-commerce sellers themselves. Is e-commerce economics sufficiently important to warrant your time and effort?

SOME E-COMMERCE MEASUREMENT ISSUES

For many people, including economists, among the most frustrating aspects of economics is that economic data are not always accurate. This can be a particularly exasperating problem for those interested in e-commerce economics.

Wide Ranges of Estimates

In fact, the B2C sales data reported in Figure 1-5 are simply the U.S. government's quarterly "best guesses" about the volumes of online business-to-consumer sales. Other knowledgeable people often come up with different guesses. For instance, at the same time the Commerce Department announced its first-ever estimate of B2C e-commerce for the fourth quarter of 1999, $5.2 billion, published estimates of

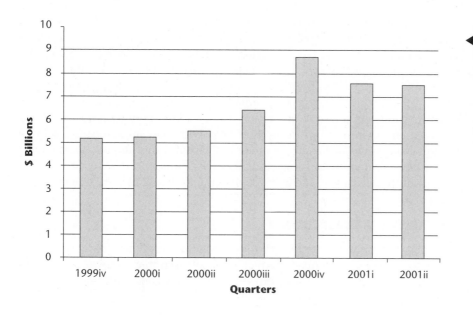

Figure 1-5:
Quarterly B2C Sales since 1999.

This chart displays the Census Bureau's estimates of quarterly retail sales generated from Web sites.

Source: U.S. Department of Commerce, Bureau of the Census.

B2C sales for that quarter by private economists and consulting groups ranged from as low as $4 billion to as high as $14 billion.

Part of the reason that private economists tend to develop higher average estimates of B2C e-commerce is that private estimates typically include estimates of online sales by travel agencies, ticket agencies, and financial brokers. One private consulting group, Forrester Research, estimated that sales excluded from the Commerce Department's B2C figures for the fourth quarter of 1999 were equal to nearly $3.5 billion. Hence, if this amount had been included in the Commerce Department's estimates, the total reported volume of B2C sales for that quarter alone would have been nearly $9 billion, or about 67 percent higher than the Commerce Department reported.

B2C Isn't All of E-Commerce

Even if e-commerce sales are really consistently as much as 67 percent higher than the Commerce Department reports, this still only pushes B2C e-commerce sales up to about 1.6 percent of total retail sales. Even if one were to accept the high-end estimate of $14 billion for the fourth quarter of 1999, B2C sales volumes would still have been less than 2 percent of total retail sales in the United States. Clearly, although absolute and relative B2C sales have grown and continue to grow, B2C e-commerce is still a blip in relation to aggregate economic activity.

B2C is not the entire story—not by a long shot. Most estimates indicate that *business-to-business (B2B)* e-commerce dwarfs B2C sales. Most estimates of B2B e-commerce volumes for 2001 were in the range of $250 billion. Furthermore, even e-commerce skeptics agree that B2B activity is growing rapidly. Private forecasts of B2B transactions for 2003 range from as low as $600 billion to as high as nearly *$3 trillion*. (By way of comparison, the total output of goods and services in the U.S. economy in 2003 will probably be on the order of $11–$12 trillion.)

In addition, there has been considerable growth of *consumer-to-consumer (C2C)* e-commerce. Unfortunately, C2C e-commerce is even harder to measure. To consider why, imagine trying to go around a large community each day to tabulate the total daily volume of transactions at neighborhood yard and garage sales. Although economists can readily tabulate the earnings that firms such as eBay receive from coordinating auctions and other C2C transactions, obtaining information about the actual volumes of the underlying transactions is very difficult.

THE GROWING DIGITAL ECONOMY

A number of economists contend that e-commerce sales figures seriously underestimate the size of the overall economic impact of electronic commerce. They argue that the current and likely future growth of electronic commerce is a driving force for broader growth of a digital economy.

Economic Spillovers from E-Commerce and E-Business

Investment Spending
Expenditures by businesses on capital goods that they use to produce more goods and services.

A significant part of aggregate annual income and product in any nation is **investment spending,** which consists mainly of business expenditures on *capital goods,* or goods that businesses use to produce additional goods and services in the future. As businesses geared up for e-commerce and e-business applications after the mid-1990s, U.S. investment spending soared. Between 1995 and 2001, annual business investment in information technology hardware more than doubled, from $161 billion to nearly $400 billion. During the same period, annual software investment increased from $82 billion to about $150 billion, or by more than 80 percent. By 2001, total information technology investment amounted to more than one-third of aggregate investment spending in the United States.

Much of this investment has been undertaken by so-called *information technology (IT) industries.* These include both industries specializing in e-commerce activities and industries that provide e-business services and associated electronic infrastructure products. IT industries account for less than 10 percent of U.S. output of goods and services, but nearly 40 percent of the nearly $55 billion total annual U.S. spending on research and development. The U.S. Department of Commerce estimates that IT industries have accounted for nearly one-third of U.S. economic growth since 1995.

Jobs, Jobs, Jobs

Good news for students learning about e-commerce economics is that growth of the digital economy has been reflected in aggregate U.S. employment figures. Job

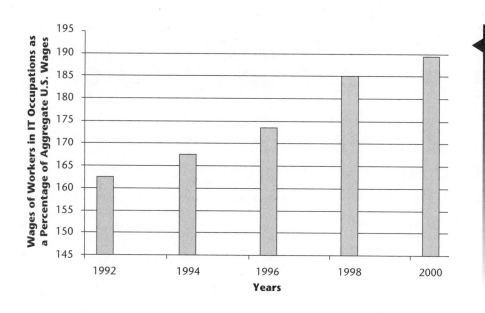

Figure 1-6:
Wages and Salaries in IT Occupations as a Percentage of Wages and Salaries in All U.S. Industries.

Workers in information-technology industries typically earn between 1.5 and 2 times the salaries of workers in other industries.

Source: U.S. Department of Commerce.

prospects are especially bright for systems analysts and computer scientists, engineers, and programmers. Total employment in software and computer services industries increased from 850,000 in 1992 to 1.6 million in 2001.

Altogether, employment in IT industries and other IT-related occupations rose from about 4.5 million in 1992 to 7.4 million in 2001. Today, more than 6 percent of U.S. workers are employed in IT industries. As Figure 1-6 indicates, these workers tend to earn higher wages than workers in other occupations. A typical employee in an IT occupation earns nearly twice as much as an average worker in the United States. (Other occupations, such as trucking, have also benefited from the development of information technologies; see on page 28 the *Management Online: How an Employment Crunch Helped Make Trucking an E-Commerce Success Story*.)

What can we conclude about the economic importance of e-commerce? First, although sales by Internet sellers are difficult to measure, current estimates indicate that they are relatively small but are growing at a steady, if not rapid, pace. Second, more reliable figures show that spending on the technologies that underlie e-commerce has grown dramatically and that overall employment in industries using these technologies has increased. Hence, electronic commerce plays an important role in today's economy, and all indications are that electronic commerce will experience both absolute and relative growth in the years to come. In the chapters that follow, you will discover the many implications of this revolutionary development in our economy.

MANAGEMENT *Online*

How an Employment Crunch Helped Make Trucking an E-Commerce Success Story

Until the late 1970s, the U.S. trucking industry was a heavily regulated business. Although there were about 10,000 U.S. trucking companies, a few big companies dominated traffic in various regions of the nation. Beginning in the early 1980s, however, the federal government lifted many legal restraints on competition, and hundreds of thousands of small trucking companies opened for business.

No Longer a Cushy Job

In the days of regulated trucking, hauling prices tended to be relatively high and stable, which all but guaranteed the profitability of the nation's dominant trucking firms. Men rushed to apply for jobs as truck drivers (only a very few women were truckers 20 years ago), because wages were relatively high, the work of driving was not too difficult, and there were several off hours each week.

After deregulation, however, competition among the multitudes of new trucking companies led to deep price cuts, and drivers had to spend days at a time on the road just to earn a living. Many drivers quit their jobs during the 1980s even as trucking price reductions helped the industry as a whole begin to grow. Trucking companies faced an employment crisis, as the average firm found itself having to replace the equivalent of its entire workforce every single year.

Attracting Good Help, and Laying a Foundation for E-Commerce

Desperate trucking firms began bidding up drivers' wages to as high as $80,000 a year. They offered more and more perks

continued

FUNDAMENTAL ISSUES ▼

1.

2.

3.

4.

4. How important is electronic commerce?

Volumes of e-commerce sales, and particularly consumer-to-consumer sales (C2C), have proved difficult to measure. Current estimates indicate that business-to-consumer (B2C) sales account for a small but growing portion of total retail sales in the United States. Business-to-business e-commerce sales volumes are several times larger than B2C sales. The development of the broader information technology infrastructure and e-business applications that accompany e-commerce activities has a more readily measurable and more quantitatively significant effect on the economy. These activities have pushed up investment spending and have created new employment opportunities in the United States.

to attract and retain drivers, such as free chiropractic care, in-cab Internet and e-mail access, special arrangements for husbands and wives to work as driving teams, and arrangements to travel with pets. In addition, companies developed new transportation systems designed to shorten truckers' trips to less than 400 miles, thereby enabling them to spend more time at home with their families. A number of trucking firms established regional hub warehouses where truckers could hand off their loads for redistribution to other trucks that would continue transporting goods on their paths to final destinations hundreds of miles farther away.

Once the warehouses were in place, in the early 1990s, trucking companies began looking for ways to use them. By chance, many Internet sellers that had just gone online around that time also happened to be looking both for ware-house space and dependable ways to fulfill online orders. By 2000, twenty-five major trucking companies had transformed themselves into e-commerce logistics operations. Now, when a B2B customer clicks on the "ship now" button in an Internet transaction, it is likely that the order is instantaneously transmitted to a trucking firm's warehouse, where employees remove the ordered good from shelves to box and label it for pickup by the next truck destined for the customer's location. Projections are that many more trucking firms will jump at the opportunity presented by e-commerce and made possible by their past efforts to find and keep good truck drivers.

For Critical Analysis:
Why are the firms' product markets and labor markets closely related?

Chapter Summary

1) **Electronic Commerce:** The term *electronic commerce* describes any process by which people use a computer-mediated electronic network to transfer ownership of or rights to use goods and services. This process is often accompanied by electronic business applications that organizations use to coordinate production, marketing, and management via electronic networks. The primary forms of electronic commerce are business-to-consumer (B2C) e-commerce, business-to-business (B2B) e-commerce, and consumer-to-consumer (C2C) e-commerce. Internet sellers and buyers engage in e-commerce transactions within an electronic marketplace, which is a location in cyberspace where they can effect exchanges using electronic networks.

2) **How Electronic Commerce Works:** E-commerce activity currently takes place on the Internet or on intranets established by companies. The Internet is a network of networks jointly developed by the U.S. government, universities, and private research facilities and operated largely within the private sector. An e-commerce shopper transmits a request to access an Internet seller's Web site using a browser program on a device such as a home computer, which, in turn, is connected to a server device operated by an Internet service provider (ISP). The ISP's server is connected to a network service provider that operates router devices that transmit the shopper's access request to the server of the Internet seller. The seller's Web server program, which the seller also uses for site updating and for compiling data, then determines how the shopper navigates the site and operates external programs that the shopper may wish to use. Like any company, an e-commerce firm must address operational problems and market and legal constraints that are fundamental to the products it produces. An e-commerce firm also faces issues that are specific to an electronic marketplace.

3) **Access to Electronic Commerce:** Income levels have proved to be central to who has online access. This helps to explain why the wealthiest nations in North America, Europe, and Asia currently contain the bulk of the world's online population. It also accounts for most of the so-called digital divide separating those with and without online access in the United States. Online access is increasing among lower-income groups and in less-developed regions, however.

4) **The Importance of Electronic Commerce:** Accurately measuring the total sales of Internet sellers is extremely difficult. This is especially true for C2C e-commerce but has also been the case for B2C and B2B e-commerce. Recent estimates of B2C and B2B sales volumes indicate that B2C transactions are a small percentage of total retail sales in the United States and that B2B sales volumes are significantly larger than B2C volumes. The more noticeable effect of e-commerce activities has been the spillover effects of related information technology and e-business applications, which have contributed to higher business investment spending and to the creation of many new jobs.

Questions and Problems

1) What distinguishes e-commerce from e-business?
2) Classify each of the following activities as either e-commerce or e-business. If it is an e-commerce activity, also state whether it is B2C, B2B, or C2C.
    (a) An information technology company establishes an intranet portal that its employees can access to process all intracompany communications and thereby eliminate most of the company's physical paperwork.

    (b) Several automakers establish a central clearinghouse for purchasing engine parts online from their longstanding network of auto parts suppliers.

    (c) A greeting card company establishes a Web site where people can, for a fee, arrange for e-mail messages and colorful, personalized attachments to be sent to family members or friends celebrating birthdays.

    (d) A baseball-card collector arranges the terms of a sale of a rare card to another collector via a company's auction site on the Internet.

3) Is there a distinction between a market and a marketplace? If so, what is the distinction?

4) Match each of the following definitions with the most closely related term among choices: ISP, cookie, TCP/IP, Internet, intranet, domain name, router, Web server

    (a) A hardware device that transmits Web site access requests to their final destinations.

    (b) A communications language used to link computers within a network.

    (c) A business that uses server devices to connect individuals and businesses to the Internet.

    (d) A text file automatically downloaded from some Web sites to a memory storage location on the device that a visitor used to access those sites.

    (e) An address that identifies the location of a Web site and thereby allows an individual to access that site using a browser program on a home computer.

    (f) Software that a company uses to track how its customers navigate through its Web site.

    (g) A network made up of other networks.

    (h) An electronic network that a company dedicates to its own internal use.

5) Some observers credit the development of electronic commerce to privatization of the Internet beginning in the 1980s. Do you agree? Why or why not?

6) Reread the *E-Commerce Today* opening to this chapter. Based on what you have learned, is the Internet more commercial because it has grown so rapidly, or does it owe its rapid growth to the ongoing commercialization of the Web? Take a stand, and support your position.

7) There is evidence that a person's level of educational attainment is strongly related to the likelihood that the individual will have Internet access. Why might this be so? Is a digital divide based on differences in educational attainment likely to be related to the digital divide stemming from income differences? Why or why not?

8) So far, which has had a more significant economic impact: e-commerce or e-business? Explain your reasoning.

9) Why are aggregate e-commerce transactions harder to measure than total traditional market transactions? Can you think of any one thing that government might do that would improve its estimates of total e-commerce sales? Are there any possible objections to such a government action?

10) A major downturn in e-commerce sales would have a direct negative effect on U.S. economic activity. Some economists believe that at present it would have an even larger indirect effect through reductions in investment and job creation that would be entailed. Does this argument make sense? Why or why not?

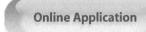

Internet URLs: http://www.iana.org, http://www.networksolutions.com, and http://www.icann.org

Titles: **Internet Assigned Numbers Authority (IANA) and Internet Corporation for Assigned Names and Numbers (ICANN)**

Navigation: Go directly to URLs that apply for each question.

Application: Perform the following operations, and answer the following questions.

1) Go to http://www.iana.org. Click on "Domain Name Services," and then click on "Generic Domains." Then click on "The Generic Domains" and next to ".com domain", click on VeriSign Global Registry Service." Read the discussion provided on this Web page. On the surface, does it appear to be difficult to register a domain name?

2) Now go to http://www.networksolutions.com, and use this search engine to check for the availability of "economics.com,"an imaginary online economics consulting business you wish to start. What happens? Now enter "economics," "economy," and "econ." What are the results?

3) Now go to http://www.icann.org. In the left-hand margin, click on "Domain Name Dispute Resolution." Read the discussion on this Web page, and then click on "Uniform Domain Name Dispute Resolution Policy," and read the more detailed explanation. If there is a dispute over a domain name, how can the parties to the dispute try resolve it? If the parties have a strong disagreement, is this process likely to be relatively costly? Why or why not?

For Group Study and Analysis: After all students have answered the above questions on their own, convene a full class discussion of the current way that domain names are assigned. Why does it make sense that there is a secondary market where people can sell domain names? Why might it be difficult to prove that someone is a "cybersquatter"? Is there a better way to allocate domain names?

Selected References and Further Readings

Greenstein, Shane. "The Evolving Structure of Commercial Internet Markets." In *Understanding the Digital Economy: Data, Tools, and Research,* by Erik Brynjolfsson and Brian Kahin. Cambridge, Mass.: MIT Press:, 2000, pp. 151–184.

Leebaert, Derek, ed. *The Future of the Electronic Marketplace.* Cambridge, Mass.: MIT Press, 1999.

McKnight, Lee, and Joseph Bailey, eds. *Internet Economics.* Cambridge, Mass.: MIT Press, 1998.

Mesenbourg, Thomas. "Measuring Electronic Business: Definitions, Underlying Concepts, and Measurement Plans," Bureau of the Census, 2000.

Turban, Efraim, Jae Lee, David King, and H. Michael Chung. *Electronic Commerce: A Managerial Perspective.* Englewood Cliffs, N.J.: Prentice-Hall, 2000.

U.S. Department of Commerce. *Digital Economy 2000.* June 2000.

Watson, Richard, Pierre Berthon, Leyland Pitt, and George Zinkhan. *Electronic Commerce.* Fort Worth: Dryden Press, 2000.

Wenniger, John. "Business-to-Business Electronic Commerce," *Current Issues in Economics and Finance.* Federal Reserve Bank of New York, 5(10), June 1999.

Westland, J. Christopher, and Theodore Clark. *Global Electronic Commerce.* Boston: MIT Press, 1999.

Wyckoff, Andrew, and Alessandra Colecchia. *The Economic and Social Impact of Electronic Commerce.* Organization for Economic Cooperation and Development, 1999.

Chapter 2

Applying Basic Economic Principles to Electronic Commerce

FUNDAMENTAL ISSUES ▼

1. What are the fundamental production and cost relationships for an e-commerce firm? ▶
2. How are prices and quantities determined in a perfectly competitive electronic marketplace? ▶
3. What are the key features of long-run equilibrium under perfect competition? ▶
4. How can economies of scale and scope matter in the electronic marketplace? ▶
5. What happens if a single firm dominates an electronic marketplace? ▶

\<E-Commerce Today\>

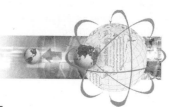

Buying Companies, or Customers?

In the nineteenth century, the town of Halfway, Oregon, was founded as a way station for travelers to water their horses during the trek between Cornucopia and Sparta, two towns at the center of the gold rush. In an effort to cash in on what appeared to be the gold rush of the new century, on December 20, 1999, the town changed its name to Half.com, thus becoming the first "dot-com" town in the United States. Its namesake was a Web site that allowed people to buy and sell used books, music, games and movies at prices at least half off from list prices. On June 13, 2000, the leading Internet auction company, eBay.com, paid nearly $400 million for Half.com. The chief executive officer (CEO) of eBay, Meg Witman, said that her company could have technically duplicated Half.com's Web site within a three-to-nine-month period, but what eBay really wanted was the "community of buyers" that had grown up around the site, which eBay viewed as consistent with its goal of being the "premier destination" for buyers and sellers on the Internet.

On the same day in June 2000, now-defunct Pets.com agreed to pay about $14 million to acquire Petstore.com. This purchase transferred the trademarks, Internet domain names, and live fish business of Petstore.com to Pets.com. The CEO of Pets.com said that there were two main rationales for engaging in the transaction. One was to acquire Petstore.com's advertising partnerships with Discovery Communications and Safeway that would help Pets.com reach more prospective buyers. The other was to obtain Petstore.com's customer lists. Naturally, Pets.com anticipated that acquiring Petstore.com would also remove a major source of online competition, thereby improving its own prospects for greater profitability.

Thus, two acquisitions of Internet sellers took place on the same day, and in both cases CEOs offered a common fundamental rationale: Access to customers. On the surface, therefore, both the acquisitions that eBay.com and Pets.com conducted were similar. There appeared to be a fundamental difference, however. In the C2C Internet auction market, eBay faced competition from thousands of rivals, with names such as UBid.com, Up4Sale.com, Haggle.com, and EWanted.com. The newly enlarged B2C retailer Pets.com, by way of contrast, faced competition from a rapidly shrinking group of online pet retailers, such as Championpuppy.com and Discounts4Pets.com. Nevertheless, Pets.com ultimately went out of business. By way of contrast, eBay solidified its dominant position within the Web auction marketplace by building its base of registered users to about 20 million.

Industry Structure
The number of and size distribution of firms within an industry.

As you will learn in this chapter, **industry structure**—the number of and size distribution of firms within the industry—can influence the production and pricing decisions of sellers. Although the number of rival sellers in an industry matters, so does the distribution of relative sizes of competing firms. As the owners and managers of Pets.com learned, becoming a dominant Internet firm selling a particular product is not necessarily a guarantee of success. At the same time, the presence of numerous fledgling rivals does not necessarily prevent one firm from dominating a marketplace, as eBay's performance demonstrated.

This chapter considers the extent to which we can attempt to apply basic concepts from principles of economics—the theories of firm production and costs, of perfect competition, and of monopoly—to the electronic marketplace. As you will learn in Chapter 3, most economists believe neither the theory of perfect competition nor the theory of monopoly apply to more than a limited range of issues within the realm of electronic commerce. Nevertheless, principles of economics can help us understand a number of essential e-commerce issues. Furthermore, the basic theories of perfect competition and monopoly are fundamental benchmarks of comparison that you will encounter in the remainder of this text. Hence, reviewing these theories and thinking about how to apply them within the electronic marketplace will prove extremely useful throughout your study of the economics of electronic commerce.

To consider an additional numerical illustration of a production function and diminishing returns, go to http://ingrimayne.saintjoe.edu/econ/TheFirm/ProductionFunct.html.

 ## Production and Costs for an Internet Seller

Production
The act of applying a technological process to inputs to manufacture a good or provide a service.

Any firm, whether it is a traditional *bricks-and-mortar company*—a firm that relies solely on traditional physical production, marketing, and distribution techniques—or a Web-based seller, engages in **production.** It does so by combining inputs using a technological process to manufacture goods or provide services and to distribute these products to consumers. A firm's production process includes not only making things or assisting people but also such activities as transporting or repackaging finished products, delivering services to various locations, and marketing and distributing products.

A FIRM'S PRODUCTION

Production Function
The relationship between the maximum output of a firm and the quantity of inputs utilized by the firm.

The relationship between the maximum physical output of a firm and the quantity of inputs that the firm uses to produce that output is called the firm's **production function.** Economists measure a firm's production as the volume of goods or services that the firm produces using inputs. Output is measured as a *rate* per unit of time, as contrasted with a level or a stock of a firm's inventories or assets at a point in time. The production function tells us nothing about how the market values either the output a firm produces or the inputs it uses.

Take a look at panel *(a)* of Figure 2-1, which displays a possible production function for an Internet-based banking firm that provides a standardized online

Figure 2-1:
Production at an Internet Bank.

Panel (a) shows that the maximum feasible number of financial-services packages that this Internet bank can provide increases as the bank hires more workers. Initially, the bank's output of financial-services packages increases more than proportionately as it hires additional workers who can specialize. Eventually, however, the law of diminishing marginal returns applies, and the slope of the production function, which is the marginal physical product of labor, declines. Thus, as shown in panel (b) the marginal product initially rises but then slopes downward.

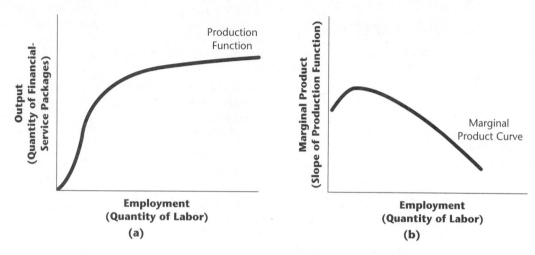

financial-service "package"—a defined set of credit-card, account-transfer, and household-bill-payment services—to actual and potential customers. Consider the bank's decisions over the **short run,** which is a period sufficiently short that the firm cannot alter the amount of at least one of its factors of production, such as labor, capital, land, and entrepreneurship. In this instance, suppose that the only variable factor of production is labor. The maximum feasible number of financial-services packages that the Internet bank can provide rises as the bank hires more employees, so the production function in panel *(a)* slopes upward over its entire range. (At one time, economists thought that e-commerce firms might view capital goods such as the number of servers or overall server capacities as variable factors of production, but short-run adjustments they made during the leveling off of U.S. economic activity in the early 2000s told a different story; see on the next page *Management Online: Short-Run Adjustments in the Virtual Marketplace Can Translate into Real Job Losses.*)

The Internet bank's production function is not, however, a straight line. At first, the bank's output of financial-services packages increases more than proportionately as it adds more employees, as indicated by the increasing slope of the production function at relatively low output rates. The reason is that there typically are gains from specialization as a firm hires additional workers. If the bank has, say, only two or three employees, then these people likely will have to

Short Run
An interval sufficiently brief that a firm cannot change the quantity of at least one of its factors of production.

MANAGEMENT *Online*

Short-Run Adjustments in the Virtual Marketplace Can Translate into Real Job Losses

E-commerce firms, such as Internet banks, online booksellers, C2C auction firms, and health-advice companies, demonstrate by their actions which factors of production are easier for them to adjust in the short run versus the long run. During the rapid growth of the electronic marketplace from the mid-1990s through the early 2000s, Internet sellers acquired large amounts of computer hardware, software, and workers. Economists began to speculate about what might happen if market downturns took place. Would the automation permitted by the computer hardware and Web servers put to use by

e-commerce firms lead them to respond by first scaling down on capital equipment while retaining their employees in the short run? Or would Internet firms behave like their counterparts in the physical marketplace, by issuing termination letters and engaging in mass layoffs?

Physical Labor Is a Variable Factor of Production Even in Virtual Markets

By late 2000 and early 2001, economists knew the answers to these questions. When U.S. economic activity began to falter and demand for products slackened off at a number of Internet sellers, job cuts mushroomed. Between July 2000 and January 2001, nearly 13,000 people lost jobs at dot-com firms. Then almost 12,000 jobs disappeared at e-commerce firms during February 2001 alone, followed by more than 9,500 job losses in March 2001.

continued

---

perform a wide variety of tasks, including Web-page design and construction, Web server monitoring, performing funds transfers among accounts, wiring funds for bill payments, and so on. As the bank hires more employees, a few can specialize in Web page development, while others can specialize in performing traditional banking functions using electronic processes. As a result, initially the bank is able to produce proportionately more output as it hires each additional worker.

Law of Diminishing Returns

An economic law that states that at some point the continued use of additional amounts of a variable factor together with fixed factors eventually results in progressively smaller increases in output.

Eventually, these gains from specialization are swamped by the **law of diminishing returns.** This economic law states that beyond some point, further increases in the amount of a variable factor such as labor, when used together with fixed factors such as capital—servers, financial-data-processing equipment, and so on—result in successively smaller increases in output. This explains why the slope of the production function in panel (b) of Figure 2-1 on page 37 declines at relatively higher employment levels. Consider, for instance, the capital constraint faced by an Internet bank's Web development team. The available capacity of the bank's Web server is fixed, as is space available on a customer's

Few of the cuts were mass layoffs. Nevertheless, at most companies they were significant relative work-force adjustments. At now-defunct Egghead.com, for instance, cutting 77 jobs in March 2001 reduced its employee base by 12 percent. When the company that owned eTown.com and ShopAudioVideo.com laid off 22 workers, the action also cut its total number of employees by about 22 percent.

Labor Laws Apply to E-Commerce Firms, Too
At some companies, the layoffs were more noticeable, both in absolute and percentage terms. When Amazon.com reduced its work force by 15 percent in February 2001, 1,300 employees lost their jobs. A 16 percent reduction at Barnesandnoble.com (http://www.bn.com) amounted to 350 workers.

Some Internet sellers got a crash course in labor law in the spring of 2001. They discovered that a federal law called the Worker Adjustment and Retraining Act applies not only to steelworkers but to Java programmers as well. Many e-commerce firms found themselves on the receiving end of dozens of lawsuits alleging that they failed to provide appropriate notification of job terminations and sufficient opportunities to retrain for other positions within the firms. Indeed, some Internet sellers found that this law makes labor not quite as variable a productive factor as they had previously thought.

For Critical Analysis:
Why might characteristics of labor versus computer hardware and software have led e-commerce firms to conclude that they should respond to a faltering economy by speedily downsizing their workforces instead of their hardware and software capabilities?

computer screen. At some point, adding more and more employees to the bank's Web development team will add little to the additional output of financial-service accounts. Likewise, with a fixed quantity of computer facilities at the bank, adding additional account-processing personnel also eventually leads to smaller increases in output of packages of financial services.

Figure 2-1 on page 37 shows two additional short-run production relationships. One of these is a curve indicating labor's **marginal product**, which is the additional output resulting from employment of an additional unit of labor along the production function. Because the slope of the production function is the "rise"—an increase in output—divided by the corresponding "run"—a given incremental increase in employment—the marginal product curve also indicates the *slope* of the production function at each possible quantity of labor. At first the marginal product curve slopes upward because of gains from specialization, but eventually it slopes downward because of the law of diminishing marginal returns.

Marginal Product
An addition to a firm's output stemming from using an additional unit of an input; the slope of the firm's production function.

A FIRM'S COSTS

A firm such as an Internet bank incurs two types of costs by engaging in production. The first is *fixed costs,* the expenses the firm incurs on its fixed factors of production, which do not change in the short run as the firm varies its output. The second is *variable costs,* the expenses the firm incurs on its variable factors. Because the Internet bank in this example has only labor as its variable factor, all variable costs are expenses on its employees.

Figure 2-2 shows how the *total costs* incurred by a firm such as an Internet bank, the sum of its fixed and variable costs, typically vary with its output. Naturally, the firm's total costs rise as it produces more output. The rate at which its costs increase varies depending on how much output the firm produces, so its total cost curve is not a straight line. At relatively low levels of output, and hence of employment (see panel *(a)* of Figure 2-1), gains in specialization allow the firm to produce more output via proportionately smaller labor expenses. Hence, at relatively low rates of output, successive increases in output result in smaller increases in the firm's total costs, so that at relatively low output rates the slope of the total cost curve decreases as the firm increases its output rate. The law of diminishing marginal returns tells us that eventually the firm can produce more output only if it incurs progressively higher labor expenses. Thus, the firm's total costs ultimately must begin to increase at a faster rate as the firm's output increases. This implies

Figure 2-2:
Cost Curves for an Internet Bank.

Panel (a) displays the total cost curve for this Internet bank. At an output rate of zero, the firm still incurs fixed costs, and it incurs variable costs as when it produces output. Initially the bank's variable costs rise at a decreasing rate as it is able to devote employees to specialized tasks. Because of the law of diminishing marginal returns, however, eventually the bank's variable costs rise at an increasing rate as it increases its output of financial-services packages. As panel (b) shows, the firm's average fixed cost declines as it increases its output. Its average variable, average total, and marginal cost curves initially slope downward as well, but ultimately both marginal and average costs increase because of the law of diminishing marginal returns.

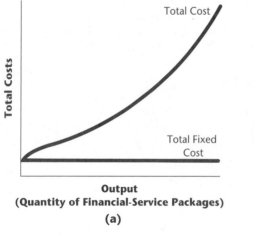

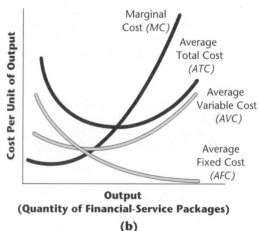

that at relatively high rates of output the slope of the total cost curve increases as the firm raises its output rate.

At each rate of output, the slope of the total cost curve in panel *(a)* is the additional cost that the firm incurs by producing one more unit of output, which economists call the firm's **marginal cost (MC).** The marginal cost curve slopes downward at first as the firm benefits from gains from specialization. Eventually the law of diminishing marginal returns applies, however, so that the marginal cost curve ultimately bends upward, as shown in panel *(b)*. For the same reason, the curve displaying **average variable cost (AVC),** variable costs divided by the firm's output, slopes downward at first but then slopes upward—at least for most bricks-and-mortar firms and for many Web-based firms (see the discussion of the economics of virtual products in Chapter 3). **Average fixed cost (AFC)** is the firm's fixed costs divided by its output, and this quantity must decline as output rises because the firm's fixed costs do not change as it varies its output. Hence, the curve displaying average fixed costs slopes downward. Finally, the firm's **average total cost (ATC)** at any given output rate is the sum of its average variable cost and its average fixed cost at that rate of output. Therefore, summing average variable cost and average fixed cost yields the points along the average total cost curve shown in panel *(b)*.

In the short run, all firms tend to have production and cost curves analogous to those displayed in Figure 2-1 and Figure 2-2. Firms' revenues and, consequently, the profits that they earn, however, depend on how their products are valued in the marketplace. In the remainder of the chapter, we examine alternative ways that firms' prices, revenues, and profits may be determined.

Marginal Cost (MC)
The additional cost that a firm incurs by producing one more unit of output; the slope of the firm's total cost curve.

Average Variable Cost (AVC)
A firm's variable costs divided by its output.

Average Fixed Cost (AFC)
A firm's fixed costs divided by its output.

Average Total Cost (ATC)
A firm's total costs divided by its output; the sum of the firm's average variable cost and its average fixed cost at that rate of output.

FUNDAMENTAL ISSUES ▼

1.
2.
3.
4.
5.

1. **What are the fundamental production and cost relationships for an e-commerce firm?**

   Like any other firm, an Internet seller's ability to produce output of goods or services in the short run, when the quantity of at least one factor of production is fixed, is determined by its production function. The production function indicates the maximum feasible amount of output that it can produce with variable and fixed factors of production. At first, the additional output produced by adding an additional unit of a variable factor such as labor rises with each unit employed, so the marginal product curve typically slopes upward at relatively low employment levels. Eventually, however, the law of diminishing returns applies, and the marginal product of labor begins to decline. This helps to account for why a firm's marginal cost initially declines as it raises its output over relatively low output rates, but then persistently rises at relatively higher rates of output.

The Electronic Marketplace: A Competitive Paradise?

During recent years it has been common to see media reports trumpeting the current and future benefits that consumers will reap from unhindered competition made possible by the Internet. Many observers argue that it has become so easy to establish a Web site that there is little to stop an intrepid entrepreneur from competing with any established company.

As we shall discuss, there are good arguments favoring and countering this position. Before you can evaluate these arguments, however, you must possess a concrete understanding of why consumers can benefit from unhindered competition with easy entry into (and exit from) a marketplace.

ESSENTIAL FEATURES OF PERFECT COMPETITION

Perfect Competition
An industry structure in which there are many consumers and many firms, each of which produces indistinguishable products, sells a miniscule fraction of total industry output, and can easily enter or leave the industry.

Perfect competition is the industry structure that those foreseeing big consumer benefits from Web-based competition have in mind. A perfectly competitive industry is composed of many firms that sell to a large number of consumers. Each firm sells a miniscule fraction of total industry output. In addition, perfectly competitive firms produce indistinguishable products. Thus, consumers are indifferent about which firm's product they purchase and consume. Finally, it is easy for firms to enter or leave the industry.

Marginal Revenue for a Perfectly Competitive Firm

The characteristics of perfect competition—many sellers and buyers, tiny portions of industry output produced by individual firms, identical products, and easy entry or exit—have a number of important logical implications. One of these is that at any quantity of output that a perfectly competitive firm may produce, its

Marginal Revenue
The additional revenue that a firm receives from selling one more unit of its product.

marginal revenue—the additional revenue that the firm can earn from selling an additional unit of its product—is always equal to the market price at which that firm and all others are able to sell each unit of output. As you shall see shortly, a firm could earn lower marginal revenue than the market price, but this would be inconsistent with maximizing the firm's profit.

Suppose that a single perfectly competitive firm in an electronic marketplace decides to stop taking customer orders at its Web site. Because this firm's output is a miniscule portion of total industry output, its departure will not have a noticeable effect on total output in the marketplace. Shoppers can simply enter the Web address of another firm in the industry and buy its product at the going market price. By implication, any action that a perfectly competitive Web-based firm might take cannot affect the market price. The firm can either keep its Web site open to customer orders at the market price, or it can suspend or close down the site.

Figure 2-3:
Profit Maximization for a Perfectly Competitive Internet Seller.

▼

In panel (a), the market price P_1 equates the total quantity demanded by all consumers in the market with the total quantity supplied by all firms in the perfectly competitive industry, Q_1. The individual e-commerce firm in panel (b) takes the market price as given and equal to the additional revenue it can earn from the sale of each additional unit of output. Thus, the firm's marginal revenue curve is horizontal at the market price. As long as the market price is higher than its minimum average variable cost, so that its total revenue at least covers its total variable cost, the firm maximizes its economic profit by producing to the point where marginal revenue equals marginal cost, or the rate of output Q_1^f. Hence, the portion of the firm's marginal cost curve above the minimum point of its average variable cost curve, or its shutdown point, is the firm's short-run supply curve. The industry supply curve is the summation of all firms' supply curves. The firm depicted in panel (b) earns a short-run economic profit equal to (P_1 − ATC_1) times Q_1^f, which is the shaded rectangular area.

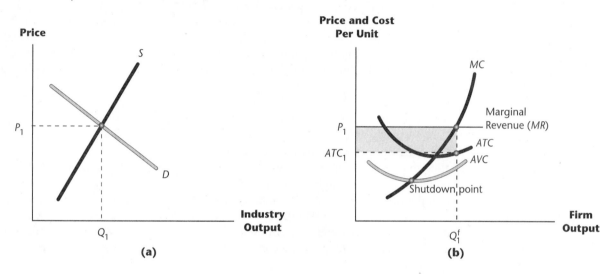

(a) (b)

Profit Maximization under Perfect Competition

A firm in any industry seeks to maximize **economic profit**—total revenue less all costs, including the opportunity cost of being in this business instead of some other business. Figure 2-3 shows how a typical Web-based firm in a perfectly competitive electronic marketplace maximizes its economic profit. In panel *(a)*, the market price of the product that the firm produces and sells, denoted P_1, is the price at which the total *quantity demanded* by all consumers equals the total *quantity supplied* by all producers. If the producer whose average and marginal cost and marginal revenue curves are displayed in panel *(b)* were to leave this industry, there would be no perceptible change in the position of the market supply curve. Hence, the market price P_1 is the per-unit revenue that the firm can earn from selling each additional unit of its output. As shown in panel *(b)*, therefore, the marginal revenue curve is horizontal at the price P_1. Each additional unit that the individual firm sells yields this additional revenue to the firm.

Economic Profit
Total revenue minus total expenses, including the opportunity cost of being in the current industry instead of an alternative industry.

Obtain the most recent estimates of U.S. firms' annual revenues and payroll expenses at http://www.census.gov/epcd/www/ smallbus. html.

To maximize its economic profit, the firm produces output to the point at which marginal revenue equals marginal cost. In the short-run situation shown in Figure 2-3, the firm's profit-maximizing output rate is Q_1^f. If it were to produce less output, marginal revenue, or the market price, would exceed marginal cost, so the firm could add to its profits by producing more units. If it were to raise its output above Q_1^f, then marginal cost would rise above marginal revenue, and the firm's profit would begin to fall. This is why Q_1^f is the output rate that maximizes the firm's profit.

Note that the firm could, in principle, charge a price different from the market price. If it chooses to charge a higher price, however, consumers will simply click on the Web sites of other firms that charge the lower, market price, and the firm will lose all its sales to its competitors. The firm could also charge a price below the market price and thereby earn a lower marginal revenue. Doing this, however, would not be consistent with maximizing the firm's economic profit. Hence, a profit-maximizing firm will not charge a price above or below the market price.

As shown in panel *(b)* of Figure 2-3, the firm's average total cost of producing Q_1^f units is ATC_1. We can find the firm's total profit, therefore, by multiplying ($P_1 - ATC_1$), the height of the shaded rectangle, by Q_1^f, the base of the rectangle. Thus, the shaded rectangle depicts a positive economic profit earned by the firm.

Supply Curves for the Firm and for the Marketplace

Note that if the market price were to rise for some reason, the individual firm in panel *(b)* would respond by equating this higher price and marginal revenue with marginal cost along its marginal cost curve, which would entail raising its rate of output. A rise in the market price, therefore, induces a movement along the firm's marginal cost curve and a consequent increase in its output. For this reason, over much of its range the perfectly competitive firm's marginal cost curve is the *firm's supply curve.*

The firm will not, however, produce over the range of the marginal cost curve that lies below the firm's average variable cost curve. Imagine what would happen if the firm continued to produce along the marginal cost curve even if the market price were less than the minimum feasible average variable cost at this firm. In this case, the product of the market price and the firm's output—its total revenue—would be less than the product of the average variable cost of this output rate and the firm's output—its total variable cost. Then the firm would experience a loss by utilizing variable inputs in production, plus it would have to pay its fixed costs. In this situation, the firm would be better off shutting down order-taking at its Web site, laying off all workers, and halting use of any other variable inputs, and paying only its fixed costs. Hence, the point where the firm's marginal cost curve crosses its average variable cost curve is the firm's *shutdown point,* and only the portion of the marginal cost curve above this point is the firm's supply curve.

The *market supply curve* in panel *(a)* of Figure 2-3 shows the total quantity supplied at every given price by all firms in the marketplace, including the individual firm in panel *(b)*. Summing the quantity supplied by this firm at each possible price, as indicated by its marginal cost curve above its shutdown point, with the quantities supplied by other firms yields this market supply curve.

FUNDAMENTAL ISSUES ▼

1.

2. **How are prices and quantities determined in a perfectly competitive electronic marketplace?**

2.

3.

In a perfectly competitive market, there are numerous consumers and many sellers, which produce essentially indistinguishable products and that can easily enter or leave the industry. Marginal revenue equals the market price for a perfectly competitive Internet seller. To maximize its economic profit—total revenue less all expenses, including the opportunity cost of being in its industry—an Internet seller produces output to the point where marginal revenue equals marginal cost. Hence, over most of its range the firm's marginal cost curve is its supply curve. Adding the quantities supplied by all firms in the marketplace yields the market supply curve. The market price adjusts to equilibrate the total quantity of the good or service supplied by all firms with the total quantity demanded by all consumers.

4.

5.

LONG-RUN EQUILIBRIUM UNDER PERFECT COMPETITION

The typical firm in the perfectly competitive market depicted in Figure 2-3 earns a positive economic profit. Thus, it earns revenues in excess of the opportunity cost of being in this industry instead of another. For instance, suppose that this firm is one of the many sites that opened to facilitate B2B exchanges during the late 1990s. The ability of this and other B2B firms to earn positive economic profits gives additional firms an incentive to enter this industry. In a perfectly competitive marketplace, it is easy for new firms to enter the industry, so entry should occur until there are no further opportunities to earn positive economic profits. Because the typical firm depicted in Figure 2-3 on page 43 earns a positive economic profit, the figure cannot illustrate a long-run equilibrium for this industry.

Producers and Consumers in Long-Run Equilibrium

As a number of additional firms enter the industry shown in Figure 2-3, the quantities that they are willing to supply at each possible price are added to the quantities by firms that were previously in the industry. As a result, the market supply curve shifts rightward. At the initial equilibrium price, there is an excess quantity supplied, and existing firms and new entrants bid down the price of their identical products. This decline in the market price pushes down marginal revenue at the typical firm in the industry. It reduces its output, and its profit begins to decline.

Figure 2-4 displays the long-run situation for the industry and for a typical firm within it following these adjustments. At the new market price P_{LR}, the firm's marginal revenue *(MR)* equals marginal cost *(MC)* at the minimum point of its average total cost curve *(ATC)*. The price it receives for each unit of output it sells just

www.

To find out how the Congressional Budget Office tries to judge whether banks engage in marginal cost pricing with automated teller machines, go to http://www.cbo.gov, and click on "Publications," then "Financial Institutions," and then "Competition in ATM Markets: Are ATMs Money Machines?"

.com

Figure 2-4:
Long-Run Equilibrium in a Perfectly Competitive Electronic Marketplace.

In a long-run perfectly competitive equilibrium, firms enter or exit the industry until each firm earns an accounting profit just sufficient to compensate for the opportunity cost of being in this industry instead of another. Hence, for a typical firm in the industry, the average total cost of producing the output, Q_{LR}^f in panel (b), just equals the long-run market price, P_{LR} that is determined by the intersection of the market supply and demand curves in panel (a), and the firm earns zero economic profit. Because the demand curve in panel (a) shows the prices that consumers would have been willing to pay for output levels up to the long-run market quantity Q_{LR}, for each unit of output up to this quantity consumers would have been willing to pay a higher price. Consequently, the triangular area shaded in panel (a) is the amount of consumer surplus received by consumers in this long-run market equilibrium.

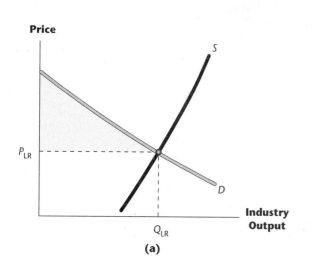

(a)

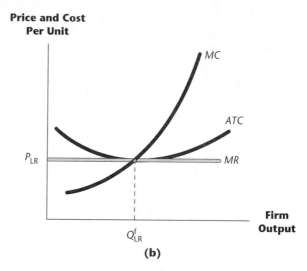

(b)

covers the average total cost of producing its output. Consequently, the typical firm in the industry earns *zero economic profit* in the long run. That is, its *accounting profit,* which equals revenues less explicit expenses, is just sufficient to cover the implicit opportunity cost of being in this line of business instead of an alternative line of business. Thus, in the long run there is no incentive for any firm to enter or leave the industry to pursue more lucrative opportunities. Furthermore, the typical firm operates at its greatest feasible **technical efficiency,** because the firm's average total cost is at its minimum feasible level.

Technical Efficiency
Production of an output rate at the minimum feasible average total cost.

Allocative Efficiency
Charging a price equal to the cost of producing the last unit of output sold; marginal cost pricing.

In addition, a perfectly competitive marketplace yields **allocative efficiency.** The market price P_{LR} is also equal to the firm's marginal cost, so that the market price that each firm charges for its product equals the additional cost of resources expended to produce the last unit that the firm sells to consumers.

Finally, the long-run equilibrium depicted in Figure 2-4 implies significant benefits to consumers, because many consumers would have been willing to pay more than the price P_{LR} for the market quantity Q_{LR}. The demand curve in panel (a) depicts the prices that consumers are willing to pay for each quantity that they might purchase. For every unit of output up to Q_{LR}, the demand curve indicates that consumers would have been willing to pay a higher price than Q_{LR}. Economists call the amount that consumers would have been willing to pay over and above the price that they actually pay for a good or service their **consumer surplus.** The total value of the consumer surplus in the long-run equilibrium for the marketplace is the shaded triangular area in panel *(a)* of Figure 2-4. This is the total amount that all consumers in this market would have been willing to pay, if necessary, to consume Q_{LR} units of output. They did not have to pay this additional amount, however, so the consumer surplus that consumers derive under perfect competition is a *welfare gain* to consumers.

Long-Run Industry Supply

Since the early 1990s a number of information-technology industries, including industries specializing in e-commerce, have grown considerably. Rising demands for the goods and services produced by these industries have spurred this growth. For instance, increased demand for computers has caused computer sales to grow significantly each year. Along the way, as the theory of perfect competition predicts, a number of firms have entered the computer industry in response to opportunities to earn economic profits. At the same time, computer prices have declined dramatically. A common measure of overall prices of computers and peripheral devices that economists use to track market prices in the computer industry has declined from a value of 61,640 in 1961 to below 35 today. This implies an average annual rate of price decline in the computer industry of about 19 percent per year.

Panel *(a)* of Figure 2-5 on page 48, illustrates why this dramatic price decline might have taken place in the computer industry. The demand for computers increased over time, from D_1 to D_2. The initial effect of this rise in demand was a movement from point E_1 to point E' and an increase in the market price to P'. As more computer producers entered the industry, however, the market supply curve shifted to the right, from S_1 to S_2. These new entrants and existing firms developed improved techniques for manufacturing and selling computers, which caused average production costs to decline significantly. As a result, on net the final equilibrium market price decreased considerably. This yields the downward-sloping curve through points E_1 and E_2. This curve, which displays the relationship between market prices and industry quantities after firms have had time to enter or leave an industry, is called **long-run industry supply.**

Because the long-run industry supply curve slopes downward in panel *(a)* of Figure 2-5, the computer industry is a good example of a **decreasing-cost industry.** In such an industry, a long-run increase in industry output brought about by entry of new firms and output expansion by existing firms brings about a reduction in the market price of the product of the firms in the industry.

Panel *(b)*, by way of contrast, illustrates an upward-sloping long-run industry supply curve for an **increasing-cost industry,** in which increases in demand for the industry's product and the rise in market supply resulting from entry of new firms and expansion of output by existing firms ultimately lead to higher average production costs and rising market prices. Panel *(c)* displays a horizontal long-run industry supply curve for a **constant-cost industry.** For such an industry, average production costs are unchanged within the industry as higher consumer demand brings about entry and output expansion.

Consumer Surplus
The amount consumers would have been willing to pay for a good or service over and above the price they actually pay in the marketplace.

Long-Run Industry Supply
The relationship between market prices and quantities in a perfectly competitive industry after firms have had time to enter or exit the industry.

Decreasing-Cost Industry
An industry in which a long-run expansion of industry output caused by entry of new firms causes a fall in the market price.

Increasing-Cost Industry
An industry in which a long-run expansion of industry output caused by entry of new firms results in an increase in the market price.

Constant-Cost Industry
An industry in which a long-run expansion of industry output caused by entry of new firms leaves the market price unchanged.

Figure 2-5:
Long-Run Industry Supply in a Perfectly Competitive Marketplace.

▼

In each of the panels, an increase in the demand for a good or service, from D_1 to D_2, causes a movement from an initial long-run equilibrium point E_1 to a new short-run equilibrium point E'. When the market price increases, existing firms begin to earn economic profits, which induces additional firms to enter the industry. Market supply increases, from S_1 to S_2, and a new long-run equilibrium results at point E_2. The curves containing the long-run equilibrium points E_1 and E_2 in each panel are long-run industry supply curves. Panel (a) shows a situation where the long-run industry supply curve slopes downward, which occurs in the case of a decreasing-cost industry. By way of contrast, panel (b) illustrates an increasing-cost industry, in which the long-run industry supply curve slopes upward. Finally, panel (c) depicts a horizontal long-run industry supply curve that arises in the case of a constant-cost industry.

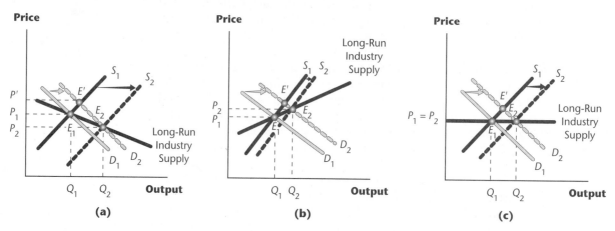

(a)   (b)   (c)

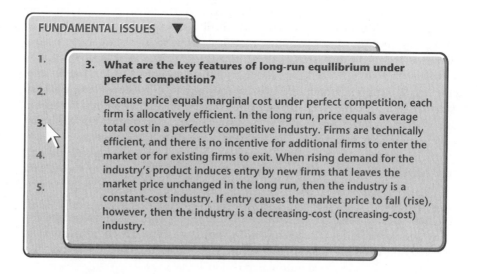

FUNDAMENTAL ISSUES ▼

1.

2.

3.

4.

5.

3. What are the key features of long-run equilibrium under perfect competition?

Because price equals marginal cost under perfect competition, each firm is allocatively efficient. In the long run, price equals average total cost in a perfectly competitive industry. Firms are technically efficient, and there is no incentive for additional firms to enter the market or for existing firms to exit. When rising demand for the industry's product induces entry by new firms that leaves the market price unchanged in the long run, then the industry is a constant-cost industry. If entry causes the market price to fall (rise), however, then the industry is a decreasing-cost (increasing-cost) industry.

In Search of Scale and Scope Economies on the Net

Naturally, costs incurred in operating a business have considerable bearing on a company's choices of how many people to hire, what types of equipment to purchase or lease, what types of goods or services to produce, and how many units to try to sell. This is as true for Web-based businesses as for traditional firms. Nevertheless, the nature of costs faced by many Internet sellers differs from those of bricks-and-mortar companies. To understand why this is so, you must understand the concepts of economies of scale and economies of scope.

ECONOMIES OF SCALE AND SCOPE

A firm incurs costs because it must purchase the services of factors of production—labor, capital, land, and entrepreneurship—to manufacture its goods or to provide its services. The firm's long-run costs change as it alters its rates of usage of all these factor services, thereby giving rise to economies of scale or scope.

Economies of Scale

The earlier discussion of perfectly competitive markets presumed that there was no perceptible difference between short-run costs and long-run costs. Of course, over a short-run horizon, firms are unable to vary at least one factor of production, such as capital. Over a long-run horizon, a fundamental factor influencing the optimal size, or *scale,* of a firm is its **long-run average cost,** which is the ratio of the firm's total production cost to its output when it is able to adjust quantities of all factors of production, including capital as well as land, labor, and entrepreneurship. Typically, firms are able to adjust their capital over a relatively long period, the *long run,* which stretches from months to years. For most firms, over relatively small ranges of output long-run average cost usually declines as they expand their ability to produce additional units of a product. When this happens, a firm experiences **economies of scale,** which arise any time that an increase in the amount of a firm's output leads to a decrease in its long-run average cost.

Economies of scale may arise because of new opportunities for specialization in the use of production factors. For instance, a larger firm might be able to reduce its long-run average cost by dividing its existing work force into separate units that focus on specific aspects of its production process. A company might be able to take advantage of physical processes that permit it to produce more output with proportionately fewer inputs. For example, consider a liquids-storage company that wins much of its business in B2B exchanges. The company specializes in storing hazardous liquids, such as chemicals or other potentially dangerous fluids. It can gain from using larger storage containers, because the volume of containers, which helps determine the company's shipping capacity, rises more than proportionately with the surface area of the containers. The surface area is a key factor in determining how much steel or plastic must be used in container construction.

Long-Run Average Cost
A firm's total cost divided by its output when the firm has sufficient time to alter its utilization of all factors of production.

Economies of Scale
A reduction in long-run average cost that accompanies an increase in output.

Diseconomies of Scale
An increase in long-run average cost that accompanies an increase in output.

Economies of scale normally are not unbounded, however. As a company continues to enlarge the scale of its operations, it encounters factors that can result in **diseconomies of scale,** or increases in long-run average cost generated by increases in its output. This occurs, for instance, when layers of supervision increase as a company's scale of operations increase, so that the costs of compiling information and maintaining communication among managers and employees grow more than proportionately with the size of the firm.

As shown in Figure 2-6, a typical company finds that as it increases its size, initially it experiences economies of scale. As it raises its scale of operations further, it will begin to experience higher long-run average costs and diseconomies of scale. The scale of operations at which economies of scale end and diseconomies of scale begin is the firm's **minimum efficient scale.** This is the firm size at which the company minimizes its long-run average cost. When all firms in a given industry have achieved their minimum efficient scale, then the industry itself operates at an overall minimum efficient scale.

Minimum Efficient Scale
The output rate at which a firm minimizes its long-run average cost.

Figure 2-6:
The Long-Run Average Total Cost Curve and the Minimum Efficient Scale.

The average total cost that a firm incurs when it is able to adjust the overall scale of its operations by varying all of its factors of production, including its capital and other inputs, is the firm's long-run average total cost. For most firms, long-run average total cost initially declines as the scale of operations increases, and over this range of output the firm experiences economies of scale. At the firm's minimum efficient scale, its long-run average total cost is minimized. If the firm were to increase its scale of operations beyond the minimum efficient scale, its long-run average total cost would increase, and it would experience diseconomies of scale.

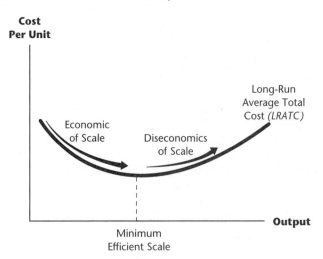

Economies of Scope

Not all firms manufacture or provide a single good or service. Economists often call companies that produce multiple goods or services *multiproduct firms.*

A company that experiences a long-run cost advantage from being a multiproduct firm takes advantage of **economies of scope.** The cost of producing two or more goods or services within that single firm is less than the combined costs that separate firms would incur if they were to produce each good or service individually.

Some multiproduct firms experience economies of scope from using common inputs to produce an assortment of goods or services. For instance, most telephone companies provide two types of services. One is switched local service, which connects one local phone with another through a computer switch in a central office. The other is switched toll service, under which the central office directs the call to a toll facility that aggregates long-distance calls and routes them to a local exchange at a distant location. Most estimates indicate that there are substantial cost savings associated with routing both types of phone traffic through a single local network instead of two separate networks.

Economies of Scope
The cost of producing two or more goods or services within one firm is lower than the combined costs at separate firms if they were to individually produce each good or service.

SCALE AND SCOPE ECONOMIES ON THE INTERNET

Economies of scale and scope affect the long-run scale of firms and the long-run mix of products that firms produce and sell. Both aspects of firms' long-run costs, therefore, have significant effects on an industry's structure.

There are good reasons to believe that economies of scale may be an important factor in many e-commerce industries. Consider companies that sell downloadable computer files, such as office productivity software, anti-virus programs, digital music, or e-books (books that can be purchased and read online). Once companies have created such products, they can produce copies at very low cost (think, for instance, how simple it is to copy a file from the hard disk of a computer to a diskette, Zip disk, or CD). This means that the average cost of producing additional output can fall rapidly—and persistently—as a firm specializing in such a product expands its output rate. Hence, the minimum efficient scale for firms in some e-commerce industries may be relatively large, thereby limiting the number of firms that may efficiently operate within the industry.

In addition, as Chapter 3 will discuss in greater detail, some e-commerce industries may have the potential to become **network industries,** in which the value that consumers place on the product that firms in the industry produce varies with the number of other people who consume the product. For example, a particular brand of office productivity software is likely to be more useful for an individual who co-authors memos or reports with a fellow worker located hundreds of miles away if the two can e-mail draft documents back and forth and alter the documents using the same word-processing software. Their task may be further eased if they can use the same data-processing software to create tables, charts, and figures to insert into the documents. Office-productivity-software

Network Industry
An industry in which the value that consumers place on the industry's product depends in part on how many other people consume the product.

companies and other e-commerce firms that can produce goods or services that are highly *interoperable*—easy for people to apply across various types of applications—can develop an advantage over other firms. In many instances, firms in network industries can also take advantage of economies of scope—for instance, using the software programming talents of existing employees to reduce the expense of developing different types of office-productivity-software products—to reduce their overall operating expenses.

FUNDAMENTAL ISSUES ▼

1.

2.

3.

4.

5.

> **4. How can economies of scale and scope matter in the electronic marketplace?**
>
> A firm experiences economies of scale when its average production cost declines as it expands its output in the long run by adjusting the quantities of all production factors. It experiences economies of scope when it can produce two or more goods or services at lower cost than separate firms could have produced the same goods or services individually. In many industries, successive increases in a firm's output eventually lead to a higher long-run average cost, so that diseconomies of scale occur. The point at which long-run average cost is minimized defines the firm's minimum efficient scale. In some e-commerce industries, it is very inexpensive to produce additional copies of firms' products, so economies of scale can be significant over a relatively large range of output. Economies of scope also may be important, especially for firms in network industries in which the willingness of a given customer to purchase a firm's products may depend on how many other people consume its products and on how well its products function when used together.

 ## Playing Monopoly, or Trying— First Movers as Dominant Firms

In the early days of e-commerce, companies rushed to set up shop on the Web. Many feared that they might fail if they were not among the first to establish an e-commerce presence. Others were convinced that getting online first would allow them to establish a dominant market position. Both perspectives were, of course, inconsistent with the implications of perfect competition. Let's consider how an initial entrant might try to establish dominance in the electronic marketplace.

BARRIERS TO ENTRY

Industries with relatively small numbers of firms exist because of **barriers to entry,** which are factors that prevent entrepreneurs from immediately creating a new firm. There are five basic types of entry barriers. One is the presence of significant economies of scale. If companies in an industry find that increasing the scale of their operations continues to reduce long-run average cost up to relatively large output rates, then it may be that only a few firms can achieve minimum efficient scale within a marketplace.

A second barrier to entry is also cost-related. It is the possibility that a new entrant might have to incur a large fixed expense to initiate operations within a market. Successful entry, for instance, might entail making a "big splash." This could require owners to raise significant initial start-up funds so that they could purchase quantities of factor services necessary to establish a noticeable presence in the industry.

A third barrier to entry is exclusive ownership of a relatively large portion of the total stock of a key resource used to produce a good or service. For many years, one diamond firm, De Beers, owned mines containing a large portion of the world's uncut diamonds. This permitted De Beers to dominate the world's diamond market until the 1990s, when other diamond discoveries occurred and new mining firms began to enter the market for uncut diamonds. This type of barrier to entry is less likely to arise in the electronic marketplace.

A fourth barrier to entry can arise from differences among products that firms produce. In some instances, it may be possible that a company has a **first-mover advantage** in an industry. During its time as the only firm in the market, the firm takes advantage of relatively low marketing costs to establish a long-term entry barrier by identifying its product as the *industry* product. It took a number of years, for example, before later entrants to the copy machine industry were able to overcome the tendency of many people to think of copying pages as "Xeroxing" them.

Fifth, governments can erect barriers to entry by sanctioning government-sponsored firms or by establishing licensing requirements for an industry and then restricting the number of licenses. (Comparing the experiences of the Internet-service-provider industries of Morocco and Tunisia helps illustrate what a difference government-erected entry barriers can make; see on the next page *Globalization Online: Mobile in Morocco.*)

Barriers to Entry
Factors hindering entrepreneurs from opening a new firm within an industry.

First-Mover Advantage
A competitive advantage that the first firm in an industry obtains because it initially faces no rivals and that it may be able to maintain if it can operate at a lower cost than potential rivals or develop good will with customers that rivals cannot readily duplicate.

MONOPOLIES AND DOMINANT FIRMS

The existence of barriers to entry makes the entry of new firms difficult in the short run and much more costly in the long run. This naturally tends to limit the number of firms in the industry. Firms protected by barriers to entry can produce rates of output that are relatively large compared with the total output of the industry, and changes in their output rates can influence the market price. As a consequence, firms protected by entry barriers can engage in *strategic pricing*. That is, when these firms set prices, they recognize that their decisions will affect the choices of consumers and the pricing decisions of rival producers.

GLOBALIZATION *Online*

Mobile in Morocco

Half of the residents of Morocco do not have access to elec-tricity or running water. Four-fifths of its villages do not have paved roads. Traditional phone lines serve only about 6 per-cent of the country's population. Nevertheless, more than 85 percent of Morocco's population of just over 28 million peo-ple has access to mobile phones. Today many of these people also have wireless access to the Internet. They are served by hundreds of Internet service providers (ISPs).

Privatization to the Rescue

Even though Tunisia was the first country in northern Africa to offer Internet access, it still only has two ISPs. Tunisia's popula-tion is less than one-third of Morocco's, but this population difference alone cannot explain the big difference in the num-ber of ISPs.

The main reason that Morocco is so far ahead in wireless phone and Internet service is that in 1999 it turned to the pri-vate sector. The Moroccan government was looking for ways to raise funds. It decided to auction off government-owned

telecommunication companies to private bidders. Then it began selling licenses to other telecommunication start-up companies. Before long, wireless telecommunication was a highly competitive business in Morocco.

A Regional Web Hub?

Bypassing traditional phone lines has allowed Morocco to leapfrog old telephone technologies that would have required years for the country's residents to develop. Because Morocco is so much more advanced in telecommunications than its neighbors, it may well become a regional hub for Internet-based commerce.

Already, several Moroccan-based satellite networks are in operation, and there is discussion of bypassing traditional tele-vision service via the wireless Web.

For Critical Analysis:

In Tunisia, the two existing Internet service providers are both closely connected to the national government. What might Tunisia learn from Morocco's experience?

Monopoly
A single producer in a marketplace.

Monopoly

One special case of strategic pricing is cooperative decision making. In principle, by working together a few firms can establish a *cartel* and restrain their output, coordinate their pricing decisions, and maximize their joint profit. Essentially, they then act as a **monopoly,** or single producer in a marketplace. True monop-oly situations involving either a single firm or a cartel are relatively rare. Never-theless, traditionally, local telephone, water, and energy services often are pro-vided by government-regulated monopolies. Cartels that mimic a monopoly are perhaps even more rare. The reason is that each cartel member typically has an incentive to cheat on a cartel agreement by expanding its production above limits established by the cartel. Thus, most cartels fail to act as a single monopoly pro-ducer for long.

Figure 2-7:
Monopolistic versus Perfectly Competitive Electronic Markets.

Under the assumption that marginal cost is constant and therefore equal to average total cost at every output rate, the short-run supply curve for each firm and for the industry as a whole is horizontal under perfect competition. The market price, P_{PC}, is equal to marginal cost, and the industry output is the quantity demanded at this price, which is Q_{PC}. The value of consumer surplus is the large shaded triangle. If the firms in this industry could coordinate their production, however, they could act as a cartel monopoly and produce only to the point where marginal revenue equals marginal cost. The marginal revenue for the cartel would slope downward, because while a price reduction tends to increase sales, it also reduces revenues on all previous units, so that marginal revenue is less than price at any given quantity. The cartel monopoly would produce Q_M units of output, which it would sell at the price that consumers are willing to pay as revealed by the demand curve, which is P_M. Under monopoly, the value of consumer surplus declines to the smaller dashed triangle.

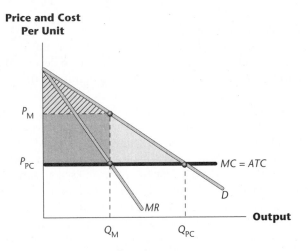

The effective operation of a cooperative cartel tends to reduce consumer welfare. To see why, look at Figure 2-7. It displays a market demand curve that is faced either by a perfectly competitive or monopolistic industry. If firms in the industry are able to form a cartel and act as a monopoly, then if the monopoly wishes to sell an additional unit of its product, it must reduce the price that it charges. One effect of a price reduction is an increase in the quantity of its product that its customers desire to consume at the lower price, which tends to raise the firm's revenues. Another effect of a price cut, however, is a reduction in revenues on the fewer units the firm could have sold at a higher price. This implies that at any quantity the cartel monopoly sells, its marginal revenue is always less than the price it charges. Hence, the cartel's marginal revenue curve lies below the demand curve. Marginal revenue declines if the firm reduces its price, so the cartel's marginal revenue curve slopes downward.

To simplify, let's assume that under perfect competition the market supply curve is perfectly elastic, which is the situation if the marginal cost of each firm in the industry is constant and identical. This automatically implies that marginal cost and average cost are equal. Under perfect competition the market price, P_{PC}, is equal to marginal cost, and total industry output is equal to the quantity demanded at this price, which is Q_{PC}. Consumer surplus, therefore, is given by the large shaded triangle in the diagram.

If this industry is monopolistic, then the cartel faces the market demand curve and the indicated marginal revenue curve. To maximize its profit, the monopoly cartel produces to the point at which marginal revenue equals marginal cost, which is the quantity Q_M in Figure 2-7. Firms within the cartel then charge the price that consumers are willing to pay, which is P_M. Consumer surplus thereby shrinks to the dashed triangle above this monopoly price. In this way, consumers are worse off. Their welfare is lower under monopoly.

The First-Mover Advantage of Amazon.com

Dominant Firm
A firm that sells the bulk of industry output and has the ability to set the market price in the face of entry by other price-taking firms.

True monopoly rarely persists, especially on the Internet. But in emerging industries, firms can sometimes use a first-mover advantage to develop a position as the **dominant firm** in a market. Like a monopoly, a dominant firm sets its price.

Amazon is one example of a dominant firm in an electronic marketplace. Amazon first cracked the bookselling market by opening up shop on the Internet in 1995. At that time, Barnes & Noble was the largest nationwide bookstore chain, with more than 11 million square feet of selling space and about 10,000 full-time and 10,000 part-time employees. Even though "Books.com" (since acquired by Barnes & Noble) was actually the first Internet bookseller, Amazon leapfrogged into an effective first-mover advantage by offering more than a million titles on its Web site. If a customer ordered a book that was not in stock, Amazon immediately submitted an order for the book to a wholesaler, which then shipped it to Amazon's distribution warehouse to be shipped on to the customer. This "just-in-time" model for filling customer orders allowed Amazon to keep its inventory expenses very low. The company also held down its operating costs by locating its headquarters in a lower-rent district in Seattle and, as the company's CEO Jeff Bezos liked to say, by "skimping on everything but people and computers."

Between December 1995 and late 1997, the average number of daily visits to Amazon's Web site increased from 2,000 to 1 million. In 1997, Barnes & Noble realized that the electronic marketplace was becoming a trading center for books, and the company developed its own colorful "virtual storefront" and Web-based book-information services. A few months later, Books-A-Million established a Web-based bookstore (http://www.bamm.com), and within the next year Borders (http://www.borders.com) and a number of independent booksellers also opened bookselling operations on the Internet. Amazon responded to these electronic-marketplace entrances by broadly expanding its list of discounted books. Today, Amazon remains the dominant Web-based bookseller. Nevertheless, its rivals have established a foothold in the electronic book market, which has experienced a rapid rise in annual book sales, from about 20 million books in 1997 to more than 60 million today.

Figure 2-8:
A Dominant First Mover and Competitive Fringe in an Electronic Marketplace.

A first mover, or dominant firm, initially faces the market demand curve D in panel (a). Suppose, however, that a fringe group of firms is able to enter the market, and is willing to provide output of the good or service at any product price above P_1 along the supply curve S in panel (b). At prices above P_1, therefore, consumers wish to purchase correspondingly less output from the dominant firm, so its effective (or residual) demand curve is D' in panel (a), and its effective marginal revenue curve is the discontinuous curve MR. The dominant firm produces output to the point where marginal revenue equals marginal cost. Consequently, the dominant firm produces Q_D^* units and charges the price P^* that consumers are willing to pay for this amount. At this price, fringe firms sell Q_F^* units.

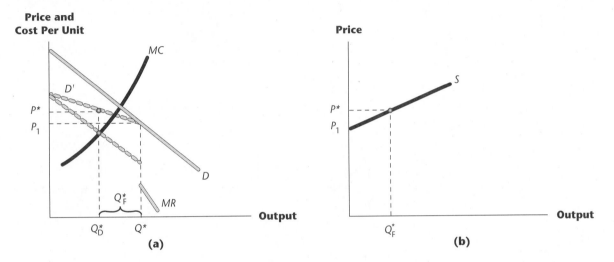

The Dominant First Mover and the Competitive Fringe

To evaluate the evolution of the electronic marketplace for books, we can apply the theory of a *dominant firm facing a competitive fringe*. In this theory, the dominant firm, such as Amazon, has a large market share, perhaps because it was the first market entrant. Initially, only the dominant firm faces the market demand, which is the straight-line demand curve *D* in panel *(a)* of Figure 2-8.

Suppose, however, that a fringe group of firms, such as Barnes & Noble, Books-A-Million, and others are able to overcome part of the entry barriers they face and establish a foothold in the marketplace. The sum of the short-run supply curves for these firms is the fringe supply curve *S* in panel *(b)*. At any product price above P_1, these firms stand ready to supply quantities along the curve *S*. From the perspective of Amazon, the dominant firm, online entry by fringe suppliers reduces the net quantity of products that customers demand by these quantities at each price above P_1. Consequently, in the presence of this competitive fringe the effective demand curve that the dominant firm faces nets out these quantities supplied by the fringe suppliers. This effective demand curve, which economists call the *residual demand curve* for the dominant firm, is D' in panel *(a)*.

Because the residual demand curve is shallower above the price P_1, its effective marginal revenue curve, *MR*, is more shallow over the corresponding range. As a

Figure 2-9:
A Dominant First Mover and Free Entry by Firms in the Competitive Fringe.

In the case where the first mover, or dominant firm, faces fringe competition from firms within a constant-cost industry, the fringe firms enter freely as long as the output price exceeds P**. Hence, the supply curve for the fringe firms, S in panel (b), is horizontal at this market price, and the dominant firms' effective (or residual) demand curve D' is horizontal at this price. In panel (a), the dominant firm produces to the point at which marginal revenue, which in this situation equals the price P**, equals marginal cost. Hence the dominant firm sells Q_D^* units. The fringe firms supply Q_F^* units.

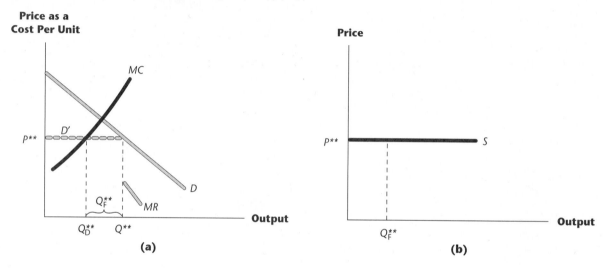

result, the marginal revenue curve has a discontinuity at the quantity correspon-ding to the price P_1. The dominant firm still maximizes its economic profit by pro-ducing to the point where marginal revenue equals marginal cost, and in this case it produces Q_D^* units of output. It charges the price that its customers are will-ing to pay. The residual demand curve indicates that this price is P^*. Under the as-sumption that the fringe firms take this price as given, they sell Q_F^* units of output. If each fringe supplier's average total cost is less than P^*, then fringe firms earn economic profits.

Suppose that the long-run fringe supply curve is horizontal, as shown in panel *(b)* of Figure 2-9, so that for fringe firms this is a constant-cost industry. For the dominant firm, the residual demand curve is horizontal at the price P^{**}, and this horizontal portion of the residual demand curve is also the dominant firm's marginal revenue curve at this price. The dominant firm produces to the point at which marginal revenue, which in this case is the price, P^{**}, equals marginal cost, and produces Q_D^{**} units to sell at this price. This leaves Q_F^{**} units for the fringe firms to supply to the marketplace. Note that this outcome depends on an impor-

MANAGEMENT *Online*

Was It Irrational for People to Pay Amazon.com More for a Book than They Could Have Paid Books.com?

How was Amazon able to retain its dominance of the Internet book market in the face of entry by many other competitors? In a study of how consumers responded to changing incentives when they first began to shop for books on the Internet, Erik Brynjolfsson and Michael Smith of the Massachusetts Institute of Technology have provided one explanation.

Higher Web Prices at Amazon.com

Brynjolfsson and Smith gathered more than 10,000 observations of the prices charged by traditional bricks-and-mortar bookstores and Internet booksellers. What they found was what most economists would predict: Lower business expenses incurred by Internet booksellers allowed them to charge about 8 percent less for a given book than traditional bookstores. Furthermore, the cost advantage of Internet booksellers allowed them to gain market share at the expense of traditional stores. (A number of bricks-and-mortar booksellers initially included in the study went out of business before the study ended!)

One finding seemed surprising, however. Even though Amazon quickly garnered an 80 percent share of all Internet-based book sales, it charged an average of $1.60 more per book than Books.com. Nevertheless, Books.com was unable to push its market share much above 2 percent during the period of the study.

The Value of Trust—and a Patent

On the surface, the fact that Amazon outpaced Books.com and other Internet booksellers, even though it charged slightly higher prices, seemingly points to irrational consumers. After all, wouldn't everyone want to choose Books.com and save $1.60 per book?

As the authors suggest, this would be true only if all factors other than price were identical across booksellers. During the period their study examined, however, all other factors were not the same. For instance, Brynjolfsson and Smith's study did not take into account differences in features of the two companies' Web sites. If people already knew how to use Amazon's Web site, then a legitimate question to ask is, would the average person learning for the first time how to shop on the Internet have considered $1.60 enough to compensate for

continued

tant assumption, which is that the dominant firm has its own separate cost curves that permit it to sell at an average total cost below the constant average cost incurred by fringe firms. This allows the dominant firm to maintain a significant market share through a superior production method, a more efficient marketing approach that gives it a goodwill advantage over its rivals, or some other source of long-term competitive advantage. (This may the situation in the Internet book market; see *Management Online: Was It Irrational for People to Pay Amazon.com More for a Book Than They Could Have Paid Books.com?*)

continued from page 59
having to learn how to order a book from another Web site?

Furthermore, Amazon spent a considerable amount on advertising to get a jumpstart on its Internet rivals. Even today, a great many Internet buyers have heard of Amazon but are unfamiliar with a number of its competitors. This made Brynjolfsson and Smith wonder if people felt confident that Amazon really would deliver but might not have as much faith in less-known Internet companies. Thus, part of the $1.60 difference in the average price of a book might have amounted to a "trust premium." If so, this is consistent with the dominant-firm model's implication that Amazon can maintain it sizable market share if it has a goodwill advantage over the competitive fringe that it faces.

Finally, at the time it entered the Internet bookselling business, Amazon patented a "one-click" purchase method that made its Web site easier to use, as compared with rival Internet booksellers. Undoubtedly this also gave Amazon a cost advantage, because any other would-be rival was stuck with trying to develop a comparable Internet shopping process—or with paying Amazon for the right to use the one-click process at the rival's own site.

For Critical Analysis:

In Figures 2-8 and 2-9, the dominant firm can earn a positive economic profit. In fact, however, Amazon only recently began to earn a positive accounting profit from selling books, and several fringe firms in the Internet bookselling business have earned accounting losses. Does this necessarily imply that neither Amazon nor fringe suppliers are profit-maximizing firms?

Limit Pricing: A Credible Threat?

In the 1950s and 1960s, long before the Internet marketplace had ever been contemplated, economists proposed a way that a dominant first mover such as Amazon might forestall entry by potential rivals. In Figure 2-9 on page 58, the dominant firm maximizes its profit by charging the price P^{**}. Suppose, however, that the dominant firm chooses instead to charge a price *below* P^{**}, thereby engaging in what economists call **limit pricing** by setting its price below the average cost of production at potential competitors.

Limit Pricing
Discouraging entry of potential rivals by setting a price below their average production cost.

Limit pricing would forestall entry by fringe firms, but it also would reduce the dominant firm's current profit, as well as its profit during each future period that it continued to keep its price artificially low. Consequently, a dominant firm that tries to engage in limit pricing performs a delicate balancing act. It must balance a future profit reduction it may experience following entry of fringe suppliers against the current profit reduction it certainly will experience if it charges a price below the profit-maximizing level in the presence of fringe firms.

Most people, including owners of a firm, discount the future relative to the present, so the most likely decision for a dominant firm is *not* to engage in limit pricing. In the real world, therefore, dominant first movers such as Amazon typically do not set prices sufficiently low to discourage the entry of fringe competitors. The common pattern is for the dominant firm to experience a gradual decline in its market share, followed by a transition to an alternative mode of competition within the marketplace that the firm no longer dominates. Hence, gaining a first-mover advantage in the electronic marketplace undoubtedly can yield considerable long-term benefits to the owners of an Internet seller. Those benefits are likely to dissipate over time, however. In the case of Amazon, its online bookselling market share has fallen from about 80 percent in 1997 to roughly 65 percent today.

FUNDAMENTAL ISSUES ▼

1.

2.

3.

4.

5.

5. What happens if a single firm dominates an electronic marketplace?

In an electronic marketplace, high start-up costs and economies of scale may be entry barriers that hinder growth in the number of firms within an e-commerce industry. A firm that first enters the marketplace may also benefit from a first-mover advantage. For a time it might even be able to function as a monopoly, which results in a higher market price, lower market quantity, and reduced consumer surplus as compared with a perfectly competitive market. A firm may remain the dominant firm in the market even following the entry of a competitive fringe if it can produce at lower cost than other competitors, if being the first mover gives it long-lasting goodwill with consumers, or if it has some other advantage. Nevertheless, maximizing its current profit usually entails pricing its product above its marginal production cost, resulting in a gradual erosion of its market share to the competitive fringe.

Chapter Summary

1) **Fundamental Production and Cost Relationships for an E-Commerce Firm:** An Internet seller's production function shows the maximum feasible amount of output that a firm can produce using fixed factors of production and various quantities of at least one variable factor of production. Initially the gain in output resulting from employing one more

unit of a variable factor such as labor increases with each unit employed. Thus, the marginal product curve typically slopes upward at relatively low employment levels. Nevertheless, the law of diminishing returns eventually holds, so that the marginal product of labor begins to decline with further increases in labor employment. As a result, a firm's marginal cost initially declines as it raises its output at relatively low rates of output but then persistently rises at relatively higher rates of output.

2) **Determination of Prices and Quantities in a Perfectly Competitive Electronic Marketplace:** In a perfectly competitive market, there are many consumers, and there are also numerous sellers, each of which produces a miniscule portion of total industry output of a product that is essentially identical across firms. For a perfectly competitive e-commerce firm, marginal revenue equals market price. Maximizing economic profit thereby entails equating price with marginal cost. The firm's marginal cost curve is its supply curve, and adding the quantities supplied by that firm to the quantities supplied by all other firms in the marketplace yields the market supply curve. At the market price, the total quantity of the good or service supplied by all firms equals the total quantity demanded by all consumers.

3) **Key Features of Long-Run Equilibrium under Perfect Competition:** In long-run equilibrium, a perfectly competitive e-commerce firm produces to the point where price equals marginal cost, so the firm is allocatively efficient. In addition, price equals average total cost in the long run, so each firm is technically efficient, and there is no incentive for firms to enter or leave the industry. If increased demand for the industry product that results in entry by new firms leaves market price unchanged in the long run, then the industry is a constant-cost industry. If entry causes the market price to fall (rise), however, then the industry is a decreasing-cost (increasing-cost) industry.

4) **How Economies of Scale and Scope Can Make a Difference in the Electronic Marketplace:** Economies of scale exist when a firm's long-run average production cost declines as it increases its output scale. A firm ultimately experiences diseconomies of scale, or higher long-run average cost with a higher output rate, beyond the firm's minimum efficient scale at which long-run average cost is minimized. In some e-commerce industries, firms can produce additional copies of their products at very low cost, so economies of scale may be significant up to relatively large rates of output. Economies of scope arise when a firm produces two or more goods or services at lower cost than separate firms could have produced the same goods or services individually. Firms in network industries may be well positioned to take advantage of economies of scope. In such industries, the willingness of a given customer to purchase a firm's products may depend on how many other people consume its products and on how well its products function when used together. The ability to produce two or more related products at lower cost than individual firms could give multiproduct e-commerce firms a cost advantage over other, single-product producers.

5) **A Dominant Firm in an Electronic Marketplace:** In an electronic marketplace, high start-up costs and economies of scale may be entry barriers that deter entry into an e-commerce industry. A firm that first enters the marketplace may also benefit from a first-mover advantage. For a time it might even be able to function as a monopoly, which results in a higher market price, lower market quantity, and reduced consumer surplus, as compared with a perfectly competitive market. It might remain the dominant firm in the market, even following the entry of firms on the competitive fringe, if it can produce at lower cost than the competitors, if being the first mover gives it long-lasting goodwill with consumers, or if it has some other advantage. Nevertheless, maximizing its current profit usually entails pricing its product above its marginal production cost, resulting in a gradual erosion of its market share to the competitive fringe

Questions and Problems

1) A large number of firms have sought to develop Web-based telephone services, called *Internet telephony,* in which phone transmissions flow over the Internet as packets of information, just like e-mail messages. Each firm offers essentially the same telephony product, but this technology has been slow to develop, and transmission quality remains spotty. The overall demand for the services provided in this industry has been relatively low. Explain why it therefore makes sense that many firms have struggled to justify keeping their operations going in the short run and to remain financially afloat in the long run.

2) Between 1997 and 1999, many dot-com businesses set up shop on the Internet. In 2000, a number of these businesses reduced the range of product offerings that they made available on the Web. Others stopped offering products entirely but maintained their sites as they searched for possible buyers or partners. Still others closed down their sites entirely. For which of these firms did product prices likely fall below their shutdown points (or in some cases, did shutdown points rise above market prices), but not sufficiently to induce them to exit the electronic marketplace? Explain your reasoning.

3) The market for digital cameras has experienced huge growth in recent years. Many people do not wish to take the time to learn how to place their photos into digital albums or to touch up photos before transmitting them to relatives and friends. Instead, they use the services of digital photo-finishing firms, which transmit raw images to companies' Web servers. The

firms then perform desired services and return the finished photos, albums, or other products.

(a) Suppose that the market for digital photo-finishing services is perfectly competitive and that firms currently in the market earn positive economic profits. Use appropriate diagrams to trace through likely future changes in the market price of these services, the equilibrium quantity of services provided in the market, and the profit-maximizing quantity of services provided by a previously existing firm.

(b) As the demand for digital photo-finishing services has expanded and the number of firms has adjusted in the long run in response to the ebb and flow of changing profit opportunities, the market price of these services has remained stable. Under the assumption that this industry is perfectly competitive, what is a key long-run characteristic of this industry?

4) Recently a company called Food.com launched operations. The company operates a Web site that lets consumers browse menus and order takeout from more than 12,000 restaurants in New York, Chicago, Los Angeles, San Francisco, and twenty-six other cities. What conditions might have helped Food.com use its first-mover advantage in this narrow market to develop and maintain a position as a dominant firm? What factors might have hindered its ability to do so?

5) One Net pharmacy, Drugstore.com (which in 2000 acquired its main rival, PlanetRX.com), accounts for well over half of the sales of Web-based pharmaceutical sales. Other Web-based rivals, such as VitaminShoppe.com and WebRX.com have tended to lag behind. To date only a few traditional brick-and-mortar Net pharmacies have made a dent in the electronic marketplace for pharmaceuticals. Speculate about what type of market structure prevails in this market and what key factors are likely to influence prices of the products sold by Web-based phramaceutical firms.

6) In the fall of 2000, the world's biggest computer processor manufacturer, Intel, cut prices on computer chips by as much as 26 percent in an effort to maintain an 85 percent market share. Its only significant rival, Advanced Micro Devices, responded with price cuts of as much as 46 percent. Does such a "price war" accord with the main predictions of the dominant-firm model? Explain your reasoning.

7) In 2000, the last of the purely Internet-based furniture retailers, Living.com and Furniture.com, both closed. These two firms had carved out a position of shared dominance, yet both failed to earn sufficient profits to remain viable. Assume that these two firms had a shared monopoly position in the market, and explain how it was possible for them to earn negative economic profits even if they had the ability to set prices for their Web-based services.

Online Application

Internet URL http://www.ebay.com

Title: **eBay Company Overview**

Navigation: Go directly to the above Web site, and click on "Community." Next, click on "About eBay," and then click on "Company Overview."

Application:

1) Read the opening "Company Overview" page, and then click on "Benchmarks" and read this section as well. Does it appear that eBay benefited from a first-mover advantage? Explain your reasoning.

2) Go back to the eBay home page. Click on "Half.com," and take a look back at the opening to this chapter. Why do you suppose that eBay has moved to merge Half.com into its regular operations? Could this decision help eBay maintain its status as the dominant Web-based auction firm?

For Group Study and Analysis: Assign groups to search the Web and compile a list of at least ten competing auction Web sites. Have students take notes on features of those sites and how they compare with those of eBay and Half.com. Reconvene the class and apply the dominant-firm theory from this chapter to evaluate eBay's prospects for continued predominance within the C2C auction market.

Selected References and Further Readings

Barnes, Anaitesh, Andrew Whinston, and Fang Yin. "Value and Productivity in the Internet Economy," *Computer,* Vol. 33, No. 5, May 2000, 102–105.

Brynjolfsson, Erik, and Michael Smith. "Frictionless Commerce? A Comparison of Internet and Conventional Retailers," MIT Sloan School of Management, August 1999.

Carlton, Dennis, and Jeffrey Perloff. *Modern Industrial Organization* 3rd Ed. Reading, MA: Addison-Wesley, 2000.

Kraemer, Kenneth, and Jason Dedrick. "Dell Computer: Using E-Commerce to Support the Virtual Company," Center for Research on Information Technology and Organizations, University of California, Irvine, June 2001.

Pepall, Lynne, Daniel Richards, and George Norman. *Industrial Organization: Contemporary Theory and Practice*. Cincinnati: South-Western, 1999.

Shepherd, William. *The Economics of Industrial Organization* 4th Ed. Prospect Hills, IL: Waveland Press, 1997.

Chapter 3

Imperfect Competition, Virtual Products, and Network Industries

FUNDAMENTAL ISSUES ▼

1. What are alternative forms of competition among evenly matched but imperfectly competitive e-commerce firms? ▶
2. How do the special production-cost characteristics of virtual products influence how they are priced? ▶
3. How do network externalities affect the demand for a product? ▶
4. How can network externalities produce market feed-back effects? ▶
5. What are common characteristics of network industries? ▶

‹E-Commerce Today›

To Dot.Com, or Not to Dot.Com?

At the height of the Asian financial crisis of the late 1990s, the economic fortunes of emerging nations such as Malaysia, Indonesia, and Thailand were on the verge of collapse. At the same time, the fortunes of e-commerce companies around the globe were skyrocketing. For instance, in 1998 a U.S. publishing company called Mecklermedia changed its name to Internet.com Corporation and promptly experienced a quintupling of the valuation of its fortunes by the stock market. Similar experiences by other information-technology companies during the late 1990s prompted then-U.S. Treasury Secretary Lawrence Summers to quip that perhaps struggling nations could reverse their economic declines by adding "dot-com" to their countries' names.

How quickly times can change. By the spring of 2001, the value of Internet.com's stock had fallen to about 4 percent of its 1998 high. Then Internet.com Corporation changed its name once again, to INTMedia Group, Inc. Removing both "Internet" and "dot-com" from its name resulted in what one stock analyst called a "double-whammy" effect. The company's share price leaped by more than 50 percent in a single day.

Basic theories of financial-asset prices indicate that the market valuation of a firm's stock reflects the stream of profit that shareholders speculate will be forthcoming from the firm's operations into the future. Shareholders naturally place more weight on a firm's profitability today and in the near future relative to prospects for profitability in the more distant future. Thus, currently perceived changes in the profitability of companies typically help to explain immediate variations in the prices of firms' ownership shares.

As economists tried to evaluate the causes of the big run-up in the average share prices of dot-com firms during the late 1990s and the significant drop that occurred in the early 2000s, they naturally focused on the role of shareholder speculations. A major part of the explanation that began to emerge was that many who had purchased stock in the e-commerce firms had speculated that these firms would offer products that would "catch on" with a sufficient number of consumers to induce other consumers to jump on the bandwagon. Speculators in e-commerce stock had gambled that entire industries would thus emerge as network industries within the realm of e-commerce. The great hope had been that this would give firms market power, allowing them to earn economic profits for some time into the future—economic profits that they would ultimately share with owners of their stock. Of course, it had not actually turned out this way for a number of dot-com firms, which helped to explain the stock-market reversals that many experienced in the early 2000s.

Why might shareholders have anticipated that economic profits could persist, at least for a time, within e-commerce industries? Why might they have guessed—albeit incorrectly in many instances—that consumers would jump on an e-commerce bandwagon by purchasing products of dot-com firms simply because other consumers were buying those products? This chapter explores these issues. In this chapter, you will learn how to evaluate situations in which an industry comprises only a few firms, as well as situations in which a number of firms sell products that are similar but sufficiently distinguishable that consumers regard them as essentially different items. You will discover why many economists believe that perfect competition rarely arises among firms that sell virtual products. In addition, you will learn about how bandwagon effects really can arise within network industries, thereby allowing at least some firms within such industries to establish the kinds of dominant positions that so many had hoped for during the dot-com stock mania of the late 1990s.

E-Commerce with Imperfect Competition— Oligopoly and Monopolistic Competition on the Web

In the previous chapter, you learned about how being a first mover might allow a company to emerge as a dominant firm within an electronic marketplace. Sometimes only a few firms are able to mount a successful challenge to a first mover. It might be that the minimum efficient scale for a typical firm in the industry is relatively large. There might be significant start-up costs entailed in entering the industry, and only a few firms may be able to raise sufficient funds to establish a market presence. Other barriers to entry, such as government licensing requirements or other legal impediments, might also discourage market entry by all but a few firms. As a consequence, just a handful of firms might make up an industry within an electronic marketplace.

E-COMMERCE OLIGOPOLIES

Oligopoly
An industry structure in which only a few firms are insulated by barriers to entry from any immediate threat of additional competition.

Economists use the term **oligopoly** to describe an industry structure in which only a few firms are protected from competition by barriers to entry. Strategic pricing and production are a distinguishing characteristic of firms in an oligopolistic industry, each of which recognizes that its own pricing and output decisions will affect the choices of their rivals in the marketplace. Economists call this *oligopolistic interdependence*.

The Anti-Virus Software Oligopoly
A good example of a largely Web-based oligopolistic industry is the market for anti-virus software for home computers. Two companies dominate this industry.

These are Symantec Corporation, which markets the Norton AntiVirus software brand, and Network Associates, Inc., which markets both the McAfee and Dr. Solomon's anti-virus software packages. Antivirus software is expensive to develop and maintain, since new viruses appear frequently, but software is easy to copy and distribute. Undoubtedly, both of these factors contribute to the fact that only two firms currently supply the bulk of the industry's output.

Symantec and Network Associates continue to distribute their programs on compact disks sold in bricks-and-mortar stores. In recent years, however, they have shifted an increasing portion of their sales to Internet product distribution. The companies offer periodic downloadable data file updates and program upgrades for software residing on the hard drives of their customers' computers. This allows them to respond rapidly to the proliferation of new viruses. Both also offer real-time access to anti-virus protection via direct Web links.

Because Symantec and Network Associates have relatively large output rates relative to the anti-virus software industry, oligopolistic interdependence is an important feature in the electronic marketplace for downloadable and real-time anti-virus protection. A Symantec decision to cut the price of Norton AntiVirus upgrades is likely to elicit a pricing response at Network Associates. Alternatively, a Network Associates strategy to focus on producing mainly downloadable versions of its McAfee product while making Dr. Solomon's a real-time-access product could induce Symantec to alter its production or pricing decisions for the Norton AntiVirus software packages it markets on the Web.

Lots of Theories, Little Agreement

A problem that economists face, however, is that there are many different theories of the quantity- and price-setting strategies that a few interdependent firms may adopt. Suppose, for instance, that two rivals who share nearly all industry output, such as Symantec and Network Associates, focus on quantity-based profit maximization. One company, for instance, might plan alternative profit-maximizing output rates under different scenarios concerning its main rival. Simultaneously, the rival firm might choose its own profit-maximizing output rates given alternative possibilities for the output rate of the first company. Their combined rate of output would be consistent with both companies' production strategies. If consumers of anti-virus software regard their products as essentially perfect substitutes, once the companies' output rates are determined, the price of downloadable upgrades or real-time access will be the amount that consumers are willing to pay at this total market output rate.

It is also possible that the two rivals could compete on the basis of the price charged for their products. One might set a schedule of different prices it would charge in response to pricing decisions of its main rival. The other might do the same. Then the pricing decisions that are consistent with both strategies would yield a market product price. The market quantity sold by the two firms would be determined by the quantity demanded at that price.

The idea that firms in oligopolistic industries might choose quantities to maximize their profits given the production strategies of rival firms was proposed in

MANAGEMENT *Online*

Shopbots—A Source of Price Stickiness in Electronic Commerce?

A key development in the continuing growth of Internet commerce is *shopbots*. These are software programs that consumers can use to search the Internet for the best available prices.

Shopbots as a Boon to Price Competition

Most observers have argued that shopbots will be a boon for consumers. The idea is that shopbots will enable consumers to flock to Web sites that post the lowest prices, thereby encouraging firms to keep their prices at the marginal cost of production. Any Internet seller that tries to raise its price above this level surely would lose customers rapidly, they argue.

If this view is correct, then shopbots should help reduce the potential for Internet sellers to engage in strategic pricing. From this standpoint, the wider use of shopbots weakens the pricing power of Internet sellers.

Using Shopbots to Discourage Rivals

According to Hal Varian, an economist at the University of California at Berkeley, it is not so clear that shopbots will help make the Internet a more competitive place. The reason is that there is nothing to stop Internet sellers from using shopbot programs, too. Indeed, some firms already are programming shopbots to keep tabs on the Web sites of rival sellers, permitting them to respond almost immediately to price cuts by competitors. If all rivals in the marketplace follow the same strategy—and know that they do—then each Internet seller knows that rivals will respond to a cut in the price of its product by cutting their prices as well. At the same time, however, the firm knows that if it raises its price, no other Internet seller is likely to follow, and it will lose its clientele as a result.

This resurrects a longstanding theory of oligopolistic behavior known as the *kinked demand curve,* in which a reduction in a firm's price will attract few new customers, so that the demand for its output is very inelastic, or price-insensitive, at prices below its current price. Rivals will not match a price increase, and the firm will lose many customers, so that demand is very elastic, or price-sensitive, above its current price. As shown in Figure 3-1 on page 71, this means that the demand curve for each firm's product is *kinked* at the current market price. The firm's marginal revenue curve therefore is discontinuous at the firm's current output. Thus, when the firm's costs change, it is not necessarily advantageous for the firm to change its price. If the wide use of shopbots by Internet *sellers* makes this theory of the kinked demand curve more relevant, then it could emerge as a

continued

the early nineteenth century by Augustin Cournot and has since been known as the Cournot approach. About four decades later Joseph Bertrand suggested that firms might instead set prices to maximize profits given the pricing strategies of competing firms. Both approaches, in turns out, are part of *game theory,* a broader approach to examining the behavior of firms that are oligopolistically interdependent. This encompassing theory examines alternative strategies and tactics that interdependent firms may utilize in an effort to maximize their profits.

A key implication of game theory is that there is a wide range of alternative strategies that oligopolistic firms may adopt. Consequently, there also are many

Figure 3-1:
The Kinked Demand Curve and Price Rigidity.

If a firm perceives that its rivals will respond to an increase in the price of its output by leaving their own prices unchanged, so that it would lose many customers, then it views the demand curve for its product as relatively elastic above its current price, denoted P_1. At the same time, if it anticipates that its rivals will cut their own prices if it reduces the price of its output, so that it would gain few customers via a price cut, then it perceives the demand curve for its product to be relatively inelastic below P_1. Hence, the demand curve is kinked at this price. This means that the marginal revenue curve, which is derived from the portions of the demand curve above and below the kink, is discontinuous. As a result, variations in the firm's marginal cost, from MC_1 to MC_2 or from MC_1 to MC_3, will not induce the firm to change its price.

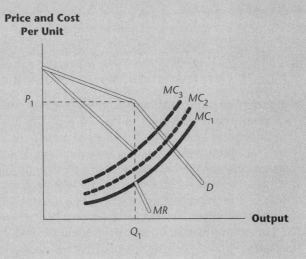

continued

different possible ways that firms in oligopolistic industries may behave. Hence, economists face something of an "embarrassment of riches" in theoretical predictions about the behavior of a firm in such an industry. At any given moment, however, it is difficult to predict what any firm will do. As we shall discuss in Chapter 11, this complicates efforts to determine appropriate regulatory policies for markets dominated by just a few firms. (Another theory of oligopoly predicts that sluggish prices could prove important in a number of e-commerce industries; see *Management Online: Shopbots—A Source of Price Stickiness in Electronic Commerce?*)

continued from page 71
rationale for increasing price stickiness in a growing virtual economy.

Varian argues that which outcome eventually prevails depends on whether consumers or producers move faster in spotting and responding to price differences. In his view, there is good reason to conclude that consumers will be at a disadvantage. After all, they will unleash their shopbots only when they happen to be shopping for a specific item. By way of contrast, producers will keep their shopbots busy,

continuously checking out rivals' prices. Many Internet sellers already engage in real-time monitoring of rivals' Web sites and *automatically* match any price cut.

For Critical Analysis:

If shopbots were to make the theory of the kinked demand curve more relevant for Internet commerce, can you make any predictions about how speedily firms would adjust their output rates to relatively small changes in demand?

PRODUCT DIFFERENTIATION AND MONOPOLISTIC COMPETITION

In many industries, there are relatively low barriers to entry and, hence, a number of competing sellers. Each seller, however, devotes considerable effort to distinguishing its products from those of its competitors. In the electronic marketplace, Internet sellers typically strive to find unique and readily recognizable Web addresses, such as Yahoo.com, Google.com, or Egghead.com, and to develop a reputation for having the most fascinating Web page, the most current and interesting links to other sites, the finest search engines and shopping features, and the best customer service.

Monopolistic Competition
An industry structure in which there are many consumers and many firms, each of which sells a miniscule fraction of total industry output and can easily enter or leave the industry, but which produces a good or service that consumers can readily distinguish.

A **monopolistic competitive** industry is one in which a number of firms sell differentiated products—goods and services that consumers can distinguish across producers. It is also an industry that is easy to enter—or to exit, as Internet sellers with otherwise catchy brand names such as Blaze.com, Soldout.com, and Deepleap.com discovered before running persistent economic losses and ultimately shutting down their operations.

Short-Run Pricing at a Monopolistically Competitive Internet Seller

Under monopolistic competition, each firm within an industry produces output at a rate that is relatively small compared with total industry output. In addition, firms in the industry produce similar, *but not identical,* products. Each is able to set the price of its own product, but demand depends on the availability of close substitutes produced by other firms in the industry.

Because a monopolistically competitive firm sells a product that is at least slightly different from the products of all other firms, there is a unique customer demand for its product. Thus, each individual firm potentially can set a price that is different from the average price charged by other firms in the industry. Nevertheless, each firm recognizes that setting a relatively high price for its product can induce some of its customers to switch to consuming the subsitute products offered by rival firms.

Panel (a) of Figure 3-2 on page 74 shows a possible short-run situation that a monopolistically competitive Internet seller might face when it takes into account production costs as well as the demand for its product and the implied marginal revenue curve. To simplify, we assume that it can always vary all factors of production, so that its long-run average cost curve applies. The other cost curve shown in the figure is the firm's marginal cost curve.

To maximize its economic profit, the firm produces to the point at which marginal revenue equals marginal cost. This is point S where the marginal revenue and marginal cost curves cross. Consequently, in the short-run situation shown in panel (a), the firm's profit-maximizing output rate is Q_S, at which marginal revenue equals marginal cost. The firm charges the price P_S that the demand curve indicates its customers are willing to pay for this amount of output. The average total cost of producing Q_S units is ATC_S. The firm's total profit, therefore, equals $(PS - ATC_S)$, which is the height of the shaded rectangle, times Q_S, which is the base of the rectangle. Thus, the shaded rectangle depicts a positive economic profit for the firm.

Long-Run Equilibrium in a Monopolistically Competitive Electronic Marketplace

In the short run, a firm in a monopolistically competitive industry can earn a *positive economic profit,* which means that its total revenue can exceed the opportunity cost of being part of that industry instead of another industry. In a monopolistically competitive industry, it is easy for new firms to enter the industry. Positive economic profits encourage other firms to enter the industry, thereby increasing the range of product choice available to consumers.

The fact that the firm depicted in panel (a) of Figure 3-2 earns a positive economic profit is a signal that revenues in this industry are more than sufficient to cover the opportunity cost of being in this industry. In the long run, additional firms will enter the industry. Panel (b) shows what happens at the previously existing firm in panel (a) following the entry of new firms. First, the demand for this firm's product declines, because some of its customers will buy similar goods from other firms. Thus, the demand curve shifts leftward. Second, the entry of new firms means that more substitute products are available, so the demand for this firm's product becomes more *elastic.* That is, a given proportionate price increase will induce a larger proportionate decrease in the quantity of the firm's product that customers wish to purchase. The new demand curve is thus represented as D'. Because the firm's marginal revenue curve stems from its demand curve, it also shifts leftward and becomes more elastic, as depicted by MR'.

Figure 3-2:
Demand, Production, and Pricing at a Firm in a Monopolistically Competitive Marketplace.

The product of a monopolistically competitive firm is distinguishable from those of numerous rival firms in the industry, so it faces downward-sloping demand and marginal revenue curves. Panel (a) depicts a short-run situation in which the firm produces to the point where marginal revenue equals marginal cost at a short-run equilibrium point S. At this point, it produces Q_S units, which it sells at the price P_S, thereby earning a positive economic profit equal to $(P_S - ATC_S)$ times Q_S. This induces other firms to enter the industry. As shown in panel (b), entry by new rivals has two effects on the demand and marginal revenue curves faced by this firm. First, the demand and marginal revenue curves tend to shift leftward as some of the firm's customers begin consuming output from new firms in the industry. Second, the availability of more substitute products causes the demand and marginal revenue curves to become more elastic. At a point of long-run equilibrium, the demand curve is tangent to the firm's average total cost curve at point L, and the firm earns zero economic profit.

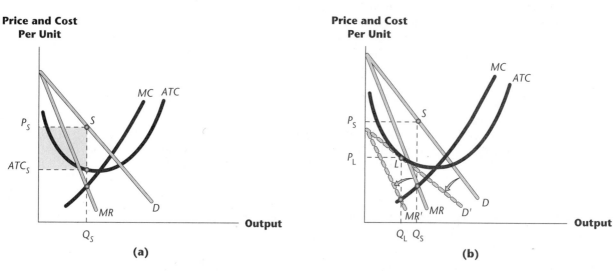

Assuming that the firm's costs are unaffected by the entry of new firms, the result is a decline in the firm's economic profits to zero in the long run. As panel (b) indicates, this occurs when the firm's demand curve shifts to a point of tangency with the long-run average cost curve at point L. At this point, the economic profit of firm falls to zero. It produces a lower rate of output, Q_L, at a lower price, P_L, and the total revenue it earns just covers the opportunity cost of being part of this industry. This removes the incentive for any more firms to enter the industry.

As new firms enter the monopolistically competitive industry and capture some of the existing firm's customers, the demand for its product declines and becomes more elastic, and its economic profit declines toward zero. As for a firm in perfectly competitive industry, the total revenue earned by a firm in a monopolistically competitive industry just covers the opportunity cost of remaining in the industry. By way of contrast to a perfectly competitive industry, firms in a monopolistically competitive firm are able to charge consumers a price above marginal cost in long-run equilibrium. In addition, if a typical firm's long-run average cost curve is U-shaped, as in panel (b), the profit-maximizing price of its product also exceeds the firm's lowest feasible long-run average cost at the minimum point of the long-run average cost curve.

Monopolistic Competition and the Electronic Marketplace: Two Perspectives

Many observers contend that a number of e-commerce industries are likely to develop monopolistically competitive structures. According to this view, the costs of establishing an e-commerce firm are relatively low in a number of industries. For many potential entrants to such industries, establishing a Web server, developing a Web site, and marketing a new or existing product could prove to be relatively inexpensive. At the same time, Internet selling offers a number of ways to differentiate products. There is the tried-and-true approach of manufacturing a "new, improved" product with different features from those offered by other competitors. In addition, an Internet seller can strive to design an intriguing home page and a distinctive shopping-navigation process. It also can advertise and set up arrangements for cross-links with Web pages of Internet sellers in other industries.

As you have learned, e-commerce firms within monopolistically competitive industries are likely to fail to produce at the lowest feasible average cost. They are also unlikely to equalize the prices of their products with the marginal cost of producing those goods or services. From one perspective, the failure to achieve minimum-average-cost and marginal cost pricing in monopolistically competitive industries are social inefficiencies. Compared with a perfectly competitive firm, a monopolistically competitive firm is allocatively inefficient, because it does not engage in marginal cost pricing. It is also technically inefficient, because in the long run it does not produce at the minimum feasible average cost. It is unclear what might be done to eliminate such inefficiencies of monopolistic competition, short of government interventions requiring that all Web pages look the same and that all Internet shopping processes operate identically.

There is an alternative perspective, however. According to this view, monopolistic competition is not really inefficient. Long-run equilibrium under monopolistic competition, after all, yields zero economic profits to all firms in the industry. Furthermore, the price of each product reflects customers' *willingness to pay* for the units that they purchased. After all, consumers will not buy the product if they are unwilling to pay the price charged by the producer, and they may be willing to pay a price that exceeds marginal cost and average cost to consume a brand with characteristics they desire. Some economists argue that the price–cost differential that arises under monopolistic competition amounts to a premium that consumers pay in exchange for the product variety that exists in monopolistically competitive industries. As discussed shortly, willingness to pay is a very important concept in the economics of electronic commerce.

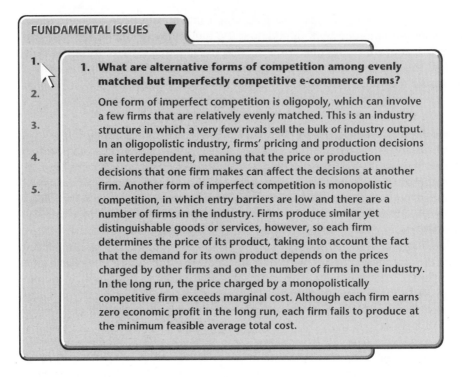

FUNDAMENTAL ISSUES ▼

1.
2.
3.
4.
5.

1. What are alternative forms of competition among evenly matched but imperfectly competitive e-commerce firms?

One form of imperfect competition is oligopoly, which can involve a few firms that are relatively evenly matched. This is an industry structure in which a very few rivals sell the bulk of industry output. In an oligopolistic industry, firms' pricing and production decisions are interdependent, meaning that the price or production decisions that one firm makes can affect the decisions at another firm. Another form of imperfect competition is monopolistic competition, in which entry barriers are low and there are a number of firms in the industry. Firms produce similar yet distinguishable goods or services, however, so each firm determines the price of its product, taking into account the fact that the demand for its own product depends on the prices charged by other firms and on the number of firms in the industry. In the long run, the price charged by a monopolistically competitive firm exceeds marginal cost. Although each firm earns zero economic profit in the long run, each firm fails to produce at the minimum feasible average total cost.

 ## The Economics of Virtual Products

Virtual Product
A digital product that is typically produced at a relatively high fixed cost but distributed for sale at a relatively low marginal cost.

A number of e-commerce products are **virtual products**, which are items offered for sale in digital form. Increasingly, virtual products are available via computer downloads. Examples include computer operating systems, office-productivity software, electronic books (*e-books*) and encyclopedias, digital music and videos, and educational and training software.

COST CHARACTERISTICS OF VIRTUAL PRODUCTS

What makes virtual products different from a number of other goods and services is that producing the first copy often entails incurring sizable up-front costs. Once the first copy is produced, however, making additional copies is nearly costless. After all, the publisher can simply take an appropriately formatted copy of the author's original digital file and make copies available for consumers to download, at a price, via the Internet.

Costs of Producing Virtual Products

To think about the cost conditions faced by the seller of a virtual product, consider the production and sale of an e-book. An e-book's author must devote many hours of labor to writing, organizing, and editing its content. Each hour of labor devoted to performing this task entails an opportunity cost. Thus, to induce someone to write an e-book, an e-book publisher typically must pay an author an upfront payment, called an *advance* because it is normally deducted from royalty payments that future sales will generate. To induce an established author or a particularly promising new author to write an e-book, the publisher might have to pay an additional lump-sum amount, often in the form of a *grant*. The sum of all up-front payments constitutes a relatively sizable *fixed cost* that the publisher must incur to generate the first copy of the e-book.

Once the author has written the e-book and the publisher has transferred its contents to an appropriately formatted digital file that is readable by special personal-computer software or e-book reading devices, the cost of making and distributing additional copies is very low. Recall from Chapter 2 that the cost that a producer incurs in producing and selling an additional unit of output is the firm's *marginal cost*. For a typical virtual product, marginal cost is often extremely low. In the case of an e-book, it is simply a matter of incurring a miniscule cost to post a downloadable file on the publisher's Web site and paying the author a royalty— a payment for each book that consumers purchase.

Cost Curves for a Virtual Product
Suppose that a publisher convinces a well-known author of science-fiction novels to write a new novel that it will release in e-book form. The publisher agrees to make a $45,000 up-front payment to the author in exchange for a "digital manuscript" of a new science-fiction novel. Then the publisher incurs a fixed cost of $2,000 to pay copy editors and company employees to clean up the writing a little and to format the manuscript for Internet downloading. The publisher has also determined that it faces a fixed opportunity cost of $3,000 for arranging a deal with *this* science fiction author instead of the next-best author it might consider inducing to write an e-book. Hence, the total fixed cost, inclusive of opportunity costs, for the e-book product is $50,000. Although royalty payments to authors normally are a percentage of a measure of total dollar sales, let's suppose that in this case, the author and publisher agree to a fixed payment of $0.50 per e-book that the publisher sells on the Internet. Consequently, the marginal cost that the publisher incurs for each copy of the e-book that consumers download is a constant amount equal to $0.50 per e-book.

Figure 3-3 on page 78 displays the publisher's cost curves for this virtual product. By definition, average fixed cost is total fixed cost divided by the quantity produced and sold. Hence, the average fixed cost of the first e-book is $50,000. But if the publisher sells 5,000 copies, the average fixed cost drops to $10 per e-book. If the total quantity sold is 50,000, average fixed cost declines to $1.00 per e-book. Hence, the average fixed cost (*AFC*) curve slopes downward over the entire range of possible quantities of e-books.

Average variable cost equals total variable cost divided by the number of units of a product that a firm sells. If this publisher sells only one copy, then the cost it incurs is the $0.50 royalty payment to the author, so the average variable cost of the first copy sold is $0.50. If consumers download 5,000 copies of the

Figure 3-3:
Cost Curves for a Producer of a Virtual Product.

If the total fixed cost of publishing an e-book is $50,000, then the cost of producing the first e-book copy is $50,000, but if the publisher sells 5,000 copies, the average fixed cost falls to $10.00 per e-book. If sales rise to 50,000, the publisher's average fixed cost decreases to $1.00 per e-book. Thus, the publisher's average fixed cost (AFC) curve slopes downward. If the per-unit cost of producing each e-book is $0.50, then both the marginal cost (MC) and average variable cost (AVC) curves are horizontal at $0.50 per e-book. Adding the AFC and ATC curves yields the publisher's short-run average total cost (ATC) curve. Because the ATC curve slopes downward, the publisher experiences short-run economies of scale.

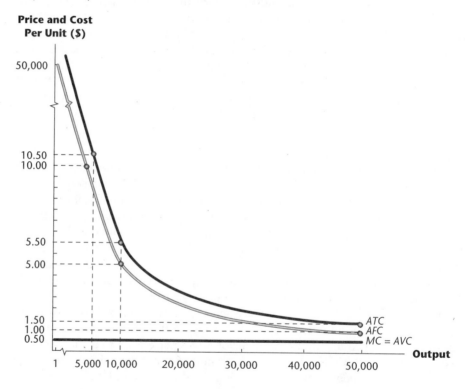

e-book from the publisher's Web site each year, then total royalty payments to the author equal $0.50 multiplied by 5,000 copies, or $2,500. The publisher's average variable cost of selling this quantity of e-books then equals its total variable cost of $2,500 divided by the 5,000 copies it produces and sells, or $0.50 per e-book. Thus, as shown in Figure 3-3, the average variable cost of producing and selling this e-book is always equal to the constant marginal cost of $0.50 per e-book that the publisher incurs. The average variable cost *(AVC)* curve is the same as the marginal cost *(MC)* curve, which for this publisher is the horizontal line depicted in Figure 3-3.

By definition, average total cost equals the sum of average fixed cost and average variable cost. The average total cost *(ATC)* curve for this e-book publisher, therefore, slopes downward over its entire range.

Recall from Chapter 2 that along the downward-sloping range of a firm's *long-run* average cost curve, the firm experiences *economies of scale*. For the producer of a virtual product such as an e-book, the *short-run* average total cost curve slopes downward. Consequently, sellers of virtual products typically experience *short-run economies of scale*. The average total cost of producing and selling a virtual product declines as more units of the product are sold. Short-run economies of scale are a distinguishing characteristic of virtual products that sets them apart from most other goods and services.

IMPERFECT COMPETITION AND VIRTUAL PRODUCTS

In the example depicted in Figure 3-3, the virtual product is a science-fiction novel distributed in e-book form via Internet downloads. There are numerous science-fiction authors and many science-fiction novels that consumers can choose among. Hence, many products are close substitutes in the market for science-fiction novels. Yet, no science fiction novel is exactly the same. This means that the particular e-book product sold by the publisher in our example is distinguishable from other competing products.

For the sake of argument, therefore, let's suppose that this publisher faces a monopolistically competitive market for this e-book. Panels *(a)* and *(b)* of Figure 3-4 on page 80 display a possible demand curve for the e-book written by this particular science fiction author.

Marginal Cost Pricing and Virtual Products

As discussed in Chapter 2, economists often regard *marginal cost pricing* as a desirable outcome. Marginal cost pricing implies allocative efficiency: The price that the consumer pays is equal to the cost incurred to produce the last unit of output sold, so that the seller's explicit and implicit opportunity costs of producing the product are just covered by the consumer's payment. Because marginal cost pricing is allocatively efficient, economists sometimes call marginal cost pricing the **first-best optimum** for society.

What if the publisher of this particular e-book were to behave *as if* it were a perfectly competitive firm by engaging in marginal cost pricing? Panel *(a)* of Figure 3-4 provides the answer to this question. If the publisher sets the price of the science-fiction e-book equal to marginal cost, then it will charge only $0.50 per e-book it sells. Naturally, a number of people desire to purchase e-books at this price, and given the demand curve in the figure, the publisher could sell 20,000 copies of this e-book.

The publisher would face a problem, however. At a price of $0.50 per e-book, it would earn $10,000 in revenues on sales of 20,000 copies. The average fixed cost of 20,000 copies equals $50,000/20,000, or $2.50 per e-book. Adding this to

First-Best Optimum
A market outcome in which the price of a good or service equals its marginal production cost, so that allocative efficiency is achieved by society as a whole.

Figure 3-4:
Marginal versus Average Cost Pricing of Virtual Products.

In panel (a), if the publisher with the average total cost and marginal cost costs curves shown in Figure 3-3 sets the price of the science fiction e-book equal to its constant marginal cost of $0.50 per e-book, then consumers will download 20,000 copies. This yields $10,000 in revenues to the publisher. The publisher's average total cost of 20,000 e-books is $2.50 per e-book, so its total cost of selling that number of copies is $3.00 times 20,000 = $60,000. The first-best social optimum of marginal cost pricing yields a $50,000 loss to the publisher, which is the total fixed cost of producing the e-book. A second-best social optimum exists at the point where the demand curve is tangent to the average total cost curve, so that the firm practices average cost pricing. At a price of $5.50 per e-book that is equal to average total cost, the publisher's revenues of $55,000 just cover its $55,000 total cost of producing and distributing the book on the Internet.

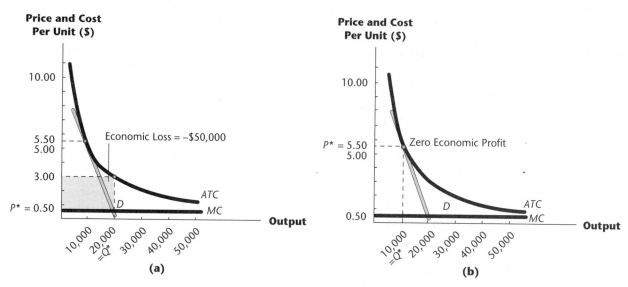

(a)   (b)

the constant $0.50 average variable cost implies that the average total cost of selling 20,000 copies is $3.00. Under marginal cost pricing, therefore, the publisher would earn an average loss of –$2.50 (price – average total cost = $0.50 – $3.00 = –$2.50) per e-book for all 20,000 copies sold. The publisher's total economic loss from selling 20,000 e-books at a price equal to marginal cost would amount to –$50,000. Hence, the publisher would fail to recoup the full amount of fixed cost of producing the e-book. It would not have ever wanted to produce the e-book in the first place if it planned to set its price equal to the e-book's marginal production cost!

The failure of marginal cost pricing to allow firms selling virtual products to cover the fixed costs of producing those products is intrinsic to the nature of such products. In the presence of short-run economies of scale in producing virtual products, marginal cost pricing is not a feasible outcome in the marketplace. Recall that marginal cost pricing is associated with perfect competition. An important implication is that markets for virtual products cannot function as perfectly competitive markets. Imperfect competition is the rule, not the exception, in the marketplace for a virtual product.

Average Cost Pricing and Virtual Products

Panel *(b)* of Figure 3-4 illustrates an alternative pricing choice for the publisher of the science-fiction e-book. The publisher sets the price of the e-book equal to its average total cost of production, thereby engaging in **average cost pricing.** Given the demand curve depicted in Figure 3-4, at a price of $5.50 per e-book, consumers are willing to purchase and download 10,000 copies. The publisher's average total cost of offering 10,000 copies for sale is also equal to $5.50 per e-book. Hence, this is the price consistent with average cost pricing.

Average Cost Pricing
Setting the price of an item equal to the average total cost of producing and selling the item.

At a price of $5.50 per e-book, the publisher's revenues from selling 10,000 copies equal $55,000. This amount of revenues is just sufficient to cover the publisher's total fixed cost of $50,000 and the $5,000 total variable cost it incurs in producing 10,000 copies at an average variable cost of $0.50 per e-book. Thus, the publisher earns zero economic profit by engaging in average cost pricing.

Economists often regard average cost pricing as a **second-best optimum** for society. The first-best optimum of marginal cost pricing of virtual products is not attainable, because sellers of such products know that marginal cost pricing would entail negative economic profits. Under average cost pricing, sellers of virtual products charge the minimum price required to cover their production costs, including the relatively high fixed costs they must incur to develop their products in the first place. Consumers thereby pay the lowest price necessary to induce sellers to provide the item.

Second-Best Optimum
The market outcome in which the price of a good or service equals its average cost of production. Consumers pay the lowest price necessary to induce sellers to provide the item.

In fact, as you learned earlier in this chapter, the situation illustrated in panel *(b)* corresponds to a long-run monopolistically competitive equilibrium in the market for science-fiction e-books. If this and other publishers face a situation such as the diagram depicts, then there is no incentive for additional publishers to enter or leave the marketplace. Consequently, in the long run for a monopolistically competitive industry composed of sellers of virtual products facing short-run economies of scale, the second-best optimum will naturally tend to emerge. In other imperfectly competitive industries, such as oligopolies where barriers to entry are significant, this is less likely to be true.

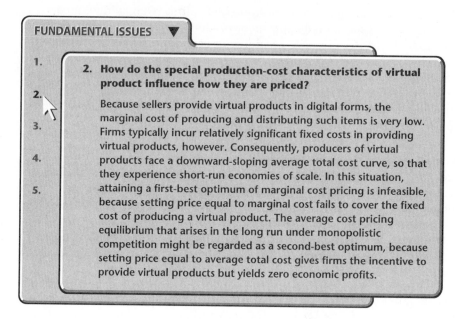

FUNDAMENTAL ISSUES ▼

1.

2.

3.

4.

5.

2. How do the special production-cost characteristics of virtual product influence how they are priced?

Because sellers provide virtual products in digital forms, the marginal cost of producing and distributing such items is very low. Firms typically incur relatively significant fixed costs in providing virtual products, however. Consequently, producers of virtual products face a downward-sloping average total cost curve, so that they experience short-run economies of scale. In this situation, attaining a first-best optimum of marginal cost pricing is infeasible, because setting price equal to marginal cost fails to cover the fixed cost of producing a virtual product. The average cost pricing equilibrium that arises in the long run under monopolistic competition might be regarded as a second-best optimum, because setting price equal to average total cost gives firms the incentive to provide virtual products but yields zero economic profits.

▶ Network Externalities

As discussed in Chapter 2, firms in certain markets compose *network industries.* In such an industry, the value that consumers assign to the good or service produced by firms depends to some extent on the number of other people who consume the product.

Network Externality
A situation that arises when the benefit that a consumer perceives to be available from using an item depends on how many others use it.

Economists say that such products are subject to **network externalities**, meaning that the benefit that a consumer anticipates receiving from a good or service depends on the number of consumers using the item. An example of such a good is a fax machine. If you were the only one who owned a fax machine, then the machine would have little value to you, except perhaps if it also functions as a copy machine. After all, you would be unable, on the one hand, to receive fax transmissions from other individuals or firms or, on the other hand, to send fax transmissions to anyone else. As more people or companies that you desire to communicate with acquire fax machines, the benefit you derive from having access to a fax machine increases.

PRODUCT DEMAND IN THE ABSENCE OF NETWORK EXTERNALITIES

To understand how network externalities can influence the demand for a product, it is helpful to explore a simple example. Table 3-1 displays alternative amounts that five consumers are willing to pay for a single copy of downloadable office

**Table 3-1: Willingness to Pay for a Software
Product without Network Externalities.**

▼

Consumer A Willingness to Pay	$50
Consumer B Willingness to Pay	50
Consumer C Willingness to Pay	60
Consumer D Willingness to Pay	70
Consumer E Willingness to Pay	80

**Table 3-2: Purchases of Software Product at Various Possible Prices
without Network Externalities.**

▼

Price	$50	$60	$70	$80	$90–190
Consumers	A, B, C, D, E	C, D, E	D, E	E	None
Quantity	5	3	2	1	0

productivity software package. Initially a fundamental characteristic of this software is that people who purchase and use it can only work with computer files located on their own personal computers. They cannot share the files with others.

Suppose that the five consumers in Table 3-1 are the only consumers in the market, denoted A, B, C, D, and E. Based on the information in Table 3-1, it is possible to tabulate quantities of the software package demanded at various prices. These price–quantity combinations are displayed in Table 3-2. If the product price is $50 per unit, then all five consumers are willing to purchase the product, because each is willing to pay at least this amount for the software. Successive price increases bring about declines in the number of consumers who are willing to buy the software. If the price is $60 per product, then consumers A and B are unwilling to buy it, so the quantity demanded in the marketplace declines to four units. If the price rises to $70 per unit, then consumers A, B, and C are all willing to purchase the product, and the total quantity demanded falls to two units. Above a price of $80 per unit, no one wishes to purchase the product, so quantity demanded equals zero.

The price–quantity combinations for the software market given in Table 3-2 appear in Figure 3-5 on page 84 as the demand schedule D_1. Because software packages are sold as single, indivisible units, this demand schedule is not a smooth curve. The law of demand holds, nonetheless: As the price of the software package increases, the quantity demanded declines. Hence, the demand relationship D_1 slopes downward.

**Figure 3-5:
The Demand for
Software Packages
without Network
Externalities.**

*If an office productivity
software package has no
facility for exchanging files
among different users, then
each potential consumer only
purchases an amount that
he or she desires to use in
isolation from other users.
In the example illustrated
in Tables 3-1 and 3-2, the
demand relationship D_1 is
the result.*

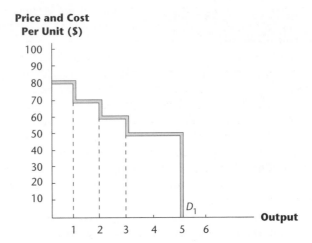

PRODUCT DEMAND IN THE PRESENCE OF A NETWORK EXTERNALITY

Now suppose that people can use the same office-productivity software to share files with others, such as spouses and other family members, friends, and co-workers. As a result, many of the applications contained in this software package—file-sharing programs, word-processing software, and the like—are more valuable to each consumer when other consumers purchase and the software package. Each consumer's willingness to pay, therefore, increases as more individuals purchase and use the software. (We assume, by the way, that the software is sufficiently copy-protected that it cannot be pirated or given away to other users, which means that all consumers must pay the purchase price to use it.)

Product Demand with a Network Externality

Table 3-3 displays how each consumer's willingness to pay varies with the number of other consumers who also choose to purchase and use the office productivity software package. The first column of Table 3-3 shows the same willingness to pay for each consumer that appears in Table 3-1. From each consumer's point of view, if he or she turns out to be the only user of the software, then the fact that file sharing is now possible makes no difference. Each consumer will have the same willingness to pay that he or she would have had if sharing files across computers remained impossible.

Table 3-4 indicates which consumers are willing, based on the information in Table 3-3, to purchase a unit of the office productivity software at various prices. If the price of the software package is $50, then naturally all five consumers are willing to purchase the product. Hence, Table 3-4 shows that the total quantity demanded in the marketplace is five units at a price of $50 per unit.

Now suppose that the price increases to $60 per unit. According to Table 3-3, consumers C, D, and E are willing to pay at least $60 per unit even if no one else buys and uses the software. These three consumers, therefore, purchase the prod-

Table 3-3: Willingness to Pay for a Software Product with Network Externalities.

Number of Users	1	2	3	4	5
Consumer A Willingness to Pay	$50	$ 60	$ 70	$ 80	$ 90
Consumer B Willingness to Pay	50	70	90	110	130
Consumer C Willingness to Pay	60	80	100	120	140
Consumer D Willingness to Pay	70	90	110	130	150
Consumer E Willingness to Pay	80	100	130	160	190

Table 3-4: Purchases of Software Product at Various Possible Prices When There Are Network Externalities.

Price	$50	$60	$70	$80	$90
Consumers	A, B, C, D, E	A, B, C, D, E	A, B, C, D, E	A, B, C, D, E	None
Quantity	5	5	5	5	0

uct. Thus, at least three people can share files among their computers. If a fourth starts using the software, then the willingness to pay for that individual and for the fifth will increase. As shown in Table 3-3, consumer A's willingness to pay increases to $80 once at least four people purchase the software. Once consumer A buys the product, so that four people can share files, consumer B's willingness to pay as a fifth user increases to $130, so this consumer also is willing to purchase the software package at a $60 price. The total quantity demanded at the higher price of $60 per unit, therefore, remains equal to five units, as indicated in Table 3-4.

A price increase to $70 per unit would induce only consumers D and E to buy the software package to use individually. Once those two purchase it, however, they can begin exchanging files, and the number of users rises to two. The willingness to pay for consumer C, as a third user, then increases to $100, so this consumer will also purchase the software package at a price of $70. Consumer B would then become the fourth user if she buys the product, and if there are four users, Table 3-3 indicates that this consumer's willingness to pay is $110, so she is willing to buy the product at the $70 price. From consumer A's perspective, therefore, joining the other four and making the total number of users equal to five raises his willingness to pay to $90, so he also is willing to buy the product at a price of $70 per unit. Thus, the total quantity of units demanded at a price of $70 is also equal to 5. In problem 6 at the end of the chapter you get the opportunity to reason out that all five consumers also wish to purchase the product at price of $80 per unit.

Now think about what happens at a price of $90 per unit. Assuming that the consumers have no way to communicate to one another the fact that each consumer's willingness to pay increases as more individuals use the software package, the first column of Table 3-3 indicates that no consumer is willing to purchase the product. As a result, total quantity demanded declines to zero, as shown in Table 3-4. The quantity demanded equals zero at or above a $90 price. (In problem 7 at the end of the chapter, you get the opportunity to contemplate what the demand relationship might look like if all consumers exchange information about willingness to pay and to purchase the software package.)

Implications of Network Externalities for Product Demand

Figure 3-6 displays both the demand relationship D_1 that we obtained in the case where there were no network externalities and the demand relationship implied by Table 3-4 when a network externality is present, denoted D_2. When consumers can use the software package to transfer and share files, then all consumers are now willing to purchase the product at any price below $90 per unit.

An immediate implication is that adding a file-exchanging capability to this particular software package induces a rightward shift in the demand relationship,

Figure 3-6:
The Demand for Software Packages without and with Network Externalities.

If the capability to share office productivity software files is added as a feature of the package, then consumers' willingness to pay for the software package increases when others also use it. Based on the example summarized in Tables 3-3 and 3-4, this gives the demand relationship D_2. In the presence of this network externality, the demand for the product increases and becomes relatively more inelastic, as compared with the original demand curve D_1 where there was no network externality.

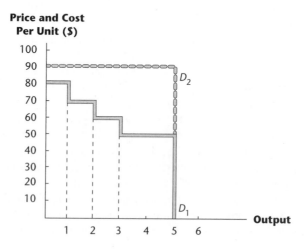

from D_1 to D_2 at every price between \$50 and \$90 per unit. That is, the presence of a network externality leads to an *increase* in the demand for the product.

This is a typical characteristic of products with network externalities. Because each consumer's willingness to pay rises as other consumers buy and use such a product, the overall demand for the product tends to differ from the level it would have exhibited if no network externality existed. In this particular example, there is a *bandwagon effect:* The presence of the network externality induces more people to consume the product at most prices where positive consumption occurs.

Another implication of Figure 3-6 is that the **price elasticity of demand—** which economists define as the absolute value of the proportionate change in quantity of a product demanded resulting from a proportionate change in the product's price—is affected by the presence of a network externality. Along the downward-sloping range of the demand relationship D_1 that applies in the absence of file-sharing capabilities, over the range of prices from \$50 to \$80, an increase in the product price causes the quantity demanded to decline. This is not true when file exchange is possible, so that a network externality is present. As the product price rises over this range of prices along the demand relationship D_2, the quantity demanded does not change, and the price elasticity of demand is zero. In this situation, therefore, the presence of a network externality makes demand *perfectly inelastic* over this price.

Hence, this example illustrates another common characteristic of products with network externalities. The price elasticity of demand for such products usually is altered when a network externality is present. In this particular example, the price elasticity of demand is relatively lower, as compared with the price elasticity of demand for the product if there were no network externalities. As you will learn in the next chapter, the price elasticity of demand can have an important bearing on a producer's decision about the profit-maximizing price to charge for its product.

Price Elasticity of Demand
The absolute value of the percentage change in quantity demanded associated with a given percentage change in the price of a product.

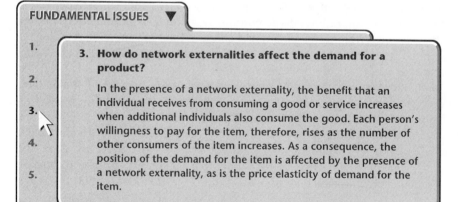

FUNDAMENTAL ISSUES ▼

1.

2.

3.

4.

5.

3. **How do network externalities affect the demand for a product?**

    In the presence of a network externality, the benefit that an individual receives from consuming a good or service increases when additional individuals also consume the good. Each person's willingness to pay for the item, therefore, rises as the number of other consumers of the item increases. As a consequence, the position of the demand for the item is affected by the presence of a network externality, as is the price elasticity of demand for the item.

Network Industries and E-Commerce

We have already discussed *network industries*. These are industries in which the value that consumers place on the firms' products varies directly with the number of consumers. That is, consumers' willingness to pay increases with the extent to which other consumers use firms' products. This means that a fundamental characteristic of network industries is that *network externalities* are present in such industries. As we shall discuss shortly, many economists suggest that network industries commonly share other characteristics that also tend to relate to the nature of their products.

NETWORK EXTERNALITIES AND MARKET FEEDBACK

Market Feedback
A tendency for a good or service to fall in or out of favor as a result of network externalities.

The bandwagon effect discussed in the last section is an example of **market feedback** that typically exists in a network industry. This is a *logrolling effect*, which can be either positive or negative, as a firm's or industry's product either "catches on" or becomes a "has-been" with consumers whose willingness to pay varies with the number of other users of the product of the firm or the industry.

Positive Feedback in Network Industries

In a situation such as the bandwagon effect involving greater purchases of a software product with file-sharing capabilities, illustrated in Figure 3-6 on page 86, a network externality induces *positive* market feedback. In the specific example we considered, introducing the ability for users to exchange files induced more people to use the product, thereby expanding demand.

Positive market feedback can affect the prospects of an entire industry. The market for Internet service provider (ISP) services is an example. The growth of this industry has roughly paralleled the growth of Internet hosts worldwide that is displayed in Figure 1-4 on page 23. Undoubtedly, positive market feedback resulting from network externalities made possible by Internet communications and interactions induced a significant logrolling effect, as more people sought online access, thereby giving additional people the incentive to obtain access to the Internet.

In addition, however, an individual firm can reap the benefits of market feedback arising from the presence of a network externality. A good example of a firm that has benefited from positive market feedback is the C2C auction firm eBay.com. An individual is more likely to use the services of an auction site if there is a significant likelihood that many other potential buyers or sellers also trade items at that site. Hence, there is a network externality in the C2C auction industry, and eBay has experienced positive market feedback as a result.

Negative Feedback in Network Industries

The presence of network externalities is not always associated with increases in demand for the product of a firm or an industry. There can also be *negative* market feedback: People can reduce their consumption of a product with a negative externality, thereby inducing others to reduce their consumption as well.

An example of an industry that has experienced negative market feedback of late is the telecommunications industry. Traditional telecommunications firms such as AT&T, Worldcom, Sprint, and the like experienced positive market feedback during the late 1980s and early 1990s as wireless phones and fax machines proliferated and individuals and firms began making long-distance phone calls from cell phones or via fax machines. Since the mid-1990s, as more people have acquired Internet access via local ISPs, e-mail communications and e-mail document attachments have supplanted large volumes of phone and fax communications. For the telecommunications industry, the greater use of e-mail and e-mail attachments by some individuals induced others to follow suit. This has resulted in a logrolling effect that has reduced the overall demand for traditional long-distance phone services.

An individual firm within a network industry can also experience negative market feedback. Many early C2C auction rivals of eBay fell by the wayside as the positive market feedback that eBay experienced reduced the rivals' share of the overall demand for Internet auction services. As more consumers utilized eBay's services, the reduction in users of other auction sites implied a fall in the number of potential buyers and sellers of any given item offered for sale on those sites. This fed a negative logrolling effect, as many rival sites were singled out by users as "has-beens." Auction volumes at those sites gradually dwindled away.

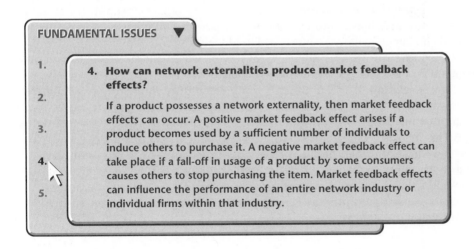

FUNDAMENTAL ISSUES ▼

1.

2.

3.

4.

5.

4. How can network externalities produce market feedback effects?

If a product possesses a network externality, then market feedback effects can occur. A positive market feedback effect arises if a product becomes used by a sufficient number of individuals to induce others to purchase it. A negative market feedback effect can take place if a fall-off in usage of a product by some consumers causes others to stop purchasing the item. Market feedback effects can influence the performance of an entire network industry or individual firms within that industry.

OTHER IMPORTANT CHARACTERISTICS OF NETWORK INDUSTRIES

Network externalities explain the existence of network industries. Economists argue that several other factors must be taken into account when evaluating choices that firms and consumers make in their interactions with firms within network industries.

Issues of Complementarity and Compatibility

When Adobe launched Acrobat 5.0 in 2001, its Web ads, marketing flyers, and CD box covers all proclaimed: "Complements Microsoft Office!" As with previous versions of the document-processing software, Adobe Acrobat had a simpler procedure for converting Microsoft Word documents to PDF form as compared with alternatives such as Corel WordPerfect documents.

Clearly, Adobe regarded Microsoft Word as the dominant product within the word-processing software industry. Thus, it chose to make its own software more **capitible** with Word rather than with WordPerfect. That is, Adobe designed its software to function more efficiently in combination with another product, namely Microsoft Word.

Economists call products that are often consumed simultaneously **complements.** Normally, we envision consumers making the choice about what products to view as complementary: for instance, bread and butter, tea and sweetener, or coffee and cream. Adobe made the choice for consumers of its product, however. Anyone who purchased and used Adobe Acrobat would have an easier time using it with Microsoft Word and other Microsoft Office programs, as compared with competing office-productivity software.

One possible indication of this decision is that Adobe regarded Microsoft Word as the **standard product** in the word-processing software industry. This is a good or service that producers of complementary products regard as the most widely used and, hence, most important for purposes of assuring compatibility with their complementary products. Failing to ensure compatibility with the standard product, firms such as Adobe might reason, would guarantee depressing the demand for their own complementary products.

Issues relating to compatibility, complementarity, and standard industry products arise naturally in network industries. In such industries, one or two firms may benefit from positive market feedback arising from network externalities. This increases the likelihood that firms producing complementary goods or services will regard their products as standard products within their industry. Of course, becoming a standard product would reinforce the positive market feedback that these one or two firms already enjoy. At the same time, failing to emerge as a standard product can be a source of negative market feedback for their rivals.

Compatibility
The ability to use one product in combination with another.

Complements
Items that are commonly consumed simultaneously.

Standard Product
An item that producers of complementary goods strive to ensure will be compatible with their products.

Switching Costs and the Potential for "Consumer Lock-In"

A common source of network externalities is a shared understanding of consumers about how to use a product. Consider, for instance, a large multinational corporation that uses a Web-based software product to provide online tutorials explaining how to develop and sharpen customer-service skills. To satisfy the corporation's exacting internal standards for providing services to its millions of customers, each one of the company's thousands of employees must provide evidence of periodic retraining using the online software. Thus, all its employees must learn how to use the educational software. A number of the tutorials also require group interactions using transferable files based on code developed by the manufacturer of the online tutorial programs. Many of the firm's employees participate in these group-training exercises within Internet chat groups that include employees of other firms using the same online training software.

If the multinational corporation were to contemplate changing to a different manufacturer of online employee-training programs, relatively large switching costs would be entailed. All its employees would have to learn how to use a new training system, which might require hiring expensive training consultants. In addition, any files that groups have used in interactive training exercises would have to be converted to a code format that is accessible within a new training system. To communicate with employees of other firms that continue to use the previous system, employees would have to reformat files. Alternatively, the company would have to sacrifice any benefits its employees have gained from their participation in group-training projects that have encompassed people in other companies.

Employee time devoted to these tasks undoubtedly would entail a substantial opportunity cost for the entire corporation. The sum of both explicit and implicit opportunity costs would constitute a significant **switching cost** for the company. (Some have argued that switching costs help to explain the configuration of computer keyboards, although there are reasons to question this interpretation; see on page 92 *Management Online: QWERTY versus Dvorak—An Example of the Importance of Switching Costs?*)

It is arguable that switching costs are likely to be particularly high for the consumers of goods or services produced by firms in network industries. In such industries, most other consumers use the same product. Thus, switching to an alternative product is likely to entail particularly high switching costs, such as the retraining costs that the corporation in the example would confront. For consumers of products of network industries, therefore, it is more likely that **consumer lock-in** may take place, meaning that the switching cost associated with consuming any item other than the product of the network industry will almost always exceed the perceived benefits from such a switch. As a result, the network industry, and perhaps one or two firms within that industry that benefit most from positive market feedback, will establish a position of dominance in the marketplace.

Switching Cost
The combined explicit and implicit opportunity cost of using one product as an alternate to another.

Consumer Lock-In
A situation in which switching costs are always higher than the perceived benefit from using an alternate product.

QWERTY versus Dvorak—An Example of the Importance of Switching Costs?

When you use your computer keyboard to surf the Net or to type a course paper, you are using a keyboard design that at least postdates the Civil War—but not by much. In 1868, Christopher Sholes patented the QWERTY (see the top five left-hand letters on your computer keyboard) layout for typewriters. Sholes had developed the keyboard layout to minimize the chances that type bars would jam when a typist hit a number of keys in rapid succession. The QWERTY layout put the keys most likely to be struck in rapid succession on opposite sides of the typewriter.

In 1936, August Dvorak patented a different keyboard layout, which he claimed permitted more rapid typing without jamming. During World War II, a U.S. Navy study concluded that the Dvorak system did work better. But no one adopted it. In the past, some economists have pointed to this as a classic example of how high switching costs can lock people into a potentially inefficient production standard. Even though individuals and companies could have quickly recov-

ered the costs of new keyboards and training, manufacturers would not switch until typists did, and individual typists would not switch until other typists switched. Thus, according to this argument, the QWERTY switching costs have remained too high to justify adopting a higher-efficiency Dvorak keyboard.

There are, however, a couple of problems with this "classic example" of a network externality with high switching costs. One is that the Navy's original study had a conflict-of-interest problem—it was directed by a lieutenant commander by the name of August Dvorak, the wartime Navy's top expert on labor-saving programs. Another is that careful studies in years since have shown that QWERTY's bad points (for instance, excess loading of common letters on the top row and unbalanced typing loads for the left and right hands) are outweighed by QWERTY's benefits (alternating hand sequences that help speed typing). This implies that incurring the cost of learning to type on a Dvorak keyboard may not, on net, be worthwhile relative to the anticipated benefit.

For Critical Analysis:
Are there any other types of computer peripherals or other associated hardware, besides keyboards, that, at least arguably, might be subject to network-externality effects?

FUNDAMENTAL ISSUES ▼

1.

2.

3.

4.

5.

5. What are common characteristics of network industries?

Issues of product compatibility often arise in a network industry. Producers of items that are complements in consumption typically seek to identify which firms within the network industry produce items experiencing positive market feedback. Producers of complementary items may design them to function most efficiently with the products of one or two companies that emerge as the standard product, thereby reinforcing positive market feedback for those firms within the network industry. Those who consume goods or services produced by a network industry often face significant costs of switching to alternative products. Consumer lock-in can occur if a number of consumers find that switching costs always exceed the perceived benefit of purchasing a substitute product.

Chapter Summary

1) **Alternative Forms of Competition among Evenly Matched but Imperfectly Competitive E-Commerce Firms:** In an oligopolistic marketplace, no more than a few firms sell the bulk of industry output. Oligopolistic interdependence results: The price or production decisions that one firm makes can affect the decisions at other firms. Under monopolistic competition, it is easy for firms to enter or leave the industry, and many firms produce similar yet distinguishable goods or services. Consequently, each firm determines the price of its product, taking into account the fact that the demand for its own product depends on the prices charged by other firms and on the number of firms in the industry. Firms earn zero economic profits in the long run, but the price charged by a monopolistically competitive firm exceeds marginal cost, and firms produce at an average cost that exceeds the minimum feasible average cost.

2) **How the Special Production-Cost Characteristics of Virtual Products Influence How They Are Priced:** Virtual products exist in digital forms that may be produced and distributed at relatively low marginal cost. Creating the product normally requires incurring a relatively sizable fixed cost. As a result, the average total cost curves of firms selling virtual products slope downward, and producers of these products experience short-run economies of scale. If a producer were to set the price of a virtual product equal to marginal cost, it would fail to recoup the fixed cost of producing the item, so the first-best optimum of marginal cost pricing is unattainable. To induce the firm to incur the fixed cost of creating the product, price must equal average cost. Economists often regard average cost pricing as a second-best optimum for society, because setting price equal to average total cost induces a firm to provide a virtual product, but at an economic profit of zero.

3) **How Network Externalities Affect the Demand for a Product:** If a good or service is subject to a network externality, this means that the benefit that a given individual receives from consuming the item rises when others also consume the good. As a result, each consumer is willing to pay more for the item as the number of other consumers of the item rises, thereby affecting the overall demand for the item as well as the price elasticity of demand for the item.

4) **How Network Externalities Produce Market Feedback Effects:** In a network industry, logrolling effects can take place in the form of market feedback effects. If a sufficient number of people purchase a product subject to network externalities to induce many others to buy the item, then a positive market feedback effect occurs. By way of contrast, if a sufficient number of people stop purchasing a product to give a number of individuals an

incentive to cut back on their purchases, then there is a negative market feedback effect. Market feedback effects influence fortunes of both entire network industries and of individual firms within those industries.

5) **Common Characteristics of Network Industries:** Product compatibility issues frequently emerge in a network industry. Firms that produce items that are complements in consumption to the products of a network industry may design the complementary items to be easiest to consume alongside the products of one or two companies experiencing positive market feedback effects. This tends to reinforce the positive market feedback effects experienced by those one or two companies, so that those firms' products emerge as the standard products within the network industry. Consumers of items produced by firms within a network industry commonly encounter significant costs of switching to substitute products. Consumer lock-in can take place if a consumer's switching costs are always greater than the perceived benefit of using the substitute product.

Questions and Problems

1) The consulting firm Forrester Research conducts regular "power" surveys of dot-com industries, in which it attempts to identify companies with the strongest opportunities for significant profitability. Key factors influencing firms' rankings are characteristics that distinguish the quality of their products and services and that set them apart from rival firms. Use appropriate diagrams to explain why successful product differentiation is likely to enhance an Internet seller's profitability.

2) There is a large market in online dating and match-making services. Each year dozens of firms enter and exit this market. The industry is composed of hundreds of sites that, in exchange for monthly subscription fees and per-message charges, provide pages where single people can provide personal information and engage in online chats. Each site attempts to distinguish itself from others by offering safe forums for unattached people to meet, often by developing special features for preserving anonymity and screening out unscrupulous customers. Take a position on how the prices of these online services are likely to be determined, and draw on one of the theories discussed in Chapters 2 and 3 to support your position.

3) Consider the e-book publisher whose cost curves are depicted in Figure 3-4. Suppose that before the publisher makes a deal with the author of this e-book, it determines that this is the long-run situation it will face if it pays

the author $45,000 in advance. The author of the e-book, however, indicates a willingness to write the book for an advance of only $25,000. Do not try to work out numerical values, but explain the basic short-run implications for the publisher's profit-maximizing price, sales, revenues, costs, and profits.

4) Suppose that, as in question 3, the e-book publisher finds that the author will settle for a smaller up-front payment to write an e-book. In addition, suppose that other publishers in the e-book marketplace find that authors accept lower up-front payments. What are the basic implications for long-run equilibrium in this monopolistically competitive industry?

5) When a firm's long-run average total cost curve slopes downward over all ranges of output, economists sometimes call the firm a *natural monopoly,* meaning that it is most efficient for a single firm to sell the product in question. Explain why firms that sell virtual products in monopolistically competitive industries are not natural monopolies.

6) Take a look at Tables 3-3 and 3-4 on page 85, and explain why all five consumers will choose to buy the software package when its price is $80.

7) Take another look back at Tables 3-3 and 3-4. Table 3-4 is constructed under the assumption that the five consumers do not share with one another information about willingness to pay. Suppose that all five consumers get together for lunch each day, and during a conversation they discover how much each one is willing to pay depending on how many others purchase and use the product at every possible price. Suppose that they act on this information by coordinating their purchases of the software package, and redo Table 3-4 under this assumption. What is the maximum price at which at least one unit of the software package is purchased in this five-consumer marketplace? What is the total number of units purchased at this price?

8) Explain why network externalities can cause the demand for a product *either* to expand *or* to contract relative to what it would be if there were no network externalities.

9) Make a list of five products that you think are subject to network externalities.
   (a) In your view, are these five products sold in network industries? Explain.
   (b) For industries in part *(a)* that you have classified as network industries, do you believe that all firms within each industry experience market feedback effects, or do just one or two firms experience market feedback effects? In your view, are the market feedback effects currently positive or negative?

10) Economies of scale normally relate to a firm's cost of production, but some economists argue that network externalities can be a source of "demand-side economies of scale" for firms within network industries. Speculate about what these economists might mean.

Online Application

Internet URL: http://www.nolo.com

Title: **Nolo.com—Law for All**

Navigation: Go directly to the above Web site.

Application

1) Most economists would argue that Nolo.com operates in either a perfectly competitive or monopolistically competitive market, because there are now many online providers of legal services that can easily enter or leave this electronic marketplace. What factors are likely to determine which of these two market structures is relevant?

2) For the sake of argument, suppose that the market for online legal services is perfectly competitive. Take a look at the large numbers of legal services offered at this Web site. What factors are likely to determine Nolo's shutdown point (see page 43 in Chapter 2) for offering any one of these services?

3) Suppose that a legal-services firm offers downloadable software that consumers can use to draft wills and other legal documents. If the firm incurs high up-front costs in designing the software but very low costs of distributing it on the Web, what can you say about the likelihood that the firm will sell this software in a perfectly competitive electronic marketplace?

For Group Study and Analysis: Assign groups to search the Web and compile a list of at least three additional online legal firms and to compare the services these firms offer. Reconvene the entire class and discuss whether the market for online legal services should be classified as perfectly competitive or monopolistically competitive.

Selected References and Further Readings

Carlton, Dennis, and Jeffrey Perloff. *Modern Industrial Organization,* 3d ed. Reading, MA: Addison-Wesley, 2000.

Choi, Soon-Yong, Dale Stahl, and Andrew Whinston. *The Economics of Electronic Commerce.* Indianapolis: Macmillan Technical Publishing, 1997.

Pepall, Lynne, Daniel Richards, and George Norman. *Industrial Organization: Contemporary Theory and Practice.* Cincinnati: South-Western, 1999.

Shapiro, Carl, and Hal Varian. *Information Rules: A Strategic Guide to the Network Economy.* Boston: Harvard Business School Press, 1999.

Shy, Oz. *The Economics of Network Industries.* Cambridge: Cambridge University Press, 2000.

Smith, Michael, Joseph Bailey, and Erik Brynjolfsson. "Understanding Digital Markets: Review and Assessment." In *Understanding the Digital Economy: Data, Tools, and Research,* ed. Erik Brynjolfsson and Brian Kahin. Cambridge, MA: MIT Press, 2000, pp. 99–136.

Varian, Hal. "Market Structure in the Network Age." In *Understanding the Digital Economy: Data, Tools, and Research,* ed. Erik Brynjolfsson and Brian Kahin. Cambridge, MA: MIT Press, 2000, pp. 137–150.

Chapter 4

Business Strategies and Conduct in the Electronic Marketplace

<E-Commerce Today>

Amazon's Big 'Pricing Mistake'

In the fall of 2000, some shoppers in the DVD section of Amazon.com's Web site noticed that prices were not always the same. The company later claimed that it was randomly raising or lowering prices to gauge how price variations were affecting customers' buying habits. A press statement said that it was all just part of a "market test."

Critics of the company accused it of experimenting with price discrimination—charging different customers different prices for the same DVDs based on their willingness to pay. After all, the critics argued, Amazon has a wealth of data about the shopping habits of its customers. From the time that a customer logs onto Amazon's site, the company's Web server can track each Web page that the customer accesses when browsing through the site or conducting searches by author, title, or subject.

In principle, Amazon could use this data to push up its profit through price discrimination practices. If a customer has made, say, a dozen purchases in recent weeks, all of which appeared to be "impulse buys" of an individual item at a time, then the company might be able to add an extra dollar or two to the price that its Web site lists for that particular customer. For a customer whose shopping habits reveal signs of considerable sensitivity to prices, the company could encourage more purchases, and hence more revenues for the company, by shaving a dollar or two off its price quote for that customer.

There is nothing novel about **price discrimination.** Long before the emergence of electronic commerce, traditional bricks-and-mortar firms learned that they could enhance their profitability by charging different consumers different prices for identical products or by charging the same consumer different prices for the same product, depending on how many units the consumer purchased. What is new is that in many ways information technology and the individualized nature of Web-based interactions between buyers and sellers have enhanced the capability of sellers to engage in price discrimination.

In this chapter you will learn why e-commerce firms can gain from price discrimination. More broadly, you will learn about the underlying economic rationales guiding alternative business strategies in the electronic marketplace.

Price Discrimination
Charging different consumers different prices for the same product or charging the same consumer different prices for different quantities of the same product.

 # Price Discrimination—Some Basics

Recall from Chapter 2 that consumer surplus arises in a market when consumers are willing to pay more for a good or service than the market price they actually pay. The idea behind price discrimination is to try to capture as much consumer surplus as possible, by charging prices that are equal to, or at least close to, the prices that individual customers are willing to pay.

PERFECT PRICE DISCRIMINATION

The best of all worlds for a producer and the worst of all worlds for a consumer exist when the firm is able to charge the maximum price that each and every consumer is willing to pay for each unit of the product that it sells. To see why this is so, take a look at Figure 4-1, which compares alternative pricing policies for an imperfectly competitive firm that can set the price of its product to maximize its economic profit. To simplify, the figure is drawn under the assumption that the firm's marginal cost is constant, so the marginal cost curve is horizontal.

A non–price-discriminating firm produces output to the point where marginal revenue equals marginal cost. Thus, it produces Q^* units and charges the price P^*. The firm's economic profit is the dark-shaded area. Consumer surplus is the dashed area depicted in the figure.

Now suppose that the firm finds a way to charge each consumer the maximum price that the consumer is willing to pay for each unit of the product. This means that at each quantity along the demand curve in Figure 4-1, the producer is able to charge the corresponding price. If a producer is able to set its price in this way, it engages in **perfect price discrimination,** which economists also call *first-degree price discrimination.* Naturally, setting prices in this manner will allow a price-discriminating firm to "steal away" consumer surplus.

Perfect Price Discrimination for a Product with Periodic Unit Sales

To understand the effects of perfect price discrimination, consider an industry in which firms sell their products as individual units on a periodic basis. Imagine, for instance, that the demand curve displayed in Figure 4-1 applies to a downloadable software product that a company sells over the Internet in versions that it upgrades quarterly. After three months of use, the software ceases to interact with any other computer software and becomes useless. Within a two-week period at the end of each quarter, the software consumer can pay to download the product again and use it for another three months. Hence, each customer must purchase a single unit of the product from the software manufacturer every three months.

Perfect Price Discrimination

Charging each consumer the maximum price that the consumer is willing to pay for each unit consumed, thereby capturing the entire amount of consumer surplus; also known as first-degree price discrimination.

Figure 4-1:
Perfect Price Discrimination.

An imperfectly competitive firm that faces the demand curve for its product and does not engage in price discrimination produces output to the point where marginal revenue equals marginal cost. It thereby produces Q^* units, which it sells at the price P^*. The firm's profit is the shaded area, and consumer surplus is the dashed area. If the firm is able to charge every consumer the maximum price that he or she is willing pay for each unit of the firm's product, it can capture the amount of consumer surplus as additional profits. Furthermore, it can engage in perfect price discrimination by producing Q^{**} units of output and adjusting the price it charges for every unit purchased according to each consumer's willingness to pay, enabling it to add the lightly shaded area to its total profit. Hence, perfect price discrimination would yield the sum of all three areas—the total region below the demand curve and above the marginal cost curve—as economic profit.

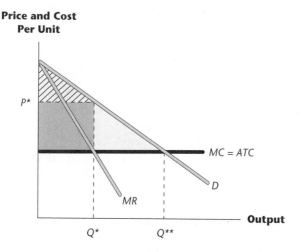

If the firm can figure out how to charge each customer the price that the customer is willing to pay, then the firm will be willing to sell its software downloads to every buyer who is willing to pay a price at least as great as the firm's presumed-constant average cost. This means that the perfect-price-discriminating firm will produce Q^{**} units of output, which is the same amount of output that would have been produced under marginal cost pricing in a perfectly competitive market for the firm's product. The firm then adjusts the price it charges for each unit of software upward from its marginal cost according to each customer's willingness to pay, which means it ratchets its price upward along the demand curve in Figure 4-1. Ultimately, the firm's profit equals the sum of all three shaded areas in the figure—the total area below the demand curve and above the firm's marginal cost curve. This is the amount that consumer surplus *would have been* under marginal cost pricing. The firm captures the entire surplus for itself and thereby significantly increases its profit.

To effectively engage in price discrimination, the firm must be able to prevent its customers from *reselling* the software. Otherwise, a consumer who was willing to pay a relatively low price—say, the price just equal to the firm's marginal cost—could download the product and then offer to sell it to another consumer. The customer who purchases the software at the lowest price might post an offer on a C2C auction site to sell the software to the highest bidder. The latter individual could turn out to be the consumer who is willing to pay the most for the product. To prevent such product resale from eroding its profits, the company can design the software to cease functioning when transferred to a computer other than the one to which it initially was downloaded.

PERFECT PRICE DISCRIMINATION FOR A PRODUCT SOLD IN VOLUME

Two-Part Tariff

Charging a lump-sum fee to consume a product and a per-unit charge based on the quantity consumed.

Many downloadable software products are distributed in the manner just described. Suppose, however, that the same software firm offers an alternative arrangement for engaging in price discrimination. Instead of selling quarterly downloads, the firm offers each customer real-time access to the software on the Internet. Rather than downloading the software to the hard drive of a computer, each customer connects to the Internet, clicks a button, and acquires the company's software product via its Web server. To prevent the potential for customer resale, the firm also develops an elaborate system for secure real-time access on a customer-by-customer basis.

In this instance, let's suppose that the demand curve in Figure 4-1 applies to an individual consumer. Instead of denoting quantities of software downloads sold by the firm, suppose that the quantity axis in Figure 4-1 refers to *software access time* purchased by the consumer. How can the firm engage in perfect price discrimination under these altered circumstances?

The answer is that the perfect-price-discriminating firm can implement a two-part pricing scheme that economists call a **two-part tariff.** The firm imposes both a lump-sum fee and a per-unit charge based on the quantity consumed. To do this, the firm can charge every customer a per-minute charge equal to its unit cost of producing the software and providing minute-by-minute access over the Internet. Because the firm knows the consumer will purchase Q^{**} units of access time in Figure 4-1, this per-minute charge guarantees that the firm covers its costs. The second part of the firm's pricing scheme is to set an "access fee" the customer pays for the right to real-time Internet access to the firm's software, irrespective of how many minutes the customer uses the software. The firm sets this access fee equal to the amount of the entire shaded area in Figure 4-1, thereby extracting the maximum available surplus that the consumer otherwise would have received under marginal cost pricing.

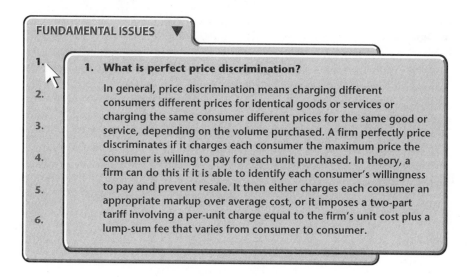

FUNDAMENTAL ISSUES ▼

1.

2.

3.

4.

5.

6.

1.   What is perfect price discrimination?

In general, price discrimination means charging different consumers different prices for identical goods or services or charging the same consumer different prices for the same good or service, depending on the volume purchased. A firm perfectly price discriminates if it charges each consumer the maximum price the consumer is willing to pay for each unit purchased. In theory, a firm can do this if it is able to identify each consumer's willingness to pay and prevent resale. It then either charges each consumer an appropriate markup over average cost, or it imposes a two-part tariff involving a per-unit charge equal to the firm's unit cost plus a lump-sum fee that varies from consumer to consumer.

IMPERFECT PRICE DISCRIMINATION

In most instances, firms have a difficult time determining exactly what each customer is willing to pay to consume any given quantity of the firm's product. For this reason, engaging in perfect price discrimination usually proves infeasible. Nevertheless, a firm may still be able to improve its profitability by practicing **imperfect price discrimination**—charging different prices to different *groups* of consumers or varying the price it charges to the same consumer depending on whether the consumer is part of a *group* that generally purchases relatively low volumes or relatively high volumes of the firm's product. Thus, a firm may be able to increase its profitability if it can find a way to categorize its customers within groups and charge different prices to those within each group.

Imperfect Price Discrimination
Charging different prices to distinct groups of consumers or charging a different price to a consumer depending on whether the consumer is classified within a group that buys relatively small or large quantities.

Differential Pricing for Different Groups of Consumers

Consider again the demand curve displayed in Figure 4-1, which is reproduced as panel *(c)* of Figure 4-2 on page 104. Now, however, we assume that the firm cannot determine each customer's willingness to pay. Suppose that it *can* separate its customers into two different groups, as shown in Figure 4-2. The demand for the firm's product by one group, called "group A," is given by the demand curve D_A in panel *(a)*. The demand by the other group, "group B," is given by the demand curve D_B in panel *(b)*. These two demand curves indicate that at the price P_1, each group consumes the quantity Q_1. Thus, the total quantity demanded at this price equals the sum of Q_1 and Q_1, or the amount $2 \times Q_1$ that panel *(c)* displays. Summing the quantities demanded by both groups at all other prices in panels *(a)* and *(b)* gives each of the other points that trace out the overall demand curve D in panel *(c)*.

**Figure 4-2:
Two Groups of
Consumers and
Demand for a Firm's
Product.**

*The total demand for a
firm's product, shown in
panel (c), equals the sum of
the demand for the product
by consumers in group A,
displayed in panel (a), and
by consumers in group B,
shown in panel (b). At the
price P_1, both groups desire
to consume the same
amount of the firm's output,
Q_1, so the total quantity
demanded at this price is
$2 \times Q_1$ in panel (c). A given
proportionate increase in the
price from P_1 would result in
a greater proportionate
response in the quantity
demanded by group A
relative to groups B. This
means that relative to the
demand by consumers
within group B, the demand
by consumers within
group A is relatively more
price-elastic.*

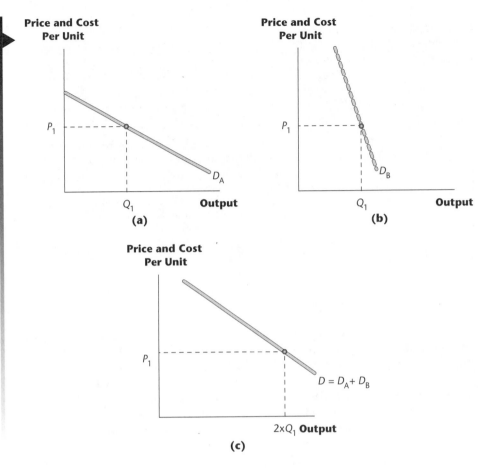

Note that if the firm were to raise its price by a given proportionate amount
relative to P_1, the quantity demanded by people within group A would decline by
a larger proportionate amount, relative to the initial quantity Q_1, as compared
with the resulting fall in the quantity demanded by people within group B. Similarly, if the firm were to reduce its price by a given proportionate amount relative
to P_1, the quantity demanded by people within group A would increase by a larger
proportionate amount, relative to the initial quantity, Q_1, as compared with the
resulting rise in the quantity demanded by people within group B. This means the
price elasticity of demand—the proportionate change in quantity demanded resulting from a proportionate change in price—is comparatively higher for consumers
in group A than for those in group B.

To consider how this firm can maximize its profit, examine Figure 4-3. As in
Figure 4-1, the firm's marginal cost is assumed to be constant. Panel *(c)* displays

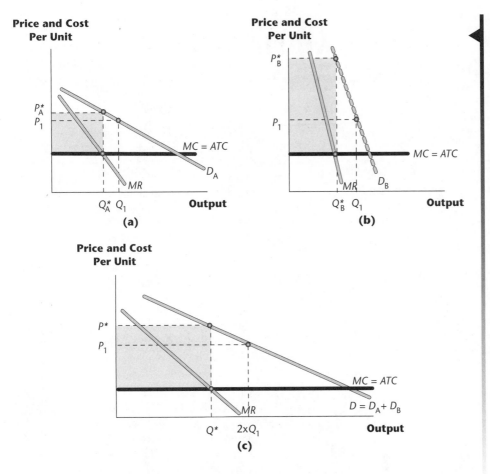

**Figure 4-3:
Alternative Pricing
Strategies for a Firm
with Two Groups of
Consumers.**

*As in Figure 4-2, the total
demand for a firm's product
in panel (c) is equal to the
sum of the demands by
groups A and B, shown in
panels (a) and (b), and the
demand by consumers within
group A is relatively more
price-elastic than the demand
by consumers within group B.
If the firm were to charge
both groups the same price,
then panel (c) shows that it
would produce Q* units and
sell them at the price P*,
earning a profit equal to the
shaded area in panel (c). If
the firm engages in price
discrimination by charging
different prices P_A^* and P_B^* to
the two groups, however, it
provides the quantities Q_A^*
and Q_B^* and earns profits
equal to the shaded regions
in panels (a) and (b). The
sum of these areas exceeds
the profit area in panel (c),
so the firm can increase its
total profit by engaging in
price discrimination.*

the firm's profit-maximizing price and output choices, P^* and Q^*, if it charges all
customers the same price. The firm produces to the point where the marginal
revenue derived from its overall market demand equals marginal cost. The
economic profit that the firm earns using this single-price strategy is the shaded
area in panel *(c)*.

If the firm engages in price discrimination, it charges group A customers and
group B customers different prices. In panel *(a)*, the firm sells output to customers
in group A up to the point where the marginal revenue derived from group A's
relatively elastic demand curve equals its marginal production cost, so it sells
Q_A^* units of output to group A and charges each customer within that group the
price P_A^*. In panel *(b)*, the firm sells output to group B consumers up to the point
where the marginal revenue derived from that group's relatively inelastic demand
curve equals the firm's marginal production cost. Consequently, it sells only

MANAGEMENT *Online*

Inferring the Elasticity of Demand from Clickstreams

You have learned that a company that wishes to increase its revenues should raise the price it charges customers with an inelastic demand for the goods it sells. By way of contrast, a firm can also increase its revenues by reducing the price it charges customers whose demand is elastic.

Increasingly, companies are using the Internet to try to have it both ways. In 1998, a California software firm developed a program that allows Internet sellers to automatically track the shopping patterns of customers who browse Web sites. Since then, a number of programs have been developed to enable Internet sellers to study Web surfers' *clickstreams*—the observed manner in which customers navigate a Web site. If a customer quickly zeroes in on a specific item and exhibits little effort to shop around for better prices, then clickstream-monitoring software targets the customer as part of a group whose demand for that item is likely to be relatively inelastic. The seller's Web server responds by quoting the customer a relatively high price that the firm has established for customers within that group. If another Web surfer who visits the site behaves like a price-sensitive shopper—perhaps by com-

paring many different products without jumping to buy—then the program concludes that the customer's demand is more likely to be relatively elastic. This signals the seller's Web server to quote a lower price.

In principle, customers could fight these pricing systems. Spendthrifts with a low price elasticity of demand could try to behave like skinflints with a high price elasticity of demand by displaying artificially cautious clickstreams. In the future, customers might do this by employing programmable shopbots to conduct masquerades—indeed, some companies have such shopbots on the drawing boards. Nevertheless, Internet sellers probably have the upper hand over people with inelastic demand. After all, by definition these are customers who are in a hurry to get what they want. They likely will not wish to waste precious time trying to program shopbots to fool Internet sellers' pricing programs.

For Critical Analysis:

What factors might discourage a prospective Internet buyer with inelastic demand from posting offers on auction sites to purchase a product from someone who has elastic demand and can thereby buy it at a lower price from a price-discriminating Internet seller?

Q_B^* units of output to group B and charges group B consumers the higher price P_B^*. Note that as in the case of a perfectly price-discriminating firm, a firm that engages in imperfect price discrimination must be able to prevent resale of its product. Otherwise, individuals within group A could profit from buying the product at the price P_A^* and reselling it to group B consumers at a price below P_B^*.

The sum of the profits earned from sales at different prices to each group, the shaded profit areas in panels *(a)* and *(b)*, exceeds the total profit earned from selling at the same price to all consumers, the shaded profit area in panel *(c)*. If the firm can find a way to price discriminate by distributing its product to members of the A and B groups at the differential prices P_A^* and P_B^*, it can enhance its profitability. (To learn how new Web server software is helping Internet sellers engage in imperfect price discrimination, see *Management Online: Inferring the Elasticity of Demand from Clickstreams.*)

Imperfect Price Discrimination with Two-Part Tariffs and Consumer Self-Selection

Simply charging different prices for the same product can raise a firm's profitability as long as it can identify groups of consumers with differing elasticities of demand, charge them different prices, and prevent resale of the product. When this is not feasible, a firm might still be able to engage in price discrimination if it can induce consumers to **self select** by inducing them to sort themselves into different groups through their own choices from among alternative pricing schemes that the firm offers.

A firm might accomplish this by offering consumers a choice between alternative two-part tariffs. To see how it can do this, let's reconsider the earlier example of a company that offers real-time access to its software. Suppose that the firm faces groups composed of two types of customers. One group consists of "type H" (high-volume) consumers who, other things being equal, tend to desire real-time access of the firm's software for relatively long stretches of time each day. The other group consists of "type L" (low-volume) consumers who typically wish to access the firm's software for relatively brief intervals each day, holding other factors unchanged.

To earn the highest profit from serving type H customers, the firm should set a relatively low per-minute charge, thereby encouraging type H customers to self select by accessing the software for lengthy periods. The firm then seeks to capture as much of the relatively large consumer surplus that results by assessing a higher fixed fee for type H customers to access its site. Alternatively, the firm should charge a relatively low fixed access fee to type L consumers to induce them to use the site, but it should set a relatively high per-minute charge for type L consumers.

The firm cannot identify the two types of consumers in advance, so its best pricing policy is to give all consumers a choice between the alternative two-part tariffs: either a low per-minute charge coupled with a high fixed access fee, or a high per-minute charge coupled with a low fixed access fee. Type H consumers who know that they will access the software for long periods will naturally be attracted by the lower per-minute charge, and type L consumers who know that they will access the software for brief periods will tend to prefer to pay the lower fixed access fee. Thus, the two types of consumers will self select into their respective groups, and the firm will enhance its profitability by imposing the different pricing schemes on each group.

Self Selection
Consumers voluntarily sort into identifiable groups by choosing among alternative pricing schemes offered by a firm.

WWW.

What are some examples of price discrimination? Review many issues relating to strategic pricing on the Web and several helpful case studies of price discrimination in "Strategic Computing and Communications Technology," by Kim Bui et. al., at http://www-inst.eecs.berkeley.edu/~eecsba1/s98/reports/eecsba1d/project3/project.html.

.com

FUNDAMENTAL ISSUES ▼

1.
2.
3.
4.
5.
6.

2. What is imperfect price discrimination?

In practice, a firm that has pricing power usually cannot identify each consumer's willingness to pay. Nevertheless, the firm may be able to engage in imperfect price discrimination by charging different prices to different groups with varying preferences, as exemplified by different elasticities of demand or volumes of purchases. If the firm can identify groups with differing price elasticities of demand, then it maximizes its profit by charging a relatively higher price to groups with relatively lower price elasticities of demand. If the firm cannot separate consumers into groups, it may be able to use a two-part tariff to induce them to sort themselves into groups that pay different prices.

 ## Other Methods of Price Discrimination

Differential pricing to identifiable groups of consumers and alternative two-part tariffs for unidentifiable groups are two common ways to engage in imperfect price discrimination. These are not the only ways that firms can price discriminate, however.

TIE-IN SALES

Tie-In Sales
Purchases of a particular product that are permitted only if a consumer buys another good or service from the same firm.

One way to practice price discrimination is to pursue **tie-in sales.** These are agreements under which a firm permits a customer to buy one good or service if the customer purchases another good or service as well.

Rationales for Tie-In Sales Unrelated to Price Discrimination
Firms may use tie-in sales for reasons that have nothing to do with efforts to engage in price discrimination. For example, firms automatically include keyboards along with many models of desktop computers. Everyone who buys a desktop computer requires a keyboard to perform the full range of functions that the computer makes possible. Therefore, as long as consumer preferences are not noticeably different across keyboards, it is more efficient to sell desktop computers and keyboards together than to sell the two goods separately.

Tie-in sales are commonplace for many information-technology products in the electronic marketplace. Both desktop computers and notebook computers typically include internal modems. Likewise, companies that sell software for creating

Web pages also commonly include separate stand-alone software that permits the user to manipulate images for placement on a Web page.

In some instances companies may require tie-in sales to ensure product quality. A B2B exchange might require a firm to purchase special security software so that both parties to a B2B transaction can be assured of correct and secure transmission of all information about pricing and delivery terms.

Firms in oligopolistic markets with implicit, or perhaps even explicit, cartel arrangements might use tie-in sales to grant secret price discounts to their customers. An oligopolistic firm might sell the cartel's product at the profit-maximizing monopoly price established by the cartel and sell a related product, such as an accessory product, at a sharply discounted price to attract customers from other firms and increase its own profits at their expense.

Using Tie-In Sales to Price Discriminate

This last example provides a foundation for contemplating how firms might use tie-in sales to engage in price discrimination. A computer software company might sell a network operating system to each corporate customer under an agreement for the corporation to purchase all its desktop office-productivity software as well. The agreement could allow unlimited installations of the network operating system on all corporate desktop and laptop computers but require the company to purchase separate copies of the office-productivity software to install on each computer. In this way, the software company effectively charges a higher price to high-volume users of its products.

The software company could also use agreements of this kind to develop separate two-part tariffs and engage in price discrimination. Consider a corporate customer who plans to intensively use the network operating system and who is predisposed to installing the office-productivity software on only the computers of a few key employees. This customer is likely to pay a relatively low lump-sum fee for the network operating system and a relatively high price for each copy of the office productivity software. Suppose that another prospective corporate customer intends to use just a few features of the network operating system to enhance certain aspects of its operations but plans to install the office productivity software on a large number of employee computers. This customer would be predisposed to pay a relatively high fixed fee for the network operating system and a relatively low price for each copy of the office productivity software. Faced with a number of prospective corporate customers of each of these types, the software company could establish separate two-part tariff schemes, let the corporations self select, and engage in price discrimination.

PRODUCT BUNDLING

A method of price discrimination that is closely related to tie-in sales (some economists do classify it as a form of tie-in sales) is **bundling**, or the joint sale of two or more products. That is, a multiproduct firm that bundles two products sells a unit

Bundling
Offering two or more products for sale as a set.

Table 4-1: Boosting Revenues via Bundling.

If the firm sells each product separately, it maximizes it revenues by setting a price of $300 for product 1 and a price of $250 for product 2, thereby earning total revenues of $550. By way of contrast, if it bundles the two products together as a package that it sells for $400, both consumers are willing to buy the package, and the firm earns total revenues of $800.

	Product 1	Product 2	Package Price
Consumer *X* Willingness to Pay	$150	$250	$400
Consumer *Y* Willingness to Pay	300	100	400

of one product to a consumer only if the consumer simultaneously buys a unit of another of the firm's products.

To see how a firm can use bundling to price discriminate, consider the example illustrated in Table 4-1. Consumer X is willing to pay $150 for each unit of product 1 and $250 for product 2. Consumer Y, however, is willing to pay $300 for product 1 but is only willing to pay $100 for product 2.

To maximize its revenues if it sells each product separately, this firm should set a price of $300 for product 1 and a price of $250 for product 2. Then its total combined sales amount to $550.

Suppose that the firm decides to sell both product 1 and product 2 as a bundle. If either consumer X or consumer Y wishes to purchase one or another of the two products, each consumer must purchase the two products as a package. In this case, both consumers are willing to pay a total of $400 each for the two-product bundle, so that the firm's combined sales amount to $800. Bundling thereby increases the firm's revenues.

Table 4-1 reveals how bundling also effectively enables the firm to engage in price discrimination. From the perspective of consumer X, the price paid for product 1 is $150, but from the perspective of consumer Y product 1's price is $300. The perceived price paid for product 2 by consumer X is $250, but the price of product 2 for consumer Y is effectively only $100.

For bundling to pay off for the firm, it must be able to prevent the resale of either product. Otherwise, consumer Y could purchase the bundle for $400 and sell product 2, which consumer Y values at only $100, to consumer X for $150. Alternatively, consumer X could pay $400 for the bundle and sell product 1, which consumer X values at $250, to consumer Y for $300. (It is possible that firms may bundle their products to extend their pricing power over one product to another; see *Policymaking Online: Software Bundling at Microsoft—Windows, Internet Explorer, and Office.*)

POLICYMAKING *Online*

Software Bundling at Microsoft—Windows, Internet Explorer, and Office

A few years back, Corel successfully marketed office-productivity software under brand names such as WordPerfect and Lotus, and Netscape was the dominant seller of Web browser software, called Navigator. Microsoft markets its own brands of office productivity software, such as Word and Excel, and it sells an alternative Web browsing program called Internet Explorer. After several years of competition with Microsoft, Corel teeters near bankruptcy, and Netscape's share of the market for Web browser software has fallen to below 25 percent.

Microsoft's rivals charged that it owed much of its success to a key advantage, namely, that more than four-fifths of the world's personal computers use its Windows operating system. Microsoft, its competitors argued, extended its near monopoly in the operating systems market to the markets for office-productivity software and Web browsers. It did so, they contended, by arranging tie-in sales of Windows and pro-

grams such as Word and Excel to computer manufacturers for installation on new computers and by bundling Windows and Internet Explorer for purchase as a package.

In May 1998, the U.S. Department of Justice took Netscape's side, arguing that "Microsoft possesses (and for several years has possessed) monopoly power in the market for personal computer operating systems." By bundling Internet Explorer within Windows, the Justice Department alleged, "Microsoft is unlawfully taking advantage of its Windows monopoly to protect and extend that monopoly." A federal judge's findings of fact in November 1999, which were partly reinforced by an appeals court, in July 2001 generally supported the Justice Department's interpretation, and Microsoft announced that it would allow computer manufacturers to separate Internet Explorer from the windows operating system.

For Critical Analysis:

Does the fact that software prices generally have fallen for a number of years necessarily imply that Microsoft actually has not had monopoly power in software markets?

FUNDAMENTAL ISSUES ▼

1.

2.

3.

4.

5.

6.

3. How can firms use tie-in sales and bundling to engage in price discrimination?

Tie-in sales allow a consumer to purchase one product only if the consumer also buys another product. Companies can use tie-in sales to implement two-part tariffs by varying the prices they charge for the separate products based on the consumption patterns of different customers. Bundling is the combined sale of one unit each of two or more products as a package product. Consumers value each unit within the bundle at different levels, and bundling raises a company's revenues. By bundling products, a firm effectively charges different prices for each product, thereby engaging in price discrimination.

Strategic Pricing in E-Commerce

In principle, both online and offline companies with the ability to set the prices of their products can practice price discrimination. Fundamental characteristics of the goods and services produced by some Internet sellers make them readily amenable to price discrimination, however. In addition, the nature of Internet interactions between e-commerce firms and their customers and the use of information technologies by Internet sellers potentially simplifies the strategic use of pricing to enhance profitability.

VERSIONING

Versioning
Selling essentially the same product in slightly different forms to different groups of consumers.

One way that Web-based firms can try to price discriminate is through **versioning**, or selling their products in slightly different forms to different groups. A typical method of versioning is to remove certain features of a product that a firm produces for sale as a somewhat "stripped-down version" of the product.

Versioning as a Method of Price Discrimination

Traditional bricks-and-mortar firms have long engaged in versioning. The basic service that Federal Express provides is to pick up packages from one location and deliver them to another. Federal Express and other delivery companies have distribution systems linking trucks to transport aircraft, and they have the capability to transmit large volumes of packages long distances within 24 hours. They can, of course, perform the same service at a slower pace.

Recall that one of the main determinants of the price elasticity of demand is the time that consumers have to adjust their expenditure patterns. People who are in a rush to get a package to a recipient typically exhibit a relatively low price elasticity of demand. For people who simply want the package transmitted but are not too concerned about how long it takes, the price elasticity of demand is relatively high.

By offering relatively high- or low-speed package delivery options, Federal Express can induce people to self-select into groups with differing demand elasticities. Then, at least in principle, it can increase profits by charging relatively high prices for next-day deliveries to relatively low-elasticity consumers and relatively low prices to consumers with relatively higher demand elasticities who opt for slower delivery schedules. If sufficient numbers of people were to fall into the latter group, the company's average package delivery time could increase due to this pricing strategy.

Versioning in the Electronic Marketplace

Many information technology companies that provide goods or services in digital formats and market these products on the Internet can also price discriminate through versioning. Good examples are anti-virus software providers (also discussed in Chapter 3). A few of these companies cater to both business and household customers. Because their livelihoods depend on smoothly functioning hardware and software, business customers typically desire the most up-to-the-minute protection from exposure to computer viruses. Many household consumers of anti-virus software, however, usually are somewhat less concerned about interruptions that viruses might cause.

Like people facing time limitations for package deliveries, business consumers of anti-virus software tend to exhibit a lower price elasticity of demand. By way of contrast, the price elasticity of demand of most household users of anti-virus software is relatively higher. In light of what you have learned about price discrimination, it should not be surprising that anti-virus software providers typically sell more than one version of anti-virus software. Consumers of anti-virus software consumers consequently face choices ranging from versions providing daily anti-virus program updates and even continual, real-time Internet protection, to versions that provide the capability for weekly downloadable updates of anti-virus software files. Businesses (and some households) with relatively low demand elasticities tend to self-select versions with speedy update options that are priced at levels well above the prices charged for versions that can be updated less frequently. Most households with a higher price elasticity of demand tend to purchase the versions of these programs that provide less frequent software updates.

Anti-virus software is a good example of an **information-intensive product**, for which a crucial factor of production used to manufacture a good or provide a service is a rapidly evolving base of knowledge. Information-intensive products are particularly amenable to versioning, because the companies that sell them can control the pace of product updates or upgrades. If the companies producing information-intensive products also have pricing power, whether because the market is concentrated or because products are easily differentiated, then versioning is an attractive method for engaging in price discrimination to enhance profitability.

A number of digital products that firms sell as downloadable computer files or programs available for real-time access are information-intensive products. Hence, consumers contemplating purchasing such products in the electronic marketplace are particularly likely to encounter versioning.

Information-Intensive Product
A good or service for which a fundamental productive input is a swiftly developing foundation of knowledge.

A Problem of Interpretation: Different Versions, or Different Products?

Not all economists agree that versioning is always equivalent to price discrimination. One perspective on versioning is that firms may initially engage in versioning in an effort to price discriminate but ultimately lay the groundwork for potentially competitive markets for product versions sufficiently distinct that consumers begin to regard them as different goods or services. Consequently, over time, different versions of the same product evolve into different products exchanged in separate markets.

Consider the package delivery companies discussed earlier. According to this alternative perspective on versioning, at one time the U.S. Postal Service (USPS) and United Parcel Service (UPS) were key rivals in the market for package deliveries within two or three days. Then Federal Express, which dominated the overnight delivery market, began to offer 24-hour and two-day versions of its delivery service in an effort to price discriminate. When USPS, UPS, and other package delivery companies recognized that Federal Express was earning economic profits by engaging in this pricing strategy, they began offering new, speedier delivery services. Eventually, consumers came to regard overnight, two-day, and multi-day delivery services as imperfectly substitutable products offered by several firms. According to this view, the differential prices for these services reflect differing cost and demand conditions in these now-separate markets.

There are signs that price discrimination in the market for Web-based anti-virus software may be evolving in an analogous manner. As noted in Chapter 3, two companies (Symantec and Network Associates) dominate anti-virus software sales to home personal computer users. The economic profits they have earned providing higher-priced anti-virus software to business customers has induced the entry of numerous fringe competitors in providing anti-virus protection to businesses. This has led to the gradual development of separate household and business markets for anti-virus software.

IS PERFECT PRICE DISCRIMINATION FEASIBLE IN THE ELECTRONIC MARKETPLACE?

Imagine searching for a particular product at the Web-shopping site of your favorite Internet retailer. Along with a product description, your search also returns, in bold letters, ". . . at the special price, *just for you* . . ." followed by your name and your special price. Later in the day, you learn that at the same time you were at the site, two friends of yours, who have placed orders at that particular Web site less frequently, happened to submit an inquiry concerning the exact same product. Your friends received almost identical responses but with crucial exceptions: Your friends' "special prices" were different from yours—and from each other's. Your favorite Internet retailer is apparently practicing individualized price discrimination.

Direct Interactions and "Personalized Information"

In principle, any Internet seller could quote different prices for the same product to customers visiting its Web site simultaneously. All that would be entailed would be pre-programming the company's Web server to recognize each individual customer—already commonplace at many companies—via a customer log-in procedure or recognition of cookies placed on customers' hard drives during earlier visits.

To determine the prices to quote, the Internet seller could conduct careful analyses of the shopping and buying habits of its customers. These, in turn, would be revealed in data collected during prior visits to the company's Web site. After all, in contrast to many shoppers who make cash payments for purchases at bricks-and-mortar retailers, an Internet customer of an e-commerce firm typically must reveal her or his identity to complete a purchase. Each time that an Internet shopper buys a good or service, the shopper provides considerable information about the shopper's buying habits. This means that the quality of information available to an Internet seller about each consumer's tastes and preferences improves with each repeat purchase.

Frequent shopping may reveal something about a customer's price elasticity of demand. On one hand, suppose that the customer visits the company's Web site often without making purchases. This behavior might indicate that the customer makes frequent price comparisons across alternative Web sites, which indicates that the customer's price elasticity of demand is relatively high. Quoting a relatively low price is more likely to generate a sale. On the other hand, suppose a different customer visits the company's site just as frequently but makes a purchase nearly every visit. Such behavior implies that the customer is relatively insensitive to the product price, indicating that the customer's price elasticity of demand is relatively low, so quoting a relatively high price to this customer is likely to be consistent with maximizing profits. Naturally, for customer buying patterns between these two extremes, intermediate prices are likely to be appropriate.

With information technologies permitting the recording and analysis of personalized data, the one-to-one interactions that e-commerce firms have with customers can allow them to charge every identifiable customer a different price. This does not, however, mean that e-commerce firms are able to practice perfect price discrimination. Recall that a firm engages in perfect price discrimination when it is able to charge each consumer the price that particular consumer is willing to pay for its product. Even though direct customer interactions and electronic data management and analysis can aid an e-commerce firm in selecting profit-maximizing prices to charge its customers, the firm still cannot precisely discern a consumer's current willingness to pay based on past buying patterns. All it can do is improve its *forecast* of each customer's willingness to pay for a product.

Nevertheless, Internet sellers have considerable advantage, in terms of their ability to engage in price discrimination, over traditional bricks-and-mortar firms. The customer-contact and information-gathering advantages inherent in Internet selling can enhance the ability of Web-based sellers, as compared with traditional brick-and-mortar firms, to capture a larger portion of consumer surplus. As we shall discuss shortly, this is one factor that helps to explain why so many brick-and-mortar companies have begun selling on the Internet.

A FUNDAMENTAL LIMITATION ON PRICE DISCRIMINATION: COMPETITION

There is an important constraint on the ability of any firm to price discriminate, whether it attempts to do so offline or online. Companies that charge relatively high prices to any group of consumers give those consumers an incentive to search for alternative products. Furthermore, if the companies' price-discrimination strategies generate significant economic profits, there is an incentive for other firms to enter the marketplace.

Firms that have the capability to price their products strategically typically must balance short-term profit gains against longer-term erosions in their ability to engage in price discrimination in the face of the entry of new rivals. The dominant-firm analysis in Chapter 2 indicates that the near-term incentive to enhance profitability by taking advantage of pricing power typically predominates over future considerations. For this reason, we can expect that most Internet sellers that have the opportunity to practice price discrimination will do so. How long they will be able to use their market power to charge different prices to different consumers will depend on the height of entry barriers into their particular industries.

FUNDAMENTAL ISSUES ▼

1.

2.

3.

4.

5.

6.

4. In what ways is price discrimination easier to practice in the electronic marketplace?

Many of the goods and services marketed by Internet sellers are information-intensive, meaning a key factor of production used to produce them is a growing body of knowledge. Thus, firms marketing these products often engage in versioning by selling different forms of the products to different groups at different times. Consumers desiring to obtain a product within relatively shorter periods of time have relatively lower price elasticities of demand. This enables a company to sell the latest versions of its product to these consumers at relatively higher prices. An additional factor contributing to the ability of Internet sellers to price discriminate is ability of sellers to keep tabs on the shopping behavior of individual buyers, which sellers can examine for clues about each buyer's willingness to pay for a given product.

Vertical Integration and Vertical Restraints On and Off the Web

A number of software producers oversee all aspects of the production and sale of their products, from the design of software applications to the creation of computer codes, to the marketing and sale of the final software products on compact disks or via Internet downloads. Thus, they are **vertically integrated** companies that handle two or more successive stages of production and distribution of their products.

Many e-commerce companies are not vertically integrated. Online drug stores, home and garden suppliers, pet stores, and grocery delivery services function solely

Vertical Integration
Incorporating two or more successive stages of production and distribution of a product within the same firm.

as retailers, selling products that they purchase in wholesale markets from other companies that oversee production processes for these goods and services.

What governs an Internet seller's choice of whether to vertically integrate each stage of production and sale of a good or service, from the initial stages of manufacture to the final sale of that good or service online? For firms that are not vertically integrated, what factors determine the prices at which goods or services change hands among producers prior to their final sale at retail prices paid by consumers? In large measure, the answers to both questions hinge on the business strategies companies pursue given the market conditions they face.

VERTICAL INTEGRATION OFFLINE AND ONLINE

There are several reasons that a firm may decide to become vertically integrated. Several of these involve potential reductions in operating costs and prices, thereby increasing consumer welfare. Other rationales for vertical integration, however, relate to enhancing pricing power and potentially reducing consumer welfare.

Vertical Integration to Reduce Costs and Improve Efficiency

CarsDirect.com, and Autobytel.com are among many online auto sales Web sites. These companies either function as brokers to market new cars directly to consumers or as providers of coordination services for the sales efforts of existing bricks-and-mortar auto dealers.

Today, about 5 percent of all consumers purchase new cars online, and this percentage is likely to grow in coming years. Traditionally, the U.S. automobile industry has been only partially vertically integrated. Auto producers obtain a significant portion of the steel and parts used to manufacture cars from a large network of steel manufactures and auto-parts suppliers. Following assembly, they distribute their products via thousands of dealerships around the country.

Some auto companies, such as the Saturn division of General Motors, have experimented with direct online selling that bypasses traditional dealers. These companies have established Web sites that permit consumers to select desired features and to place an order for production and delivery, sometimes directly to their front door. In this regard, the auto manufacturers are following the example of Dell Computer and various other companies that have vertically integrated online distribution into their overall operations.

A key motivation for vertically integrating online product distribution is to reduce operating costs. By giving auto buyers the opportunity to place Internet orders for new cars, manufacturers reduce the number of cars they produce with features that turn out to be undesirable, such as color schemes, seating arrangements, or hubcap designs that suddenly go out of style. As a result, online distribution of new cars can help reduce manufacturers' inventory costs, thereby boosting profits while keeping prices low and benefiting consumers. (There are signs that vertical integration online also may begin to become more important in the production and sale of books, as discussed in *Management Online: Are Web Booksellers Destined to Be the Publishers of E-Books?*)

MANAGEMENT *Online*

Are Web Booksellers Destined to Be the Publishers of E-Books?

In many respects, online bookselling has been mainly a technical advance in book marketing and distribution via Web companies such as Amazon.com and Barnesandnoble.com. Although authors now turn in completed book manuscripts in electronic form and publishers have found ways to print books on ever thinner and cheaper paper, the process of producing books remains largely the same as in years past.

The Advent of E-Books

Recent developments indicate the potential for this state of affairs to change, however. Computer manufacturers have developed "eye-friendly" display monitors for reading text at long stretches, and software makers have developed "reading" software programs that sharpen the appearance of text on any computer screen.

Now publishers have begun offering electronic versions of top-selling novels and nonfiction in the form of digitalized *e-books*. Textbook publishers are also marketing electronic versions of their books, often with highlighting, underlining, and notetaking capabilities available for student readers.

Vertical Integration in Online Bookselling

Both Amazon and Barnes and Noble have taken steps toward vertical integration of e-books. Their efforts were spurred by the initial success of direct e-book sales by the horror-fiction author Stephen King, who proved that people were willing to read books on their desktop and laptop computers. Both companies are now exploring becoming online publishers, taking books straight from edited "e-manuscripts" to final online products.

Online booksellers and e-publishing seem like a good fit. Nevertheless, vertical integration shows signs of going both directions. Random House, the largest English-language publishing company in the world, recently announced plans to publish new fiction and nonfiction as e-books. Time Warner has also entered the e-book market. Both companies indicated that e-publishing would allow them to keep pace with growing pressures to publish books quickly while saving on printing, warehousing, and shipping costs.

For Critical Analysis:

Why might publishers continue to market both physical and virtual books, even in the face of continuing improvements in e-publishing capabilities?

Will the Internet Bring About the Demise of the Industrial-Age Corporation?

Back in 1937, the British Nobel-prize-winning economist Ronald Coase asked a very basic question: Why do firms exist? That is, he sought to understand why it was that each person, at every stage of production and delivery, is not an independent profit center.

Coase concluded that the reason was **transaction costs**, which are all the costs that people incur when they exchange products, assets, and information, when they negotiate contracts, and when they monitor contractual agreements to ensure that the terms of agreements are enforced. A firm exists, he decided, to internalize these various activities within an umbrella organization of individuals,

Transaction Costs
All the costs associated with economic exchanges, including the costs of acquiring and disseminating information, plus the costs of negotiating and enforcing contracts.

thereby reducing the number of exchanges, contract negotiations, and contractual enforcement actions required to produce, market, and distribute products.

The Internet greatly reduces many transaction costs by giving large and diverse sets of people easy and timely access to relatively inexpensive knowledge required to make informed decisions and to coordinate complex activities. This makes it possible for more individuals and small groups to establish independent profit centers. Individual specialists and small companies concentrating on specific tasks in production, marketing, or distribution may be able to do a better job of adding value to a good or service than large, vertically integrated firms. As the Internet economy expands, negotiating separate deals among networks of individuals or small companies becomes more reasonable. Consequently, widespread vertical integration, as exemplified by the big industrial-age corporations of the twentieth century, may diminish in the years to come.

Vertical Integration in Search of a Market Niche

Companies may decide to integrate online product distribution into their operations in an effort to enhance the potential sales of products that otherwise might be overlooked in the marketplace. For instance, International Business Machines Corporation (IBM) recently established an online patent exchange operation that enables users to search for, learn about, and buy, sell, or license patents (see Chapter 7 for more discussion of issues relating to patents and e-commerce). This naturally increased the likelihood that others might purchase or license IBM's existing patents, thereby bringing the firm new streams of revenue. At the same time, however, establishing the patent exchange broadened the market for patents, arguably benefiting both owners and users of patents.

Firms may also vertically integrate online distribution efforts in an effort to capture actual or potential economic profits available to current firms in the electronic marketplace. Traditional bricks-and-mortar booksellers and book publishers have responded to the success of Amazon by establishing online distribution operations of their own, thereby seeking to combat Amazon's dominance of the electronic marketplace for books. Early in the development of the market for Internet service access, local ISPs earned economic profits that encouraged telephone and cable television providers to vertically integrate ISP services into their business operations. Vertical integration thereby contributes to greater competition in e-commerce and to increased consumer welfare. (Producers can also vertically integrate online in an effort to combat pricing power possessed by buyers of their products; see on page 120 *Management Online: Reducing the Pricing Power of the Press*.)

Vertical Integration to Enhance Pricing Power

In some situations, a firm that has pricing power over a product may vertically integrate in an effort to extend or enhance its ability to engage in strategic pricing. For instance, a firm with pricing power as a supplier of an input used to produce a good might attempt to do this by vertically integrating into marketing and distribution of the final product. Alternatively, a dominant producer of a final product might seek to become the dominant distributor as well, perhaps by opening a Web site for marketing and selling the item.

MANAGEMENT *Online*

POLICY MAKING   GLOBALIZATION   **MANAGEMENT**

Reducing the Pricing Power of the Press

Many people still obtain broad news coverage from their local newspaper. Even though there are more than 1,500 newspapers throughout the United States, most of them face no competition from other newspapers. Furthermore, regional corporations own groups of newspapers in a number of locales. This makes newspapers a big block of buyers of news reports provided by news services such as the Associated Press, Reuters, and Dow Jones Newswires. Traditionally, this concentration of buying power has given local and regional newspaper corporations the ability to exercise a certain degree of *monopsonistic* pricing power.

Monopsony and Marginal Factor Cost

A pure **monopsony** is a single buyer of a product. As indicated in Figure 4-4, a monopsony faces the market supply curve alone. A monopsony has the power to determine both the price it pays and the quantity of the product that it purchases. It thereby determines its own **marginal factor cost,** which is the additional cost of consuming another unit of a good or service that the firm uses as an input in its own production process. When a monopsony increases the price that it pays for an input to induce producers to supply additional units, it raises not only the additional cost of the additional units it buys but the cost of all other units purchased from suppliers. Thus, for the monopsonist, marginal factor cost exceeds the price of the input at each quantity it consumes, which means that its marginal factor cost curve lies above the supply curve, as shown in Figure 4-4.

To maximize economic profit, a monopsonist purchases an input to the point where marginal factor cost equals **marginal revenue product,** or marginal revenue times the input's marginal product (see Chapter 2), which is the additional revenue generated by an additional unit of a factor of production. Figure 4-4 shows that the monopolist then pays a price suppliers of the input are willing to accept. This price, however, is less than the additional revenue that the monopsonist derives from using the input that the suppliers produce, thereby "exploiting" its monopsony power to enhance its own profitability.

Online News Gradually Erodes Newspaper Monopsony Power

Local and regional newspaper groups are not pure monopsonies. News services also sell their stories to other news media, including radio and television. Nevertheless, as a big purchasing block within the print news business, newspapers have possessed considerable monopsony power.

Recently, news services have fought back by selling more of their news reports to online news sites. Beginning in the mid-1990s, the Associated Press responded to the relatively low prices that newspapers were offering for its stories by marketing to Web news start-ups. So did Reuters, the main news-service rival of the Associated Press. Reuters now sells news stories to more than 900 worldwide Web sites, which together provide more than 60 percent of Reuters' revenues from media sources other than newspapers. These and other news services were struggling in the 1980s and early 1990s, but the gradual erosion of newspapers' monopsony power has helped boost their revenues and profits.

continued

Monopsony
A single buyer in a market.

Marginal Factor Cost
The additional cost that a firm incurs from employing an additional unit of a factor of production.

Some critics argued that the 2000 America Online–Time Warner merger amounted to an attempt to vertically integrate in pursuit of market power. Critics contended that a simultaneously proposed merger of Time Warner with EMI, which owns a large portion of the world's recorded music, would, for example, have allowed an AOL–Time Warner combination to extend its market power in the music industry to the ability to engage in strategic pricing in the market for downloadable music. Time Warner also owns a number of cable television companies, and some observers worried that it would couple its local and regional

Figure 4-4:
Monopsonistic Pricing of an Input.

A single buyer of an item, or monopsony, faces the market supply curve and has the ability to determine both the price it pays and the quantity it buys. When the monopsony raises the price it pays for an input, it raises both the additional cost of that unit and the cost of all other units it purchases, so the additional cost it pays—its marginal factor cost—exceeds the price of the input at each quantity it purchases. Thus, the marginal factor cost curve faced by the monopsony lies above the supply curve. The additional revenue that the monopsony earns from purchasing an additional unit of this input equals marginal revenue times the inputs marginal product, or its marginal revenue product. The marginal revenue product curve is downward sloping, because the marginal product declines as it uses more units of the input. To maximize its profit, the monopsony purchases the input to the point where marginal factor cost equals marginal revenue product. Hence, it buys Q_1 units and pays a price P_1 that is less than the marginal revenue product of the input, MRP_1, thereby exploiting its monopsony power.

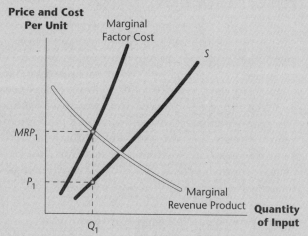

For Critical Analysis:
Several news services have taken tentative steps toward vertical integration by establishing their own online news sites funded by advertisements. Why do they continue to sell news stories to newspapers and other news media?

market clout in cable television with AOL's looming presence in Internet access to develop a dominant position in providing Internet services.

The main difficulty in evaluating the effects of vertical integration is that it often can have conflicting effects on firm behavior and market outcomes. Many aspects of vertical integration can help to reduce the overall cost of making, marketing, and distributing a product, rendering firms more efficient and placing downward pressure on prices. At the same time, vertical integration can enhance a firm's pricing power. We shall return to this issue in Chapter 11.

Marginal Revenue Product

Marginal revenue times marginal product of a factor of production, which is the contribution to a firm's total revenue of an additional unit of that input.

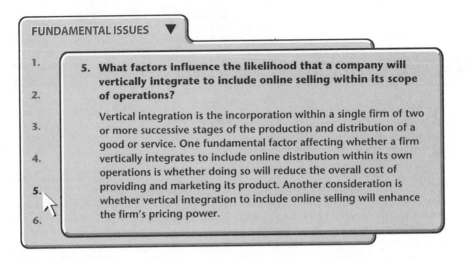

FUNDAMENTAL ISSUES ▼

1.

2.

3.

4.

5.

6.

5. What factors influence the likelihood that a company will vertically integrate to include online selling within its scope of operations?

Vertical integration is the incorporation within a single firm of two or more successive stages of the production and distribution of a good or service. One fundamental factor affecting whether a firm vertically integrates to include online distribution within its own operations is whether doing so will reduce the overall cost of providing and marketing its product. Another consideration is whether vertical integration to include online selling will enhance the firm's pricing power.

VERTICAL RESTRAINTS IN E-COMMERCE

Many manufacturers of goods or providers of services rely on independent firms to market and distribute their products. A common rationale is that the costs of monitoring employees at marketing offices or distribution centers exceed the costs associated with dealing with independent distributors.

Nevertheless, companies that utilize independent distributors often seek to limit the range of activities of distributors by imposing **vertical restraints.** These are binding contractual limitations that a nonintegrated firm places on the behavior of another firm from which it buys or to which it sells. As in the case of vertical integration, some vertical restraints may be anticompetitive and thereby reduce consumer welfare, while others may enhance efficiency and thereby raise consumer welfare.

Vertical Restraint

A legally binding limitation that a nonintegrated firm places on another firm from which it buys or to which it sells.

Vertical Restraints as Anticompetitive Tools

Homestore.com is a company with five housing-related Web sites. In addition to providing general information about arranging mortgages, planning moves, and other aspects of the home buying and relocation process, Homestore gives a visitor access to an online real-estate database covering the roughly 1.5 million houses and condominiums available for sale in the United States at any given time. Homestore is majority-owned by the National Association of Realtors, and the National Association of Home Builders has a minority stake in the online company.

At first glance, it is tempting to regard Homestore as part of the final marketing and distribution stage in a vertically integrated process that begins with housing construction, continues with listings through local realtors, and proceeds to a national clearinghouse on the Web. In fact, conditions in local and regional real-estate markets are primarily influenced by local and regional factors. For this reason, there is not a truly "national" housing industry subject to complete vertical integration.

Indeed, Homestore faces competition from several fronts, including other online real-estate listing services operated by companies such as Yahoo.com and Microsoft. Compared with Homestore, however, these rival online services have much smaller real estate listings. A key reason is that Homestore obtains more than half of its listings through arrangements in "Gold Alliance" contracts with about 200 multiple-listing services in major U.S. metropolitan areas. In return for 10 percent of the revenue generated from advertising on Homestore's Web sites, plus shares in Homestore or options to purchase its shares, these listing services have agreed not to share their property listings with other national listing services. As a result, the only way that Yahoo, Microsoft, and other companies that offer online real-estate services can obtain information about available housing is by contacting thousands of individual real estate agents and firms around the country.

It is at least arguable that Homestore's exclusive contract arrangement with local and regional listing services may be an example of an anticompetitive vertical restraint. According to its rivals, Homestore's owners created the company's Golden Alliance contracts to limit their ability to offer competing online listing services. Other critics argue that Homestore's exclusive contracts also create barriers to entry by additional online competitors. From this perspective, discouraging competition from existing or potential rivals is a rationale for establishing vertical restraints with suppliers, as may be true in the case of Homestore.

Companies may also try to protect competitive positions by establishing vertical restraints limiting the distribution of their products. For instance, in addition to trying to restrain online competition in new car sales by integrating online selling into their car distribution systems, automobile manufactures have included limitations on online selling by car dealers. In 2000, General Motors sent letters to its 7,700 U.S. dealers reminding them of a clause in their franchise agreements prohibiting them from selling vehicles to third-party intermediaries. General Motors also refuses to replace new vehicles that dealers sell to online brokers and makes dealers engaging in such activities ineligible for the various sales incentives it periodically offers. (Some companies have found that discouraging competition via vertical restraints on online distribution of their products does not always pay off; see on the next page *Management Online: Blocking Internet Ticket Sales*.)

In some instances existing firms might also be able to use vertical restraints to perpetuate cartels. If a group of manufacturers wishes to collude, they could enforce the agreement by requiring the sale of their products at identical retail prices, which they could maintain via vertical restraints. To do this, they can require online retailers to sell their products at specified prices that cannot be discounted, thereby engaging in a practice that economists call **resale price maintenance.** Web sites are open to view by anyone, including cartel participants, simplifying efforts to police the cartel agreement. This feature of online retailing could make cartel arrangements easier to establish and maintain.

Resale Price Maintenance
Setting a minimum price that retailers are permitted to charge for a product.

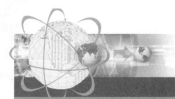

MANAGEMENT *Online*

Blocking Internet Ticket Sales

In 1998, Delta Airlines became the first major airline to offer its inventory of unsold tickets for sale via Priceline.com, the online discount ticket seller. Nevertheless, its pact with Priceline initially included stringent limitations over how and whether Priceline could sell Delta tickets. As other airlines linked up with Priceline, Delta gradually reduced the restrictions it had imposed, but it retained one key clause. Delta specified that Priceline could sell only Delta tickets for travel through the Hartsfield Atlanta International Airport, which is the world's busiest airport and also happens to be the southeastern hub for Delta flight connections.

A Vertical Restraint Sets Off a Price War

The Priceline deal turned out to be a gold mine for Delta, which received Priceline stock that rose in value to nearly $800 million. This allowed Delta to generate a big cash infusion when it sold the stock in the summer of 2000.

Nevertheless, Delta's vertical restraint on online ticket distribution set off a bitter feud with rival carrier Northwest Airlines. In protest of Delta's protection of its Atlanta hub, Northwest ran a special fare sale on its on Web site. Northwest also posted print and Web advertisements criticizing

Delta's restriction of online ticket discounting. Delta's initial reaction was to launch a return salvo by price discounts on tickets for flights that competed with Northwest airline routes. In particular, Delta offered deep discounts for flights to Northwest's key airport hubs in Minneapolis and Detroit.

Peer Pressures Induce a Reversal

By the fall of 2000, Delta faced a new problem. It sought admittance to Hotwire.com, another online site for marketing unsold tickets developed by several airlines, including United, Continental, American—and Northwest. To gain entry, Delta would have to permit online ticket discounters to get equal access to tickets for all airlines in all locations.

Delta faced a choice. It could either protect its turf in Atlanta, or it could continue its unprofitable price war with Northwest and lose admission to Hotwire. Quietly, the airline stopped blocking Priceline from selling cheap tickets for Atlanta flights offered by its competitors, including Northwest.

For Critical Analysis:

In the near term, Delta's action clearly offered Priceline an opportunity to generate additional sales of airline tickets, but was Delta's action necessarily in Priceline's long-run interest?

Alternative Rationales for Vertical Restraints

Free-Rider Problem
Failure of an agent that benefits from the provision of a product to contribute to the provision of the product.

There are several reasons that firms might impose vertical restraints that do not necessarily have anything to do with efforts to expand their pricing power. One reason that companies establish exclusive contracts has to do with the **free-rider problem,** which exists whenever one agent benefits from the provision of a good or service by another agent without having to contribute to the provision of that good or service. Suppose, for example, that a drug manufacturer recently launched a major advertising promotion touting the benefits of a new hair-growth tonic to combat baldness. It might require an online drug seller to market only *its* hair-growth tonic to prevent the online retailer from marketing a competing brand on the same Web page and getting a free ride from its efforts to promote hair-growth tonic.

Likewise, an online retailer might worry about other online sellers free riding on its marketing efforts on behalf of a specific manufacturer's brand. To prevent its online retail competitors from gaining sales of the product through its own efforts to promote the product, the online retailer might require an exclusive contract to market the product.

Finally, manufacturers and distributors alike might enter into exclusive contracts to ensure coordination of joint sales efforts. The manufacturer of an anti-baldness hair-growth tonic might have decided to emphasize positive messages in its advertising—alleging that it simply makes consumers look more youthful, for instance. Its advertising effort might be less effective if multiple online retailers posted their own ads with different, perhaps contradictory messages. Thus, exclusive contracts sometimes are a way to make sure that both manufacturers and online retailers are "on the same page" in providing marketing information about products. In the next two chapters, you will learn many more ways in which product information and advertising pose important issues in e-commerce economics.

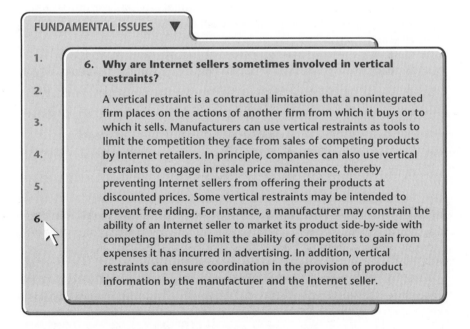

FUNDAMENTAL ISSUES ▼

1.

2.

3.

4.

5.

6.

6. Why are Internet sellers sometimes involved in vertical restraints?

A vertical restraint is a contractual limitation that a nonintegrated firm places on the actions of another firm from which it buys or to which it sells. Manufacturers can use vertical restraints as tools to limit the competition they face from sales of competing products by Internet retailers. In principle, companies can also use vertical restraints to engage in resale price maintenance, thereby preventing Internet sellers from offering their products at discounted prices. Some vertical restraints may be intended to prevent free riding. For instance, a manufacturer may constrain the ability of an Internet seller to market its product side-by-side with competing brands to limit the ability of competitors to gain from expenses it has incurred in advertising. In addition, vertical restraints can ensure coordination in the provision of product information by the manufacturer and the Internet seller.

Chapter Summary

1) **Perfect Price Discrimination:** A firm engages in price discrimination by charging different consumers different prices for the same good or by charging the same consumer different prices, depending on the quantity the consumer buys. To accomplish perfect price discrimination, a firm must charge each consumer the maximum price the consumer is willing to pay for each unit sold to the consumer, thereby capturing the entire amount of consumer surplus in the market. This requires determining each consumer's willingness to pay, preventing resale, and then either charging each consumer an individualized markup over average cost or a two-part tariff involving a per-unit charge equal to the firm's unit cost plus a lump-sum fee that applies to each individual consumer.

2) **Imperfect Price Discrimination:** In most instances, a firm that can engage in strategic pricing is not able to determine every consumer's willingness to pay. A firm may still be able to engage in imperfect price discrimination, however, if it charges different prices to groups with different elasticities of demand or distinctive purchase patterns. A firm that is able to single out groups with differing price elasticities of demand can enhance its profitability by charging relatively higher prices to groups with relatively lower price elasticities of demand. If the firm cannot separate consumers into groups, it may be able to use a two-part tariff to induce them to sort themselves into groups that pay different prices.

3) **How Firms Use Tie-In Sales and Bundling to Engage in Price Discrimination:** When a firm permits a customer to buy one product only if the customer also purchases another product, it requires tie-in sales. The firm can use tie-in sales requirements to impose two-part tariffs by altering the prices charged on the products in a tie-in sale arrangement based on the volumes of sales to different customers. When a firm bundles products for sale, it sells individual units of two or more products together as a package to increase its total revenues. Because consumers value each unit within the bundle at different levels, the firm essentially practices price discrimination by charging different prices to consumers.

4) **Reasons that Price Discrimination May Be Easier to Practice in the Electronic Marketplace:** A number of e-commerce firms sell information-intensive products that the firms can update as the body of knowledge used to produce them changes. Consequently, firms selling these products can engage in versioning by marketing distinctive forms of the products to different groups. Because consumers wishing to obtain a product within relatively shorter periods of time have relatively lower price elasticities of demand, a firm can sell the latest versions of its product to these consumers at relatively higher prices. Another characteristic of the electronic marketplace that adds

to the potential for price discrimination is the capability of sellers to use information technologies to track the shopping behavior of individual consumers in search of evidence concerning each consumer's willingness to pay for goods and services.

5) **Factors Affecting the Likelihood that a Company Will Vertically Integrate to Incorporate Online Selling within Its Scope of Operations:** When a company vertically integrates, it includes two or more successive stages of the manufacture and distribution of its product as part of its overall operations as a firm. A key factor influencing whether a firm engages in vertical integration by including online distribution of its product within its own scope of operations is whether online selling will bring about a decrease in overall production and distribution costs. In addition, the firm will take into account whether vertically integrating by becoming an Internet seller will increase the firm's ability to strategically set the price of its product.

6) **Why Internet Sellers Are Sometimes Involved in Vertical Restraints:** Firms that are not vertically integrated may impose vertical restraints, which are legally binding limits on the behavior of another firm from which it buys or to which it sells, in an effort to reduce competition from sales of competing products marketed by Internet retailers. Firms also use vertical restraints to engage in resale price maintenance by keeping Internet retailers from selling their products at discounted prices. Nevertheless, certain vertical restraints prevent free riding. An Internet retailer may insist on the exclusive right to sell a manufacturer's product to prevent other Internet sellers from benefiting from its own efforts to promote the manufacturer's product. Manufacturers and distributors may also use vertical restraints to ensure coordination of advertising or of the release of product information.

Questions and Problems

1) The price elasticity of demand is less than 1 along the lower, inelastic range of a downward-sloping demand curve, and as the price of an item rises over this range of the demand curve, a firm's revenues increase. Further boosts in the item's price along the upper range of the demand curve where the price elasticity of demand exceeds 1 lead to declining revenues. Recently, the person-to-person payments firm PayPal (http://www.paypal.com) began collecting fees on various payments services that previously had been free, and its revenues rose from $7 million to $8 million. Assuming that no other factors affected its revenues, was PayPal operating along the elastic or inelastic portion of the demand curve for its services? Was the price elasticity of demand greater than or less than 1?

2) Assume that the firm discussed in question 1, PayPal, charged the same fees to all customers. Describe a general scheme for how PayPal might use a two-part tariff to increase its revenues, in which the company's customers to engage in self-selection behavior. How difficult would it be for PayPal to implement your scheme?

3) When people buy new products and register them for warranties and other benefits, product-registration Web sites often ask visitors and purchases to provide their e-mail addresses and other personal information. How could firms use this information to aid their efforts to engage in price discrimination?

4) The C2C auction firm eBay offers several "packages" of auction services. In early 2001, the company implemented a program designed to hinder efforts by some of its customers to choose the least-expensive online service packages and work together offline to develop deals for negotiating and settling various aspects of their deals. Why do you think that eBay developed this program?

5) To navigate through Web pages at most companies' Internet sales sites, customers must permit the companies' Web servers to place cookies on the hard drives of their computers. How might consumers frustrate companies' efforts to track customer clickstreams and to categorize their customers into different groups for purposes of engaging in price discrimination? Why might relatively few consumers be willing to go to the trouble?

6) How might a company that manufactures operating-system software engage in tie-in sales for its various Web-downloadable software products, such as office-productivity, anti-virus, and Internet-firewall software? What factors will aid or hinder its efforts to develop a scheme for tie-in sales?

7) In 1998, AT&T embarked on a business strategy to sell consumers a bundle of four services: home telephone, wireless, Internet, and television.
   (a) What considerations could have motivated AT&T to adopt this bundling-of-services strategy?
   (b) By the end of 2000, AT&T's strategy had failed when many consumers instead opted to obtain telephone, wireless, Internet, and television services from separate providers. What factors do you think ultimately undermined AT&T's business strategy?

8) Give one real-world example, other than newswire services, of how vertical integration might enable a firm to develop monopsonistic pricing power in the market for an input. Explain how the firm would set the price of the input.

9) Initially, the big toy retailer Toys "Я" Us tried to vertically integrate Web sales into its operations. Eventually, however, it gave up on this idea and developed an affiliate relationship with Amazon. What factors potentially played a role in management's decision to do this?

10) Government regulators often investigate whether B2B exchanges jointly operated by producers of products such as automobiles and computers require agreements that prevent price discounting. What type of behavior do regulators wish to prevent? Why?

Online Application

Internet URL: http://www.meigloal.com

Title: **Mars Electronics International (MEI)**

Navigation: Go directly to the above URL, and in the drop-down menu under "Region," click on United States.

Application: Perform the indicated operations, and answer the following questions.

1) Click on "Product Application," and examine the variety of products marketed by this company. How many types of vending machines does this company market? Why do you think there are so many models to choose from?

2) Click on "Soft Drink Vending." MEIGlobal recently purchased the vending management software business of Rutherford & Associates. Go to its home page, http://www.ruthsx.com and click on "Products," and then click on "Vending." What various functions does the software of Rutherford & Associates permit vending machines to perform? Could any of these allow venders to adjust the prices of their products based on differing price elasticities of demand?

For Group Study and Analysis: If a vending machine is equipped with a temperature sensor and a computer chip, soft-drink prices can be increased in hot weather. Prices can also be changed during periods of the day when people are most likely to be in buildings or near kiosks where vending machines are located. Furthermore, connecting a fiber-optic cable to the machine would permit an Internet connection to the central offices of a vending company. Then its employees could track data about which drinks are selling best and in which locations. From a distance, therefore, they could set a slightly higher price for a more popular brand or raise prices of items in stock if other brands are temporarily out of stock. Discuss which of these strategies would entail responding to changes in demand versus actively engaging in price discrimination.

Selected References and Further Readings

Bakos, Yannis, and Erik Brynjolfsson. "Aggregation and Disaggregation of Information Goods: Implications for Bundling, Site Licensing, and Micropayment Systems." In *Internet Publishing and Beyond,* ed. Brian Kahin and Hal Varian, Cambridge, MA: MIT Press, 2000, pp. 114–137.

Chuang, John Chung-I, and Marvin Sirbu. "Network Delivery of Information Goods: Optimal Pricing of Articles and Subscriptions." In *Internet Publishing and Beyond,* ed. Brian Kahin and Hal Varian, Cambridge, MA: MIT Press, 2000, pp. 138–166.

DeLong, J. Bradford, and A. Michael Froomkin. "Speculative Microeconomics for Tomorrow's Economy." In *Internet Publishing and Beyond,* ed. Brian Kahin and Hal Varian, Cambridge, MA: MIT Press, 2000, pp. 6–44.

Ming, Susan, and Peter White. "Profiting from Online News: The Search for Viable Business Models." In *Internet Publishing and Beyond,* ed. Brian Kahin and Hal Varian, Cambridge, MA: MIT Press, 2000, pp. 62–96.

Shapiro, Carl, and Hal Varian. *Information Rules: A Strategic Guide to the Network Economy.* Boston: Harvard Business School Press, 1999.

Varian, Hal. "Versioning Information Goods." In *Internet Publishing and Beyond,* ed. Brian Kahin and Hal Varian, Cambridge, MA: MIT Press, 2000, pp. 190–202.

Westland, J. Christopher, and Theodore Clark. *Global Electronic Commerce.* Boston: MIT Press, 1999.

Wiseman, Alan. "Economic Perspectives on the Internet," Bureau of Economics, Federal Trade Commission, July 2000.

Unit Two

Information, Advertising, and Innovation in the Electronic Marketplace

Chapter 5

Searching for Information in Electronic Markets

FUNDAMENTAL ISSUES ▼

1. What is asymmetric information, and what types of problems can it generate? ►
2. What is the lemons problem, and what are some potential solutions? ►
3. Why can a firm gain from providing more information, and how does a firm determine how much information to provide to consumers? ►
4. How does a consumer determine the best price of a product and how much product price and quality information to acquire? ►
5. What makes a market efficient, and how efficient is the electronic marketplace? ►
6. What is the role of market intermediaries, and what are important intermediaries in the electronic marketplace? ►

<E-Commerce Today>

Looking Ahead to a Brave New World of Web Shopping

It has been a long day. The commute to work was held up by a software malfunction in the city's traffic-management network, and a scheduled video conference with other managers at various points around the world was much more intensive than expected. In addition, there were some tough decisions to make about the best way to go about placing information about a new product on the company's Web site.

Now that you are home, however, you dread making still more decisions. You will have to determine what set of groceries to have delivered tomorrow by an Internet grocer, and you also need to decide what birthday gift to purchase for a favorite relative. In addition, the hacker-prevention system for your personal computer needs an upgrade.

After grabbing a cool drink from the refrigerator, you sit down in front of the screen of the central computer console of your home office network. After double-clicking an icon and entering a password, you connect to the "intelligent shopping agent" you had forward a series of Web searches before you left for work this morning. To your relief, you find that your shopping agent has already used data transmitted by your refrigerator to compose a tentative grocery list for you to check, update, and approve. The shopping agent has also found two possible gifts for your relative. In addition, it determined the single best upgrade option for your hacker-prevention system, which has already been purchased and installed in your home computer system. In just a couple of minutes you will finally be able to relax.

It is conceivable that this scenario may be possible not too many years from now. All that is required are a few technological developments and confidence in the ability of an "intelligent shopping agent" to gather information you accept as reliable.

We are not there yet, however. Today we still engage in labor-intensive information searches before deciding about what goods and services we wish to purchase. Your own experience undoubtedly has taught you that not all information you receive is reliable. All of us have heard rumors, confronted opinions masquerading as facts, and encountered overblown claims of "high quality." This means that a rational consumer should not rely on information received from all available sources.

In addition, from time to time you have probably found yourself in a state of information overload. Sometimes so much information, even conflicting information, is available from so many different sources that it can become difficult simply to recollect and recall the information you have obtained.

Furthermore, you probably have experienced situations in which few information sources are readily available. Sometimes this information can be costly to obtain.

Consumers typically face all three types of informational difficulties—the potential for information to be unreliable, to be difficult to process, or to be hard to find. In this chapter, you will learn about how these information-related problems can arise in the electronic marketplace and how some types of e-commerce intermediaries try to address these issues.

Imperfect Information about Product Quality

Asymmetric Information
Information possessed by one party in a transaction but unavailable to another party.

Adverse Selection
A situation in which a number of the products offered for sale in a market are those with the worst quality or in which many of those who offer to purchase a product have bad characteristics.

Moral Hazard
The potential for either the buyer or seller of a product to exhibit undesirable behavior after arranging or completing an exchange.

Consumers often encounter a lack of knowledge about how much quality varies among products of different firms. This is the problem of **asymmetric information**, in which one party to a transaction possesses information that is not available to the other party. Two types of problems can arise as a result from asymmetric information. One is **adverse selection**, in which many or perhaps all of the products offered in the marketplace are those with the worst quality or in which at least some of the producers or consumers who offer to sell or buy a product are those possessing undesirable characteristics. Another is **moral hazard**, which is the possibility that either the buyer or seller may engage in undesirable behavior after arranging or completing a transaction.

Incomplete information about the quality of a firm's product or its service gives rise to these asymmetric-information problems, which have the potential to hinder the smooth functioning of the electronic marketplace. Let's consider how.

ADVERSE SELECTION AND THE MARKET FOR "LEMONS"

The colloquial "lemon" is a product with undesirable features that limit its usefulness. A recently purchased used car that exhibits persistent engine problems is a classic example.

Adverse Selection in C2C Auctions

Used cars are not the only goods that can turn out to be lemons. Suppose that a college student who is an aspiring amateur astronomer, but who has a limited budget, decides to shop for a backyard telescope at C2C auction sites. The student knows enough about astronomy to realize that a telescope equipped with a clock drive is essential to serious amateur astronomy. A clock drive is a motor that powers gears that move the body of the telescope along its mount as the Earth rotates on its axis, so that the image of a planet, star, or other astronomical object will remain centered in the eyepiece.

Consequently, the student searches online auction sites for telescopes that have this feature. After finding one with a clock drive plus several other desirable features, the student offers what seems to be a relatively low price of $800 for the telescope and is pleased when the bid wins. The student arranges payment and receives the telescope from a delivery service. Soon, however, the student discovers that the telescope's clock drive makes a subdued, but audible, grinding noise. One gear seems to move only grudgingly, and the image of the student's favorite astronomical object persistently drifts out of the field of vision as the Earth turns on its axis. The clock drive with the used telescope, it turns out, will require expensive repair work, or perhaps replacement.

This student is a victim of the adverse selection problem. Because people have incomplete information about products such as telescopes, they can overvalue bad products while undervaluing good products.

A Consequence of Adverse Selection: Bad Products Can Drive Good Products Out of the Electronic Marketplace

Suppose that potential buyers of used telescopes at C2C auction sites believe that half the used telescopes in the market are lemons (such as the one purchased by the student in our example), which they value at $400. They believe that the other half of used telescopes of a given quality for serious amateur astronomical observing have a value of $1,200. This means that the average value assessment of a randomly selected used telescope offered for sale at a C2C auction site by a typical consumer equals ($\frac{1}{2} \times$ $400) + ($\frac{1}{2} \times$ $1,200) = $200 + $600 = $800. Consequently, a buyer is willing to pay $400 more than the assessed value of a lemon telescope because there is a 50–50 chance that the telescope might be a good one. At the same time, a buyer is only willing to pay $400 less than the assessed value of a good-quality telescope because of the even chance that it might turn out to be a lemon.

Now suppose that all potential sellers of used telescopes understand that this situation governs the market. An owner of a used telescope in good condition realizes that typical buyers will be willing to offer only $800 for the telescope, even though its inherent value is $1,200. Thus, an owner of a high-quality telescope is much less likely to offer it for sale at a C2C auction site. By way of contrast, a person who owns a used telescope that barely functions and thereby has an inherent value of only $400 is pleased to sell it for $800. This means that relatively few people with good used telescopes are likely to offer them for sale at C2C auction sites, while many people with low-quality telescopes are likely to do so.

Eventually, potential used-telescope buyers may begin to recognize that the probability of finding a good used telescope for sale on a C2C auction site is as high as the probability of having a meteor land in their backyards. That is, their belief that a good used telescope will be offered for sale may drop close to zero. If so, the market price of a used telescope will drop to $400, the assessed price of a low-quality telescope, because only lemon telescopes will trade in this electronic marketplace. In this case, the likely presence of bad used telescopes drives high-quality used telescopes from Internet auction sites.

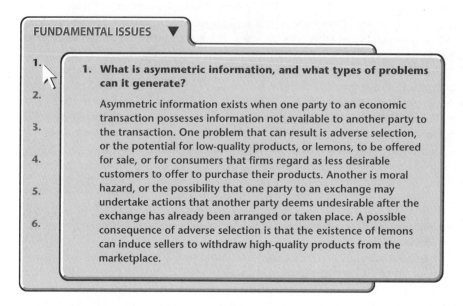

FUNDAMENTAL ISSUES ▼

1.
2.
3.
4.
5.
6.

1. What is asymmetric information, and what types of problems can it generate?

Asymmetric information exists when one party to an economic transaction possesses information not available to another party to the transaction. One problem that can result is adverse selection, or the potential for low-quality products, or lemons, to be offered for sale, or for consumers that firms regard as less desirable customers to offer to purchase their products. Another is moral hazard, or the possibility that one party to an exchange may undertake actions that another party deems undesirable after the exchange has already been arranged or taken place. A possible consequence of adverse selection is that the existence of lemons can induce sellers to withdraw high-quality products from the marketplace.

AVOIDING THE LEMONS PROBLEM

Lemons Problem
The possibility that adverse selection leads to a general reduction in product quality in a marketplace.

If some sellers of high-quality products pull their products from a market, then the overall level of quality in the market will decline. Economists call this potential outcome of adverse selection the **lemons problem.** It is important to keep in mind that the lemons problem refers to a *tendency* for asymmetric information to result in a reduction in the quality of goods and services. The characteristics of some goods and services are readily observable and difficult for sellers to hide from buyers. Other goods, such as telescopes with clock drives and automobile with engines and drive trains, have features that are not easy to observe and evaluate. Nevertheless, for products susceptible to the lemons problem, there are various ways to limit, or even eliminate, the scope of the lemons problem in the electronic marketplace.

Guarantees and Warranties

Internet sellers can attempt to convey their own faith in the quality of their products by extending guarantees and warranties. For instance, a company that sells computer speakers online may offer a money-back guarantee if the customer is not satisfied, or a warranty promising repair or replacement of any defect.

Companies normally place time limits on guarantees and warranties. The reason is that promising refunds, repairs, or replacements exposes the companies to a moral hazard problem, because they cannot observe how consumers treat products following their sale. Granting unlimited guarantees or warranties can give consumers an incentive to use products recklessly and expose companies to considerable expense in living up to their promises. (Sometimes companies feel

MANAGEMENT *Online*

POLICY MAKING   GLOBALIZATION   **MANAGEMENT**

PayPal Pays Up

PayPal.com is a leader in online person-to-person payment services. On a typical day, PayPal processes more than 150,000 transactions. The average transaction that the company processes is about $50. So far, the company has issued about 5 million customer accounts.

To open a PayPal account, a customer provides basic personal information, such as name, address, phone number, and e-mail address. Then the customer can send a payment to anyone else via e-mail by inserting a dollar figure into an electronic form at the PayPal Web site (http://www.paypal.com). When the customer sends the e-mail, PayPal automatically charges it to the sender's credit card or bank account.

Buyer Beware

PayPal is one of a growing number of online-payment services. These services have proliferated as more people purchase goods and services at C2C auction sites, because they simplify the task of finalizing payments from winning bidders to the sellers of items placed into auction.

In the summer of 2000, however, one customer used PayPal's service to transmit $418 to pay for seven computer hard drives that he bought at the auction site operated by Yahoo.com. Then the customer confronted the ultimate adverse selection problem: The recipient of his PayPal payment

never sent the hard drives. The customer was a victim of fraud, and he got even worse news: Like other online-payment services, PayPal had a policy of not reimbursing fraud victims.

Guaranteeing Transactions

Confronted with this case and numerous other frauds perpetrated on its customers, PayPal faced a dilemma. On the one hand, reversing its policy and reimbursing customers who experience fraudulent transactions would have entailed incurring significant expenses to track down fraud perpetrators and to file charges. That, of course, was the reason it had established the policy in the first place. On the other hand, continuing the policy would have risked a loss of faith on the part of its customers. The ultimate lemons problem of fraud threatened the company's future.

Ultimately, the company decided that retaining its customers was crucial to its future prospects. Thus, PayPal became the first online person-to-person payment company to guarantee that it would stand behind all person-to-person transactions. Now many other firms in this industry offer similar transaction guarantees.

For Critical Analysis:

Why is fraud a potentially significant lemons problem in e-commerce?

---

obliged to offer guarantees to customers who are exposed to asymmetric-information problems relating to possible bad behavior by third parties; see *Management Online: PayPal Pays Up.*)

Industry Standards and Product Certification

Offering guarantees and warranties may not fully overcome consumer concerns about the potential for acquiring lemons if a firm's other competitors sell low-quality products. Indeed, because information is imperfect, the production and

What kinds of standards have Web firms developed on their own? For information on this topic, visit the site of the Computing Technology Industry Association at http://www.comptia.org.

Industry Standards
Measurable or identifiable criteria that a group of firms in an industry indicate their products should satisfy to merit purchase.

Certification
A verification process for determining if a product's quality meets industry standards.

Information Intermediaries
Companies or organizations that specialize in evaluating the quality of goods and services produced by firms in various industries.

How do manufacturers develop certification standards? Find out by visiting the site of the National Center for Manufacturing Sciences, http://www.ncms.org.

sale of bad products by even a few firms in an industry can put the entire industry under a cloud of suspicion.

In an effort to prevent the actions of a few firms from giving an entire industry a collective black eye, several firms may decide to work together to establish **industry standards.** These are quantitative or qualitative criteria that the industry's products should satisfy to merit a positive decision by consumers to buy them.

Of course, consumers might suspect such efforts to be aimed more at promoting certain firms' products over others in the industry, thereby curtailing competition from lower-cost competitors charging lower prices. To alleviate such concerns, firms wishing to establish industry standards often seek external **certification** in the form of scientific reports supporting the proposed standards and bearing witness that the products of certain firms in the industry meet those standards. To legitimize a product-certification process, firms typically hire outside companies or groups to issue these reports. (Sometimes, however, efforts to obtain independent product certification can backfire by revealing that industry standards actually are intended to be anticompetitive or not truly open to outside scrutiny; see *Policymaking Online: How* Not *to Gain Certification of Internet-Snooping Technology*.)

Reputation and Information Intermediaries

A long-standing approach used by traditional bricks-and-mortar firms to distinguish their products from low-quality goods or services produced by competitors has been to try to establish a reputation for providing high-quality products. If a firm can establish such a reputation, then it can reduce its own exposure to ill effects relating to asymmetric information.

Once a firm establishes a reputation for producing high-quality goods or services, it has an incentive to maintain that reputation in an effort to induce repeat purchases. Hence, a company places value on its reputation. Customers know this, which, in turn, helps generate repeat purchases.

When contemplating purchases of products, consumers may also solicit the services of **information intermediaries,** which are firms or organizations that specialize in evaluating goods and services produced by other firms and publishing and distributing product or company ratings. Consumers often are willing to pay information intermediaries to monitor and report on the reputation of products and companies. Some consumers, for example, seek to keep up with changing ratings by subscribing to publications such as *Consumer Reports,* a product-rating magazine issued by the Consumers Union (see http://www.consumerreports.org).

C2C auction sites that coordinate the auctions of items such as astronomical telescopes, baseball cards, or previously purchased but unused clothing often provide information-intermediation services in the form of buyer-feedback pages. This gives buyers the opportunity to gauge the reputation of a seller who previously has sold items through such sites.

Legal Liability and Government Licensing

Sometimes laws provide consumers with protections similar to those provided by company guarantees and warranties. For example, following the 1999 Christmas

POLICYMAKING *Online*

POLICY MAKING GLOBALIZATION MANAGEMENT

How *Not* to Gain Certification of Internet-Snooping Technology

There is a dark side to the Internet. Unscrupulous people use it to perpetrate scams, to identify possible victims of all manner of nefarious activities, to arrange sales of illegal goods or services, and even to "launder" funds received from these illegal sales. In an effort to monitor such activities, the Federal Bureau of Investigation designed an e-mail-snooping program called Carnivore. Soon after unveiling the program, the FBI realized that this forbidding name only added to fears of government intrusion into the privacy of U.S. citizens. Some Internet service providers refused to install Carnivore in their systems out of a concern that the quality of their service could also be adversely affected by software conflicts.

Faced with a public outcry, the U.S. Department of Justice decided that it needed to reassure the public that the FBI and other agencies of the federal government would not use this new "government service" to engage in unwarranted privacy invasions or to complicate ISP systems. The Justice Department solicited bids from scientists at top universities for a consulting contract to evaluate Carnivore and certify it as fit for cyber-crime-fighting activities. A problem quickly emerged, however. University scientists read the fine print in the certification contract the government proposed, and many determined that it granted the government the authority to withhold any and all negative conclusions that consulting scientists might reach. Many top universities refused to submit bids, and it was soon obvious that the Carnivore certification process was unlikely to allay the privacy and software-conflict concerns of many U.S. citizens.

For Critical Analysis:

Does the government's attempt to certify the reliability of Carnivore offer any lessons for private industries wishing to benefit from independent certification of their products?

---

holiday, the Federal Trade Commission charged several Internet sellers, including the online divisions of Toys "Я" Us and KB Toys, with violating laws governing mail-order sales dating from the early 1970s. These firms had failed to deliver packages within the time frame promised their customers. Mail-order laws make certain firm guarantees mandatory. Such laws often force firms that desire to distinguish the quality of their products from those of other firms to go well beyond offering simple guarantees and basic warranties.

Federal and state governments also get involved in consumer protection by issuing licenses granting companies the legal right to engage in certain businesses only if they meet minimum standards specified by governmental authorities. Although licensing may successfully eliminate low-quality goods, there are two related problems associated with licensing. One is that licensing requirements often limit the number of providers, irrespective of product quality. This gives established firms a helping hand with pricing power in the marketplace. The other is that governments often turn to existing producers to help in drafting licensing requirements, and these firms have strong incentives to recommend low quality standards for themselves but high quality standards for new entrants.

How does your university rate? You can take a look at opinions about your college or university, or just about any other product, at http://www.epinions.com.

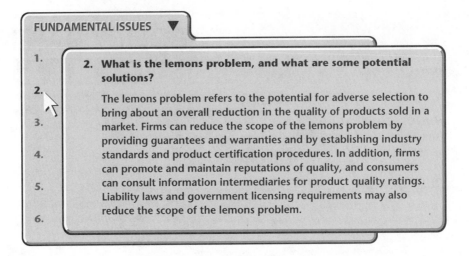

FUNDAMENTAL ISSUES ▼

1.

2.

3.

4.

5.

6.

2. What is the lemons problem, and what are some potential solutions?

The lemons problem refers to the potential for adverse selection to bring about an overall reduction in the quality of products sold in a market. Firms can reduce the scope of the lemons problem by providing guarantees and warranties and by establishing industry standards and product certification procedures. In addition, firms can promote and maintain reputations of quality, and consumers can consult information intermediaries for product quality ratings. Liability laws and government licensing requirements may also reduce the scope of the lemons problem.

Quality Signaling and Product Information

To this point, we have assumed that it is in the interest of a firm with relatively high-quality products to find a way to reveal this fact to consumers and that it is in the interest of a firm that produces relatively low-quality products to keep this information from consumers. Next let's consider the economic rationales for these producer preferences that we have assumed. Then let's contemplate how much effort a firm will put into signaling the quality of its product to potential buyers.

PRICE, QUANTITY, AND PROFIT EFFECTS OF ASYMMETRIC INFORMATION ABOUT PRODUCT QUALITY

Because product quality information matters most to consumers who are choosing from among various products with differing characteristics, a useful framework to employ in considering the incentives that firms face to signal product quality is monopolistic competition. As you learned in Chapter 3, this is an industry structure featuring many consumers and a large number of firms, each of which sells an insignificant portion of total industry output and can easily enter or leave the industry.

Nevertheless, each monopolistically competitive firm produces a good or service that consumers can distinguish, so it individually faces the demand for the product it produces. The demand for the firm's product depends on a number of factors, such as consumers' tastes and preferences, consumers' incomes, and the prices of substitutes and complements. Another factor affecting the demand for the firm's product is the perceived quality of its product, which depends on the information about product quality available to consumers.

Figure 5-1:
Product Demand and Firm Profitability with Asymmetric versus Complete Information.

The demand curve for a truly high-quality product and the associated marginal revenue curve lie in relatively low positions, D_a and MR_a, in the presence of asymmetric information. The profit earned by the producer of this item, therefore, would be the shaded area in the figure. If consumers had complete information about actual product quality, however, the demand and marginal revenue curves would be D_c and MR_c. In this situation, the firm would earn a higher profit equal to the dashed area. Consequently, the firm could increase its profit if it could find a way to provide more information to consumers and induce them to raise their demand from D_a toward D_c.

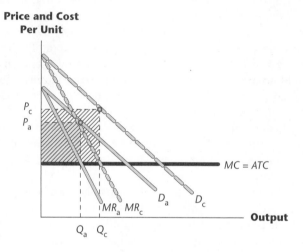

To evaluate how information affects product demand and influences the price of a good or service, take a look at Figure 5-1. The figure is drawn under the assumption that a firm's marginal production cost is constant. Let's suppose that the firm in the figure produces a high-quality product. In the presence of *asymmetric information,* however, consumers think there is at least a chance that the product's quality is lower than it actually is. Consequently, the product demand curve D_a and corresponding marginal revenue curve MR_a lie below the demand curve D_c and marginal revenue curve MR_c that the firm would observe if consumers had *complete information* about product quality.

As Figure 5-1 indicates, the firm maximizes its economic profit by producing to the point where marginal revenue equals marginal cost. Compared with the case of complete information, when confronted with asymmetric information, the firm produces less output (Q_a instead of Q_c) and charges a lower price (P_a instead of P_c). Its revenues are also lower. Because the firm produces less output at the same average cost, its total cost is lower under asymmetric information. Nevertheless, on net the firm's economic profit is lower under asymmetric information.

This implies that the firm could boost profitability if it could effectively inform consumers about the true quality of its product, thereby inducing them to increase their demand. Providing information is not a costless activity, however. Thus, if a firm wishes to signal the true quality of its product to potential customers, it must balance the additional profits it can gain against the cost of providing that information.

HOW MUCH INFORMATION SHOULD A FIRM PROVIDE?

Suppose that the firm in the situation in Figure 5-1 on the previous page is a Web-based landscape-design company. In contrast to traditional landscape designers who make house calls to look over a home or business and its surroundings to form a plan for the best types of trees and shrubs to plant in particular locations, this company makes its recommendations to customers over the Internet. Customers submit electronic files containing scanned (or digital) photos and a surveyor's drawing of their lot. Employees of the company then construct a digital map of the building and yard and design a computerized landscape layout, which they send back to the customer in exchange for a payment sent electronically or billed to the customer's credit card.

The problem this firm faces is that it is relatively new to the market and has no established reputation. Potential customers may be wary of doing business with the firm, even though it employs top landscape specialists and has a newly patented process for producing high-quality landscape designs. For this reason, the firm earns a lower profit than it would if consumers had complete information about the firm's product. (It is also possible that firms with low-quality products can enhance their profitability by providing *disinformation;* we leave it to you to examine how firms could do this in problem 1 at the end of the chapter.)

The Marginal Benefit of Providing Information

Figure 5-1 indicates that the firm can improve its profitability by providing more information to potential customers, thereby inducing a shift in the demand curve, from D_a in the direction of D_c. It might, for instance, begin by employing language arts experts such as linguists to write the clearest possible explanations of its product to post on its home page. (E-commerce has been kind to linguistics specialists; see *Management Online: The Growing Value of a Linguistics Degree.*) Then the firm might run banner advertisements at frequently visited Web sites that link potential customers to these explanations of its high-quality landscape-design service. It might also run advertisements in the print media to better inform potential customers who read newspapers or magazines. Finally, the company could purchase commercial time on radio or television. Undertaking each successive form of information dissemination provides more information and induces successive increases in the demand for the company's product, thereby increasing the firm's economic profit.

MANAGEMENT *Online*

POLICY MAKING   GLOBALIZATION   **MANAGEMENT**

The Growing Value of a Linguistics Degree

Once a linguistics degree was among the least marketable of academic credentials. Linguists traditionally studied shades of meaning in languages spoken by peoples in far-flung lands, so their average earnings were on the low end among professions. Jobs, when they were available—mostly for Ph.D. linguists in academia—typically paid at most a little over $35,000 per year.

During the past few years, dozens of technology start-ups have begun commercializing linguistics research. Today, a number of linguists have their pick of jobs as "lexicographers," "vocabulary engineers," and "vocabulary resource managers." For linguists with doctoral degrees, starting salaries now average around $60,000 (not including stock options). For those with more training and experience, annual salaries often exceed $100,000.

Two factors have accounted for this upsurge in the demand for linguists. First, linguistics experts help businesses in their e-commerce efforts by building so-called natural-language processing systems that can respond to typed requests for information transmitted over the Internet. Using databases that linguists develop, these systems can distinguish among multiple word meanings, relate words by concept, and narrow the scope of a search by asking questions of the site visitor.

America Online, Amazon.com, eBay.com, and other online firms have made expanding into developing and emerging economies top business priorities. Having the ability to distinguish between shades of meaning in words has a market value it did not have before.

For Critical Analysis:
Are there any other traditionally "low-paying" areas of academic study in which graduates might encounter growing opportunities in e-commerce?

The firm can derive a **marginal benefit** from providing information about product quality, which is an additional benefit to the firm resulting from each additional unit of information it provides, equal to the profitability enhancement generated by each additional unit of information the firm offers to consumers. As shown in Figure 5-2 on page 144, the marginal benefit tends to decline as the firm provides more and more product information. After all, many of those who see the landscape-design company's banner ads at Web sites also are likely to see advertisements it places in print media or on television. Although multiple exposures to ads may help raise the demand for the firm's product among a few consumers, for most it constitutes duplicated efforts to spread information that will yield progressively smaller gains in profitability.

Marginal Benefit
An additional benefit, perhaps in the form of higher firm profitability or increased consumer satisfaction, from an activity such as distributing product information or searching for product price and quality information.

Determining the Amount of Information to Provide

We noted earlier that spreading information is not costless. Simply posting information at a home page may be a relatively low-cost endeavor. The additional cost

Figure 5-2:
Determining the Amount of Product Information to Provide.

▼

Each additional piece of information that a firm with a high-quality product provides about the product can help induce an increase in consumer demand and boost the firm's profit. Hence, there is a positive marginal benefit to providing additional information. As the firm provides more and more information, however, the additional benefit per unit tends to decline, so the marginal benefit curve slopes downward. The marginal cost of providing information rises as the firm releases more information through an increasing number of mechanisms, so the marginal cost curve slopes upward. If the firm provides I_1 units of information, then the marginal benefit is greater than the marginal cost of the last unit provided, so the firm will increase the amount of information provided. It would not release I_2 units of information, however, because then the marginal cost of the last unit exceeds the marginal benefit it yields to the firm in higher profit. Thus, the firm will provide information up to the point where the marginal benefit equals the marginal cost, at $I*$ units of information provided about its product.

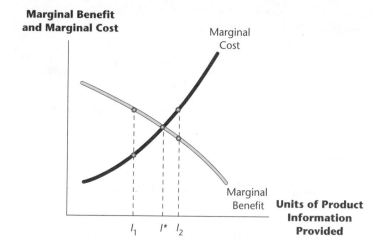

of transmitting additional information rises, however, as a firm expands the quantity of information it releases. Thus, the marginal cost of providing information usually rises as a firm disseminates more information through an increasing number of mechanisms, such as Internet, print, radio, or television ads. For this reason, in Figure 5-2 the marginal cost curve slopes upward.

If the firm provides I_1 units of information, then the marginal benefit to the firm, in terms of enhanced profitability, exceeds the marginal cost of the last unit of information provided. This encourages the firm to continue providing additional information. If the firm provides I_2 units of information, however, then the marginal cost of the last unit of information the firm provides exceeds the marginal benefit. Thus, it is not in the best interest of a profit-maximizing firm to provide as many as I_2 units of information.

The firm will release information about the quality of its product to the point where marginal benefit equals marginal cost. This is the point at which the marginal benefit curve crosses the marginal cost curve in Figure 5-2. Hence, this particular firm chooses to provide I^* units of information to potential customers. Factors that affect the marginal benefit or marginal cost of spreading product information can alter the amount of information that a firm seeks to transmit to potential customers. You will learn about several of these factors in our investigation of the economics of e-commerce advertising in Chapter 6. For now, let's consider some situations faced in the electronic marketplace by imperfectly informed consumers.

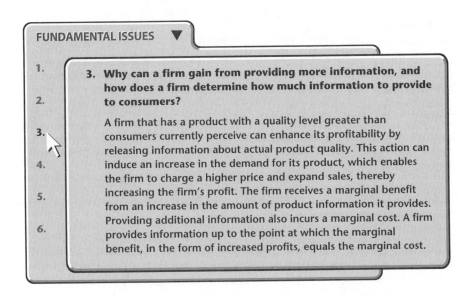

FUNDAMENTAL ISSUES ▼

1.
2.
3.
4.
5.
6.

3. **Why can a firm gain from providing more information, and how does a firm determine how much information to provide to consumers?**

A firm that has a product with a quality level greater than consumers currently perceive can enhance its profitability by releasing information about actual product quality. This action can induce an increase in the demand for its product, which enables the firm to charge a higher price and expand sales, thereby increasing the firm's profit. The firm receives a marginal benefit from an increase in the amount of product information it provides. Providing additional information also incurs a marginal cost. A firm provides information up to the point at which the marginal benefit, in the form of increased profits, equals the marginal cost.

Consumer Decision Making with Incomplete Information about Quality and Prices

Even as Internet sellers determine how much product information to provide to potential customers, consumers must decide how much information they wish to acquire about the quality of the various products available in the electronic marketplace. Consumers face an additional problem, however: They must determine the alternative prices at which they can acquire an item they wish to purchase.

BALANCING PRODUCT PRICE AND QUALITY IN THE ELECTRONIC MARKETPLACE

In a world of nearly complete information, consumers still face choices among similar products with differing prices and varying ranges of quality. When browsing among bricks-and-mortar apparel stores at a shopping mall, you can feel and try on different clothing, which you cannot do when using an electronic device. Nevertheless, you often must choose among relatively low-priced clothes made with inexpensive polyester fabric versus relatively high-priced clothes made with fabric containing high percentages of cotton or wool. Even when good information about product quality is available to a consumer, the individual still must make a decision about how to balance price and quality when purchasing a good or service. Let's consider how a consumer makes this choice before we contemplate the additional difficulty posed by imperfect information about either product quality or prices in the electronic marketplace.

The Price–Quality Trade-Off

As you learned in Chapter 3, when a monopolistically competitive industry is in long-run equilibrium, firms earn zero economic profits. That is, each firm earns an accounting profit just sufficient to cover the opportunity cost of allocating resources to that industry instead of an alternative industry.

This does not necessarily mean that monopolistically competitive firms charge the same prices, however. The reason is that because monopolistically competitive firms produce differentiated items, the quality of the item produced by each firm can differ. Producing items with higher quality typically requires firms to incur higher costs.

As shown in panel (a) of Figure 5-3, this means that two monopolistically competitive firms in long-run equilibrium may charge different prices. The firm depicted in panel (a) faces the demand curve $D_1(q_1)$ for its good or service that has a relatively low level of quality, denoted q_1. This monopolistically competitive firm's average total cost curve is ATC_1, and in long-run equilibrium (see Chapter 3) the firm earns zero economic profit, thereby producing output to the point where the demand curve and average total cost curve are tangent, at point A. It produces Q_1 units of output and charges the price P_1.

The other firm in panel (b), however, produces a similar good or service that has a higher quality level, q_2. If we assume that consumers can perceive this quality difference and that all other factors are unchanged, the higher quality of the second firm's product yields a higher demand for its product, $D_2(q_2)$, in panel (a). To produce a higher-quality product, the second firm must incur a higher average total cost, so its average total cost curve, ATC_2, lies above the average total cost curve of the first firm. Even though both firms produce and sell the same quantity of output and earn zero economic profits in the long-run equilibrium situations depicted in panels (a) and (b), the second firm charges a higher price for the higher-quality good or service it produces. This price is P_2, at point B.

Panel (c) shows the implied relationship between price and quality in a monopolistically competitive market. Firms in the industry producing a good or service of relatively low quality, such as the first firm at point A in panel (c), charge lower prices than firms producing goods or services of relatively high quality, such as the second firm at point B. Consequently, any consumer of good or service produced by firms in this industry faces the upward-sloping relationship between price and product quality in panel (c), which for simplicity is depicted as a straight

Figure 5-3:
The Price–Quality Trade-Off Faced by a Consumer.

Panel (a) shows a long-run equilibrium position for a monopolistically competitive firm that sells a product with a relatively low quality level denoted q_1, and which thereby experiences a relatively low level of demand but can produce output at a relatively low per-unit cost. By way of contrast, the firm depicted in panel (b) produces an item that is substitutable for the first firm's product but has a relatively higher quality level denoted q_2. There is relatively higher demand for this second firm's product, but the firm experiences a relatively higher per-unit cost of production. Panel (c) shows that because the price of the higher-quality product, P_2 is higher than the price of the lower-quality product, P_1, consumers of the products in this monopolistically competitive industry face an upward-sloping price–quality trade-off.

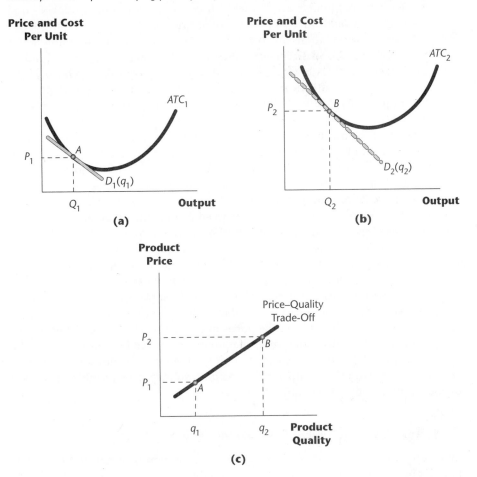

Price–Quality Trade-Off
Implied relationship between price and quality in a monopolistically competitive market.

line. This is the **price-quality trade-off** faced by a consumer of the good or service produced by firms in this monopolistically competitive industry.

Determining the Best Price–Quality Combination

A consumer who wishes to purchase a unit of a good or service produced by firms in a monopolistically competitive industry must select a point along the price–quality trade-off curve shown in panel *(c)* of Figure 5-3. The consumer does this in light of her own tastes and preferences.

Consider panel *(a)* of Figure 5-4, in which the price–quality combination available by purchasing the good or service from one firm is P_1 and q_1 at point C. Now suppose that the consumer considers buying a product with a higher quality level, q_2. To remain equally satisfied with the price–quality combination P_1 and q_1 at point C, she would have to pay a higher price, such as P_2. Economists call points C and D choices where this consumer is indifferent. There are many other such choices along the **indifference curve** IC_1 that includes points C and D. This indifference curve is bowed downward, because a consumer typically perceives diminishing benefits from successively higher product quality. Hence, she is willing to pay only slightly higher prices for each successive degree of product improvement.

Indifference Curve
A curve displaying combinations of choices among which a consumer is indifferent, because each choice yields the same satisfaction.

Of course, if the consumer could attain the higher level of product quality q_2 at the lower price P_1, at point F in panel *(a)*, then she clearly would be better off than at point C. Furthermore, because the consumer is indifferent between the price–quality combinations at points C and D, she would be better off at point F than at point D. Point F, in turn, lies on an indifference curve IC_2 below and to the right of IC_1. The consumer is indifferent between point F and all other price–quality combinations along IC_2, which means that the consumer prefers all combinations along IC_2 to combinations that lie along IC_1. Consequently, the consumer would like to purchase products with price–quality combinations along successively lower indifference curves that tend to have lower prices and higher levels of quality.

Panel *(b)* depicts this consumer's choice of the best price–quality combination available when choosing among the products offered by firms in this monopolistically competitive industry. Given the price–quality trade-off, the consumer attains the greatest possible satisfaction from the product produced by a firm offering the price-quality combination $P*$ and $q*$ at point E. At point E, she attains the indifference curve $IC*$, which is as far downward and rightward as possible, given the available price–quality trade-off.

HOW MUCH WILL CONSUMERS SEARCH FOR THE BEST PRICE?

By assumption, Figures 5-3 and 5-4 apply to a situation in which the consumer has complete information about the price–quality trade-off in a monopolistically competitive industry. As discussed previously, the consumer must face the problem of asymmetric information about product quality. In addition, most consumers also are imperfectly informed about the prices charged by the many firms in a monopolistically competitive industry.

Figure 5-4:
The Consumer's Choice of the Best Price–Quality Combination.

In panel (a), a consumer initially considers buying a product with the quality level q_1 that sells at a price P_1, at point C. If she buys a product with a higher quality level, she will be equally satisfied consuming either product only if she also pays a higher price P_2, at point D. Because points C and D yield the same satisfaction to the consumer, they are on the same indifference curve IC_1. The indifference curve is bowed downward because a the additional amount that a consumer is willing to pay for successive quality improvements tends to decline as the level of quality increases. If the consumer could purchase a product at the original price P_1 but at the higher quality level q_2, at point F she would be at a higher level of satisfaction along the indifference curve IC_2. Panel (b) shows this consumer's choice of the product with the best available price-quality combination given the price–quality trade-off she faces in the monopolistically competitive marketplace. This is point E, where the indifference curve IC^* is tangent to the price-quality trade-off. There, she chooses to purchase the product with the quality level q^* at the price P^*.

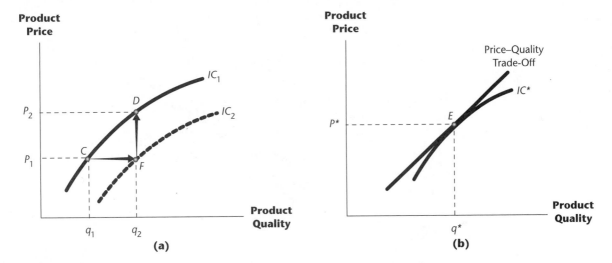

Improving Perceptions with Better Information

In the real world, a typical consumer makes a decision based on a *perception* of the price–quality trade-off. The *true* price–quality trade-off may differ from the one that the consumer perceives given available information. Indeed, because of asymmetric information, some firms may be able to charge different prices for identical products.

Take a look at Figure 5-5 on page 150 to see how the acquisition of information can potentially affect a consumer's perceived price–quality trade-off. In the example illustrated, this consumer initially perceives that prices offered by firms vary considerably in response to steady increases in quality. His initial perception is that the price–quality trade-off is relatively steep, as depicted by *P-q*. The price–quality combinations at points A, B, and C in the figure correspond to those he perceives to be available at firms A, B, and C. As a result, the customer's initial preference is to purchase the good or service produced by firm B that he believes offers the price–quality combination P_B and q_B, at point B. This is the point of tangency of the lowest feasible indifference curve, IC^*, with the price–quality trade-off that he perceives to be available.

Figure 5-5:
Altering the Perceived Price-Quality Trade-Off with Improved Information.

Given the amount of information that a consumer initially possesses, his perception of the price quality trade-off is denoted P-q. The price–quality combinations A, B, and C are those he perceived to be available from firms A, B, and C, and given his initial information he decides to purchase the product of firm B with the quality level q_B at the price P_B. After making this initial decision, however, the consumer acquires information indicating that causes him to change his perception of the price-quality trade-off in this industry to (P-q)'. This means that he can attain a higher level of satisfaction at point C' along the indifference curve IC'. Searching for information thereby helps the consumer determine the best price consistent with his preferences regarding product quality.*

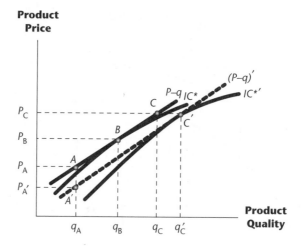

Suppose that after reaching the tentative conclusion that the product with a price P_B and perceived level of quality q_B is his best choice, this consumer decides to gather more information. After searching through firms' product descriptions, advertisements, independent reviews in magazines or trade journals and at Web sites, the consumer's perception of the price–quality trade-off changes. He discovers that even though his perception of the quality of the product produced by firm A was correct, he was wrong about his perception of firm A's price, which he finds actually is slightly lower, $P_{A'}$ at point A'. In addition, the consumer finds that while his earlier view of the price charged by firm C was correct, the quality of firm C's product is significantly higher, at $q_{C'}$, than he had realized before his search for more information. Thus, point C actually is now perceived by this consumer as his best quality choice at the price P_C.

Overall, gathering more information about the choices available for these and other firms in the industry has resulted in the lower price–quality trade-off line (P-q)' depicted in Figure 5-5. The consumer now discovers that he can attain an indifference curve IC*' that lies below and to the right of IC*. Consequently, the consumer's effort to collect more information about prices and quality levels

Figure 5-6:
Determining How Much Information to Acquire When Searching
for the Best Price.

Each additional unit of information that a consumer collects helps improve her perception of the price–quality trade-off available in the marketplace, thereby yielding a positive marginal benefit. The additional benefit gained from acquiring more information declines as she acquires additional information, however, so the marginal benefit curve slopes downward. The consumer must devote time to acquiring information, and the opportunity cost time she spends searching for more information tends to increase as she devotes more and more time to her search efforts. Consequently, the marginal cost curve slopes upward. The consumer acquires information to the point where the marginal benefit from information equals the marginal cost.

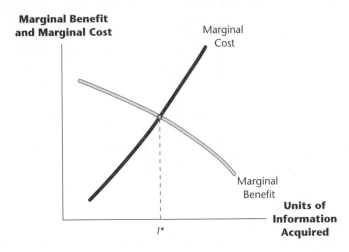

available within this industry has allowed him to reach a higher level of satisfaction, at point C', where he consumes the higher-quality product of firm C instead. Even though the product of firm C has a higher price than the product offered by firm B, the perceived quality level of firm C's product is sufficiently high to improve the consumer's satisfaction. Hence, this consumer is better off after conducting a search for more information: He has found his own **best price**—the lowest price consistent with the consumer's preferences concerning product quality.

Deciding How Much Information to Acquire

In fact, a consumer nearly always benefits from searching for additional information about product prices and quality levels. This means a consumer typically receives a positive marginal benefit from every bit of information obtained via shopping activities. Nevertheless, as shown in Figure 5-6, the marginal benefit from each additional amount of information tends to decline as the consumer acquires more information. The initial moments spent shopping at the home pages of Internet sellers typically yield the most information about prices and

Best Price
The lowest price available for a good or service that is consistent with a consumer's preferences regarding product quality.

product quality. The extent of new information uncovered over longer periods of time tends to decline, as does the additional benefit.

Searching for information on the Internet takes time, which has value to a consumer. For one consumer, a given hour spent shopping for price and quality information about a product might be time that he could alternatively allocate to playing a computer game at a favorite Web site, reading a book, or watching a video. For another consumer, this might be time that she could otherwise devote to consulting work performed in her home office. In both cases, each additional hour spent gathering information about a product has an **opportunity cost**, which is the value of the best alternative use of that hour. The opportunity cost of each additional hour of shopping is the marginal cost that a consumer incurs when searching for additional information about product prices and quality levels. As a consumer allocates more time to shopping activities, the effort to gather more information begins to interfere with alternative activities that the consumer also values. The marginal cost of time of additional information gathered during time spent shopping for the best price increases, as shown in Figure 5-6.

The consumer acquires information about the best price to the point at which marginal benefit equals marginal cost. In Figure 5-6, this is the point where the marginal benefit and marginal cost curves cross. This particular consumer acquires an amount of information equal to I^*. Based on this information, she forms her perception of the price–quality trade-off and decides which particular product to purchase, given her tastes and preferences.

Opportunity Cost
The value of the next best alternative.

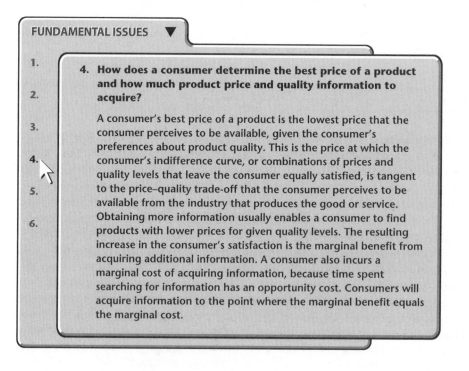

FUNDAMENTAL ISSUES ▼

1.

2.

3.

4.

5.

6.

4. How does a consumer determine the best price of a product and how much product price and quality information to acquire?

A consumer's best price of a product is the lowest price that the consumer perceives to be available, given the consumer's preferences about product quality. This is the price at which the consumer's indifference curve, or combinations of prices and quality levels that leave the consumer equally satisfied, is tangent to the price–quality trade-off that the consumer perceives to be available from the industry that produces the good or service. Obtaining more information usually enables a consumer to find products with lower prices for given quality levels. The resulting increase in the consumer's satisfaction is the marginal benefit from acquiring additional information. A consumer also incurs a marginal cost of acquiring information, because time spent searching for information has an opportunity cost. Consumers will acquire information to the point where the marginal benefit equals the marginal cost.

Price Comparisons and Market Efficiency

You now have the background you need to understand how economists evaluate how well a market functions. Our main interest, of course, is in the performance of the electronic marketplace. Nevertheless, economists use the same methods to judge the performance of the electronic marketplace that they apply to traditional markets.

MARKET EFFICIENCY

Economists say that a market is an **efficient market** when there are numerous competing products, so consumers are very sensitive to price changes, as reflected in a relatively high price elasticity of demand for any given firm's brand. In a truly efficient market, the prices of an industry's products are responsive to changes in the tastes and preferences of consumers and to variations in the operating costs of producers. If firms charge a product price equal to the marginal cost they incur, then all firms also are technically efficient. Thus, they sell their product at the same price that reflects the minimum feasible cost of production. Finally, identical products have the same price in an efficient market.

Efficient Market
A market in which consumers are very sensitive to price changes, firms' prices respond quickly to changes in consumer demand and firm operating costs, and prices equal both marginal production costs and average production costs.

Information and the Price Sensitivity of Demand

Fundamental factors influencing consumers' price elasticity of demand are the marginal benefits and costs they encounter in their efforts to acquire information. To see why this is so, consider Figure 5-7 on page 154. Suppose that initially both consumers paid a price equal to P' for identical quantities of product, Q', that have a quality level equal to q'. Now, all firms in the industry have raised their prices, although by potentially different amounts, at all possible quality levels. Consumers must adjust their perceptions according to the new price–quality trade-off they face.

Panel *(a)* depicts marginal benefit and marginal cost curves for two different consumers, consumer 1 and consumer 2. Both wish to reduce their purchases to the same number of units of the product, Q'', following the price change. They begin with identical information and the same perceptions about the price–quality trade-off they confronted following the industry-wide price increase. Their marginal benefits and costs of acquiring information differ, however. The marginal benefit *(MB)* and marginal cost *(MC)* curves MB_1 and MC_1 apply to consumer 1, and the MB_2 and MC_2 curves apply to consumer 2. Because Consumer 2 obtains a larger marginal benefit for any given amount of information acquired while incurring a lower marginal cost, the consumer chooses to acquire only $I_2 > 0$ unit of product price and quality information, whereas consumer 1 obtains $I_1 = 0$ units of information.

Figure 5-7:
Informational Differences and Implications for the Price Elasticity of Demand.

In panel (a), consumer 1 and consumer 2 face different marginal benefit and marginal cost curves. Both initially consume the same number of units of the product, Q' in panel (c), with the same quality, q', at the initial price P'. After a price increase, both also wish to consume the same quantity Q". They begin with identical information and the same perceptions about the price–quality trade-off that they confront following the industry-wide price increase, so they have the same initial perception of the price–quality trade-off, $(P-q)_1$ in panel (b). Because consumer 2 obtains a larger marginal benefit for any given amount of information he acquires while incurring a lower marginal cost, he chooses to acquire $I_2 > 0$ unit of product price and quality information, whereas consumer 1 obtains $I_1 = 0$ units of information. By acquiring more information, however, consumer 2 revises his perception of the price–quality trade-off to $(P-q)_2$, so that consumer 2's best price, P_2, is below the best price of consumer 1, P_1. Thus, in panel (c), less-informed consumer 1 is willing to pay a higher price, P_1, for the same quantity, Q". Thus, consumer 1 is willing to pay a proportionately higher price after reducing the quantity consumed by the same proportionate amount as consumer 2. This implies that the demand for this product by consumer 1 is relatively less elastic than the demand of consumer 2.

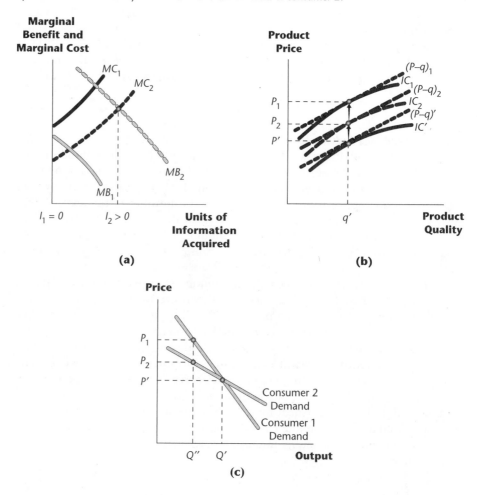

Because both consumers begin with the same information and the same preferences, the price–quality trade-off $(P\text{-}q)_1$ in panel *(b)* initially applies to both consumers. By acquiring more information, however, consumer 2 revises his perception of the price–quality trade-off to $(P\text{-}q)_2$. If both consumers purchase the same number of units of a product with a given quality level q', consumer 2's best price, P_2, is below the best price of consumer 1, P_1. Hence, consumer 1 is willing to pay a higher price for the same quantity of the product with the quality level q'. As panel *(c)* indicates, this means that consumer 1's demand is relatively less elastic than the demand of consumer 2.

Thus, any consumer like consumer 1, who receives a lower marginal benefit or incurs a higher marginal cost from the act of searching for information, tends to exhibit relatively more price-inelastic demand. This means that factors affecting the marginal benefits and costs of acquiring additional information about product prices and quality levels for consumers are key determinants of the overall price elasticity of demand in a marketplace. For instance, suppose that most consumers of a particular product are relatively high-income individuals who place significant value on the time they spend shopping for the best price. Other things being equal, the marginal costs of information acquisition are relatively high for consumers in the market for that product, so the demand for the product is relatively inelastic. As a result, the market is relatively inefficient. Hence, high costs of consumer search for product price and quality information contribute to market inefficiency.

Market Structure, Menu Costs, and the Responsiveness of Prices

As you learned in Chapters 2 and 3, market structure is a fundamental determinant of the responsiveness of prices to changes in market demand conditions or variations in the operating costs of firms within an industry. Holding other factors unchanged, firms with first-mover advantages in industries with relatively sizable barriers to entry will be slower to adjust their prices than firms confronting a host of competitors.

Firms in less-competitive markets will have pricing power and thereby will balance profit gains from adjusting prices to the fixed costs of adjusting their prices, which economists call **menu costs.** Firms with pricing power may adjust their prices less frequently because the gains from price adjustment may be too small relative to the menu costs they would incur. Hence, markets with relatively large numbers of rival sellers with limited pricing power that face relatively low menu costs are likely to be more efficient than markets with just a few firms.

Menu Costs
Fixed costs of adjusting prices.

Marginal Cost Pricing, Technical Efficiency, and the Law of One Price

Recall from Chapter 2 that in the long run, firms in a perfectly competitive industry charge the same market price, a price that equals both marginal cost and the minimum feasible average total cost of production when amounts of all inputs can be varied. Thus, perfectly competitive markets satisfy two key requirements of an efficient market: *allocative efficiency,* or marginal-cost pricing, and *technical efficiency,* or a price equal to minimum long-run average total cost.

Law of One Price
An economic law that in a perfectly competitive market, all firms should sell their products at the same price.

In addition, a perfectly competitive industry yields product prices that are consistent with the **law of one price**, which states that perfectly competitive producers should sell at an identical price. It is a "law," however, only when an efficient market is in long-run equilibrium. Finding the same product offered for sale at different prices by various sellers is relatively commonplace and may simply reflect incomplete adjustment of prices to changes in market conditions.

The *variation* in prices of similar products among firms should be relatively small if the market is relatively efficient. For this reason, another way to gauge whether consumers and firms interact in an efficient market is to examine the range of prices charged for essentially identical products. A relatively narrow range of prices indicates significant competition among firms and considerable access to product price and quality information on the part of consumers. By way of contrast, a wide dispersion of prices is an indicator that firm rivalry may be low or that consumers face high costs of acquiring information, both of which reduce market efficiency.

IS THE ELECTRONIC MARKETPLACE LIKELY TO BE MORE OR LESS EFFICIENT THAN TRADITIONAL MARKETS?

Because electronic commerce is a relatively new phenomenon, economists are just beginning to form their own perceptions of the efficiency of the electronic marketplace relative to traditional markets. This has not kept them from speculating about the likely effects of Web-based market interactions, however.

Consumer Price Sensitivity in Cyberspace

Key determinants of the price elasticity of demand for a good or service are the time that consumers have to adjust to price changes, the expenditures on that good or service as a share of total expenditures, and the availability of close substitutes. Increases in any of these factors tend to raise the price elasticity of demand.

Most observers presume that the potential ease with which shoppers can compare the prices and quality levels of substitute goods and services sold over the Internet should definitely lead to a relatively higher price elasticity of demand in the electronic marketplace, as compared with traditional markets. There are reasons to think that Internet consumers might have a lower price elasticity of demand, however. Although Internet shopping allows consumers to obtain large volumes of price-comparison information over the course of numerous visits to various Web sites, thereby increasing demand elasticities, it is also easy to engage in impulse buying when shopping on the Web, which tends to reduce the price elasticity of demand.

Furthermore, information about product quality viewed on a computer screen can be less accurate than information obtained from physical observation. Adjustments to perceptions of price–quality trade-offs by consumers in response to price changes could steepen as a result. As discussed previously, this will tend to reduce consumers' price elasticity of demand.

Hence, the price elasticity of demand could be either higher or lower in the electronic marketplace as compared with traditional markets. Currently, there is limited evidence about this issue, which economists will continue to explore as they evaluate market efficiency in electronic commerce.

Market Price Flexibility in Electronic Commerce

To date, the evidence is also preliminary regarding the evolving structure of the electronic marketplace. A limited number of studies of the likely importance of menu costs in electronic commerce as compared with traditional markets have been conducted.

Menu costs are hard to measure directly. Economists have concentrated on comparing the propensity for Internet sellers and traditional sellers to make frequent but small price changes. By definition, small price changes entail menu costs just as large price changes would. Yet small price changes bring a small profitability effect, so a firm will make such price changes only if menu costs have little impact on profits. Studies to date indicate that menu costs probably are very small for e-commerce companies, because most firms just have to change the prices posted on their Web pages.

Are Market Prices Charged by Internet Sellers Lower?

Measuring the extent to which prices reflect either allocative or technical efficiency is already a challenge in traditional bricks-and-mortar industries. Economists can rarely observe firms' marginal costs directly, so they typically must infer them. Likewise, they must also infer the minimum feasible average total cost faced in the long run within a given industry. Under the big assumption that they can accurately make both inferences, economists then can try to evaluate whether market prices are significantly different from marginal cost and minimum long-run average total cost.

Electronic commerce is so new that the data required to make cost inferences are very sparse or virtually nonexistent. For this reason, most studies concentrate on evaluating the relative efficiency of e-commerce firms compared with traditional sellers. The few studies making this comparison have yielded mixed conclusions. Those looking at most recent data on prices, however, indicate that prices are lower in the electronic marketplace, even after taking into account shipping and handling charges borne by Internet consumers and sales taxes faced by bricks-and-mortar firms. Lehman Brothers economists Joseph Abate and Ethan Harris conducted a survey comparing e-commerce prices for more than 100 items to those at moderately priced retail outlets and found that prices at Web-based retailers were 13 to 15 percent lower. This reinforces studies of Internet retail prices of specific products that have found comparable price discounts on the Internet relative to traditional markets. Thus, there is some limited evidence that e-commerce firms are at least as efficient, in terms of overall levels of product prices, as traditional companies.

MANAGEMENT *Online*

Is Price Discrimination Always Inconsistent with Greater Market Efficiency?

As you learned in Chapter 4, firms can improve their profitability by engaging in *price discrimination*—charging different buyers different prices or charging the same buyer different prices depending on the quantity purchased. Price discrimination is incompatible with the traditional perspective on market efficiency on at least three grounds: It is inconsistent with marginal cost pricing, with setting prices equal to minimum feasible average total costs, and with satisfying the law of one price. Nevertheless, some economists argue that under certain circumstances price discrimination may be more consistent with attaining allocative efficiency than alternative pricing schemes.

Purchases Don't Happen Unless Consumers Are Willing to Buy

The basis for the "pro-price-discrimination" view is that in markets with high entry barriers, such as large fixed costs and significant economies of scale, marginal-cost pricing may not be feasible. After all, at output rates where average total cost is declining, marginal cost is always less than average total cost. Thus, if average total cost declines over a large range of output rates, a firm that sets price equal to marginal cost can only earn an economic loss.

When a firm that experiences economies of scale sets only one price for its product, it produces to the point where marginal revenue equals marginal cost and charges the single price that customers as a single group are willing to pay for that quantity of output. If this is a relatively high price, consumers may be unwilling to purchase the product. Those

continued

Price Dispersion in the Electronic Marketplace

Evidence to date indicates that there are even larger spreads in prices for the same products in the electronic marketplace. For example, Erik Brynjolfsson and Michael Smith of the Massachusetts Institute of Technology found that prices for identical books and compact disks at Internet retailers differed on average by 33 percent. Some prices differed by as much as 50 percent. In a study of airline tickets sold by online travel agencies, Eric Clemons, Il-Horn Hann, and Lorin Hitt of the University of Pennsylvania found an average price differential of 28 percent.

One possible reason for the wide dispersion in prices for identical goods and services sold online could be a lack of information for consumers to improve their perceptions of the price–quality trade-offs they face in the electronic marketplace. It is also possible that some Internet sellers have become adept in price discrimination. If so, this would help to account for the wide variations in prices. (Some economists believe that price dispersion generated by online price discrimination should not always be interpreted as evidence of inefficient markets; see *Management Online: Is Price Discrimination Always Inconsistent with Greater Market Efficiency?*)

who choose not to buy the product at this single price obtain no consumer surplus.

If the same firm engages in price discrimination, it establishes two or more prices. The firm may charge one group a relatively high price and another group a relatively low price. It is possible in this situation that the result is that more people end up buying the product than before. It is also possible that more people obtain consumer surplus, and it is even feasible for consumer surplus to be higher than it would have been in the absence of price discrimination.

"Willingness to Pay" as an Efficiency Criterion?

Because consumer surplus can actually increase when a price-setting firm engages in price discrimination, some economists, such as Hal Varian of the University of California at Berkeley, have promoted replacing the standard marginal-cost pricing criterion for market efficiency with a **marginal-willingness-**

to-pay condition. Varian argues that a market should be judged allocatively efficient when the marginal cost of producing a product is equal to the additional amount that a consumer is willing to pay for that product. The reason is that when this condition holds in many industries, more consumers are willing and able to purchase the product, and obtain consumer surplus, than would be the case if price were equal to marginal cost.

As discussed in Chapter 3, firms that sell virtual products often experience high fixed costs and short-run economies of scale. Varian contends that the marginal-willingness-to-pay condition is the most sensible criterion to apply when evaluating allocative efficiency in the electronic marketplace.

For Critical Analysis:

Under what circumstances are the marginal-willingness-to-pay condition and marginal-cost pricing identical concepts?

FUNDAMENTAL ISSUES ▼

1.

2.

3.

4.

5. ⬉

6.

> **5. What makes a market efficient, and how efficient is the electronic marketplace?**
>
> A market tends to be more efficient when consumers become more sensitive to price changes, firms adjust their prices more readily to changes in consumer demand and their own operating costs, and prices move toward equality with both marginal production costs and average production costs. So far, the evidence on the price elasticity of demand in the electronic marketplace is scanty. Studies have shown, however, that e-commerce firms face low menu costs and adjust their prices quickly and that prices of goods and services in the electronic marketplace tend to be lower than the prices of those same products in traditional markets. Nevertheless, prices charged for identical products sold on the Internet tend to be very dispersed, perhaps because of relatively poor consumer information or price discrimination by e-commerce firms.

Marginal-Willingness-to-Pay Condition
A condition that some economists promote as a criterion for evaluating allocative efficiency in an industry with relatively high entry barriers such as large fixed costs or significant economies of scale.

E-Commerce Intermediaries

As noted earlier, information intermediaries can reduce the scope of the lemons problem. These and other market intermediaries improve market efficiency, so it is not surprising that intermediaries have carved out several niches in the electronic marketplace.

MARKET MIDDLEMEN

Market intermediaries function as *market middlemen* that specialize in lowering transaction costs faced by buyers and sellers. Whenever producers do not sell their products directly to the final consumer—that is, whenever firms are not completely vertically integrated (see Chapter 4)—there are, by definition, one or more middlemen involved in production and distribution of a good or service.

A market intermediary performs a specific type of market-middleman role: They concentrate on bringing together buyers and sellers. A good example of a market intermediary is a *broker.* This is an individual or institution that specializes in matching buyers and sellers. Brokers are active in markets for financial instruments such as bonds and stocks. They also perform an important role in markets for commodities such as oil, natural gas, and other mineral resources.

INTERMEDIATION ON THE WEB

Three important types of intermediaries have emerged in the electronic marketplace: search engines, B2B exchanges, and shopbots. Let's consider the current and potential roles of each of these intermediaries.

The Role of Search Engines

Search Engines
Software programs that Internet users can access via Web sites to search other Web sites for key words, names, or phrases.

One of the first developments following the creation of the Wide World Web was the creation of **search engines,** which are software programs that a visitor to the Internet can access via Web sites to engage in searches from among millions of Web sites using key words, names, or phrases. Search engines are important e-commerce intermediaries. Many Internet shoppers use search engines, sometimes also known as *information aggregators,* to help identify both products and producers.

Today, most search engines are based on the search system developed by the creators of the Google.com search engine. When a person enters a word or phrase into this search engine, the Google system searches for sites that have received the most "hits" in past searches, treating the site essentially as the winner of an election based on "votes" cast for the site when people choose to visit it.

The system does not treat all votes, equally, however. To rule out efforts to manipulate the search system by having people visit sites over and over again to help the sites score "hits," Google's search engine gives greater weight to links

MANAGEMENT *Online*

Will "Reputation Managers" Earn Trust in Cyberspace?

How can you decide what companies to trust on the Internet? One way is to shop only at the Web sites of companies with established reputations. Nevertheless, getting the best value may require considering a purchase from a relative newcomer to the electronic marketplace.

Establishing Trust

Early on, Internet sellers recognized that potential customers would encounter the problem of trust in transactions. To combat it, companies established rudimentary systems for letting customers provide feedback that would be visible to other shoppers.

For years Amazon has included a "customer reviews" feature accompanying the description of every book, so that shoppers could have the opportunity to see what other consumers thought about it. At the eBay.com auction site, buyers and sellers rate each other and earn stars once they have accumulated a sufficient number of positive reviews. Through their willingness to post customer feedback at their sites, both companies contributed to their reputations.

Reputation Managers as Information Intermediaries

Today there are a growing number of Web sites specializing in monitoring the reputations of Internet sellers. These sites rely on *reputation managers,* which are software programs designed to establish the overall reliability of a product or a company based on potentially huge amounts of customer feedback.

There are different approaches to designing reputation managers. The simplest is a one person–one vote system that simply adds up favorable and unfavorable evaluations to establish a net reputation score. More sophisticated systems, however, allow a user to search for product and company reviews and to provide feedback about which were most helpful. In this way, the reviewers themselves develop reputations, so that future reviews that they contribute receive more weight in determining the overall rating for a product or a company.

For Critical Analysis:

Could the time and effort required for a consumer to determine the reputation of a relatively new Internet seller constitute a barrier to entry into the electronic marketplace?

---

from sites that also receive large numbers of visits. (E-commerce firms seeking to establish trust in their products have applied this approach by developing interactive mechanisms for customers to post product reviews for other prospective customers; see *Management Online: Will "Reputation Managers" Earn Trust in Cyberspace?*)

Many people set their browser to load up a Web search engine as the opening page when they log onto the Internet. E-commerce firms realize this, so the home pages of search engines have also become the homes of much of the commercial advertising on the Web (see Chapter 6 for more on this issue) and to multiple links to other sites. Owners of the search engines earn revenues from these advertisements and links. Just as brokers compete against one another to improve their abilities to match buyers and sellers of financial instruments or commodities, the owners of search engines compete on the capabilities of their search systems to

How do reputation managers work? Learn more about them at http://www.isrg.freeuk. com.

direct consumers to Web sites that best fit their queries. Success in this endeavor induces consumers to keep returning to their search-engine sites, thereby helping convince other companies to keep paying to maintain their ads and links.

B2B Exchanges and Referral Services

Companies that are not vertically integrated must purchase from other suppliers or rely on retailers to market and distribute their final products. Many B2B sites perform an intermediary role by matching buyers and sellers in the markets for factors of production.

In traditional marketplace, brokers often become *dealers* as well. Dealers specialize in buying and selling goods or assets on their own account. They earn profits when they are able to buy low and sell high. Some B2B exchanges have begun acting as dealers as well as brokers. So far, such activities have been relatively limited, because dealers must maintain inventories of goods or assets. Thus, with the exception of those dealing in information-based goods that can be stored in digital form, dealers in B2B merchandise require more than a virtual presence.

Many B2B exchanges have sought to become *market makers.* Like stock exchanges that have traditionally profited from providing a common physical location for stockbrokers and dealers to trade financial securities, B2B exchanges such as FastParts.com, Ironmall.com, and Medicalbuyer.com aim to provide a common location on the Internet for companies to conduct exchanges.

Internet customer referral services also form a brokerage function. For instance, Autobytel.com and similar Web services match prospective automobile consumers with automobile dealers. A study by Fiona Scott Morton of Yale University, Jorge Risso of J.D. Power and Associates, and Florian Zettelmeyer of the University of California at Berkeley has found that the average Internet consumer using Autobytel pays about 2 percent less, or $450, for her car as compared with traditional consumers. The reasons for the lower price, they conclude, are the lower costs of serving consumers online, the fact that Web-based matching services tend to pair consumers with lower-price dealers, and the ability of referral services to establish bargaining power with dealers.

Shopbots and Intelligent Agents

Shopbot
A software program that searches large volumes of information contained in networks for answers to questions posed by a potential consumer of a product; also known as an intelligent agent.

In the perhaps not-so-distant future, both consumers and businesses are likely to rely increasingly on **shopbots,** also known as *intelligent agents.* The term is a shortened form of "shopping robot." Shopbots essentially are software tools for digging through data. They act as agents for those wishing to undertake a virtual search by giving the shopbot directions and wait for it to search the Internet for answers.

Data Mining
The process of searching for patterns in large masses of information.

The reason shopbots are also called intelligent agents is that their purpose is to engage in informed **data mining,** or searching out relevant patterns in enormous quantities of information. Data mining typically entails conducting series of searches, and effective data mining often requires refining investigative techniques during the course of information searches. An "intelligent" shopbot is able to make decisions based on past experiences, thereby rapidly narrowing the focus of its explorations among potentially billions of pieces of information available about a search topic on the Web.

Rudimentary shopbots are already in use. For instance, eFoods.com employs intelligent agents to help restaurant owners and managers customize Web sites enabling customers to order food via wireless devices while in transit to lunch or dinner. In addition, the advertising measurement firm Media Matrix offers a service called AdRelevance that allows marketing and advertising executives to track where, when, how, and how much rival firms are advertising online.

Initially, shopbots such as BidFind, DealTime, and GreaterGood were envisioned as competitors to Internet search engines. In fact, most search engines either purchased or developed their own shopbot technologies. You can access shopbots either via their own Web sites or by using shopping-comparison programs available at Yahoo.com and other search engine sites.

Some observers envision a time when a typical Web shopper has an individually tailored shopbot residing on his or her personal computer, wireless online device, or other system for accessing the Internet. In such a world, shopbots will gather product price and quality information for a consumer, taking into account the consumer's tastes and preferences, while the consumer works, exercises, or relaxes. When the consumer goes back online, the shopbots will display a narrowed set of best-price choices available—or perhaps might already have made a purchase on the consumer's behalf.

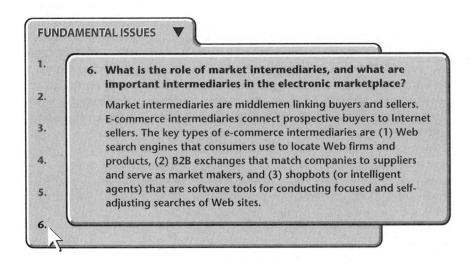

FUNDAMENTAL ISSUES ▼

1.

2.

3.

4.

5.

6.

6. What is the role of market intermediaries, and what are important intermediaries in the electronic marketplace?

Market intermediaries are middlemen linking buyers and sellers. E-commerce intermediaries connect prospective buyers to Internet sellers. The key types of e-commerce intermediaries are (1) Web search engines that consumers use to locate Web firms and products, (2) B2B exchanges that match companies to suppliers and serve as market makers, and (3) shopbots (or intelligent agents) that are software tools for conducting focused and self-adjusting searches of Web sites.

Chapter Summary

1) **Asymmetric Information and Problems It Can Cause:** A situation of asymmetric information arises when one party to an exchange has information not possessed by another party to the exchange. This can result in adverse selection, or the potential for sellers to offer only low-quality products (lemons) to customers or for customers that firms regard as less desirable to buy goods or services. In addition, moral hazard can arise—or the possibility that one party to an exchange may undertake actions that another party deems undesirable after the exchange has already been arranged or taken place. A potential outgrowth of the adverse selection problem is that a widespread perception of large number of lemons in the marketplace can depress prices and cause sellers to withdraw high-quality products.

2) **The Lemons Problem and Possible Solutions:** The possibility that adverse selection can bring about an overall reduction in the quality of products sold in a market is known as the lemons problem. To reduce the potential scope of the lemons problem, producers can provide guarantees and warranties, develop industry standards and product certification procedures, and attempt to establish and maintain reputations of quality. In addition, consumers can use information intermediaries to obtain product quality guidance. Liability laws and government licensing requirements may help screen out low-quality products.

3) **Why a Firm Can Gain from Providing More Information, and How a Firm Determines How Much Information to Provide to Consumers:** If consumers perceive that a product has a lower quality than it really does, then the firm can increase its profitability by providing additional information about the true quality of the product. By doing so, the firm's action will increase the demand for its product. This allows the firm to charge a higher price and expand its sales. The firm receives a marginal benefit, in the form of a profit increase, from an increase in the amount of product information it provides. The firm provides information up to the point where this marginal benefit equals the marginal cost of disseminating information to consumers.

4) **How a Consumer Determines the Best Price of a Product and How Much Product Price and Quality Information to Obtain:** The best price for a consumer is the lowest price that the consumer perceives to be consistent with the consumer's preferences about product quality. At this price, the consumer's indifference curve, which indicates combinations of prices and quality levels that leave the consumer equally satisfied, is tangent to the consumer's perceived price–quality trade-off. This trade-off, in turn, is the set of price–quality combinations that the consumer views to exist within

the industry that produces the good or service. Typically, gathering additional information allows the consumer to identify products with lower prices at given quality levels, thereby raising the consumer's satisfaction and yielding a marginal benefit from the added information. Time spent searching for information entails an opportunity cost, so a consumer also incurs a marginal cost of acquiring information. A consumer searches for information to the point where the marginal benefit equals the marginal cost.

5) **What Makes a Market Efficient, and the Efficiency of the Electronic Marketplace:** Market efficiency increases if the price elasticity of demand increases, if firms change prices more readily in response to variations in consumer demand and their own operating costs, and if prices move toward equality with both marginal production costs and average production costs. It is too early to state whether the price elasticity of demand is higher or lower in the electronic marketplace. There are indications that Internet sellers face low menu costs and adjust their prices quickly. In addition, studies indicate that prices charged for products sold in the electronic marketplace tend to be lower than the prices of identical products in traditional markets. There are, however, relatively large spreads between the highest and lowest prices charged for identical products sold on the Internet. This may be because of weaker information or successful efforts on the part of Internet sellers to engage in price discrimination.

6) **The Role of Market Intermediaries and Important E-Commerce Intermediaries:** A market intermediary is a middleman who connects buyers and sellers. Intermediaries in the electronic marketplace lead prospective buyers to firms that offer products for sale on the Web. There are three important e-commerce intermediaries. One is Internet search engines, which many consumers use to find the home pages of Internet sellers. A second is B2B exchanges, which match companies to suppliers and serve as market makers. The third is shopbots, or intelligent agents, which are software programs that consumers use to conduct sophisticated searches for information about product prices and quality levels.

Questions and Problems

1) Figure 5-1 on page 141 shows how a firm with a relatively high-quality product could enhance its profitability by providing more information to consumers. Use an appropriate diagram to show how a firm that produces a relatively low-quality item could also increase its profit by providing false information indicating that it sells a high-quality product. What are the implications of this finding?

2) At one time, companies were in a rush to outbid each other for the rights to Web site names that were common nouns, such as "pets," "garden," "mortgage," "jewelry," and "furniture."
   (a) Based on what you learned in this chapter, why did many businesspeople regard common-noun names as potentially valuable names for Web sites in the electronic marketplace?
   (b) Eventually, companies named Pets.com, Jewelry.com, and Furniture.com failed to earn profits and shut down their first attempts at online retailing. Does this necessarily imply that common-noun names are unlikely to be successful in e-commerce? Why or why not?

3) What types of asymmetric-information problem(s) might be encountered by consumers and producers of online dating and matchmaking services for college students?

4) Explain how the asymmetric-information problems you discussed in question 3 might generate a potential lemons problem for firms providing online dating and matchmaking services for college students. What steps might these firms take to reduce the scope of the lemons problem that they face?

5) Suppose that a firm finds that posting a special Web page providing information about any given product it sells pushes up the demand for that product. Use an appropriate diagram to explain how this is likely to affect the number of informational Web pages the firm posts at its Web site.

6) The firm discussed in question 5 upgrades its Web server and finds that it is much less expensive to develop and post additional informational Web pages on its site. Redraw the completed diagram from your answer to question 5 and use it to help determine how this development is likely to affect the number of informational Web pages the firm posts at its Web site.

7) Is an Internet consumer's perception of the "best price" of a good or service necessarily the lowest available price?

8) Suppose that a decade from now most automobile owners use Internet-connected wireless telephone devices equipped with software that allows them to find the "best price" for gasoline.
   (a) What factors might drivers take into account when determining the "best price" of gasoline?
   (b) Is whether the car is currently in an urban, suburban, or rural area likely to influence how much information about gas prices the driver acquires using the wireless Internet connection and gas-price-search software? Explain.

9) Suppose that Microsoft and other makers of personal computer software were to end distribution of software on CDs and other physical media and make their software available only via Internet downloads. Other things being equal, would this action raise or lower the price elasticity of demand for downloadable software? Why?

10) As noted in the chapter, there are relatively wide spreads between highest and lowest prices of products sold on the Internet. Why might there also be

noticeable spreads between the prices of identical products marketed and distributed online and in the physical marketplace?

11) What should happen to spreads between the highest and lowest prices of identical products sold on the Web as the use of shopping agents and other intermediaries becomes more common? Is it possible that there will always be a noticeable spread between the highest and lowest prices of identical products marketed by Internet sellers? Why?

Online Application

Internet URL: http://www.infotoday.com/lu/jul99/rudich.htm

Title: **Link-Up: "Shopbots,"** by Joe Rudich

Navigation: Go directly to the above URL.

Application: Read the article, and answer the following questions.

1) What type of shopbot appears most likely to assist consumers in gathering price and quality information?

2) Why might Internet sellers block access to their sites by shopbots? Why might they be willing to permit shopbot access?

For Group Study and Analysis: Divide the class into groups, and have each group explore the features of shopbots mentioned in the article. List ways that shopbots promote competition. In addition, discuss how firms might use shopbots to engage in noncompetitive pricing activities.

Selected References and Further Readings

Brynjolfsson, Erik, and Michael Smith, "The Great Equalizer? Consumer Choice Behavior at Internet Shopbots," Massachusetts Institute of Technology Sloan School of Management, Cambridge, MA, July 2000.

Camp, L. Jean. *Trust and Risk in Internet Commerce.* Cambridge, MA: MIT Press, 2000.

Carlton, Dennis, and Jeffrey Perloff. *Modern Industrial Organization.* 3d ed. Reading, MA: Addison-Wesley, 2000.

Choi, Soon-Yong, Dale Stahl, and Andrew Whinston. *The Economics of Electronic Commerce.* Indianapolis: Macmillan Technical Publishing, 1997.

Choo, Chun Wei, Brian Detlor, and Don Turnbull. "Information Seeking on the Web: An Integrated Model of Browsing and Searching," *First Monday* 5 (February 7, 2000) (http://www.firstmonday.dk/issues/issue5_2/choo/index.html).

Clay, Karen, Ramayya Krishman, and Eric Wolff. "Prices and Price Dispersion on the Web: Evidence from the Online Book Industry," National Bureau of Economic Research Working Paper 827, May 2001.

Friberg, Richard, Mattias Ganslandt, and Mikael Sandström, "E-Commerce and Prices—Theory and Evidence," SSE/EFI Working Paper 389, Stockholm School of Economics, June 2000.

Johkheer, Kees, "Intelligent Agents, Markets, and Competition: Consumers' Interests and Functionality of Destination Sites," *First Monday* 4 (June 7, 1999) (http://www.firstmonday.dk/issues/issue4_6jonkheer/index.html).

Morton, Fiona Scott, Florian Zettelmeyer, and Jorge Risso. "Internet Car Retailing," NBER Working Paper No. 7961, October 2000.

Smith, Michael, Joseph Bailey, and Erik Brynjolfsson. "Understanding Digital Markets: Review and Assessment." In *Understanding the Digital Economy.* Cambridge, MA: MIT Press, 2000.

Varian, Hal. "Differential Pricing and Efficiency," *First Monday* 1 (August 5, 1996) (http://www.firstmonday.dk/issues/issue2/different/).

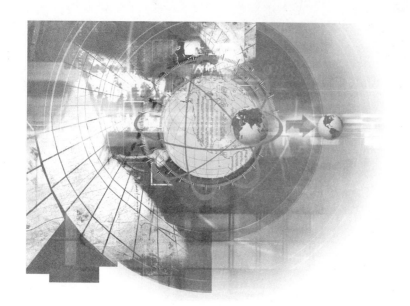

Internet Advertising

<E-Commerce Today>

The Winner of the Yahoo Book-Ad Battle Is . . .

Two pioneering companies, Yahoo.com and Amazon.com, had maintained a relationship since the earliest days of electronic commerce. In autumn 2000, Amazon decided to call it quits, opting instead to run online ads exclusively through America Online's service. No longer would Internet surfers see ads pop up on their computer screen inviting them to shop at Amazon for books relating to topics they had entered into the Yahoo search engine.

Yahoo, which had already experienced a slight drop-off in Web advertising revenue during the previous year, immediately struck a deal with Barnesandnoble.com (http://www.bn.com). This second-largest Internet bookseller had been struggling to become more than just a fringe competitor in the electronic marketplace for books. Even though Barnes and Noble had been selling books on the Web for several years, many consumers remained unaware of its existence. Hence, the Yahoo-Amazon split was a godsend for the struggling online unit of the company. Soon its ads for books, CDs, DVDs, and other products began popping up on computer screens around the globe.

The commercialization of the Internet began in earnest when Yahoo.com and Amazon.com first established an advertising relationship at the end of 1996. Other companies jumped into the electronic marketplace soon afterward, and even traditional bricks-and-mortar firms began to see the Internet as a new medium for advertising.

In any medium, **advertising** is the distribution of information promoting consumption of a particular good or service. A credit-card company might, for instance, place a sign on a billboard, or it might run a display ad in a newspaper or a commercial on radio or television. To market its credit-card services to college students, the company might even set up a booth outside a college or university bookstore manned by a salesperson. The simple presence of the booth serves as an ad for the credit-card company. In addition, students can obtain information from the employee staffing the booth. Students can also apply for a credit card at the booth or obtain an application form to fill out later. Hence, this traditional form of advertising allows for a variety of promotional interactions with consumers.

For many advertisers, the promise of the Internet is its potential to turn personal computers into an advertising booth for every residence. Indeed, for many firms this potential has been realized. The electronic marketplace has already developed into an important advertising medium.

Advertising
The act of distributing information intended to promote a consumer's purchase of a product.

E-Commerce as a Marketing Revolution

The Internet has significantly broadened the scope for firms to engage in interactive selling. In principle, the Web server of a credit-card company and an Internet site that it supports can do everything an employee-staffed booth can accomplish. The site can serve as a display ad for the company's credit-card services, with additional informational pages that a potential customer's Web browser can access. Furthermore, the company's Web server can monitor the site for informational questions by potential customers, and it can either provide automated answers or forward the queries to customer-service representatives to answer via e-mail.

If you have spent much time browsing the Web, you are well aware of the fact that companies have gone far beyond simply establishing Web sites. A few years ago, the opening page of an Internet search engine site was relatively bare. Today, someone browsing the Internet confronts a steady stream of advertisements at the site of a typical search engine.

What are current and future prospects for Web advertising? Find more information about Web advertising at the Interactive Advertising Bureau at http://www.iab.net.

THE GROWTH OF INTERNET ADVERTISING

The advertisements that now almost cover a computer screen when some Web pages are displayed provide superficial visual evidence of the significant growth of Internet advertising. Figure 6-1 furnishes more concrete evidence of this growth. Panel *(a)* shows quarterly spending on Internet-based ads since 1996, when total spending on Internet advertising in the United States was only a little over a quarter of a billion dollars. By 2001, annual expenditures on ads placed on the Internet had increased to nearly $9 billion.

Panel *(b)* displays the implied annual rates of growth expenditures on Internet advertising. Although the growth rate has slowed, as compared with the late 1990s, it is still several times the rate of growth that many industries might regard as phenomenally successful.

WHAT IS DIFFERENT ABOUT INTERNET ADVERTISING?

What explains the sizable growth of Internet advertising? To answer this question, let's begin by considering alternative ways in which firms market their products to consumers.

Direct Marketing
Advertising targeted at specific consumers, typically in the form of postal mailings, telephone calls, or e-mail messages.

Mass Marketing
Advertising intended to reach as many consumers as possible, typically through television, newspaper, radio, or magazine ads.

Marketing Methods
Figure 6-2 on page 174, shows the current distribution of advertising expenses among the various advertising media. Today, as in the past, firms primarily rely on two approaches to advertising their products. One is **direct marketing,** in which firms engage in personalized advertising using postal mailings, phone calls, and e-mail messages. The other is **mass marketing,** in which firms aim advertising messages at as many consumers as possible via media such as televisions, newspapers, radio, and magazines.

Figure 6-1:
Internet Advertising Spending Since 1996.

Panel (a) shows that spending on Internet ads now exceeds $2 billion every three months. As shown in panel (b), annual Internet advertising spending has increased by at least 90 percent a year every year since 1996.

Source: Internet Advertising Bureau (http://www.iab.net) and author's estimates.

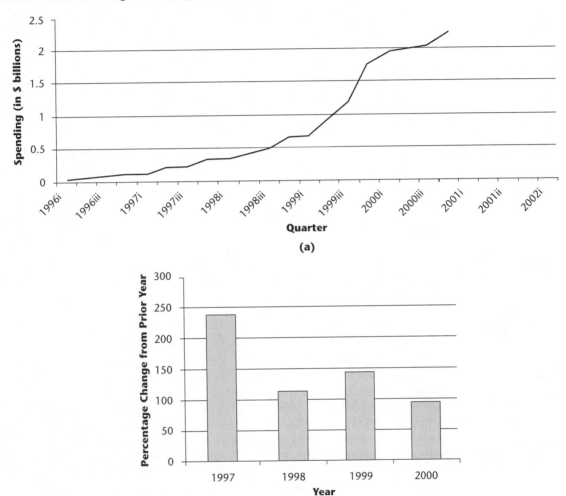

(a)

(b)

Figure 6-2:
Spending on Internet Advertising versus Traditional Advertising Channels.

Total expenditures on traditional forms of advertising continue to exceed spending on Internet ads.

Sources: *Advertising Today, Direct Marketing Today,* and Interactive Advertising Bureau.

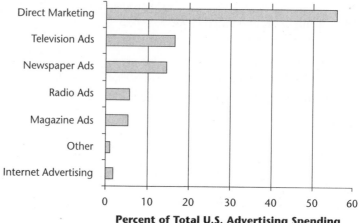

Percent of Total U.S. Advertising Spending

Interactive Marketing
Advertising that permits a consumer to follow up directly by searching for more information and placing direct product orders.

A third advertising method is called **interactive marketing.** This advertising approach allows a consumer to respond directly to an advertising message, often by permitting the consumer to search for more detailed information and to potentially place an order as part of the response. The earlier example of a marketing booth staffed by an employee of a credit card company is a form of interactive marketing.

Most Internet advertising is a form of interactive marketing. As Figure 6-2 indicates, spending on Internet advertising remains a small portion of total advertising expenditures. Nevertheless, the Internet's advertising share has increased rapidly each year as more companies opt to place ads on Web pages alongside or in place of alternative means of advertising.

Banner Ad
An Internet advertisement that appears as a graphic display on a Web page and that is linked to the advertiser's home page.

The most common type of advertising on the Internet is **banner ads,** which appear as graphic displays on Web pages to provide links to the advertiser's home page. One function of banner ads is to provide a mass-marketing message, much like a billboard on the highway. In addition, banner ads are links to more information that can be found on the Web pages of firms that purchase the ads. Unlike a billboard, a newspaper ad, or a television commercial, when a consumer clicks a banner ad posted on a Web page, the result is a direct connection to the company. Furthermore, the firm that placed the banner ad can get an idea of how effective the ad is from the ad's so-called *click ratio,* or the number of times consumers click the ad to establish a link divided by the total number of times that they access the Web site where the ad appears. (Ad click ratios can vary dramatically across various age groups; see *Management Online: What the Powerpuff Girls and Scooby Doo Have in Common Online.*)

Pros and Cons of Internet Advertising

Table 6-1 on page 176 lists the most important advantages and disadvantages of Internet advertising. There are obviously several ways that advertising on the Internet is advantageous as compared with many mass-marketing and direct-marketing

MANAGEMENT *Online*

What the Powerpuff Girls and Scooby Doo Have in Common Online

A big question for Internet advertisers in recent years has been determining what groups among the general population of Internet surfers are most likely to click on banner ads. To the surprise of many observers, the answer is children under 11. The average click ratio for kids in this age group hovers between 0.8 and 0.9 percent—that is, out of every 100 times a Web page containing an ad appears, a child typically clicks on the ad 0.8 times. By way of contrast, the click ratio for the overall Internet audience is between 0.4 and 0.5 percent.

Not surprisingly, among the kinds of ads that attract kids are Cartoon Network fare, such as interactive sites featuring characters from popular television cartoon shows and contain-

ing even more banner ads for Nintendo games and Hershey candy offerings. Some companies have developed Web-based games that also function as advertisements, such as Trident Gum's "Adventures of Supertooth," which drew the most clicks among Web ads one month.

An interesting phenomenon is that the ad click ratio plunges when a typical child reaches the age of 12. For the age group 12–17, the click ratio falls to between 0.1 and 0.2 percent, the lowest of all age groups. Internet advertisers are still scrambling to try to figure out how to hold onto kids when they graduate from elementary school.

For Critical Analysis:

What economic factors might help to account for the drop in the ad click ratio for teenagers? (Hint: How do opportunity costs change for kids when they become teenagers?)

---

alternatives. The ability to use click ratios or other measures of response to ads is one example. So is the ability to change ad content at any time with relative ease.

Just as a billboard has advantages over television commercials because consumers can see it alongside a highway any time of day or night, banner ads are present on Web pages 24 hours per day. Unlike billboards and most other forms of advertising, Internet ads also offer direct interactivity with potential customers.

Like mass-marketing ads, significant economies of scale can be realized though Internet advertising. After all, people with Internet access can view Internet ads without limit, so the expense of putting the ads in place can be divided by a large number of consumers to yield a lower average cost to reach each individual consumer.

One advantage of Internet advertising is the possibility of customizing ads and targeting them to selected individuals or groups. When Internet visitors can be identified using cookies (see Chapter 1) or other mechanisms, information about their Internet browsing and buying patterns can help determine what ads they see on their computer screens. (Of course, as discussed in Chapter 11, this raises some privacy issues.)

Table 6-1: Advantages and Disadvantages of Internet Advertising.

Advantages	Disadvantages
Content of advertisements can be updated relatively easily.	Ads may require frequent content changes to maintain consumer interest.
There is a possible means of establishing direct customer relationships.	Interactivity with consumers requires consumers to initiate contact.
Customers can view advertisements at any given second within a day.	In absence of consumer clicks, it can be difficult to measure effectiveness with consumers.
It is feasible to target ads to specific individuals.	Fixed costs of developing effective Internet advertising are potentially high.
Advertising response rates can be measured and updated automatically.	Aside from click ratios and affiliate sales, it can be hard to judge overall market impact of ad.
Economies of scale: average cost per consumer declines as more access ads.	It can be difficult to determine the actual average cost per consumer.

Where are additional Web advertising resources? Check out the links available at http://www.iab.net/ tools/content/ industryinfo.html.

There are also some drawbacks associated with advertising on the Internet. For some companies, the fixed costs of developing Web advertising content can be significant. In addition, even though there is the promise of economies of scale in Internet advertising, lack of knowledge of how many people are likely to view a given ad on the Internet can make it hard to determine the actual average cost of reaching customers. (Recently companies have developed ways to pay only for advertising that generates sales; see *Management Online: Banner Ads Meet Affiliate Marketing*.)

An important concern in the online business community is that for sellers to realize the promise of advertising interactivity on the Internet, consumers must make an active decision to initiate interactions. In recent years one of the troubling questions raised about Internet advertising is that the proposed advantage of interactivity may have been overestimated, because many consumers choose to bypass ads as they surf the Net.

The rapid growth of Internet advertising indicates that so far many companies have determined that the advantages of Internet advertising tend to outweigh the disadvantages. This poses important economic considerations:

MANAGEMENT *Online*

POLICY MAKING   GLOBALIZATION   **MANAGEMENT**

Banner Ads Meet Affiliate Marketing

From the perspective of a firm seeking to generate additional sales of its product, Web banner ads have two big advantages. They make prospective customers aware of the firm's product, and they provide a channel for directly connecting that individual with a mechanism—usually Web shopping pages at the firm's Internet site—for purchasing the firm's product.

Payment for Performance

For several years, companies such as Amazon.com and CDNow.com have used **affiliate marketing** programs, in which the advertising merchant provides a flat fee or a commission to owners of sites providing Web links that result in purchases. For instance, a Web site devoted to scuba diving often contains links to retailers that sell boats, diving equipment, and Caribbean vacations. If an Internet surfer clicks on the link and buys merchandise from the retailer, the retailer pays the owner of the scuba diving site a fee or commission.

Like banner ads, affiliate-marketing links help to increase consumer awareness of a company's product. In contrast to banner ads, companies using affiliate-marketing programs pay nothing to the site that posts Web links unless sales actually take place.

Affiliate-marketing programs are not successful unless they involve links to a large number of Web sites. A basic rule of thumb that retailers use when developing a new affiliate-marketing programs is that typically only 20 percent of affiliate sites will generate about 80 percent of actual transactions with consumers. Only after such programs have been in place for some time can a retailer determine which affiliate sites have proved most effective in generating sales. Consequently, Internet sellers setting up new affiliate-marketing programs typically launch their campaign on about 10,000 affiliate sites.

An Increasing Presence in Online Marketing

According to Nielsen Net Ratings, about three consumer mouse clicks to connect with Internet sellers will result for every 1,000 Web banner ads, yielding a click ratio of only 0.3 percent. Affiliate links, by way of contrast, yield about three successful connections of potential buyers to online retailers for every 100 affiliate links, yielding a much higher click ratio of 3 percent. Hence, affiliate ads are about ten times more effective in linking Internet sellers to prospective customers.

Currently affiliate-marketing programs now generate nearly 15 percent of online sellers' revenues. Companies are become more adept at implementing such programs, so many Internet advertising experts expect this percentage to increase significantly during the next several years.

For Critical Analysis:

Given that affiliate marketing is ten times more effective in generating potential sales, why do you suppose that online sellers have not completely abandoned banner ads in favor of affiliate-marketing programs?

- What types of goods should companies advertise on the Internet?
- What kinds of ads should they place on the Web?
- How much advertising should they do?
- Are there any rationales for placing legal limitations on their advertising activities?

These are the key topics addressed in the remainder of this chapter.

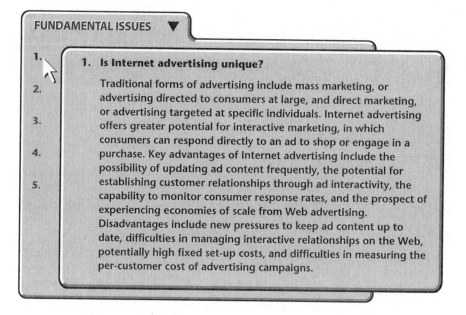

1. Is Internet advertising unique?

Traditional forms of advertising include mass marketing, or advertising directed to consumers at large, and direct marketing, or advertising targeted at specific individuals. Internet advertising offers greater potential for interactive marketing, in which consumers can respond directly to an ad to shop or engage in a purchase. Key advantages of Internet advertising include the possibility of updating ad content frequently, the potential for establishing customer relationships through ad interactivity, the capability to monitor consumer response rates, and the prospect of experiencing economies of scale from Web advertising. Disadvantages include new pressures to keep ad content up to date, difficulties in managing interactive relationships on the Web, potentially high fixed set-up costs, and difficulties in measuring the per-customer cost of advertising campaigns.

Marketing Search Goods and Experience Goods on the Web

As you learned in Chapter 5, there are good reasons for firms to engage in advertising. A banner ad can provide consumers with useful information about a new products or a recent price cut. It may simply give consumers better information about the likely quality of a good or service. Information from advertising can improve the consumer's perception of the market price–quality trade-off and can benefit the producer by raising the demand for its product.

At the same time, there are incentives for sellers to inform consumers of product strengths while withholding information about weaknesses. For example, firms selling products that are lemons (see Chapter 5) have an incentive to disguise the true quality of their products behind deceptive or even untruthful advertising.

Search Good
A product with characteristics that enable an individual to evaluate the product's quality in advance of a purchase.

Experience Good
A product that an individual must consume before the product's quality can be established.

DISTINGUISHING SEARCH GOODS FROM EXPERIENCE GOODS

To consider the informational aspects of firm advertising, economists have traditionally classified products into two groups. One is **search goods**, which are goods and services possessing qualities that are relatively easy for consumers to assess in advance of their purchase. The other is **experience goods.** These are products that people must actually consume before they can determine their qualities.

Search Goods: "Naturals" for Internet Marketing?

A basic quality that a search good possesses can be summed up by "seeing is believing." That is, many search goods are products that consumers evaluate simply by visual inspection. Apparel items, for example, have this property. The color and style of an article of clothing is almost as apparent in high-quality photographs as it is on a hanger or shelf located in a bricks-and-mortar retail outlet. Likewise, a photograph of a filing cabinet accompanied by a description of its dimensions (height, depth, and width) and components (heavy-duty steel versus lightweight metal alloys) can provide considerable information about its functionality and durability.

Because search goods have characteristics that consumers can readily evaluate from photographs and written descriptions, some observers have argued that they are particularly marketable on the Internet. Not all search goods have characteristics that can be judged solely on the basis of visual examination and careful reading of product descriptions, however. Some are products possessing characteristics that customers can best assess by touch or smell, for instance.

Consider the example of online furniture sales. In February 1999 Amazon announced that a start-up firm called Living.com, an Internet seller of furniture, would be a featured partner on its Web site. Within seven months, Living.com had shut down its site, and much of the value of Amazon's 18 percent stake in the company had evaporated. Although crowded competition in the furniture market undoubtedly was a key factor in explaining the company's exit from the marketplace, another problem was that many consumers are hesitant to purchase furniture online. As you may have experienced yourself, some leisure chairs or loft beds may look wonderful on paper or on a screen but actually provide poor back support.

Selling Experience Goods Online

There are also good reasons to regard some experience goods, such as soft drinks, packaged foods, and software programs as good candidates for online marketing. People who have experienced consumption of these types of products are already familiar with their characteristics. The focus of their market search is often on finding the highest-quality products at the best available prices. Internet advertisements for such items can help consumers identify both products and prices, thereby aiding in efforts to generate sales.

Traditionally, major advertising efforts for experience goods have functioned as signals of the quality of the producer. Firms that launch large advertising campaigns for experience goods often do so in the hope that consumers will infer that they are reputable companies and not fly-by-night manufacturers. To the extent that the Internet reduces the cost of launching marketing efforts for experience goods, this "reputation effect" may be diminished. (Psychotherapy services are an experience good that some providers have had recent, but somewhat controversial, success in marketing and distributing on the Internet; see *Management Online: Is Internet Psychotherapy the Wave of the Future?*)

MANAGEMENT *Online*

Is Internet Psychotherapy the Wave of the Future?

In a widely read book of the early 1970s entitled *Future Shock*, the pop-sociology writer Alvin Toffler envisioned a future time—namely, today—in which rapid technological changes would create social and cultural upheavals. Many individuals would, he predicted, experience trying personal times and struggle with psychological depression in the face of the demands that these changes placed on their careers, their spiritual lives, and their interpersonal relationships.

Enter Internet Counseling

The technology of mental health has adapted in ways that Toffler's sociological analysis did not contemplate, however. The traditional technique of psychotherapy—one-on-one discussions between therapists and patients suffering from depression and other cognitive disorders—has been comple-

mented by a broad array of psychoactive medications, such as Prozac, that influence the brain's chemistry and provide relief from a number of mental health difficulties. Some medications were such effective treatments that during the 1990s many health-care providers began to regard psychoactive medications as a *substitute* for psychotherapy services. Some in the health-care industry even began to speculate that the market for psychotherapy services would ultimately disappear with the development of even more effective medications.

So far, people have maintained their demand for psychotherapy services. Millions of people continue to seek traditional psychotherapy treatment from psychiatrists, clinical psychologists, and licensed counselors. Today, however, some people do not go to an office to discuss their mental health problems. An increasing number of people seek help on the Internet, where thousands of Web sites offer mental health education, teen crisis counseling, and online programs for dealing with personal problems at home or in the workplace.

continued

FUNDAMENTAL ISSUES ▼

1.

2.

3.

4.

5.

2. What is the difference between search goods and experience goods, and does either predominate in Internet marketing?

Search goods are products with characteristics that are easy to assess before consumers buy them. Experience goods are goods and services that people must actually purchase and consume in order to evaluate their qualities. Products that are particularly suited to Internet marketing are search goods with features that are relatively easy to assess in photographs, drawings, and written descriptions. Nevertheless, many producers of search goods requiring evaluation of other characteristics and of experience goods also have engaged in Internet advertising. Hence, goods of both types are marketed on the Internet.

In addition, a growing number of psychiatrists offer online employee assistance programs to corporations. For $35 to $40 per year, participating companies can give their workers access to a variety of online mental health programs. Some of these programs now include one-on-one therapeutic counseling over the Internet. Many psychotherapists have built private practices around online provision of their services. Some even specialize, with sites devoted to group therapy, Freudian psychoanalysis, and analysis of dreams.

The Pros and Cons of Internet Therapy

Why would people seek treatment for mental health problems from a faceless therapist via the Internet? One reason might be the traditional response of many people with chronic depression problems who do not seek assistance: a desire to keep their problems secret from others. In addition, hours spent in psychotherapy are costly to a patient in terms of both the fees paid to providers and the opportunity cost of time spent obtaining care. Online therapy can reduce the latter

cost significantly by eliminating time spent traveling to and from a therapist's office each week. In addition, providing therapy online reduces providers' costs by eliminating expenses for waiting rooms, furniture, and other accruements of a bricks-and-mortar psychotherapy business.

There are some potential drawbacks, however. A traditional tool that counselors use to evaluate a patient's mental health is the so-called "nonverbal clues" of the patient's condition, including general demeanor, the state of their physical health, and so on. In addition, there is a huge potential for a lemons problem in online therapy. As unqualified therapists stream online in search of profits, many people could end up being treated by unqualified, nonprofessional providers of psychotherapy services.

For Critical Analysis:

In what ways might reputable therapists effectively market and distribute their services on the Internet?

MARKETING SEARCH GOODS AND EXPERIENCE GOODS: INFORMATIONAL VERSUS PERSUASIVE ADVERTISING ON THE WEB

A key determinant of how a firm goes about advertising its product is that particular product's characteristics. The forms of advertising that firms use to market a search good are likely to be considerably different than those employed in the marketing of an experience good. A firm is more likely to use **informational advertising** describing the features of its product if it is a search good. By way of contrast, a firm is more likely to engage in **persuasive advertising** intended to influence a consumer's tastes and preferences, thereby inducing the consumer to try its product, if that product is an experience good.

Informational Advertising
Advertising that emphasizes the transmission of knowledge about the features of a product.

Persuasive Advertising
Advertising that is intended to alter a consumer's tastes and preferences and induce the consumer to purchase a particular product.

Must Internet Advertisers Choose between Informational and Persuasive Ads?

By and large, informational ads are passive in nature. Web sites that describe product features, list product prices, and compare the advertiser's prices to those charged by rivals are passive forms of advertising that mainly transmit information to prospective customers. Initiating an interaction between a seller and a

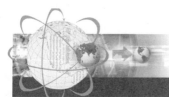

MANAGEMENT *Online*

POLICY MAKING   GLOBALIZATION   MANAGEMENT

The Future Meets the Past— Internet-Order Catalogs

More than a century ago, the Sears catalog appeared in American homes. City and rural residents alike had a new shopping option: They could search the catalog to review the company's offerings, mail an order, and anticipate delivery within a few days.

When Paper Beats Out Web Pages

In recent years, a number of Internet retailers, such as Delias.com, a marketer of women's sportswear, and Garden.com, a seller of home and garden products, have begun sending glossy catalogs to targeted customers. Naturally, one motivation for these and other Internet sellers to launch catalog operations is to broaden the scope of their business by attracting consumers who are still reluctant to use the Internet because of security or privacy worries.

Marketing surveys conducted by many Internet sellers indicate that a number of potential customers—in particular, those without access to high-speed cable modems or digital service lines—were frustrated by the long download times required to access high-quality images of products from the Internet. These consumers browse through images of products displayed in paper catalogs in less time than would be required to go through many Web pages. At that point they turn to the company's Web page to place their orders on the Internet.

A "Fresh" Way to Go After Internet Customers—And a Big Market

Many Internet sellers that continue to distribute paper catalogs to potential customers hope to achieve broader objectives than just attracting customers who are reluctant to shop on the Web or who are hobbled by slow-speed access to the Internet. Distributing catalogs is a useful way to provide information about their operations to people who have not come across their Web sites during the course of conducting Internet searches.

Traditional catalogs generate in excess of $100 billion in sales every year. This volume of sales provides a significant incentive for many Web-based retailers to try to get a foothold in this market. In this way, catalog sales have become another area within the traditional economy that faces competition from close substitutes offered via the Internet.

For Critical Analysis:

What factors might motivate a consumer to place a catalog order on the Internet instead of by mail or phone?

---

consumer requires the consumer to respond actively to such sites, perhaps by clicking on an icon next to a phrase such as "Add to Shopping Basket." (An old-fashioned form of informational advertising, paper catalogs, has recently been rediscovered by a number of Internet sellers; see *Management Online: The Future Meets the Past—Internet-Order Catalogs.*)

Firms that engage in persuasive advertising also often initiate interactions with consumers. One way to do this on the Internet is to apply tried-and-true mass-market techniques. A favorite approach to persuasive advertising used by many traditional sellers is to mail cards, letters, and brochures to consumers in an effort to persuade them to try various products. From a consumer's perspective, of course, this is "junk mail." Nevertheless, many companies regard mass mailings as part of the lifeblood of their business.

Web-based sellers might try to engage in persuasive advertising by blanketing Internet consumers with e-mail messages advertising new experience goods with allegedly or novel product features. This sort of "junk e-mail" is known as **spam.** Several states and the federal government have moved to enact laws intended to limit spam (see Chapter 11). There are also court cases in progress testing the theory that existing federal laws against sending unsolicited faxes should also apply to e-mail spam. In many legal jurisdictions, unsolicited e-mail advertising remains permissible under the law.

Spam
Mass marketing via unsolicited e-mail messages to numerous recipients.

Spam has fallen into such disfavor among consumers that relatively few companies use this type of mass-marketing approach. Most try to take advantage of the unique features of the Internet to *combine* elements of both informational and persuasive advertising. Web banner ads are an example. Left unclicked, banner ads are passive reminders of the existence of a good or service and of its manufacturer or provider. When a consumer clicks an ad, Web links automatically route the customer to pages that may provide informational content, persuasive content, or both.

It is arguable that Internet advertising does not fit neatly into the traditional categories of informational advertising and persuasive advertising. Nevertheless, there are good reasons for e-commerce firms to emphasize informational or persuasive approaches to advertising their products. These relate to the incentives firms face, given the characteristics of their products and market conditions.

Successful versus Unsuccessful Informational Advertising

Recall from Chapter 5 that a company provides information about its product to the point where the marginal benefit, in the form of enhanced profitability resulting from a rise in product demand generated by the provision of information, equals the marginal cost of information dissemination. A key factor determining how much a firm engages in informational advertising is the size of the marginal benefit compared with the marginal cost of providing informative ads.

An important determinant of the marginal benefit of a firm's informational advertising is how effectively the advertising distinguishes that firm's product from those of rivals. To see why this is so, consider Figure 6-3 on page 184. Both panels illustrate alternative situations faced by a monopolistically firm, which is initially in long-run equilibrium. In both cases, the firm initially produces an output rate at which the price it charges for its product, point *A*, which yields a marginal revenue equal to marginal cost, equals the average cost of producing that quantity of the product, so that the firm's economic profit equals zero.

Now suppose that the firm engages in advertising that accomplishes two things. First, as shown in panel *(a)*, the firm's ads convince more consumers that the firm provides a high-quality product, so the demand for the firm's product increases. Second, its ads successfully distinguish its product from those of other firms, because the ad succeeds in distinguishing the firm's product from items sold by rival firms. As a result, consumers perceive that the products of other firms are imperfectly substitutable for this firm's product, so the demand for the firm's product becomes relatively more inelastic. The firm increases its output to the point where the new marginal revenue curve crosses its marginal cost curve, at point *B*.

Figure 6-3:
Successful and Unsuccessful Advertising Outcomes.

Panel (a) depicts a situation in which advertising by a monopolistically competitive firm both induces customers to desire to purchase more of its product and convince them that there are fewer close substitutes for its product. As a result, the demand for the firm's product both increases from D_1 to D_2 and becomes relatively more inelastic, so that the firm's economic profit rises from zero to a positive amount equal to the shaded area. In panel (b), however, the firm's advertising efforts succeed only in highlighting substitutability of firm's product with those of its rivals, so that the new demand for the firm's product, D_2 becomes more elastic relative to the original demand D_1. The firm remains in a long-run equilibrium with zero economic profit, so advertising generates no benefit in the form of increased profit.

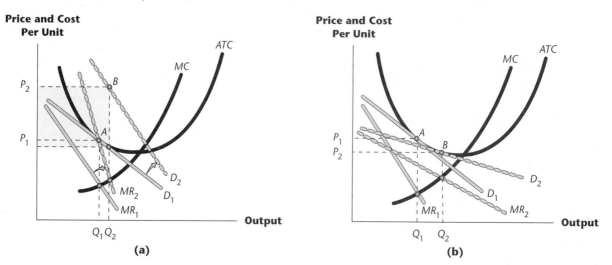

(a)   (b)

It is able to charge a higher price, and it earns an economic profit equal to the shaded area in panel *(a)*. In this case, advertising unambiguously raises the firm's profitability, and this increase in profits is the marginal benefit that the firm derives from engaging in advertising.

Now consider a situation in which advertising provides information that induces consumers to buy more of the *industry's* product without necessarily convincing them that there is anything distinguishable about the firm's own product. In a "worst case" situation for a firm, the information in its ad actually highlights the ease with which consumers can find a variety of brands that are close substitutes for its own product. This situation is illustrated in panel *(b)*. Although the firm's advertising efforts succeed in altering the demand for its own brand, they also make consumers more aware of substitutes for its brand and generate a relative increase in the elasticity of demand. In the worst-case situation depicted in panel *(b)*, the result is that the firm sells additional units but continues to earn an economic profit of zero. Because the firm's profitability remains unchanged, there is no marginal benefit to advertising in this instance.

Hence, a fundamental determinant of the effectiveness of informational advertising for a firm is how well the advertising maintains a distinction between its products and those of other firms. For a firm with a truly "different" product, this may not be a difficult task. In a monopolistically competitive industry in which several brands may be close substitutes, however, informational advertising might yield only modest profit gains.

Can Persuasive Advertising Alone Succeed on the Internet?

Trying to successfully distinguish its product from those of competitors requires a firm to walk a fine line. On one hand, the firm must emphasize a quality advantage over rival products, highlight price differences, or both. On the other hand, the firm must avoid overemphasizing the presence of competing products and thereby giving customers an incentive to identify brands that are close substitutes.

To accomplish this balancing act, Internet companies often supplement informational advertising with at least some elements of persuasive advertising as part of their marketing efforts. For instance, a Web site promoting a particular brand of athletic shoes may include an endorsement of that specific brand by a well-known celebrity athlete. Alternatively, companies may choose to remove most information content from their ads and opt for purely persuasive advertising. Thus, a Web site promoting a specific brand of athletic shoe may include several celebrity endorsements and focus on the benefits of buying that particular shoe, such as how "cool" that shoe will look to your friends.

Economists question whether this kind of purely persuasive advertising, which is commonly practiced in other media, is likely to succeed on the Internet. Certainly, an Internet seller can post banner ads containing celebrity endorsements or "cool shoes" messages, thereby designing banner ads to persuade in the same way that highway billboard ads persuade. The likeliest route to sales, however, is a high click ratio, and consumers searching for price and quality information are more likely to click an ad that they anticipate will link them to a Web site with informative content.

For this reason, some companies have tried an alternative approach to attracting consumers to Web pages offering persuasive advertising. They have sought to make their Internet advertising entertaining. Companies have discovered that while potential customers watch television to be passively entertained, they surf the Internet to actively *do* something. Thus, companies are still seeking the right Web entertainment formulas. Coca-Cola, for instance, set up a Cherrycoke.com Web site as an entertainment gateway to interesting sites around the Internet, but the company determined that the average visitor stayed at its Cherrycoke.com site no more than 90 seconds before surfing away. Now, typing http://www.cherrycoke.com sends you directly to Coca-Cola's home page (http://www.coca-cola.com). Pursuing the formula pioneered by radio and television, Bell Atlantic Corporation tried running a weekly soap opera on its Web site. After finding scant evidence that anyone was following the plotline, the company canceled the project. (Some companies now go to considerable lengths to determine what aspects of their Web sites catch consumers' attention; see *Management Online: Turning the Art of Persuasion into a Science.*)

Turning the Art of Persuasion into a Science

Have you ever wondered how an Internet seller determines whether a Web page is "eye catching"? Most companies simply post a site, wait to see whether it attracts customers, and then re-evaluate the site if it fails to generate many revenues. Typically companies rely on in-house Web designers, who may seek external reviews of their sites and conduct consumer surveys to try to learn what they like and dislike about navigating Web pages.

Some high-tech marketing research firms have developed more sophisticated techniques for evaluating the reactions of visitors to companies' sites. For instance, Web marketing research firms have created various types of headgear equipped with devices that follow test subjects' eye movements as they scroll through and scan Web pages. The equipment, which ranges in price from $8,000 to nearly $20,000,

tracks subjects' shifting gazes and measures pupil expansions and contractions.

The big advantage of eye-tracking devices are that they generate quantitative data that is not subject to interviewer manipulations or self-reporting biases of qualitative survey approaches. Companies can use data they collect from these devices to decide if a new site is likely to succeed in attracting customers or if an old site is growing stale with regular customers. Of course, these devices cannot tell a company *why* an Internet surfer decides to make a quick glance at one page but loiter at a second page. To get answers to these questions, companies that use eye-tracking devices usually conduct follow-up interviews with test subjects.

For Critical Analysis:
If Internet sellers find that the use of eye-tracking devices makes a big difference to their sales, could their relatively high cost pose a barrier to entry for small Web start-ups?

FUNDAMENTAL ISSUES ▼

1.

2.

3.

4.

5.

3. What distinguishes informational advertising from persuasive advertising?

Informational advertising emphasizes descriptions of the features of a product, whereas persuasive advertising aims to influence a consumer's tastes and preferences and induce the consumer to try a product. In general, a firm is more likely to engage in informational advertising if the product it sells is a search good, while a firm that produces a search good is more likely to practice persuasive advertising. Successful persuasive advertising on the Internet both increases the demand for a firm's product and causes consumers to regard the firm's product as having few close substitutes. Many items marketed on the Web have properties of search goods, which is likely to limit the extent to which purely persuasive advertising can succeed on the Internet. Nevertheless, some firms use entertainment sites and other techniques to try to promote experience goods on the Web.

Can Internet Sellers Do Too Much Advertising?

As we noted in Chapter 1, many of the original founders of the Internet contend that the medium has become overly commercialized. When companies first began advertising on the Web, some consumer advocates even pushed for laws and regulations to make Web advertising illegal. Internet marketing, consumer advocates argued, makes consumers worse off, because it clutters the Web with ads inducing consumers to buy "unneeded" products. This contention, of course, parallels similar criticisms levied against radio advertising beginning in the 1920s and television advertising since the 1950s.

Both radio and television programming contain considerable advertising, so critics clearly failed in their efforts to halt commercialization of these media. Is it possible that today's version of the same criticism may be relevant when applied to Internet advertising? Let's give some consideration to this question.

HOW MUCH ADVERTISING BENEFITS SOCIETY?

Some economists argue that, at least in principle, there is a "socially optimal" amount of advertising. Others contend that how much society might or might not benefit from advertising depends on the nature of firms' advertising efforts.

Measuring Gains from Additional Advertising

To understand the basis of the argument that firms can advertise "too much," consider Figure 6-4 on page 188. Advertising that increases the propensity of consumers to purchase a firm's product, either because it provides helpful information or because it is sufficiently persuasive, shifts the demand and marginal revenue curves rightward. Let's assume that the relative elasticity of the firm's new demand curve is not particularly higher or lower.

Under the simplifying assumption that the firm's marginal cost is constant and thus equal to average cost at any given quantity produced, the firm increases its profit-maximizing output from Q_1 to Q_2. The firm's profit-maximizing price rises from P_1 to P_2, and its profits rise by the sum of areas A, B, and E. Thus, additional advertising provides a benefit to the firm in the form of a higher economic profit.

The area denoted A in Figure 6-4 is a portion of the additional profit the firm earns on the original Q_1 units of output that it initially produced and sold. Before advertising raised demand, this dark-shaded area A was part of consumer surplus, so it represents a transfer from consumers to the firm after the firm engages in additional advertising. Although the firm is better off and consumers are worse off because of the transfer of consumer surplus from these Q_1 units of output, net social welfare is unaffected by this portion A of the profit increase resulting from the firm's increased advertising.

Figure 6-4:
Advertising and Social Welfare.

If advertising successfully induces an increase in the demand for the product of a firm with a constant marginal production cost, then the firm's profit-maximizing price rises from P_1 to P_2, and it raises its output from Q_1 to Q_2. The area A represents a transfer of previous consumer surplus to the firm in the form of higher profit, and the area B is a net increase in firm profit arising from the consumption of $Q_2 - Q_1$ additional units, given consumers' original willingness to pay before the increase in demand from D_1 to D_2. The area E is a net increase in profit that arises from an increased willingness to pay for these additional units, and the area F is an increase in consumer surplus that occurs if we take into account consumers' higher willingness to pay for all Q_2 units that they purchase following the increase in demand.

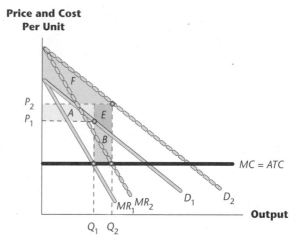

The sum of the areas denoted B and E is additional profit, over and above the area A, that the firm earns from selling both the original Q_1 units and $Q_2 - Q_1$ more units of output at a higher price after the demand for its product increases. The area B, so economists who worry about too much advertising contend, is the appropriate measure of the social gain from the additional advertising. This area, they argue, represents an amount that consumers are willing to pay, based on their original demand curve D_1, for the additional $Q_2 - Q_1$ units that the firm's advertising effort convinces them to purchase. This amount is captured by the firm as higher profit, but it is an amount consumers are willing to transfer to firms based on their pre-advertising preferences.

Can More Advertising Be Bad for Society?

To complete the foundation of the anti-advertising argument, let's suppose that an Internet firm incurs a cost in increasing its advertising that is equal to C. It will engage in more advertising as long as the profit gain it experiences, which equals $A + B + E$, is not less than the cost of additional advertising, C. For society as a whole, however, more advertising is beneficial only if the net gain to society, B, is at least equal to the advertising cost C. The firm's total additional profit $A + B + E$ will likely be significantly larger than the proposed social gain B. This means, according to the anti-advertising argument, that there is a considerable likelihood that the profit gain $A + B + E$ is at least equal to C, so that the firm desires to advertise more, even if B is less than C. As a result, society is worse off.

Now it is possible to figure out why some people, and, indeed, some economists, argue that firms can engage in too much advertising. Recall from Chapter 5 that a firm will provide additional information—in this case, advertise more—to the point where the marginal benefit equals the marginal cost. In the above example, the firm's marginal benefit from advertising is the profit increase $A + B + E$. The marginal cost is the cost of more advertising, which is C. Hence, the situation in Figure 6-4 actually will arise only if $A + B + E = C$. Then the marginal benefit from additional advertising equals the marginal cost.

Because the firm advertises to the point where $A + B + E = C$, this means that B is less than C. That is, the social gain from additional advertising by the firm fails to cover the marginal cost of advertising. Society is worse off from the additional advertising, argue some economists, even though the firm will experience a net benefit and hence will engage in more advertising.

A Flaw in the Anti-Advertising Argument?

On the surface, this argument seems to lead to the inescapable conclusion that more advertising leads to a net reduction in social welfare. Before you conclude that additional advertising is always bad for society, it is important to recognize that other economists are strongly critical of the argument.

To understand their logic, suppose that the rise in product demand depicted in Figure 6-4 took place simply because the firm significantly improved the quality of its product, and already well-informed consumers figured this out without additional advertising by the firm. In addition, suppose that the cost C was the expense that the firm incurred in enhancing the quality of its product. In this situation, Figure 6-4 and the above discussion of its apparent implications would still apply. Yet the interpretation would change: The conclusion would be that efforts to improve product quality reduce social welfare!

This counterintuitive conclusion illustrates an area of disagreement among economists. In the case of major improvement that increases the demand for a firm's product, all economists agree that this justifiably increases the consumers' *willingness to pay*. At any given quantity, including the original Q_1 units purchased in Figure 6-4, a product improvement causes consumers to regard the item as "better" and hence a product they are willing to pay a higher price to purchase. As a result, even though a portion of the consumer surplus for the Q_1 units purchased is transferred to firms as part of the area A, consumer surplus also expands by the area F. Hence, following a product improvement, consumers are certainly better off. Taking into account consumers' increased willingness to pay after the rise in demand, society also gains the entire amount of increased profit to firms on the additional $Q_2 - Q_1$ units produced, which is the total area $B + E$. Hence, a product improvement actually raises social welfare by firm profits by $A + B + E + F$. Because the firm advertises to the point where $A + B + E = C$, there is definitely a social gain from the product improvement equal to the rise in consumer surplus equal to the area F.

The key to the anti-advertising argument, therefore, is the assumption that the rise in willingness to pay on the part of consumers associated with the rise in demand from D_1 to D_2 should not be used to evaluate welfare effects of advertising. This lies behind their exclusion of areas E and F from part of society's gain from advertising. Presumably, this reflects a judgment by opponents of advertising that the gains that consumers *believe* they experience by increasing their desired consumption of the firm's product are simply a result of effective advertising that *fools* those consumers.

Other economists question this presumption. After all, they ask, if consumers *perceive* they are better off, as revealed by their choice to buy more of the advertised product, how can economists conclude they not *truly* better off? Moreover, if a product that a firm advertises to be "new and improved" really has been improved, then informing consumers of that fact via advertising certainly implies that the areas E and F are part of the social gain from the firm's advertising. Then advertising definitely yields a social gain.

JUDGING THE SOCIAL DESIRABILITY OF ADVERTISING

A fundamental point that emerges from the disagreement between those who advance the anti-advertising argument illustrated in Figure 6-4 and those who question the scope of its relevance is that some forms of advertising are likely to be more beneficial for society than others. On one hand, the anti-advertising argument most likely applies to advertising intended to convince people to buy an existing good or service in a form that its producer has not altered. On the other hand, the anti-advertising argument is less applicable to informational advertising that notifies consumers of a new, high-quality product or of a previously existing good or service that a producer has successfully improved.

In recent years, some consensus has emerged concerning a relative undesirability of purely persuasive advertising of existing goods and services as opposed to a relative desirability of purely informational advertising of truly improved products. There is considerable agreement that persuasive advertising promoting the sale of inferior goods and services tends to worsen the lemons problem discussed in Chapter 5, because the unambiguous result of this form of advertising is lower consumer and producer welfare.

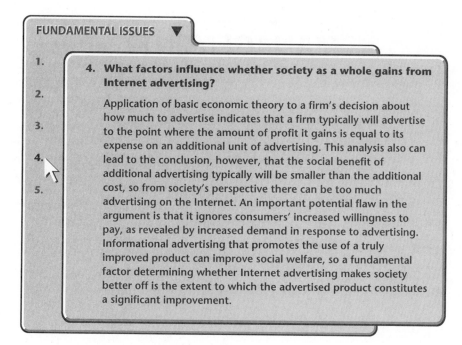

FUNDAMENTAL ISSUES ▼

1.

2.

3.

4.

5.

4. What factors influence whether society as a whole gains from Internet advertising?

Application of basic economic theory to a firm's decision about how much to advertise indicates that a firm typically will advertise to the point where the amount of profit it gains is equal to its expense on an additional unit of advertising. This analysis also can lead to the conclusion, however, that the social benefit of additional advertising typically will be smaller than the additional cost, so from society's perspective there can be too much advertising on the Internet. An important potential flaw in the argument is that it ignores consumers' increased willingness to pay, as revealed by increased demand in response to advertising. Informational advertising that promotes the use of a truly improved product can improve social welfare, so a fundamental factor determining whether Internet advertising makes society better off is the extent to which the advertised product constitutes a significant improvement.

Some Legal Limits—But Do They Have Intended Effects?

The conclusion that some forms of advertising unambiguously reduce social welfare has led the U.S. Congress and numerous state legislatures to adopt laws governing the nature of advertising in various media. The Federal Trade Commission (FTC) enforces most federal advertising laws in the United States, and state legal departments enforce state legislation governing advertisements.

ANTIFRAUD AND DISCLOSURE REQUIREMENTS FOR INTERNET ADVERTISING

The most dramatic example of a lemon is a product that a consumer never receives after placing an order and authorizing payment. Other examples are products that fail to perform in ways promised by advertisements or that sell for higher prices than ads lead consumers to believe. Because these are the most overt lemon situations that consumers confront, many advertising regulations aim to combat deceptive advertising and related forms of fraudulent business activities. (Of

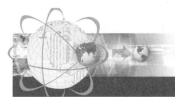

MANAGEMENT *Online*

Just How Big of a Problem Is Internet Fraud?

According to a recent ActivMedia Research survey of more than a thousand businesses that sell both offline and online, about 2 percent of companies with e-commerce operations considered fraud to be "somewhat of a problem," and only 1 percent indicated that fraud was a "substantial problem." Based on figures provided by the companies, fraud-related losses experienced in selling goods and services offline were about 1.5 percent of total sales. Proportionate losses due to fraudulent online sales were not significantly different from this figure.

The electronic marketplace is still young, so this is only one piece of evidence on fraud. Furthermore, the dollar amount of online losses due to fraud is a sizable amount of nearly $10 billion per year. Nevertheless, this survey evidence indicates that the proportionate incidence of fraudulent activities may not be any greater for e-commerce than for bricks-and-mortar commerce.

For Critical Analysis:

Contemplate the incentives that e-commerce firms face when asked to answer survey questions about fraud they experience, and offer a possible rationale for why some economists are hesitant to put faith in surveys such as this one.

course, fraud can go both ways; sometimes consumers perpetrate frauds against businesses in B2C e-commerce or against other consumers in the C2C marketplace. The costs associated with fraud may not be any higher in e-commerce than in traditional commerce; see *Management Online: Just How Big of a Problem Is Internet Fraud?*)

The Rationale for Regulating Advertising

There is a strong argument for why firms would choose to be truthful in advertising even in the absence of federal or state regulations. Consumers have good reason to investigate the truthfulness of a firm's advertising claims, and they certainly can make judgments after buying a product. A firm that makes untrue claims is unlikely to get repeat business from customers. Unhappy customers are likely to spread word of deceptions to others they know, further reducing the firm's ability to market its product.

For a firm that produces a relatively high-quality product, there is a strong incentive to engage in extensive advertising. The reason is that such a firm anticipates repeat business. Thus, the marginal benefit of having a consumer try its product is likely to be relatively higher as compared with the marginal benefit of advertising at a firm that produces a lower-quality product that will not attract repeat business. As shown in Figure 6-5, this means that if all other things are equal, the firm with the higher-quality product will engage in more advertising. Because this firm's products are of higher quality, its ads will truthfully state that fact.

Figure 6-5:
Relative Amounts of Advertising at High- versus Low-Quality Firms.

High-quality firms anticipate gaining greater demand and generating greater current and future profits by advertising the true characteristics of their products. Consequently, it is arguable that the marginal benefit from providing information via advertising is likely to be greater at any given amount of advertising for high-quality firms than for low-quality firms. If this argument is correct, then high-quality firms will provide more information via a greater amount of advertising.

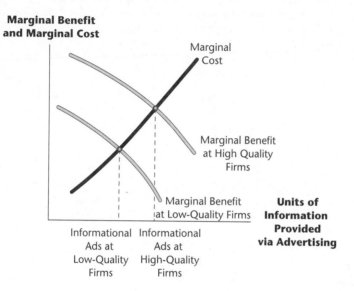

The potential problem is that the situation will not necessarily be the same for both types of firms. A firm with a lower-quality product is also likely to incur lower production costs, as compared with the production costs incurred by a firm that markets a higher-quality good or service. This means that the firm with the lower-quality product might anticipate higher short-term profits. Even if it anticipates fewer future sales, the firm with a lower-quality product can experience a marginal benefit from advertising that is as high as the marginal benefit of a firm with a higher-quality product. For a while, it may engage in just as much advertising, thereby potentially succeeding in flooding the market with lemons. This provides the main justification for federal and state laws regulating advertising.

Legal Rules for Internet Advertising

In principle, Internet advertisers can attempt to engage in self-regulation. They can establish minimum industry standards, implement ad certification procedures, and engage in other efforts to combat deceptive advertising. To date, most developments along these lines in the electronic marketplace have proceeded through traditional advertising associations.

Table 6-2: FTC's Internet Advertising Guidelines.

FTC's legal jurisdiction	The same consumer protection laws that apply to commercial activities in other media apply online. The FTC act's prohibition on "unfair or deceptive acts or practices" encompasses Internet advertising, marketing, and sales. In addition, many FTC rules and guides are not limited to any particular medium used to disseminate claims or advertising and, therefore, apply to online activities.
Disclosure requirements	Disclosures that are required to prevent an ad from being misleading, to ensure that consumers receive material information about the terms of a transaction, or to further public policy goals, must be clear and conspicuous. In evaluating whether disclosures are likely to be clear and conspicuous in online ads, advertisers should consider the *placement* of disclosure in an ad and its *proximity* to the relevant claim.
Standards for disclosure	To make a disclosure clear and conspicuous, advertisers should do the following: • Place disclosures near, and when possible, on the same screen as the triggering claim. • Use text or visual cues to encourage consumers to scroll down a Web page when it is necessary to view a disclosure. • Make disclosure hyperlinks obvious. • Display disclosures prior to purchase, and not necessarily only on order page. • Creatively incorporate disclosures in banner ads or Web pages to which they link, and display disclosures long enough for consumers to read them. • Make disclosures prominent so that other elements of the ad do not distract consumers' attention. • Use audio disclosures when making audio claims.
Redefining legal terminology	FTC rules and guides that use specific terms, such as "written," "writing," "printed," or "direct mail," are adaptable to new technologies: • Rules and guides that apply to written ads or printed materials also apply to visual text displayed on the Internet. • If a seller uses e-mail to comply with FTC rule or to guide notice requirements, then the seller should provide e-mail information in a form consumers can retain. • Direct mail solicitations include e-mail. If an e-mail invites consumers to call the sender to purchase goods or services, then the telephone call and subsequent sale must comply with rules governing telephone sales.

Source: Federal Trade Commission, "Dot Com Disclosures," May 4, 2000 (http://www.ftc.gov/bcp/conline/pubs/buspubs/dotcom/index.html).

To a large extent, the federal government has already preempted these efforts. In May 2000, the Federal Trade Commission issued a set of guidelines governing Internet advertising. Table 6-2 summarizes the main points contained in these guidelines. As you can see, the guidelines essentially extend existing rules to the Internet and indicate standards that the FTC applies when judging whether an Internet ad complies with federal advertising restrictions.

To some extent, the FTC polices the Internet to screen ads for potential violations of its rules. There are many ads in cyberspace, however, so the FTC's ability to engage in such activities depends largely on the size and quality of its staff. Given the limitations it faces, the FTC relies heavily on consumer complaints to direct it toward identifying potential violators of advertising restrictions.

DO ANTIFRAUD AND DISCLOSURE LAWS ALWAYS HAVE INTENDED EFFECTS?

Of course, declaring an activity to be illegal does not necessarily dissuade people from engaging in that activity. The only way to prevent producers of lemons from falsely advertising their products as higher-quality goods and services would be to raise the marginal cost of their activities to a sufficiently high level. Federal and state laws attempt to do this by establishing penalties for violations of advertising regulations and setting up enforcement agencies, such as the FTC and state regulatory bodies. (Different national laws governing advertising can sometimes complicate the advertising efforts of e-commerce firms based in other countries; see on page 196 *Globalization Online: In France, Has U.S.-Style E-Commerce Mass Marketing Met Its Match?*)

It is possible that laws providing for relatively minor penalties or only moderately effective enforcement can lead to worse outcomes. Under these circumstances, consumers who in the past have been more cautious in their interpretations of advertising claims may feel assured, falsely, that governmental regulations have eliminated "lemon ads."

Thus, relatively low penalties or relative lax enforcement of regulations could, in principle, make consumers worse off than they would have been in the absence of such regulations. In a sense, governments enacting such laws but failing to follow through with sufficiently high penalties or strong enforcement would have engaged in deceptive practices, because they would have ineffective and misleading "lemon laws" on the books.

On one hand, many consumer advocate groups claim that there is a danger that this could happen to Internet consumers. They argue that regulators such as the FTC are ill equipped to police the entire Internet for false and deceptive advertising practices. Others contend that penalties for violations are too light to deter misleading claims. Consequently, these groups argue, federal and state regulations governing Internet advertising should be considerably toughened, and the budgets of regulators should be increased so that they can better do their jobs, which would include surveillance of the Internet.

On the other hand, there are critics who reach a strikingly opposite conclusion. These critics contend that the Internet is so difficult to police for violations of advertising rules that it is fruitless to attempt to do so. The best the FTC and other regulators can do, they argue, is to respond to consumer complaints. Thus, according to this argument, consumers themselves should be the regulators' sources of information. The job of regulators should be to follow up by investigating allegations and

GLOBALIZATION *Online*

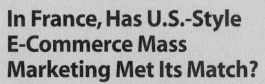

POLICY MAKING   GLOBALIZATION   MANAGEMENT

In France, Has U.S.-Style E-Commerce Mass Marketing Met Its Match?

As discussed in Chapter 1, the United States has a big lead in electronic commerce, and only recently have producers in other nations begun to catch up. As they do, Web-based firms located in the United States have opened marketing sites in languages ranging from German to Cantonese. In an effort to persuade populations that are new to e-commerce to go on-line and take a look at the available products, U.S. Internet sellers have launched big media ad campaigns worldwide. Most have found television ad campaigns particularly effective, so in most countries, television has been the key advertising medium for launching new local-language Web sites.

In France, however, a 1992 law may stand in the way of applying the standard mass-marketing techniques of U.S. e-commerce firms. This law prohibits television advertising by any retailers, media and film companies, and publishers.

Officially, the law is intended to protect French culture from foreign influences. When Amazon.com attempted to enter the online bookselling market in France, one possible side effect of the law emerged: hindering exposure of the

French e-commerce marketplace to international competition. The top French "cultural goods" retailer FNAC (http://www. fnac.com) had just established its own online bookselling operation, as had Alapage.fr, which is owned by France Telecom. Both of these companies already dominated the French online bookselling market, so in this market Amazon was a new fringe competitor.

As it awaited an official judgment about whether the French advertising restriction applied to U.S. e-commerce firms, Amazon began advertising its presence in newspapers and magazines. French Internet consumers immediately gained a benefit from Amazon's entry into the French online bookselling market when FNAC responded with a new promotion promising 24-hour delivery of most items in its online catalog. As a result, one customer-service advantage that Amazon had hoped to promote in mass-marketing ads disappeared while the French government delayed its decision about whether such ads would be legal.

For Critical Analysis:
Why do you suppose that Internet sellers entering another country's market for the first time often rely on traditional mass-market advertising?

imposing penalties, so there is no reason for taxpayers to fund what effectively would be an "Internet police force."

As you will learn in Chapter 11, this argument arises with respect to many potential forms of e-commerce regulation. In the next chapter, you will contemplate a specific area of government intervention in electronic commerce, which is assigning and enforcing intellectual property rights on the Internet.

FUNDAMENTAL ISSUES   ▼

1.

2.

3.

4.

5.

5. **Why is Internet advertising regulated, and how is it regulated?**

An Internet seller with a high-quality product has a profit incentive to provide information about the true quality of its product so as to induce an increase in demand. Even though the producer of a low-quality product will lose repeat customers if it provides misleading information about its product, its operating costs are lower than those of a high-quality producer. A low-quality Internet seller's anticipation of relatively higher short-term profits also gives it an incentive to provide misleading information in ads. Governments typically regulate advertising in an effort to limit the lemons problem that can result. The Federal Trade Commission has issued guidelines for Internet ads that parallel those applying to ads in the physical marketplace. Firms violating these guidelines can be fined and subjected to criminal prosecution.

Chapter Summary

1) **Unique Features of Internet Advertising:** Traditional bricks-and-mortar firms have relied on mass marketing, or advertising broadly disseminated to all consumers, and direct marketing, or advertising aimed at specific individuals. In principle, both Internet sellers and traditional firms can use Internet advertising to engage in interactive marketing that allows consumers to respond directly to an ad to examine or order products. Advantages of Internet advertising include being able to keep ad content current, to enhance interactive relationships with customers, and to track consumer response rates. Potential disadvantages include constant demands to update ad content, pitfalls in managing interactive customer relationships, significant fixed costs of designing Web content, and difficulties in determining the per-consumer cost of Internet ads.

2) **The Difference between Search Goods and Experience Goods, and Internet Marketing of Both Types of Goods:** Search goods are goods and services with features that consumers have a relatively easy time assessing in advance of purchase. Experience goods are products that consumers must actually buy and use before they can determine the products' qualities. Search goods with features that are relatively easy to assess visually or by reading product descriptions are especially well suited to Internet marketing. Nevertheless, a number of firms market other types of search goods on the Internet and also advertise experience goods in Web ads.

3) **Informational Advertising versus Persuasive Advertising:** Informational advertising highlights a product's features. Persuasive advertising seeks to alter a consumer's tastes and preferences and to convince a consumer to try its product. Firms that produce and market search goods are generally more likely to practice informational advertising, while firms that sell search goods are more likely to engage in persuasive advertising. Persuasive Internet advertising that brings about both an increase in the demand for a firm's product and a reduced price elasticity of demand for that product is more likely to successfully increase a firm's profitability. A large portion of goods and services sold on the Internet possess search-good characteristics, and this tends to reduce the likelihood that purely persuasive Internet advertising will become widespread. A number of firms that market experience goods nonetheless have attempted to use Web inducements such as free access to entertainment sites in an effort to market their products.

4) **Factors Influencing Whether Society as a Whole Gains from Internet Advertising:** A firm advertises to the point where the amount of profit it gains from additional advertising equals the expense it incurs from this activity. Basic economic theory indicates that the resulting social benefit of additional advertising typically could be lower than the additional advertising cost. It is arguable, therefore, that from the broad viewpoint of society as a whole, there can be too much advertising on the Internet. A potentially significant problem with this argument, however, arises in the case of a product improvement that would yield a clear benefit to society at large if more units were consumed. Because a major product improvement can change the nature of the demand for the item, the standard analysis supporting the anti-advertising conclusion ignores the fact that informational advertising encouraging the use of a truly improved product can improve social welfare.

5) **Why and How Internet Advertising Is Regulated:** An Internet seller with a high-quality product has a profit incentive to provide information about the true quality of its product so as to induce a rise in demand. Even though the producer of a low-quality product will lose repeat customers if it provides misleading information about its product, its operating costs are lower than those of a high-quality producer. Hence, a low-quality Internet seller's anticipation of relatively higher short-term profits also gives it an incentive to provide misleading information in ads. Governments typically

regulate advertising in an effort to limit the lemons problem that can result. The Federal Trade Commission has issued jurisdiction and disclosure guidelines for Internet ads that parallel those applying to ads in the physical marketplace. Firms violating these guidelines can be fined and are subject to criminal prosecution.

Questions and Problems

1) AdRelevance, a company that analyzes Internet advertising, reports that the fraction of the top 200 online adverters that are e-commerce firms that either originated on the Web or depend on the Internet for their existence has increased from just over one-half in 1999 to more than two-thirds today. What factors might account for this change? Does the change necessarily imply that the Internet is relatively more important as an advertising medium than it was in 1999?

2) One of the fastest-growing forms of Internet advertising is e-mail marketing, in which companies send e-mail ads to specifically targeted individuals who agree to receive them (thus distinguishing e-mail marketing from the transmission of spam). What basic form of marketing is this? In what ways might this type of Internet advertising entail lower costs than analogous marketing efforts using alternative media to the Internet?

3) As noted at the beginning of the chapter, for several years whenever Web surfers using the Yahoo search engine entered key words, accompanying the Web pages that popped up were banner ads directing them to buy books at Amazon relating to that topic. Now a banner ad for Barnes & Noble appears instead. What are the pros and cons of this form of Internet advertising?

4) AdRelevance reports that Web banner ads with the highest click ratios related to sales of books, music, movies, flowers, gifts, greeting cards, computer hardware, and computer software. Do your best to classify each of these as either experience goods or search goods.

5) In 2000, instead of running advertisements to promote its various products, Microsoft shifted the majority of its ad budget to selling Microsoft itself. A Microsoft manager said that the main idea behind the ad campaign was to make people perceive the company as "warm and approachable." Undoubtedly politics figured into this advertising approach, because Microsoft was in the midst of appealing a negative antitrust judgment. Are there other good reasons that Microsoft might run ads seeking to convince potential customers that it offers an "approachable brand"? Explain.

6) A couple of years ago, Volvo decided to advertise a new automobile model almost exclusively online. The company conducted no radio, television, or print campaigns, and it ran only a couple of ads in magazines for auto

enthusiasts. Instead, the company posted banner and column advertisements on various pages available to the nearly 25 million people who connect to the Internet via America Online. The ads directed Web surfers to a special Web site for the new vehicle, which was the company's third new model launched during the year. The site provided basic information about the car and emphasized free options for America Online subscribers, a contest to win one of the vehicles, and various other promotions. Some critics of the car argued that it was not dramatically different from existing models. Evaluate whether this online advertising campaign was most likely to be informational or persuasive in nature.

7) British Airways recently began running "superstitial" ads on the Internet, in which video-like images similar to television commercials appear when a user moves from one part of a Web site to another, thereby filling "dead time" while a browser waits for a Web page to download. Rather then focusing on British Airways' prices and services, the ads emphasized consumer options for relatively expensive first class and club seats on the company's planes. In your view, are airline services experience or search goods? Does this potentially help explain the nature of the company's Internet advertising?

8) An annual poll of Internet advertisers by the Association of National Advertisers has consistently indicated that a major purpose of Internet advertisements is to provide product information and increase consumers' awareness of online buying options. Every year, more advertisers indicate that they seek to develop and improve brand loyalty via Internet advertising. In your view, which advertising objective is likely to be more consistent with improving social welfare? Why?

9) A few years ago, the C2C auction company eBay began embedding advertisements for online retailers within postings of goods for sale by consumers. It halted this practice, however, after many consumers threatened to stop using the site. Instead, it began running more unobtrusive ads. Why might some people have been bothered by eBay's initial foray into selling advertising space on its site?

10) In June 2000, the FTC reached consent agreements with several traditional and online retailers that it had charged with violating advertising laws. In one case, an online ad indicated that a home computer system could be purchased at a total price of $269. The ad also mentioned that Internet access was part of the deal for a separate, clearly indicated monthly charge. Nowhere in the ad was there mention of the total price including Internet access, which exceeded $1,000. In your view, was this a case in which the online advertiser committed fraud or engaged in deceptive advertising, or was it simply a situation of potentially unclear disclosure of pricing terms? Justify your position.

Online Application

Internet URLs: http://www.coca-cola.com and http://www.pepsi.com

Title: **Coca-Cola.com** and **Pepsiworld.com**

Navigation: Go directly to the above URL.

Application: Perform the following operations, and answer the following questions.

1) Go to Coca-Cola's home page at http://www.coca-cola.com.
   (a) Click on *"Business Today,"* and then click on "Community." In pop-down menu of search-engine topics, click on "Environment." Why do you suppose that Coca-Cola is so interested in convincing visitors to its site that it is an environment-friendly corporation? Do you think that this discussion is aimed at consumers, investors, or both? Why?
   (b) Does the advertising at this site appear to be mainly informational or persuasive? Why might this be the case?

2) Now go to the home page of Pepsico, the maker and distributor of Pepsi Cola and related soft-drink products.
   (a) In what ways does this home page differ from the home page of Coca-Cola? Does this Web site appear to be oriented more toward consumers or investors?
   (b) Without clicking your mouse, move it up and down across the list of topic areas in the top-left portion of the home page. Do you now see any similarities between the marketing approaches in the two companies' Web sites? Are there still apparent differences in the companies' approaches to marketing their products on the Web?

For Group Study and Analysis: Why do Coca-Cola and Pepsi have Web sites? Is Internet advertising really likely to affect whether a typical consumer buys Coke or Pepsi? If so, what types of Internet ads are more likely to be effective? If not, why not?

**Selected References
and Further Readings**

Carlton, Dennis, and Jeffrey Perloff. *Modern Industrial Organization.* 3d ed. Reading, MA: Addison-Wesley, 2000.

Choi, Soon-Yong, Dale Stahl, and Andrew Whinston. *The Economics of Electronic Commerce.* Indianapolis: Macmillan Technical Publishing, 1997.

Federal Trade Commission. "Dot Com Disclosures," May 4, 2000.

Hoffman, Donna, and Thomas Novak. "Advertising Pricing Models for the Wide World Web." In *Internet Publishing and Beyond,* ed. Brian Kahin and Hal Varian. Cambridge, MA: MIT Press, 2000, pp. 45–61.

Pepall, Lynne, Daniel Richards, and George Norman. *Industrial Organization: Contemporary Theory and Practice.* Cincinnati: South-Western, 1999.

Shepherd, William. *The Economics of Industrial Organization.* 4th ed. Prospect Hills, IL: Waveland Press, 1997.

Zeff, Robbin, and Brad Aronson. *Advertising on the Internet.* 2d ed. New York: John Wiley & Sons, 2000.

Chapter 7

Innovation, Intellectual Property Rights, and the Internet

<E-Commerce Today>

Topping the Billboard Charts—Offline or Online?

A recent fad in the music-recording industry pitted Metallica, Dr. Dre, and Elton John against Courtney Love, Chuck D, and the Beastie Boys. The fad didn't concern any new rhythms, instrumentations, or controversial lyrics. It was the growing use of Web-based file-swapping programs that enabled Internet surfers to exchange favorite songs in downloadable formats.

According to the members of Metallica, Dr. Dre, and Elton John, companies offering access to music-file-swapping software on their Web sites were stealing from traditional recording companies. As a consequence, these entertainers received fewer royalty fees. They argued that sites providing music-file-swapping services should be banned.

Other musicians, such as Love, contended that the ability to market their songs on the Internet offers them an alternative to paying high recording and manufacturing fees to traditional music-recording companies before receiving royalties. These musicians argued that new singers, rappers, and bands must sign contracts favorable to the music-recording industry to first get their music recorded and released on tapes and CDs. Then they end up hiring prominent entertainment attorneys to help get them out of bad contracts once they make it big. Permitting people to transfer digital music files on the Web, the musicians maintain, gives a new artist, or even one trying to break out of a mid-career slump, the opportunity to market music directly to fans, thereby cutting out middlemen and associated costs.

The dispute about the legitimacy of Web exchanges of digital music files is not fully resolved. At issue are the rules governing the payoffs that creators of music, art, and literature receive as compensation for their efforts. Together, the availability of new information technologies and the existence of computer networks such as the Internet have dramatically altered the nature of the problems that creative people face in protecting the rights to such payoffs. This chapter explains why payoffs are likely to be required to induce individuals to invent new ideas, products, and processes. It also examines the overlap between the law and economics of protecting individual rights to returns on such creative activities.

 ## Invention and Innovation

We tend to think of technological progress as, say, the invention of the microprocessor. **Invention**, or the development of a new productive process, a novel business model, or a unique good or service, is only the first step toward altering

Invention
Creation of a new process for producing a good or service, a novel business organization method, or a unique product.

the nature of market activities within an economy. Many inventions never achieve widespread adoption. They fail the test posed by the harsh realities of the marketplace. Inventions alone do not alter the direction of national or global economic activity. Also required is **innovation,** or the transformation of an invention into something that reduces production costs, makes business organizations more efficient, or provides concrete benefits that induce consumers to purchase products.

Innovation
Transforming an invention into something that lowers costs of production, reduces the costs of operating a business, or provides concrete benefits inducing consumers to buy a product.

FUNDAMENTALS OF INNOVATION

The act of invention is a *technical* process. A scientist or an engineer, for instance, might spend years in a laboratory developing a better production technique or a new good or service. Innovation is an *economic* process that moves inventions from the drawing board to the production floor, the office, and the marketplace.

Classifying Innovations

Economists classify innovations into two separate categories. One category includes **process innovations,** which often involve the development of new technologies for producing existing goods or services. Implementing a novel method of organizing existing production processes is also a type of process innovation. Typically, these forms of process innovation succeed in the marketplace because they reduce the costs of producing, marketing, or distributing existing goods or services.

Process Innovation
Development and market introduction of a new technology for producing existing goods or services or a new method of organizing businesses.

Successful process innovations need not always make businesses more cost-efficient. Some process innovations pass the market test because they assist firms in generating larger streams of revenues. Innovations in marketing processes that simplify the task consumers face in searching among, shopping for, or ordering existing products could conceivably raise a company's overall expenses. If such innovations lead to even higher streams of revenues, however, they can enhance the firm's profitability nonetheless, and may succeed in the marketplace as a result.

Product Innovation
The creation, production, marketing, and distribution of an entirely new good or service.

The other category of innovations is **product innovations,** which entail the creation, production, marketing, and distribution of entirely new goods or services. Developing a new product frequently requires inventing and implementing a new production, marketing, or distribution process. Thus, there can be overlap between a process innovation and product innovation. Nevertheless, all innovations that yield new goods or services are classified within the category of product innovations.

Major Innovation
A process or product innovation that brings about a significant change in an existing market or the creation of a new market.

Minor Innovation
A process or process innovation that results in relatively small cost reductions or revenue enhancements or that primarily allow firms to differentiate their products.

Within the broad categories of process and product innovations, economists often attempt to classify innovations into additional subcategories. They classify process or product innovations that entail significant changes in existing markets or the creation of new markets as **major innovations.** Process or product innovations that yield relatively slight cost efficiencies, that generate slender revenue enhancements, or that mainly enable firms to differentiate their products from those of market rivals are classified as **minor innovations.** It is not always easy to classify innovations within either of these subcategories. Some innovations—such as electric power, the microprocessor, the personal computer, and the

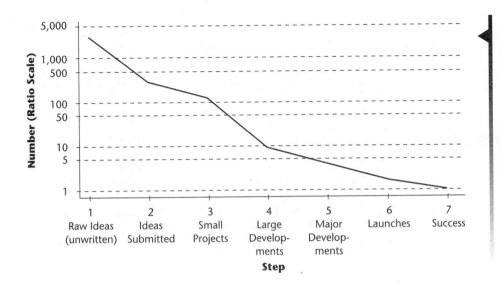

Figure 7-1:
The Process of Moving from Ideas to the Marketplace.

Only a fraction of new ideas are actually studied seriously, and a small percentage of these become research and development projects. Very few ultimately emerge as new products or processes.

Internet—are easily classified as major innovations. Others that yield relatively insignificant profitability enhancements or product changes are readily placed in the subcategory of minor innovations.

The Process of Innovation

Any innovation begins with an idea for a new process or product. Within a company, discussion among employees eventually leads to proposals. Following evaluation of such proposals, firms identify projects they think are the best bets for expending resources for formal research projects. Of these projects, some appear worthy of additional process or product development, and a portion of these reach the stage of being significant developments within the firm. Some innovations then reach the marketplace or generate a production reorganization within firms, and a few become market success stories.

Figure 7-1 depicts this process by which raw ideas are transformed into development projects that ultimately emerge as true process or product innovations. Typically, only a few initial ideas actually lead to the adoption of new processes or products in the marketplace. (Some entrepreneurs hope to profit from using the Web to enlarge the number of ideas, however; see on the next page *Management Online: An Electronic Marketplace for Ideas*.)

ALTERNATIVE THEORIES OF INNOVATION

For some time, economists have tried to understand what factors determine the extent to which firms are able to successfully introduce novel processes or products into the marketplace. Two basic hypotheses have emerged concerning the sources of innovation. One credits the process and product designers of firms with

MANAGEMENT *Online*

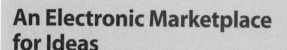

POLICY MAKING   GLOBALIZATION   **MANAGEMENT**

An Electronic Marketplace for Ideas

Do you think that you have a novel idea for a minor innovation that could improve a firm's product or that might help streamline the firm's production process? If so, one place to try to sell your idea is Ideas.com (http://www.ideas.com). At this Web site, anyone can offer to sell a suggestion for a new product or process to a major corporation, such as Coca-Cola or Sears, in exchange for a cash "bounty" that could amount to several thousand dollars.

In exchange for a 30 percent commission from companies that purchase unsolicited ideas submitted at Ideas.com, the site's owners offer a mechanism for arranging legal transfer of product or process ideas. On the one hand, people who

think they have good ideas but do not wish to develop them can submit them online via legal release forms and binding "digital signatures." On the other hand, companies that wish to review submitted ideas must legally bind themselves to paying an individual who transmits an idea to Idea.com's Web site.

In the electronic marketplace for ideas, anyone with a good idea can try to sell it. Companies searching for suggestions that could trim operating costs or enhance sales can locate and purchase them.

For Critical Analysis:

Why might it prove easier to match people who have good ideas for minor improvements in products or processes with companies searching for suggestions using the Web, as compared with alternative mechanisms?

---

providing the impetus for most innovative activities. The other hypothesis places consumers and firms' marketing staffs at the forefront of the innovation process.

The Technology-Push Hypothesis

The theory of innovation that focuses on the role of a firm's process or product designers is the **technology-push hypothesis.** According to this view, a firm's research staff initiates innovations by bringing advances in basic scientific or engineering knowledge to the attention of the firm's senior marketing managers for possible commercialization.

A good example of an innovation that fits the technology-push hypothesis is the laser. Scientists first conceived of lasers in the 1950s. After determining the feasibility of laser technology, scientists then built the first lasers in the 1960s. At that time, lasers had no known commercial applications. Only later did lasers emerge as process innovations in the markets for surgeries, scanning devices, and digital network-connection mechanisms.

The Demand-Pull Hypothesis

According to the **demand-pull hypothesis,** managers and employees who deal with customers are the driving force for innovative activity within firms. From this

Technology-Push Hypothesis
A theory of innovation that emphasizes the potential role of companies' research staffs in initiating process or product innovations.

Demand-Pull Hypothesis
A theory of innovation in which managers and employees initiate process and product innovations based on observations of factors influencing customer demand in the marketplace.

perspective, those within firms who are most intimately involved with the problem of satisfying customers with new, lower-priced, or higher-quality products make firms' research staffs aware of a perceived "need" for innovation. In this sense, it is customer demand, instead of researchers' scientific quests, that provides the impetus for innovative activity.

Most economists believe that the bulk of process and product innovations intermingle technology-push and demand-pull forces. For instance, consider again the laser. Profit opportunities eventually arose from more effective treatment of diseases to the eye and other organs, more automated ways to enter prices at checkout counters, and higher-speed and more-efficient means of connecting remote computers within networks. In the absence of such opportunities, laser technology undoubtedly would have been an invention lacking a marketable use.

As you learned in Chapter 1, the Internet first developed simply because government and researchers wanted to find a speedier way to communicate using available computer technologies. In this regard, the technology-push hypothesis helps to explain the development of networks that have made electronic commerce feasible. At the same time, however, the desire by both consumers and businesses for better ways to search for information, shop, order products, and track orders provided a demand-pull impetus for further innovation.

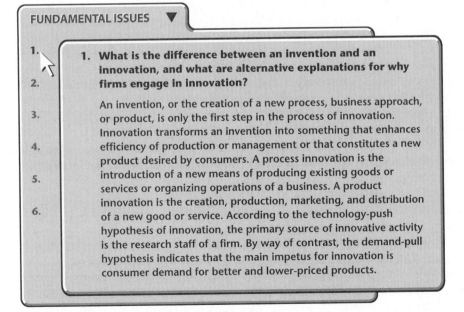

FUNDAMENTAL ISSUES ▼

1.
2.
3.
4.
5.
6.

1. **What is the difference between an invention and an innovation, and what are alternative explanations for why firms engage in innovation?**

    An invention, or the creation of a new process, business approach, or product, is only the first step in the process of innovation. Innovation transforms an invention into something that enhances efficiency of production or management or that constitutes a new product desired by consumers. A process innovation is the introduction of a new means of producing existing goods or services or organizing operations of a business. A product innovation is the creation, production, marketing, and distribution of a new good or service. According to the technology-push hypothesis of innovation, the primary source of innovative activity is the research staff of a firm. By way of contrast, the demand-pull hypothesis indicates that the main impetus for innovation is consumer demand for better and lower-priced products.

Firm Size, Market Structure, and Innovation

There is a general consensus among economists that both the technology-push and demand-pull hypotheses for innovation have important implications for how firm size and market structure may influence the pace of innovation. Many economists also believe that the pace of innovative activity can influence both firm size and market structure.

The economist most identified with the idea that market structure plays a fundamental role in innovation is Joseph Schumpeter (pronounced "shoom-pater"), who studied this subject during the first half of the twentieth-century. Schumpeter first identified both firm size and market structure as two key factors influencing how rapidly innovation alters the scale and scope of markets for goods, services, and factors of production. (Schumpeter also helped to develop a broader theory indicating that innovations generally appear in clusters and in somewhat regular cycles; see *Management Online: Riding the Waves of Innovation*.)

FIRM SIZE AND INNOVATION

Schumpeter and economists who built on his ideas recognized that both the technology-push and demand-pull hypotheses typically are relevant for understanding innovative activities. Both hypotheses have similar implications about how firm size may influence innovation: Large firms have an innovation advantage over smaller firms.

Consider the technology-push hypothesis, which indicates that the fundamental source of innovation is inventive and development research by scientists and engineers. If this is so, then a firm with relatively large research staff and facilities will have a natural advantage over one with a smaller staff and facilities. A larger research staff, after all, will be able to cover a broader base of emerging scientific knowledge in search of commercial applications, thereby giving the firm possessing this staff an edge in more rapidly identifying new processes and products. The firm with the larger research staff also may be able to take advantage of specialization within its research staff, which can allow it to more rapidly develop such processes and products.

According to the demand-pull hypothesis, a firm's marketing managers and sales force encounter customer desires for improved processes and products, which they communicate to managers and employees who are responsible for the firm's research and development activities. In the context of this perspective, there are two ways that a large firm has an innovation advantage over a smaller firm. First, a large firm has a larger marketing team and customer base, so it is more likely to readily identify potential niches for new processes or products. Second, for the same reasons discussed with respect to the technology-push hypothesis, a large firm with a big research and development staff may be better equipped to respond with solutions to perceived profitable opportunities for new processes or products.

Hence, both hypotheses indicate that there is likely to be a positive relationship between firm size and the speed of innovation. Increases in firm size are,

MANAGEMENT *Online*

POLICY MAKING   GLOBALIZATION   **MANAGEMENT**

Riding the Waves of Innovation

Schumpeter coined the term creative destruction to describe innovative activity within an economy that experiences market upheavals, with some firms or even entire industries disappearing as new firms and industries appear as a consequence of widespread technological innovations. Building on earlier writings of a Russian economist named Nikolai Kondratieff, Schumpeter proposed that innovative activity takes place in cycles that each last roughly 50 to 60 years. Figure 7-2 on page 212 illustrates the cycles he had in mind, which economists since have called Kondratieff waves of innovation.

In Schumpeter's view, clusters of new industries typically dominate cycles of creative destruction. These clusters emerge after sufficient time has passed for entrepreneurs to determine how best to apply new technological discoveries and innovations in the marketplace. Schumpeter argued that an initial wave of technological innovations took place in the late eighteenth century following the development of new technologies in textile manufacturing, water power, and construction

using iron. He dated the beginning of a second innovation wave, centered around steam power, steel fabrication, and rail transportation, to be the start of the twentieth century, and he proposed that a third wave began about 50 years later after the adoption of technologies driven by the harnessing of electricity, advances in chemical engineering, and widespread adoption of the internal-combustion engine. Economists agree that at the time of Schumpeter's death in 1950, a fourth wave had emerged, generated by innovations in oil and natural gas as energy sources, the broad use of electronic appliances in homes and businesses, and jet aircraft as a key mode of air transport.

A number of economists believe that a fifth wave, depicted in Figure 7-2 on page 212, may have begun in the early 1990s. This wave, they argue, has resulted from innovations in digital networks, computer software, new-media technologies, and e-commerce. It has resulted in the emergence of yet another set of industry clusters that are seeking to provide the infrastructure for the Internet and intranets, to develop new software applications, to offer interactive media linking households and firms, and to market and distribute

continued

other things being equal, more likely to lead to innovative activities that pass the market test by bringing about increased profitability via greater efficiencies or revenue enhancements.

It is important to recognize, however, that neither theory necessarily implies that ever-greater firm size always improves the potential for successful innovative activities. After all, in the absence of increased coordination efforts, larger marketing and research staffs may encounter bureaucratic inefficiencies that could end up slowing the pace of innovation. Effective coordination of large staffs, in turn, is a costly activity, so as a firm's size increases, the costs it incurs through such coordination efforts could eventually begin more than proportionately, making its innovative activities less efficient.

Hence, while the technology-push and demand-pull hypotheses provide a strong rationale for why large firms may have an advantage in innovation, the argument is not ironclad. Some small firms may be very successful in process and product innovation. Nevertheless, the advantages of size tend to increase the probability of greater innovative success at larger firms.

continued from page 211
goods and services via electronic networks. Some of the economists who subscribe to Schumpeter's views argue that the information technologies that have fueled this proposed new wave of innovation have made it easier for scientists and engineers to bring additional inventions into the marketplace at a rapid pace. If they are correct, the pace of innovation could increase, and their proposed fifth wave could well be shorter than the 40-year wave that preceded it.

For Critical Analysis:
Not everyone gains from innovation. What groups were most likely to have lost out in the marketplace during the waves of innovation depicted in Figure 7-2?

Figure 7-2:
Waves of Innovation.

Building on the ideas of Nikolai Kondratieff, the economist Joseph Schumpeter argued that periods of "creative destruction" arising from sweeping technical developments in various industries lead to periodic waves of economic growth that span decades.

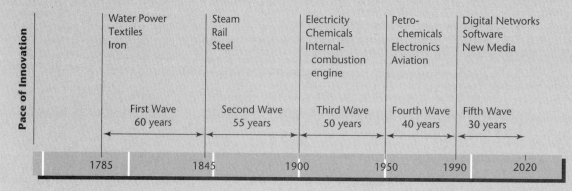

MARKET STRUCTURE AND INNOVATION

As compared with predictions about the importance of firm size for innovative activity, the implications of the technology-push and demand-pull hypotheses for the role of market structure are less clear-cut. Schumpeter recognized this fact. He argued that the *evolution* of market structure is a crucial factor affecting the pace of innovation within an economy. Early in the process of adopting an innovation, Schumpeter argued, society gains from the possession of market power by a few

Figure 7-3:
Market Structure and Product Innovation.

Consumer surplus is greatest (the entire shaded area between the demand curve and marginal and average cost curve) if perfect competition prevails, so that there is marginal-cost pricing at PPC and producers earn zero profits producing Q_{PC} units. This provides little incentive to create new products, however. The incentive to engage in product innovations is greatest when the innovating producer knows that it will be able to restrict output to Q_M and set a monopoly price P_M, thereby earning the darkly shaded area as profit, yielding a lower amount of consumer surplus equal to the dashed triangle.

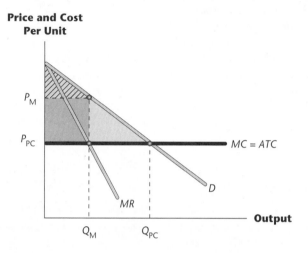

firms, or perhaps by a single firm. Later on, however, society is more likely to come out ahead if markets become more competitive.

To understand the basis of Schumpeter's argument, take a look at Figure 7-3. Let's limit ourselves to considering a product innovation, and let's suppose that marginal production cost is constant and equal to average cost. Once a new product is available, consumer surplus is greatest—the entire shaded area in the figure— if the many perfectly competitive producers have the unhindered right to imitate the product and sell essentially perfect substitutes under their own company names. As a result, the price of the product, P_{PC}, is equal to marginal cost across the industry, and the quantity produced equals the quantity demanded at this price.

Now let's consider the innovation process from the perspective of the technology-push hypothesis. It indicates that a perfectly competitive outcome can arise only if the product is available in the first place. The perfectly competitive outcome entails zero economic profits once the product goes into production: Operating revenues are just sufficient to cover total explicit production expenses and opportunity costs. But this means that incurring any up-front costs of product innovation is an activity that goes unrewarded. Because there is no inducement for a firm to incur a potentially sizable cost of inventing and developing the product, the firm may never introduce it into the marketplace in the first place!

Now suppose that a firm with a new product is the single seller of this product. As a consequence, it sets the monopoly price, P_M. This shrinks consumer surplus to the dashed triangle shown in Figure 7-3. The economic profit earned by the patent's owner, the darkly shaded area, is a transfer from society to the single firm that invented and developed the product.

From the perspective of the demand-pull hypothesis, however, the presence of economic profits in this market signals to other potential firms that there is a profit opportunity available if they can introduce their own product offerings to compete with the product sold by this monopoly firm. These potential competitors may seek to introduce a rival product using lower-cost techniques, or they may try to develop a higher-quality product.

This reasoning provides the basis for Schumpeter's hypothesis. In his view, innovation initially is spurred by market power that permits innovators to obtain a reward for their efforts. To induce firms to innovate, therefore, society must be willing to allow these firms to earn positive economic profits for a time. Later on, however, the interests of society are better served by entry of additional firms into the marketplace. In many instances, Schumpeter concluded, the initial entrants launch major innovations, and those that follow fill in available market niches with minor innovations.

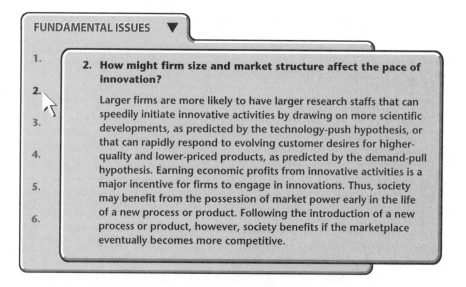

FUNDAMENTAL ISSUES ▼

1.

2.

3.

4.

5.

6.

2. How might firm size and market structure affect the pace of innovation?

Larger firms are more likely to have larger research staffs that can speedily initiate innovative activities by drawing on more scientific developments, as predicted by the technology-push hypothesis, or that can rapidly respond to evolving customer desires for higher-quality and lower-priced products, as predicted by the demand-pull hypothesis. Earning economic profits from innovative activities is a major incentive for firms to engage in innovations. Thus, society may benefit from the possession of market power early in the life of a new process or product. Following the introduction of a new process or product, however, society benefits if the marketplace eventually becomes more competitive.

Intellectual Property, Patents, and E-Commerce Processes

By inventing new products, implementing new production processes, and organizing new ways of marketing, selling, and delivering goods and services, scientists, engineers, and businesspeople contribute to economic development and growth. To encourage the efforts of these individuals, governments often act to protect

intellectual property rights, which are legal rules governing the ownership of creative ideas.

SAFEGUARDING INTELLECTUAL PROPERTY RIGHTS

Today people use information technologies to copy and transfer Web pages and digital text and data files with increasing ease. For this reason, a significant issue arising in the electronic marketplace is determining an appropriate framework to govern rights to intellectual property.

Forms of Intellectual Property Rights

There are three ways that governments ensure rights to intellectual property. One is by issuing **copyrights,** which grant authors exclusive privileges to reproduce, distribute, perform, or display creative works. Copyrights cover works such as articles, stories and novels, computer programs, audio recordings, and cinematographic films.

Governments also protect intellectual property by establishing rules governing **trademarks.** These are words or symbols that companies use to identify their goods or services and distinguish them from goods or services produced by other firms.

Patents are a third type of intellectual property protection. These are legal documents granting an inventor the exclusive right to make, use, and sell an invention for a specified number of years.

Currently, many nations abide by international standards for intellectual property rights established by a multilateral agreement called the *Agreement on Trade-Related Aspects of Intellectual Property Rights,* or *TRIPS*. Nations that do not currently meet these standards—mainly the least-developed nations of the world—have agreed to meet them by January 2006. TRIPS establishes a 50-year minimum standard for copyright protection, common rules governing international trademark protections, and a minimum term of patent protection of 20 years.

The Intellectual Property Balancing Act

The rationale for granting intellectual property rights is based on Schumpeter's reasoning concerning the interaction between market power and innovation. Assigning intellectual property rights in the form of copyright, trademark, or patent protection bestows market power on inventors and innovators. They can earn economic profits that compensate them for incurring process or product development costs. In the absence of intellectual property rights, there would be less incentive for inventors and innovators to develop new products and technologies.

Nevertheless, if people are free to imitate the creative ideas of others, then society gains from the speedy diffusion of products and processes that results. Competition among firms in industries using these ideas, however, leads to zero economic profits. In this case, there is no return beyond covering the opportunity cost of being in the industry to compensate inventors for the time and effort they invested in developing the new product or process.

Intellectual Property Rights
Laws regulating ownership of creative ideas that is typically granted in the form of a copyright, trademark, or patent.

Copyright
An author's legal title to the sole right to reproduce, distribute, perform, or display creative works, including articles, books, software, and audio and video recordings.

Trademark
A company's legal title to a word or symbol that identifies its product and distinguishes it from the products of other firms.

Patent
An inventor's legal title to the sole right to manufacture, utilize, and market an invention for a specific period.

By granting intellectual property rights, governments seek to balance this trade-off between the interests of consumers and producers. Granting a patent to the inventor and developer of a process or product allows this firm to charge a monopoly price to those who would like to use the new product or process. The innovating firm earns compensation for incurring the up-front expenses required to make the new process or product available to society. When the term of the patent expires, others can freely imitate the process or product, effectively reallocating social welfare gains back to consumers.

In principle, the terms of copyrights, trademarks, and patents should be determined on a case-by-case basis, based on the costs of developing processes or products, as well as the demand and operating-cost conditions in the relevant marketplace. In practice, innovation costs and market conditions are difficult to evaluate on a case-by-case basis. This is why governments typically establish fixed terms of protection of intellectual property rights. (The extent of international protection of intellectual property rights in the electronic marketplace has not yet been determined; see *Globalization Online: Should Developing Nations Agree to Protect Intellectual Property Rights in the Electronic Marketplace?*)

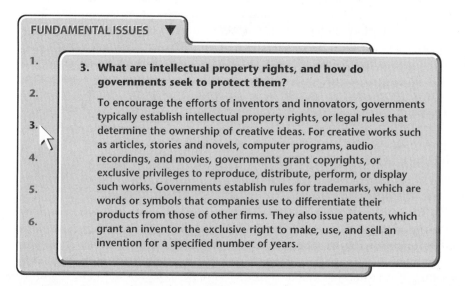

FUNDAMENTAL ISSUES ▼

1.

2.

3.

4.

5.

6.

3. What are intellectual property rights, and how do governments seek to protect them?

To encourage the efforts of inventors and innovators, governments typically establish intellectual property rights, or legal rules that determine the ownership of creative ideas. For creative works such as articles, stories and novels, computer programs, audio recordings, and movies, governments grant copyrights, or exclusive privileges to reproduce, distribute, perform, or display such works. Governments establish rules for trademarks, which are words or symbols that companies use to differentiate their products from those of other firms. They also issue patents, which grant an inventor the exclusive right to make, use, and sell an invention for a specified number of years.

PATENTING E-COMMERCE PROCESSES

The U.S. government grants patents for new and useful designs, products, processes, or substances. Under some circumstances, it is also possible to patent significant improvements to products, processes, and substances. Obtaining a patent requires an applicant to prove that the invention is useful, that it is novel, and that it will function as claimed.

Rules Governing Patents

It is not enough for someone desiring a patent to prove novelty, however. To obtain a patent, an individual or a firm must also provide a publicly available de-

GLOBALIZATION *Online*

Should Developing Nations Agree to Protect Intellectual Property Rights in the Electronic Marketplace?

In late 2000, the U.S. government proposed an ambitious plan for agreements covering both open trade and intellectual property rights protections in electronic commerce. This proposal led to initial international negotiations of this subject. If the past is any guide, most nations ultimately will participate in some type of agreement governing rights to intellectual property in the electronic marketplace. Panel *(a)* of Figure 7-4 on pages 218–219 displays significant increases in the numbers of nations participating in various international conventions for assuring common standards for the protection of international property rights.

Winners and Losers from Current Property Rights Protections

Increased protection of intellectual property rights has immediate benefits for current owners of intellectual property. For those who wish to incorporate new ideas and processes into their businesses, strengthening intellectual property rights is likely to push up business expenses by forcing them to make payments to owners of copyrights, trademarks, and patents.

Currently, most owners of intellectual property reside in the United States and Western Europe. As shown in panel *(b)* of Figure 7-4, this means that residents located in these re-

gions are most likely to realize immediate gains from the growing globalization of intellectual property rights. Producers in other regions, most of which are less developed, experience immediate losses.

Incentives to Adopt International Protections

Nearly all of the recent additions to the memberships of international conventions for protecting intellectual property rights have been developing nations, however. Some of these nations undoubtedly felt pressured by U.S. threats of trade retaliation if they did not join these conventions. Similar pressures may induce developing nations to enter into agreements governing intellectual property rights in the electronic marketplace.

Presumably, a number the nations already participating in international conventions for intellectual property rights have also decided that it is in their best interest to incur near-term losses in return for potentially significant future gains. These, they may have decided, and may yet decide in the case of e-commerce, are likely to come in the form of greater development and higher economic growth that access to both traditional and electronic markets will afford.

For Critical Analysis:

What mechanisms might national governments develop to ensure enforcement of international rules governing intellectual property protection in the electronic marketplace?

continued

scription of a novel design or of a new or substantially improved product, process, or substance. This permits others to use the invention, as long as they pay the patent owner for doing so. The patent owner may file legal claims against the revenues earned by any individual or firm that fails to do so and that thereby engages in *patent infringement*.

For years, a guiding principle of determining whether an inventor could apply for a process patent was that the process had to transform objects in the real

continued from page 217
Figure 7-4:
Increased International Protection of Intellectual Property Rights and the Immediate Winners and Losers.

As panel (a) indicates, there has been a significant increase in the numbers of nations that are members of treaties or conventions protecting intellectual property rights. Panel (b) shows that the immediate gains from these arrangements go to developed nations that own the largest numbers of patents, copyrights, and trademarks. Source: Keith Maskus, Intellectual Property Rights in the Global Economy, Washington, D.C.: Institute for International Economics, August 2000.

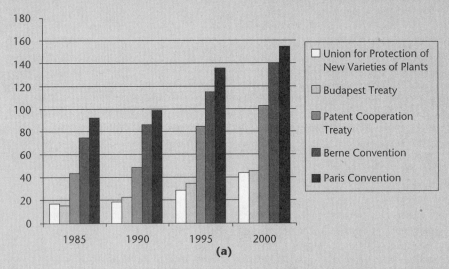

Legend:
- Union for Protection of New Varieties of Plants
- Budapest Treaty
- Patent Cooperation Treaty
- Berne Convention
- Paris Convention

(a)

continued

world. This ruled out mere mental processes, which courts had long determined to be ineligible for patent protection.

In 1994, however, the line dividing a patent-eligible invention from a mental process became more blurred. A federal appeals court ruled that the U.S. Patent

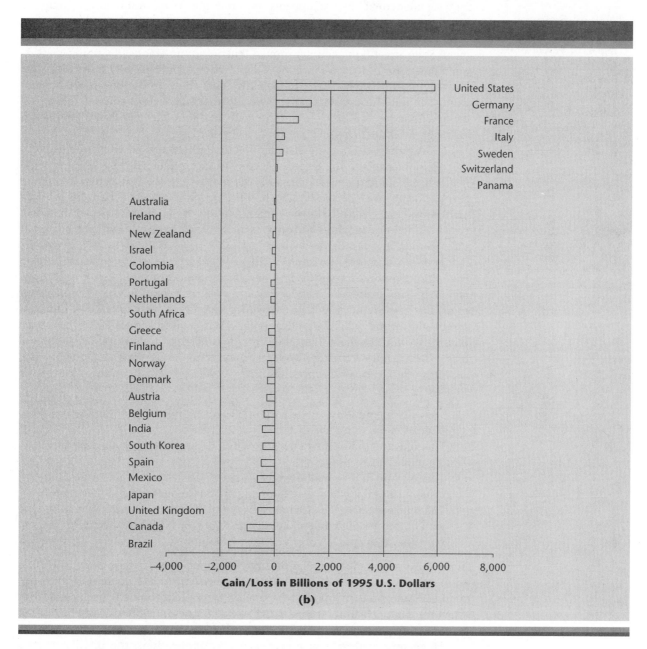

Gain/Loss in Billions of 1995 U.S. Dollars

(b)

and Trademark Office had improperly rejected an application for improving the images on oscilloscopes, which project images of waves on cathode-ray tubes. The court ruled that because the invention was implemented as a computer, it did not amount to purely an abstract idea.

What are the various e-commerce programs of the U.S. Patent and Trademark Office? To find out, go to http://www.uspto.gov, click on "Activities & Education," and then click on "eBusiness Center."

Business Method Patents
Patents for process innovations that involve the use of computer software and methods of organizing business operations.

Business Method Patents and the Great E-Commerce Patent Race

The court decision regarding a computer-linked scientific instrument set the stage for a another crucial federal appeals court ruling in 1998. In this case, a company called Signature Financial Group obtained a patent for a data processing system designed to determine the market value of a specific type of mutual fund arrangement. State Street Bank counter-argued that Signature Financial Group was seeking a patent for a mental process. A federal district court initially sided with State Street Bank, but then a federal appeals court ruled that Signature Financial Group's mutual-fund-system patent was legitimate because it enabled the user of the invention to produce a "useful, concrete, and tangible" result in the form of a mutual fund share price.

Shortly thereafter, another federal court upheld the patent eligibility of a process for enhancing the records of long-distance phone calls by adding a data field into the standard message record. The court remarked that its new interpretation of patent law reflected a "sea change" in technology and the legal environment for patents. Indeed, this new interpretation of patent law opened the floodgate for **business method patents,** or patents that typically combine computer software with business methodologies.

In the e-commerce marketplace, the new patent rules were significant. Walker Digital, a company owned by Priceline.com's founder Jay Walker, patented the reverse-auction procedure used by Priceline. Walker Digital now owns patents for many business methods such as procedures for online sale of options on financial assets and airline tickets. The license fees that Walker Digital earns from such patents account for the bulk of the company's operating revenues. Other companies sought to follow Walker's lead, setting off a run on business method patents.

To obtain a business method patent, the following conditions must be satisfied:

1) The software and/or method cannot be a law of nature, a natural phenomenon, or an abstract idea.
2) The software and/or method must be useful. It must ultimately provide a "tangible" result.
3) The software and/or method must be novel. It must have some aspect that distinguishes it in some way from all previous knowledge and inventions.
4) The software and/or method must be nonobvious, which means that someone with ordinary skills could not easily think of it. It must be a "concrete" invention that goes beyond a mere mental process.

Table 7-1 gives recent examples of controversial business method patents relating to the electronic marketplace that the U.S. Patent and Trademark Office has granted. Amazon.com's patent for one-click shopping gained special notoriety when the company won an injunction forcing BarnesandNoble.com to halt use of a similar one-click shopping method at the height of a Christmas season.

To keep up with a deluge of new patent applications, the U.S. Patent and Trademark Office hired more than a thousand additional patent examiners within a two-year period. Although this increased its staff of examiners by about 25 percent, waits of a year or longer following the initial submission of a patent

Table 7-1: Examples of Controversial E-Commerce Patents.

Microsoft Patent #5,860,073	The use of style sheets in electronic publishing systems
Amazon Patent #5,060,411	A method and system for placing an order to purchase an item via the Internet "in response to only a single action being performed" (that is, one-click shopping)
Sony Patent #5,978,807	An apparatus and method of automatically downloading and storing Web pages
Amazon Patent #6,029,141	A method for rewarding affiliated companies for sales generated via links from their Web sites

Source: Bureau of National Affairs, *Computer Technology Law Report,* vol. 1, no. 1 (May 19, 2000).

application are not uncommon. When there are many existing patents or applications for patents relating to that application, attempting to determine whether an individual application satisfies the requirement for a business method patent can be a major task. Critics of business method patents argue that patent examiners typically lack the backgrounds required to evaluate the novelty of proposed "new" business methods. (Recently, bank and import/export firms have complained that too many patents of ordinary banking, international trade, and Internet download processes are being granted; see *Policymaking Online: Patent Pending—Does the U.S. Patent and Trademark Office Know What It's Doing?*)

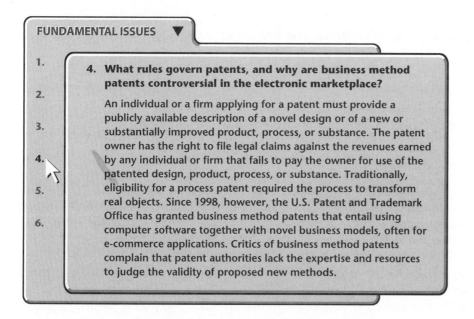

FUNDAMENTAL ISSUES ▼

1.

2.

3.

4.

5.

6.

4. What rules govern patents, and why are business method patents controversial in the electronic marketplace?

An individual or a firm applying for a patent must provide a publicly available description of a novel design or of a new or substantially improved product, process, or substance. The patent owner has the right to file legal claims against the revenues earned by any individual or firm that fails to pay the owner for use of the patented design, product, process, or substance. Traditionally, eligibility for a process patent required the process to transform real objects. Since 1998, however, the U.S. Patent and Trademark Office has granted business method patents that entail using computer software together with novel business models, often for e-commerce applications. Critics of business method patents complain that patent authorities lack the expertise and resources to judge the validity of proposed new methods.

POLICYMAKING *Online*

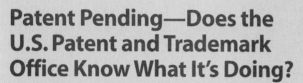

POLICY MAKING   GLOBALIZATION   MANAGEMENT

Patent Pending—Does the U.S. Patent and Trademark Office Know What It's Doing?

In July 2000, the U.S. Patent and Trademark Office issued a patent to a new system for managing banking payments, giving owners of the patent rights to collect payments from every bank that used the system. There was a problem, however. The newly patented technology had been in place at banks for years. Within short order, the U.S. Patent and Trademark Office agreed to participate in an emergency meeting with representatives of the American Bankers Association, the National Automated Clearinghouse Association, and other banking groups. It was time, the Patent Office agreed, for patent examiners to get some lessons in banking.

Problems of this kind were not supposed to happen. Just four months earlier, the Patent Office had embarked on a series of changes intended to improve the review process for applications for patents relating to computerized business methods. It had added a new layer of review and doubled the number of applications automatically receiving a final screening by the most highly experienced patent examiners.

Nevertheless, in August 2000 a small Virginia company called DE Technology began warning other firms that it would soon be demanding a fee equal to 0.3 percent of the value of every cross-border trade deal arranged using computers. DE Technology had just received a letter from the U.S. Patent and Trademark Office indicating that it would soon obtain a broad patent covering "a process for carrying out an international transaction . . . using computer-to-computer communication."

continued

 ## Copyrights, Trademarks, and Digital Products

Perhaps the most contentious issue relating to intellectual property rights in the electronic marketplace concerns the protection of copyrights to materials that people can easily store in digital forms and transfer across networks. To recognize why this is so, it is important to understand the nature of copyrights.

COPYRIGHT BASICS

Since 1897, the U.S. Copyright Office, a division of the Library of Congress, has overseen the registration and cataloging of books, movies, music, architectural drawings, and similar creative works. Until recently, the Copyright Office staff worked in relative obscurity, mainly handling paperwork.

Copyrights in the United States

The U.S. Constitution first laid out the notion of copyright protection, and at the urging of the dictionary author Noah Webster, Congress passed the first copyright

If DE Technologies received the patent, and if courts interpreted it as applying as broadly as the company claimed, nearly everyone using computer-to-computer links to arrange international trade would have to pay DE Technologies. Based on current computer-processed international trade transactions and the patent rate DE Technologies indicated it planned to charge, the company would stand to earn hundreds of millions of dollars in patent fees each year.

DE Technology's primary owner had applied for the patent in the early 1990s. In the meantime, businesses all over the world were already using computer-to-computer trade processes. Forwarders of international freight had implemented various computer-based processes for streamlining international trade shipments. An active computer-software market for these processes also had developed. The use of computers for processing trade was taken for granted.

Not long afterward, yet another company began demanding royalty payments for a business method that seemed obvious to a lot of people. Sightsound.com launched a lawsuit against N2K, a company that retails digital music files on the Web. Sightsound.com had obtained a patent that it claimed covers the sale of *any* audio or video recording over the Internet. After it filed its lawsuit, Sightsound.com also contacted other prominent sellers of music on the Web to demand a royalty on every sale.

For Critical Analysis:

Analysts' estimates of the patent royalties that DE Technologies might receive were based on total trade processed using computer links in the absence of payment of fees to DE Technologies. Why did some economists argue that these estimates probably were too high? (Hint: Remember the law of demand: An increase in the price of any item reduces the quantity demanded.)

---

laws in the late eighteenth century. These granted copyright protection up to 28 years for books, charts, and maps.

Today the duration of a copyright extends to 70 years beyond an author's death. Copyright Office staffers must sift through, rule upon, and catalog in excess of 800,000 copyright applications each year. Creators of works that receive copyrights then can determine under what circumstances works are published. (Copyright owners can, of course, grant permission for individuals or organizations to reproduce written works without compensation; see on page 224 *Globalization Online: Publishing Online Medical Information in Bangladesh.*)

The Rationale for Copyright Protection

Most works that creators copyright are *information-intensive products*. As you learned in Chapter 4, an information-intensive product is an item produced using a potentially rapidly developing foundation of knowledge. Many information-intensive products can be created only if the producer incurs high fixed costs. In the Internet environment, however, the per-unit costs of reproducing these works can be extremely low.

Before writing an economics textbook, an author spends years studying the foundations of economic analysis. In addition, the author must sift through huge

What are the latest developments in U.S. copyright rules regarding digital copies? Find out by going to http://www.loc.gov/copyright and clicking on "Digital Transmissions."

GLOBALIZATION *Online*

Publishing Online Medical Information in Bangladesh

Until the late 1990s, medical schools in Bangladesh were fortunate to own a single computer. The country's top medical school, Dhaka Medical School, could afford current subscriptions to only one or two medical journals at a time. Consequently, doctors were in the dark about the latest medical developments in treating serious illnesses and injuries.

MEDINET to the Rescue

Health-care professionals in Bangladesh responded to this problem by establishing Medinet, a nonprofit online medical-information network. Medinet began with two digital phones. System operators downloaded medical information from professional journals via the Web on a regular basis. With the permission of journal publishers, they placed data in a central computer system, from which they produced paper reports that six offices regularly distributed at no charge to 17 organizational users, including the nation's medical schools, and 60 individual users.

Today, a growing number of Bangladesh medical schools have access to electronic mail. A doctor trying to determine the best way to treat a particular condition can send an e-mail request to Medinet, which assists the doctor in electronically retrieving articles concerning the latest treatment techniques.

A Virtual Training Ground

Gradually, medical schools in Bangladesh have used basic e-mail access to develop a network built around the Medinet system. Today, Medinet serves as the center for the distribution of national public health information.

It also has become a major resource for training new physicians. Six up-to-date medical courses are accessible on the Medinet system, and more than 200 medical students have used these courses to supplement their training.

For Critical Analysis:

What would happen to the dissemination of new medical knowledge if every medical practitioner, like those in Bangladesh, could get access to the latest articles on medicine without paying for the information? (Hint: Why do scientific and professional journals charge subscription fees to libraries and to individual subscribers?)

You can explore Medinet at http://www.angelfire.com/ak/medinet.

volumes of theories, facts, and data, synthesize that information, and compose a text that succeeds in transmitting this synthesized knowledge to the reader. Although computer hardware and software can simplify the process of writing a textbook, it remains very labor-intensive. Consequently, the fixed costs of textbook writing, which include both the explicit cost of compiling information and the opportunity cost of time spent sifting through and synthesizing the information, are significant.

Nevertheless, once an economics textbook has been published, the cost of reproducing it is relatively low. In the absence of copyright protection, a group of students taking a class could buy a single copy of the book and photocopy the pages to distribute to all members of the group. If enough students were to do this, the publisher of the book would not earn a sufficient return to justify marketing the book and compensating the author for the effort. Eventually, very few textbooks would be written.

Today, preventing this outcome has become a greater challenge. After all, someone could scan each page of a textbook and post the pages on a Web site—thereby transforming a physical, paper-based product into a pirated *virtual product* (see Chapter 3). The student might even try to charge other students to access the site, though naturally at a total price less than the price of the book. A student engaging in such activity would violate current U.S. copyright laws and would be subject to prosecution.

THE CHALLENGE OF COPYRIGHT PROTECTION IN A NETWORK ECONOMY

In the electronic marketplace, obscure and arcane copyright rules have suddenly emerged as major policy issues. Should owners of Web sites be able to wall off their sites so that university researchers cannot access them to conduct studies? How much should firms—sometimes called Webcasters—that sell musical recordings as downloadable files or as real-time digital transmissions have to pay musicians to sell their compositions or performances? Can someone store television shows recorded from cable or broadcast transmissions in digital form and then charge others to view them at a separate Web site? During the past few years, Congress, the Copyright Office, and the courts have scrambled to find answers to these and other questions concerning copyright protection on the Internet.

The Hazy Legal Boundaries of Copyright Protection in Cyberspace

To try to address some of these questions, in 1998 Congress enacted the *Digital Millennium Copyright Act*. This legislation strengthened existing copyright law with respect to accessing and storing information on computers and distributing it via networks.

The Digital Millennium Copyright Act seeks to place boundaries that distinguish between a copyright owner's right to restrict access to digitally encoded information and the constitutional rights of citizens to seek out and publish reports for the public at large. It also includes an "anti-hacking" provision that specifies criminal penalties for breaking through passwords, encryptions, and other technological defenses companies use to guard their Internet content.

At the same time, Congress gave the Copyright Office the discretion to grant exemptions to the provision against breaking through such technological defenses. For instance, in 2000 the Association of American Universities requested an exemption for digital versions of scholarly journals, newspaper archives, and databases. This group argued that otherwise a publisher of such digital products could charge a fee each time a professor or student accessed a research study, a news article, or a set of data on the Internet. (Book publishers are already experimenting with fee-based schemes for accessing digital books; see *Management Online: Renting E-Textbooks—The Future of Copyright Protection in Electronic Publishing?*) Other groups also have requested exemptions, which publishing companies have opposed on the grounds that granting such exemptions would effectively remove

MANAGEMENT *Online*

Renting E-Textbooks— The Future of Copyright Protection in Electronic Publishing?

Web surfers now have access to software that allows them to swap digital files. Consequently, companies that hope to earn profits from marketing books in digital form, or e-books, are seeking ways to protect the intellectual property rights of authors.

The Self-Destructing Textbook

The newest e-books cannot be sold, loaned out, or given away. They also do not remain patiently on a computer's hard drive while you put off reading them. Instead, they demand payments from time to time. Failure to make the requested payments induces the e-books to self-destruct.

At many universities, students in professional schools increasingly use digital textbooks. For instance, dental students at several universities have used an electronic textbook stored on a videodisk. Students cannot purchase the e-book, however. They must pay a recurring annual fee to rent the e-textbook. If a student fails to make the payment when it is due, the e-book's software automatically eliminates further access to the e-textbook's content. Only good programmers might be able to get around an added protection: Additional software code automatically closes off access to the e-textbook if someone tries to make a digital copy. Designers of future e-textbooks hope to make it hard for students to use printers to make hard copies of pages.

Market Power, Access, and the Joy of Reading

Advocates of this model for e-books argue that it allows publishers to impose stringent conditions on electronic access and digital file transfers, thereby protecting publishers' copyrights.

continued

copyright protections. In the end, the Digital Millennium Copyright Act did not fully lay out the boundaries of copyright protection, although it did increase the discretionary powers of the U.S. Copyright Office.

Copyright Violations and the Lost Revenues of Copyright Owners

One of the Web sites that has often appeared in the top 50 most visited by Internet browsers is Napster.com (http://www.napster.com). This company's downloading software allows visitors to exchange digital music files. It has been estimated that as many as 25 million users have engaged in digital-music swaps at this site.

According to the music-recording industry, digital music swapping amounts to outright theft each time a user downloads a digital music file without paying royalties. Media reports often indicate that the music-recording industry loses hundreds of million of dollars in annual revenues as a result of the activities of Napster, MP3.com, and thousands of other music-file swapping sites. One technology-research firm, Forrester Research, Inc. (http://www.forrester.com), has concluded that the music-recording industry could lose as much as $3 billion in

For professionals, students, and those who simply enjoy the pleasure of reading, however, some important issues arise. First, many dentists, doctors, and other professionals desire to keep their physical textbooks as references that they can refer to periodically. They would have to pay for continual access to e-textbooks, however.

Second, professors often require specific textbooks. The restrictive nature of access to e-textbooks precludes searching for close substitutes available from other textbook publishers at lower prices. In addition, because e-textbooks are continually updated, there will be no market for used versions of current or older editions. Thus, stringent restrictions on access to e-textbooks could add to publishers' market power, permitting them to charge higher prices.

Finally, although better software has improved the readability of e-books on computer screens, some critics question whether an e-book is likely to appeal to general book consumers who, unlike professional students, are not captive buyers. Curling up in bed to read and study an e-book is feasible, at best, only using laptop computers with smaller screens or with smaller, specially designed e-book-reading devices. Otherwise, a reader restricted to using an e-book on a personal computer must sit at a desk for hours on end—which, critics argue, is unlikely to improve the quality of an individual's reading experience.

For Critical Analysis:
If higher prices of e-textbooks significantly reduce the quantity demanded, then why might publishers continue to sell or rent them at those higher prices nonetheless?

revenues each year. It also estimated that book publishers lose about $1.5 billion annually in unauthorized transfers of material published in copyrighted books.

Economists tend to be skeptical of such predictions, which are often based on estimates of total downloads of copyrighted materials that take place at an explicit price of zero. (Of course, the true price to any individual of downloading copyrighted materials is always somewhat greater than zero, because the person accessing them must devote time and effort to the undertaking.) To predict total revenues lost to copyright violations, those performing studies often multiply this estimated quantity by the average market price of legally traded copies of a musical performance or a publication. Basic economics, however, tells us that these cannot truly be the revenues that copyright owners lose from sales of unauthorized copies, because at least some of those who trade unauthorized copies at an explicit price of zero would not have purchased them at the market price.

Take a look at Figure 7-5 on page 228. The demand curve D_1^a in panel (a) depicts the total demand for, say, legally authorized songs performed by popular rock musicians. When music-swap Web sites opened, this undoubtedly induced a

Figure 7-5:
Determining How Many Revenues Sellers of Rock Music Recordings Lose as a Result of Unauthorized Releases.

Panel (a) depicts initial demand and supply curves, D_1^a and S^a, in the market for authorized releases of musical recordings. Panel (b) shows the demand for unauthorized digital copies of musical recordings, D_1^u. If these unauthorized copies are available at no explicit charge on the Internet, then the amount of copies consumed equals the satiation consumption level Q_s^u in panel (b). These individuals thereby cut back on their consumption of authorized recordings, so the demand for authorized releases to shift leftward, to D_2^a. The resulting revenue loss to producers of authorized recordings is the shaded area in panel (a).

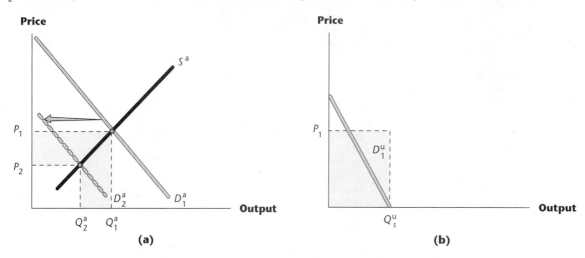

decline in the number of consumers in the market for legally released rock-music recordings, as some people began downloading unauthorized copies of recordings from Web sites. Hence, the quantity demanded of authorized rock-music recordings fell at any given price, so that the demand curve in the market for legal recordings of rock music shifted to the left, to D_2^a. Panel *(b)* shows the resulting demand curve D_1^u in the newly created market for unauthorized rock-music recordings. At the explicit price of zero, those who seek music-recordings in this market obtain the quantity Q_s^u by downloading the recordings from Web sites. Economists call this quantity the **satiation consumption level,** because at the explicit price of zero this is the maximum quantity that consumers desire to buy in this market for unauthorized recordings.

Satiation Consumption Level
The maximum feasible quantity of a good or service that consumers desire to purchase at an explicit price of zero.

This does *not*, however, mean that the amount of revenues that music-recording companies lose equals the original market price P_1 times the Q_s^u, or the shaded area in panel *(b)*. After all, at this market price the quantity demanded by these consumers at the original price P_1 in the market for authorized recordings is equal to the smaller quantity Q_1^u in panel *(b)*. That is, the quantity of recordings consumers obtain at an explicit price of zero in the market for unauthorized recordings is larger than it would have been if they had been required to pay the true market price. Hence, multiplying the original market price by the satiation consumption level does not really indicate the revenues that music companies lose from unauthorized releases of rock-music recordings. Indeed, this approach could considerably overstate the revenue losses that these companies experience.

To see why this is so, note that the *true* revenue loss is the shaded area depicted in panel *(a)* of the figure. The decline in demand for authorized rock-music recordings causes both the market price and the equilibrium quantity consumed in the marketplace to fall. Owners of copyrighted rock music undeniably lose revenues from the loss of customers who purchase authorized releases of song albums. The amount of this revenue decrease, the shaded area in panel *(a)*, is likely to be less than the product of the original market price times the satiation consumption level in the market for unauthorized releases, the shaded area in panel *(b)*.

Another Complication for Evaluating Revenue Losses from Copyright Violations

There is another twist to evaluating revenues losses for copyright owners as a result of unauthorized copying and distributions of their works on the Web. In Figure 7-5, the position of the demand curve D_2^a that prevails after some consumers seek to obtain unauthorized recordings of rock music is assumed to be permanent. It is possible, however, that many people who obtain individual rock songs in the market for unauthorized releases may do so simply to listen to samples of the songs of new performers, or perhaps of performers whom they previously had not noticed. When they discover performers with musical styles that match their tastes and preferences, some of these people may desire to obtain more than just one or two songs via the Internet. They may want full sets of songs that are most readily obtained on complete albums offered for sale by recording companies in the market for authorized releases.

The ability to sample individual songs at Web sites reduces the search costs that consumers face when shopping for music, books, and other copyrighted works. As we discussed in Chapter 5, this leads to an increase in the amount of information that consumers acquire, which can cause their demand for products that they judge to be of high quality to increase. Although some consumers with relatively low opportunity costs of their time may be willing to spend hours searching for all of the songs of particular artists that they can download at a zero explicit price, others who face higher opportunity costs may choose to purchase complete albums in the market for authorized releases of music recordings. This would lead to at least a partial reversal of the leftward shift in demand illustrated in panel *(a)* of Figure 7-5. As a result, the revenues lost from unauthorized Web file transfers of copyrighted works would be smaller.

It is even conceivable that on net the demand for authorized music releases could rise beyond its initial level at D_1. In this case, the availability of downloadable songs on the Web could actually *increase* the revenues of music-recording companies. Indeed, Napster, MP3.com, and other music-sharing Web sites advanced these arguments when traditional music companies complained about

MANAGEMENT *Online*

"Do Unto Others . . ." at Napster.com?

When the music-recording industry began to complain that consumer file-sharing was infringing on copyrights and cutting into the industry's revenues, Napster publicly stated that people were simply using the technology it was providing to "share" their favorite songs. Napster's president said, "Napster . . . is a return to the original information-sharing approach of the Internet.

A Hypocritical Stance?

Nevertheless, when a punk-rock band began selling T-shirts displaying the "Napster" logo, the company immediately sent the band a cease-and-desist order. Napter rescinded the order when it received a flood of criticism for its alleged hypocrisy. Nevertheless, in early 2001 Napster also filed a trademark-infringement suit against a California merchandising company for selling caps and shirts depicting its logo.

Napster refuses to share technical information about its software code. The company also alters the code from time to time to prevent people from linking other software to its own. Furthermore, Napster blocks computers from other Web sites from accessing its database containing hundreds of thousands of songs.

Where to Draw the Line?

In court, Napster has contended that its actions were consistent with copyright laws. It has based this stance on a 1984

continued

their activities. (At the same time, however, Napster was itself very sensitive to violations of its own intellectual property; see *Management Online: "Do Unto Others . . ." at Napster.com?*)

Cracking Down on Alleged Copyright Violations—And Moving Toward Fee-Based Access of Digital Files

In spite of the claims of the Web-based music-file-swapping industry, MP3.com and Napster have confronted legal challenges to their activities. In September 2000, a federal court ruled that MP3.com would have to pay legal damages of $25,000 for each of the 5,000 to 10,000 compact disks that it copied into digital files for the use of visitors to its Web site. A typical CD contains twelve or thirteen songs, so this award amounted to an average of about $2,000 per song.

This damage award was significantly less than the damages of $45,000 per CD that Universal, one of the five music-recording companies that sued MP3.com

U.S. Supreme Court ruling concerning videocassette recorders. The Supreme Court ruled that a technology that might be used for piracy and other copyright violations cannot be banned as long as it also capable of "substantial noninfringing uses" that were legal. It is one thing, the company claimed, to offer a technology that can be used for copyright infringement, but it is another thing when someone actually engages in such infringement.

The company's legal argument has consistently been that, just as the introduction of videocassette recorders was not in itself a violation of copyright laws, its music-file-swapping technology has both legitimate and illegitimate uses and, therefore, cannot be banned. Copying the company's own software, however, is a consciously illegitimate act, the company claims, which would indisputably violate copyright laws.

So far courts have not agreed with Napster's arguments. In the spring of 2001, a federal judge required Napster to take steps to block access to unauthorized copies of recordings. In July 2001, a district court judge ruled that Napster could not enable file transfers until it could ensure 100 percent success in screening out "noticed works." The legal battle is not over yet, but so far the chances that Napster will emerge unscathed appear to be relatively small.

For Critical Analysis:
In your view, was Napster's argument reasonable, or was it simply self-serving?

under federal copyright laws, had requested. Nevertheless, the total damages awarded by the judge amounts to between $125 million and $250 million.

It is important to recognize that these damage awards were based in large part on **statutory penalties,** or dollar penalties prescribed by law. Although judges and juries can take into account economists' estimates of the true losses experienced by owners of violated copyrights, laws typically specify minimums, ranges, and limitations of damages that courts may award copyright holders.

After another federal court ruled that Napster had also violated copyright laws through its Web-based music-file-swapping business, both MP3.com and Napster initiated settlement talks with traditional music-recording companies. One result was that the two sides began to work out approaches to fee-based distribution of copyrighted works on the Internet. This may mean that the days of "free Web music" have neared an end, although there is some indication that the music-recording industry may permit some free sampling of songs as part of authorized marketing efforts.

Statutory Penalties
Pecuniary penalties authorized by laws, which may or may not reflect actual losses caused by intellectual property violations in the marketplace.

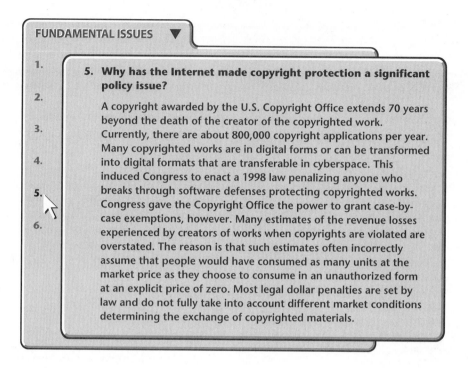

FUNDAMENTAL ISSUES ▼

1.

2.

3.

4.

5.

6.

5. Why has the Internet made copyright protection a significant policy issue?

A copyright awarded by the U.S. Copyright Office extends 70 years beyond the death of the creator of the copyrighted work. Currently, there are about 800,000 copyright applications per year. Many copyrighted works are in digital forms or can be transformed into digital formats that are transferable in cyberspace. This induced Congress to enact a 1998 law penalizing anyone who breaks through software defenses protecting copyrighted works. Congress gave the Copyright Office the power to grant case-by-case exemptions, however. Many estimates of the revenue losses experienced by creators of works when copyrights are violated are overstated. The reason is that such estimates often incorrectly assume that people would have consumed as many units at the market price as they choose to consume in an unauthorized form at an explicit price of zero. Most legal dollar penalties are set by law and do not fully take into account different market conditions determining the exchange of copyrighted materials.

TRADEMARKS AND THE VALUE OF A "PRODUCT IDENTITY"

Companies use trademarks—words, symbols, and logos—to distinguish their product brands from goods or services that rival firms produce. Consumers associate these trademarks with products, so companies regard their brands as valuable private property.

Brand Value and Trademarks

Naturally, a firm's product sales generate current profits and, as long as the firm is viable, future profits. A company's value in the marketplace, or its purchase value, depends largely on its current profitability and perceptions of its future profitability.

Table 7-2 gives the market values of the world's most valuable brands. These valuations are based on the market prices of publicly traded shares of stock in these companies.

Recall from Chapter 5 that brand names can convey information to consumers about product quality. Because brand names, symbols, and logos relate to consumers' perceptions of products, companies desire to protect their trademarks from misuse by registering them with the U.S. Patent and Trademark Office. Approval of trademark applications gives companies the right to seek legal damages if someone makes unauthorized use of a company's brand name, spreads false rumors about the company, or engages in other activities that can reduce the value of the company's brand.

Table 7-2: The Values of the Top Twenty Brands.

Brand	Brand Value in 2000 ($ billions)
Coca-Cola	69.0
Microsoft	65.1
IBM	52.8
General Electric	42.4
Nokia	35.0
Intel	34.7
Disney	32.6
Ford	30.1
McDonald's	25.3
AT&T	22.8
Marlboro	22.1
Mercedes-Benz	21.7
Citibank	19.0
Toyota	18.6
Hewlett-Packard	18.0
Cisco Systems	17.2
American Express	16.9
Gillette	15.3
Sony	15.0
Merrill Lynch	15.0

Source: Interbrand Annual Survey, 2001, http://www.interbrand.com.

Warding Off "Brand Crimes"

There are a number of ways that trademark abuse can occur online. Just as a company that makes blue jeans can deceive consumers into believing they are purchasing a "name" brand by attaching a patch displaying a logo that is very similar to that of the "name" brand of jeans, a Web seller can place a logo or other image on its site that similarly deceives an Internet shopper. In addition, a company might use another company's name, symbol, or logo on its own site in a way that questions the integrity of the competitor's brand. Or it might even engage in unauthorized **framing,** which includes a rival's Web site within its own Web site.

Framing
Including a company's Web site within a Web site operated by another individual or company.

Table 7-3: Examples of Online Disinformation Regarding Company Brands.

Tommy Hilfiger clothing	In 1997, a rumor began spreading via Internet chat rooms and e-mail messages that this clothing designer and manufacturer had stated on the *Oprah Winfrey Show* that his clothing lines were not intended for wear by African Americans, inducing Winfrey to cut a commercial, change her clothes, and switch to a different subject for the show. Even though Hilfiger and Winfrey have repeatedly denied that Hilfiger has ever even appeared on the show, some groups have threatened to organize boycotts against Hilfiger products.
Mrs. Fields Cookies	Shortly after a jury declared former football star O.J. Simpson not guilty of murder in the famous 1995 trial, an anti-Simpson Web site targeted Mrs. Fields for a consumer boycott, claiming that the company had supplied free cookies for a post-verdict "victory party" at Simpson's home. The TV show *Hard Copy* reported the Web site's claims. Although the Web site and *Hard Copy* retracted their statements when they were proven false, Mrs. Fields suffered a measurable sales decline for several months afterward.
McDonald's	In response to a McDonald's libel suit against Greenpeace when it handed out leaflets entitled "What's Wrong with McDonalds," in 1996 a British couple set up a Web site called "McSpotlight." This site, which included the McDonald's logo, provided unfavorable news stories about the company, access to file downloads of the text of the Greenpeace leaflets, and shopping pages for anti-McDonald's T-shirts.
Procter & Gamble	In 2000, a widespread Internet chat rumor encouraged people not to purchase a Procter & Gamble's odor-controlling spray with the brand name "Febreeze." According to the rumor, which pet organizations verified to be entirely false, the spray was hazardous to dogs, cats, and birds. Nevertheless, Procter & Gamble received thousands of phone calls and e-mail messages about the rumor.

Source: Beth Snyder Bulik, "The Brand Police," *Business 2.0* (November 28, 2000), pp. 145–255, © 2000 Time, Inc. All rights reserved. Used with permission.

Meta Tag

An HTML software code that provides an Internet search engine with information that will link a Web site to a Web search request.

Companies have been known to include a company's name or product brand name in **meta tags,** which are HTML software codes that give an Internet search engine information required to link a Web site in response to a search request initiated by a Web surfer. A company might place a competing firm's brand name in a meta tag so that when a Web surfer enters that rival firm's brand name into a search engine, the search engine will display that company's Web site as well as the Web site of the rival. In most cases, unauthorized use of company or product names in meta tags is an online trademark violation.

Sometimes people spread false information about a company or its product that can alter consumer perceptions and affect the value of a brand. Disseminating information that a company supports controversial social causes might induce large numbers of consumers to stop purchasing the company's product. This would cause the demand for the firm's product to decline, resulting in lower revenues and profits. Table 7-3 details examples of online disinformation that caused problems for several brands in recent years.

A company can file libel suits to halt the spread of false information about its product. Convincing a court to issue a cease-and-desist order or even order payment of damages, however, can entail incurring considerable legal expenses. For this reason, many companies have begun establishing procedures for monitoring and responding to false Internet claims about their brands.

Some firms have made monitoring the Web for trademark violations and libelous statements part of the job tasks of some of their employees. A few have even established positions dedicated solely to this task. Others hire firms that specialize in this task. Indeed, there is now an e-commerce marketplace in brand-protection services. Companies such as Cyveillance, eWatch, GenuOne, and NetCurrents provide Web-monitoring services to detect violations and to notify companies when they occur. Then it is up to companies to determine if they should file claims of trademark infringement or libel.

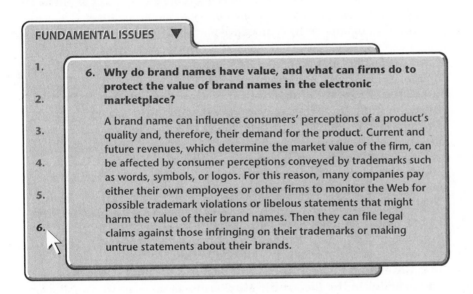

FUNDAMENTAL ISSUES ▼

1.
2.
3.
4.
5.
6.

6. Why do brand names have value, and what can firms do to protect the value of brand names in the electronic marketplace?

A brand name can influence consumers' perceptions of a product's quality and, therefore, their demand for the product. Current and future revenues, which determine the market value of the firm, can be affected by consumer perceptions conveyed by trademarks such as words, symbols, or logos. For this reason, many companies pay either their own employees or other firms to monitor the Web for possible trademark violations or libelous statements that might harm the value of their brand names. Then they can file legal claims against those infringing on their trademarks or making untrue statements about their brands.

Chapter Summary

1) **The Difference between an Invention and an Innovation, and Alternative Explanations for Why Firms Engage in Innovation:** An invention is the creation of a new process, business approach, or product. Innovation is the transformation of an invention into something that enhances efficiency of production or management or that represents a new product that satisfies consumers' tastes and preferences. A process innovation

is a novel way to produce existing goods or services or to organize a business's operations. A product innovation is the development, provision, marketing, and distribution of a new good or service. The technology-push hypothesis of innovation indicates that the key inducement to innovation is a firm's research staff, while the demand-pull hypothesis emphasizes the role of consumer preferences for new and less expensive products.

2) **How Firm Size and Market Structure May Affect the Pace of Innovation:** The technology-push hypothesis for innovation predicts that larger firms are more likely to have bigger research staffs that can initiate innovative activities by specializing and drawing on a larger body of scientific developments. The demand-pull hypothesis predicts that bigger research staffs at larger firms can innovate more rapidly in response to evolving customer desires for higher-quality, lower-priced products. A crucial incentive for invention and innovation to occur is for creators of new processes or products to reap rewards from their efforts in the form of economic profits. Consequently, an imperfectly competitive market structure may be required for new processes and products to emerge. Society tends to benefit from greater competition, however, after these processes and products become more standard features of the marketplace.

3) **Intellectual Property Rights, and How Governments Try to Protect Them:** Governments attempt to encourage the firms to engage in invention and innovation by establishing intellectual property rights, which are legal rules assigning ownership to creative ideas. Governments award copyrights to creators of works such as articles, stories and novels, computer programs, audio recordings, and movies, giving those individuals or firms exclusive privileges to reproduce, distribute, perform, or display such works. They provide a means for firms to register words or symbols, known as trademarks, that firms use to distinguish their goods or services from those of other firms. Governments also grant patents that give an inventor the exclusive legal right to make, use, and sell an invention for a specified number of years.

4) **Rules Governing Patents, and Why Business Method Patents Are Controversial in the Electronic Marketplace:** Someone who applies for a patent must provide a publicly available description of a novel design or of a new or significantly improved product, process, or substance. If the application is approved, the individual or firm owning the patent can claim a portion of the revenues earned by anyone who uses the patented design, product, process, or substance. In the past, eligibility for a process patent required the process to transform real objects, but since 1998 the U.S. Patent and Trademark Office has granted business method patents. These cover processes that combine computer software with novel business models, typically in e-commerce applications. Critics of business method patents contend that patent examiners do not have sufficient business background to award such patents.

5) **Why the Internet Has Made Copyright Protection a Significant Policy Issue:** The U.S. Copyright Office grants about 800,000 copyrights per year that extend up to 70 years past the death of the creator of the

copyrighted work. Because many copyrighted works are in digital formats or can be converted to digital forms, in 1998 Congress enacted a law specifying penalties for anyone who breaks through encryption barriers to copyrighted works, unless the Copyright Office grants an exemption. A number of studies overestimate the revenue losses caused by copyright infringements, because they often are based on the faulty assumption that people would have consumed as many units at the market price as they consume in an unauthorized form at an explicit price of zero. Laws establish most dollar penalties for copyright infringement. Although they allow for some judicial flexibility, copyright laws do not fully take into account different market conditions affecting the terms of exchange of copyrighted materials.

6) **Why Brand Names Have Value, and What Firms Can Do to Protect the Value of Brand Names in the Electronic Marketplace:** Because a brand name affects consumers' perceptions of product quality, it influences the demand for a firm's product, and hence the firm's current and future revenues. Anticipated revenues into the future determine the market value of the firm, so trademarks such as words, symbols, or logos are valuable to the firm. This is why a number of companies pay either their own employees or other firms to monitor the Web for possible trademark violations or false statements that might adversely affect consumers' brand perceptions. Firms can then ask courts to halt such activities and, in some cases, award legal damage payments from the perpetrators.

Questions and Problems

1) Arthur C. Clarke, the science and science fiction author, first proposed the use of satellites before World War II, and the development of satellites for wireless communications began in the 1960s. Today satellites are used to beam telephone calls, pager messages, television signals, Internet transmissions, and other communications. In your view, does this innovation best fit the technology-push hypothesis or the demand-pull hypothesis?

2) The basic telephone technology that we use today—albeit now structured around computer technology—has been available for more than a century. Recently, however, "Internet telephony" emerged on the scene. Voice transmissions of digital data can be transmitted over the Internet as data packets just like e-mail messages. So far, the quality of Internet voice transmissions has been relatively low. Nevertheless, many companies continue in their efforts to market Internet telephony services. In your view, does this innovation best fit the technology-push hypothesis or the demand-pull hypothesis?

3) The business world typically regards "infant industries" as those that are new to the scene and comprised of two or three trail-blazing firms with rapidly

soaring profitability. "Mature industries," by way of contrast, usually have many firms offering numerous competing brands, most of which experience relatively stable profitability. How does this perspective appear to mesh with Schumpeter's view of the relationship between market structure and innovation?

4) If a government chose to limit itself to issuing only patents, copyrights, or trademarks in the electronic marketplace, which form of intellectual-property-right protection do you believe it should choose? Support your position.

5) For years, people have used videocassette recorders to make copies of programs and movies channeled through their television sets via cable, satellite, or wireless transmissions. A federal judge recently ruled, however, that a fledgling company could not market software it developed that would have allowed people to make copies of digital DVD files of programs and movies that they could play on their personal computers. In your view, should digital DVD files deserve more legal protection than videotape? Explain your reasoning.

6) Even though Amazon has vigorously defended its one-click shopping patent, its chief executive officer, Jeff Bezos, has argued that business method patents should last only 3 to 5 years. Can you think of any arguments for why it might be socially desirable for business method patents to last fewer years than other types of patents? Do you find these arguments compelling, or do you feel that a full 20 years is reasonable for a business method patent? Support your position.

7) Option contracts, which permit people to buy or sell a good, service, or financial asset whenever its price falls within a certain specified range, have been around for centuries. Nevertheless, Jay Walker of Walker Digital holds a business method patent on how to use option contracts on the Internet. In your view, is this a sufficiently innovative idea to merit a patent? Why or why not?

8) A couple of years ago, Motorola, Inc. charged several individuals with using the C2C auction site eBay.com as a center for marketing illegally copied software used with IBM-compatible computers to program two-way radios. In your view, who should be responsible for policing the trading of intellectual property rights at online auction sites: the companies who own those rights, the auction sites, or the government? Explain your reasoning.

9) Recently Ticketmaster.com filed a copyright-infringement suit against Tickets.com, which had established hyperlinks to Ticketmaster's site so that consumers could make direct price comparisons. In your view, did Ticketmaster have a legitimate complaint when it argued that the Tickets.com was using the hyperlinks to save itself from having to develop its own Web content, thereby infringing on Ticketmaster's intellectual property rights? Or should the potential benefits for consumers outweigh this intellectual-property-rights concern? Support your position.

10) Although Ford's Model T automobile went out of production in 1927, the company has the Model T trademark registered for everything from air

fresheners to postcards. Ford recently filed a trademark-infringement suit against the online automotive marketplace Model E Corporation over what Ford regarded as a violation of the Model T trademark. Where do you think courts should draw the line in cases such as this one? Is similarity of trademarks sufficient to constitute infringement, or should exact duplication be the standard? Explain your reasoning.

Online Application

Internet URL: http://www.uspto.gov/web/menu/busmethp/index.html

Title: **USPTO White Paper: "Automated Financial or Management Data Processing Methods (Business Methods)**

Navigation: Go directly to the above URL; or start at the home page of the U.S. Patent and Trademark Office (http://www.uspto.gov), and then click on "Patents." Under the "Resources" heading, click on "Business method-related patent issues." Then click on "Business Methods White Paper" (already highlighted).

Application: Perform the following operations, and answer the following questions.

1) According to this white paper, are business method patents really all that new?
2) Who are the "customers" of the USPTO?

For Group Study and Analysis: After students have read the USPTO white paper, have them also read the summary and analysis by Steve Shumaker, located at http://www.fr.com/publis/whitepaper.html. Then divide the class into two groups. Assign each group to take a side in a debate over the question: "Should the USPTO budget be 'upsized' to allow it to do a better job with business method patents, or should business method patents be eliminated and the USPTO's powers remain more limited?"

Selected References and Further Readings

Carlton, Dennis, and Jeffrey Perloff. *Modern Industrial Organization.* 3d ed. Reading, MA: Addison-Wesley, 2000.

Hunt, Robert. "Patent Reform: A Mixed Blessing for the U.S. Economy?" Federal Reserve Bank of Philadelphia *Business Review* (November/December 1999), 15–29.

Kamien, Morton, and Nancy Schwartz. *Market Structure and Innovation.* Cambridge, U.K.: Cambridge University Press, 1982.

MacKie-Mason, Jeffrey, and Juan Riveros. "Economics and Electronic Access to Scholarly Information." In *Internet Publishing and Beyond,* ed. Brian Kahin and Hal Varian. Cambridge, MA: MIT Press, 2000, pp. 203–230.

Maskus, Keith. *Intellectual Property Rights in the Global Economy.* Washington, D.C.: Institute for International Economics, August 2000.

Pepall, Lynne, Daniel Richards, and George Norman. *Industrial Organization: Contemporary Theory and Practice.* Cincinnati: South-Western, 1999.

Shepherd, William. *The Economics of Industrial Organization.* 4th ed. Prospect Hills, IL: Waveland Press, 1997.

Shy, Oz. "The Economics of Copy Protection in Software and Other Media." In *Internet Publishing and Beyond,* ed. Brian Kahin and Hal Varian. Cambridge, MA: MIT Press, 2000, pp. 97–113.

Tucker, Robert. "Information Superhighway Robbery: The Tortious Misuse of Links, Frames, Metatags, and Domain Names," *Virginia Journal of Law and Technology* 8 (Fall 1999), pp. 1522–1687.(http://www.vjolt.net/vol4/v4i2a8-tucker.html).

Internet Finance, Online Banking, and E-Money

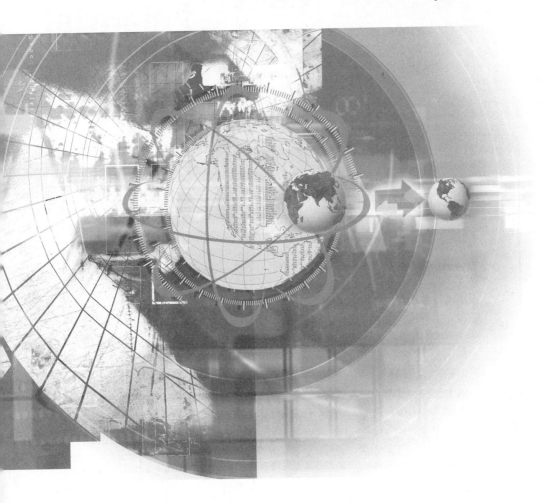

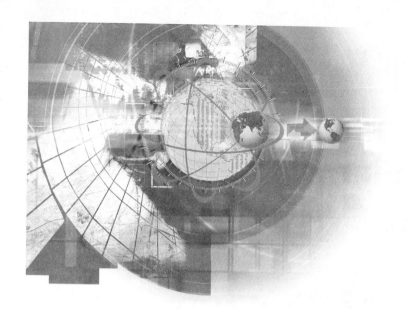

Chapter 8

Online Financial Markets

FUNDAMENTAL ISSUES ▼

1. How was financial trading becoming more automated before the Internet, and how has the Internet contributed to automated trading? ▶

2. What factors have contributed to the growth of online stock trading, and what are the pros and cons of trading stocks online? ▶

3. Why did online bond trading initially progress more slowly than Internet stock trading, and what is the status of online bond trading? ▶

4. What are the prospects for the trading of international currencies and derivative securities to shift to the Internet? ▶

5. What issues does online trading pose for regulators of financial markets? ▶

<E-Commerce Today>

Trading Floors versus Trading Screens

Since 1995, the value of "seats," or memberships, permitting an individual or firm to execute trades in the New York Stock Exchange, the Chicago Board of Trade, and the Chicago Mercantile Exchange have fallen 30 to 60 percent. In August 1999, a seat on the New York Stock Exchange sold for $2.65 million. Less than a year later, a seat sold for only $1.7 million—barely enough at the time to purchase a small two-bedroom apartment on New York's Park Avenue.

The number of seats in each exchange has not changed, so the market price of a seat has not been pushed down by a big boost in supply. It is a fall in the demand for seats on exchanges that is responsible. There are fewer people purchasing seats on traditional exchanges, and those who have an interest to own a seat desire to pay less compared with years past.

What happened is that there are online substitutes for traditional financial exchanges. Before the Internet appeared, many traders were already switching to automated trading. Use of transactions on the Internet has hastened the exodus to electronic trading. For instance, when a Paris financial futures exchange, MATIF (Marché à Terme International de France) introduced electronic trading, it retained traditional floor trading so the market could eventually decide which approach would predominate. Within two weeks almost everyone was executing electronic trades. Six weeks later, MATIF ended floor trading entirely.

Many stock trades are still initiated on traditional trading floors. Most people still use the services of stockbrokers based in bricks-and-mortar offices. Nevertheless, individuals and firms participating in *financial markets*—markets that facilitate the lending of funds from saving to those who wish to use those funds to finance various undertakings—have long led the way toward greater use of electronic mechanisms for conducting exchanges. In recent years they have also been at the forefront of developing an online marketplace for financial assets.

Automated Financial Markets

What do "CORES" and "CATS" have in common? The answer is that like the French Matif system, these are automated systems for trading **securities**—legal claims that those who lend savings have on the future earnings of borrowers who apply those funds to engage in business operations. CORES, or the Computer-Assisted

Security
A financial claim requiring a borrower to make future payments to those who have provided funds used by the borrower to finance its activities.

How has MATIF adjusted to the increasing integration of European financial markets? To learn the answer to this question, visit MATIF at http://www.matif.fr.

Order Routing and Execution System, is a completely automated system based in Tokyo that links buyers and sellers of government securities, corporate bonds, and equity shares. CATS, the Toronto-based Computer-Assisted Trading System, performs the same basic functions. These trading systems, plus others in such locales as Denmark, Singapore, Sweden, the United Kingdom, and the United States, all permit traders in financial markets to place orders for purchases and sales of securities via computers.

MECHANICS OF AUTOMATED FINANCIAL TRADING

Each automated trading system has unique characteristics. In general, however, traders linked via computer connections use system-specific software programs to access information on current market quotes of securities. The software displays on the trader's computer screen the best bid and offer with the amounts involved, the most recent sale price and quantity traded, and related spot market prices. A trader then may use the computer's keyboard to interact with the system to attempt to make trades via appropriate commands.

Making an Automated Trade

Suppose that a trader observes a bid for a share of stock that she would like to accept. She places a sell order into the system. The system then automatically launches a verification procedure.

First, the system verifies that earlier offers to sell have not been received. Then it checks to see that this sell order is at a price equal to or less than outstanding buy orders. Finally, it verifies that the quantities of buy and sell offers are compatible.

If these conditions are met, the system automatically places orders "in line," based on the times they arrived. Finally, the system transmits information on the trade it arranges to the clearinghouses of individual exchanges, which execute the trade.

Hand in Hand: Automation and Globalization of Financial Trading

Automated trading has made possible around-the-clock securities trading. When financial markets open in Tokyo, Hong Kong, Australia, and Singapore, it is evening of the previous day in New York and Chicago. A trader in Tokyo may see an acceptable asking price for a security in New York and initiate a transaction to purchase the security. If the security is a U.S. Treasury security, ownership is transferred and payment is settled the next business day in the United States. A transaction arranged, for instance, on Wednesday in Tokyo—Tuesday night in New York—would settle on Thursday in New York, about a day and a half later.

Because U.S. Treasury securities are held in virtual form as electronic "book entries" in accounts at Federal Reserve banks, one of these institutions processes the ownership transfer and payment. A Federal Reserve bank does this by transferring balances from the account of the Tokyo dealer's bank to the account of the seller's bank, presumably in New York.

AUTOMATION IN FINANCE IS NOTHING NEW

Stocks, also known as corporate equities, are shares of ownership in corporations. Corporate equity shares are traded in stock exchanges. Members of stock exchanges function both as *brokers* and as *dealers*. As **brokers,** these stock exchange members earn fees by trading on behalf of others. As **dealers,** they seek to earn profits from trading on their own accounts.

Stock Exchanges and Electronic Trading

Traditionally, **stock exchanges** have been organized as physical locations that function as marketplaces for stocks. One of these, the New York Stock Exchange, began operating in 1792. The New York Stock Exchange (NYSE) lists the shares of more than 3,000 companies and handles nearly half of U.S. stock trades. There are 1,366 membership positions in the NYSE, called *seats* in the Exchange. Securities firms own more than 500 seats, and about a third of these firms are so-called *specialists* that are responsible for laying out and honoring basic ground rules for orderly trading activity in the Exchange. Another traditionally important stock exchange, the New York-based American Stock Exchange, handles the shares of more than 700 companies. There also are regional stock exchanges in such cities as Chicago, San Francisco, and Boston.

Since the early 1970s, however, a number of corporations have chosen not to be listed on the organized exchanges. Shares in these corporations are **over-the-counter (OTC) stocks** traded on electronic networks that link traders around the world.

In the United States, most OTC stocks are traded on the National Association of Securities Dealers Automated Quotation (Nasdaq) system. Nasdaq began operations in February 1971 as a tiny network of 100 or so securities firms with $25 million worth of interconnected "desktop devices" to trade about 2,800 over-the-counter stocks. At the time, trading in the financial world was done largely through phone calls, with runners on foot even distributing some information on stock prices. Indeed, the screens displaying the over-the-counter stock prices on Nasdaq's "desktop devices" were not even known as computer screens, because the devices did not actually compute anything. The system simply displayed stock quotes and the phone number of the broker to call to trade. Today, Nasdaq links about 500 dealers via true computers, and the market is home to nearly 5,500 stocks, including those of such companies such as Microsoft, Intel and Cisco. In March 1998, Nasdaq passed the New York Stock Exchange to become the largest U.S. stock exchange.

A Short Step to the Internet

About a third of the average daily transaction volume on Nasdaq is processed on **electronic communications networks (ECNs).** These Internet-based auction networks link buyers and sellers of stocks around the world. Moving stock trading to the Internet offers several advantages for investors. One is the ability to trade more hours each day. The two largest ECNs, Instinet and Island, are open 24 hours per day.

Broker
A financial institution that specializes in matching buyers and sellers of securities in secondary markets.

Dealer
A financial institution that specializes in selling securities from its own portfolio and earning profits from this activity.

Stock Exchanges
Organized marketplaces for corporate equities and bonds.

Over-the-Counter (OTC) Stocks
Equity shares offered by companies that do not meet listing requirements for major stock exchanges but instead are traded in decentralized markets.

Electronic Communications Networks (ECNs)
Internet-based networks that use computer software to match buyers and sellers of shares of stock.

What are the latest information-technology innovations at Nasdaq? To find out, visit the National Association of Securities Dealers at http://www.nasd.com.

ECNs also offer investors the ability to consider stocks from multiple exchanges simultaneously. Instinet, for instance, lists stocks from sixteen different exchanges. Island lists stocks from both Nasdaq and the New York Stock Exchange.

Another advantage for investors using ECNs is fewer problems with asymmetric information (see Chapter 5). Although individual investors must have an account with a broker–dealer subscriber before their orders can be routed to an ECN for execution, anyone can access an ECN system using personal computers, laptop computers, or any other Internet-ready devices. Any interested party can look up buy and sell orders for any Nasdaq stocks at ECN Web sites. By way of contrast, NYSE specialists have exclusive access to information concerning all buy and sell orders that come to the trading floor for their stocks. Thus, ECNs arguably offer investors more transparency than traditional stock exchanges.

ECNs specialize in executing trades on behalf of so-called institutional investors, such as equity funds and pension funds. They do not offer their services directly to private individuals. A big advantage of an ECN for an institutional investor is that trades executed on an ECN are anonymous. ECN transaction records list only the price and amount traded, not the trader's identity. This protects institutional investors from a practice called front running, in which traders somehow learn that an institutional investor plans to buy or sell stock and trades in advance in an effort to profit from small price changes that might result from the institutional investor's later transaction.

ECNs typically charge brokers fees ranging from between $1 per trade to $1 per hundred shares traded, which is significantly below the fees charged by the traditional order execution systems employed by broker-dealers. This is why more than 30 percent of all stock trades now take place on ECNs, even though they have only been in existence since 1992.

FUNDAMENTAL ISSUES ▼

1.
2.
3.
4.
5.

1. How was financial trading becoming more automated before the Internet, and how has the Internet contributed to automated trading?

Before development of the Internet, investors had already found ways to buy and sell securities using computer connections with system-specific software programs. Initially, the sale of over-the-counter stocks on the Nasdaq system did not involve computers but simply used desktop devices that displayed stock quotes and the phone number of the broker to call to make a trade. Using the Internet, however, allows investors to trade more hours each day in more than one market simultaneously. Today, about a third of Nasdaq trades take place on Internet-based auction networks linking buyers and sellers of stocks, which are known as electronic communications networks (ECNs).

MANAGEMENT *Online*

POLICY MAKING   GLOBALIZATION   **MANAGEMENT**

At Toyota's Web Site, Keep Track of Your Car's Tune-Ups—and Your Stock Portfolio

Toyota's Web site Gazoo.com has more about a half million subscribers and more than a million visitors each month (http://gazoo.com/eng will take you to the English version). Toyota has promoted Gazoo as a comprehensive e-commerce shopping mall where consumers can purchase goods and services associated with the company. Individuals who subscribe to the site can search for prices and alternative configurations of Toyota's automobiles. They can also obtain information about car tune-ups and repairs.

When Toyota found that about one in seven of Gazoo's new subscribers typically buy cars within six months, the com-

pany decided to expand the Web site. The company now offers a "Gazoo media mall." At that site, consumers can shop for books, music CDs, and DVD videos.

Toyota has also added a "Gazoo financial mall" to the Web site, where consumers can buy auto insurance and arrange financing for new vehicle purchases. Gazoo Financial Mall also encourages visitors to open a brokerage account and buy and sell shares of stock. Thus, Toyota has joined the flood of firms rushing into the online stock brokerage business.

For Critical Analysis:

Why might it be easier for a company to sell very different products, such as automobiles and stock brokerage services, online as compared within a traditional bricks-and-mortar environment?

 ## It's a Natural—Internet Stock Trading

Increasingly, however, the Internet is linking individual investors directly to brokers and transforming the functioning of stock markets. This development began in the mid-1990s with the establishment of E*Trade.com, Ameritrade.com, and Schwab.com These companies offered something never before available: the capability to buy shares of stock online. (Today many companies compete to offer online stock-trading services; see *Management Online: At Toyota's Web Site, Keep Track of Your Car's Tune-Ups—and Your Stock Portfolio*.)

TRADING IN PRIMARY VERSUS SECONDARY MARKETS

A **primary market** is a financial market in which a newly issued security is purchased and sold. For instance, a newly formed business that wishes to sell shares of stock offers these shares for sale in the primary market. The first attempt by a

Primary Market
A market for the exchange of newly issued securities.

business to issue ownership shares to the public in the primary market is called an *initial public offering (IPO)*. Most securities sold in primary markets have maturities ranging from several months to many years. Stock shares in firms have no set maturities, because firms in principle could last "forever," as long as they are going concerns.

At some point beyond the initial purchase of ownership shares, the original purchaser may not wish to hold them any longer. The original owner may then sell the shares in a **secondary market.** This is simply a market for securities that were issued at some point in the past. Secondary markets contribute to the efficient functioning of primary markets. The ability to buy or sell previously issued securities gives these securities more **liquidity.** That is, those who hold securities that they can readily sell in a secondary market know that it will be relatively easy to convert the security into cash at short notice and at low risk of loss of nominal value. Persons contemplating purchasing shares of ownership in a fledgling company are more likely to buy shares if they know there is a readily available market in which they can sell them. (Most online stock trading takes place in the secondary market, but Internet IPOs are becoming more commonplace; see *Management Online: Funding a Start-Up Company on the Internet*.)

Secondary Market
A market for the exchange of previously issued securities.

Liquidity
The ease with which a person can sell or redeem an asset for a known amount of cash at short notice and at low risk of loss of nominal value.

BENEFITS OF ONLINE TRADING

Internet stock trading sites offer low brokerage fees to those trading in the secondary market. To buy 100 shares of stock in IBM from a traditional brokerage firm entails fees in the neighborhood of $100. By way of contrast, online brokers typically charge about $15 to make the same transaction. The result is predictable: Online securities trading has taken off; in 2001, there were more than 17 million online trading accounts, totaling more than $1 trillion. Figure 8-1 on page 250 displays the distribution of assets held in online brokerage accounts. Many observers expect that by 2003 the number of online stock-trading accounts will increase to more than 20 million, with at least $1.5 trillion in online trading via those accounts.

These estimates could prove to be low. They take into account only "hardwired" trading via desktop and laptop computers, and they do not include online trading by customers of several traditional brokerage firms, such as Merrill Lynch, that now allow online trading. Furthermore, some firms have recently introduced online securities trading systems that use cellular telephones, two-way pagers, and hand-held devices connected to wireless modems. Today, there are more than 200 million mobile telephone subscribers worldwide, and that figure is expected to exceed 500 million by 2003. Thus, there is significant potential for even more growth in online securities trading.

Naturally, the greatest appeal of online trading for many individuals is the low price of a trade, which usually is 50 percent to 90 percent less than the price charged by a full-service stock brokerage. Online trading also helps make the stock markets more efficient by broadening market access. When people face high

MANAGEMENT *Online*

Funding a Start-Up Company on the Internet

Getting a business off the ground requires more than hard work—it requires raising hard cash. Many small businesses have trouble raising seed money to get started. But those that succeed can seek out venture capital firms for additional financing. Eventually, new firms can "go public" by floating a stock issue in an IPO.

Firms traditionally have paid investment banks, which are financial firms specializing in marketing ownership shares issued by new businesses, to conduct IPOs on their behalf. Today, however, a business can go public on the Internet by selling initial shares of stock on the Web. In 1995, Spring Street Brewing Company made history as the first company to conduct an initial public offering over the Internet. It made history again in March 1996 when the Securities and Exchange Commission (SEC) permitted Spring Street to trade its

shares via its Web site without registering as a broker–dealer. The SEC only required Spring Street to use an independent agent, such as a bank or escrow agent, to process the funds it raised.

The SEC estimates that going public via the traditional, non-Internet route takes about 900 hours of work. Most of this time is devoted to preparing a prospectus prior to the sale of stock. Companies also hire specialized attorneys and use an underwriter, who normally charges a fee equal to about 10 percent of the value of the IPO. The cyber-based alternative is to buy a computer program that automates the process of compiling the offer documents. By posting these documents on a Web site, a company can sell shares directly to investors over the Internet.

For Critical Analysis:

Does anyone stand to lose if Internet IPOs become commonplace events?

---

trading costs, some choose not to buy stocks or bonds they believe have upside potential, while other refrain from selling stocks or bonds they feel are headed down in value. With lower online trading costs, both types of investors will choose to trade, so that the market price more fully reflects general perceptions of the likely future fortunes of companies whose shares trade in the stock market.

Nevertheless, the social benefits of online trading may not be as large as the difference between the conventional broker's fee and the fee charged by online brokers. For one thing, online traders typically devote more of their own time and computer resources to engage in Internet stock purchases and sales. Suppose, for example, that for a trade of 2,000 shares of stock the fee charged by a traditional stockbroker is $500, while the online fee is $100. The $400 difference is only the pecuniary cost saving for the individual initiating the trade. If the individual incurs an opportunity cost of $50 by devoting his time to research and uses his computer to complete the online trade, then the net resource saving on the trade is actually $50 less, or $350. Of course, when added up over millions of trades that

Figure 8-1:
Distribution of Assets
at Online Brokerages.

Schwab and Fidelity are the major providers of online brokerage services, although TWE Online, E*Trade, and Ameritrade are also important online brokerage firms.

Source: Securities and Exchange Commission.

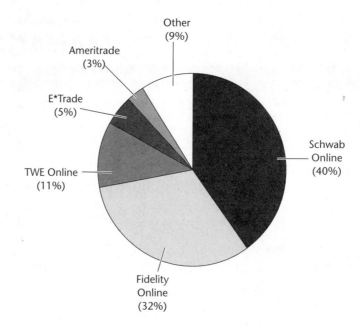

online traders make each day, the aggregate resource savings are still likely to be significant.

Net social gains will arise even if lower trading costs induce individuals to engage in more trades than they would otherwise, thereby increasing total trading volumes and fees paid to stockbrokers. If the number of trades increases sufficiently and the demand for stock trading services is elastic, then the net effect of the lower effective fee per trade will be higher spending on stock trading. Nevertheless, individuals will not trade a given volume of shares of stock unless they benefit. The net cost of engaging in online trading simply enhances the net benefits that traders receive.

HOW TRADING SPEED MATTERS

Online trading does not just reduce the net expense of making a trade. It is faster, too. Anyone can reach Internet-based brokerage accounts from a computer with a secure Web browser. Today, literally at one's fingertips are hundreds of sites offering investment research sources and trading capabilities—all of which help make the Web a logical fit with the fast-paced, high-tech financial world of Wall Street.

To connect to an online-trading site, an Internet trader punches in an ID and account password. Typically, the trader then has access to a package of services that might otherwise be quite costly if purchased separately. These include portfolio-tracking software and databases containing information about the market capitalization and earnings growth of listed companies. After conducting market research, an Internet trader can scan her portfolio of holdings, search for key information on companies whose stock she owns, and send an order to buy or sell more stock. Moreover, she can do all this in a few minutes.

Most online brokers now offer to sell information about and evaluations of stocks, and some now offer this service as part of an overall online trading "package." This makes it possible for online traders to devote less time to stock research, as compared with years past. The result is a reduction in the opportunity cost that traders incur when they buy or sell stocks online, which further raises the potential net social saving from Internet stock trading.

THE CHALLENGE OF EXECUTING ONLINE TRADES

Internet trading also benefits the brokerage firms that offer it to their customers. Internet-based brokerage firms and traditional stockbrokers that have added Web-based services, can get by sending fewer printed marketing materials to clients, employing smaller customer-service staffs, and establishing fewer physical branches.

Adjusting to the electronic marketplace has not always been a smooth process for online brokers, however. For instance, on July 16, 1996, just a few months after online trading experienced its first burst of growth, U.S. stock prices suddenly dropped. Stock prices then recovered somewhat, while thousands of people followed the events online. For many brand-new Internet brokers, that day turned out to be a supreme test of the capacities of their systems.

Some brokerage firms almost failed the test, however. People across the nation reacted to the sudden fluctuation in stock prices by turning on their home computers to conduct a speedy online reshuffling of their portfolios. Many discovered they were frozen out of their Internet trading accounts. One New Jersey trader indicated that he found himself "stuck in Never-Never Land" for two hours on that day. He was unable to log onto his account, check his stock-account status, obtain stock-price quotes, or even check the values of market indexes such as the Dow Jones Industrial Average. He was finally able to get connected later in the day, but even then the system reported incorrect stock prices. Ultimately, his online broker sent him a negotiated payment to try to compensate for its inability to handle the unexpectedly large volume of Internet traffic it experienced that day.

Nowadays, Internet brokers are much better equipped to handle huge trading volumes. Nevertheless, the July 1996 experience showed that Internet traders are unable to rule out the possibility of a new kind of stock-market crash: the crash of an online system along with the market itself. When Internet traders crowd online at once, computer systems can fail to handle the overflow. As a result, active traders who like the minute-to-minute control offered by online trading actually might find themselves completely frozen out of the market.

DOES DAY TRADING PAY?

The average customer of a traditional stockbroker makes just over four transactions in a typical year, which works out to about 0.01 trades per day. As Figure 8-2 on page 252 shows, at firms that offer online brokerage services, the average

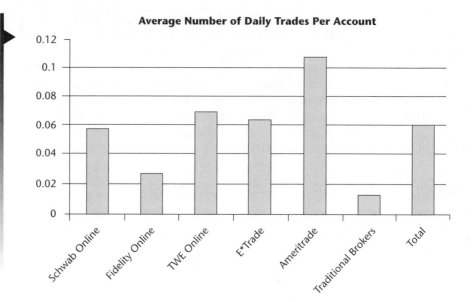

Figure 8-2:
Average Number of Daily Trades Per Account at Online Brokerages.

The average investor instructs a traditional brokerage firm to make about four trades per year, or about 0.01 trade per day. Average daily trades at online brokers typically are many times greater.

Source: Securities and Exchange Commission.

customer makes several times more trades per day. The annual trading volumes for the average customer of an Internet stockbroker exceed fifteen per year. At some online brokerages, the average customer makes more than twenty-five trades per year.

Day Trader
A person who conducts many securities transactions each day, with the goal of earning a living from trading profits.

Some Internet traders, known as **day traders,** conduct numerous securities trades each day with a primary goal of earning a living through the profits derived from their activities. Many day traders buy and sell securities from their homes, but a number also engage in their trading activities at so-called *day-trading firms,* which offer day traders access to services such as real-time data feeds and up-to-the-minute news links. Fees range from $50 per month to in excess of $600 per month. Day-trading firms also charge day traders commissions ranging from $15 to $25 per trade. Traders who use such services must take these costs into account when calculating their profits. Figure 8-3 shows the trading revenues day traders at such firms must earn each month to break even under alternative fee structures. For instance, if a day trader who pays a day-trading firm just $50 a month and a commission of $14.95 per trade engages in fifty trades per day, he must earn net revenues of $15,000 on his trades just to cover his explicit costs.

Unfortunately for some day traders, as well as for others who trade frequently online, researchers Terrance Odean and Brad Barber of the University of California at Davis have found evidence that people who engage in more stock purchases and sales tend to earn lower overall returns on their portfolios. Odean and Barber studied the trading behavior and earnings of more than 1,600 investors who switched from phone-based trading through brokers to online trading be-

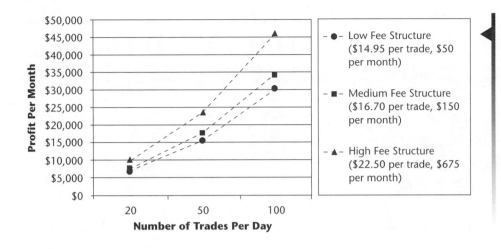

Figure 8-3:
Monthly Revenues that Day Traders Using Services of Day Trading Firms Must Earn to Break Even.

This chart plots the monthly trading revenues that a day trader must earn based on alternative fees and daily trading volumes.

Source: Securities and Exchange Commission.

tween 1992 and 1995. They found that the average returns on the stock portfolios of these individuals declined from about 2 percent above the market average to about 3 percent below the market average. Odean and Barber blamed this on more active and speculative purchases and sales of stocks when people started trading online. That is, some who trade online may have a tendency to act impulsively, resulting in more trading, hasty decision-making, and lower earnings. (Evidence from pension funds that allow people to reshuffle their stock portfolios online indicate that Internet access tends to lead to considerably more stock trading; see on the next page *Management Online: Phone Calls versus Mouse Clicks—The Effects of Online Access to Pension Funds.*)

The spontaneity of Internet trading could make some people worse off. Many of us know reasonable people who sometimes act as impulsive consumers, wasting hard-earned income on goods or services they realize later they did not really "need." Likewise, some impulsive Internet stock traders can end up losing hard-earned savings by buying stocks that perform worse than expected.

Currently, only a little more than one out of ten people who trade stocks do so online. Furthermore, the $1.5 trillion in funds allocated for online trading predicted for 2003 would make up less than 10 percent of the total volume of securities trading likely to take place. These figures indicate that people have not given up on traditional stockbrokers. Thus, a two-tiered stock market is emerging. One group of savers will trade on their own accounts in the electronic marketplace. The other group of savers will continue to rely on traditional brokers in bricks-and-mortar offices, both to offer advice and to execute transactions on their behalf.

MANAGEMENT *Online*

Phone Calls versus Mouse Clicks—The Effects of Online Access to Pension Funds

In the booming economy of the late 1990s, corporations competed to retain employees through both wage boosts and improved benefits. One new benefit at many companies is the ability to trade stocks held within the portfolios of their individual corporate 401(k) pension plans. Many pension plans have set up ways for contributors to initiate portfolio changes using their telephones. A number of pension plans also set up

Web sites where contributors could reallocate their individual pension stock portfolios at no charge and at any time of day or night.

James Choi and David Laibson of Harvard University and Andrew Metrick of the University of Pennsylvania compared the trading activity by employees in two large companies that allowed Internet access to pension stock accounts to trading by employees at companies of similar size that offered only telephone access. They found that within 18 months, trading frequency at the companies allowing Web access was twice as high compared with companies where employees used

continued

FUNDAMENTAL ISSUES ▼

1.

2.

3.

4.

5.

2. What factors have contributed to the growth of online stock trading, and what are the pros and cons of trading stocks online?

The main factor contributing to the growth of online securities trading has been that cost efficiencies available to online brokers permit them to charge trading fees that are much lower than those of full-service brokers. Even though people trading online often must devote more of their own time to researching the characteristics of securities, lower fees and speedier trade execution induce them to trade on the Internet. Online brokerage firms have struggled to keep up with the growing volumes of Internet stock trading, particularly during periods of rapid stock-price swings that have generated big increases in trading activity. This has exposed some online traders to problems when online systems have crashed. There is evidence that online trading of securities tempts some people, and particularly many day traders, to buy and sell with a frequency that actually reduces their average returns.

phones to make trades. The rate of share turnover—the rate at which an average employee's portfolio changed its composition—for employees with Web access increased by 50 percent. In addition, people who could reshuffle stock allocations in their pension funds on the Web were more likely to reverse relatively small trades.

Frequent trading and greater portfolio turnover are not necessarily "bad." Indeed, increased trading can make financial markets more efficient. The reason is that if people respond more rapidly to shifting profit opportunities by directing resources to companies more likely to succeed—and away from companies that are not—then society benefits because resources are directed more speedily to higher-valued uses.

For Critical Analysis:

If greater trading frequency and portfolio turnover at the individual level translate into greater volatility of desired holdings of stocks at the aggregate level, what are the possible implications of greater online trading for the stock market as a whole?

 ## Bond Trading on the Internet

Corporations do not always fund capital expansions by issuing shares of stock. Sometimes they borrow by issuing legal forms of IOUs, or corporate debt securities in the form of *bonds*. Although the adoption of online bond trading has lagged behind Internet stock trading, an increasing number of bond traders are engaging in primary and secondary trades of bonds and other types of corporate debt securities on the Internet. (In recent years, sites for trading all sorts of IOUs have popped up on the Web; see on the next page *Management Online: Selling Distressed Debt at "Vulture Sites."*)

BONDS AND COMMERCIAL PAPER

Companies issue debt securities with both relatively long and relatively short terms to maturity. Debt securities with relatively long terms to maturity are *bonds,* while those with relatively short terms to maturity are *commercial paper.*

Borrowing in the Capital Market

One way companies borrow is by issuing **corporate bonds,** which are debt securities of corporations that have a maturity exceeding 1 year. A typical corporate

Corporate Bonds
Long-term debt securities of corporations.

MANAGEMENT *Online*

Selling Distressed Debt at "Vulture Sites"

What can Sprint Corporation do with more than $100 million in unpaid bills for long-distance calls that it does not want to go to the trouble to collect? How can Bank One Corporation try to convert more than $200 million in delinquent credit-card bills into cash? The answer for both companies has been to join Internet shoppers by surfing the Web for potential buyers of their "distressed debts"—a catchall term for problem debts such as unpaid bills for services rendered, overdue rental payments, delinquent mortgage payments, and uncollected lawsuit settlements.

Sprint put its unpaid phone bills up for sale to the highest bidder at DebtAuction.com, while Bank One chose to try to unload its unpaid credit-card bills at Debtforsale.com. Other sites where companies try to sell off IOUs that they would prefer to avoid trying to collect themselves include E-Debt.com, DistressDebt.com, and CollectionsX.com.

In the past, bad-debt brokers have specialized in matching companies seeking to sell distressed debt to collection agencies, lawyers who specialize in suing debtors, and so-called *vulture firms* that specialize in buying defaulted loans so they can take control of indebted businesses. Bad-debt brokers provided potential buyers of distressed debt detailed information about the nature of debts, the age of the debts, and previous efforts to collect the debts. In the past, typical fees charged by brokers for these services were commission rates ranging from 5 percent to 15 percent of resulting debt collections.

Internet-based debt brokers, which some call *vulture sites,* make considerable information about distressed debts available to potential buyers at the click of a mouse. Several sites even provide standardized ratings of the quality of distressed debt that owners put up for sale. Because the electronic marketplace offers a more efficient way for buyers and sellers of distressed debt to find each other, Web brokers charge commission rates of only 0.5 percent to 1 percent. Not surprisingly, large amounts of distressed debts now change hands online, though usually at small fractions of the nominal amounts of the debts. Sprint, for instance, received only about 2 cents for each dollar of uncollected phone bills that it auctioned online.

For Critical Analysis:
Instead of selling distressed debts, why don't companies that own the debts simply collect the debts themselves?

---

bond pays a fixed amount of interest twice each year until maturity. Some corporate bonds are *convertible,* meaning the holder has the right to convert them into a certain number of stock shares prior to maturity. Corporations that offer such a convertibility feature usually do so to make the bonds more attractive to potential buyers.

Another feature that can make corporate bonds attractive to potential holders is the degree of liquidity that they offer, as compared with stocks. Corporate bonds typically are liquid securities because they are traded in secondary markets. Most corporations that issue these bonds must have relatively strong credit ratings to encourage secondary market trading. Corporate bonds usually are issued in denominations of $1,000 and are traded alongside equity shares in the major stock exchanges.

Bonds trade alongside stocks and other securities with maturities of one year or more in **capital markets.** U.S. Treasury securities, including Treasury notes with terms of 1 to 10 years and Treasury bonds with terms longer than 10 years, also trade in capital markets. Other securities exchanged in capital markets are state and local municipal bonds, home mortgages, and bank commercial and consumer loans.

Capital Market
Market for a security with a maturity of one year or more.

Borrowing in the Money Market

Sometimes companies seek to obtain short-term funding, perhaps to meet a payroll or to pay for raw materials. One way to obtain such funds is by issuing commercial paper, which is a short-term debt security. For businesses, **commercial paper** has become an important substitute for borrowing directly from banks.

Commercial Paper
A short-term debt security issued by businesses in lieu of borrowing from banks.

Issuers normally offer commercial paper in maturities from 2 to 270 days. Only the most creditworthy banks and corporations are able to sell commercial paper to finance short-term debts.

The commercial paper market is a **money market,** where securities with short-term maturities of less than 1 year are traded. Money markets also include certificates of deposit with maturities ranging up to a year that are issued by banks and interbank loans (called *federal funds*) with maturities ranging from a day to a few weeks. Money market trading is very active, with many traders entering the market with offers to buy or sell each day. As a result, money market securities tend to be very liquid. Because there are so many potential buyers, a seller of a security in a money market has a greater chance of finding someone who is willing to buy that security at a mutually agreeable price.

Money Market
Market for a security with a maturity of less than one year.

A very important debt security that trades actively in U.S. money markets is *Treasury bills* (T-bills), which are U.S. government-issued securities with maturities of less than a year. Since 1998, the federal government has issued Treasury bills (T-bills) with minimum denominations of $1,000. T-bills have terms to maturity of 91 days (3 months), 182 days (6 months) and 52 weeks (12 months). The government sells T-bills at discounts from the face-value denominations. It sells T-bills with 91-day and 182-day maturities in auctions each week and sells 52-week T-bills every 4 weeks.

THE CURRENT STATUS AND FUTURE PROSPECTS OF ONLINE TRADING OF DEBT SECURITIES

Only recently has online trading in corporate debt securities such as bonds and commercial paper become relatively widespread. The speediest adoption of Internet bond trading took place in the market for U.S. government securities.

Government Bonds on the Web

Active bond trading on the Internet began in 1998 when the U.S. Treasury Department began taking Internet orders for Treasury securities purchased in the primary market. To purchase a Treasury bill, note, or bond online, an individual establishes a "TreasuryDirect" account. Once an individual has an authorized account, he can access the Treasury Department's "BuyDirect" Internet service using his TreasuryDirect account number and taxpayer identification number. After logging onto the BuyDirect system's "virtual lobby," he can enter bids for recently issued Treasury securities.

At present, a person can only make a noncompetitive bid online. *Competitive bids* are bids that the Treasury Department solicits to determine the market price at which it will sell its securities in its weekly and monthly auctions. People making competitive bids must still file these only in paper form, although plans are in the works for Web-based competitive bidding when government establishes a mechanism for validating electronic signatures of those making competitive bids. An individual who submits a noncompetitive bid online simply agrees to purchase a certain quantity of Treasury securities at the same price as the competitive bids that end up winning the auction.

Online Trading of Corporate Bonds

Various factors have slowed adoption of online trading of debt securities in primary bond markets and in the secondary market. One is that dealers traditionally market new bonds in the U.S. primary market through a relatively inefficient system of offering private quotes to customers. There has been no equivalent to the open pricing system for new stock issues. Hence, developing online mechanisms for distributing newly issued corporate bonds entails both the creation of a trading apparatus and the establishment of an altogether novel approach to marketing these securities.

In secondary markets, the key impediment to online bond trading arises from the fact that corporate bonds are less liquid than shares of stock. Many individuals and companies that purchase corporate bonds hold them to maturity. Consequently, relatively few bonds issued by specific corporations are available for sale in the secondary market on any given day.

Another factor that initially slowed adoption of online bond trading was the wariness of established Wall Street firms to consider Internet trading mechanisms. Indeed, some critics of the first launches of Internet trading at traditional firms suggested that these efforts mainly involved minimal interactions with rival firms to give customers less reason to explore the sites of new online competitors.

Finally, throughout the 1990s, stock returns often outpaced bond returns. Investors arguably had a greater incentive to develop online trading mechanisms in stock markets. The potential to earn significant returns from trading bonds online was not as great.

Nevertheless, the significant profits earned by traditional bond dealers provided a major incentive for such competitors to enter the electronic marketplace. These included online bond exchanges such as Tradebonds.com, BondConnect, TradeWeb, which link buyers and sellers in the secondary market for Treasury and corporate bonds, Deutsche Bank's DBConvertibles.com, which offers online trading of convertible bonds, and Asiabondportal.com, an online bond exchange for bonds issued in a number of Asian countries.

Unlike traditional bond exchanges, online bond-trading sites openly post buy and sell prices. Their bond-auction formats also seek to replicate the trading floors of stock exchanges, including a requirement to make quick decisions so that bond prices can adjust rapidly to changing market conditions. On the TradeWeb exchange, for instance, customers must execute a transaction at a displayed price within an "on-the-wire period" that lasts only 3 to 5 seconds.

Today about one out of three bond investors engages in online trades. Figure 8-4 displays the estimated percentages of investors that trade specific types of bonds on the Internet. Online trading of U.S. Treasury notes and bonds is most commonplace, although trading in money market securities such as Treasury bills and commercial paper is growing. Trading of commercial paper in particular is shifting to the Internet, because even though trading volumes in the commercial paper market are often heavy, most exchanges are relatively easy to automate. Since 2000, a company called Prescient Markets has had a contract with nineteen large issuers of commercial paper, including GE Capital and General Motors Acceptance Corporation, to sell their issues at its cpmarket.com Web site. Traditional Wall Street firms such as Goldman Sachs also offer automated commercial trading online. In addition, online bond exchanges such as TradeWeb are beginning to offer commercial paper trading.

In 1999, the dollar volume of Internet trading of debt securities amounted to $1.5 trillion, and in 2001 it more than doubled to more than $3 trillion in total online transactions. Many large investors prefer to haggle over terms of exchanges over the phone, so trades by smaller and medium-sized investors make up most of these transactions. As has been true in stock markets, online trading of debt securities tends to broaden the markets for these securities and to increase the competition among exchanges, which has the potential to make these markets considerably more efficient.

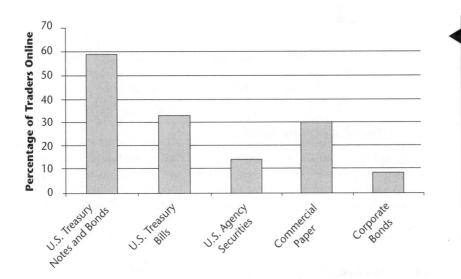

Figure 8-4: Estimates of the Portions of Bondholders Who Engage in Online Trading.

Currently, most online bond trading involves short- and medium-maturity U.S. government securities and commercial paper.

Source: Securities and Exchange Commission

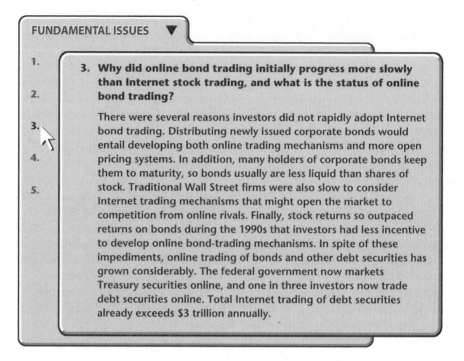

FUNDAMENTAL ISSUES ▼

1.

2.

3.

4.

5.

3. **Why did online bond trading initially progress more slowly than Internet stock trading, and what is the status of online bond trading?**

There were several reasons investors did not rapidly adopt Internet bond trading. Distributing newly issued corporate bonds would entail developing both online trading mechanisms and more open pricing systems. In addition, many holders of corporate bonds keep them to maturity, so bonds usually are less liquid than shares of stock. Traditional Wall Street firms were also slow to consider Internet trading mechanisms that might open the market to competition from online rivals. Finally, stock returns so outpaced returns on bonds during the 1990s that investors had less incentive to develop online bond-trading mechanisms. In spite of these impediments, online trading of bonds and other debt securities has grown considerably. The federal government now markets Treasury securities online, and one in three investors now trade debt securities online. Total Internet trading of debt securities already exceeds $3 trillion annually.

Web Trading of Foreign Exchange and Derivative Securities

Foreign Exchange Market
A system of private banks, foreign exchange brokers and dealers, and central banks through which households, businesses, and governments purchase and sell currencies of various nations.

Among the world's most active financial markets is the **foreign exchange market,** a system through which private banks, brokers, and dealers buy and sell about $1.5 trillion in international currencies *daily.* Other very active financial markets are markets for **derivative securities,** in which individuals and firms trade securities with returns that depend on the returns of other securities. Increasingly, trading in these financial markets also is moving online.

Derivative Security
A security with a return that depends on the return of another security.

TRADING CURRENCIES ON THE INTERNET

In the United States alone, the growth rate of foreign exchange trading has exceeded 13 percent a year since the early 1990s. By 2001, the average daily foreign exchange trading volume in the United States exceeded $450 billion. A large fraction of foreign exchange transactions involves the U.S. dollar, although significant volumes of foreign exchange trading involve the European Monetary Union's euro, the Japanese yen, the British pound, and the Swiss franc.

Online Links for the Major Foreign Exchange Traders
Banks are heavily involved in foreign exchange trading. Nearly all banks trade currencies, but the business is largely dominated by U.S. money-center banks such

as Citibank, J. P. Morgan Chase, and BankAmerica, and a few European banks such as Deutsche Bank and ABN Amro. These five banks alone typically account for more than one-fourth of the foreign exchange transactions that take place in the United States.

Bank of America recently joined an alliance of fourteen worldwide foreign exchange dealers in establishing FXall.com, a Web-based currency-trading site linking multinational corporations, institutional investors, and investment funds that wish to trade currencies (http://www.FXall.com). The FXall exchange permits traders to enter offers to buy or sell currencies online. The Web exchange then executes orders automatically. AM Amro participates in a competing online currency exchange, called Currenex (http://www.currenex.com). This Web site links traders to the foreign exchange operations of 25 major banks.

Foreign exchange dealers affiliated with these Web sites do not use their systems to trade with each other. Instead, the sites are virtual locations where banks' clients gain immediate access to banks' quotes in a competitive auction environment and obtain speedier settlement of transactions. About 15 percent of foreign exchange trading is estimated to take place online, and some forecasts indicate that this percentage could double within the next five years.

Web-Based Currency Exchange for Smaller Firms and Individuals

Single trades conducted on FXall and Currenex often amount to tens of millions of dollars. A relatively "small" foreign exchange trade amounts to hundreds of thousands of dollars. Nevertheless, a growing number of medium-sized and small businesses are becoming involved in importing or exporting goods and services, so the portion of foreign exchange market trading associated with smaller currency transactions is likely to increase in future years.

A company called GainCapital (http://www.gaincapital.com/flash/main.html) has sought to establish an electronic marketplace for pricing foreign exchange trades as low as $100,000 and no larger than $10 million and for selling market research to clients that typically execute foreign exchange trades within this range. Another Web site plans to eventually allow traders to buy and sell the most popular currencies in amounts as low as $1. These and other companies are betting that smaller currency transactions will become more commonplace as e-commerce spreads across the globe. (In fact, some companies are already developing ways to process payments requiring more than one currency in "real time" on the Internet; see on the next page *Globalization Online: Shrinking the World Marketplace via Multicurrency Payment Processing*.)

TRADING DERIVATIVE SECURITIES ON THE WEB

Many currency trades that FXall and Currenex process are transactions in the **spot market** for foreign exchange. In general, traders in a spot market deliver a financial asset immediately after they reach an agreement concerning the price and quantity that they will exchange. Hence, in the spot market for foreign exchange, the demand for and supply of a nation's currency determines the rate of exchange at which buyers and sellers will transact an immediate currency exchange.

Spot Market
Market for immediate exchange of financial assets.

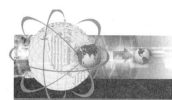

GLOBALIZATION *Online*

Shrinking the World Marketplace via Multicurrency Payment Processing

Imagine the following scenario. It is 2015, and Internet access has spread to such far-flung locales as India, Morocco, and Bolivia. Many small manufacturers and retailers in nations around the globe have set up shop on the Web. A U.S. resident is searching among Web sites for a special gift for a close friend. At each site, she is able to click a button that automatically converts product descriptions to English translations and prices of the gifts to dollars. She settles on a gift handcrafted in a remote Icelandic village, enters her credit-card number, and submits her order. Her credit-card transaction is automatically processed in dollars, but payment is made to the seller's bank in the Icelandic currency, the krona.

In fact, this scenario could become possible much earlier than 2015. One company, Planet Payment (http://www. planetpayment.com), has already signed up about 300 merchants in 30 countries to develop multilingual versions of their

Web sites. The company also offers software that automatically converts prices in local currencies to other countries' currencies at the exchange rate prevailing at the moment the customer submits an Internet order. Thus, a buyer literally would be able to compare the dollar price of a handcrafted gift in Pakistan to the price of an item made in Iceland.

Planet Payment also offers a facility for multicurrency processing of credit-card transactions conducted over the Internet. Payments are automatically routed among a network of international banks that translate payment debits to buyers' accounts and payment credits to sellers' accounts. Both debits and credits take place in local currency terms, however, so that a transaction that once required an advance exchange of foreign currencies to take place can now bundle together the purchase and exchange of currencies.

For Critical Analysis:
If the dollar value of the Icelandic krona rises considerably just before a U.S. customer is about to submit an order on a site using system such as the one operated by Planet Payment, thereby changing the terms of the transaction, will the U.S. customer be more or less likely to click on the "order submit" button?

Forward Market
A market for the exchange of a financial asset at a future date.

Foreign exchange market transactions frequently take place outside the spot market, however. For instance, many currency transactions occur in the **forward market** for foreign exchange. In a forward market, traders of a financial asset agree on the price at which they will trade a particular amount of a commodity, a security, or—in the case of a forward market for foreign exchange—a currency, on a particular date. In the forward market for a currency, traders negotiate the terms of *forward contracts* for currency delivery. A forward contract is an example of a *derivative security*. Table 8-1 lists this and other fundamental types of derivative securities.

In addition to offering currency traders a virtual marketplace for engaging in spot currency trades, online foreign currency exchanges such as FXall and Currenex facilitate trading in forward currency contracts. These sites also permit customers to sell currency options. Hence, trading in derivative securities denominated in foreign currency has begun to shift to the electronic marketplace.

Table 8-1: Basic Derivative Securities.

Forward contract	A financial contract requiring delivery of a financial asset at a specified price on a certain date
Futures contract	An agreement to deliver to another a given amount of a standardized commodity or financial asset at a designated future date
Option	A financial contract giving the owner the right to buy or sell an underlying financial instrument at a certain price within a specific period of time
Futures options	Options to buy or sell futures contracts
Swap	A contract entaining an exchange of payment flows between two parties

Online derivatives trading is increasingly catching on with those who buy and sell other types of derivatives securities. For instance, Deutsche Boursche and the London International Futures and Options Exchange, the two key European futures and options exchanges that compete with the Chicago Mercantile Exchange and the Chicago Board of Trade, have begun merging their operations. One organizational plan that the two European exchanges have considered would entail maintaining separate trading centers by linking the existing exchanges via the Internet. Indeed, some industry experts anticipate that within a few years most trading in derivative securities will take place on the Internet.

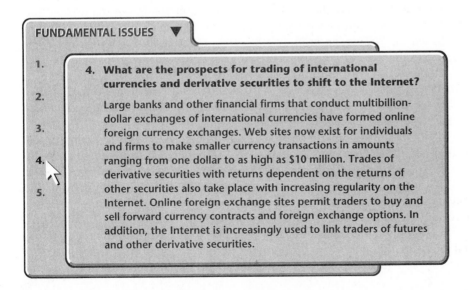

FUNDAMENTAL ISSUES ▼

1.

2.

3.

4. ▸

5.

4. What are the prospects for trading of international currencies and derivative securities to shift to the Internet?

Large banks and other financial firms that conduct multibillion-dollar exchanges of international currencies have formed online foreign currency exchanges. Web sites now exist for individuals and firms to make smaller currency transactions in amounts ranging from one dollar to as high as $10 million. Trades of derivative securities with returns dependent on the returns of other securities also take place with increasing regularity on the Internet. Online foreign exchange sites permit traders to buy and sell forward currency contracts and foreign exchange options. In addition, the Internet is increasingly used to link traders of futures and other derivative securities.

Financial Regulation and Internet Trading

At what online trading sites should consumers especially be on the lookout for potentially fraudulent activities? Explore the consumer advisories issued by the CFTC at http://www.cftc.gov/cftc/cftccustomer.htm#advisory.

In September 2000, the Securities and Exchange Commission (SEC), the federal agency that Congress charges with maintaining the integrity of U.S. securities markets, reached settlement with a 16-year-old boy from New Jersey who had used Internet message boards to manipulate stock prices. The boy, who had shown a knack for online stock trading since he was in the eighth grade and had been a contributor to a financial Web site, allegedly talked up the value of companies to convince others to buy shares. Then he allegedly sold his own shares in those companies at a profit. Under the terms of the boy's settlement with the SEC, he gave up about $285,000 in illegal trading profits. Following the settlement, the SEC claimed a major victory against online fraud.

Critics of the settlement pointed out that the boy had managed to keep at least $500,000 in earnings from questionable trades that the SEC could not prove to be related to the boy's allegedly illegal activities. These critics argued that, in fact, a teenage boy had shown U.S. securities regulations to be ineffective in the electronic marketplace for financial assets.

KEY FINANCIAL REGULATORY AUTHORITIES

The electronic marketplace for trading in stocks, bonds, foreign exchange, and derivative securities is giving investors new freedoms. It also poses new risks. Containing these risks is a fundamental objective of financial regulation.

U.S. securities market regulation dates from 1933, when Congress passed the Securities Act requiring companies issuing stocks and bonds to make public statements that would help traders assess the risks of those securities. Essentially, the 1933 legislation required **market transparency,** or the wide availability of information about the risk characteristics of stocks and bonds. On the heels of this law, the next year Congress passed the Securities Exchange Act of 1934. This law established the SEC as the primary federal regulator charged with enforcing the 1933 legislation and charged the SEC with regulating securities brokers, dealers, and exchanges. (Other countries have regulatory authorities similar to the SEC, and offering cross-border exchange of stocks and bonds sometimes causes complications for online brokers; see *Globalization Online: For Foreign Securities Regulators, "Out of Sight" Doesn't Mean "Out of Mind."*)

In 1974, Congress sought to provide government oversight for trading in derivative securities. That year, it created the Commodity Futures Trading Commission (CFTC), an independent agency that regulates U.S. futures and options markets. Although the explicit mandate for the CFTC is to regulate futures and options for commodities such as pork bellies and gold, the CFTC also plays a role in regulating trading of financial derivatives such as currency futures and options.

In addition, individual states have their own laws governing trading in financial markets. Although there is an umbrella organization of state securities called the North American Securities Administrators' Association, each state has specific

Market Transparency
The availability of detailed information about the various risk characteristics of securities.

GLOBALIZATION *Online*

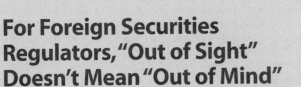

POLICY MAKING **GLOBALIZATION** MANAGEMENT

For Foreign Securities Regulators, "Out of Sight" Doesn't Mean "Out of Mind"

For the myriad financial firms setting up shop on the Internet, the promise of avoiding the costs of physical offices has been perceived as a key advantage. Nevertheless, the online broker E*Trade.com ran into a snag in the late 1990s when it attempted to offer its services for trading U.S. securities to investors located in Australia, Canada, New Zealand, and the United Kingdom.

As a U.S.-based company, E*Trade considered itself to be bound by U.S. laws and regulations established by the Securities and Exchange Commission. From its perspective, the online broker regarded itself in compliance with U.S. trading rules governing brokerage services relating to U.S. stocks.

To its chagrin, E*Trade found that securities regulators in other nations were tied to rules designed for the age of bricks-and-mortar brokering. Australian, Canadian, and New Zealand regulators told the company it would have to open physical offices before it would have the legal right to do any business in their countries.

The United Kingdom's Securities and Investments Board (SIB) even threatened to require E*Trade to locate some of its computers within Britain. The SIB was unconvinced by E*Trade's argument that cyberspace is both everywhere and anywhere. The British agency noted that the United Kingdom has laws forbidding solicitation by unauthorized foreign securities firms. It ruled that a Web site alone constitutes "solicitation." Indeed, the SIB claimed that whenever a British-based computer was used to make offers to buy or sell securities over the Internet, those offers were legally made in Britain. The SIB concluded that anyone posting financial-trading Web sites must comply with British laws. Otherwise, they face penalties of prison or a fine.

For Critical Analysis:

Should national securities regulators compel companies such as E*Trade to abide by their home rules, or should they authorize companies in other nations to sell their services across borders under the rules of the nations in which the companies themselves are based?

---

rules determining what types of trading activities are legal within the borders of that state.

ADAPTING FINANCIAL REGULATION TO THE ONLINE TRADING REVOLUTION

Under federal and state laws, the SEC, the CFTC, and state securities regulators are at the forefront of efforts to adapt securities and derivatives regulation to the electronic marketplace. Unfortunately for these regulatory agencies, there is no clear agreement among the brokers, dealers, and exchanges, investors and traders, and members of Congress and state legislatures concerning the most appropriate regulatory stance toward market automation and online trading.

One view is that close regulation of financial markets explains why most U.S. financial markets account for at least half of global trading volumes. According to this perspective, tight regulation gives investors confidence that U.S. markets are "safe havens" for their funds. Proponents of this view argue that some innovations

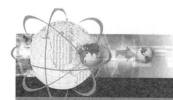

POLICYMAKING *Online*

Should Just Anyone Be Able to Broker Internet Currency Trades?

Do you think you have the know-how to profit from trading dollars for euros, euros for yen, or yen for dollars? If so, Web sites with names such as Foreigncurrencytrading.com and Forex4all.com have offered individuals the opportunity to set up trading accounts starting with as little as $500 and to engage in online currency trading.

The Regulatory Void in Online Currency Trading

Studies of Web-based currency trading operations have found that the majority of these sites do not have licenses required by law. A number of companies offering such sites also extend credit at high rates of interest to allow online traders to trade multiples of their own funds in foreign exchange markets. In some cases, currency trading sites have turned out to be complete scams.

For instance, one Web site claimed to accept orders to buy or sell currencies. When it accepted funds, it transmitted receipts indicating that trades that should have generated profits had instead yielded 100 percent losses. Site owners actually were simply stealing the funds.

Federal law does not encompass online currency trading. Because securities do not change hands in spot currency

trades, the SEC has no role. Neither does the CFTC, because it can only regulate activities relating to foreign currency futures or options. This has left prevention of fraudulent online currency trading largely to state regulators.

What's So Special about Foreign Exchange?

Some regulators attempted to completely shut down online trading of foreign exchange. When asked what might be wrong with foreign currency trading on the Internet, an official with the California Department of Corporations, which establishes rules governing financial trading in that state, answered, "That it exists."

A number of foreign-currency-trading sites, however, are legitimate business operations. Owners of these sites argue that just as online brokers that allow small investors to trade stocks and bonds, they provide a service to small currency traders who want to try their hand at profiting from movements in exchange rates. In their view, efforts by state regulators to halt their operations are really intended to help protect banks and other large dealers of foreign exchange from new competition made possible by the Internet.

For Critical Analysis:

Some observers have argued that online currency trading currently suffers from a "lemons problem." In the absence of a regulatory solution, what might online currency brokers do on their own initiative to try to overcome this problem?

in online trading, increase the inherent riskiness of U.S. financial markets. They conclude that the appropriate role of financial regulation is to preempt efforts to adopt certain trading innovations in the electronic marketplace that would increase financial market risks. (In some cases, proponents of this view have argued that preemptive actions might include making certain forms of online trading illegal; see *Policymaking Online: Should Just Anyone Be Able to Broker Internet Currency Trades?*)

A contrasting view is that financial regulators should largely stay out of the way and permit competitive forces to shape the new online marketplace for financial assets such as stocks, bonds, foreign exchange, and derivative securities.

Those favoring this laissez-faire perspective argue that online trading in stocks and bonds has already reduced trading commissions and fees incurred by investors. In their view, such consumer gains justify a more hands-off approach to regulating online financial trading. According to adherents of this perspective, regulatory authorities such as the SEC, CFTC, and state regulators should try to fix problems only after they arise, not before. Otherwise, they risk substituting government rules that contribute to market inefficiencies in place of private incentives that can enhance market efficiencies.

This dispute about whether financial regulators should be rule-makers or should police existing rules is likely to become increasingly relevant as more financial activities move to the Internet. As you will learn in the next chapter, similar regulatory issues are rapidly emerging in a major part of the financial system, the banking industry.

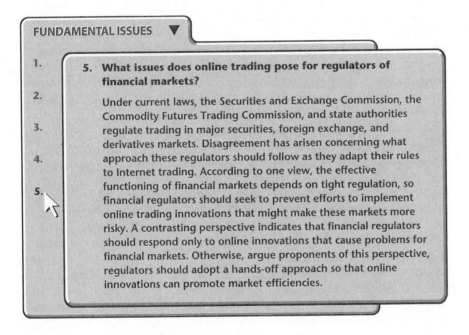

FUNDAMENTAL ISSUES ▼

1.

2.

3.

4.

5.

5. What issues does online trading pose for regulators of financial markets?

Under current laws, the Securities and Exchange Commission, the Commodity Futures Trading Commission, and state authorities regulate trading in major securities, foreign exchange, and derivatives markets. Disagreement has arisen concerning what approach these regulators should follow as they adapt their rules to Internet trading. According to one view, the effective functioning of financial markets depends on tight regulation, so financial regulators should seek to prevent efforts to implement online trading innovations that might make these markets more risky. A contrasting perspective indicates that financial regulators should respond only to online innovations that cause problems for financial markets. Otherwise, argue proponents of this perspective, regulators should adopt a hands-off approach so that online innovations can promote market efficiencies.

Chapter Summary

1) **How Financial Trading Was Becoming More Automated Before the Internet, and How the Internet Has Contributed to Automated Trading:** Prior to the existence of the Internet, securities exchanges used computer connections with system-specific software programs that allowed

traders to buy and sell securities. The original Nasdaq system enabled trades of over-the-counter stocks through linked desktop devices that displayed stock quotes and brokers' telephone numbers. Using the Internet, however, traders can interact 24 hours a day and buy and sell securities in more than one market at the same time. Now traders in the Nasdaq exchange can use Internet-based auction networks linking buyers and sellers of stocks. These electronic communications networks (ECNs) currently process about one-third of all Nasdaq stock trades.

2) **Factors that Have Contributed to the Growth of Online Stock Trading, and the Pros and Cons of Trading Stocks Online:** The key factor fueling the growth of online securities trading is the lower trading fees offered by Internet brokers. Lower fees are made possible by the cost efficiencies Internet brokers experience relative to full-service brokers. People who trade online typically use more of their time to study the features of securities they trade, but for those who choose online trading, lower fees and speedier trade execution more than compensate. The rapid growth of online trading has sometimes posed problems for the capability of Internet brokerage firms to keep up with the growing trading volumes. Sudden large changes in stock prices have generated big increases in trading activity, and some Internet brokers' systems have become overloaded, causing problems for online traders. Some economists have argued that the ability to trade stocks online encourages day traders to buy and sell stocks with a frequency that tends to yield lower overall returns on their holdings of stocks.

3) **Why Online Bond Trading Initially Progressed More Slowly than Internet Stock Trading, and the Status of Online Bond Trading:** Several factors slowed the initial adoption of Internet bond trading. For one thing, marketing corporate bonds in the relatively inefficient primary market for bonds would require simultaneous development of both online trading mechanisms and more open pricing systems. Furthermore, those who hold corporate bonds tend to keep them until maturity, and as a result corporate bonds are generally less liquid than stocks. Wall Street bond dealers also were hesitant to adopt Internet trading mechanisms that would expose them to competition from online rivals. In addition, average returns on shares of stock were often much higher than bond returns during the 1990s, which reduced the incentive to develop online bond-trading mechanisms. Despite these factors, online trading of bonds and other debt securities has increased during recent years. The U.S. Treasury sells all of its securities online. One in three investors now trade both government and private debt securities on the Internet, and total annual online trading volumes for these securities now exceeds $3 trillion.

4) **The Prospects for Trading of International Currencies and Derivative Securities to Shift to the Internet:** Currency dealers such as large banks have already created Web-based exchanges for trading billions of dollars in international currencies. Sites now exist on the Internet where

individuals and firms can engage in currency trades in amounts as low as $1 or as high as $10 million. Traders increasingly use the Internet to trade derivative securities that have returns hinging on the returns of other securities. Foreign exchange sites allow traders to buy and sell forward currency contracts and foreign exchange options, and traders of futures and other derivative securities increasingly use the Internet to buy and sell these securities.

5) **Issues That Online Trading Pose for Financial Market Regulators:** The primary regulators of trading in securities, foreign exchange, and derivatives markets are the Securities and Exchange Commission, the Commodity Futures Trading Commission, and state authorities. There currently is no consensus among these regulators on adapting uniform rules for financial trading in the electronic marketplace. One perspective emphasizes the importance of strict regulatory oversight to risk containment in financial markets. According to another view, however, efforts to restrain online trading and related innovations in financial markets can prevent the achievement of greater market efficiency. Thus, proponents of this view argue that financial regulators should respond to online innovations that actually cause problems for investors.

Questions and Problems

1) As noted in the chapter, electronic communications networks (ECNs) currently link brokers, dealers, and institutional investors. Who would stand to gain or lose if ECNs began offering their services directly to individual investors via the Internet?

2) Develop a list of the advantages and disadvantages of conducting initial public offerings online instead of through traditional bricks-and-mortar investment-banking channels.

3) Chuck is a financial analyst whose time is worth $120 per hour. Maria is an accountant whose time is worth $40 per hour. FSB, a bricks-and-mortar service brokerage, offers to make stock trades for its clients on the following basis: For each trade there is a fee of $25, plus ten cents per share for each share traded. InterStock offers to make trades for a flat rate of $50 per trade, regardless of how many shares are traded. Because people using InterStock's Web site must do their own research and analysis, it takes 30 minutes more to execute a trade with InterStock than to execute with FSB.

   (a) If Chuck and Maria are separately considering a trade involving 100 shares, with whom will each person execute the trade?

   (b) If Chuck and Maria are separately considering a trade involving 500 shares, with whom will each person execute the trade?

(c) If Chuck and Maria are separately considering a trade involving 1,000 shares, with whom will each person execute the trade?

(d) In general, how will the value of a person's time affect the choice of using InterStock or FSB? Explain.

4) Given the information in question 3, will larger or smaller trades generally be executed with InterStock or with FSB?

5) Compose lists of the pros and cons associated with trading stocks online. Based on your tabulation, do you think that it is inevitable that the bulk of stock trading ultimately will move to the Internet, or do you believe that bricks-and-mortar brokerage operations will continue to predominate? Explain your reasoning.

6) Stock prices broadly declined in late 2000 and into 2001. Explain why this helps to explain the notable slowdown in the pace of growth of online trading during this interval.

7) How might the inherent risk differences between government securities and privately issued securities have contributed to the speedier growth of online trading in U.S. government securities, as compared with commercial paper and corporate bonds?

8) Is there any reason that regulators should regard Web sites offering individuals the opportunity to trade foreign currencies online as any more or less "anti-consumer" than brokerages that give individuals the capability to trade stocks online? Why or why not?

9) Is there any reason that regulators should regard Web sites offering individuals the opportunity to trade derivative securities online as any more or less "anti-consumer" than brokerages that give individuals the capability to trade stocks online? Why or why not?

10) Who would gain or lose if online financial trading were subjected to more stringent regulations than financial trading in the traditional physical marketplace?

Online Application

Internet URL: http://www.nyse.com/public/educate/6a/6a3/6a3.htm

Title: **The New York Stock Exchange: How the NYSE Operates**

Navigation: Begin at the home page of the New York Stock Exchange (http://www.nyse.com). In the left margin, click on "About the NYSE." Next, click on "Education." Then, in the left-hand margin click on "You and the Investment World." Next, click on Chapter 3: How the NYSE Operates.

Application: Read the chapter, and answer the following questions.

1) According to the article, the price of a seat on the NYSE currently can sell for more than $1 million. Why do you suppose that someone would be willing to pay this much for a seat? [Hint: Think about the potential ways to generate earnings from holding an NYSE seat.]

2) List the key functions of a stock-exchange specialist. Why would online access to the "Point-of-Sale Display Book" likely be particularly useful for a specialist?

For Group Study and Analysis: Divide the class into groups, and have each group examine and discuss the description of how NYSE trades are executed. Ask each group to compose a listing of the various points at which Internet trading may be a more efficient way to execute a trade, as compared with trading via a traditional brokerage firm. Then go through these as a class, and discuss the following issue: In the New York Stock Exchange, what people cannot be replaced by new information technologies?

Selected References and Further Readings

Barber, Brad, and Terrance Odean. "Online Investors: Do the Slow Die First?" Working Paper, University of California at Davis, October 2000.

Barber, Brad, and Terrance Odean. "Trading is Hazardous to Your Wealth: The Common Stock Investment Performance of Individual Investors," *Journal of Finance* 55 (April 2, 2000), pp. 773–806.

Choi, James, David Laibson, and Andrew Metrick, "Does the Internet Increase Trading? Evidence from Investor Behavior in 401(k) Plans," NBER Working Paper No. 7878, September 2000.

Claessens, Stijn, Thomas Glaessner, and Daniela Klingebiel. "Electronic Finance: Reshaping the Financial Landscape Around the World," World Bank Financial Sector Strategy and Policy Group, 2000.

McAndrews, James, and Chris Stefandis. "The Emergence of Electronic Communications Networks in the U.S. Equity Markets," *Current Issues in Economics and Finance* 6 (October 12, 2000).

Securities and Exchange Commission, Division of Market Regulation. "Electronic Communication Networks and After-Hours Trading." June 2000.

Securities and Exchange Commission, Office of Compliance Inspections and Examinations. "Report of Examinations of Day-Trading Broker-Dealers." February 2000.

Securities and Exchange Commission. "Online Brokerage: Keeping Apace of Cyberspace." November 1999.

The Economics of Online Banking

<E-Commerce Today>

Online Banking Meets Online Fraud

A few years ago, a newly formed company established itself in a small North Carolina community and announced its intention to provide full-scale banking operations over the Internet. The company proclaimed its right to provide such services under U.S. constitutional law, and its Web site said that its deposits were backed by a policy issued by a major insurance company. The company had a "fax-on-demand telephone line" through which prospective customers could order an application to open an account. To attract deposits, the new bank promised to pay annual interest rates up to 20 percent on savings accounts and 10 percent on checking accounts, at a time when most traditional banking institutions were offering rates slightly above 5 percent. The Internet bank also said that it would offer small-business loans, "with no credit checks," at one to two percentage points above the prime rate.

The Office of the Comptroller of the Currency (OCC), the federal agency charged with regulating national banks, investigated the new bank's claims. It learned from the "major insurance company" that it had never made an arrangement to back the bank's deposits. The OCC immediately pointed out to the new company's owners that federal banking laws prevent institutions from accepting deposits without a formal bank charter. Nevertheless, the OCC had to turn to the Federal Trade Commission (FTC) to enforce the law and stop the new company from opening its banking operations, because the OCC has power to enforce actions only against institutions that do have federal banking charters.

At about the same time, the Federal Deposit Insurance Corporation (FDIC), which administers federal deposit insurance and regulates many state-chartered banks, took control of a Kentucky-based Internet bank called BestBank. This legally chartered bank had raised many of its deposits on the Internet, and its low-cost operations—the bank had only 23 employees at a single location—had permitted it to become five times more profitable than the average bank. What BestBank had not told its depositors was that it had used their funds to issue a half-million credit cards with $600 borrowing limits. A precondition for receipt was for the cardholder to join a Florida-based travel company at a fee of $543, which the bank charged to each cardholder's account before sending out the card, leaving only $57 of available credit. Many of the bank's credit-card customers, however, failed to pay off their loan balances. By the time the FDIC seized the bank, the bulk of the bank's cardholders had defaulted, and the bank was insolvent—its liabilities exceeded its assets by nearly $100 million.

B ank fraud is an old problem. Because banks and other financial institutions are so important, various U.S. government agencies examine and supervise these institutions in an effort to limit social losses from fraudulent activities. As these examples indicate, online banking is further complicating regulators' efforts. At the same time, online banking promises to contribute to greater competition and efficiency within the financial system.

Bricks-and-Mortar Financial Institutions Meet the Web

When savers allocate funds to a company by purchasing a newly issued corporate bond through a traditional Wall Street firm or via a Web site, they effectively lend directly to the company. That is, they take part in *directly financing* capital investment or other activities that the company wishes to undertake. The process of financing business investment is not always so direct, however. Consider a situation in which a saver holds a deposit with a bank that uses the deposit funds of this and other savers to purchase the same company's corporate bonds. In this instance, *indirect finance* has taken place, and the saver's bank has served as a **financial intermediary,** which is an institution that stands between savers and ultimate borrowers.

Financial Intermediary
An institution that serves as the "middleman" in channeling funds from savers to borrowers.

Traditionally, banks and other financial institutions have led the way in adapting information technologies to the process of indirect finance. Not surprisingly, financial intermediaries also led the way in efforts to incorporate the Internet into their regular business dealings.

FINANCIAL INTERMEDIATION AND FINANCIAL INSTITUTIONS

Figure 9-1 depicts the distinction between direct and indirect finance. In the case of direct finance, a financial intermediary such as a bank is not involved in the process. A saver lends directly to parties who invest. In the case of indirect finance, however, some other institution allocates savers' funds to borrowers of those funds.

Why Financial Intermediaries Exist

Why do many savers choose to hold their funds at a financial intermediary instead of lending them directly? Most economists agree that one key reason is *asymmetric information* (see Chapter 5) in financial markets. For instance, *adverse selection* problems often arise in financial transactions. If a resident of Portland, Oregon, is considering a relatively high-yield municipal bond issued by a town in Rhode Island, this individual might worry that the bond offers a high return because the town intends to direct funds it raises to a risky project. Only municipal leaders in the Rhode Island community know for sure, which makes it hard for the Portland resident to compare the yield on this bond with yields on alternative securities.

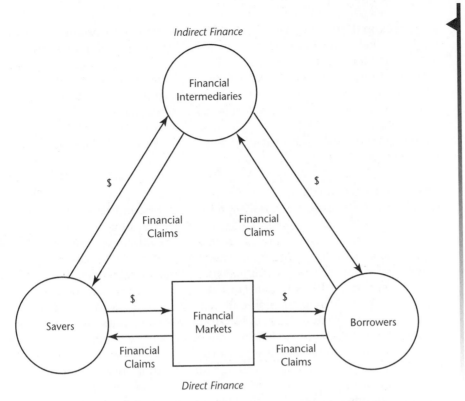

Indirect Finance

**Figure 9-1:
Indirect Finance
through Financial
Intermediaries.**

*Those savers who lend funds
directly to those who invest
undertake* direct finance.
*Financial intermediaries
make* indirect finance
*possible by using funds that
they obtain from savers to
extend to borrowers that use
the funds to finance
investment projects.*

In addition, *moral hazard* problems often exist in financial markets. When they first issue bonds, leaders of the Rhode Island town might have a good-faith intention to make good use of funds they raise. After selling their bonds, however, an event such as electoral turnover might bring new leaders to power who decide to use the funds for less worthy projects that will reduce the return to bondholders.

One way for the Portland resident to deal with adverse selection and moral hazard problems is to make several trips to assess and monitor the Rhode Island community's uses of funds raised from bond sales. This would be a time-consuming and costly endeavor. Instead, the Portland investor could make use of the services of a financial intermediary that specializes in collecting information on behalf of savers. Financial intermediaries cannot completely eliminate the adverse selection and moral hazard problems resulting from asymmetric information. Nevertheless, they can reduce those costs by specializing in gathering information about the likely prospects of securities and in monitoring the performance of those who issue them.

Another key reason for the existence of financial intermediaries is *economies of scale* in financial markets. These arise whenever average costs of engaging in financial transactions decline as a trader's scale of operations increases. Some financial intermediaries assist people in pooling their funds, thereby increasing the amount of funds that are saved. Pooling of funds allows intermediaries to manage the larger volume of funds, which can reduce average fund management costs below those that people would incur if they otherwise managed their savings individually. If intermediaries can manage funds for many savers at a lower average cost than all the savers would face if they managed their funds alone, then financial economies of scale exist. One cost to risk-averse savers arises from volatility of returns on savings, and diversification made possible by pooling larger sums and spreading them among a greater range of investments also offer economies-of-scale benefits to savers.

Types of Financial Institutions

Financial circumstances for various firms and individuals vary widely, which is why there are so many different kinds of securities and financial markets. There are many ways that asymmetric information problems or opportunities to experience economies of scale can arise in financial markets. Consequently, many different types of firms, or *financial institutions,* function as financial intermediaries.

One set of financial institutions includes *insurance companies,* which specialize in trying to limit adverse selection and moral hazard problems by offering to insure against possible future risks of loss. Insurance companies issue *policies,* which are promises to reimburse the holder for damages suffered in the event of a "bad" event. There are two types of insurance companies. *Property and casualty insurers* cover risks relating to property damage and liabilities arising from injuries or deaths caused by accidents or adverse natural events. *Life insurance companies* charge premiums for policies that insure people against the financial consequences associated with death. The prices that consumers pay for property-casualty and life insurance policies reflect both the risks that insurers face and the market demand for their policies. (There is evidence that the ability of consumers to obtain more information about insurance has had a significant effect on the prices of insurance policies; see *Management Online: Internet Access and Life Insurance—More Information Plus Greater Competition Equals Lower Prices.*)

Traditionally important financial institutions in the capital markets are *investment banks.* These institutions specialize in marketing initial stock offerings of new businesses. Investment banks typically *underwrite* such issues, meaning that they guarantee the businesses' initial fixed share prices by temporarily purchasing the shares of the businesses. Then they attempt to resell them in the primary market at a slightly higher price. They keep the difference between purchase price and resale price as a profit.

Pension funds are another type of financial institution. These institutions specialize in managing funds that individuals save to draw upon when they retire from jobs and careers. One reason people use the services of pension funds instead of saving funds on their own is asymmetric information, because those who operate pension funds may be better informed about securities and markets than those who save for retirement. A more important reason is probably economies of scale. Many people would find it very costly to monitor the securities that they hold on a day-by-day basis throughout their lives. Pension funds do this for many people at the same time, thereby spreading the costs across large numbers of individuals.

MANAGEMENT *Online*

Internet Access and Life Insurance—More Information Plus Greater Competition Equals Lower Prices

Three online developments have affected the insurance business in recent years. First, most established companies have begun posting detailed information about their policies on the Internet. Second, some nontraditional companies, such as Web-based Priceline.com, have begun selling insurance online. Third, some insurance sales companies have opened so-called Web "aggregation" sites, where consumers can provide information about desired areas of risk coverage and purchase the lowest-cost policies covering various types of risk offered by different insurance companies. Using aggregation sites, consumers can maintain separate insurance policies with various companies instead of buying all their policies from a single insurer.

In a recent study, Jeffrey Brown of Harvard University and Austan Goolsbee of the University of Chicago examined how access to such online insurance sites has affected the market prices of insurance policies since the mid-1990s. They examined term life insurance, in which a policy insures an individual's life only during a limited period.

Brown and Goolsbee concluded that each 10 percent increase in the share of people who are able to access Web sites using the Internet is associated with a 5 percent reduction in the average price of term life insurance. They determined that the total price reduction for term life insurance since the mid-1990s generated by increased Internet access was at least 8 percent and potentially as high as 15 percent. The researchers estimated that the result for consumers was a significant gain in consumer surplus ranging between $115 million and $215 million.

For Critical Analysis:

What kinds of risks are insurance companies likely to be more or less willing to insure via online sales of policies? (Hint: What kinds of risks can be verified by written documentation, and what kinds require evaluation through visual inspection?)

Another type of financial institution is *mutual funds.* These financial institutions issue shares are backed by portfolios of securities they hold, which typically include stocks and corporate and government bonds. Mutual funds usually are operated by investment companies, which charge shareholders fees to manage the funds. Today there are more than 7,000 mutual funds in operation. Like pension funds, mutual funds take advantage of financial economies of scale. Mutual fund shareholders typically pay lower fees to investment companies than they might have to pay brokers to handle their funds on a personal basis. The reason is that mutual fund managers can spread the costs of managing shareholders' funds across all the shareholders. (Mutual funds are now available on the Internet; see on the next page *Management Online: Will E-Funds Catch On?*)

Finance companies are financial institutions that specialize in making loans to individuals and businesses. They use the funds invested by their owners or raised through issuing their own debt securities to finance these loans. Many finance companies specialize in making loans that depository institutions regard as too risky.

MANAGEMENT *Online*

Will E-Funds Catch On?

There are all sorts of mutual funds—money market funds with portfolios composed of Treasury bills, commercial paper, and other money market instruments, bond funds that hold mainly Treasury notes and bonds, municipal bonds, and corporate bonds, and equity funds that maintain portfolios dominated by stocks. Now there are also "e-funds," mutual funds that cater exclusively to online customers.

E-funds offer various advantages over traditional mutual funds. Most investment companies require customers to maintain sizable minimum balances in their mutual funds. For instance, the Vanguard equity fund charges a $20 annual fee whenever a customer's balance in its Standard & Poor's 500 stock index fund falls below $2,500. At some e-funds, however, there are no minimum-balance requirements. Traditional mutual funds normally meet minimum legal disclosure re-

quirements and provide information about their portfolios every six months, but the e-funds at StockJungle.com, TDe-Funds.com and MetaMarkets.com post online trades on their Web sites immediately and publish frequent management reports at Web pages that are accessible 24 hours per day.

Whether e-funds will really make a big dent in the mutual-fund business will depend on their ability to keep costs low. Most e-funds require customers to accept only electronic statements concerning their accounts. At e-funds, customers can face sizable fees if they request a service that is standard fare at traditional mutual funds: postal delivery of paper account statements.

For Critical Analysis:

Why are efforts to cut costs by limiting paper statements likely to prove crucial to the ultimate success of e-funds?

The federal government also operates or subsidizes financial institutions, such as the Federal Financing Bank, which intermediates loans issued by government agencies using funds made available by the U.S. Treasury from some of the Treasury's tax receipts. The U.S. Farm Credit Administration supervises the Banks for Cooperatives, Federal Intermediate Credit Banks, and Federal Land Banks. In addition, the Federal National Mortgage Association (FMMA, or "Fannie-Mae"), the General National Mortgage Association (GNMA, or "Ginnie-Mae"), the Federal Home Loan Banks (FHLBs), and the Federal Home Loan Mortgage Corporation (FHLMC, or "Freddie-Mac") seek to make mortgage markets more liquid by buying mortgages with funds that they raise by selling debt securities called mortgage-backed securities.

A particularly important group of financial institutions includes various types of *depository institutions*. These institutions issue IOUs called deposits from which people can transfer funds and finalize purchases of goods, services, or financial assets. Depository institutions must hold funds on deposit with Federal

Reserve banks, and the federal government insures a large fraction of the deposits they issue. One type of depository institution is *commercial banks,* which are depository institutions that specialize in sizing up the risk characteristics of business borrowers. In addition, there are *savings institutions,* such as savings banks and savings and loan associations, which traditionally have specialized in extending mortgage loans to individuals who wish to purchase homes. Finally, *credit unions* accept deposits from and extend loans only to a closed group of individuals. They specialize in making consumer loans and some types of mortgage loan business. All told, the depository institutions in the United States include more than 8,000 commercial banks, 2,000 savings institutions, and 11,000 credit unions.

THE DEVELOPMENT OF ONLINE BANKING

The act of conducting financial intermediation on the Internet is broadly known as **online banking.** The first efforts to move financial intermediation online were spurred by the efforts of developers of home financial-management software. These companies wanted to include features in their software packages to make them more desirable to consumers, so they offered to help software users consolidate bills and initiate payments over the Internet. To make this possible, financial-software companies formed alliances with banks, because bill payments typically had to be issued from bank accounts.

Online Banking
Providing financial intermediation services on the Internet.

Financial institutions soon recognized that there might be fee income to be earned by providing these services themselves. Soon many rushed to develop their own Web-based services, and online banking was born.

Types of Online Banking Services

People who engage in online banking use three kinds of services. One of the most popular is the original online service of bill consolidation and payment. This service allows consumers to lump many of the bills they pay each month into a single account for automatic payment via electronic deductions from their bank deposit accounts.

Another form of online banking uses Web sites to transfer funds among accounts. This eliminates the need to make trips to a bank branch or *automated teller machine (ATM)* to conduct such transfers. (Automated teller machines would not necessarily disappear following an eventual widespread adoption of online banking; see on the next page *Management Online: Transforming ATMs into "Smart ABMs."*)

In addition, people can engage in online banking to apply for loans, insurance policies, and the like. Although customers typically have to appear in person to finalize terms of a financial transaction such as a loan or purchase of an insurance policy, they can save some time and effort by starting the process at home or at work.

WWW.

What banks offer the latest automated bill payment services? One place to check is the search engine offered by Banxquote at http://www.banx.com. At the opening page, select "Banking, Trading & Deposits," and then click on "Online Banking, Bill Pay & Trading—Saver's Scoreboard."

.com

MANAGEMENT *Online*

Transforming ATMs into "Smart ABMs"

Currently, there are more than 200,000 automated teller machines in the United States and Canada. ATM networks have been a huge investment for the North American banks, but they have yielded a big payoff. An average ATM machine is used for about 100,000 transactions each year. Most of these ATM transactions are cash withdrawals and account transfers, many of which require customers to pay small access fees that add billions of dollars to total bank revenues each year.

Under one scenario, widespread consumer adoption of online banking, together with digital payment systems (see Chapter 10), would make all these ATMs largely obsolete. Many banks have not waited for this dark scenario to play out. In 1997, Canadian Imperial Bank of Commerce became the first North American bank to deploy "smart automated banking machines (smart ABMs)" that included Internet access. Since then, several large banks with big networks of ATMs, such as Bank of America and Wells Fargo, have been upgrad-

ing their existing ATM networks with smart ABM technology, including Pentium processors, color-touch screen monitors, sound cards, Web software, and thermal printers to issue receipts and coupons. Eventually, a consumer on the go will be able to access smart ABMs to pay bills, verify receipts and transmissions of online payments, send and receive messages, buy or sell stocks, and view updated portfolios. Many smart ABMs will let people download music from the Internet, buy movie tickets, purchase toiletries and greeting cards, and a host of other functions. Of course, customers will have to pay a small fee to access many of these online services, thereby continuing the stream of billions of dollars of revenues to banks.

For Critical Analysis:
Banks are also in the process of providing wireless access to online banking services. If this approach to online banking were to catch on, under what circumstances might smart ABMs remain an economically viable investment for banks?

There are two important activities that few people currently do online: depositing and withdrawing funds. As you will learn in Chapter 10, funds can be transmitted online, but such activities are in their early stages of development. Many observers believe that the lack of widespread standards for how to transmit digital payments is a key innovation that must precede the fullest possible adoption of online banking.

Nevertheless, many financial institutions have decided that there are two good reasons to promote online banking, irrespective of the adoption of technologies for transferring payments online. One is that online banking offers many opportunities for financial institutions to gain from cost efficiencies. If customers interact directly with automated systems and computers that take only a few people to maintain, financial institutions can save on some of the significant expenses of opening and maintaining large systems of branch offices. The cost savings of online banking can be difficult to quantify, but this has not stopped many financial institutions from adopting aggressive targets for converting their customers to Internet-based banking services. A number of financial institutions have adopted explicit targets for portions of their customers that they wish to convert to online banking services within the next few years.

Competitive Pressures for Online Banking

Another fundamental incentive that financial institutions have for developing online services is that if they do not, someone else may steal away their customers. For example, many new commercial banks began operating exclusively on the Internet by the early 2000s. These **Internet banks** have no physical branch offices, so they accept deposits through physical delivery systems, such as the U.S. Postal Service or Federal Express. This sharply reduces the costs incurred by Internet banks, and these institutions promise to pass on part of the cost savings to customers in the form of lower fees and interest rates. Some even offer customer choices that were unheard of in the traditional banking world, including free checking with very low minimum deposits, such as $100, and zero-fee money market accounts with average monthly balances of $2,500 or more.

Internet Bank
A bank that operates exclusively on the Internet, without physical branch offices.

Internet banks are not the only online source of competition faced by traditional banks. Today there are several Internet loan brokers, such as Quicken Loans, E-Loan, Lending Tree, and Microsoft's HomeAdviser. Each of these broker systems use software that matches consumers with loans. The consumer supplies information to the program, which then searches among available loan products for the best fit. The loans are available from lenders with which the broker has a contractual relationship.

Internet loan brokers' biggest forays into the banks' turf have been in credit-card and mortgage markets. In the credit-card business, Internet brokers have been especially successful in providing credit-card debt consolidation services. They do not always compete with banks, because often they act as marketers for traditional credit-card-issuing banks. Credit-card issuers pay the brokers' fees to match with new customers, thereby saving them from having to develop lists of potential prospects and develop and mail card offers.

The competition is more direct in the mortgage market. Indeed, Internet loan brokers often take the place of the traditional loan officer at a banking institution that makes mortgage loans. When mortgage rates fell in the late 1990s, people who wished to refinance their houses flooded the telephone lines of traditional banking institutions, only to get lots of busy signals, long waits on hold, and slow responses from loan officers. This led many to turn on their computers and surf the Internet. One Internet broker reported that visitors to its Web site increased from about 35,000 per month to more than 500,000 per month. Recently it has been a bumpy road for Internet mortgage sites, but many real-estate specialists continue to believe that within a few years at least 10 percent of U.S. mortgage-loan refinancings will be initiated through the Internet.

FUNDAMENTAL ISSUES ▼

1.

2.

3.

4.

5.

6.

1. What do financial institutions do, and what factors led them to offer online banking services?

Many financial institutions function as intermediaries that address problems arising from asymmetric information. One of these problems is adverse selection, or the potential for the least creditworthy borrowers to be the most likely to seek to borrow. Another is moral hazard, or the possibility that an initially creditworthy borrower may become less creditworthy after receiving a loan. A number of financial institutions also take advantage of economies of scale by spreading costs of managing funds across large numbers of savers. Several forms of banking services offered by financial institutions can be performed online, including bill consolidation and payment, account transfers, and loan applications, and ways to transfer funds on the Internet are being developed. The main incentives for financial institutions to offer online banking services are to earn fee income from providing these services and to try to offset competition from other online banking-service providers.

 ## Can Internet Banks Go It Alone?

In theory, Internet banks were to be the cutting-edge leaders in the electronic marketplace for banking services. Because the marginal cost of online banking transactions is a tiny fraction of the marginal cost of operating bricks-and-mortar bank branches, many observers expected Internet banks to proliferate. Some even speculated that Internet banks eventually might rise to a predominant position in the banking industry.

In fact, there are now many Internet banks. To a large extent, however, Internet banks that have made the most headway have succeeded by establishing a "market niche." Some Internet banks have established a mainstream banking presence, but Internet banks are far from a position of dominance. Today, some banking experts even question whether Internet banks will survive in a heavily regulated industry already populated by more than 20,000 primarily bricks-and-mortar competitors.

THE PROMISE AND EXPERIENCE OF INTERNET BANKING

Internet banks have managed to become a simultaneous story of success and failure. Just as some e-commerce firms in nonfinancial markets, such as Amazon.com and eBay.com, have established a solid market presence while others, such as Living.com and Pets.com, have collapsed, some Internet banks have thrived while others have faltered. What remains to be seen is whether the model of an Internet bank as a standalone institution will become the norm or the exception.

The Growth of Online Banking

When Internet bank start-ups first appeared in the marketplace, the promise of big profits beckoned. As increasing numbers of people began surfing the Web, enterprising Internet bankers concluded that many of those individuals would embrace online bill payment services, access to account transfer services from their homes and offices, and the convenience of applying for and finalizing loan terms on personal computers.

The willingness of banking customers to adopt online banking was the single greatest concern of owners and managers of Internet banks. In fact, bankers' hopes for customer acceptance of online banking have been surpassed. In the mid-1990s, all but the most optimistic Web-banking pioneers expected that a decade might pass before 50 percent of U.S. banking customers would be willing to use online banking services. As Figure 9-2 indicates, by 2001 at least 30 million U.S. households already used at least some type of online-banking services.

The Challenges of Stand-Alone Internet Banking

What Internet banks failed to anticipate, however, was that many households who were willing to use online banking services would not do so at Internet banks. Inducing banking customers to defect from traditional institutions has proved to be a hard sell.

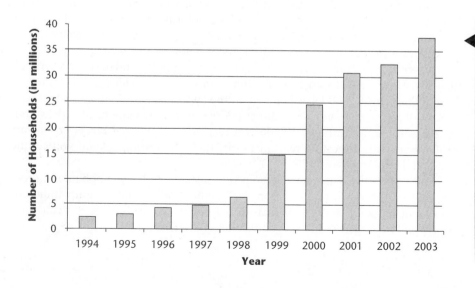

**Figure 9-2:
U.S. Households Using
Online Banking Services.**

The number of households engaging in online banking has increased steadily.

Source: Comptroller of the Currency and author estimates.

What progress are Internet banks making in the marketplace? Read a free sample issue of Online Banking Report and find links to Internet banks and credit unions at http://www.netbanker. com.

The decline of the stand-alone Internet bank has been a global phenomenon. An early pioneer in Internet banking, WingspanBank.com, struggled to earn profits, even as a wholly owned subsidiary of a bricks-and-mortar institution, Bank One. WingspanBank remained a going concern only by sharing its information-technology facilities with its parent institution. Bank One then offered selective online-banking services on a piecemeal basis to supplement the traditional banking services it offered its customers. In like manner, the Irish Internet Bank First-E.com laid off a portion of its staff to cut expenses before eventually becoming a subsidiary of a traditional Spanish banking firm. Softbank.com, a Japanese Internet bank, attracted considerable attention in the media before nearly going broke.

What Internet banks discovered was that they faced significant hurdles in their efforts to establish a foothold in banking markets. First, a fundamental promise of online banking was supposed to be the convenience it would offer consumers. At some Internet banks, however, providing reliable service turned out to be a challenge. An Internet user might become mildly irritated when a retailer's Web site is unavailable because a server crashes, but for a bank customer who is counting on making a transfer to close a financial deal in 30 minutes, such an event could prove disastrous. Furthermore, to obtain certain banking services, such as quotes on loan rates, some customers have found it quicker and easier just to make a phone call than to locate a Web page containing the desired information.

Second, Internet banks learned that many banking consumers have a stubborn attachment to face-to-face financial dealings. In particular, many consumers are reluctant to send funds to a bank with a physical location they have not seen. According to the president of the bank Nexity.com, a prospective customer from California who happened to be in Alabama on a business trip made a special side-trip to visit Nexity's physical office in Birmingham simply to verify that the Web bank offering relatively high deposit rates was "for real."

The higher deposit rates that Nexity offered point to a third challenge faced by it and other Internet banks. By definition, Internet banks begin as new institutions with no customers. To be successful in establishing a market foothold, they must rapidly recruit customers. Internet banks that had anticipated profiting from big cost advantages over traditional bricks-and-mortar competitors have quickly discovered that to attract customers, they must pay higher interest rates on their deposits. Figure 9-3 displays recent index measures of average rates paid on 12-month certificates of deposit offered online by Internet banks as compared with selected traditional bank competitors, relative to the average of all bricks-and-mortar banking institutions. As you can see, the rate Internet banks pay a rate online deposits is almost 20 percent higher than the average of rates offered by traditional banking rivals.

Fourth, Internet banks have struggled to offer the full range of banking products that customers can obtain from bricks-and-mortar banks. Competing with traditional banking institutions has turned out to be much more difficult than owners and managers of Internet banks had ever envisioned.

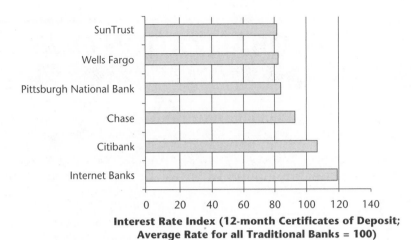

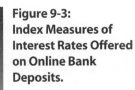

Figure 9-3:
Index Measures of Interest Rates Offered on Online Bank Deposits.

Internet banks typically offer interest rates on certificates of deposit that are well above the average rates paid by traditional banking institutions.

Source: Office of the Comptroller of the Currency.

Interest Rate Index (12-month Certificates of Deposit; Average Rate for all Traditional Banks = 100)

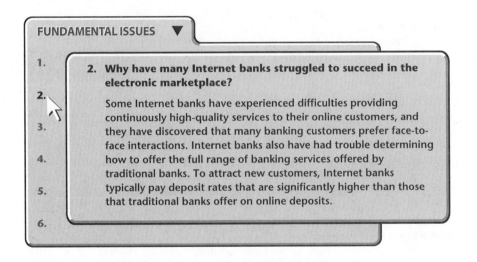

FUNDAMENTAL ISSUES ▼

1.
2.
3.
4.
5.
6.

2. Why have many Internet banks struggled to succeed in the electronic marketplace?

Some Internet banks have experienced difficulties providing continuously high-quality services to their online customers, and they have discovered that many banking customers prefer face-to-face interactions. Internet banks also have had trouble determining how to offer the full range of banking services offered by traditional banks. To attract new customers, Internet banks typically pay deposit rates that are significantly higher than those that traditional banks offer on online deposits.

BRICKS, CLICKS, OR BOTH?

In the early 1990s, the *Wall Street Journal* ran a series of articles questioning the future of the U.S. banking industry. The industry appeared to be populated, authors contended, with aging dinosaurs that might never adapt to the challenges posed by new information technologies. To the contrary, many traditional banking institutions have proved to be surprisingly nimble competitors in the electronic marketplace.

GLOBALIZATION *Online*

Brazilian Banks Drum Up New Customers by Connecting Them to the Internet

Only about 46 million of Brazil's 170 million residents are in households with bank accounts. Thus, about three-fourths of Brazil's population is "unbanked"; they use no bank services and conduct the bulk of their transactions with cash.

To induce more people to use their services, Brazilian banks have opted to go online. This poses a new challenge, however: fewer than 5 percent of Brazilians have Internet access. To address this problem, one institution, Banco Bradesco, began selling basic personal computers to all employees and current and new customers for $43 per month for a total of 24 months. In a nation in where *monthly* interest rates on credit card purchases are about 12 percent, this monthly payment plan was a tremendous bargain. Employees and customers have been snapping up Banco Bradesco's computers. The bank, which was the third bank in the world to

offer online banking services, also provides limited free access to the Internet as part of the deal. In addition, it has transformed its Web site into a portal where customers can connect to more than 300 online retailers, buy and sell stocks, invest in mutual funds, and apply for credit cards. People who cannot afford to buy Bank Bradesco's computers can shop online at kiosks it has installed in its 2,500 branches. The bank's services also are available through cellular phones and Web TV.

Other Brazilian banks, such as Banco Itau and Banco Unibanco, are striving to keep pace by offering Internet-related deals to their own customers. Banco Itau purchased a 12 percent share of America Online's Latin American unit so that it can offer its customers unlimited free Internet access. Banco Unibanco also provides free access to entice new customers, and it offers a special credit card product called *e-card*, which customers can use to make payments for goods and services purchased on the Internet.

For Critical Analysis:
What incentives might motivate Brazilian banks to try to expand online access for both existing and new customers?

Traditional Banks Meet the Internet

In 2000, a study of the business plans of British Internet banks found that together they intended to attract 3.5 million customers by the end of 2002. This finding revealed an immediate problem: only about 2 million new consumers of banking services were likely to emerge in the United Kingdom. To succeed in accomplishing their goals, British Internet banks would have to attract every one of those new banking consumers and steal away 1.5 million customers from established banking institutions in the United Kingdom, even though most of those institutions were already offering online banking services to their customers. (Banks around the globe, and particularly in Brazil, are adding online banking services to their line of financial products; see *Globalization Online: Brazilian Banks Drum Up New Customers by Connecting Them to the Internet.*)

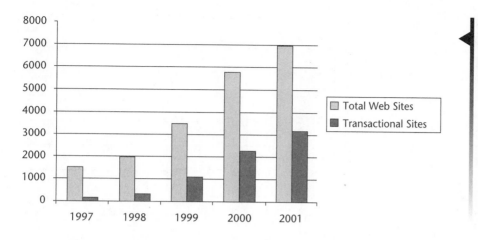

Figure 9-4:
Internet Access to Banks in the United States.

Thousands of banks throughout the United States now have Web sites, and an increasing number also offer the ability to conduct deposit and loan transactions via the Internet.

Source: Office of the Comptroller of the Currency and author's estimates.

The situation faced by start-up Internet banks in the United Kingdom reflects the experience of Internet banks throughout the world. Even as Internet banks sought to enter the electronic marketplace, they met immediate competition from previously established banking firms. As Figure 9-4 illustrates, many bricks-and-mortar depository institutions now have Web sites, and a growing number also offer transactional services at their sites. Online banking has been spreading through the entire U.S. banking industry. As a consequence, Internet banks have been unable to develop the first-mover advantages considered in Chapter 2.

Can Internet Banks Compete?

The basic problem that Internet banks face in their efforts to compete with traditional banks is illustrated by the experience of WingspanBank. After WingspanBank was opened by Bank One in June 1999, the Internet bank launched a new slogan: "If your bank could start over, this is what it would be." A year later, WingspanBank had fewer than 150,000 accounts, while Bank One had 500,000 regular online customers. In July 2001, Bank One folded WingspanBank's operations into its own Internet-banking business.

To remain viable in the face of online competition from traditional rivals, many Internet banks have, like WingspanBank, resorted to merging with or forming business alliances with traditional financial institutions. For instance, during 2000 Telebank.com sold out to E*Trade, Netbank.com partnered with a Fidelity Investments affiliate, Compubank.com established an affiliation with General Electric, and USABancshares.com developed an alliance with Palm Pilot. These banks continue to function as standalone operations, but their business partnerships and alliances allow them to offer a broader range of products so that they

Figure 9-5:
Shares of Banks Offering
Online Banking Services
in Selected Nations.

Online banking is being
offered by relatively large
percentages of institutions in
various nations of the world.

Source: Bank for
International Settlements.

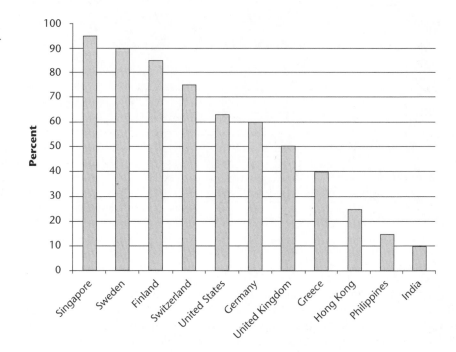

can effectively compete with mainstream banking firms that also offer online banking services.

In their quest to maintain viability as independent companies, other Internet banks have sought to establish specialized market niches. PointpathBank.com, for instance, specializes in making mortgage loans to newlywed couples. Virtual-Bank.com caters to high-salaried workers employed by information-technology companies. Another Internet bank, UmbrellaBank.com concentrates on pooling investments from corporations to rehabilitate apartments for low-income people struggling to enter the job market.

Today, an increasing number of Internet banks, such as Everbank.com and Principal.com, began operations as divisions or wholly owned subsidiaries of other financial institutions. Others have thrown in the towel and decided to become more like traditional banks. Some banks that previously operated only on the Internet, such as VirtualBank.com, and First-E.com, have begun opening physical branches. It may be that when it comes to banking, the issue is not whether "bricks" or "clicks" will win out in the end. Future success in banking may entail an ability to succeed in both the physical and virtual domains of financial intermediation. As Figure 9-5 shows, online banking services have become a common feature in the banking systems of many nations. The global future of banking may entail both bricks *and* clicks.

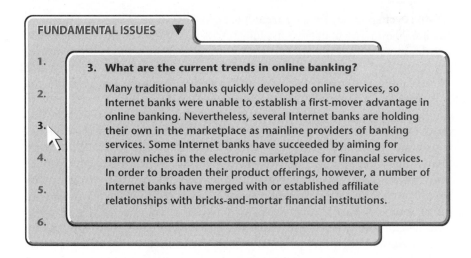

FUNDAMENTAL ISSUES ▼

1.

2.

3.

4.

5.

6.

3. What are the current trends in online banking?

Many traditional banks quickly developed online services, so Internet banks were unable to establish a first-mover advantage in online banking. Nevertheless, several Internet banks are holding their own in the marketplace as mainline providers of banking services. Some Internet banks have succeeded by aiming for narrow niches in the electronic marketplace for financial services. In order to broaden their product offerings, however, a number of Internet banks have merged with or established affiliate relationships with bricks-and-mortar financial institutions.

Testing the Limits of "Banking" on the Web

Banking has traditionally been a heavily regulated business. Most nations, including the United States, restrict the availability of licenses, called **charters,** to open and operate depository institutions that engage in traditional banking practices. Institutions that obtain such charters are granted the power to issue deposits that people can use to make payments, and they automatically qualify for examination and supervision by government regulators.

Charter
A license to operate a depository financial institution such as a commercial bank.

As banks have begun offering an increasing array of financial services online, so have other companies. These include other financial institutions, such as insurance companies, pension funds, and finance companies. Also joining the rush to offer financial services online are a number of traditionally nonfinancial companies, including the likes of Microsoft, Intuit, and General Electric. Many of the financial services offered by these and other firms are close substitutes for online banking services.

THE INTERNET AND AN ALREADY CHANGING FINANCIAL STRUCTURE

Nonbank financial institutions had begun to compete with banks before the Internet came along. Online access to financial services has only hastened the process of making U.S. financial institutions look more and more alike.

The Growing Overlap among Financial Institutions Expands Online

For instance, Merrill Lynch, the nation's largest brokerage firm with more than 12,000 brokers and more than 6 million client accounts, is also the second-largest mutual fund company and the largest investment banking underwriter. In addition, it has become a significant force in the commercial lending business. Beginning in the 1980s, Merrill Lynch jumped into small business lending, which was a growing loan market that many large banks had ignored and that smaller banks lacked resources to exploit to its fullest potential. Merrill Lynch now has established a reputation as a major competitor in the market for small business loans, and it owns subsidiaries that offer accounts with checking privileges, which the Federal Deposit Insurance Corporation insures alongside traditional bank deposits. Merrill Lynch offers a fully integrated financial services package that permits clients to make online transfers among their various stock, bond, mutual fund, and deposit accounts.

Commercial banks have also made inroads into markets that traditionally were the province of other financial institutions, such as sales of insurance policies and mutual funds. A number of commercial banks in the United States now deal in stocks and bonds, typically through subsidiary or affiliate companies. Many of these banks, like Merrill Lynch, permit customers to shift funds among various accounts on the Internet.

The Altered Legal Landscape in U.S. Banking

There is a reason that different types of U.S. financial institutions have only recently been confronting each other in various financial markets. For 66 years, the Glass–Steagall Act of 1933 governed range of permissible activities for U.S. financial institutions. In 1999, however, the growing similarity among services provided by various types of financial institutions convinced the U.S. Congress that the Glass–Steagall Act had outlived its usefulness.

By passing the *Financial Services Modernization Act of 1999,* also called the *Gramm-Leach-Bliley Act,* Congress swept away a number of the provisions of the Glass-Steagall legislation. There were two key provisions of this law, however, that overshadowed all others:

1) Securities firms and insurance companies are permitted to own commercial banks.
2) Banks are empowered to underwrite insurance and securities, including shares of stock.

Thus, securities brokers and dealers, investment banks, and insurance companies can now compete directly with commercial banks. In addition, commercial banks can compete directly with traditional insurers, brokers and dealers, and in-

MANAGEMENT *Online*

Making Islamic Financial Services Available on the Internet

The Shariah is the Islamic legal code. It forbids the roughly 1.2 billion Muslims of the world from entering into financial contracts that entail payments of interest, which rules out dealings with most conventional financial institutions. This code generally requires Muslims to enter into financial contracts that grant payments based on shares of ownership.

An estimated 20 million Muslims are online, and that number is expected to increase to 100 million by 2003. Consequently, most observers expect an upsurge in Web sites offering financial services geared toward Muslims.

These sites are likely to follow the example of London-based IslamiQ.com, which has existed since early 2000 under the guidance of a Shariah board comprising four Middle Eastern scholars. At this site, which offers services in both English and Arabic, Islamic believers can obtain information on financial institutions that comply with the Shariah. A companion site is IslamiQstocks.com, which provides real-time quotes from global stock exchanges, as well as information and links to Islamic banking, finance, and insurance products and services.

For Critical Analysis:

Of the types of financial institutions surveyed earlier in this chapter, which appear to offer products that best fit the requirements of the Islamic Shariah?

vestment banks. This new competition can take place both offline, in the traditional physical marketplace, and online, at Web sites on the Internet.

The Gramm–Leach–Bliley Act also laid the foundation for the growing affiliations between Internet banks and nonbank financial institutions such as brokerages, mutual funds, and insurance companies. Access to consumers of banking services via Internet sites operated by financial institutions of all stripes promises to vastly expand the scope of competition in markets for these services. (Even though it is now legal for many different financial institutions to offer traditional banking services online, for some people secular legality does not overcome spiritually based rules against consuming certain financial services; see *Management Online: Making Islamic Financial Services Available on the Internet*.)

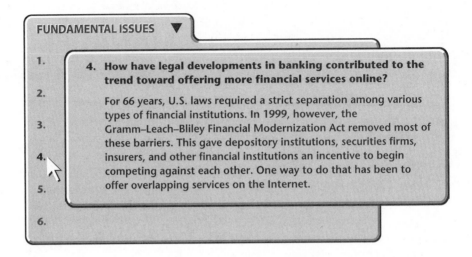

FUNDAMENTAL ISSUES ▼

1.

2.

3.

4.

5.

6.

4. **How have legal developments in banking contributed to the trend toward offering more financial services online?**

For 66 years, U.S. laws required a strict separation among various types of financial institutions. In 1999, however, the Gramm–Leach–Bliley Financial Modernization Act removed most of these barriers. This gave depository institutions, securities firms, insurers, and other financial institutions an incentive to begin competing against each other. One way to do that has been to offer overlapping services on the Internet.

CAN BANKS TURN AN ONLINE THREAT INTO AN OPPORTUNITY?

Initially, many owners and managers of banks and other depository institutions viewed both offline and online competition from other financial institutions with alarm. In the end, however, most decided that the increasingly overlapping functions of financial institutions presented banks with an opportunity to sell financial services as bundled products. During the past several years, banks have rushed to launch sales of insurance, mutual funds, and stock-trading services both in traditional branches and on the Internet. Indeed, part of the reason many banks have embraced the Internet is that they hoped to profit from bundling products for sale to customers online.

THE PROMISE OF WEB-BASED "CROSS SELLING"

Cross Selling

Marketing financial products in bundles, thereby engaging in price discrimination in an effort to enhance an institution's revenues and profits.

In banking, the product bundling considered in Chapter 4 is called **cross selling.** This is the act of marketing additional financial products to current customers, such as current depositors or borrowers, in an effort to expand a financial institution's overall sales and profits.

By engaging in cross selling, bankers bundle financial services into sets of products tailored to individuals. For instance, a bank might offer a current depositor the opportunity to purchase life insurance policies within alternative packages offering choices from among different interest payments on deposit funds and fees on online banking services. Customers would then choose from among different bundles, resulting in potentially enhanced revenues for banks.

Pricing financial product bundles in this way could, as you learned in Chapter 4, allow banks to engage in *price discrimination*. By taking into account differing elasticities of demand for various financial services they can now legally provide offline and online, banks hope to boost revenues and profits. (Some banks have gone beyond online cross selling to multilingual Web operations; see *Globalization Online: A California Bank Reprograms Its Web Site from the Ground Up—In Chinese.*)

GLOBALIZATION *Online*

POLICY MAKING GLOBALIZATION MANAGEMENT

A California Bank Reprograms Its Web Site from the Ground Up— In Chinese

After East West Bancorp of San Marino, California finished the first version of its online banking site, it did not bother to advertise its existence. The reason was that the first version was in English.

It was the follow-up version, which was translated entirely into Chinese, that the bank actively promoted. The reason is that 90 percent of the bank's customers are either Chinese or Chinese Americans. The Chinese version of the bank's Web site also included links to Chinese-oriented Web sites and contained ads for products intended to appeal to Chinese speakers.

East West initially marketed its new Web site to Chinese-American residents by running local radio, television, and newspaper ads and running banner ads—in English—on Web sites of other companies. Ultimately, however, the bank hopes to use the site to help build its overseas customer base, which currently accounts for more than 16 percent of its deposits. By offering people who prefer to communicate in Chinese the opportunity to do so in their financial dealings, the bank hopes to garner their business as both savers and borrowers.

For Critical Analysis:
Under what conditions would a North American bank such as East West stand to profit from duplicating its Web sites in other languages, such as Chinese, Spanish, or French?

Aggregators: A Death Knell for Cross Selling?

Among the most recognizable names on the Web are Yahoo.com and America Online. In recent years, many observers of the financial electronic marketplace have viewed these companies as potential providers of banking services. They could join Web portals such as Microsoft's MoneyCentral, Intuit's Quicken, and General Electric's GE Financial Network, which offer an individual the opportunity to manage all of his finances—deposit accounts, stock and bond portfolios, insurance policies, and pension funds—on a single Web site.

Some firms have jumped into this market by becoming online **aggregators**, sometimes called "screen scrapers." These Internet firms, which include companies such as Yodlee.com, obtain a customer's permission to collect all online financial data available from their banks, stockbrokers, insurers, and pension funds. For a fee, an aggregator places those data on a single Web site, which saves the customer from having to go to several different Web sites to keep track of these various accounts. This gives an aggregator access to considerable information about financial institutions, including how they do business, the types of service features they offer to their customers, the interest rates they charge on loans and pay on deposits, and the fees they charge for services.

Aggregators are bad news for banks that had counted on the Web for marketing bundled financial services to customers. The reason is that just as Web portals

Aggregators
Also known as "screen scrapers," these companies give their customers the capability to download all online financial information from Web sites operated by institutions such as banks, insurance companies, and stockbrokers for access at a single Web site.

can serve as e-commerce intermediaries that direct consumers to higher-quality, lower-price sites for goods and services, aggregators potentially can provide their customers with information about the best prices on various financial products. Then, instead of choosing among product bundles offered through banks engaging in cross selling, customers of aggregators can select products offered by various financial institutions. Effectively, they can create their own bundles at the Web set an aggregator provides them. By doing so, they can avoid banks' efforts to engage in price discrimination via cross selling.

Some banks have tried to combat aggregators by denying them access to customers' Web sites. Others have taken a more subtle approach by requiring aggregators to jump several hoops before accessing their customers' accounts. These banks require aggregators to sign contractual agreements that bind aggregators to identifying themselves when pulling data from a customer's account, thereby providing trails for bank auditors to follow. On one hand, such requirements help to protect the security of the bank's customers' accounts. On the other hand, the requirements also allow banks to keep tabs on what kinds of information aggregators obtain, which can help them track how the information may ultimately be used. Of course, such requirements also raise the operating costs of aggregators, and the prices aggregators charge consumers for their services ultimately reflect these higher costs. (Even the U.S. Postal Service is trying to become an aggregator; see *Mangement Online: Finally, the U.S. Postal Service Pays Complete Attention to Benjamin Franklin.*)

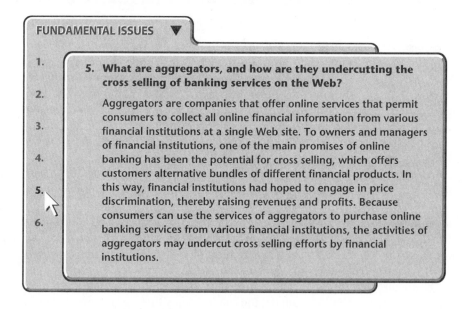

FUNDAMENTAL ISSUES   ▼

1.

2.

3.

4.

5.

6.

5. **What are aggregators, and how are they undercutting the cross selling of banking services on the Web?**

Aggregators are companies that offer online services that permit consumers to collect all online financial information from various financial institutions at a single Web site. To owners and managers of financial institutions, one of the main promises of online banking has been the potential for cross selling, which offers customers alternative bundles of different financial products. In this way, financial institutions had hoped to engage in price discrimination, thereby raising revenues and profits. Because consumers can use the services of aggregators to purchase online banking services from various financial institutions, the activities of aggregators may undercut cross selling efforts by financial institutions.

MANAGEMENT *Online*

POLICY MAKING   GLOBALIZATION   **MANAGEMENT**

Finally, the U.S. Postal Service Pays Complete Attention to Benjamin Franklin

Every young child knows that Benjamin Franklin was among the first people who attempted to determine the properties of electricity. Only those well versed in history know that Benjamin Franklin was also the first postmaster general, the official who manages the nation's postal service. Since Franklin's day, the U.S. Postal Service (USPS) has specialized in moving envelopes and boxes from one point on a map to another. In recent years, however, the USPS has been slow to confront the fact that e-mail mes-

sages may be displacing an estimated one-half of first-class mail, which accounts for about a third of USPS revenues.

There is nothing the USPS can do to stop e-mail. The agency has, however, sought to find new sources of revenues. One source it has in mind is the electronic marketplace. Its Web-based eBillPay service allows people to transmit payments to anyone in the United States, either electronically through a network of nearly 300 companies that accept electronic payments or by printing out paper checks ordered up online but transmitted through standard first-class mail service. Like aggregators, the USPS has become yet another source of competition for online banking services.

For Critical Analysis:
Does its status as a quasi-governmental agency give the USPS an "unfair advantage" over private online bill-payment firms?

 ## Regulating Online Banking

Important privacy and security issues are associated with the activities of financial aggregators. For this reason, bank regulators have explored whether they have the power to regulate the activities of aggregators. More broadly, bank regulators have struggled to adapt to the world of online banking, which arguably is beginning to look surprisingly similar to banking back in horse-and-buggy days—a time when banks were much less regulated than they are today.

BANK FRAUD: AN OLD PROBLEM WITH A NEW FACE

During a large portion the nineteenth century, U.S. banks issued their own **banknotes,** which were privately issued paper money redeemable in gold. Those who used the services of banks learned to be wary of so-called "wildcat banks,"

Banknotes
Privately issued paper currency.

however. Wildcat banks were institutions that allegedly established gold-redemption offices in locales where wildcats, not the humans who might wish to redeem the banknotes, were located. Essentially, these banks were fly-by-night operations that pocketed customers' deposits of gold and other marketable assets and departed. Although there is considerable evidence that this practice was not as widespread as some twentieth-century historians contended, there is also plenty of evidence that at least some wildcat banking existed.

Looking Back at Free Banking

Free Banking Laws
State laws in force in many U.S. states between 1837 and 1861 that allowed anyone to obtain a charter authorizing banking operations.

Wildcat banking was made possible by the **free banking laws** that many U.S. states adopted after 1836. These laws allowed any group of investors to secure a broad corporate charter allowing them to engage in banking practices. Before 1836, and within some states even after that date, a bank could incorporate only if the state legislature gave special permission. Requirements for obtaining a charter varied from state to state.

Free banking was not quite "free." States typically required free banks to purchase and deposit state-issued bonds with state banking authorities. This meant that banks in some states were risky propositions if the bonds issued by their state governments had uncertain prospects for full repayment or if the prices of the bonds fluctuated. Free-banking laws also required banks to pay gold or other specific assets in exchange for their banknotes. In most states, free banks had to restrict business to a single office, nor could they branch across state lines.

Is the Online Banking Free-for-All a Free-Banking Parallel?

In many states free banks faced few other restrictions on their activities. Recent research has shown that despite this relative lack of state oversight and the considerable latitude for entry or exit, the notes of free banks generally were quite safe. Many free banks were long-lived institutions, and among free banks that closed down at one time or another between 1837 and 1860, few depositors experienced losses. In addition, failures of free banks tended to be localized, and they rarely led to failures of other banking institutions. Hence, the evidence is that most free banks were easy-going, conservative housecats, not fly-by-night wildcats.

When anyone can post a Web site seeking deposits of funds and offering to pay depositors a rate of return, this nineteenth-century experience with free banking may have some modern-day relevance. When contemplating the role of bank regulation in a world of online banking, a big issue is whether Internet banks are more likely to be like housecats or wildcats.

REGULATING INTERNET BANKING

In light of new risks such as online bank fraud, should governments regulate all online financial services that overlap with services traditionally offered by regulated banks? Before addressing this question, let's first think about why governments might wish to regulate banking institutions.

The Rationales for Bank Regulation

Banks have always faced regulation. The traditional justification for regulating banks has been that if the government were to leave them alone, socially "bad" outcomes might result. In the worst case of a banking panic, many customers might lose their life savings.

Certainly, in the broad sweep of world history many such events have occurred. In the United States between the 1830s and 1930s, national banking panics seemed to occur in nearly regular cycles of fifteen to twenty years, with significant panics taking place in 1837, 1857, 1873, 1893, 1907, and 1929–1933. The severity of the last of these panics motivated much of the federal regulation of depository institutions that exists today. It also lies behind some of the current efforts to regulate online banking technologies.

Traditionally, governments have regulated banking institutions to pursue four essential goals:

1) **Maintaining depository institution liquidity**—A large portion of the liabilities of banking institutions are checking accounts and other types of deposits, which depository institution customers have the legal right to access almost immediately. Any banking institution that finds itself without sufficient cash on hand to meet the needs of its depositors suffers from **illiquidity.** Such illiquidity inconveniences the institutions' customers. If a large number of banks are illiquid simultaneously, then the result can be a serious disruption in the nation's flow of payments for goods and services, with potentially broader negative effects on the economy.

Illiquidity
A situation in which a banking institution lacks the cash assets required to meet requests for depositor withdrawals.

2) **Assuring bank solvency by limiting failures**—An overriding goal of bank regulaton is to reduce the likelihood of widespread bank failures. Any business, including a bank, typically fails and declares bankruptcy when it reaches a pont of **insolvency,** when it is unable to pay debts as they mature. Although an insolvent business may have positive net worth, it is insolvent if it cannot meet its financial obligations. Because many of a bank's assets are financial instruments that are more liquid than most assets of nonfinancial businesses, bankruptcy and insolvency are generally used as synonymous terms. Consequently, a depository institution generally is considered to have reached a point of insolvency if the value of its assets falls below the value of its liabilities, so that the value of its *equity,* or net worth, is negative. A key feature of depository institution regulation typically is the periodic *examination* of institutions' accounting ledgers to verify that the institutions are solvent. Another aspect normally is the *supervision* of these institutions via the publication and enforcement of rules and standards with which the institutions must comply. A purpose of regulatory supervision is to make insolvency and failure a rare occurrence.

Insolvency
A situation in which the value of a bank's assets falls below the value of its liabilities.

3) **Promoting an efficient financial system**—Another key rationale for bank regulation is to promote an environment in which banking institutions provide services at lowest possible cost. Achieving cost efficiency minimizes the total resources that society expends on services that banks provide,

thereby freeing up the largest possible amount of remaining resources for other social uses.

4) **Consumer protection**—Throughout history, many leading Americans have mistrusted banks. Thomas Jefferson said they were more dangerous than standing armies. When Andrew Jackson lost considerable personal wealth to banks from foreclosed loans after suffering big losses on land speculation, he made bank-bashing a national pastime. The U.S. Congress has consistently heeded the calls of constituents by passing consumer-protection legislation intended to protect them from possible misbehavior by bank managers. Hence, consumer protection is another fundamental goal of bank regulation. (Some federal laws single out specific groups of consumers for protection; see *Policymaking Online: Internet Banks Confront the Community Reinvestment Act.*)

The Problem of Conflicts among Regulatory Goals

The depository institution regulators described in Table 9-1 struggle to achieve all four goals simultaneously. Typically, achieving one objective may entail sacrificing another. For instance, a problem that regulators often face is distinguishing illiquidity from insolvency. It is possible for a banking institution to be illiquid temporarily yet to be solvent otherwise, just as it is possible for an otherwise wealthy individual to experience temporary "cash flow" difficulties. Bank regulators, and particularly a central bank such as the Federal Reserve, can assist institutions suffering from short-term liquidity problems by extending them credit. The difficulty is that illiquidity can be a symptom of pending insolvency. Extending such loans could keep otherwise insolvent institutions operating when they really

Table 9-1: Federal Regulators of Depository Institutions.

Office of the Comptroller of the Currency (OCC)	A unit of the Department of the Treasury that supervises and examines all commercial banks with charters granted by the federal government
Federal Reserve (Fed)	Regulates all state-chartered banks that are members of the Federal Reserve System; also regulates bank holding companies that own commercial bank subsidiaries
Federal Deposit Insurance Corporation (FDIC)	Regulates all state-chartered banks that are not members of the Federal Reserve System
Office of Thrift Supervision (OTS)	A unit of the Department of the Treasury that regulates federally chartered savings banks and savings and loan associations
National Credit Union Administration (NCUA)	Supervises and examines all federally chartered credit unions

POLICYMAKING *Online*

Internet Banks Confront the Community Reinvestment Act

A key consumer protection law is the Community Reinvestment Act (CRA) of 1977. This legislation calls for every bank to provide evidence that it follows a "CRA planning process" intended to promote lending to all individuals regardless of race, ethnicity, or gender. The act requires bank managers to collect detailed data concerning lending applications, acceptances, and denials and to provide analyses of how these data relate to the characteristics of the populations within "service areas" surrounding the bank's offices and branches.

In addition, CRA directs bank regulators to evaluate each institution's record in lending to populations that it serves and to provide banks with ratings of their performances in meeting the credit needs of all groups. Banks that fail to meet CRA requirements to the fullest can experience difficulties when they contemplate mergers and acquisitions. Recently, bank regulators have even proposed incorporating a bank's CRA ratings into their evaluations of its overall safety and soundness.

An emerging issue is how, for the purposes of CRA evaluations, to define the "service area" of a bank that operates exclusively in cyberspace. Some Internet banks, such as Atlanta-based Netbank.com, have reached agreements with regulators to serve low- and middle-income communities within specific regions near the buildings that house their management offices. Others, such as Houston-based Com-

pubank.com, were able to gain designations as "limited-purpose banks" with scaled-down CRA obligations in exchange for promises to lend directly to minority-owned businesses and to provide those businesses with computers that allowed them to access the bank's services online.

Nevertheless, as Internet banks begin to gain competitive footholds in markets outside the immediate geographic vicinities of their offices, they are likely to come under increasing pressure to meet CRA requirements everywhere their customers may be located. Already there is a movement among consumer groups to require Internet banks to regard their "service area" as any regions where Internet banks make loans. Exactly what this might entail is unclear. Under a literal interpretation of the law, it could well mean that an Internet bank based in, say, Ohio could find itself developing "CRA planning processes" that encompass such far-flung locales as Yuma, Arizona, and Columbus, Mississippi. After all, if borrowers in those locales successfully point and click their way to a loan from the bank, then its "service area" will extend a considerable distance from its Ohio office. So will the obligation of Internet banks to compile paperwork to satisfy CRA's requirements.

For Critical Analysis:
Critics argue that the paperwork requirements of meeting CRA's requirements—a time cost of 50 to 600 hours per year for every bank and an industrywide dollar cost estimated at about $35 million— considerably raise bank costs. Who ultimately pays these costs: banks, consumers, or both?

---

ought to close. Efforts to promote liquidity of banks can thereby permit poorly managed, insolvent banks to run up even more debts, worsening the extent of their insolvency.

In addition, because earning high profits helps banks avoid liquidity and insolvency difficulties, governmental regulators often are tempted to find ways to protect banks from competition. At the same time, banks are more likely to operate as efficiently as possible when exposed to rivalry from other financial institutions. Competition, however, drives down bank profitability, so that unexpected shocks to the economy or financial system can cause them to operate at significant losses, thereby threatening their liquidity and solvency levels.

Innovation May Be Stifled

Laws designed to protect bank customers from potentially unscrupulous bank managers can interfere with the development of innovative banking practices that might improve customer service. For example, suppose that a reputable bank develops the ability to post an Internet Web site that a visitor can use to apply for a loan without going to the trouble to drive to a bank and conduct a long-winded interview with a bank loan officer. The bank gains, because it reduces the amount of time that loan officers have to allocate to such personal interviews. To prevent *unscrupulous* banks from taking advantage of unwary consumers on the Internet, however, government regulators may require this reputable bank to meet a number of standards in posting its Web site. It may also require the bank to file detailed reports about each application it receives. The costs of meeting the government's consumer-protection regulations might very well offset the efficiency gains the bank hoped to achieve, inducing it to drop its plans to provide the new service. In this way, protecting consumers reduces bank efficiency.

The Pros and Cons of Regulating Online Banking

A key issue of bank regulation is determining how best to trade off progress toward achieving one regulatory goal against sacrificing progress in accomplishing greater efficiency. Undoubtedly, this will prove to be a challenge as banking continues to move across corridors within cyberspace.

On one hand, a traditional way to limit the potential for insolvency of banks is to require periodic audits of their accounts. To ease the task of auditing banks, regulators typically require them to follow industry and regulatory standards in their business practices. Applying this same approach to online banking would necessitate placing limits on "permissible" online banking business practices. Although such regulatory restraints might be consistent with easing the task regulators face in limiting the potential for bank insolvency, they would not be consistent with allowing banks to experiment with new ways of operating that might achieve significant cost savings.

On the other hand, unhindered adoption of new ways of banking via the latest information technologies might, under some circumstances, induce bank managers to engage in riskier practices. In addition, entry in banking-related businesses via the Internet could greatly increase the potential for widespread illiquidity—or even insolvencies, if the result is poorly implemented plans conceived by entrepreneurs unskilled in the arts of banking. Many people could lose their savings as a result, and society as a whole could bear significant costs.

These considerations indicate that decisions about whether or how to regulate online banking technologies involve the same trade-offs that bank regulators have always faced. The main difference is that governmental bodies charged with pursuing the traditional goals of bank regulation must keep up with an ever more rapidly changing financial environment.

FUNDAMENTAL ISSUES ▼

1.

2.

3.

4.

5.

6.

> **6. What are the rationales for regulating online banking?**
>
> The reasons for contemplating regulation of online banking mirror those typically offered for regulating traditional banking activities: preventing illiquidity, limiting insolvencies, promoting efficiency, and protecting consumers. An important issue is whether online banking poses unique problems, including greater security concerns and an increased potential for bank fraud, which may justify special regulation. Nevertheless, regulators contemplating restrictions on online banking are likely to face trade-offs among their broad regulatory objectives that are similar to those they face in regulating traditional banking activities.

Chapter Summary

1) **What Financial Institutions Do, and Factors That Led Them to Offer Online Banking Services:** Many financial institutions function as intermediaries that address problems arising from asymmetric information. These include adverse selection, or the potential for the least creditworthy borrowers to be the most likely to seek to wish to borrow, and moral hazard, or the possibility that an initially creditworthy borrower may become less creditworthy after receiving a loan. A number of financial institutions also take advantage of economies of scale by spreading costs of managing funds across large numbers of savers. Several forms of banking services offered by financial institutions can be performed online, including bill consolidation and payment, account transfers, and loan applications. Banks also are developing ways to transfer funds on the Internet. The main incentives for financial institutions to offer online banking services are to earn fee income from providing these services and to try to offset competition from other online banking-service providers.

2) **Why Many Internet Banks Have Struggled to Succeed in the Electronic Marketplace:** One problem that some Internet banks have strived against is the challenge of providing high-quality services to online banking customers on a continuous basis. Internet banks have also encountered a customer preference for face-to-face interactions and have experienced difficulties in offering the full range of banking services available from traditional banks. To induce customers to use their services, Internet banks normally have to pay deposit rates significantly above the rates that traditional banks offer on online deposits.

3) **Current Trends in Online Banking:** Because many bricks-and-mortar banks were quick to offer online services, Internet banks did not establish a first-mover advantage. Many Internet banks continue to provide mainline banking services exclusively online, however, and some Internet banks have experienced success in narrow niche markets. Nevertheless, a number of Internet banks have merged with or developed affiliate relationships with traditional financial institutions in an effort to broaden the range of financial services that they can provide.

4) **How Legal Developments in Banking Have Contributed to the Trend Toward Offering More Financial Services Online:** From 1933 to 1999, the activities of U.S. financial institutions were legally separated. Passage of the Gramm–Leach–Bliley Financial Modernization Act in 1999 altered the U.S. banking environment in a way that favored more online competition by giving banks, insurance companies, securities firms, and other financial institutions a greater incentive to offer overlapping services on the Internet.

5) **How Aggregators Are Undercutting the Cross Selling of Banking Services on the Web:** Aggregators are firms that provide services allowing their customers to transfer financial information from various online accounts at financial institutions to a single Web site. A major promise of online banking for financial institutions has been the possibility to engage in cross selling by offering consumers alternative bundles of various financial products, which would permit price discrimination that would push up the institutions' revenues and profits. Aggregators' services allow consumers to buy online-banking services from different institutions, however. This reduces the incentive for consumers to respond favorably to cross selling by financial institutions.

6) **The Rationales for Regulating Online Banking:** The traditional justifications for regulating traditional banking activities—preventing illiquidity, limiting insolvencies, promoting efficiency, and protecting consumers—are the same rationales commonly offered for online banking restrictions. Some observers also argue that unique security concerns and an increased potential for bank fraud justify special regulation of online banking. Online banking regulators are likely to face trade-offs among regulatory objectives that are similar to those they experience in traditional regulation of banking institutions.

Questions and Problems

1) Consider the rationales for the existence of financial intermediaries. Do these rationales apply any more or less to Internet-based financial intermediaries than they do to traditional bricks-and-mortar intermediaries? If so, in what respects? If not, then what are the rationales for Web-based intermediation over intermediation within the physical marketplace?

2) Does your answer to question 1 relate to recent trends in Internet banking? Based on your answer, do you predict more of a movement toward niche-related Internet banks or more consolidation of online banking services within traditional banking firms?

3) As noted in the chapter, Internet banks offer higher deposit rates than those paid by traditional banks. Provide arguments for why this could be regarded as evidence favoring the view that Internet banks face either higher or lower costs in operating and in attracting customers.

4) How might tough regulatory restrictions on banking have either slowed or speeded the development of online banking?

5) In what ways might the Gramm–Leach–Bliley Financial Modernization Act of 1999 promote the speedier development of online financial services? Are there any ways that it could hinder the development of these services?

6) How might the Internet contribute to greater consolidation among various types of financial-services firms? Provide concrete examples.

7) Is it possible that the Internet could contribute to greater specialization among some types of financial intermediaries? Why or why not?

8) How might banks protect their bundling efforts from the services provided by aggregators? Are there competitive forces that might complicate such efforts?

9) In what ways might bank fraud be easier to perpetrate using online banking methods instead of traditional banking practices? Explain.

10) Deposits up to $100,000 at traditional banking institutions are federally insured.

   (a) Recently Merrill Lynch and other brokerage firms have purchased banks and begun allowing investors to intermingle funds in both offline and online brokerage accounts and money market deposit accounts that are eligible for federal deposit insurance protection. How might this complicate federal efforts to regulate brokerage firms and banks as separate institutions?

   (b) Suppose that commercial firms such as auto and computer producers eventually are allowed to own Internet banks. In what ways might this complicate federal deposit insurance and bank regulation?

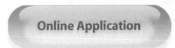

Online Application

Internet URL: http://www.firstib.com

Title: **First Internet Bank of Indiana**

Navigation: Go directly to the above URL.

Application: Perform the following operations, and answer the following questions.

1) Click on "Personal Accounts," and then click on "Personal Accounts FAQs." What issues arise with online banking that do not arise at traditional banks? In what ways are these advantages or disadvantages for Internet banks?

2) Back up to the "Personal Accounts" page and review the personal banking services that First Internet Bank provides. Then back up again and click on "Business Accounts" and review those services. Can you think of any basic banking services traditionally available from bricks-and-mortar banks that this Internet bank does not provide?

For Group Study and Analysis: Divide the class into two groups, and have both groups compare the online banking services and interest rates available from First Internet Bank of Indiana and another Internet Bank, Nexity Bank of Birmingham, Alabama (http://www.nexity.com). Reconvene the class, and discuss factors that might contribute to different approaches at these two Internet banks.

Selected References and Further Readings

Brown, Jeffrey, and Austan Goolsbee. "Does the Internet Make Markets More Competitive? Evidence from the Life Insurance Industry," Working Paper No. 7996, National Bureau of Economic Research, November 2000.

Claessens, Stijn, Thomas Glaessner, and Daniela Klingebiel. "Electronic Finance: Reshaping the Financial Landscape around the World," World Bank, Financial Sector Strategy and Policy Group, 2000.

Couch, Karen, and Donna Parker. "'Net Interest' Grows as Banks Rush Online," Federal Reserve Bank of Dallas, *Southwest Economy* (March/April 2000).

Cronin, Mary J., ed. *Banking and Finance on the Internet.* New York: Wiley, 1998.

Furst, Karen, William Lang, and Daniel Nolle. "Who Offers Internet Banking?" Office of the Comptroller of the Currency, *Quarterly Journal* (June 19, 2000), pp. 27–46.

"Online Finance: The Virtual Threat." *The Economist* (May 20, 2000), pp. 5–31.

Chapter 10

Digital Cash and Electronic Payments

FUNDAMENTAL ISSUES ▼

1. What are the primary means of payment in the United States, and how important are electronic payments? ▶
2. What distinguishes payment systems that use stored-value cards, debit cards, and smart cards? ▶
3. What is digital cash, and what effects might its widespread use have on the payment system? ▶
4. Is digital cash less secure than physical cash? ▶
5. What factors are likely to determine whether smart cards and digital cash receive widespread adoption in the electronic marketplace? ▶

<E-Commerce Today>

A Mouse Replaces a Machine Gun

It is June 30, 1934. John Dillinger, the U.S. Federal Bureau of Investigation's (FBI's) "Public Enemy Number One," has received information that the South Bend, Indiana, post office will deposit more than $100,000 (more than $1.25 million in today's dollars) at Merchants National Bank. He targets the bank for his gang's next big holdup. Everything goes wrong, however, including brave efforts by a teenager and an elderly man to thwart the robbery. Gang member Baby Face Nelson fires bursts of machine-gun bullets at police officers on a street crowded with innocent citizens, and the five gangsters manage to complete a desperate escape in their getaway car. After Dillinger's gang reaches its lair in Illinois, Baby Face Nelson divides the money into neat piles. Dillinger's face falls when he sees his share of the loot: $4,800 (more than $60,000 in today's dollars), or less than 5 percent of the sum he had anticipated. Dillinger decides to postpone his plans to flee to Mexico; to finance the lifestyle he wants there, he will have to commit more robberies. Three weeks later, however, FBI agents thwart his plans by gunning him down outside a Chicago theater.

Now fast forward almost exactly 61 years later, to a day when Citibank's top security officials are working feverishly in a special bank "war room" in Manhattan. From this command center, the officials are closely monitoring Citibank's global funds transfer system so that they can provide customers with early warnings of unauthorized funds transfers that recently have plagued the bank's payment network. So far, all the Citibank officials know is that a computer hacker has accessed secret codes and procedures that have permitted him to transfer funds between Citibank computers in Buenos Aires and New York. Finally, computer experts in the war room find a way to trace a $400,000 transfer to a BankAmerica account in San Francisco, and this turns out to be the break FBI investigators have been seeking to crack the case. Eventually, law enforcement officials arrest Russian gang members not only in New York and San Francisco, but also in Britain, Israel, and the Netherlands. The leader of the gang of modern-day bank robbers turns out to be a biochemistry graduate in St. Petersburg, Russia. He and his fellow computer gangsters used no weapons, took no hostages, and had no getaway cars, but Citibank discovers they had managed to transfer about $12 million out of Citibank customer accounts. The modus operandi for bank robberies will never be the same.

These contrasting "true crime" episodes illuminate the dramatic changes that have taken place in the global payment system. Banks no longer are isolated storehouses for cash and checks. Today, banks in the smallest communities have access to computer and communications systems that permit them to electronically transfer funds to nearly any other financial institution on the planet. In addition, small, medium-sized, and large companies are increasingly linked to these payment networks. In this chapter we shall discuss current and emerging payment systems in modern-day electronic banking.

 ## Electronic Money Isn't New

Whenever you use currency to pay for a good or service, the exchange is final at the moment that the transaction takes place. By way of contrast, for many other means of payment, such as checks, exchanges are final only after depository institutions transfer funds from the account of the purchaser to the seller. Hence, to use some means of payment to make a transaction, people must rely on depository institutions as intermediaries in the nation's **payment system.** This is the institutional structure through which individuals, businesses, governments, and financial institutions make payments.

Payment System
A term that broadly refers to the set of mechanisms by which consumers, businesses, governments, and financial institutions exchange payments.

AN OVERVIEW OF THE U.S. PAYMENT SYSTEM

Today's payment system is a fascinating mix of old and new. There are two main components of the overall U.S. payment system. The first consists of the various mechanisms for processing **retail payments,** which are funds transfers for transactions of relatively "small" value—tens of thousands of dollars or less. Consumer transactions with merchants account for the bulk of retail payments. The second consists of **wholesale payments,** which are large-value transactions typically denominated in hundreds of thousands or millions of dollars.

Retail Payments
Transfers of funds amounting to tens of thousands of dollars or less.

Wholesale Payments
Transfers of funds amount to hundreds of thousands of dollars or more.

Nonelectronic Payments
Within the retail and wholesale payment categories, there are two methods of delivering payments: nonelectronic, paper-based means of payment and payments transmitted electronically. As panel *(a)* of Figure 10-1 indicates, about 98 percent of all transactions in the United States are accomplished using these nonelectronic means of payment.

By far the most popular means of retail payment in the United States, in terms of number of transactions, is nonelectronic paper notes and coins. These currency transactions alone make up more than three-fourths of *total* U.S. payments. In spite of all the available information technologies, the bulk of transactions in the U.S. economy remain very low-tech. Nevertheless, individual currency transactions are quite small on average—so small that together they compose less than 0.5 percent of the total dollar value of all exchanges in the United States. Think of all the times you make minor purchases of such low-ticket items as ink pens or hamburgers, and you will understand why this is so.

Figure 10-1:
Electronic versus Nonelectronic Payments.

As panel (a) indicates, nonelectronic transactions account for nearly all payments in the United States. Panel (b), however, shows that the bulk of the dollar value of exchanges is accomplished through electronic means of payment.

Source: Author's estimates.

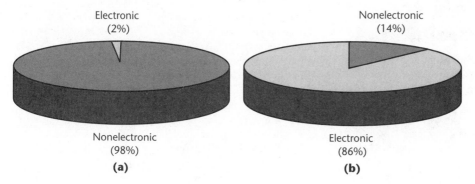

The second most used means of payment is checks, which account for about one-fifth of all transactions. Depository institutions clear millions of checks each day, for a total of more than 70 billion in a year. This is possible because nearly all checks have magnetic ink encryptions that special machines can read to sort and distribute checks automatically. Machines also can process information for crediting and debiting of accounts. Large-scale automation of check sorting, accounting, and distribution has kept the per-check cost of clearing checks very low.

Other nonelectronic means of payment include money orders, traveler's checks, and credit cards. Together these make up less than 1 percent of the total number of transactions and of the dollar value of all transactions.

Electronic Payments

Although panel *(a)* of Figure 10-1 shows that the bulk of payment *transactions* are nonelectronic, panel *(b)* indicates that approximately 86 percent of the *dollar value* of all payments is transmitted in electronic transactions. U.S. residents continue to use currency and checks for the large number of low-value transactions they make each day, but these and other paper-based payments account for just 14 percent of the total value of payments.

Most of the dollars that people exchange in the United States are transacted electronically. These large volumes of funds are transmitted in a very small share of total transactions—the 2 percent of payments shown in panel *(a)* of Figure 10-1. Consequently, many of these electronic payments are much, much larger than those transmitted by consumers. (If the owners of some Web sites have their way, in future years there will be so many goods and services traded without money

MANAGEMENT *Online*

Can Barter Make a Comeback on the Internet?

Barter is the direct exchange of goods and services without the use of money. Normally engaging in barter requires a high opportunity cost in finding others willing to exchange items directly. Completing any barter transaction requires a "double coincidence of wants." Hence, the costs of finding a partner to an exchange are prohibitively high. This provides the traditional explanation for why societies past and present eventually opt to use money.

On the Internet, however, searching for an exchange partner only requires meandering through Web *barter exchanges.* These are sites where people and companies can engage in bartering just as easily as they can transmit online bids at C2C sites such as eBay.com and QXL.com. At barter exchanges with names like All Business, users simply sign up, agree to a credit check, and begin searching for trading part-

ners. A company that operates an oil refinery can, for instance, obtain materials it requires to upgrade its operations by offering to refine an oil producer's petroleum without any cash trading hands.

These are just two of more than 400 regional barter exchanges in the United States, and they are also only two of many that now offer their services online. On these exchanges, individuals and firms trade books for services such as tax advice, airline tickets for advertising space, and the like.

There is one important sign that barter exchanges do not believe they will eventually drive money from existence. Typically, barter exchanges charge both sides of a barter transaction a fee of up to 4 percent of the amount traded—measured in dollars.

For Critical Analysis:
Under what circumstances could barter transactions ever become more commonplace than exchanges settled with money?

---

that measuring "dollar values" of exchanges will be problematic; see *Management Online: Can Barter Make a Comeback on the Internet?*)

ELECTRONIC RETAIL PAYMENT SYSTEMS

Before the Internet came into existence, there were several consumer-oriented electronic payments mechanisms. Even though these payment mechanisms have not involved a large portion of the value of U.S. payments, they have long processed consumer payments in digital formats.

Automated-Teller-Machine Networks

Most U.S. consumers have experience using *automated teller machine (ATM) networks,* which are depository institution computer terminals activated by magnetically encoded bank cards. Many consumers use ATM networks to make deposits, obtain cash from checking and savings accounts, and transfer funds among accounts.

A sizable number of consumers also pay some of their bills using ATM networks. A recent innovation in ATM technology is the "Personal Touch" ATM, which offers visual contact with depository institution employees at another location. Using such ATM links, consumers can apply for loans and mortgages, purchase mutual funds, and obtain information about loan and deposit terms and rates.

Automated Clearing Houses

Another type of consumer-oriented electronic payments mechanism is the **automated clearing house (ACH).** ACHs are computer-based clearing and settlement facilities for the interchange of credits and debits via electronic messages instead of checks. ACHs process payments within one or two days after the request for a transfer of funds. Common ACH transfers are automatic payroll deposits, in which businesses make wage and salary payments directly into employees' deposit accounts. The federal government makes large use of ACH facilities. In particular, the Social Security Administration distributes many payments to Social Security beneficiaries via ACH direct-deposit mechanisms.

The government also disperses a growing portion of welfare and food stamp payments using an *electronic benefits transfer (EBT) system.* EBT functions like an ACH system but looks a lot like an ATM network to welfare and food stamp beneficiaries, because beneficiaries receive their welfare funds or food stamps from special cash or food stamp disbursement machines.

Point-of-Sale Networks

Since the 1970s technology has permitted the use of **point-of-sale (POS) networks.** These systems of direct computer links between banks and retailers that allow customers to pay for items by authorizing direct deductions from their deposit accounts at depository institutions. POS networks have not developed as quickly as some observers had expected, given that most large chains of department stores and other retail outlets use networks of cash-register terminals that have the capability to process POS payments.

The cost of setting up POS systems can be significant, and it has never been clear who would be willing to incur these costs. Check-processing costs have remained so low that depository institutions have little incentive to switch to POS networks, and retailers have little desire to bear the cost of installing such systems. For POS networks to become more widespread in the future, consumers will have to desire to use them—and to be willing to pay for them. Recent trends toward greater consumer use of online banking via the Internet may lead to increased consumer interest in POS networks.

Where the United States Stands in Electronic Retail Payments

In spite of all these developments, U.S. consumers use paper-based, nonelectronic means of payment much more than people in most other high-income nations. As Table 10-1 indicates, an average U.S. resident made 234 such transactions each

Automated Clearing House (ACH)
A computer-based facility for clearing and settlement facility that replaces check transactions by interchanging credits and debits electronically.

Point-of-Sale (POS) Networks
Systems in which consumer payments for retail purchases occur through direct deductions from their deposit accounts at depository institutions.

WWW.

How do ACH systems function? Find out by visiting the Web site of the National Automated Clearing House Association at http://www.nacha.org, where you can click on "About NACHA" for a summary and links to many other informative web sites.

.COM

Table 10-1: Annual Noncash Transactions Per Person in Selected Countries.

Country	Number of Transactions Per Person		Percent Electronic Payments
	Paper-Based	**Electronic**	
Italy	23	6	20%
Japan	9	31	78
Switzerland	2	65	97
Sweden	24	68	74
Norway	58	40	41
Belgium	16	85	84
United Kingdom	57	58	50
Finland	40	81	67
Denmark	24	100	81
Canada	76	53	41
Germany	36	103	74
the Netherlands	19	128	87
France	86	71	45
United States	234	59	20

Source: David Humphrey, Lawrence Pulley, and Jukka Vesala, "Cash, Paper, and Electronic Payments: A Cross-Country Analysis," *Journal of Money, Credit, and Banking* 28 (November 1996, Part 2), pp. 914–939.

year in the mid-1990s, which amounted to between 3 and 100 times more than average residents of other nations.

Table 10-1 shows that most non–U.S. residents, except for those in Italy, use electronic means of payment more regularly than U.S. residents. One popular retail payment mechanism in many European nations is *electronic giro* systems, in which banks, post offices, and other payment intermediaries transfer funds by telephone lines or via other forms of electronic communication. This eliminates the need for paper checks and for automated clearing house networks.

ELECTRONIC WHOLESALE PAYMENTS

Although consumer-oriented electronic payment systems account for a growing portion of both the number of transactions and the dollar value of such transactions, the bulk of the dollars that flow through the U.S. payments system are wholesale payments. Delivery systems for processing wholesale payments are **large-value wire transfer systems,** which are designed and operated specifically to manage electronic transfers of large sums.

The Federal Reserve's Wire Transfer System

In the United States there are two large-value wire transfer systems. One of these is **Fedwire,** a wire transfer system that the Federal Reserve System operates. All depository institutions that hold reserves at Federal Reserve banks have access to Fedwire, although fewer than 2,000 institutions regularly use the system. Depository institutions pay fees for the wire transfer services that Fedwire provides, and they use Fedwire mainly for two specific kinds of transfer.

One important type of Fedwire funds transactions is book-entry security transactions. The Fed operates book-entry security systems on behalf of the U.S. Treasury Department. Fedwire is the means by which depository institutions pay for securities they purchase using these systems. The second primary type of Fedwire transactions is funds transfers among reserve deposit accounts that depository institutions maintain at Federal Reserve banks. When depository institutions extend or repay federal funds loans to other depository institutions, they send the funds on Fedwire. The average Fedwire payment is about $3 million, and the total average *daily* payment volume on the Fedwire system is nearly $1 *trillion.*

Other Large-Value Payment Systems

The other major large-value wire transfer system in the United States is the **Clearing House Interbank Payment system (CHIPS).** This is a privately owned system operated by the New York Clearing House Association, which has about 90 member depository institutions. These institutions typically transfer funds for foreign exchange and Eurodollar transactions using CHIPS, and the average value of a CHIPS transaction is about $6 million. The average daily payment volume on the CHIPS system is about $1.5 trillion.

Table 10-2 on page 314 lists the world's major large-value wire transfer systems and provides estimates of transactions and flows of funds on these systems, which are similar in structure to Fedwire and Chips. For instance, the Bank of Japan's BOJ-NET system is analogous to Fedwire, and the British CHAPS system performs functions similar to those provided by CHIPS. The European Monetary Union's TARGET system is a new major wire transfer system, and its payment volumes likely will increase significantly following a complete switchover to the euro as the European Monetary Union's circulating currency in 2002.

Large-Value Wire Transfer Systems
Payment systems such as Fedwire and CHIPS that permit the electronic transmission of large dollar sums.

Fedwire
A large-value wire transfer system operated by the Federal Reserve that is open to all depository institutions that legally must hold reserves with the Federal Reserve.

Clearing House Interbank Payment System (CHIPS)
A large-value wire transfer system linking about 90 depository institutions and permitting them to exchange large dollar sums electronically.

How many Fedwire transactions took place in the latest quarter? To track Fedwire data, go to the Federal Reserve's home page at http:// www.federalreserve. gov, click on "Banking System," and then click on "Fedwire and Net Settlement."

Table 10-2: The World's Key Large-Value Wire Transfer Systems.

Country/Payment System	Transactions (Millions)	Value ($ Trillions)
France		
SAGITTAIRE	1.3	5.3
Germany		
ELS	13.5	22.4
EAF	22.5	107.0
Italy		
ME	11.5	47.4
Japan		
FEYCS	11.2	81.6
BOJ-NET	5.3	329.2
Switzerland		
SIC	134.4	32.0
United Kingdom		
CHAPS	18.0	68.8
United States		
Fedwire	98.1	328.7
CHIPS	59.1	350.4

Source: Bank for International Settlements, 2000.

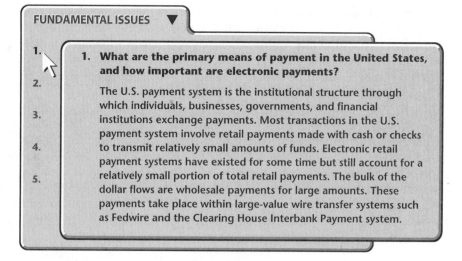

FUNDAMENTAL ISSUES ▼

1.

2.

3.

4.

5.

1. **What are the primary means of payment in the United States, and how important are electronic payments?**

    The U.S. payment system is the institutional structure through which individuals, businesses, governments, and financial institutions exchange payments. Most transactions in the U.S. payment system involve retail payments made with cash or checks to transmit relatively small amounts of funds. Electronic retail payment systems have existed for some time but still account for a relatively small portion of total retail payments. The bulk of the dollar flows are wholesale payments for large amounts. These payments take place within large-value wire transfer systems such as Fedwire and the Clearing House Interbank Payment system.

Stored-Value, Debit, and Smart Cards

According to the Bank for International Settlements, an institution that coordinates policymaking among the central banks of the world's most developed nations, U.S. residents make more than 300 billion individual cash transactions every year. Of these, 270 billion are in dollar amounts of less than $2. It is easy to see why people use paper currency and coins to purchase a soft drink, a candy bar, or a hamburger. Why would they consider using electronic money instead of coins and paper currency?

STORED-VALUE SYSTEMS

To understand the incentives for using electronic money (e-money) instead of real cash, we must first contemplate exactly how e-money transactions take place. First, let's think about the simplest kind of e-money system, which is a **closed stored-value system.** In this type of system, cards containing pre-stored currency values entitle the bearer to purchase specific goods and services offered by the card issuer. Many college and university libraries contain copy machines that faculty and students operate after inserting a plastic card that has a magnetic strip on the back. Each time they make a copy, the machine automatically deducts the fee. If the balance on a student's card runs low in the middle of copying an article, the student can replenish the balance by placing the card in a separate machine and inserting real cash. The machine stores the value of the cash on the card. Then the student can go back to a copy machine, reinsert the card, and finish copying the article.

Some closed stored-value cards, such as pre-paid telephone cards, are disposable. Cards with magnetic strips or other means of electronic-data storage have a broader range for other uses, however. Banks and other issuers now can issue reusable cards for use in **open stored-value systems**, in which the bearer of a card may use it to purchase goods and services offered by a number of participating merchants.

DEBIT CARDS

Another type of card that functions in open systems is the **debit card.** This card essentially adapts the technology used by stored-value cards to permit authorization of funds transfers between accounts of consumers and merchants.

How Debit-Card Systems Work

Figure 10-2 illustrates a sample transaction flow within a debit-card system. In this example, issuing banks, denoted bank A and bank B, provide cards to

Closed Stored-Value System
An e-money system in which consumers use cards containing pre-stored funds to buy specific goods and services offered by a single issuer of the cards.

Open Stored-Value System
A system in which consumers buy goods and services using cards containing pre-stored funds offered by multiple card issuers and accepted by multiple retailers.

Debit Card
A plastic card that allows the bearer to transfer funds to a merchant's account if the bearer authorizes the transfer by providing personal identification.

Figure 10-2:
A Debit-Card System.

*Holders of cards issued by
Bank A and Bank B can
arrange for funds transfers
from their accounts via card
authorizations. Retailers in
turn transmit claims to
Bank C and Bank D. These
banks then transmit their
claims for funds to the
operator of the system. The
system operator transmits
the claims to Bank A and
Bank B and arranges account
settlements among the four
banks.*

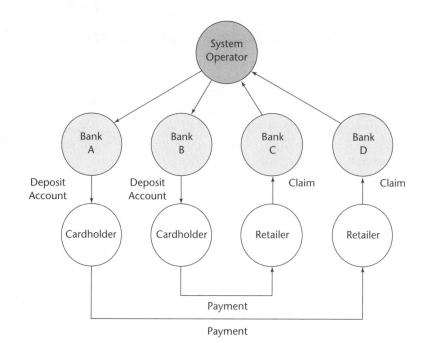

customers. Cardholders use the cards to authorize transfers of funds from their checking or savings deposits, so that they can buy goods and services from retailers that participate in the system. At retail outlets, electronic cash-register terminals record the values of purchases and the routing numbers of issuing banks.

At some point—either instantly or later in the day—the retailers submit the recorded transactions data to the banks where the retailer's own deposit accounts are located, denoted bank C and bank D. These banks then forward claims for funds to the system operator, which in turn transmits these claims to the issuing banks, bank A and bank B. Once banks A and B honor their obligations to banks C and D, the latter banks credit the deposit accounts of the retailers.

An important aspect of Figure 10-2 is that it could also illustrate the workings of our current system of paper checks. Instead of using debit cards to buy goods and services from retailers, bank customers could use checks to make their purchases. Then the retailers would send the checks to their banks, which would submit them to a clearinghouse for payment. The clearinghouse then would process payments among banks, and the retailers would eventually receive final payment of funds. Thus, a debit-card system effectively amounts to electronic checking. As with standard paper check clearing, behind the scenes there are a number of clearinghouse transactions that must take place to finalize a transaction.

Are Debit-Card Systems Really "New"?
In addition, the mechanisms that debit-card systems use to ensure security make these systems somewhat cumbersome to use, as compared with paper currency and coins. When a cardholder presents a typical debit card to a retailer, the re-

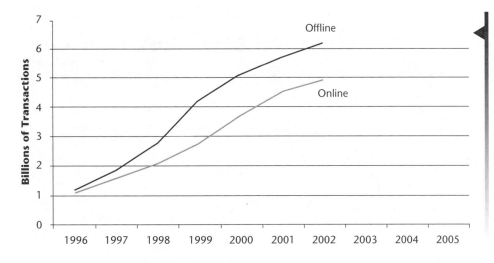

Figure 10-3:
Total U.S. Debit-Card
Transactions.

The use of debit cards has grown at a fast pace in recent years. Nevertheless, the majority of debit-card transactions take place offline instead of online.

Source: Bank for International Settlements and author's estimates.

tailer's electronic cash register automatically routes a request for authorization to the issuing bank. After checking the cardholder's account number against a file of lost or stolen cards and verifying that funds are available in the customer's account, the bank sends confirmation of payment authorization.

This authorization system enhances the security of the system to both the cardholder (perhaps the person trying to make a purchase stole the card) and the retailer (bank authorization guarantees receipt of funds). Nevertheless, the telecommunication costs of standard online authorizations range normally from 8 cents to 15 cents per transaction, which is much higher than the per-transaction cost of paper currency and coins.

In addition, retailers who strive for speed in delivery of goods and services—such as grocery stores and fast-food restaurants—do not want other customers to stand in line waiting as a customer provides personal identification numbers and employees await payment authorizations. For this reason, as Figure 10-3 indicates, the majority of debit-card transactions actually take place offline. Many retailers simply store transactions during the day and transmit requests for payment from banks during off-hours—just as they do with the checks their customers write.

For these reasons, debit cards represent a purely technical innovation in retail payments. Barring major developments making them more cost-effective, debit-card systems are unlikely to alter the nature of retail payments. (In some countries, stored value and debit cards have emerged as a safe way to make electronic payments, see on the next page *Globalization Online: Stored Value and Debit Cards May Be the Ticket to E-Commerce in Russia.*)

SMART CARDS

A more fundamental innovation has been the development of **smart cards**, which have embedded computer chips that can store much more information than a magnetic strip. The microchip on a smart card can do more than maintain

Smart Card
A card containing a microprocessor that permits storage of funds via security programming, that can communicate with other computers, and that does not require online authorization for funds transfers to occur.

GLOBALIZATION *Online*

Stored-Value and Debit Cards May Be the Ticket to E-Commerce in Russia

In Russia, B2C electronic commerce began to show progress for the first time beginning in 2000. Some forecasts indicate that by 2002, Web-based retail purchases may be as much as 0.5 percent of total Russian national expenditures—if Russian residents can find a way to arrange payment for goods and services that they shop for online.

The Russian Federation has a population of nearly 150 million people, yet there are only about 5 million active credit-card accounts. Even though a significant portion of the people holding these accounts are Internet users, many indicate they are so worried about fraud that they hesitate to use their credit cards to make online purchases.

One answer to this concern may be the STB debit card, which is issued by more than 100 banks. The heaviest users of the STB card are students, who already use the cards at cash machines and shops around the country. Now, through a Russian Internet payment system called Assist, STB cards can be used for Web purchases as well.

A 1998 financial crash wiped out big chucks of Russians' savings, however, and discouraged many people from using debit cards. For these people, a key alternative for e-commerce transactions is the old-fashioned stored-value card. For instance, a standalone Moscow-based payment-processing company called Avtocard issues the "e-port" card, which holders can use at a virtual mall composed of more than 100 Russian retailers.

For Critical Analysis:

Why do you suppose that Russians are using stored-value cards on the Web, but relatively fewer U.S. residents do?

---

a running cash balance in its memory. These tiny silicon chips function as micro-computers that can carry and process security programming.

The Potential for Greater Reliability

The communications capability of smart cards gives them an advantage over the magnetic strip on stored-value cards. Magnetic-strip cards have a failure rate—a typical rate of failure to process a transaction correctly—of about 250 per million transactions. For smart cards, the failure rate is less than 100 per million. Continuing improvements in microprocessor technology promise to push this failure rate even lower.

Microprocessors on smart cards also can authenticate the validity of transactions. When a cardholder initiates a transaction with a retailer, the chip in the retailer's electronic cash confirms the authenticity of the smart card by examining a unique **digital signature** stored on the card's microchip. This authentication is

Digital Signature
Software algorithms that guarantee the authenticity of the digital cash held on a smart card or other digital-cash storage and communications device.

Figure 10-4:
Digital Encryption and Electronic-Payment Security.

An electronic payment instruction starts out in a form readable by a human being, called "plaintext." When this instruction is entered into a computer, it is secured, or encrypted, using an "encryption key," which is a software code. In computer-readable form, the payment instruction is called "ciphertext," which the computer transmits to another location. A computer at the other location uses another software code, called a "decryption key," to read the data and turn it back into a plaintext form that a human operator can read.

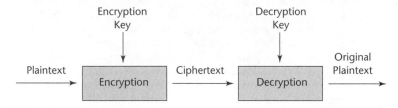

generated by software called a *cryptographic algorithm*, which is a secure program loaded onto the microchip of the card. It guarantees to the retailer's electronic cash register that the smart card's chip is genuine and that it has not been tampered with by another party—such as a thief. Figure 10-4 illustrates how digital encryption helps to guarantee the security of electronic payments.

Convenience and Anonymity

Widespread adoption of smart cards would pave the way for development of an **open smart-card system** for payment transfers. In such a system, there would be numerous smart card issuers, holders, and participating retailers.

In an open smart-card system, a cardholder does not have to provide a personal identification number. Just as with physical cash, the user of a smart card can remain anonymous. There is no need for online authorization using expensive telecommunication services. Each time a cardholder uses a smart card, the amount of a purchase is deducted automatically and credited to a retailer. The retailer, in turn, can store its electronic cash receipts in specially adapted point-of-sale terminals. The retailer can then transfer accumulated balances to its bank at the end of the day by means of telephone links. This permits completion of payments within just a few seconds.

Open Smart-Card System
An electronic system in which consumers use smart cards with embedded microprocessors, which may be issued by a number of institutions, to purchase goods and services offered by multiple retailers.

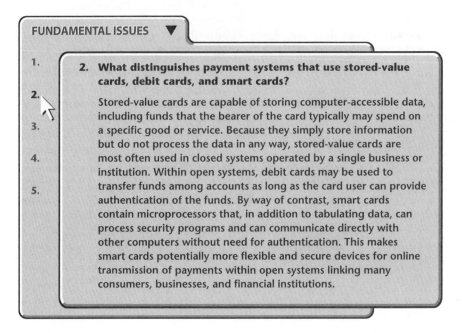

FUNDAMENTAL ISSUES ▼

1.

2.

3.

4.

5.

2. What distinguishes payment systems that use stored-value cards, debit cards, and smart cards?

Stored-value cards are capable of storing computer-accessible data, including funds that the bearer of the card typically may spend on a specific good or service. Because they simply store information but do not process the data in any way, stored-value cards are most often used in closed systems operated by a single business or institution. Within open systems, debit cards may be used to transfer funds among accounts as long as the card user can provide authentication of the funds. By way of contrast, smart cards contain microprocessors that, in addition to tabulating data, can process security programs and can communicate directly with other computers without need for authentication. This makes smart cards potentially more flexible and secure devices for online transmission of payments within open systems linking many consumers, businesses, and financial institutions.

Digital Cash

What quality does a smart card possess that paper currency and coins do not? The answer is potentially even more convenience. Smart cards permit people to use **digital cash,** which consists of funds contained on the algorithms stored on microchips and other computer devices. Smart cards' microchips can communicate with any device equipped with appropriate software. Besides automated teller machines and electronic cash registers, this includes any computer with sufficient memory and speed to operate the software, including personal computers.

Digital Cash
Funds contained on computer software, in the form of secure algorithms, which is stored on microchips and other computer devices.

The Network Functionality of Digital Cash

Unlike paper currency and coins, checks, and stored-value cards, which require physical space to process transactions, digital money can be stored on smart cards or other devices with smart-card-type microchips and sent across cyberspace. Consequently, consumers can use smart-card technology to purchase goods and services from Internet-based retailers.

For instance, suppose that a classical-music enthusiast wants to hear the latest rendition of a favorite performer. The classical-music enthusiast must have a smart-card-reading device connected to his personal computer—or pre-loaded digital cash onto a program located on the hard drive of the computer. The performer's recording company also must have the necessary software. If both conditions are met, then the classical-music enthusiast can enter a designated location on the recording company's Web site, point, click, and download the music as a digital file. The classical-music enthusiast's computer automatically sends digital cash as payment for this service. Then the classical-music enthusiast can listen to the latest release on the computer's speakers.

WHAT MIGHT DIGITAL CASH REPLACE?

Presumably, in a digital-cash environment consumers would have less desire to use other means of payment. To understand why, consider Table 10-3 on page 322, which lists the key characteristics of checks, government-issued currency, debit cards, and digital cash.

When people contemplate what means of payment to use, they trade off features that each offer. Consider a comparison of currency with checks. If a pickpocket steals a man's billfold containing cash and checks, then he can contact his depository institution to halt payment on all stolen checks. Currency payments are final, however, so the pickpocket can spend the cash he has taken. Hence, checks promise greater security. An individual can send checks through the mail, but using currency requires face-to-face contact. Currency transactions are anonymous, and under some circumstances this may be desirable. In some situations, checks are not accepted in payment for a transaction, and a check payment is not final until the check clears. Check transactions also are more expensive to process. In light of these features of currency and checks, it is not surprising that people commonly choose to use *both* means of payment.

In comparing debit cards with checks, however, it is clear why the use of debit cards is growing. The costs of debit-card payments are somewhat lower, and in other respects the features of debit-card payments parallel those of checking transactions. For many people the only advantage of checks over debit cards is that they automatically generate paper records of transactions.

People likewise compare the features that digital cash offers with features currently offered by government-provided currency, checking accounts, and debit cards. As Table 10-3 indicates, at present the extent of digital-cash acceptability is uncertain. In an environment with widespread adoption of digital cash, this means of payment would be nearly as acceptable as government-provided currency. After all, digital cash held on smart cards without special security features such as personal identifications numbers will be as susceptible to theft as government currency. At the same time, digital cash may be stored on devices, such as laptop computers or even wristwatches (Swiss watch manufacturers have already developed watches with microchips for storing digital cash), requiring an access code before a microchip containing digital cash can be accessed. Thus, digital cash is likely to be more secure than government-provided currency, though not as secure as check transactions.

Transactions involving digital cash are likely to be less costly, because people will not have to go to bank branches or ATMs to obtain digital cash (although

What are the latest developments in smart card technology? Learn more about the evolution of and newest innovations in smart-card technology at http://www.cardshow.com/EN/Public/Welcome.html.

Table 10-3: Features of Alternative Means of Payment.

Feature	Currency	Checks	Debit Cards	Digital Cash
Security	Low	High	High	High(?)
Per-Transfer Cost	Medium	High	Medium	Low
Payment Final, Face-to-Face	Yes	No	No	Yes
Payment Final, Non-Face-to-Face	No	No	No	Yes
Anonymity	Yes	No	No	Yes
Acceptability	Wide	Restricted	Growing	Uncertain

Source: Aleksander Berentsen, "Monetary Policy Implications of Digital Money," *Kyklos* 51 (1998), pp. 89–117.

they undoubtedly will be able to do this if they wish). In addition, consumers also will have the capability of accessing digital cash at home on their personal computers, and they will be able send digital cash from remote locations using the Internet. Digital-cash transactions will be instantaneously final. In contrast to transactions using currency, digital-cash transactions need not be conducted on a face-to-face basis. Nevertheless, digital-cash transactions will be just as anonymous as payments made using currency.

In many ways, therefore, digital cash compares most favorably with government-provided currency. Certainly, for some time to come a number of items—canned soft drinks and candy in vending machines, for instance—will be easiest to purchase using government-provided currency. Many economists, however, believe that widespread adoption of privately issued digital cash ultimately will "crowd out" government-provided currency. In the future, even vending machines are likely to have smart-card readers.

DIGITAL CASH IN GLOBAL MARKETS

Europe has different technical standards for videos and videocassette players, so most U.S. videos will not play on European videocassette players, and vice versa. This means that a U.S. resident whose company has transferred her to Europe for the next two years cannot take along her collection of videocassettes. If the transfer were to happen at a future time in which the use of smart cards and digital cash is widespread, she might have another problem. Her U.S.-issued smart cards, card-reading equipment, and software for downloading digital cash might not allow her to purchase more videocassettes in Europe because it has a different set of standards for smart cards. Thus, if she wishes to have the same convenient access to digital-cash technology in Europe, she will have to obtain new smart cards, rent or lease additional card-reading equipment, and purchase new software to use during the period of her stay. Otherwise, she will have little choice but to use old-fashioned paper currency, coins, and credit cards for transactions.

Settling on World Digital-Cash Standards

The potential for a mismatch in systems for means of payments is very real. Just as U.S. videotapes cannot work on European videocassette players, some day U.S. residents who travel to Europe may discover that their smart cards do not work in European equipment or with European software. Or they may find that their smart cards will not function in online systems installed in Japan, China, or South Africa.

At a minimum, avoiding cross-border incompatibility of digital-cash systems will require nations to coordinate international certifications of digital signatures.

Certificate Authorities for Digital Cash

Currently, every open smart-card system has its own digital-cash **certificate authority,** which is a designated group that administers and regulates the terms under which people legitimately engage in e-money transactions. For instance, JapanNet is the key certificate authority overseeing most digital-cash transactions in Japan. One of its principal functions is to approve and implement standards for digital signatures of smart cards. Every certificate authority designs its standards to be consistent with the legal requirements binding purchases and sales that occur within its own nation. Thus, JapanNet's standards for digital signatures and *authentication protocols,* or terms under which digital-cash transfers are considered legally binding, are based on Japanese laws. Although these laws are similar to laws that govern exchanges in other nations, certain points of legal interpretation—what a layperson calls "legal technicalities"—are particular to Japan, and JapanNet's digital-cash authentication protocols reflect this fact.

In recent years, JapanNet and certificate authorities for smart-card systems based in other nations have developed agreements for e-money **cross-certification,** which is an authentication technique that permits digital-cash algorithms from one system to recognize and verify digital signatures certified by another system. The other system might be based in another country, such as Denmark. Once the certificate authorities of the two nations' systems have agreed to permit cross-system smart-card transactions, cross-certification software linking the systems permits an individual with a Japanese smart card to use the card to transmit digital cash to a Danish company. If cross-certification becomes widespread, then global trade of digital cash will become a reality.

Certificate Authority
A group charged with supervising the terms governing how buyers and sellers can legitimately make digital-cash transfers.

Cross-Certification
A process by which digital-cash algorithms used on one e-money system may be recognized and verified as authentic digital cash by another e-money system.

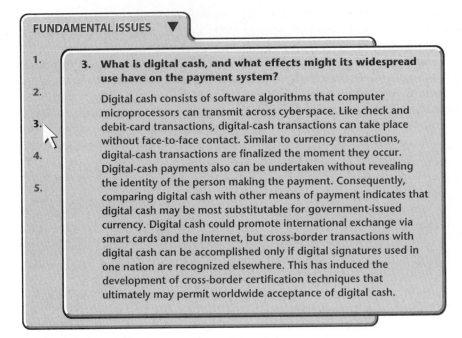

FUNDAMENTAL ISSUES ▼

1.

2.

3.

4.

5.

3. What is digital cash, and what effects might its widespread use have on the payment system?

Digital cash consists of software algorithms that computer microprocessors can transmit across cyberspace. Like check and debit-card transactions, digital-cash transactions can take place without face-to-face contact. Similar to currency transactions, digital-cash transactions are finalized the moment they occur. Digital-cash payments also can be undertaken without revealing the identity of the person making the payment. Consequently, comparing digital cash with other means of payment indicates that digital cash may be most substitutable for government-issued currency. Digital cash could promote international exchange via smart cards and the Internet, but cross-border transactions with digital cash can be accomplished only if digital signatures used in one nation are recognized elsewhere. This has induced the development of cross-border certification techniques that ultimately may permit worldwide acceptance of digital cash.

 ## The Security of Digital Cash

Digital cash makes some people nervous for the same reasons that slow adoption of any new technology. Until they have time to evaluate new technologies, people often assume the worst.

It remains to be seen whether people will find digital cash more convenient than other means of payment. As we have already discussed, there are reasons to think that many people ultimately will desire to use digital cash. An overriding concern in the minds of most potential users of digital cash is the *security* of this means of payment.

DIGITAL COUNTERFEITING

Smart cards and other storage and transmission mechanisms for digital cash will not be 100-percent secure even if equipped with authentication software. Time and time again, criminals have found ingenious ways to steal hard-earned funds from honest but unsuspecting consumers and businesses. In principle, there are a number of ways they might find to steal digital cash.

The Threat of Reverse Engineering

One conceivable way that a criminal could pilfer digital cash is through the old-fashioned but potentially very lucrative illegal operation known as counterfeiting. The most obvious way to counterfeit might be to produce smart cards that look, feel, and function just like legitimate smart cards and that contain counterfeit digital cash.

Potential returns from digital counterfeiting could be high—possibly high enough to encourage well-trained engineers and computer scientists to join a digital counterfeiting ring. These counterfeiters could, in theory, analyze and *reverse-engineer* smart cards by taking the cards apart and analyzing their software to determine how they are constructed. The criminals could then experiment with loading value onto fraudulent cards (or trying to fool computers into accepting fake cryptographic algorithms they have placed on the cards' microprocessors). Ultimately, they could attempt to spend the fraudulent digital funds.

Defending Against Counterfeiting

In Asia, members of Chinese and Malaysian gangs have enlisted retail clerks, or taken jobs as clerks themselves, to gain access to customers' credit cards. When customers offer their cards for payment, the clerks covertly swipe them a second time on small devices called "skimmers" that store data on the cards. Later, the gangs scan this information onto counterfeit cards and go on big spending sprees.

Issuers of smart cards have undertaken defensive measures to limit the success of counterfeiting efforts aimed at smart cards. To make counterfeit smart cards easier to recognize, issuers typically place holographic images on their own legitimate cards, just as credit-card issuers do. Issuers also design the computer code on microprocessors so that data stored in memory cannot be accessed or changed except through predefined authorization and access software protocols. These software commands, in turn, are stored in a portion of the microprocessor's memory that can be changed only by altering its internal functions.

To help prevent unauthorized reading of data on the cards, smart cards are equipped with physical barriers to inhibit optical or electrical analysis or physical alteration of the microprocessor's memory. Most smart-card chips also are coated with several layers of wiring, installed in such a way that unauthorized removal of the chip is difficult to accomplish without damaging the chip beyond repair.

PILFERING DIGITAL CASH OFFLINE AND ONLINE

It has become increasingly common for people to engage in thefts by driving a pickup truck through the front window of a bank branch or supermarket, quickly lifting an ATM into the back of the truck, driving to their hideout, and removing the cash. This illustrates the *modus operandi* for *off-line thefts* of digital cash, in which thieves would break into a merchant's establishment, physically remove electronic devices used to store value from customers' smart cards, and download these funds onto their own cards.

Recently some thieves have acted more covertly by inserting microprocessor chips into computerized cash registers. The chips scan data from credit- and debit-card transactions. Later, the thieves regain access to the machines, remove the chips, and download the data for use or for sale to the highest bidder.

Even more sophisticated thieves might attempt *online theft* by intercepting payment messages as they are transmitted from smart cards and other electronic-funds-storage devices to host computers. For instance, if thieves learn the time of day a large, up-scale department store transmits its receipts to a central computer, they could try to tap into the transmission line and steal the funds. These kinds of online theft are most likely to be "inside jobs," in which employees commit *internal theft*—pilfering their own companies' funds—using their knowledge of the companies' systems for transmitting cybercash.

GIVING DIGITAL CASH A "COLD"

Counterfeiting, robbery, and internal theft are old problems. To steal digital cash, self-interested thieves only have to possess more technical ability than John Dillinger and Baby Face Nelson did in the 1930s. One security problem with digital cash, which arguably exposes it to special dangers, is its dependence on correctly functioning microprocessors and software.

In the classic James Bond film, *Goldfinger,* the super-criminal by that name plots to blow up a small nuclear device within Fort Knox. He reasons that this would make the gold stored there radioactive and, consequently, worthless, enabling him to reap substantial capital gains on his own hoards of gold. In a world of digital cash, it would be hard to profit financially from the wholesale destruction of outstanding stocks of digital cash. Not all people care solely about their own financial status, however. A person who is fanatically wedded to some political or personal "cause" and who also happens to possess a talent for creating computer viruses potentially could transform himself into a cyber-terrorist. A virus that damages the input–output mechanisms of smart-card microprocessors and other digital-cash storage and communications devices or that erases data stored on such e-money mechanisms potentially could create financial havoc, thereby attracting considerable attention to the terrorist's cause.

MALFUNCTIONING PAYMENTS

Physical cash can wear out, and magnetic-ink-scanning devices can misread checks. Nevertheless, people can still exchange physical units of money during electricity outages. Power failures or other equipment breakdowns, by way of contrast, can bring e-money transactions to a grinding halt.

This means that consumers and retailers may face a trade-off in their use of digital cash. As compared with currency and checks, e-money systems are speedier, less costly, and more efficient. Just as air travel is, on average, the quickest

and safest way to traverse a long distance, when digital cash works it is comparatively the most effective way to conduct transactions. Yet when an airplane fails to
operate correctly, the result can be a spectacular crash. Likewise, the gain from
using information technologies to transfer payments comes at the cost of exposure
to new risks of loss.

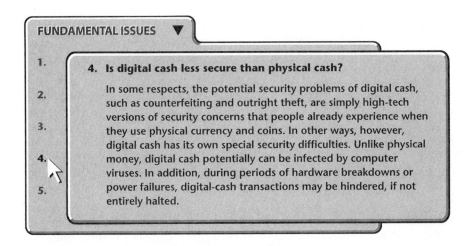

FUNDAMENTAL ISSUES ▼

1.

2.

3.

4.

5.

4. Is digital cash less secure than physical cash?

In some respects, the potential security problems of digital cash,
such as counterfeiting and outright theft, are simply high-tech
versions of security concerns that people already experience when
they use physical currency and coins. In other ways, however,
digital cash has its own special security difficulties. Unlike physical
money, digital cash potentially can be infected by computer
viruses. In addition, during periods of hardware breakdowns or
power failures, digital-cash transactions may be hindered, if not
entirely halted.

Where Will Digital Cash Fit Into the Existing Payment System?

Just because people have the capability to adopt a technology does not mean they
actually implement it. For instance, the basic technology for stored-value cards
has been available since the 1970s, but only recently have U.S. residents used
stored-value cards to buy such items as telephone calls. As far back as the 1960s,
economists recognized that electronic banking transactions would be much less
costly than transactions at physical branches. Figure 10-5 on page 328 shows that
the least-expensive ways of making financial transactions is on the Internet.

As you learned in Chapter 9, a widening array of banking services are available online. Nevertheless, the most common type of banking transactions—deposits and withdrawals—cannot be accomplished using the Internet unless people
use digital cash. So far, few people have chosen to do so.

A CHICKEN-OR-EGG PROBLEM: NETWORK EXTERNALITIES

Even when online-payment systems have been structured so that digital cash can
be used, a fundamental difficulty has tended to arise. Banks and other financial
institutions have been hesitant to install online systems for processing digital-cash

**Figure 10-5:
Costs of Alternative
Types of Banking
Transactions.**

*The average cost of an
Internet banking transaction
is much lower than the
transaction costs using
alternative mechanisms.*

Source: Bank for
International Settlements.

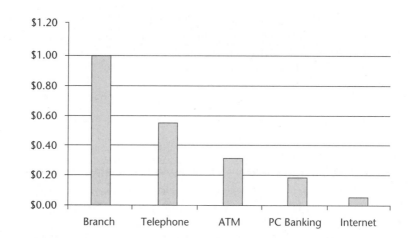

payments unless retailers that would use them share in the cost. Retailers, however, are not willing to incur such costs until more customers use the systems. But many customers indicate they will not consider using digital-cash systems until more merchants are online.

Network Externalities

As you learned in Chapter 3, firms in certain markets comprise *network industries.* In such an industry, the value that consumers assign to the good or service produced by firms depends to some extent on the number of other people who consume the product, so that *network externalities* are an important feature of the marketplace in which a good or service is bought and sold.

Network externalities likely play a role in the context of digital cash. Depositing and withdrawing funds is feasible using smart cards or other digital devices, which people can use to upload and download digital cash, thereby transforming their personal computers into home ATMs. Undoubtedly, this would provide incentive to bank from home via the Internet. At the same time, however, many believe that online banking is the way to introduce people to digital cash and induce them to use smart cards. This is a chicken-or-egg problem, as bank customers wait for widespread acceptability of smart cards before exploring home-banking options, while banks wait for more customers to choose online banking before making big investments in smart-card technology.

Economists have long recognized that means of payment, such as currency, checks, and the like, are particularly subject to network externalities. By definition, a means of payment will come into increasing use if more people accept it in exchange for goods and services. This is as true of digital cash as was the case at one time for gold coins, government currency, checks, and, more recently, stored value and debit cards.

Following the Example of Frequent-Flyer Miles: Virtual Points

One way that companies promote the development of network externalities is to create online payment programs that benefit both retailers and consumers. Companies such as E-centives.com, MyPoints.com, and now-defunct Flooz.com and Beenz.com have offered Internet payment systems that parallel frequent-flyer programs.

At Beenz, for instance, consumers were able to sign up to earn virtual points called "beenz," each of which was worth one-half cent, every time they viewed retailers' Internet ads or filled out retailers' online marketing surveys. Consumers benefited because they could use accumulated beenz to purchase goods and services from participating retailers. In August, 2001 Beenz called it quits when use of its currency declined in the midst of stagnant economic activity. So far, My-Points has survived by offering a similar program and permits people to "cash out" by converting accumulated "virtual points" to cash that can be deposited into their deposit accounts or credited to balances on their credit-card accounts.

Retailers can also benefit from virtual-points programs. Like frequent-flyer programs, these online payments programs promise to help retailers lock in customers by offering them product discounts for making repeat purchases. Hence, companies offering online virtual-points programs hope to develop into a network industry.

A Developing Network Industry: Person-to-Person Payments

Today, a fast-growing online payment system involves the transmission of e-mail messages. Firms such as PayPal.com, Billpoint.com, eMoneyMail.com, and MoneyZap.com permit consumers to authorize billing their credit-card account to finance a payment e-mailed to another recipient. If the recipient does not already have an account with the firm, then one is created. The person-to-person payment firm gives the recipient the option of leaving the account active for later use in transmitting a payment, receiving the payment via a check, or arranging for electronic deposit of the funds into the recipient's bank account.

Increasingly, people are choosing to maintain accounts with person-to-person payment firms. At one point during 2000, PayPal was adding new accounts at the rate of 20,000 per day, as more and more people found person-to-person digital payments widely accepted by others. People who participate in online auctions at C2C sites in particular have adopted person-to-person payment systems offered by online firms.

Person-to-person payments offered by these firms are not formally digital cash. That is, they are not computer algorithms that function as standalone money. Essentially, they are claims on funds in accounts at banks and other financial institutions. Accounts that people hold on deposit with PayPal and other firms are money that is fully backed by dollar deposits elsewhere in the nation's payment system.

Billpoint.com is partly owned by Wells Fargo Bank, and eMoneyMail is a unit of Bank One. PayPal and various other systems are not, however. Hence, the first widely traded forms of digital deposit and payment systems have engendered competition from outside the banking industry. It remains to be seen whether banks will emerge as dominant payment intermediaries in cyberspace as well as in the traditional financial system. (Traditional banks are losing out to convenience

GLOBALIZATION *Online*

In Japan, Corner Shops Become Web Banks— and E-Commerce Package Pick-Up Centers

In the United States, the widespread ownership of bank-issued credit cards has provided the foundation for most Internet payments. Alongside, there is a highly competitive market for package delivery services. In other countries, the lack of Internet payment options and less-developed delivery systems is holding up the development of the electronic marketplace.

Paying in Cash at the Store Down the Street

Among the most important Japanese retailers are the *konbini,* which are discount convenience stores connected to high-

tech information-processing networks. Several *konbini* chains have sought to establish a business linking e-commerce sellers and consumers.

Seven-Eleven, which operates 8,000 Japanese outlets, or almost three times the number of stores operated by Wal-Mart, has placed Internet kiosks in its stores so their customers can surf the Web and order products. To pay for goods ordered, consumers can use cash obtained from automated teller machines located in the stores. They hand the cash over to store clerks, who transmit the payment electronically to Internet sellers to complete the sales. Thus, customers who rely on cash instead of credit cards can still shop in the electronic marketplace.

Furthermore, this service allows customers to bypass banks by effectively choosing Seven-Eleven as their payment intermediary. Some *konbini* are taking an additional step by

continued

stores as Internet payment intermediaries in Japan; see *Globalization Online: In Japan, Corner Shops Become Web Banks—and E-Commerce Package Pick-Up Centers.*)

THE STATUS OF SMART CARDS AND DIGITAL CASH

Recently, the village of Ennis, in County Clare, became Ireland's "Information Age Town." About 6,000 Ennis households were equipped with voice mail, personal computers, and Internet access. The town's residents also received smart cards they could use to store data, process computer messages, and communicate with cell phones, screen phones, personal computers, parking meters, and vending machines. Department stores, supermarkets, gas stations, taxicabs, and pubs were equipped with smart-card devices. Participating banks deployed card-accessible, cash-loading stations in parking lots, shopping centers, schools, and bank branches. This grand experiment was designed to find out what aspects of smart-card technology would and would not work in an ordinary community.

Many Pilot Projects

The Ennis experiment has been one of many pilot projects involving smart cards. In July 1995, Mondex, a company majority-owned by MasterCard International, applying for banking licenses permitting them to accept deposits and issue debit cards. This would save customers the trouble of getting cash from ATMs. It would also save store clerks the time and effort entailed in recycling cash back into the ATMs for other customers to withdraw.

Carrying the Goods Home
The entry of *konbini* into the banking industry promises to make the Japanese banking system much more competitive. The *konbini* also simplify the process of obtaining goods ordered online.

The Japanese market for delivery of envelopes containing tickets ordered from an airline's Web site or packages of books purchased on the Internet is not very competitive. Market prices for deliveries are relatively high, which has discouraged online shopping. The *konbini*, however, permit consumers to arrange for pickup of envelopes and packages at the stores where they placed Internet orders, thereby cutting out high-priced package delivery services.

For Critical Analysis:
Some observers of Japanese markets have speculated that the *konbini* might eventually begin making home deliveries of items their customers order at Internet kiosks. What factors might limit their ability to begin competing with delivery companies as well as with banks?

introduced an e-money system in Swindon, a city of 100,000 located south of London, England. Three years later, there were 13,000 cards in circulation, below Mondex's initial lofty estimates but above the projections of e-money pessimists.

Undeterred, Mondex followed up with fifteen more pilot e-money systems in five other countries. At the same time, Visa introduced fifty-five pilot projects in seventeen nations. Examples of these pilot projects were developed by Chase Manhattan (with Mondex cards) and Citibank (with Visa Cash cards), which issued smart cards to 50,000 consumers and 500 merchants on the upper-west side of Manhattan.

Will the Fast-Food Business Get Smart Cards Rolling?
Smart cards have caught on much more rapidly in Europe. Europeans are particularly fond of using stored-value cards to pay for telephone service. In Norway, the use of stored-value and smart cards has risen from about one-tenth of check transactions in 1989 to about *five times* the volume of check transactions today. Since 1998, McDonald's Inc. has accepted smart cards at all 870 fast-food restaurant locations it operates in Germany. McDonald's developed the smart-card system with the German association of savings banks, which have issued more than 40 million cards. The company has a corporate commitment to accept smart cards on a global scale.

This is just one sign that fast-food restaurants could prove the first setting for commercially viable smart-card systems. One reason is that fast-food chains have a predisposition to couple card use with "loyalty rewards," such as free meals after a certain number of purchases. As part of its effort to distinguish J. P. Morgan Chase's Mondex card from the Visa Cash card offered by Citibank, Burger King restaurants in the Long Island suburbs of New York City began to offer such customer incentives. This led McDonald's to offer to automatically add "loyalty points" to Mondex cards whenever its customers loaded value onto the cards, which entitled customers to automatic discounts on McDonald's products. McDonald's went a step further by using the Mondex system as a way to market its products. The system sends "marketing messages" to customers as they add value to their cards. McDonald's uses Internet connections to manage the programs and marketing messages centrally.

Can Banks Get into the Act?

Payment Intermediary
An institution that facilitates the transfer of funds between buyer and seller during the course of any purchase of goods, services, or financial assets.

A key function of banks has been to serve as **payment intermediaries,** or institutions that serve as go-betweens in processing funds transferrals that occur during the course of any purchase of goods, services, or financial assets. Since the Middle Ages, banks have served as storehouses for means of payment—gold, other precious metals, and the like—that people have accepted as money. More recently, they have processed payments authorized by checks. When one person buys a good or a service from another individual, thereby initiating a person-to-person transaction, the banking system intermediates the transaction by clearing the check—behind the scenes, debiting the account of the person who writes the check and crediting the account of the person who receives it.

Banks continue to strive to maintain their traditional dominance of payment intermediation. Through membership in such card-industry groups as Mondex, Visa International, or American Express, many banks indirectly are part of the Global Chipcard Alliance, which has promoted the *standardization* of smart-card technology. *Smart-card dial tones* are new, sophisticated algorithms allowing any smart card to be accepted by any card-reading terminal. Such standardization is necessary for worldwide adoption of smart cards to be feasible.

In an effort to promote the adoption of smart-card technology, many banks have begun including microprocessors in credit cards. For instance, in recent years FleetBoston and Providian Bank have marketed credit cards that include a computer chip for online authentication, providing credit information for Internet purchases, and keeping track of points in purchase loyalty programs.

Some credit-card issuers have sought to establish an online-payment niche by sticking with basic credit-card services while trying to address consumer privacy worries and concerns about security of credit card information on the Web. American Express has developed a disposable credit card for use on the Internet. An American Express cardholder can register for the service at a special Web site and download special software. When the cardholder wishes to purchase an item online, the software automatically connects the cardholder's browser to the American Express Web site, where the cardholder obtains an authorization number unique to the transaction—essentially a different credit-card number available for one-time use. This means that the customer is anonymous to the Web retailer and that the retailer cannot reuse the account number the customer provided. This payment product entails no costs for retailers, and the costs to cardholding consumers are minimal. More important for American Express, banks, and other credit-card issuers, this type of online payment arrangement keeps them at the center of the online payment intermediation process.

The *digital wallet* is another system for online payments pursued by a number of banks. Under this type of online payment system, banks recruit retailers and equip them with software that can communicate with the software of online banking customers. Then, whenever a customer wishes to purchase an item online from a participating Web retailer, the amount of the purchase is billed automatically to the credit-card account number stored in the customer's digital wallet.

Unfortunately for banks, they face considerable competition in offering digital wallets from nonfinancial online intermediaries. In fact, Yahoo.com has become the leader in digital wallets. Its system includes more than 11,000 participating online merchants, far more than digital wallet systems developed by any bank. Other nonfinancial companies that offer digital wallets to consumers include Microsoft and America Online. In this area, like many others, banks face a number of new payment-intermediary rivals.

FUNDAMENTAL ISSUES ▼

1.

2.

3.

4.

5.

5. What factors are likely to determine whether smart cards and digital cash receive widespread adoption in the electronic marketplace?

Means of payment are subject to network externalities, meaning that the benefit a consumer anticipates receiving from using them depends on how many others use them. This gives rise to the potential for issuers of smart cards and digital cash to face a chicken-or-egg problem: Retailers will not desire to adopt these means of payment unless many consumers wish to use them, while consumers are less likely to use smart cards or digital cash unless a large number of retailers accept them. Trials are under way in various locales to identify successful ways of structuring smart-card systems. Recent efforts to develop means of online payment that address the network-externalities problem include person-to-person payments, virtual points systems, virtual credit-card payments, and digital wallets.

Chapter Summary

1) **The Primary Means of Payment in the United States, and the Relative Importance of Electronic Payments:** The institutional structure through which individuals, businesses, governments, and financial institutions transmit payments is the overall payment system. In the U.S. payment system, most transactions are retail payments transmitted using cash or checks involving relatively small amounts of funds. Although electronic retail payment systems have existed for years, these systems continue to account for a relatively small fraction of total retail payments. The bulk of dollar flows transmitted within the U.S. payment system are wholesale payments involving sums of hundreds of thousands of dollars or more. Most wholesale payments are transmitted through large-value wire transfer systems such as Fedwire and the Clearing House Interbank Payment system.

2) **The Distinctions among Stored-Value Cards, Debit Cards, and Smart Cards:** Consumers can use stored-value cards to maintain balances of electronic money that they can use to purchase specific goods or services. Stored-value cards are most often used in closed systems operated by a single business or institution. Within open systems, debit cards may be used to transfer funds among accounts as long as the card user can provide authentication of the funds. Smart cards contain computer microchips that permit them to communicate directly with other computers to process software programs containing algorithms that store and transmit cash. In contrast to debit cards, transferring funds with smart cards can be done anonymously. As a result, smart cards are potentially a more flexible and secure means of transmitting online payments within open systems linking consumers, sellers, and financial institutions.

3) **Digital Cash and Its Possible Effects on the Payment System:** Digital cash consists of software algorithms that computer microprocessors can transmit across cyberspace. Because digital-cash transactions can occur without face-to-face contact, this means of payment has the same advantage over government-issued currency that is possessed by checks and debit cards. Digital-cash transactions are superior to those accomplished using checks and many debit cards because, like currency transactions, they are final at the instant they occur and can be accomplished anonymously. A comparison of digital cash with other means of payment indicates that digital cash may be most substitutable for government-issued currency. As long as digital signatures used in one nation can be recognized by a digital-cash system used in another, digital cash can flow internationally. In light of this fact, efforts are under way to develop cross-border certification methods intended to allow worldwide use of digital cash.

4) **The Security of Digital Cash:** Counterfeiting and theft are potential problems with digital cash, just as they are for physical currency and coins. Digital cash is subject to special security threats, however. One is the potential for theft to occur during online transmissions. Another threat is the potential susceptibility of digital-cash systems to computer viruses. In addition, power outages or hardware malfunctions can prevent digital-cash payments from being completed.

5) **Factors That Are Likely to Determine Whether Smart Cards and Digital Cash Are Widely Adopted in the Electronic Marketplace:** The benefit that a consumer anticipates receiving from using a particular means of payment depends on how many others use it. Consequently, means of payment are subject to network externalities, so issuers of innovative means of payment such as smart cards and digital cash confront a chicken-or-egg problem. That is, retailers typically will not want to accept digital-cash payments via smart cards or online transmissions unless many consumers wish to use these means of payments, whereas consumers are less likely to use these new means of payments unless many retailers accept them. Issuers of smart cards are experimenting with systems using these means of payment in various locales. Banks and other companies seeking to become online payment intermediaries have developed systems involving person-to-person payments, virtual points systems, virtual credit-card payments, and digital wallets.

Questions and Problems

1) What is the distinction between retail payments and wholesale payments?
2) In what ways is a debit card a direct substitute for paper checks? Is there any way it is an improvement on paper checks?
3) In what ways is a smart card a "more flexible" payment instrument than a stored-value card? Explain.
4) A key governmental concern about smart cards is that they may engender a increase in *money laundering,* or the funneling of cash into and out of bank accounts for purposes of hiding taxable transactions (as well as otherwise illegal exchanges). Based on what you learned about smart cards in this chapter, does this seem to you to be a legitimate concern? Take a stand, and support your answer.
5) According to one Federal Reserve economist, "the current paper-based system doesn't have much to recommend it, other than it works great, is cheap, reliable, and we trust it." Use this statement for evaluating the relative merits of a digital-cash system versus the current system based on the use of currency and checks in most retail transactions.

6) In what ways is digital cash more convenient to use than physical cash? Explain.

7) In what ways is digital cash less secure than physical cash? Explain.

8) How might greater competition in providing means of payment generate efficiency gains for the economy? Be specific.

9) Is it possible that smart cards will never develop sufficient network externalities to be widely adopted? What factors do you think might tip the balance toward widespread acceptance of smart cards?

10) Of the various types of online payment mechanisms discussed in this chapter, which do you think has the greatest potential for success during the next few years? Why?

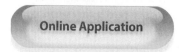

Online Application

Internet URL: http://www.echeck.org

Title: **What Is eCheck?**

Navigation: First, go to the eCheck home page (http://www.echeck.org). Click on "overview," and then click on *What Is eCheck?*

Application: Read the explanation of eCheck, and then answer the following questions.

1) People are likely to use digital cash in place of government-issued currency and coins. Would people be more likely to use eChecks in place of traditional paper checks?

2) Based on the discussion in the article, who are likely to be the main providers of eCheck technology?

For Group Study and Analysis: The article indicates that consumer acceptance of eCheck technology could "set the stage" for more widespread consumer use of other electronic delivery systems. As a group, review the arguments in favor of this view. Identify some arguments that run counter to this perspective. Does the banking industry have a vested interest in echecks catching on?

Selected References and Further Readings

Bank for International Settlements. *Clearing and Settlement Arrangements for Retail Payments in Selected Countries.* Committee on Payment and Settlement Systems, September 2000.

Board of Governors of the Federal Reserve System. *Report to the Congress on the Application of the Electronic Fund Transfer Act to Electronic Stored-Value Products.* Washington, D.C. (March 1997).

Choi, Soon-Yong, and Andrew Whinston. "Smart Cards: Enabling Smart Commerce in the Digital Age," Center for Research in Electronic Commerce, University of Texas at Austin, May 1998.

Group of Ten. *Electronic Money: Consumer Protection, Law Enforcement, Supervisory and Cross-Border Issues.* Report of the Working Party on Electronic Money, April 1997.

O'Mahony, Donal, Michael Peirce, and Hitesh Tawari. *Electronic Payment Systems.* Boston: Artech House, 1997.

Organization for Economic Cooperation and Development. *The Economic and Social Impact of Electronic Commerce.* Paris, 1999.

Osterberg, William, and James Thomson. "Network Externalities: The Catch-22 of Retail Payment Innovations," Federal Reserve Bank of Cleveland, *Economic Commentary* (February 15, 1998).

Schreft, Stacey L. "Looking Forward: The Role for Government in Regulating Electronic Cash," Federal Reserve Bank of Kansas City, *Economic Review* 82 (4, Fourth Quarter 1997), pp. 59–84.

Sheehan, Kevin P. "Electronic Cash," *FDIC Banking Review* 11 (2, 1998), pp. 1–8.

Weiner, Stuart. "Electronic Payments in the U.S. Economy: An Overview," Federal Reserve Bank of Kansas City, *Economic Review* 84 (4, Fourth Quarter 1999), pp. 1–12.

Wenninger, John. "The Emerging Role of Banks in E-Commerce," Federal Reserve Bank of New York, *Current Issues in Economics and Finance* 6 (March 2000).

Policy Implications of Electronic Commerce

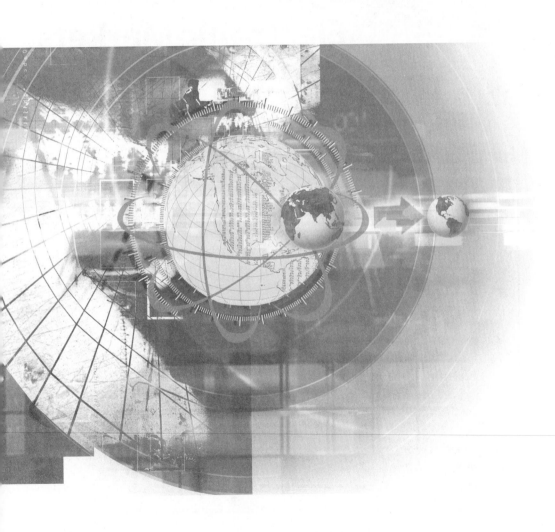

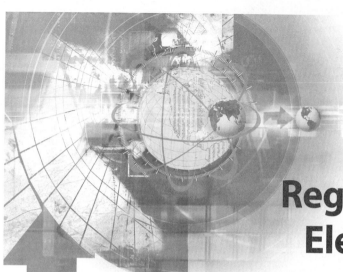

Chapter 11

Regulatory Issues in Electronic Markets

<E-Commerce Today>

New Web Retailers Confront Old Mail-Order Laws

The 1999 holiday season was a milestone for e-commerce retailing. Internet shoppers spent nearly $6 billion, which was roughly double the amount they spent online the preceding year. During the second week of December alone, consumers placed online orders for more than $1.2 billion in merchandise. For some Web retailers, this good news was more than they had anticipated. Many companies suddenly found their inventories of the most popular toys, gifts, and other items of holiday cheer depleted. In addition, some retailers were so swamped with orders that they simply did not have enough employees to handle packaging and shipping of items they had in stock. Office workers and managers at Amazon.com found themselves at the company's warehouses, shoving boxes into trucks parked at loading docks.

Several retailers, such as Macys.com, ToysRUs.com, KBKids.com, and CDNow.com, failed to fill online orders in time for the holidays. One result was a large number of unhappy customers. Another result was $1.5 million in fines assessed by the Federal Trade Commission (FTC). In July 2000, the FTC ruled that Web retailers are subject to the Mail or Telephone Order Merchandise Rule, a federal regulation that spells out ground rules for promises concerning shipment time frames, customer notification of shipment delays, and customer refunds. Under this regulation, if a retailer that takes orders via the mail, phone, or—under the FTC's legal interpretation—Internet fails to ship merchandise within 30 days, the retailer must inform the customer and give the customer an option to agree to a new shipping date or to cancel the order. In settlements with the FTC, retailers found to be in noncompliance with the regulation paid fees ranging from $45,000 to $350,000 and pledged to file periodic reports to the FTC detailing their efforts to comply with federal rules. They also agreed to finance an advertising campaign projected from their own Web sites informing consumers of their rights under the law.

"Consumer Beware!" was once the operative warning in business–consumer interactions. Today, however, the U.S. government requires companies to meet specified minimal standards in dealings with customers. The FTC and other government agencies now search the Web for failures to abide by regulations governing distance shopping, for evidence of Internet scams, for activities that look suspiciously like attempts to restrain competition, and for other violations of a huge body of laws, rules, and regulations. In this chapter, you will learn about several issues relating to government regulation within the realm of electronic commerce.

POLICYMAKING *Online*

POLICY MAKING   GLOBALIZATION   MANAGEMENT

Helping Consumers Distinguish Cyberdocs from Cyberquacks

The nation's largest health maintenance organization, Kaiser, now has a Web site that allows its 9.2 million members to register for office visits, send e-mail questions to nurses and pharmacists, learn about the results of lab tests, and refill prescriptions. The for-profit health site called Drkoop.com has former U.S. Surgeon General Dr. C. Everett Koop as its namesake. Thousands of people visit the Mayo Clinic's "Health Oasis" Web site each month. All told, at least $150 million in venture capital has been invested in Net-related health-care companies, and estimates indicate that at least 30 million people per year search the Internet for information or assistance with a health problem.

The Promise of Web-Based Health-Care Services

Health-related Web sites offer a wide array of medical research and news, as well as links to databases that explain diseases and drugs in layman's terms. Some offer online chats with physicians and nurses, personal medical pages with customized data, and risk-assessment services that rate a person's health based on lifestyle and medical information. A growing number of sites sell health-related products ranging from vitamins to health insurance.

Some medical experts hope that the Web ultimately will link together physicians, patients, and insurers much like human nerve cells are linked to form the body's nervous system. Creating a Net-based "electronic nervous system" for the health-care industry, they argue, could avoid wasting funds on unnecessary and duplicated medical treatments, thereby

continued

The Economics of Consumer Protection in Electronic Commerce

Why do governments get involved in protecting the interests of Internet consumers? To answer this question, let's consider the various reasons that governments engage in any form of regulation and then evaluate how these rationales might also extend to electronic commerce.

COMPENSATING FOR INCOMPLETE INFORMATION

A standard argument favoring government intervention in business-consumer interactions is that consumers may possess incomplete information. As a result, sellers of products may have an advantage that requires government involvement to correct.

This rationale for regulation relates to the problem of asymmetric information that you first encountered in Chapter 5. Recall how asymmetric-information saving as much as a third of the more than $1 trillion that Americans spend annually on health care.

Confronting the Lemons Problem

Nevertheless, there are hazards to Net-based health advice and care. Recall the *lemons problem* discussed in Chapter 5: If consumers do not know the details about the quality of a product, they may be willing to pay no more than the price of a low-quality product, even if a higher-quality product is available at a higher price. There are now at least 15,000 health-related Web sites, and undoubtedly some of these charge consumers for bad or misleading information. It is likely that some cyberspace health practitioners market low-priced "remedies" that do little to cure diseases. Some may even push products that could cause harm.

One approach to combating this problem is industry self-regulation and certification. The nonprofit Health on the Net Foundation, for example, certifies and monitors health-related Web sites.

Nevertheless, the U.S. government has begun providing consumers with improved online health-care information. The Department of Health and Human Services has set up a Web site, http://www. healthfinder.gov, which is aimed at helping consumers distinguish legitimate sites from those that practice cyberquackery. The department has also requested additional funding from Congress to promote more active governmental regulatory and enforcement mechanisms in the area of Web-based health-care services.

For Critical Analysis:

What are the pros and cons of allowing a free market in the sale of health-care information, services, and products on the Internet?

difficulties arise through *adverse selection*. Businesses that manufacture particularly poor-quality products can be among those with the greatest incentive to misrepresent the attributes of their products in an effort to sell them.

To generate sales, some businesses also succumb to the temptation to misrepresent customer services they will provide after a sale takes place. Hence, there is a potential for *moral hazard*. A seller may act in an "immoral" (from a consumer's perspective) manner after a sale takes place.

These asymmetric-information problems provide a rationale for governments to establish minimal standards for product quality and customer service. These problems also can provide rationales for government agencies, such as the FTC, to offer consumer-protection services. Agencies such as the FTC act both as a "consumer watchdog," in an effort to minimize the adverse selection problem, and as an "industry policeman," with the goal of combating the moral hazard problem. (For instance, the U.S. government recently has become more active in these areas in the face of booming growth in Internet health-care services; see *Policymaking Online: Helping Consumers Distinguish Cyberdocs from Cyberquacks.*)

CORRECTING EXTERNALITIES IN THE ELECTRONIC MARKETPLACE

In Chapter 2, you learned about how firms with market power can profit from restraining their output. Even under perfect competition, too few or too many resources are sometimes allocated to certain economic activities. Such situations are **market failures,** which prevent the attainment of economic efficiency. Traditionally, many economists have argued that addressing market failures requires governmental intervention. Today some economists speculate that market failures will become more commonplace on the Internet and that more government regulation is likely to emerge to address these failures.

Market Failure
Inability of unhindered private market processes to produce outcomes that are consistent with economic efficiency, individual freedom, or other broader social goals.

Internet Externalities

Economic efficiency results only when individuals know and take into account the full opportunity costs associated with their decisions. In some circumstances, the price that someone actually pays for a good or service can be higher or lower than the opportunity cost that society as a whole incurs as a result of its provision. This can occur if actions by the buyers or sellers have *spillover effects* on others not directly involved in their transactions. Such market spillovers are called **market externalities.**

Market Externality
A spillover effect influencing the welfare of third parties not involved in transactions within a marketplace.

Suppose, for instance, that a C2C auction site allows collectors of World War II memorabilia to offer Nazi artifacts to be displayed for sale. For many people, such displays at these auction sites arguably would be a form of visual pollution that generates psychic costs for those who chance across them during visits to auction sites.

Let's examine the implications that follow. In Figure 11-1, the market for C2C auction services is presumed to be perfectly competitive, and D and S are the private-market demand and supply curves for these services. The private-market price is P_1, and the quantity of auction services provided and consumed is Q_1.

By assumption, the visual display of Nazi artifacts on computer screens of people who visit auction sites creates negative spillover costs for many Web surfers, so that there is a net social cost created by their presence. This means that the private-market supply curve in Figure 11-1, which is the sum of the short-run supply curves of individual producers of Internet auction services, fails to account for the social costs these sites create through their display of Nazi artifacts. If C2C auction sites were to take into account the additional social costs caused by this display, they would provide any given quantity of auction services only at a higher price. Thus, the market supply curve would shift upward, from S_1 to S_2. As a result, Internet consumers would pay the higher market price P_2, and auction sites would provide Q_2 units of services.

Negative Market Externality
A situation in which accounting for all social costs associated with production of a good or provision of a service would reduce the quantity forthcoming in the marketplace.

Figure 11-1 illustrates an example of a **negative market externality.** The quantity of auction services provided when all social costs are taken into account is lower than the quantity that emerges in the private marketplace. From society's perspective, too many resources were allocated to C2C auction services at the private market price of these services.

Figure 11-1:
A Negative Market Externality in the Market for Internet Auction Services.

Left to its own devices, the private market for Web auction services yields the market price P_1 and the equilibrium quantity of services Q_1. If auctions involving items that some visitors to C2C auction sites deem offensive create spillover costs for these individuals, however, then it is arguable that providers of Internet auction services fail to take these costs into account. If they did, then their marginal costs would be higher, so that the short-run market supply curve would shift upward, from S_1 to S_2, resulting in an increase in the market price, to P_2, and a reduction in the equilibrium quantity of Web auction services, to Q_2. Hence, in the presence of a negative market externality there can be an overallocation of resources to the provision of these services.

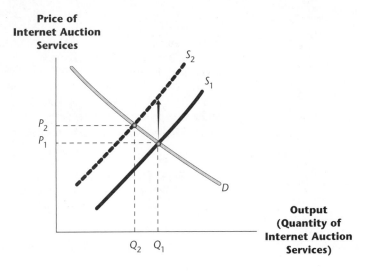

To bring about the socially preferable outcome of fewer auction services, which might even entail curtailing production of those services creating the negative market externalities, a government could enact policies limiting the proliferation of auction services. In principle, one approach might be to restrain the types and amounts of auction services made available on the Internet, in an effort to reduce overall production to the socially preferred level.

Many economists, however, doubt that it would be possible to successfully fine-tune quantity-focused policies that yield exactly the socially preferred production level of a good or service that creates negative market externalities. Consequently, economists generally have advocated imposing taxes on producers of such items. If governmental policymakers could determine the per-unit amount of the social cost resulting from the polluting effects of Nazi-artifact displays at C2C auction sites, then they might impose a per-unit tax equal to this cost. The policymaker might then channel the funds to reimburse those who demonstrate harm from the visual pollution.

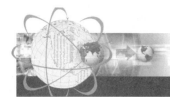

GLOBALIZATION *Online*

POLICY MAKING   **GLOBALIZATION**   MANAGEMENT

A French Judge Tries to Correct a Perceived Negative Market Externality

In April 2000, several groups joined in filing a lawsuit in a French court against Yahoo.com. The argued that Yahoo's willingness to host auctions of Nazi artifacts amounted to a "banalizing of Nazism." In fact, selling or displaying any items that might incite racism is illegal in France. The groups that brought the lawsuit argued that Yahoo should not be permitted to offer auction services on a Web site that any French residents might visit.

Making Yahoo.com Pay

Yahoo responded to the lawsuit by pointing out that it did not permit exchange of Nazi artifacts on its French auction site. French residents who found displays of these artifacts offen-

sive, the company argued, should avoid visiting its U.S. auction site, where such auctions were allowed.

On May 22, 2000, however, a French judge concurred with the groups that had filed the lawsuit. The judge appointed a panel of experts to determine the technical feasibility of preventing French Web users from accessing Yahoo's U.S. auction site. After the panel provided its conclusions in November 2000, the judge ordered the company to incur the costs of implementing a special filtering system. This system would identify French visitors to Yahoo's auction site using their Internet protocol addresses and prohibit them from accessing the site. Failure to abide by the order within 90 days, the judge declared, would result in a fine of $13,000 per day.

Shortly thereafter, eBay.com announced that it would no longer permit trading of Nazi artifacts via its C2C auction site, and several other firms announced similar policies. Hence, the French judge's efforts to force Yahoo to incur the cost of clean-

continued

Alternatively, the policymaker might induce the same outcome by requiring owners of the sites to incur these costs. This would have the effect of shifting the market supply curve by exactly the amount shown in Figure 11-1, thereby pushing up the private market price and inducing a cutback in service provision. Producers required to take into account the full costs associated with their auction services might even voluntarily halt the provision of specific services that cause the negative externality problem. (In a path-breaking decision, a French court attempted to force Yahoo.com to incur costs required to halt French access to Nazi artifacts that it judged offensive to all French residents; see *Globalization Online: A French Judge Tries to Correct a Negative Market Externality*.)

Positive E-Commerce Externalities and the Potential Role of Government

Not all market externalities are negative. There are also **positive market externalities.** These exist whenever there are social benefits associated with produc-

Positive Market Externality
A situation in which accounting for all social benefits associated with production of a good or provision of a service would increase the quantity forthcoming in the marketplace.

ing up the perceived negative externality induced other firms to voluntarily cut back on the provision of certain services.

The Problem of Regulatory Jurisdiction

This situation revealed two problems concerning the correction of Internet externalities. First, in this situation one person's "historical memorabilia" was another person's "offensive artifact." Unlike air or water pollution, which anyone surely agrees are negative market externalities, the Nazi artifacts are visual pollution to some but not to others. Some who purchased such items online contended that even though they detested Nazi ideas, they were interested in the historical significance of certain Nazi artifacts.

Second, the situation highlighted the problem of determining what countries have regulatory jurisdiction over electronic commerce, which in principle knows no boundaries. When Amazon.com received complaints about its willingness to sell Adolf Hitler's radical book, *Mein Kampf,* it responded by refusing to sell the book for shipment to a German address. If a ruling similar to that of the French judge had applied in the case of Hitler's book, Amazon would have had to filter the book's availability from view by German consumers. Undoubtedly governments of many nations would like to restrain Amazon and other Internet booksellers from offering to sell certain books. A dictator, for instance, might desire to prevent residents of his or her nation from being able to view a book containing writings about freedom and democracy by Thomas Jefferson or James Madison. If more governments follow the example established by this French judge, operating costs for e-commerce firms could rise dramatically in coming years.

For Critical Analysis:

How might a government go about determining that a negative market externality exists and should be corrected?

tion of a good or provision of a service that the private market fails to take into account.

For instance, increased Internet shopping for Christmas-season gifts adds to the number of package-delivery trucks on the road. Nevertheless, it can contribute to a net reduction in holiday traffic if many individuals who might have driven cars to shopping malls stay at home and surf through Web retailers' sites instead. This reduction in traffic congestion can benefit drivers who are on the roads for other reasons. Some of those who experience less traffic might not have ever used a computer to surf the Internet. Hence, there are potential benefits from e-commerce shopping that extend beyond those who buy and sell in Web-based retail markets.

To consider the implications of positive market externalities from e-commerce retailing, take a look at Figure 11-2 on page 348. Internet shoppers benefit directly from the services of Web retailers, and D_1 is their private-market

Figure 11-2:
A Positive Market Externality in the Market for Internet Auction Services.

The interaction between demand and supply in the private market for Web-retailing services yields the market price P_1 and the equilibrium quantity of services Q_1. If the availability of Web-retailing services helps reduce traffic congestion by reducing the number of shoppers on roads and highways, then society as a whole would benefit if the demand curve for Internet-based retailing services were to shift rightward, from D_1 to D_2, resulting in a rise in the market price, to P_2, and an increase in the equilibrium quantity of Web retailing services, to Q_2. Hence, in the presence of a positive market externality there can be an underallocation of resources to the provision of these services.

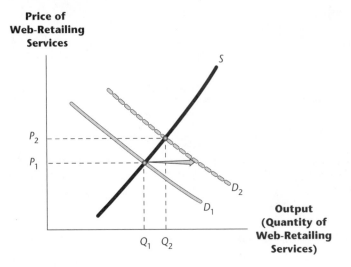

demand curve for Web-retailing services during the holiday season. Others also benefit from reduced holiday traffic congestion resulting from Internet shopping, so society as a whole prefers the demand curve D_2. Then the market price of services provided by Internet sellers would rise from P_1 to P_2, which would induce private producers to supply more services during the holiday season. Thus, the total quantity of Web-retailing services would increase from Q_1 to Q_2.

To push the amount of Web-retailing services up to Q_2, a government might provide Web-based shopping services directly. For instance, to relieve local road congestion, a city government might offer subsidies to consumers to give them a greater incentive to purchase computers or other devices to access the Internet and to pay for access via Internet service providers. Alternatively, a government might set up an online "shopping mall" and establish regulations requiring local retailers to provide Web links to its online mall.

1. What factors can induce government regulators to seek to safeguard consumers, and in what ways can regulators try to protect the interests of Internet consumers?

Because firms often have more information than consumers about the quality of their products and customer service, there is a potential for adverse selection or moral hazard problems to exist. Governments may enact regulations establishing minimal standards for quality or service, and they may establish agencies such as the Federal Trade Commission to enforce those standards both offline and online. In addition, governments may seek to address perceived market failures arising from market externalities relating to electronic commerce. In the case of a negative market externality that leads to an overallocation of resources to production and sale of a particular item, the government might directly restrict production or try to force firms creating the externality to incur the cost of addressing it. A positive market externality arises when there is an underallocation of resources to a productive activity, and governments may respond by subsidizing consumption of an item or establishing regulations inducing firms to provide more of the item.

Privacy, Discrimination, and Electronic Commerce

A computer network routes online transactions through servers, which also record the transactions in data files. Companies may retrieve these data for use in gauging consumer tastes, preferences, and habits. This has given rise to concerns about whether firms might use data in ways that violate the privacy of consumers.

THE INTERNET'S PRIVACY PROBLEM

The underlying structure of the Internet makes privacy an issue. Recall from Chapter 1 that the basic HyperText Transfer Protocol (HTTP) governs the way a browser requests pages from a Web server. For a Web server to transmit a Web page to a remote computer, the Web server must know the Internet Protocol (IP) address of the recipient. Browsers, therefore, typically transmit an individual's IP address every time he or she requests a Web page.

MANAGEMENT *Online*

Could the Web Reveal *Where* You Are, as Well as *Who* You Are?

Currently, it is easiest for owners of Web sites to identify the *Internet* address of a user. As more and more people begin accessing the Internet using wireless technologies, however, operators of Web sites may find ways to determine the *physical* locations of users.

Wireless Phones and "e911"

Recently the Federal Communications Commission (FCC) embarked on a program called "e911." Once this program is implemented, someone who enters 911 on a cell phone's keypad will not have to give public safety officials verbal directions to his or her location. The phone will take care of that, so all the caller will have to do is to state the nature of the emergency.

Two types of systems will allow the e911 program to function. One relies on triangulating a phone's signal among different cell-phone towers. Another entails placing miniature devices within the phones that would access signals from U.S. military satellites and permit pinpointing each phone's location using the U.S. government's Global Positioning System. Cell phones connected to the Global Positioning System could reveal a user's location within a range of accuracy approximately the size of a tennis court.

A Trade-Off between Safety and Privacy?

Even as the e911 system has been developed, there has been an increase in wireless Internet access using cell phones. Many

continued

Tracking Virtual Footprints

It is possible to use an individual's IP address to track that individual's Web activities. The reason is that whenever an individual provides personal information at a Web site, the owner of that site can link the user's name to his or her IP address.

Browsers also transmit a *remote host identifier* that tags the user's computer using strings of letters and numbers. Typically remote host identifiers reveal the user's Internet service provider, but they do not normally reveal the individual user. Nevertheless, the individual user can be identified when the user is logged onto another network. An internal company network, for instance, may automatically assign the user's name to remote host identifiers.

In addition, whenever a user types a name, term, or phrase into a search engine, the act of clicking on one of the sites that appears forwards the name, term, or phrase to that site. Together with the IP address, the owner of that site could use this information to compile a profile of the user associated with that IP address.

Furthermore, *cookies,* the short text files containing coded identifiers that Web sites place on users' hard disks to enable them to browse back and forth among various pages at those sites, can aid in tracking a user's interests or preferences. The reason is that the company that transmitted the cookie to the user's hard disk financial institutions, for instance, permit customers to conduct a number of online banking transactions on the Web via their cell phones. Many Web sites allow people to perform a broad range of function using cell phones, from sending e-mail to ordering airline tickets.

Once the e911 system is in place, it will be feasible—at least, in theory—for Web site operators to determine the locations of people accessing their sites using cell phones. Some cell-phone Internet service providers already assign the numbers of cell phones as the IP addresses of users. Matching those phone numbers to locations available via the e911 sys-

tem would thereby make it possible to know almost exactly where a person surfing the Web is located. This, in turn, would be more information that could be added to a company's "user profile" for that individual.

For Critical Analysis:
Under what circumstances might firms value information about the locations of people surfing the Web? What are examples of situations in which people might regard this as an invasion of their privacy?

can use them to store the user's "clickstream" as he or she browses the Internet. (A clickstream reveals an individual's *virtual* pathway through Web sites and Web pages, but wireless technologies offer the potential for Internet firms to track a customer's *physical* movements; see *Management Online: Could the Web Reveal Where You Are, As Well As Who You Are?*)

Privacy Regulations

To retailers and marketers, the information available through their e-commerce transactions with customers constitutes a treasure trove of data concerning consumers' incomes, wealth, and creditworthiness. Hence, online transactions information possessed by Internet sellers has a potentially significant market value.

The difficulty, of course, is that private information about an individual arguably is also the private property of that individual. Basic legal principles governing the transfer of property typically require firms to give individuals the opportunity to authorize use of their property. It is arguable that information about individual's tastes, preferences, or other traits gleaned from clickstreams are possessions of those individuals. Viewed from this perspective, firms that sell this information violate basic laws governing the exchange of property.

Firms devote their own resources to compiling data about their customer's clickstreams. Hence, another perspective is that information about customers' Web-surfing habits belongs to the companies that devote resources to compiling it.

The U.S. Congress is still in the process of sorting out these arguments. Federal rules governing the use of customer information obtained online are generally based on privacy protections granted prior to the growth of electronic commerce. Most of these rules, which the Federal Trade Commission enforces, are *liability laws:* If a company invades someone's privacy, the company can be sued. Current U.S. privacy protections require companies to post privacy statements at their sites, to provide information about how they intend to use information they collect, and to honor commitments made to consumers. When Web retailer Toysmart.com, which had issued a promise not to share any customer data, went bankrupt in 2000 and tried to raise funds to pay its debtors by selling customer data, the FTC intervened to force the company's owners to honor its agreement. This action helped scuttle a deal to sell the company, because most potential buyers valued its customer data more than other assets of the company.

Congress has, however, taken a concrete stand regarding the privacy rights of children who visit commercial Web sites. In 1998, Congress passed the Children's Online Privacy Protection Act. Under this law, sites must prominently disclose what personal information they collect from children, how it is used, and whether it is shared with third parties. Most importantly, the law requires sites to obtain "verifiable parental consent" before collecting any information from pre-teen children and to monitor Internet chat rooms or e-mail services to protect children from teen or adult predators.

To comply with this law, companies that collect data from children must process parental consent forms. They must also hire employees to monitor Internet chat rooms that they provide for children to, say, talk about Lego train set-ups they have constructed on their computer screens or layouts of virtual Barbie doll houses. Hundreds of companies operating Web sites geared to children have found that the total expenses entailed in complying with the Children's Online Privacy Protection Act amounted to between $50,000 to $200,000 per year. Some companies decided these expenses made offering online chat or e-mail services to children unprofitable. A number of companies simply shut down such services rather than comply with the law. Some companies even closed their sites. (Although the law required prompt compliance by businesses, government agencies have been slow to adapt their own Web practices to the spirit of the law; see *Policymaking Online: Internet Privacy and the Federal Government—"As We Say, Not As We Do!"*)

An Open Marketplace for Personal Data?

Privacy experts have estimated that the average U.S. resident is profiled in at least 25, and perhaps as many as 100, different databases. Opinion surveys indicate that many consumers realize shopping on the Internet improves the odds that data indicating their tastes and preferences will end up on such databases. Even though an increasing number of Web sites let consumers "opt out" from collection and distribution of their personal data, many consumers continue to indicate in such surveys that these concerns discourage them from shopping on the Internet.

POLICYMAKING *Online*

POLICY MAKING   GLOBALIZATION   MANAGEMENT

Internet Privacy and the Federal Government— "As We Say, Not as We Do!"

The Children's Online Privacy Protection Act requires companies operating Web sites to take specific steps to minimize potential intrusions into the privacy of children. The act obliges posting privacy statements, obtaining parental consent, and providing an opportunity to remove any collected information.

Failing to Protect Kids' Privacy at the White House

Congress aimed this legislation at commercial Web sites. After the law was passed, however, the president's Office of Management and Budget ordered federal agencies to comply with its provisions.

Nevertheless, several government agencies failed to abide by this order. Sites operated by the Environmental Protection Agency and the National Aeronautics and Space Administration, for instance, collected personal information from children who submitted artwork to be posted on their sites. Then both agencies displayed each child's name, age, and hometown alongside posted drawings. Even the White House Web site failed to comply with the law for months after its

passage. It invited children to submit their names, ages, and addresses to the president and the first family.

Government Cookies and Information Sharing

A presidential executive order also banned the use of cookies by federal agencies operating Web sites, unless visitors were informed that their activity was being tracked. Nevertheless, for months afterward agencies such as the U.S. Customs Service, the Federal Aviation Administration, and the Office of National Drug Control Policy remained in violation of the directive. The U.S. Forest Service even gathered information from clickstreams of visitors to its site and shared it with a private organization.

In 2000, a study by the Congressional General Accounting Office (GAO) found that very few government Web sites were in compliance with basic regulations issued by the Federal Trade Commission. Of a total of 65 government Web sites examined by the GAO, only 2 satisfied the FTC's rules.

For Critical Analysis:

Information from clickstreams often has a market value, so who directly or indirectly benefited or incurred a cost as a result of the free but restricted release of information that the U.S. Forest Service gathered from cookies?

According to some estimates, privacy concerns cost Internet sellers billions of dollars in lost revenues.

From this standpoint, privacy concerns pose a potential *lemons problem* for the electronic marketplace (see Chapter 5). If a sufficient number of consumers are convinced that their overall satisfaction with electronic commerce will be lower because of a loss of privacy, the result could be a reduction in the number of consumers willing to engage in Internet transactions. Only people willing to accept an anticipated reduction in privacy would continue to participate. Furthermore, firms would recognize that consumers' worries reduce the demand for products online. This could reduce the number of firms entering the electronic marketplace. Overall, therefore, privacy concerns could depress electronic commerce.

GLOBALIZATION *Online*

Is European Privacy Protection Synonymous with European Competition Protection?

U.S. regulations simply *limit* the use of data about consumers that companies obtain online. By way of contrast, European Union (EU) privacy rules *prohibit* the transferal of online consumer data.

The EU Data Privacy Directive

The European Union's privacy rules were adopted in October 1998 in personal privacy guidelines known collectively as the *Data Protection Directive*. These privacy restraints are much more stringent than those in the United States. Under the EU

Data Protection Directive, before a company can transfer any data it has obtained about a customer to any other firm, it must obtain written permission—online permission will not do—from that customer.

EU regulations apply to both offline and online interactions among individuals and companies, but they have especially important implications for ongoing efforts by U.S. Web firms to do business in Europe. EU rules require U.S. companies to develop separate systems for their online dealings with customers in both parts of the world.

Protecting EU Markets from Foreign Competition?

To satisfy EU rules, U.S. companies doing business with EU consumers essentially have had to develop a separate "track" for EU marketing, sales, and customer service. For instance,

continued

One way to address this potential lemons problem might be to establish more laws and rules forbidding companies from collecting private information in the e-commerce realm. A less radical approach is the current legal scheme in which companies can be held liable for misusing consumer data.

Another approach might be to move in an entirely different direction, by laying legal foundations for an open marketplace for personal information. According to proponents of this idea, the problem is that rights to personal information are too hazy. If the ownership of personal data were clearly established, they argue, then companies would have to receive permission any time they used personal information and pay consumers for the right to do so. (European nations moved partway in this direction, although some U.S. companies have questioned whether privacy concerns are the motivation for tough privacy rules in those countries; see *Globalization Online: Is European Privacy Protection Synonymous with European Competition Protection?*)

In a market for personal information, companies seeking to profit from the use of such information would be willing to purchase more data at a lower price, whereas consumers would be willing to provide more data at a higher price. In this proposed open market for information, consumers would receive a market price for each bit of personal data they might choose to release for use by product designers, marketers, and distributors. At that market price, it would be up to consumers to decide how much personal information they wish to sell.

U.S. firms have had to develop European advertising efforts that satisfy EU guidelines. U.S. firms also must use separate "European contracts," which are legally enforceable promises to European consumers that they will not share data with other companies. By way of contrast, fledgling European on-line firms do not face a requirement to expend resources on separate marketing, sales, and customer-service "tracks" for EU and U.S. consumers.

Some U.S. critics have contended that privacy protection in Europe may really be designed to increase the height of barriers to entry by foreign firms—otherwise known as "protectionism." In their view, privacy protection laws in Europe may have as much to do with discouraging U.S.-based Internet sellers from entering the European electronic marketplace as they do with protecting the privacy of European residents. According to this contention, European governments realize that U.S. Internet sellers have a first-mover advantage in marketing to European residents. By slowing up U.S. firms and raising their costs, critics allege, the European Union hopes to give European companies a chance to catch up.

For Critical Analysis:
Which residents of Europe gain or lose if the costs of meeting the Data Protection Directive discourage a significant number of U.S. firms from offering to sell their products online in Europe?

FUNDAMENTAL ISSUES ▼

1.

2.

3.

4.

5.

6.

2. Why is privacy a major issue in the electronic marketplace, and what are possible ways to address the e-commerce privacy issue?

The Internet creates privacy concerns because providing personal information on a Web site permits the site's owner to link the user's name to an IP address. In addition, a company may be able to track an individual's Web-surfing behavior through remote host identifiers, search-engine queries, and cookies. The Children's Online Privacy Protection Act of 1998 lays out strict rules governing the online collection of personal information from children, but online adult privacy protections are in a state of flux and are largely confined to enforcement of general laws governing liability for misuse of information. Some economists argue that consumers would gain if personal information were classified as personal property that consumers can sell. Then a private market in personal information could develop, and consumers could determine how much information they wish to sell at current market prices.

ANTI-DISCRIMINATION POLICIES AND THE INTERNET

Throughout history, people within some groups have treated persons within other groups differently. There are documented historical examples of differing treatment of males and females or of members of different racial, ethnic, or religious groups.

A major policy issue in recent years has been the extent to which such differential treatment may occur in markets for goods, services, credit, labor, and so on. Congress has enacted laws addressing this issue. Furthermore, Congress has charged various government regulators with monitoring and enforcing these laws. Some of these regulations have implications for the electronic marketplace, particularly in the area of financial services.

The "Cultural Affinity" of Buyers and Sellers?

Recently, economists have developed theories to help explain why race, gender, ethnicity, or other factors may influence trade among individuals. One theory proposed as potentially useful for understanding possible racial and ethnicity factors affecting the behavior of buyers and sellers is called the **cultural affinity hypothesis.** This theory proposes that sellers find it easier, and consequently less costly, to interact with buyers who share similar characteristics.

Cultural Affinity Hypothesis
A theory that sellers experience lower costs in interacting with buyers who share their characteristics.

Of course, providing a theory for differential interactions on the basis of different characteristics does nothing for those who feel their racial, ethnic, or gender status causes them to lose out on earnings. For instance, if a white customer asks an African-American salesperson if a different salesperson can assist the customer, the African American might suspect that race was an issue. Likewise, when a white banker turns down an African-American loan applicant, there is always the chance that race made a difference.

The market for credit is an area where some economists believe the cultural affinity hypothesis may be particularly applicable. If the hypothesis is correct, a lender may identify more with applicants of the same race, gender, ethnicity, and so on, thereby increasing the likelihood that the lender will extend credit to someone who shares the lender's own characteristics. Likewise, applicants for loans might prefer to apply for loans at banks owned and managed by people who share characteristics of the applicants. Studies of bank lending have shown that there is a greater propensity of African Americans to apply for loans at banks that are majority-owned by other African Americans. This may help to explain the otherwise puzzling fact that African-American–owned banks tend to have *higher* rejection rates for African-American loan applicants as compared with banks that are majority-owned by people without African-American ancestry.

Does the Electronic Marketplace Require Anti-Discrimination Rules?

One of the promising features of electronic commerce is that it could contribute to reductions in both actual and perceived discrimination on the basis of race. Someone who applies for a loan on the Internet, for instance, looks for the best terms irrespective of whether the bank is primarily owned by males or females, by people whose racial characteristics might be classified as black, white, oriental, or Native American, or by individuals who are Jewish, Muslim, Christian, agnostic, or atheist. At the same time, a loan officer handling an Internet-based loan application does not physically see the applicant before ruling on the loan. Loan officers who wish to discriminate might have some success using names to identify an applicant's gender or, in some instances, the applicant's ethnicity. Names, however, provide weak clues about race. Consequently, arranging a loan on the Internet is, in principle, more likely to be free of racial bias and, perhaps to a lesser extent, other forms of discrimination on the part of lenders.

Beyond credit markets, the Internet increasingly is providing African-American entrepreneurs a means to avoid racial discrimination they otherwise might have experienced. For instance, AutoNetwork.com is a Web site that offers auto broker services and leasing information. An Asian woman looking for a good deal on an auto lease does not necessarily know that the site is owned by an African-American man who earns more than $200,000 per year in advertising revenue from operating the site. Likewise, all a college biology student cares about is whether Cyberstudy101.com can help him do better in class. The fact that an African-American woman founded this successful online business is unlikely to be an issue.

There is considerable promise that electronic commerce may break down racial, ethnic, or gender barriers that otherwise might exist if people were limited to trading in the physical marketplace. People who worry about the potential to be on the receiving end of discrimination arguably have a powerful incentive to participate in the electronic marketplace.

Nevertheless, some economists worry that existing regulations originally designed for the pre-commerce world could actually erase some of these advantages. Again, consider the market for credit. Provisions of the Home Mortgage Disclosure Act of 1975 and the Community Reinvestment Act of 1977, for instance, require lenders to collect information about an applicant's race, ethnicity, and gender. Thus, Internet loan applications ask people applying for credit to submit this information, thereby defeating a key advantage of using the Internet as a means of obtaining credit. After all, under these laws a loan officer who wishes to discriminate against people with particular characteristics now finds those characteristics openly listed on an application form.

www.

Should individuals who have disabilities be concerned about being shut out of the electronic marketplace? You can learn more about issues relating to accessibility and equal opportunities in electronic commerce at the home page of the Web Accessibility Initiative at http://www.w3.org/WAI.

.com

FUNDAMENTAL ISSUES ▼

1.

2.

3.

4.

5.

6.

3. As compared with the physical marketplace, do people interacting in the electronic marketplace face fewer problems with discrimination?

In principle, electronic commerce should be relatively blind to the race, ethnicity, or gender of buyers and sellers. For this reason, antidiscrimination regulations may be less applicable to the electronic marketplace as compared with the physical marketplace. Nevertheless, existing anti-discrimination regulations apply to the electronic marketplace. In some cases, existing regulations could reduce the potential for electronic commerce to reduce discrimination, particularly if regulations require people to reveal information about their race, ethnicity, or gender.

**Market Power and Public Policy
in the Electronic Marketplace**

As you learned in Chapter 2, consumers benefit from increased rivalry among producers. In years past, this has led to public policy efforts to try to encourage increased competition in markets for goods and services. More recently, policymakers have been exploring the extent to which such efforts should be extended to the electronic marketplace.

ANTITRUST LAWS

Antitrust Laws
Statutes designed to achieve benefits of competition for consumers and producers.

Governments seek to influence the extent of market competition using **antitrust laws.** These legal statutes are aimed at ensuring that consumers and producers benefit from market competition. Antitrust laws govern the marketing, sale, and distribution of products, whether they are sold offline or online.

The Objectives of Antitrust Laws

Traditionally, a fundamental goal of antitrust laws has been to limit the pricing power available to firms. Because cartels have an incentive to enrich participating firms at the expense of consumer welfare and economic efficiency, antitrust laws in most countries, including the United States, explicitly prohibit efforts by combinations of firms to restrain market competition. Most national antitrust laws make it a crime even to try to form a monopoly.

It is also common for antitrust laws to restrict *price discrimination.* As you learned in Chapter 4, one type of price discrimination entails charging different consumers different prices for identical goods. Another involves charging the same consumer different prices for the same good, depending on number of units that the consumer purchases. Antitrust laws do not outright forbid charging different prices to different consumers, but they typically require such price differentials to reflect actual distinctions in the costs of providing goods or services to different consumers.

Predatory Pricing
A situation in which a firm sets artificially low prices intended to induce competitors to leave the industry and to dissuade potential rivals from entering the industry.

Many nations also prohibit efforts to engage in so-called **predatory pricing**, in which firms allegedly reduce their prices to drive competitors out of business and dissuade potential rivals from entering the marketplace. Antitrust laws seeking to restrain price discrimination and predatory pricing often generate controversy, because it is not unusual for enforcement of these laws to raise market prices.

U.S. Antitrust Rules and Enforcement

As you can see in Table 11-1, antitrust laws in the United States seek to address each of these public-policy objectives. The Sherman Act of 1890 bans coordinated efforts to obtain pricing power. The Clayton Act of 1914 and the Robinson–Patman Act of 1936 limit the scope of permissible price discrimination. The Robinson–Patman Act and the Federal Trade Commission Act also provide legal restraints against predatory pricing aimed at reducing the extent of competition.

Table 11-1: Key U.S. Antitrust Laws.

Sherman Antitrust Act of 1890	Forbids any contract, combination, or conspiracy to restrain trade or commerce within the United States or across U.S. borders. The law holds any person who attempts to monopolize trade or commerce criminally liable.
Clayton Act of 1914	Prohibits specific business practices deemed to restrain trade or commerce. The law bans discriminating in prices charged to various purchasers when price differences are not due to actual differences in selling or transportation costs. It also forbids a company from selling goods on the condition that the purchaser must exclusively deal with that company. In addition, the act prevents corporations from holding stock in other companies when this may lessen competition.
Federal Trade Commission Act of 1914 (and 1938 Amendment)	Outlaws practices that contribute to actions that reduce the extent of competition, such as business practices involving cutthroat pricing intended to drive rivals from the marketplace. It also established the Federal Trade Commission and empowered it to issue cease and desist orders in situations where it determines "unfair methods of competition in commerce" exist. The 1938 amendment added deceptive business practices to the list of illegal acts.
Robinson–Patman Act of 1936	Bans selected discriminatory price cuts by chain stores that allegedly drive smaller competitors from the marketplace. In addition, it forbids price discrimination through special concessions in the form of price of quantity discounts, free advertising, or promotional allowances granted to one buyer but not to others, if these actions substantially reduce competition.

Individuals, firms, state governments, the U.S. Department of Justice, and the Federal Trade Commission can file legal challenges against business practices they allege violate any one or more of these antitrust laws. Each year hundreds of antitrust suits are filed in courtrooms across the nation. Every day that courts are in session, judges and juries find themselves trying to determine whether companies have engaged in business practices that harm consumers. Firms may have done so either directly via overt efforts to restrain push up prices by restraining production or indirectly through discriminatory or predatory pricing policies.

INFORMATION TECHNOLOGY MEETS ANTITRUST LAW

In 1998, a head of the Antitrust Division of the U.S. Department of Justice stated, " . . . there is nothing so different about . . . new technology-based markets that could possibly support abandoning this nation's longstanding belief—a belief

www.

What are the costs of being sued under provisions of the Robinson–Patman Act? Find out about the estimated costs of a price discrimination lawsuit at http://www. lawmall. com/rpa/rpaexpen.html.

.com

based on lots of experience—that competitive markets work best for consumers and that antitrust enforcement is essential for sustaining markets." This statement served notice to e-commerce firms that this antitrust enforcement authority was going to pay attention to the electronic marketplace. The Federal Trade Commission, state authorities, and individuals and firms who participate in these markets also have been examining the applicability of antitrust laws to electronic commerce.

Traditional Antitrust Issues Applied to Electronic Commerce

The first and arguably most important antitrust law, the Sherman Act, does not define monopoly. Economic principles discussed in Chapter 2 indicate that in principle a single firm can be a monopoly, or a group of firms can act together as a monopoly. Furthermore, the Sherman Act does not lay out a detailed definition of "restraint of trade." Again, basic economic analysis provides some guidance. It indicates that firms with market power can increase their profits and potentially reduce consumer welfare by reducing their output. As you learned in Chapter 4, principles of economics also indicate that firms possessing market power are positioned to engage in price discrimination that may be illegitimate under federal laws.

Traditionally, therefore, antitrust enforcement has emphasized two areas:

1) **Detecting and negating efforts to create monopolies**—Under the Sherman Act, any active attempt to form a monopoly situation in any market is illegal. Such an attempt does not necessarily have to succeed to constitute a violation, although in this case an accuser must be able to marshal evidence of a conspiracy or other effort to control production and pricing in a market. In the case of a successful attempt to monopolize a market, simply proving that a monopoly situation exists is sufficient to justify remedies that can include breaking the offending firm into separate companies. (This excludes situations in which firms are exempt from antitrust laws, a situation that has led to double-charging for some Internet services; see *Policymaking Online: Paying Twice for Internet Services in Markets with Legalized Monopolies.*)

2) **Assessing how various business practices relate to market power**— Economic theory implies that absolute size does not necessarily determine a situation in which a firm has market power. Instead, it indicates that it is the *relative* sizes and numbers of competitors that influence the extent of competition within an industry. Hence, antitrust authorities typically track measures of relative competition within markets in an effort to identify industries that deserve the greatest degree of enforcement scrutiny.

Measuring Market Power   Under both of these traditional focus areas of antitrust enforcement, it is of considerable importance to find a way to measure the relative predominance of a few firms within a market. Economists have often measured whether a few firms account for a large portion of industry output using **concentration ratios,** which are the portions of total industry sales accounted for by the largest firms. The most commonly examined concentration ratio is the four-firm

Concentration Ratio
The share of total industry sales by the top few firms.

POLICYMAKING *Online*

POLICY MAKING　　　GLOBALIZATION　　　MANAGEMENT

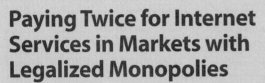

Paying Twice for Internet Services in Markets with Legalized Monopolies

Numerous laws exempt various industries and organizations from antitrust legislation. Examples include professional baseball, hospitals, public transit and water systems, and labor unions. A particularly important example is public utilities, such as electric, gas, and telephone companies.

For some businesses, high-speed Internet access is an indispensable key to success of their business plans. Nowadays, two channels for obtaining high-speed Internet access are satellite Internet access, which is made available by various relatively unregulated companies, and digital service line (DSL) service provided mainly by telephone companies. Under federal law, telephone companies are designated to be "common carriers," meaning they are required to offer competing firms access to their lines. As a result, hundreds of DSL-based Internet service providers vie for customers.

In many locales, however, broadband, high-speed access to the Internet is available only from traditional cable-TV providers that local governments have deemed to be public utilities eligible to be legal monopolies. Cable-TV providers are *not* legally designated to be common carriers, and at a number of these cable firms, Internet access automatically includes a bundled package of e-mail and Web-surfing services. This means that if a company that purchases Internet access from one of these cable companies desires to use what it perceives to be superior e-mail and Web-surfing services offered by other companies, it must pay *twice* for e-mail and Web-surfing services.

Access to the Internet has become a major issue in light of consolidation among companies that provide broadband access services *and* e-mail and Web-surfing services. For instance, Time Warner is a major stakeholder in Road Runner, one of the nation's two largest cable-access companies. At the same time, however, America Online (AOL) is the nation's largest provider of e-mail and Web-surfing services. Both of these companies merged in 2001, which set the stage for an end to double charging for both types of services. Nevertheless, it also became clear that the AOL–Time Warner combination would automatically have significant market power in areas with limited (or no) choice among broadband access services.

To gain approval of their merger from federal antitrust authorities, the two companies agreed to terminate exclusive agreements with e-mail and Web-surfing service providers and to open their cable services to multiple providers of these services. Many observers agree that this agreement may have laid a foundation for eventual passage of legislation extending common-carrier status to cable access providers.

For Critical Analysis:
What are possible rationales for exempting some businesses and organizations from antitrust laws?

concentration ratio, or the percentage of total sales at the top four firms in the market.

An obvious problem with concentration ratios is that they can fail to capture important differences among structures of different industries. For example, suppose each of the top four firms in two different markets has a 20 percent share, so the four-firm concentration ratio for each industry is 80 percent. In one of the markets, however, there might be just one more firm, so that rivalry within the market is limited to a total of five firms. In the other market, there might be ten more firms equally sharing the remaining 20 percent of industry sales and attempting to actively compete with the top four companies.

Partly in response to this and other perceived problems with simple concentration rations, beginning in the early 1980s the U.S. Department of Justice and Federal Trade Commission began emphasizing a different concentration measure. This measure, called the **Herfindahl–Hirschman index,** is the sum of the squared market shares for all firms in an industry. For the example of a five-firm industry with a 20-percent market share at each firm, this would yield a Herfindahl–Hirschman-index value of 2,000. For the case of the industry in which the top four firms have 20-percent market shares while ten others each have a 2-percent share, the value would be 1,640. The lower index value for the latter industry would thereby reflect its greater potential for more broad-based competition among a larger set of producers.

Herfindahl–Hirschman Index

The sum of the squares of the market shares of each firm in an industry.

The Biggest Issue: Determining the Relevant Market   It is a subjective decision to determine how high a concentration ratio or Herfinadahl–Hirschman-index value must be to indicate that individual firms are likely to have enough power to affect market prices. Even more problematic is that concentration ratios or Herfindahl–Hirschman-index values have meaning only if they are calculated using correctly defined markets.

For instance, one might find that the four-firm concentration ratio for the cable modem Internet-access industry is very high in many areas. Indeed, in most areas where cable modem service is available, there are likely to be fewer than five providers of cable-modem Internet access, so a four-firm concentration ratio of 100 percent is likely to be common. Most economists would agree, however, that this ratio would be meaningless, because the **relevant market**—the true economic marketplace taking into account the availability of all products that directly influence product prices at individual producers—surely includes other providers of Internet access, such as traditional phone-dial-up providers, providers of Internet direct service lines, and satellite-service providers.

Relevant Market

The extent of the marketplace containing all available products that directly impinge on the prices charged by individual firms.

In electronic commerce, defining the relevant market is a particularly thorny issue. The reason is that many products sold in the electronic marketplace are available from bricks-and-mortar firms. For instance, about 10 percent of all books in the United States are now sold over the Internet, but traditional booksellers remain the dominant outlets for books. Any published book, such as *E-Commerce Economics,* is identical whether it is purchased over the Internet or at a bricks-and-mortar bookstore.

So is the relevant market for judging the extent of competition an overall national market for books? Or are there two relevant markets—one an electronic marketplace for books and the other a bricks-and-mortar marketplace—in which firms sell separate, albeit highly substitutable, products? If one believes there is a single national book market, then Amazon.com's sales share within that overall marketplace for books is about 6.5 percent. Viewed from this perspective, Amazon is a relatively small player in the book market. If one determines that there are separate e-commerce and bricks-and-mortar markets, however, then Amazon's share of the e-commerce book market is about 65 percent, implying dominant-firm firm status (see Chapter 2) for the company in the electronic marketplace.

Bricks versus Clicks   To date, there is no clear-cut conclusion regarding whether e-commerce and bricks-and-mortar markets are indeed separate markets. Since the advent of e-commerce, the bulk of companies that initially established Web-based operations—eToys.com, Amazon, E*Trade.com, Petsmart.com, PlanetRX.com, Priceline.com, and so on—specialized in Internet marketing and selling. Even previously established bricks-and-mortar firms—Toys "Я" Us, Barnes & Noble, Merrill Lynch, and the like—avoided integrating e-commerce operations directly into their businesses. Toys "Я" Us, for instance, initially developed a "spin-off" company for Internet toy sales. Barnes & Noble also initially separated its Internet operations from its traditional network of retail stores, choosing to operate its Web site as a separate company.

From the "supply side" of the marketplace, the electronic marketplace and the physical marketplace have tended to remain separate entities. Nevertheless, in recent years, bricks-and-mortar companies have begun to integrate their Internet activities into their basic operations. For instance, Barnes & Noble ultimately recombined with Barnesandnoble.com, and, as you learned in Chapter 9, traditional financial institutions have begun integrating online services within their regular product lines. Furthermore, some companies that initially were exclusively Web-based have added bricks-and-mortar operations. E*Trade, for example, now owns a network of automated teller machines and has begun establishing physical branch offices in various locations.

On the "demand side" of the marketplace, a fundamental issue in judging the relevant market is whether consumers regard the products they purchase from e-commerce firms as *distinctive,* even if they can purchase the same items from bricks-and-mortar companies. That is, groups of consumers and firms interact in separate electronic and physical markets if the products traded in those markets are imperfect substitutes.

In principle, economists can try to judge whether consumers products are imperfect substitutes by examining the **cross price elasticity of demand,** which is the percentage change in the quantity of an item demanded resulting from the percentage change in the price of a related item. Suppose that there is a relatively low value for the cross price elasticity of demand for, say, books purchased from Amazon following an increase in the books prices at traditional booksellers. This might indicate that consumers regard the bundle of shopping experience, service package, and book delivery offered by Amazon as distinctive from those available from a bricks-and-mortar bookstore, even though the books offered by both are identical. In this case, economists might judge that there are two relevant markets—electronic and physical—in the bookselling business, each of which should be evaluated separately for purposes of antitrust enforcement.

Unfortunately, there is little definitive evidence on the values of cross price elasticities for the large numbers of products available in both the electronic marketplace and the physical marketplace. Economists and policymakers have tended

Cross Price Elasticity of Demand
The percentage change in the quantity of an item demanded resulting from the percentage change in the price of a related item.

to rely on less reliable measures of whether consumers regard electronic and physical markets as distinct, such as survey evidence concerning the portion of goods and services that consumers in various identifiable groups say they purchase online. There is also even less trustworthy evidence about consumer shopping preferences provided by consumer surveys.

Hence, antitrust authorities have relatively little guidance for determining the relevant markets for products sold in both electronic and physical markets. This is likely to emerge as a pressing issue in antitrust enforcement as the electronic marketplace continues to expand.

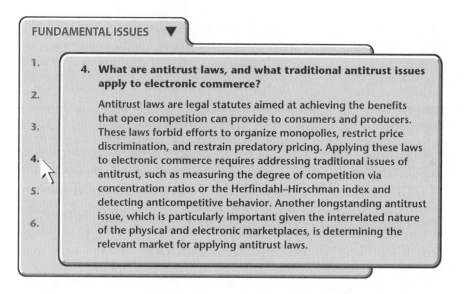

FUNDAMENTAL ISSUES ▼

1.
2.
3.
4.
5.
6.

4. What are antitrust laws, and what traditional antitrust issues apply to electronic commerce?

Antitrust laws are legal statutes aimed at achieving the benefits that open competition can provide to consumers and producers. These laws forbid efforts to organize monopolies, restrict price discrimination, and restrain predatory pricing. Applying these laws to electronic commerce requires addressing traditional issues of antitrust, such as measuring the degree of competition via concentration ratios or the Herfindahl–Hirschman index and detecting anticompetitive behavior. Another longstanding antitrust issue, which is particularly important given the interrelated nature of the physical and electronic marketplaces, is determining the relevant market for applying antitrust laws.

Nontraditional Issues in E-Commerce Antitrust

There are other important, but less commonplace, antitrust issues associated with electronic commerce. One arises because electronic commerce is borderless. The other relates to the potential for *network industries* to develop within the electronic marketplace.

1) **Antitrust enforcement in markets without physical borders**—How should national antitrust authorities define the "relevant market" if AT&T decides it wishes to merge with British Telecommunications, or if Germany's Deutsche Telecom wants to acquire Sprint? What should they do if America Online and Time Warner, each of which has a global presence in markets for Internet access, instant messaging, cable communications, and entertainment, wish to merge? How should they react if Time Warner

simultaneously attempts to merge with EMI, one of the world's largest recorded-music companies?

These are not just rhetorical questions, as U.S. and E.U. antitrust authorities learned in 2000 and 2001 when all these issues actually surfaced. The emergence of cross-border markets for many goods and services has increasingly made antitrust policy a global undertaking.

So far, U.S. antitrust authorities have ruled that a number of international combinations in markets for physical products, such as a merger between Daimler-Benz of Germany and Chrysler Corporation of the United States and an acquisition of U.S.-based Banker's Trust by Germany's Deutche Bank, were globally based, so that these combinations would not have anticompetitive consequences for U.S. consumers. European antitrust authorities, however, raised so many objections to the proposed Time Warner–EMI merger that the two parties called it off. It remains to be seen how antitrust authorities might address antitrust issues relating to future proposals for cross-border mergers or acquisitions involving e-commerce firms.

2) **Addressing market power gained from network externalities**—As you learned in Chapter 3, network externalities arise when products become more valuable to individual consumers when they are more widely used by other consumers. Producers of an item that is subject to network externalities comprise a *network industry.*

As discussed in Chapter 2, firms in network industries may experience an *interoperability* advantage over other firms. Producers of complementary products, such as software applications, may design their products to be usable only with the dominant product offered by firms within the network industry, such as a computer operating system. If network externalities are sufficiently strong, then a "winner-take-all" situation can arise, in which a single firm is able to become the dominant firm within the network industry. It may be more cost-efficient for consumers and firms producing complementary goods or services to use its product, or the costs of switching to an alternative technology may be prohibitively high.

In such a situation, it is possible that antitrust authorities may have trouble determining whether the price of a good or service provided by a network industry in the electronic marketplace would rise or fall if more competition were forced on the marketplace. On one hand, if the firm or firms dominating a network industry have taken advantage of their market power and there are relatively significant cost efficiencies from network externalities, then the price might decline. On the other hand, if their network externalities bring about big cost savings, then breaking up dominant firms could actually push up the market price paid by consumers.

To date, antitrust authorities have not taken a firm stand on how to apply antitrust laws in the electronic marketplace. Recently, however, a Justice Department report reached the following conclusion:

How much do antitrust policies vary across countries? To evaluate international differences in antitrust policies, go to the U.S. Department of Justice's worldwide antitrust links at http://www.usdoj.gov/atr/contact/otheratr.htm.

[C]yberspace will undoubtedly increase market-based competition. However, the need for antitrust enforcement will remain important as some firms may try to use anticompetitive practices to forestall competition from new e-commerce entrants or, alternatively, firms that use e-commerce may still have opportunities to exploit their market power and engage in anticompetitive activities.

There is good reason to believe that antitrust authorities will continue to emphasize traditional views on the role of antitrust laws in maintaining a competitive e-commerce environment.

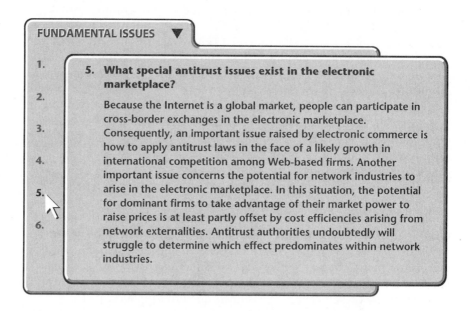

FUNDAMENTAL ISSUES ▼

1.

2.

3.

4.

5.

6.

5. What special antitrust issues exist in the electronic marketplace?

Because the Internet is a global market, people can participate in cross-border exchanges in the electronic marketplace. Consequently, an important issue raised by electronic commerce is how to apply antitrust laws in the face of a likely growth in international competition among Web-based firms. Another important issue concerns the potential for network industries to arise in the electronic marketplace. In this situation, the potential for dominant firms to take advantage of their market power to raise prices is at least partly offset by cost efficiencies arising from network externalities. Antitrust authorities undoubtedly will struggle to determine which effect predominates within network industries.

Protecting E-Commerce Security— Web Crime and Cybercops

A company called ActiMate markets a toy version of "Barney," the purple dinosaur. The toy can be controlled by a personal computer via radio signals for use with interactive educational software. To determine how difficult it might be for computer hackers to break into wireless computer communications, a Xerox laboratory spent weeks intercepting the radio traffic between a computer and an Acti-Mate Barney doll. Eventually, engineers at the lab were able to decipher the communications protocol in the software and take control of the doll's motor functions (though not its voice) from a remote computer, thereby demonstrating that a hacker potentially could "steal" software code or other digital information over the airwaves.

THE ECONOMICS OF CYBERCRIME

Why might there be a concern about the potential for hackers to intercept, decode, and make use of digital data transmitted by radio? As you learned in Chapter 10, billions of dollars already flow over telephone lines, fiber optic cables, and other wired connections throughout the United States and the rest of the world. Increasingly these data flows are likely to be transmitted via the airwaves as well. Whether electronic communications take place via wired or wireless connections, these large flows of funds provide a considerable incentive to *cybercriminals* lying in wait for the opportunity to pilfer large sums.

The Benefits and Costs of Cybercrime

The potential to obtain big dollar sums is one obvious inducement to try to hack into computer transmissions. As the world learned in 2000, when a student in the Philippines planted the so-called "I Love You" virus that infected millions of computers at an estimated worldwide cost of $10 billion, some people apparently gain only implicit benefits from such activities.

The two panels of Figure 11-3 on page 368 depict possible *marginal benefit* curves for individuals who may contemplate engaging in illicit computer network activities. This is the expected return individuals anticipate receiving, whether measured in dollars or in units of satisfaction. Someone who considers committing crimes first seeks to engage in activities he or she anticipates will yield the greatest potential gain. Additional activities tend to have lower anticipated payoffs. Hence, the *marginal benefit* curves for individuals engaging in illegal activities on the Internet or other computer networks typically slope downward, as shown.

Anyone contemplating committing cybercrime also faces a *marginal cost* of engaging in illegal activities. One reason is that even a cybercriminal's time has a positive opportunity cost. Each hour that such an individual devotes to trying to break into a computer network has value, because the person could, after all, alternatively earn a market wage engaging in legal activities. In addition, an individual engaging in criminal activities may experience personal, psychic costs arising from feelings of guilt. Furthermore, if caught, an individual who attempts to hack into a computer system faces potential penalties. Because the chances of getting caught increase as the individual undertakes more efforts to hack into a wired or wireless system, the individual's expected cost of engaging in additional criminal efforts increases. This means that the marginal cost curves slope upward in both panels of Figure 11-3.

Any individual determines how much to engage in criminal activities by doing so to the point where the marginal benefit is equal to the marginal cost. For many individuals, the marginal cost of criminal activity is so high that it always is at least as great as the marginal benefit. This is the situation depicted in panel (a) of the figure. Such an individual therefore undertakes no criminal activities. For a few people, however, the marginal benefit of engaging in illicit activities exceeds the marginal cost over some range, as in panel (b). A person in this situation will take part in illegal activities such as trying to hack into network security

Figure 11-3:
The Marginal Benefit and Marginal Cost of Cybercrime.

Panels (a) and (b) display possible marginal benefit and marginal cost curves associated with engaging in criminal activities on the Internet. The marginal benefit curve slopes downward, because someone contemplating committing crimes typically aims initially to engage in illicit activities with the greatest payoffs. As people engage in more illegal activities, opportunity cost rises. In addition, the chances of getting caught and suffering a penalty increase. Hence, the marginal cost curve slopes upward. Panel (a) depicts the situation that arises for an individual who chooses not to commit cybercrimes. For such a person, the marginal cost always exceeds the marginal benefit. As shown in panel (b), however, for some people the marginal cost is less than the marginal benefit over at least some range of cybercriminal activities. Hence, a person such as the one in panel (b) will choose to engage in an amount of criminal activities equal to C*.

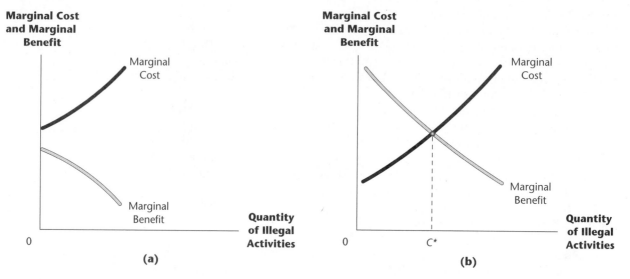

systems to the point where the marginal benefit just equals the marginal cost. Beyond this point, engaging in further criminal activity results in a cost that exceeds the expected return, so the individual halts his or her efforts. Thus, C^* is a positive amount of criminal activities that the individual will choose to undertake.

Punishment, Expected Rewards, and Crime

Comparing the two panels in Figure 11-3 indicates that one way to deter a budding cybercriminal is to raise the marginal cost of taking part in illicit pursuits such as planting viruses or hacking into computer systems. Governments might, for instance, establish laws that specify tough penalties. They might also establish official agencies charged with enforcing these laws and provide funding for these enforcement efforts. One reason that the creator of the "I Love You" virus may have transmitted it over the Internet was that there were no enforcement mechanisms, penalties, or even laws concerning computer hacking in the Philippines at the time. In fact, the student who transmitted the virus ultimately was not charged with any crime, despite the multibillion-dollar property damage he caused.

Another way to cut the amount of illicit computer activities would be to reduce the marginal benefit that a cybercriminal could anticipate receiving. Those who store valuable data on computer files and transmit these data over the Internet, intranets, and other computer networks can reduce the probability that a criminal can successfully intercept and use the data by implementing security protections. As discussed in Chapter 10, people can encrypt data they transmit or find other ways to "scramble" data transmissions. To protect themselves from viruses, they can also purchase anti-virus software. Of course, people storing and transmitting valuable digital data also face marginal benefits and marginal costs associated with efforts to protect the information. Thus, there are limits to the extent to which individuals and firms will seek to reduce the expected reward from engaging in cybercrime.

WEB SECURITY AND ENFORCEMENT

A typical Web surfer probably owns and uses anti-virus programs. Many Internet consumers also obtain software that establishes *firewalls* to protect their computers from hackers.

At the same time, not every Internet consumer has the expertise to determine the best methods for protecting their digital information. In light of this potential for consumers to be incompletely informed, governments worldwide increasingly are establishing laws, regulations, penalties, and enforcement agencies relating to criminal activities within the sphere of electronic commerce.

Currently, such efforts in the United States relate to enforcement of the National Information Infrastructure Protection Act of 1996. This law amended the Computer Fraud and Abuse Act, which already dealt with hacking into Web sites, pilfering data transmissions, and spreading computer viruses, by toughening penalties and strengthening federal enforcement efforts. The 1996 legislation also made it illegal to engage in so-called **distributed denial-of-service attacks,** in which individuals or groups attempt to overload companies' servers via large numbers of simultaneous and repeated acquisitions of Web sites. Such attacks took place, for instance, in February 2000, when prominent Web sites such as those operated by Yahoo, E*Trade, Amazon, and eBay were each temporarily overloaded and shut down.

Distributed Denial-of-Service Attacks
Efforts by individuals or groups attempt to overload companies' servers and shut down access to their Web sites.

This law also established the National Infrastructure Protection Center to coordinate enforcement efforts by various agencies, such as the Federal Bureau of Investigation, the Federal Trade Commission, and the National White Collar Crime Center. Private firms can participate in projects operated by the National Infrastructure Protection Center, which Congress also assigned the task of helping to distribute information about Web security.

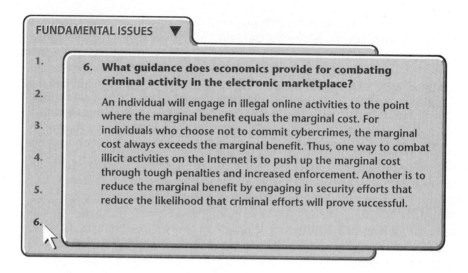

FUNDAMENTAL ISSUES ▼

1.

2.

3.

4.

5.

6.

6. **What guidance does economics provide for combating criminal activity in the electronic marketplace?**

An individual will engage in illegal online activities to the point where the marginal benefit equals the marginal cost. For individuals who choose not to commit cybercrimes, the marginal cost always exceeds the marginal benefit. Thus, one way to combat illicit activities on the Internet is to push up the marginal cost through tough penalties and increased enforcement. Another is to reduce the marginal benefit by engaging in security efforts that reduce the likelihood that criminal efforts will prove successful.

Chapter Summary

1) **Factors That Can Induce Government Regulators to Seek to Safeguard Consumers, and Ways That Regulators Can Try to Protect the Interests of Internet Consumers:** Producers typically possess more information than consumers concerning the quality of their products and customer service. Thus, adverse selection or moral hazard problems can arise, and governments may respond by establishing regulations setting out minimal standards for quality or service. In addition, governments may create agencies such as the Federal Trade Commission to enforce those standards in both the physical and electronic marketplaces. Governments may also try to deal with perceived market failures arising from negative or positive market externalities. A negative market externality leads to an overallocation of resources to producing an item, so a government might try to restrict production or to require firms creating the externality to incur costs in addressing it. In the case of a positive externality that leads to an underallocation of resources to producing an item, governments might choose to subsidize consumption of an item or to establish regulations inducing firms to provide more of the item.

2) **Why Privacy Is a Major Issue in the Electronic Marketplace, and Possible Ways to Address the E-Commerce Privacy Issue:** The way the Internet is structured gives rise to privacy concerns. Entering personal information at a Web site allows the site owner to link the user's name to an IP address. Companies may be able to track an individual's tastes and

preferences using remote host identifiers, search-engine queries, and cookies. The main law directly affecting personal information on the Internet is the Children's Online Privacy Protection Act of 1998, which establishes strict guidelines for the online collection of personal information from children. Adult Internet privacy protections are currently unsettled, however. They largely entail enforcement of existing laws covering liability for misallocation and misuse of information. Some economists contend that consumers might be better off if personal information were classified as personal property. In a private market in personal information, consumers could decide for themselves how much information they desire to sell at current market prices.

3) **Discrimination Issues in the Electronic Marketplace, as Compared with the Physical Marketplace:** There are good reasons to believe that transactions in the electronic marketplace should be less influenced, as compared with the physical marketplace, by racial, ethnic, or gender differences among buyers and sellers. From this standpoint, it is arguable that antidiscrimination regulations may have less usefulness when applied to electronic commerce. Existing antidiscrimination regulations apply to the electronic marketplace with the same force that they apply in the physical marketplace. Under certain circumstances the application of existing regulations could weaken the potential for electronic commerce to reduce discrimination. A particular problem arises if regulations require people to reveal information about their race, ethnicity, or gender, because this information could promote rather than discourage discriminatory behavior on the Internet.

4) **Antitrust Laws and How Traditional Antitrust Issues Apply to Electronic Commerce:** Antitrust laws are statutes established to provide consumers and producers with benefits available from unhindered competition. They forbid organizing monopolies, engaging in price discrimination not justified by distance or cost considerations, and practicing predatory pricing intended to enhance market power. A traditional antitrust issue that arises in applying these laws to electronic commerce is how to measure the degree of competition via concentration ratios or the Herfindahl–Hirschman index and how to determine if firms have engaged in anticompetitive practices. An especially important issue in light of the potential overlap between the physical and electronic marketplaces is determining the relevant market to which antitrust laws ought to apply.

5) **Antitrust Issues Special to the Electronic Marketplace:** The worldwide expanse of the Internet means that the electronic marketplace literally spans the globe. A key antitrust issue for electronic commerce is how to apply antitrust laws to markets likely to become increasingly international in scope. In addition, a fundamental antitrust issue in the electronic marketplace concerns the potential for network industries to develop. If the products of some firms possess strong network externalities, then these firms may establish dominant positions. On one hand, these firms might take advantage of their market power to raise prices. On the other hand, network

externalities can contribute to lower costs and, therefore, lower prices. Antitrust authorities will have to determine which of these effects is likely to prove most important.

6) **The Guidance Economics Provides for Combating Criminal Activity in the Electronic Marketplace:** An economic analysis of criminal activities indicates that a person will engage in illicit online activities to the point where the marginal benefit equals the marginal cost. To induce people not to take part in these activities, the marginal cost must be sufficiently high relative to the marginal benefit that it is not in a person's best interest to commit cybercrimes. In principle, this can be accomplished by establishing strong penalties and enforcement mechanisms that push up the marginal cost of engaging in illegal online activities. In addition, efforts to improve online security reduce the likelihood that criminal activities will yield a reward to the perpetrator, thereby reducing the marginal benefit of engaging in such activities.

Questions and Problems

1) List the key rationales for market regulation reviewed in this chapter. Of these, which do you believe is most likely to apply to the electronic marketplace? Which of these do you think is least likely to apply? Support your answer.

2) Children's Internet search queries sometimes inadvertently lead them to sites that nearly all adults would agree are unsuitable for children. Does this situation fit any of the rationales for regulation reviewed in this chapter? If so, can you propose a possible regulatory solution to the problem? Explain how your solution might be implemented.

3) There is a booming market for hardware and software that permit parents to monitor the online activities of their children. Some Web-based applications even allow parents to use audio and video equipment to monitor their children's offline activities. Proponents of an open marketplace in personal information point to the market prices parents are willing to pay for such information as strong evidence that there likely would be an active market for personal information if one were to develop. Do you agree with this assessment? What types of market failures, if any, do you think might arise in a market for personal information? Explain your reasoning.

4) When Living.com, an online furniture retailer, went bankrupt and closed down its operations, it attempted to sell its customer database. Authorities in the state of Texas, where Living.com was headquartered, intervened and reached a settlement that granted former Living.com customers the option to have their personal information deleted from the company's database. This

settlement did not give customers the opportunity to request payment for retaining their information in the Living.com database. Do you think former customers of Living.com might have been willing to accept payment for inclusion in the company's database? If so, who would have stood to gain or to lose if this option had been available?

5) Companies have developed software that can track every Web site a person visits and build a "digital silhouette," or a profile based on those choices. Thus, after a person successively visits sites relating to travel, history, and museums, companies might begin feeding pop-up window ads from travel agencies, book clubs, and museum shops to the individual's IP address. One company, Predictive Networks, Inc., has developed a system that requires consumers themselves to download software onto their personal computers. In exchange for receiving a specified number and type of online advertisements relating only to their interests as revealed by their digital silhouettes, consumers grant the company the power to sell the data it collects to online advertisers. Does this constitute the beginning of an open market for personal information? If so, what is the "market price" of personal information in this market?

6) As a follow-up to question 5, consider another real-world example in which a software company called Encirq Corporation offered to pay financial institutions for each customer who signs up to have Encirq's digital-silhouette software loaded onto their computers alongside online-banking software. Whenever a customer reviews his or her financial statements online, the company's software automatically provides banner ads for and links to home pages of merchants for which bills appear on billing statements, offering incentives for customers to shop with those merchants again. The company providing this arrangement has publicly argued that there are no personal privacy problems associated with it, because the digital profiles never leave the consumer's computer. Do you agree? Why or why not?

7) There are thousands of real estate agents in the United States. In cities and even in local communities, there is considerable rivalry among Realtors. Nevertheless, nearly all belong to the National Association of Realtors, which is the majority owner of Homestore.com. This Web-based real estate company has a network of sites related to the housing industry, including Realtor.com, Homebuilder.com, and Homefair.com. In 2000 Homestore purchased a rival site, Move.com, which left Microsoft Network's Homeadvisor as its only remaining key rival. Around the same time, the U.S. Justice Department initiated an antitrust investigation of the Homestore network. How might the Justice Department go about determining the relevant market for Realtor services provided online and/or offline?

8) Suppose a staff economist with an antitrust agency determines that when the price of women's clothing at traditional bricks-and-mortar retail stores rises by 10 percent, the quantity of women's clothing purchased from Web clothing retailers increases by 1.5 percent. By way of contrast, the economist determines that when the price of toys at traditional bricks-and-mortar retail

stores increases by 10 percent, the amount of toys purchased from Internet toy sellers increases by 15 percent. Calculate the implied values of the cross price elasticities of demand. In which of these cases is it more likely that the electronic marketplace is a relevant market for antitrust considerations?

9) In recent years, eBay has sought to make its technology for Internet-based C2C auctions the favorite of software programmers, and it has begun licensing its technology to other Web sites. EBay's managers have publicly stated their goal is for eBay's auction system to become the "operating system" of all auction applications on the Internet. What factors are likely to determine whether eBay is successful in this effort? Are there any potential antitrust issues related to the company's efforts? If not, why not? If so, what are the issues?

10) America Online is by far the largest provider of instant-messaging services, with more than 140 million registered users. The company has resisted efforts by competitors such as Microsoft and Yahoo to permit users of their instant-messaging system join America Online's popular "buddy list" feature that lets an individual know when co-workers or friends are currently using the Internet. Why might America Online have a strong incentive to keep this feature off-limits to users of competing instant-messaging systems? Is there any reason that this action should concern antitrust authorities? Explain.

11) Suppose there eventually is widespread adoption of digital cash, which people begin transmitting in large quantities over the Internet. Shortly after this occurs, the economy is buffeted by a recession that hits information-technology firms especially hard, and many highly trained individuals are unable to find gainful employment in the information-technology industry. Apply the basic economic model of crime to determine what is likely to happen to the marginal benefit and marginal cost of illegal activities. Can you predict whether cybercriminal activities are likely to increase or decrease?

Online Application

Internet URL: http://www.ftc.gov/opa/2000/10/b2breport.htm

Title: **Federal Trade Commission: "Entering the 21st Century: Competition Policy in the World of B2B Electronic Marketplaces"**

Navigation: Go directly to the above URL, and read the brief summary. In the right-hand margin, click on "Text of the Report." In the outline that appears, click on the PDF download entitled "Antitrust Analysis of B2Bs."

Application: Review the first twelve pages of this portion of the report, and answer the following questions.

1) What aspects of B2B e-commerce tend to raise concerns of antitrust authorities? Why?

2) According to the report, what actions can B2B exchanges take to satisfy antitrust authorities that their sites do not promote anticompetitive behavior? Why do you think that taking these actions would help alleviate antitrust concerns?

For Group Study and Analysis: Separate the class into "pro-B2B" and "anti-B2B" groups, and instruct each group to develop arguments promoting their assigned positions. Under ground rules established by the instructor or the class, conduct a debate of the following position: "B2B exchanges enhance economic efficiency and pose no legitimate antitrust concerns."

Selected References and Further Readings

American Bar Association. "Achieving Legal and Business Order in Cyberspace," Global Cyberspace Jurisdiction Project, 2000.

Balton, David. "Emerging Antitrust Issues in Electronic Commerce," Bureau of Competition, Federal Trade Commission, November 12, 1999.

Braithwaite, John, and Peter Drahos. *Global Business Regulation.* Cambridge, U.K.: Cambridge University Press, 2000.

Camp, L. Jean. *Trust and Risk in Internet Commerce.* Cambridge, MA: MIT Press, 2000.

Cronin, Mary. "Privacy and Electronic Commerce." In *Public Policy and the Internet: Privacy, Taxes, and Contract,* ed. Nicholas Imparato. Hoover Institution Press, 2000.

Department of Justice International Competition Policy Advisory Committee. *Final Report,* Chapter 6: "Preparing for the Future," 2000, pp. 281–302.

Federal Trade Commission. "Protecting Consumers Online," December 1999.

Garicano, Luis, and Steven Kaplan. "The Effects of Business-to-Business E-Commerce on Transaction Costs," National Bureau of Economic Research, Working Paper 8017, November 2000.

Sholtz, Paul. "Economics of Personal Information Exchange," *First Monday* (September 4, 2000) (http://www.firstmonday.dk/issues/5_9/sholtz/index.html).

The Public Sector and the Electronic Marketplace

FUNDAMENTAL ISSUES ▼

1. What are the essential arguments for and against ▶ exempting electronic commerce from taxation?
2. In what ways can electronic commerce influence ▶ tax revenues, and how has it actually affected tax collections?
3. If Internet sales were taxed, who would pay? ▶
4. What effects would taxation have on electronic ▶ commerce?
5. Should the government boost the provision of ▶ e-commerce services?

<E-Commerce Today>

Kentucky's Governor Pays His Web Taxes, Don't You?

Thousands of Kentucky taxpayers break the law every year when they fail to pay taxes on purchases they make on the Internet. Like the other forty-five U.S. states that impose at least some form of sales tax, Kentucky requires its residents to pay a use tax on all purchases from out-of-state retailers, including online sellers based in other states. Kentucky taxpayers are supposed to report out-of-state purchases for which they did not pay sales taxes on their state income tax forms. Then they are supposed to calculate the use tax they owe. Most, however, rarely do.

As a result, the governor of Kentucky has argued, the approximately $700,000 in use taxes that the state currently collects fails to compensate for millions of dollars in revenues that the state has lost every year since people began shopping on the Internet. Two-thirds of the sales and use taxes that Kentucky residents pay are used to fund public education. The remainder provides a big chunk of the funding for other basic state services. According to the state's governor, the state either will have to do a better job of collecting use taxes that its residents legally owe or will have to join with other states in convincing the federal government to coordinate a nationwide system of state sales taxes on online purchases.

Kentucky's governor is not alone. The governors of forty-two U.S. states are on record as opposing the current federal moratorium on e-commerce taxation. Unless the moratorium is lifted, they contend, state and local tax revenues will fall by tens of billions of dollars nationwide. Eventually, they worry, state sales-tax revenues may wither to a fraction of their current levels as more and more people become online shoppers.

In a famous statement criticizing what he regarded as federal over-intrusiveness, former president Ronald Reagan complained that too often the U.S. government's attitude could be summed up as follows: "If it moves, tax it; if it still moves, regulate it; and if it stops moving, subsidize it." So far, the government's treatment of electronic commerce only partly fits President Reagan's observation. As you learned in the previous chapter, it is certainly true that the electronic marketplace has been subjected to various regulations. You will learn later in this chapter that some countries have subsidized certain e-commerce activities. Nevertheless, to date only a small portion of electronic commerce has been subjected to taxes in the United States. Evaluating the rationales for and ramifications of this policy is one of the main topics of this chapter.

The Great Tax Debate

Sales Taxes

Taxes assessed on the value of purchases of goods and services from firms located within the nexus that applies for sales taxes.

Nexus

A geographic overlap between a company's physical location and the location of its customers.

Use Taxes

Taxes assessed on the value of purchases of goods and services from firms located outside the nexus that applies for sales taxes.

The expansion of electronic commerce has engendered a fundamental debate about the issues of whether and how to apply state and local **sales taxes**—taxes levied on the value of purchases of goods and services—to "remote sales." A series of U.S. Supreme Court opinions have determined that a state cannot compel a firm selling to consumers within its borders to collect and remit sales and use taxes without a substantial **nexus,** or geographic overlap between the firm's physical location and the location of consumers who make purchases from the firm.

The Supreme Court rulings have led lower courts to interpret "substantial nexus" as implying a physical presence of the firm within any state that seeks to collect sales taxes on purchases from that firm by that state's residents. States have responded by imposing **use taxes,** or taxes levied on the value of purchases of goods and services from firms located outside the nexus that applies for sales taxes. Most states, however, have chosen to collect use taxes primarily from businesses. (Few households around the nation pay use taxes. See *Policymaking Online: Why Don't States with Use Taxes Make Households Pay Up?*)

Supreme Court decisions consistently indicate that Congress has the power to impose e-commerce taxes if it chooses to do so. After the electronic marketplace began to develop rapidly in the mid-1990s, however, the U.S. Congress passed the Internet Tax Freedom Act of 1998. This legislation exempted electronic commerce from *federal* taxation and restraining state governments from imposing *Internet-specific* taxes. In 1999 Congress established an Advisory Commission on Electronic Commerce, and in 2000 the Commission filed a report recommending an extension of the e-commerce taxation ban. Congress responded with a short-term extension of the tax moratorium with "grandfather clauses" allowing eleven states to continue charging Internet access taxes established before its original action. Since then, Congress has continued to study and debate the merits of Internet taxes.

ANTI-TAX ARGUMENTS

The congressional moratorium on Internet taxes applies only to *interstate* e-commerce transactions. A number of states already require firms with a physical presence within their borders—for instance, Wal-Mart, Barnes & Noble, and other retailers with bricks-and-mortar outlets—to charge sales taxes on online purchases. Nevertheless, most states have refrained from trying to tax all the sales of Web-based firms, in some cases even when those companies have a physical presence inside those states.

There are three basic arguments in support of continuing minimal e-commerce taxation:

Giving Governments Fewer Funds to Spend

One argument offered in opposition to bringing electronic commerce under the umbrella of about 7,500 tax authorities is the view that these governmental enti-

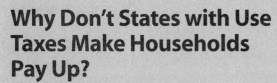

POLICYMAKING *Online*

POLICY MAKING   GLOBALIZATION   MANAGEMENT

Why Don't States with Use Taxes Make Households Pay Up?

Many consumers in states with use taxes are entirely unaware of the existence of the tax. Undoubtedly, more would become aware if states actively enforced their use-tax rules. Yet states rarely go to the trouble to do so.

When a state agency decides whether to enforce tax laws, it weighs the expected gain against the anticipated cost of enforcement. Suppose that each year a typical household that buys goods and services online and via mail-order catalogs spends $400 on these items. If a state's use tax rate is 5 percent, then that household should pay $20 in use taxes for the year. This relatively small sum is the state tax agency's gain if it were to notify the household that it owes a use tax, require the household to fill out forms reporting the household's online and catalog purchases, verify the household's full

compliance with the law, and collect the full amount of the household's tax liability.

All of these enforcement activities would require expenditures of state funds. The cost of enforcing a use-tax requirement would easily mount to several dollars per household. So the state's net gain from collecting use taxes from each household that owes taxes is likely to be relatively small.

A number of people buy few items from Web firms or catalog retailers, and an agency's annual "take" from these households is likely to be much less than $20. In many situations, therefore, a state agency would spend more trying to enforce the use tax than it would collect. Undoubtedly, most states have concluded that overall they would probably experience a net revenue *loss* if they tried to require universal household compliance with use-tax laws.

For Critical Analysis:
If states so rarely choose to require households to pay use taxes, why do you suppose that household use taxes exist?

---

ties tax and spend too many funds. According to this perspective, governments are already "too big" relative to local, state, and national economies. By withholding the authority to tax electronic commerce, citizens protect themselves from further growth of "big government."

Underpinning this argument is the view that government budgets should be smaller, perhaps because governments use the funds they raise to encroach on private market activities or because they use the funds inefficiently or even spend some of them wastefully. Whether there is any validity to this view is, of course, a value judgment. Nevertheless, this is one rationale for favoring the current moratorium on Internet taxation.

Slowing the Spread of an Already Regressive Tax System

A more common argument against taxing Internet sales focuses on a longstanding problem with sales taxes. A sales tax is a **regressive tax**, meaning that as the incomes of individuals paying the tax increase, the tax payments tend to be a smaller portion of people's incomes. In other words, sales tax payments for low-income people tend to be a relatively larger portion of their incomes as compared

Regressive Tax
A system of taxation in which a lower percentage of income is taxed as income increases.

with sales tax payments by higher-income people. By way of contrast, taxes on incomes, such as the federal income tax that generates most of the U.S. government's revenues, typically are designed to be **progressive taxes.** Income tax rates normally are greater at higher income levels.

Progressive Tax
A system of taxation in which a higher percentage of income is taxed as income increases.

Many opponents of applying sales taxes to Internet sales simply desire to halt the spread of further sales taxes. Indeed, some opponents of e-commerce taxation have expressed the hope that so many transactions will move online that state sales tax revenues will shrink away, thereby forcing states to find more progressive taxes to replace their sales-tax systems.

Protecting an Infant Industry

The reason given most often for limiting taxation of transactions in the electronic marketplace is the **infant industry argument.** This is a contention that e-commerce industries are still at their earliest stages and should be given an opportunity to develop further before being subjected to taxation.

Infant Industry Argument
The contention that an industry in its earliest stages of development should be exempted from taxation.

As you will learn later in this chapter, taxation has associated *economic burdens* that tend to push up market prices and to reduce production and sales. Hence, the infant industry argument essentially proposes protecting e-commerce industries from these economic burdens until they have developed into fully viable industries within the economy. Only at that point, proponents of this view maintain, should governments consider imposing taxes on exchanges that take place in the electronic marketplace.

PRO-TAX ARGUMENTS

There are also arguments in favor of taxing electronic commerce. Naturally, these are on the opposite sides of the anti-tax arguments.

Reducing the Ability to Provide Government Services

In the United States, about 7,500 state and municipal governments impose sales taxes on their residents. The average nationwide sales-tax rate is almost 5 percent. Sales taxes are approximately a third of the revenues of state governments and about 11 percent of the revenues of municipalities. Thus, the tax-free status of electronic commerce originating beyond state borders potentially threatens an important revenue source for many states, counties, cities, and towns around the nation.

Making the Sales Tax Even More Regressive

As noted in Chapter 1, higher-income people are more likely than lower-income individuals to have online access. This means that higher-income people who purchase goods and services online are more likely to take advantage of the tax-free status of the Internet. As a result, exempting electronic commerce from taxation may shift a relatively larger portion of the overall burden of paying sales taxes to lower-income people.

Failing to tax online purchases could make the existing sales tax on offline purchases even more regressive. Certainly, states might be able to address this problem in other ways, such as adding progressive income taxes or making existing income tax systems more progressive. Nevertheless, many state leaders argue that the most straightforward way to deal with the problem is to subject electronic commerce to the same system of sales taxes that applies to offline purchases in the physical marketplace.

Failing to Establish a Level Playing Field

Those who favor taxing electronic commerce emphasize that taxing offline purchases while failing to tax online transactions effectively raises the after-tax price of exchanges in the physical marketplace relative to purchases in the electronic marketplace. This naturally gives people even more incentive to undertake Web-based transactions.

The Internet tax exemption can also induce companies to operate in ways that otherwise would be inefficient. An example is when Barnes & Noble initially established Barnesandnoble.com as a standalone Internet firm. One factor contributing to that decision was that Barnes & Noble had outlets in 49 of the 50 states and therefore had to charge sales taxes throughout the nation, whereas Amazon.com did not. Because Barnesandnoble.com did not have a physical presence beyond a single state, it did not have to charge state sales taxes.

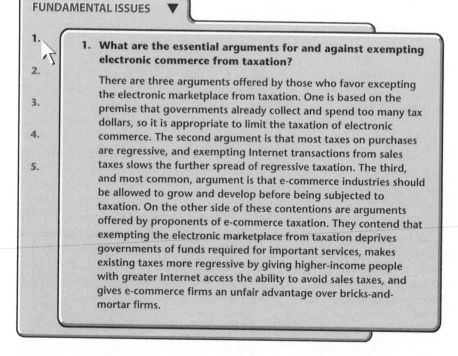

FUNDAMENTAL ISSUES ▼

1.
2.
3.
4.
5.

1. What are the essential arguments for and against exempting electronic commerce from taxation?

There are three arguments offered by those who favor excepting the electronic marketplace from taxation. One is based on the premise that governments already collect and spend too many tax dollars, so it is appropriate to limit the taxation of electronic commerce. The second argument is that most taxes on purchases are regressive, and exempting Internet transactions from sales taxes slows the further spread of regressive taxation. The third, and most common, argument is that e-commerce industries should be allowed to grow and develop before being subjected to taxation. On the other side of these contentions are arguments offered by proponents of e-commerce taxation. They contend that exempting the electronic marketplace from taxation deprives governments of funds required for important services, makes existing taxes more regressive by giving higher-income people with greater Internet access the ability to avoid sales taxes, and gives e-commerce firms an unfair advantage over bricks-and-mortar firms.

Can Governments Get by without Taxing E-Commerce?

Governments collect tax revenues to fund their operations. As e-commerce industries have developed, state and local governments have cast a wary eye on Internet firms and Web operations of traditional companies. Some governments perceive an opportunity to enhance their revenues by taxing electronic commerce. Most, however, worry about the potential for tax revenues to shrink if their taxing authority is not extended to the electronic marketplace.

APPLYING SOME TAX FUNDAMENTALS

Tax Base
The value of goods, services, incomes, or wealth subject to taxation.

To collect taxes, such as sales, income, or property taxes, governments first establish a **tax base,** which is a value of goods, services, incomes, or wealth subject to taxation. Then they develop a schedule of **tax rates,** which are percentages applied to the relevant tax base to determine the amount of taxes that an individual or company is legally obliged to pay to the government.

Tax Rate
The fraction of a tax base an individual or company is legally required to transmit to the government.

Tax Rates and Tax Revenues: The Static View

The total tax revenues a government collects are equal to the tax rate multiplied by the tax base. Thus, if the tax rate is a fraction equal to t and the tax base is an amount equal to B, then the government's total tax revenues are $T = t \times B$. Figure 12-1 depicts this equation, which is a straight line extending from the origin. The equation implies that a change in tax revenues, ΔT, which is measured along the vertical axis in the diagram, equals the tax rate t times a change in the tax base, ΔB, which is measured along the horizontal axis. Hence, $\Delta T = t \times \Delta B$. Rearranging this equation yields $t = \Delta T / \Delta B$. The slope of the *tax schedule* graphed in Figure 12-1, therefore, or the "rise" divided by the "run," is the tax rate t.

When considering the effects of taxing electronic commerce or exempting Internet transactions from taxes, a key issue is how tax revenues, the tax rate, and the tax base are related. One perspective is the *static view,* which is based solely on the tax function in Figure 12-1. To understand the static view and how it applies to sales taxes, take a look at Figure 12-2, in which a state government desires to collect a total amount of sales taxes equal to T^*. This revenue objective may be an amount of funding required to build new schools or provide various social services.

In a situation in which both offline and online purchases were subject to the same sales-tax rate t and the resulting tax base is equal to B_1, the government would achieve its tax revenue objective T^* at point A by establishing a tax rate equal to t_1. Setting this tax rate would ensure that the tax schedule crosses point A, thereby achieving the desired level of tax collections T^* given the tax base B_1 that is comprised of both online and offline sales.

Figure 12-1:
The Tax Schedule.

The tax schedule is a graph of the equation $T = t \times B$, in which T is the government's tax revenues, B is the tax base, and t is the tax rate. The tax rate is the slope of the tax schedule, which is the "rise," ΔT, divided by the "run," ΔB.

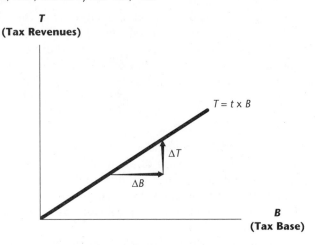

Figure 12-2:
Attaining A Tax Revenue Objective by Adjusting the Tax Rate.

If both offline and online purchases were subject to the same sales-tax rate t, then the tax base is equal to B_1, and the government could achieve a tax revenue objective T^* at point A by setting a tax rate equal to t_1. Because most online purchases are not taxed, however, the tax base is lower by the amount of untaxed Web sales. If the lower tax base equals B_2 at point C, then the government's tax collections fall to T_2. From a static view of the relationship between the tax rate and tax revenues, the government can respond to this situation by raising the sales-tax rate t_2, which raises the slope of the tax function and pushes tax collections back up to T^* at point D. According to the dynamic view on this relationship, however, a tax-rate increase is likely to induce consumers to shift more of their purchases online, thereby pushing the tax base even lower.

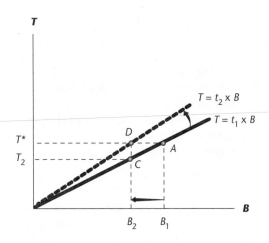

Because most online purchases are not taxed, the tax base is lower by the amount of untaxed Web sales. If only offline sales are subject to taxation, which implies a lower tax base equal to B_2 at point C, tax collections fall below the tax revenue objective T^*, to the quantity T_2.

According to the static view of taxation, the government can respond to this situation by raising the sales-tax rate. As shown in Figure 12-2, a sufficient increase in the tax rate, to t_2, raises the slope of the tax function. At the lower offline tax base, B_2, this higher tax rate yields tax collections equal to T^*, at point D. Thus, increasing the tax rate can allow the government to attain its tax revenue objective even if it continues to tax only offline transactions in the physical marketplace.

Tax Rates and Tax Revenues: The Dynamic View

There is a problem with the static view of the relationship between the tax rate and actual tax collections: It ignores the incentives that consumers face to respond to a higher tax rate on offline purchases by buying more goods and services on the Web. The *dynamic view* of the relationship between tax rates and tax revenues takes this incentive into account.

To consider the dynamic view, take a look at the situation at point D in Figure 12-2, following an increase in the sales-tax rate to t_2. This tax-rate increase is likely to induce at least some consumers to start ordering more products on the Internet to avoid paying the higher sales tax they face if they purchase goods and services offline. Thus, they shift some of their spending to the electronic marketplace from the physical marketplace. Spending in the physical marketplace is, however, the source of the government's sales-tax base. This means that the tax base will begin to decline. How much it declines will depend on the size of the proportionate reduction in consumer spending in the physical marketplace in response to the increase in the sales-tax rate.

The government's tax revenues once again will begin to fall below T^* as the tax base declines. If cutting public spending is not regarded as a feasible option, then the government has only three choices:

1) **Increase the tax rate again**—This action would essentially duplicate the steps illustrated in Figure 12-2. As the dynamic view makes clear, however, this is likely to lead to a further shift in spending from physical transactions that are taxed to Web exchanges that are not taxed.
2) **Rely on a different system of collecting taxes**—The government could, for instance, raise existing income-tax rates and/or property-tax rates.
3) **Broaden the tax base to include online purchases**—This would remove the incentive for people to shift their spending from bricks-and-mortar outlets to companies located on the Web.

In principle, governments could opt for either or both of the first two choices. It is not "necessary" to tax Internet sales.

In fact, individual state governments have tended to shy away from taxing electronic commerce. In 2000 the California legislature voted in favor of extending the state sales tax to Internet transactions, but the state's governor vetoed the measure. Nevertheless, the dynamic view of taxation helps explain why pressure continues to build in California and elsewhere to subject electronic commerce to the same taxes that apply to the physical marketplace.

ASSESSING THE CURRENT AND FUTURE TAX IMPLICATIONS OF ELECTRONIC COMMERCE

The static view of taxation indicates that failing to tax Internet sales reduces the tax base for sales taxes, thereby reducing tax revenues. The dynamic view suggests that seeking to boost tax collections by raising rates is likely to lead to a further reduction in the tax base. An important issue for state governments, therefore, is to determine exactly how much exempting electronic commerce from the tax base for sales taxes reduces their revenues at existing tax rates. Another key issue is to assess how responsive consumers would be to tax-rate boosts intended to raise additional revenues from the existing bricks-and-mortar tax base. In addition, state governments that contemplate imposing sales taxes on residents' Internet purchases in future years must evaluate how much additional tax revenue would be generated by the resulting expansion of the tax base.

Evaluating the Revenue Effects of the E-Commerce Sales-Tax Exemption

Unfortunately for state governments, coming up with hard-and-fast conclusions about dollar amounts is a thorny problem. Figures 12-1 and 12-2 assume that the tax base is a known quantity. In fact, the tax base for sales taxes is the total value of goods and services purchased by consumers and businesses. How much people decide to purchase depends on factors including their tastes and preferences and the market prices of items subject to taxation. Another key factor is consumer incomes, which depend on the overall health of the economy. During business expansions, the sales-tax base expands as incomes rise and consumer spending increases. During business recessions, however, consumer incomes fall, causing a drop-off in consumer purchases and a reduction in the sales-tax base.

This means that economists can, at best, only provide rough estimates about the effects of e-commerce tax exemptions on state sales-tax revenues. To try to sharpen such estimates, economists base their estimates on the assumption that tastes and preferences, market prices, and general economic conditions will remain essentially unchanged.

Panel (a) in Figure 12-3 on page 386 displays three different estimates of total dollar losses to state governments in tax year 2000 resulting from the *de facto* exemption of Internet purchases from state tax bases for sales taxes. These estimates range from $0.3 billion to $3.8 billion, which are low- and high-range estimates developed by the U.S. government's General Accounting Office. A separate study by Donald Bruce and William Fox of the University of Tennessee provides a middle-range estimate of $2.7 billion in sales-tax revenue losses arising from failure to tax Internet purchases in 2000. The study by Bruce and Fox projects that by 2003, state governments stand to lose more than $10 billion in tax revenues if they fail

Figure 12-3:
Estimates of Sales-Tax
Reductions Resulting
from Failing to Collect
Taxes on Internet
Purchases.

Panel (a) shows estimates of
total annual state-tax
revenue losses from failure to
collect taxes on Internet
purchases. Panel (b) relates
these estimated tax losses to
total state sales-tax revenues.

Sources: Donald Bruce and
William Fox, "E-Commerce
in the Context of Declining
State Sales Tax Bases,"
Center for Business and
Economic Research,
University of Tennessee,
April 2000, and General
Accounting Office, "Sales
Taxes: Electronic Commerce
Growth Presents Challenges;
Revenue Losses are
Uncertain," Report to
Congressional Requesters,
June 2000.

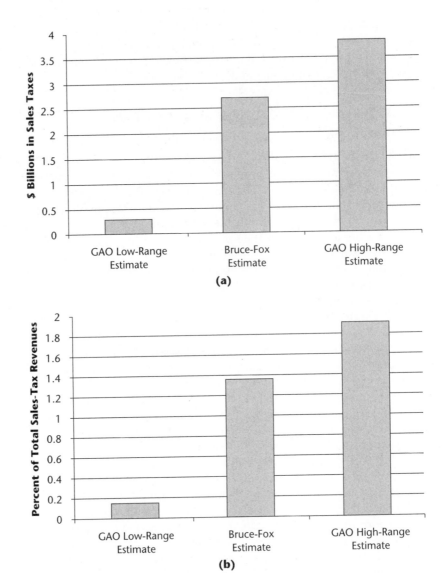

either to collect use taxes on Web purchases by their residents or to expand their sales-tax bases to include the value of goods and services purchased from Internet sellers.

All told, U.S. states collect more than $200 billion in sales taxes each year. Although $0.3 billion to $3.8 billion in potential revenue losses from failure to tax e-commerce transactions are certainly sizable amounts, panel *(b)* of Figure 12-3 shows that these revenue losses were relatively small percentages of total sales-tax collections in 2000. Even if states forgo more than $10 billion in sales-tax

Figure 12-4:
U.S. Sales-Tax Base as a Percentage of Personal Income.

The total sales-tax base has steadily declined relative to aggregate personal income in the United States.
Source: Donald Bruce and William Fox, "E-Commerce in the Context of Declining State Sales Tax Bases," Center for Business and Economic Research, University of Tennessee, April 2000; U.S. Economic Report of the President, various issues; and author's estimates.

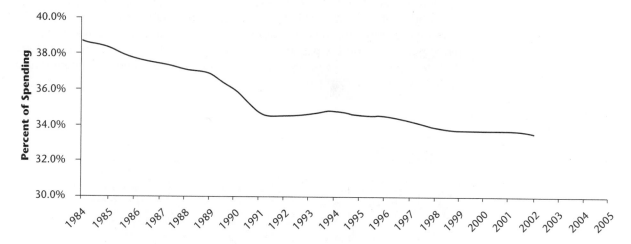

revenues in 2003, this amount likely will account for little more than 5 percent of total sales taxes collected.

E-Commerce Taxes to the Rescue?

After a look at panel *(b)* of Figure 12-3, it is tempting to conclude that sales-tax revenue losses in such small percentage terms are relatively unimportant. Nevertheless, the range of estimated tax losses in panel *(a)* indicate that the average state with sales taxes could gain from about $6 million to more than $80 million from taxing electronic commerce. Every state government undoubtedly would be pleased to have millions of additional dollars available to supplement other sources of revenue.

Hence, there is considerable interest among state policymakers in including Internet purchases within their sales-tax base. Some state officials view this as a simple way to increase their sales-tax revenues. Others are concerned that if they fail to gain authorization to tax electronic commerce, an increasing portion of the existing sales-tax base may shift to the untaxed Internet sector.

As Figure 12-4 indicates, however, the sales-tax base for all U.S. states has been declining steadily relative to aggregate personal income since the end of the 1970s, well before the Internet appeared on the scene. Two factors account for most of this decline. The main reason is that many states include most purchases of physical goods within the sales-tax base but exclude a number of services. Hence, as the consumption of services relative to goods has increased, the share of personal consumption expenditures subject to sales taxes has declined.

The second factor contributing to the relative decline in the national sales-tax base is remote sales, including catalog and telephone sales that took off in the 1980s. Remote sales via electronic commerce are just the latest aspect of an overall trend toward evading state sales taxes.

In light of the nationwide downward trend in the sales-tax base, it may be that state governments are overestimating both the potential gain from taxing Internet purchases and the possible threat faced if they fail to do so. It seems likely that state governments will continue to pressure the U.S. Congress to permit a coordinated national effort to tax electronic commerce.

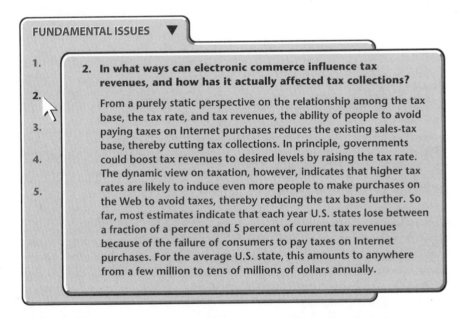

FUNDAMENTAL ISSUES ▼

1.

2.

3.

4.

5.

2. In what ways can electronic commerce influence tax revenues, and how has it actually affected tax collections?

From a purely static perspective on the relationship among the tax base, the tax rate, and tax revenues, the ability of people to avoid paying taxes on Internet purchases reduces the existing sales-tax base, thereby cutting tax collections. In principle, governments could boost tax revenues to desired levels by raising the tax rate. The dynamic view on taxation, however, indicates that higher tax rates are likely to induce even more people to make purchases on the Web to avoid taxes, thereby reducing the tax base further. So far, most estimates indicate that each year U.S. states lose between a fraction of a percent and 5 percent of current tax revenues because of the failure of consumers to pay taxes on Internet purchases. For the average U.S. state, this amounts to anywhere from a few million to tens of millions of dollars annually.

 ## Who Would Bear an E-Commerce Tax Burden?

Tax Incidence
The effect of a tax on the distribution of income or wealth, or the burden created by a tax.

Taxes impose a burden on those who pay them, because they redistribute the income of private taxpayers to governments. A fundamental issue in assessing the potential effects of current or future taxes on electronic commerce is **tax incidence.** This is the term economists use when discussing who actually bears the burden of a tax.

EVALUATING THE BURDENS OF E-COMMERCE TAXATION: TAX INCIDENCE IN THE ELECTRONIC MARKETPLACE

There are two types of tax incidence. One is **statutory incidence,** which refers to who is legally responsible for transmitting tax payments to the government. The other is **economic incidence,** which refers to the manner in which incomes are redistributed within the marketplace as a result of a tax. In the case of a sales tax, the statutory incidence of the tax falls on firms responsible for tabulating sales data and transferring required tax payments to state and local governments. This does not necessarily mean that the economic incidence of a sales tax falls upon firms, however. If firms are able to raise prices in equal proportion to the tax, then consumers will bear the full burden of the tax. Only if firms are unable to pass some of the tax along via higher prices do firms bear any burden of the tax.

Statutory Incidence
The determination of the party that is legally responsible for transmitting a tax payment to the government.

Economic Incidence
The determination of the relative burden of a tax that is borne by parties to market transactions.

Determining Who Pays a Tax

Because companies attempt to incorporate sales taxes into the prices they charge, determining the economic incidence of a tax requires evaluating how the market price will respond when the tax is assessed. To examine this relationship, let's first consider how the statutory incidence of a sales tax on electronic commerce would affect an Internet seller's production costs. Recall from Chapter 2 that a typical firm has an upward-sloping short-run marginal cost curve, such as MC_1 in Figure 12-5, which crosses the minimum point of its short-run average total cost curve, ATC_1. Sales taxes normally are assessed as a percentage of the price of the firm's product price, but to simplify the diagram let's assume that the sales tax is assessed as a fixed per-unit tax equal to τ (the Greek letter "tau"). This raises the firm's cost of producing each unit of output. As a result, both the marginal cost curve and the average total cost curve shift upward by exactly the amount τ, to MC_2 and ATC_2 in the figure.

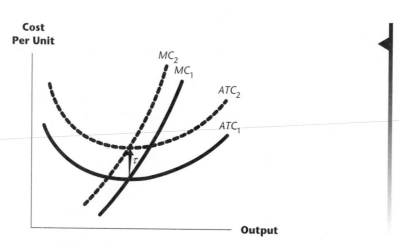

Cost Per Unit

MC_2
MC_1
ATC_2
ATC_1
τ

Output

**Figure 12-5:
The Effects of a Per-Unit Sales Tax on a Firm's Short-Run Marginal and Average Costs.**

The imposition of a per-unit tax equal to τ that a firm must collect and transmit to the government causes an increase in the firm's marginal and average total cost at every feasible output rate. Thus, the firm's marginal and average total cost curves shift upward by the amount of the tax.

How this change in this firm's marginal and average costs will affect the market price of its product depends on the structure of the marketplace in which it sells that product. Let's assume this particular firm sells its output in a perfectly competitive market. (You have an opportunity to consider the likely effects of this tax in an imperfectly competitive market in Problem 5 at the end of the chapter.) Remember from Chapter 2 that in the case of perfect competition, most of the firm's marginal cost curve is its short-run supply curve. Because imposing a per-unit sales tax equal to τ causes each firm's short-run supply curve to shift upward by this amount, the market supply curve shifts up by the amount τ, as shown in each of the three panels of Figure 12-6. To be induced to supply any given quantity of output, such as Q_1 in each panel, firms must receive a price higher than the original price by exactly enough to compensate them for the per-unit sales tax τ that they must transmit to the government.

Panels (a), (b), and (c) display identical initial equilibrium market prices and quantities. In panel (a), demand is perfectly inelastic, so that consumers do not alter their consumption when confronted with any proportionate change in price. In this case, the market demand curve is vertical. As a consequence, the upward shift in the market supply curve after the tax is imposed causes the equilibrium product price to increase by exactly the amount of the tax. This means that even though the statutory incidence of the tax falls on the firms that sell the product, if demand is perfectly inelastic, firms are able to pass the full burden of the tax onto consumers in the form of higher prices. The economic incidence of the tax falls entirely on consumers when demand is perfectly inelastic.

Panel (b) of Figure 12-6, by way of contrast, illustrates a situation in which demand is perfectly elastic, so that even the smallest proportionate increase in the product's price induces consumers to stop purchasing the item. In this case, the equilibrium price does not change, so the equilibrium quantity supplied by firms at the unaltered price declines to Q_2. Because the price remains unchanged, consumers do not pay the sales tax. Thus, the economic incidence of the tax falls on firms, which fully incur the amount of the tax as an additional per-unit cost and thereby cut back on production.

Finally, panel (c) illustrates an intermediate case with a normal downward-sloping demand curve. In this situation, the market price increases to P_2 following the imposition of the tax. The increase in price is less than the amount of the tax, so consumers bear part of the burden of the tax and reduce their consumption somewhat. Because firms are unable to shift the entire burden onto consumers, they incur part of the tax as a higher per-unit cost and cut back on production. As a result, the equilibrium quantity consumed declines to Q_2. The economic incidence of the tax falls on both consumers and producers.

Who Would Pay E-Commerce Taxes?

The examples in Figure 12-6 imply that the price elasticity of demand is a fundamental determinant of the economic incidence of taxes on electronic commerce. As long as the demand for an item sold in the electronic marketplace is neither perfectly inelastic nor perfectly elastic, then consumers and producers typically would share the prospective burden of e-commerce taxation.

Figure 12-6:
Effects of a Per-Unit Sales Tax on the Market Price
in a Perfectly Competitive Market.

Because the imposition of a per-unit tax equal to τ shifts every firm's marginal cost curve upward by the amount of the tax, the market short-run supply curve shifts upward by this amount in all three panels. In panel (a), demand is perfectly inelastic, so the market price rises by the full amount of the tax. Thus, consumers bear the entire amount of the tax. In panel (b), demand is perfectly elastic, so the market price does not change. Instead, the economic burden of the tax falls on firms, and the equilibrium quantity they produce declines. Panel (c) depicts an intermediate situation with a downward-sloping demand curve, in which both consumers and firms share the burden of the tax.

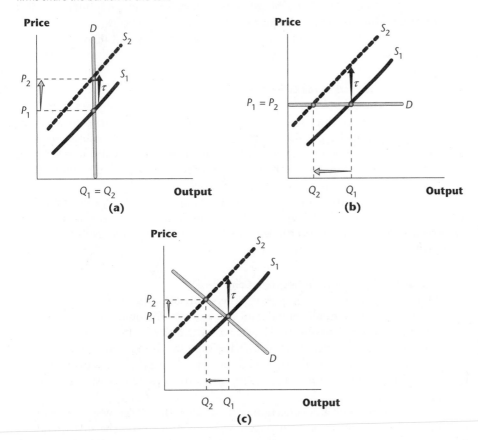

Other things being equal, if demand is relatively inelastic, consumers would bear a greater share of the burden of any taxes imposed on Internet purchases. If demand is relatively elastic, most of the burden of e-commerce taxation would be borne by producers.

The main determinant of the price elasticity of demand for any product is the extent to which close substitutes for that item are available. Hence, demand is more likely to be elastic for e-commerce products that have many close substitutes elsewhere in both the electronic marketplace and the physical marketplace. Firms producing these items will have less ability to shift the burden of e-commerce taxation onto consumers in the form of higher prices.

By way of contrast, the demands for products offered by Internet sellers that have few close substitutes are likely to be more inelastic. Producers of these items should be able to push up prices, thereby transferring much of the burden of any taxes on Internet sales to consumers.

BEARING THE COSTS OF E-COMMERCE TAX COLLECTIONS

Because the statutory incidence of sales taxes falls on firms, an Internet seller would not be able to entirely escape the effects of e-commerce taxes, even if the demand for its product is completely inelastic. The reason is that there are costs of collecting taxes.

Nothing Is Free: The Costs of Tax Collection

States that impose sales taxes require companies to report total sales, to collect taxes based on the statutory sales-tax rate, and to transmit the taxes to sales-tax authorities. Firms in the physical marketplace that are already subject to sales taxes have systems in place for tabulating and transferring sales taxes. Large firms have automated much of this process, but for both large and small companies there is considerable paperwork required.

The various costs associated with collecting and transmitting sales taxes are *fixed costs*. That is, these costs typically do not fluctuate very much with short-run changes in sales volumes. Nevertheless, they must be added to a firm's total operating costs.

Just Another Cost of Engaging in Electronic Commerce?

Recall that the direct effect of imposing a per-unit sales tax on a firm's costs is a rise in its marginal cost and average total cost equal to the amount of the per-unit tax. Incurring fixed tax-collection costs would have no effect on an Internet seller's marginal cost curve, which is affected only by changes in the firm's variable costs. New tax-collection costs would, however, raise the firm's average total cost at any given output rate. Hence, the firm's average total cost curve would shift upward.

Taking into account tax-collection costs implies that there would be two effects of e-commerce taxes on firm's average production costs. The first would be the direct effect of the tax itself. To the extent that firms can pass along the tax to their customers through higher taxes, they can transfer some of this first burden to consumers. The second effect would be an increase in average total cost arising

POLICYMAKING *Online*

The German Government Gives Up on a Novel Approach to Taxing Electronic Commerce

To try to attract workers, companies in many countries constantly search for ways to offer tax-free benefits to their employees. At the same time, government tax collectors persistently strive to detect employee perks to which a monetary value can be assessed, thereby allowing the government to assess income taxes on that value.

The Proposed Web-Surfing Tax
In Germany, the government determined that many employees were using their companies' computers to engage in private Web surfing. As in other countries, German employees often send personal e-mail messages via corporate e-mail accounts, search the Internet for information relating to personal health issues, and shop for family gifts at Web retailers.

Some government accountants looked at estimates of the number of hours that people were surfing the Web on their employers' computers and—as government accountants are adept at doing—immediately spotted a source of tax revenues. The German government proposed applying existing

laws to impose taxes on the *implicit income* it said German workers earn from being able to use their companies' computers to surf the Internet. The government announced a plan to tax office workers who spent enough time on the Internet to receive an implicit compensation of at least 25 euros per month. The standard income-tax rate, the German Finance Ministry stated in a special tax directive to businesses, would be applicable to implicit income over that amount.

A Tax that Looked Good in Theory Confronts a Harsh Reality
The new Web-surfing tax immediately bumped up against a major problem, however. To determine the implicit income workers received from getting to visit Web sites from corporate computers, the government had to know two things: how much each company spent providing Internet access to every employee and how much time each employee spent engaging in Web surfing that was not related to the company's business. Gathering these two pieces of information for each employee would require companies to monitor their employees' time on the Internet, to track the various Web sites they visited, to keep careful records, and to file detailed reports to the government tax authorities.

When German firms found out just how much time, effort, and expense they would have to devote to helping the

continued

---

from fixed tax-collection costs. Firms cannot readily shift these costs onto their customers; typically, firms must "eat" higher fixed costs and settle for reduced profitability. (Recently German companies faced the prospect of a government e-commerce tax mandate that would have significantly boosted their fixed costs; see *Policymaking Online: The German Government Gives Up on a Novel Approach to Taxing Electronic Commerce.*)

continued from page 393

government collect its proposed Web-surfing tax, there was an explosion of opposition to the Finance Ministry's tax plan. This opposition gained momentum when a government study determined that the costs firms would incur gathering the information required to enforce the Web-surfing tax would greatly exceed the revenues the tax would generate for the government. Within weeks, the Finance Ministry rescinded its

directive. Thus, the world's first Web-surfing tax never quite got off the ground.

For Critical Analysis:

Does the German government's experience with its proposed Web-surfing tax point to broader issues associated with taxation in the electronic marketplace?

FUNDAMENTAL ISSUES ▼

1.

2.

3.

4.

5.

3. If Internet sales were taxed, who would pay?

The statutory incidence of sales taxes would fall on Internet sellers required to report their sales volumes, collect taxes, and transmit the funds to state and local governments. A fundamental determinant of the economic incidence of such taxes, or the determination of who ultimately would bear the burden of the taxes, is the price elasticity of demand for items sold in the electronic marketplace. For those goods and services with few close substitutes, demand is likely to be relatively inelastic. In this case, the upward shift in the supply curve caused by the tax would tend to push up the market price, shifting much of the burden of the tax onto consumers. By way of contrast, demand is likely to be relatively elastic for items with many substitutes, and imposing a tax on Internet sales of such items would lead to relatively little change in the market price. Then Internet sellers would bear most of the economic burden of the tax. In every case, e-commerce firms would incur fixed costs of collecting taxes that many of them currently avoid incurring.

Can E-Commerce Get by If It Is Taxed?

Given the predisposition for federal, state, and local governments to raise and spend large volumes of tax dollars, many observers argue that Internet sellers are fighting a losing battle to prevent governments from taxing their activities. It remains to be seen if this turns out to be true.

IS TAXATION A LOOMING TRAIN WRECK FOR ELECTRONIC COMMERCE?

Many e-commerce firms are very concerned about potential ill effects that their industries might experience if the current tax environment changes. Let's consider the limited available information about how taxes might affect the fortunes of industries based in the electronic marketplace.

The Supply-Side Effects of E-Commerce Taxation

As already discussed, there would be a direct effect from imposing a per-unit tax on an item sold over the Internet: The market supply curve would shift upward and leftward. As long as the market demand curve is not perfectly inelastic, this would result in a fall in the equilibrium quantity of that product. In addition, as long as the market demand curve is not perfectly elastic, there would be an increase in the equilibrium price.

An additional effect would arise from the statutory obligation of Internet sellers to report, collect, and transmit taxes to governments imposing the taxes. Incurring such tax-collection costs would raise firms' fixed operating costs. This increase in fixed costs would leave the firms' short-run average variable cost and marginal cost curves unaffected, thereby having no bearing on their decisions concerning whether to produce and how much to produce in the short run. In the long run, however, some firms in various e-commerce industries might well find continued operations unprofitable. These firms would exit their e-commerce industries. The result would be further reductions in market supply in those industries.

The Demand-Side Effects of E-Commerce Taxation

As noted earlier, the dynamic view of taxation indicates that higher tax rates applied to purchases in the physical marketplace induce consumers to shift their purchases to the electronic marketplace. Undoubtedly, imposing sales taxes on electronic commerce would lead many consumers to shift expenditures from the electronic marketplace back to the physical marketplace. Thus, taxing online transactions would reduce purchases of e-commerce products. That is, as the supply of e-commerce products shifts leftward, when the product demand curve has its typical downward slope, the quantity of items purchased on the Web likely will decline, as shown in panel *(c)* of Figure 12-6 on page 391.

Just how many consumers might desert the electronic marketplace if their purchases were subjected to sales taxes? To answer this question, Austan Goolsbee of the University of Chicago studied the behavior of about 25,000 Internet consumers. He found that people residing in states and cities with relatively high sales-tax rates on purchases in the physical marketplace were significantly more likely to purchase goods and services online, as compared with consumers residing in locales with lower tax rates. A 10 percent rise in the after-tax price of a good or service in the physical marketplace induced by a higher sales-tax rate, Goolsbee found, was likely to induce decreases in purchases of goods and services from Web-based firms ranging from 20 percent to more than 40 percent.

After taking various other factors that affected consumers' choices into account, Goolsbee used estimates of the responsiveness of Internet consumers to off-line sales taxes to try to determine the likely effects of extending current sales taxes to online purchases. He found that as many as 24 percent of current Internet consumers would stop purchasing items online if governments imposed sales taxation.

The Net Price and Quantity Effects of E-Commerce Taxation

Figure 12-7 depicts the likely net effects that taxes on Internet transactions would have on the price and quantity in the market for an item sold in the electronic marketplace, under the assumption that the market demand curve is neither perfectly inelastic nor perfectly inelastic. As discussed earlier, one effect is that the market supply curve for the product would decline, both as a direct response to the tax and as some firms' profits decline sufficiently to induce them to leave the industry.

These reductions in supply would likely induce a decline in desired purchases of the item on the Web. A number of consumers would shift their expenditures away from the electronic marketplace as the price of the item increased. Thus, the equilibrium quantity would fall. A typical e-commerce industry would shrink as a result of Internet taxation.

EMERGING TAX ISSUES IN A GLOBAL ELECTRONIC MARKETPLACE

The prospect of market shrinkage from Internet taxes helps explain why e-commerce firms continue to resist ongoing efforts by various state and local officials to extend sales taxes to the electronic marketplace. Still another tax issue looms on the horizon. Because the electronic marketplace has no physical borders, people located in other countries also purchase items from domestically based Internet sellers. Other nations' governments, however, have not been as willing as the U.S. government to give their e-commerce industries breathing room from taxation.

Figure 12-7:
Typical Market Effects of Taxing Electronic Commerce.

Imposing taxes on the sales of Web firms would have two effects. One would be a reduction in supply, from S_1 to S_2, following the imposition of taxes. The other would be another fall in supply, from S_2 to S_3, resulting from a long-run reduction in the number of firms in the marketplace after some firms choose to exit when higher costs of collecting and transmitting taxes to the government push down their profitability. The net effects would be an overall increase in the price of items sold by e-commerce firms and an overall reduction in the output of these firms.

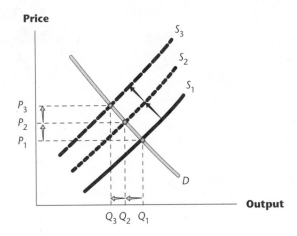

This means that U.S. Internet sellers increasingly must take into account difference in tax laws around the globe. (An ongoing area of disagreement between the United States and the European Union, for instance, has arisen from their differing tax treatment of electronic commerce; see on the next page *Globalization Online: Should U.S. Internet Sellers Have to Collect European Taxes?*) Selling a product to consumers residing in an Asian country, for instance, may entail developing a separate system for collecting and transmitting sales taxes to national, state, or local governments located within that country. This is one important reason that most U.S.-based Internet sellers that market their products abroad have established separate Web sites and operating subsidiaries. Marketing and distributing products internationally entails considerable tax complications, as well as other issues explored in more detail in Chapter 13.

GLOBALIZATION *Online*

POLICY MAKING   **GLOBALIZATION**   MANAGEMENT

Should U.S. Internet Sellers Have to Collect European Taxes?

In April 2000, the Advisory Commission on Electronic Commerce that the U.S. Congress had established to review various issues relating to e-commerce issues recommended a 5-year extension of an existing moratorium on subjecting Internet sales to taxes. Congress hastened to enact that recommendation into law. This U.S. action has not, however, stopped other countries from pursuing efforts to tax electronic commerce.

The European Union's Online Tax Proposal

Nations of the European Union (EU) rely heavily on *value-added taxes (VAT)* to provide revenues to fund government expenditures. Unlike sales taxes, which are assessed solely on the final sales price in a transaction, a VAT is applied to each stage of production in which value is added to a good or service, including final assembly or the provision of a final service to a consumer.

In July 2000, the EU's Executive Commission proposed requiring U.S. companies with annual sales on Internet-downloadable products within EU nations exceeding $96,000 to register in at least one EU nation. Companies selling downloadable goods and services—including software, videos, music, and computer games—would have to collect a VAT of 15 to 25 percent for payment to that nation's government.

Are EU Governments Needy, or Simply Greedy?

The EU's Executive Commission offered two rationales for their proposal. First, EU online sellers must collect a VAT on each

continued

FUNDAMENTAL ISSUES ▼

1.

2.

3.

4.

5.

4. What effects would taxation have on electronic commerce?

The immediate effect of making Internet transactions subject to taxes would be a short-run reduction in market supply as the supply curve shifted upward by the amount of the tax. In the long run, there could be an additional decline in supply if the higher fixed costs of tax collection sufficiently reduces the profitability of some e-commerce firms and leads them to exit the electronic marketplace. The resulting increase in the market price would induce a number of current Internet consumers—perhaps as many as 20 percent or more—to shift at least a portion of their purchases to the physical marketplace. The equilibrium volume of e-commerce transactions would decline, except in the few industries producing items with very inelastic demand.

downloadable product they sell. If U.S. companies are able to sell downloadable products tax-free while EU companies are not, then U.S. companies will have an "unfair competitive advantage" over their European rivals. Second, EU governments undertake considerable social welfare spending, and they desire the additional revenues.

U.S. firms blasted the EU proposal. The U.S. government's response was more diplomatic and muted. Nevertheless, a Treasury undersecretary noted that at least some of the tax rates that the EU was proposing to use were higher than the tax rates that EU governments charge on the same products when sold offline. Some economists speculated that the EU planned to charge higher online taxes to push up the effective price of the online products predominantly sold by

U.S. firms—thereby effectively placing a tariff on EU imports of downloadable U.S. products. The EU proposal remains under very quiet discussion at relatively low levels within the EU and U.S. governments. Nevertheless, the broad issue of how to deal with different national approaches to taxing online commerce is unlikely to go away. China recently announced that it also will be taxing e-commerce transactions, and it is already exploring ways to tax the sales of both domestic and foreign Web firms.

For Critical Analysis:
Should a sales tax or a VAT apply based on the location of the seller or on the location of the buyer? Why does it matter?

 ## Electronic Commerce: A Public Good?

Imagine if you could update your driver's license and transmit the associated fees and taxes on the Web. Later on, if a police officer tickets you for speeding, the officer scans your license, records your transgression in a government database, assesses the fine, and automatically bills the fine using a point-of-sale terminal linked to the Internet via a wireless connection in the police car. When you sell your car or trade it in for a newer model, the transfer is automatically recorded in yet another government database. Later, government employees upload data concerning the ownership transfer to other authorities who maintain catalogs for tracking automobiles on a government-operated system within the overall global positioning system. That way, if someone uses the car you have sold to commit a crime within the new few weeks, police officers will not be directed to your residence to make an arrest.

A brave new world of law enforcement is emerging in some areas. Law enforcement and the provision of a wide array of other government services are undergoing a transformation as federal, state, and local governments strive to integrate e-business and e-commerce technologies into their operations. What remains to be determined, however, is just how involved governments should be in the provision of goods and services via the Web. As has long been true in the physical marketplace, citizens are struggling to evaluate the appropriate role of government in the electronic marketplace.

PUBLIC GOODS, MERIT GOODS, AND THE INTERNET

Private Good
An item that can only be consumed by one person at a time.

Most goods and services are **private goods** that can be consumed by only one individual at a time. Thus, private goods are subject to the **principle of rival consumption:** One person's consumption of a private good necessarily reduces the amount of the item available for consumption by another individual.

Principle of Rival Consumption
The principle that individuals are rivals in consuming private goods, because consumption of such items by one person reduces the ability of another person to consume those items.

Public Goods

Individuals can simultaneously consume a number of goods and services, such as the entertainment services provided by a band or orchestra concert. Among these goods and services, a few cannot be provided to some consumers without others being able to derive benefits from them. In addition, some have the property that when provided, additional people can consume the goods or services at no additional cost. Furthermore, it is difficult, if not impossible to deny the benefits of these goods or services to an individual who fails to pay for it. A good or service that satisfies these criteria is a **public good.**

Public Good
Any good or service that can be consumed by many people at the same time, cannot be consumed by one individual without others also consuming it at no extra cost, and cannot be withheld from a person who has not contributed to funding its production.

A public good is subject to the **exclusion principle:** No one can be excluded from the benefits of a public good, even if that person has not paid for it. This means the private sector of the economy faces a difficult task in providing a public good. After all, if no one can be excluded from using a public good, it may be difficult to provide the item in sufficient amounts and simultaneously devise a system for collecting sufficient funds to pay for its provision. (Some goods are illegal to buy or sell on the Internet; see *Policymaking Online: Is a Vote a Private Good or a Public Good?*)

Exclusion Principle
The principle that no one, including someone who has failed to pay for an item's provision, can be excluded from the benefits of the item if that item is a public good.

Most economists agree that there are public goods, but it is often difficult to find widespread agreement about specific examples. For instance, one of the most commonly proposed examples of a public good is a lighthouse. Arguably, many seafarers can use the services of a lighthouse simultaneously, and once a lighthouse is in place, additional ship navigators can use it at no additional cost. In the thirteenth century, however, French King Louis IX erected a 105-foot tower with a dual purpose. In addition to serving as a lighthouse, it also was a revenue enhancer. From the lighthouse, the King's men could spot ships sailing close enough to view its light. Speedy ships of the king's navy would then prevent the masters of these ships from escaping payment for the lighthouse's services. Thus,

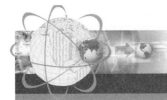

POLICYMAKING *Online*

Is a Vote a Private Good or a Public Good?

In November 2000, a college student posted flyers on trees along New York's Park Avenue that read, "BUY MY VOTE—Struggling Student Is Willing To Sell Vote in This November 7th Election—$1,000 or Best Offer." Undercover officers contacted the student at his e-mail address that he also printed on the flyer. They arrested him after he agreed to accept $600 and to videotape the ballot in the voting booth to confirm his choice.

Auctioning Votes on the Internet

This student's effort to sell his vote was decidedly low-tech as compared with more organized activities that popped up on the Internet before the 2000 election. At least seven vote-swapping sites, such as a site called Voteexchange2000.com, appeared on the Web in the weeks preceding the election.

Particularly active sites helped connect people across the country who wanted to support Ralph Nader, the third-party environmentalist presidential candidate, without harming the chances that Democratic candidate Albert Gore would lose the national election. For instance, a voter residing in California, which Gore was on the way to winning handily in the weeks before the election, could use a vote-swapping site to strike a bargain to vote for Nader. Someone residing in Gore's home state of Tennessee, where the race was much tighter, might then agree to vote for Gore.

Is Swapping a Vote the Same as Selling a Vote?

As the New York student learned, selling a vote is illegal under federal and state laws. In California, the California secretary of state threatened criminal legal action against Internet vote-swapping sites, and several shut down.

The owner of California-based Voteexchange2000.com, however, filed suit against the California government, arguing that the 1973 federal law that forbids selling a vote for "something of value" applies only to receipts of financial payments. California law, however, does not specify whether money must be involved in vote exchanges, and it provides for penalties as harsh as a three-year prison term. It will be up to a California state court to determine whether vote swapping violates the law.

For Critical Analysis:

Evaluate a vote's properties as a "good." Is there anything to the argument that it has properties of a public good, or is it more properly viewed as a private good?

---

this French king found a way to try to ensure that everyone paid for the service they received from his lighthouse.

Several goods and services often appear on lists of national or regional public goods. These include national or regional defense, forest fire suppression, groundwater pollution cleanup, flood control, and animal disease control. Some people like to include parks, rivers, waterways, and highways.

Many people have added the Internet to their list of public goods. Most economists classify these items, as well as the Internet, as "impure" public goods. The reason is that it is possible to prevent people who do not pay from using them.

After all, if someone will not pay for access to the Internet, it is easy enough to deny them access by preventing them from attaining a physical or wireless link and refusing to assign them the IP address they need to navigate the Web.

There are also a number of goods and services on lists of **global public goods** that arguably benefit people worldwide, including ocean pollution cleanup, weather forecasting, protection of the world's ozone layer, and disease eradication. Lists of global public goods also differ from person to person. Some observers include items such as world satellite orbits, continental and oceanic ship and air transport corridors, and allocations of bands of the electromagnetic spectrum.

Increasingly, some observers also list the Internet as a global public good, because it spans national borders. To reiterate, however, most economists are hesitant to categorize the Internet as anything more than an impure public good, because it is also possible to prevent people from having access to the Internet if they fail to pay for that access.

Merit Goods

It is important to distinguish public goods from goods and services that government entities sometimes choose to provide. For instance, some observers classify health care as a national, regional, or even global public good, from an economist's standpoint, it is incorrect to classify health care as a public good, because it is a simple matter to deny access to health care when people will not or cannot pay for the care. Nevertheless, many national governments around the world either partially or fully fund health care. Some even provide relatively large amounts of health care services directly. In these countries, health care has been deemed a **merit good** that societies promote through government intervention in the marketplace.

Many citizens and government officials around the globe have promoted the view that the Internet and associated e-commerce products should be regarded as merit goods. Without public funding, they argue, society will fail to reap many of the rewards the Internet offers for use in education, the provision of government services, and even business applications. Proponents of the Internet as a merit good commonly argue for complete access to the Internet by all citizens.

In addition, many governments have included the Internet, intranets, and related networks among industries benefiting from **industrial policies** that actively promote the development of specific economic sectors. For instance, in 2000 the Japanese government decided that a key national goal is for Japan to have the world's foremost Internet infrastructure by 2005. This obliged the government to establish a regulatory framework consistent with attaining global leadership for its mobile phone and broadband-Internet industries.

Many economists question the wisdom of industrial policies, arguing that private market forces normally direct resources to the most socially desirable activities, which governments cannot necessarily identify successfully. In addition, in-

Global Public Good
A good or service that yields benefits to the world's people simultaneously, cannot provide benefits to one person without others around the world deriving benefits at no additional cost, and cannot be withheld from a person who has failed to contribute to its provision.

Merit Good
A good or service that residents of a nation determine, typically through a political process, to be socially desirable.

Industrial Policy
A government policy designed to assist the development of specific national industries.

POLICYMAKING *Online*

Giving Big European Companies Taxpayers' Euros to Set Up Shop on the Internet

It is called the "Content and Multimedia Tools Unit" of the European Commission. This office provides 30 million euros (about $27 million) per year to eight or nine European companies interested in trying to push forward the development of an electronic marketplace in Europe. Companies can use the funds to support collaborative efforts among service providers, content producers, and new media designers. Top priorities for receiving the funds are small to medium-sized enterprises that otherwise might be dissuaded by the potential risk that an Internet venture might not establish viability in the marketplace. Nevertheless, the European Parliament hoped the funds might help encourage the development of relatively small but nimble companies that could compete with the many Internet start-ups in the United States and Asia.

The Content and Multimedia Tools Unit ran into a problem soon after it was established in 1995, however: Many of the companies interested in getting government funds to as-

sist in setting up shop on the Internet were huge, bureaucratic corporations. These companies often were spending more than 30 million euros on efforts to establish operations on the Internet. They were happy, though, to receive government funds to supplement their own annual expenditures on long-term e-commerce research and development projects.

By 1998, big companies were submitting nearly half of all requests for EU funding, and it had become clear that only a few of the intended recipients of government funds were actually receiving those funds. The European Parliament responded by shortening the period a company is eligible for funding to 5 years and changed various rules of the program so that only companies truly looking for a quick "jump start" for their Internet efforts would qualify. Immediately, the percentage of requests from large corporations fell to about 25 percent. Nevertheless, a few million euros of government funds still make their way each year to big, lumbering European companies, some of which are already partly owned by governments of member states of the European Union.

For Critical Analysis:
What are some pros and cons associated with offering government subsidies to companies seeking to develop Internet operations?

---

dustrial policies can become entangled with antitrust enforcement to the benefit of producers, because by pursuing these policies governments often facilitate interactions among competing firms. This can lay the groundwork for implicit governmental sanctioning of cartel arrangements. (As residents of the European Union have learned, it can also entail transferring taxpayers' funds to companies that are already big and profitable; see *Policymaking Online: Giving Big European Companies Taxpayers' Euros to Set Up Shop on the Internet.*)

What constitutes a public good or a merit good worthy of public support is often in the eye of the beholder. This poses problems in determining how to obtain funding to support provision of the item through governmental efforts.

The Free-Rider Problem

A common feature of any item that society deems worthy of public support is the *free-rider problem*. This problem is particularly acute for goods and services subject to the exclusion principle. After all, when it is impossible to exclude anyone from reaping benefits from the provision of a good or service, many people will presume that others will pay for the item. Consequently, each person will feel confident that it is possible to avoid paying a share of the cost of providing the item, because others will bear the cost.

If a sufficiently large number of people attempt to be free riders, it may prove difficult to fund provision of a public good. This is a key reason most tax systems are compulsory. It is also a reason taxation is a hotly debated subject everywhere in the world. After all, if a country's citizens disagree about which goods or services to classify as public goods or merit goods, then they are unlikely to agree about how many taxes they should contribute to fund the provision of these goods or services.

The Internet: A Network for Tax Avoidance?

For those who view the Internet as either an impure public good or a merit good that deserves public support, the free-rider problem emerges as a significant barrier. Indeed, contemplating the public provision of various goods and services takes us full circle to the issue of using the Internet to engage in tax avoidance. To some observers, it is apparent that governments should assess taxes on Internet access, e-commerce sales, and other Web-based transactions, so that the funds raised can be funneled back into the development of an even more widespread, ever-more-accessible, global Internet.

For instance, a few years ago the United Nations discussed a proposal for assessing special taxes on each bit of information transferred on the Internet. The funds raised from this global "Internet tax" would be used to expand the worldwide infrastructure of the Internet, including within less developed and emerging nations. When developed nations refused to agree, some UN officials criticized them as free riders.

Undoubtedly, the number of and the breadth and depth of issues relating to the proper role of the public sector in electronic commerce will only increase during the years to come. Achieving a consensus about whether Web-based communication infrastructures, e-commerce capabilities, and the like are public or merit goods and whether people should be taxed to use those infrastructures and capabilities may prove to be a major challenge for our society.

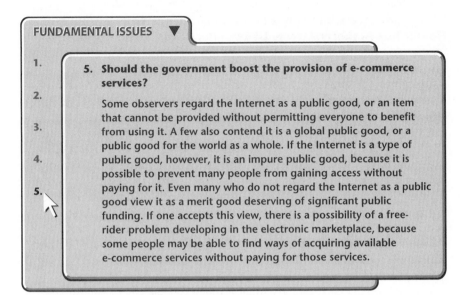

FUNDAMENTAL ISSUES ▼

1.

2.

3.

4.

5.

5. Should the government boost the provision of e-commerce services?

Some observers regard the Internet as a public good, or an item that cannot be provided without permitting everyone to benefit from using it. A few also contend it is a global public good, or a public good for the world as a whole. If the Internet is a type of public good, however, it is an impure public good, because it is possible to prevent many people from gaining access without paying for it. Even many who do not regard the Internet as a public good view it as a merit good deserving of significant public funding. If one accepts this view, there is a possibility of a free-rider problem developing in the electronic marketplace, because some people may be able to find ways of acquiring available e-commerce services without paying for those services.

Chapter Summary

1) **The Essential Pros and Cons of Exempting Electronic Commerce from Taxation:** Some of those who favor exempting the electronic marketplace from taxation argue that doing so limits the ability of governments to collect and spend taxes. Others contend that most taxes assessed in the physical marketplace are regressive sales taxes, so that exempting Web sales from taxation prevents this form of regressive taxation from spreading to electronic commerce. Many other proponents of limiting Internet taxation argue that e-commerce industries should be permitted to grow and develop before being taxed. Those who oppose exempting electronic commerce from taxation contend that doing so causes governments to lose funds needed for crucial public services. They also claim that higher-income individuals with Internet access are most able to use the electronic marketplace as a haven from sales taxes, thereby making the existing taxation of sales at bricks-and-mortar firms even more regressive. Other critics argue that the failure to collect taxes on most electronic commerce gives Internet sellers an unfair advantage over traditional retailers.

2) **Ways That Electronic Commerce Can Influence Tax Revenues, and How It Has Actually Affected Tax Collections:** The static view on the relationship among the tax base, the tax rate, and tax revenues indicates that people can shift purchases subject to sales taxes to the electronic marketplace, thereby reducing the existing sales-tax base and decreasing tax revenues. Governments might try to recover lost tax revenues by raising the tax rate, but the dynamic view on taxation implies this action is likely to induce even more people to become Internet consumers. This would further erode the existing sales-tax base. Most estimates to date indicate that U.S. states lose a fraction of a percent to 5 percent of current annual tax revenues because of their failure of enforce use-tax regulations that apply to Internet purchases. As a consequence, each year the average U.S. state fails to collect a few million to tens of millions of taxes.

3) **Who Would Pay If Internet Sales Were Taxed:** The statutory incidence of sales taxes would fall on Internet sellers. Web-based firms would be legally obliged to report sales and collect and transmit taxes to state and local governments. A key factor influencing who ultimately would bear the economic burden of e-commerce taxes is the price elasticity of demand for items sold in the electronic marketplace. Demand is likely to be relatively inelastic for items sold on the Web that have few close substitutes, so that an upward shift in the supply curve caused by imposing a tax would boost the market price and shift much of the burden of the tax onto consumers. For items with many close substitutes and relatively elastic demand, the imposition of a tax on electronic commerce would lead to relatively little change in the market price. In this instance, Internet sellers would bear most of the economic burden of the tax. Irrespective of who would bear the direct burden of e-commerce taxation, many Internet sellers that currently have avoided incurring fixed costs of collecting taxes would have to bear these expenses.

4) **Effects of Taxation on Electronic Commerce:** The direct effect of extending existing taxes to electronic commerce would be a short-run reduction in the market supply of items sold on the Web, because the supply curve for each item would shift upward by the amount of the tax. There also could be an additional decline in supply in the long run if increased fixed costs of tax collection reduce profitability at some Internet sellers sufficiently to induce them to exit the electronic marketplace. In response to higher market prices, a number of current Internet consumers would shift their consumption to the physical marketplace. Some estimates indicate that 20 percent or more of existing Internet consumers might desert the electronic marketplace. This undoubtedly would reduce the equilibrium volume of purchases from e-commerce firms, except for those in industries producing items with very inelastic demand.

5) **Evaluating a Potential Government Role in Boosting the Provision of E-commerce Services:** Some argue that the Internet is a public good, which is an item that cannot be provided without permitting everyone to

experience benefits from the item. A few observers also contend that the Internet is a global public good that benefits people worldwide, even if they fail to pay for it. Most economists regard the Internet as at most an impure public good, however, because it is possible to prevent many people from gaining access to the electronic marketplace unless they pay for it. Nevertheless, many regard the Internet as a merit good deserving of tangible public support. If so, then a free-rider problem could develop in the electronic marketplace as people discover ways to acquire e-commerce services without paying for those services.

Questions and Problems

1) Why might states hesitate to give up on sales taxes in the age of electronic commerce?

2) Some proponents of applying sales taxes to the Internet argue that these taxes should be imposed on both buyers and sellers. For instance, in a Web transaction involving a consumer in New York and a company based in California, the New York consumer would pay a New York Internet sales tax, while the California firm would pay a California Internet sales tax. What are the pros and cons associated with this proposal?

3) In your view, would it be easier or harder to enforce Internet sales taxes, as compared with sales taxes assessed on sales by bricks-and-mortar firms? Support your answer.

4) How does the failure to tax many Web sales have both static and dynamic consequences?

5) Suppose that all Internet sellers subjected to a per-unit sales tax equal to τ are monopolistically competitive. Use an appropriate diagram to trace through the effects of this tax on the price that a typical firm charges and on the firm's output. Does the price elasticity of demand influence who bears the burden of the tax? Explain.

6) List three physical goods marketed on the Internet. Next to each good, make a judgment about whether the price elasticity of demand is likely to be "relatively high" or "relatively low" based on the availability of close substitutes offered either online or offline. If Internet purchases of each good were subjected to sales taxes, who do you predict (based on your elasticity estimations) would bear most of the burden of taxation: Internet sellers or Internet consumers?

7) List three types of services sold on the Internet. Next to each service, make a judgment about whether the price elasticity of demand is likely to be "relatively high" or "relatively low" based on the availability of close substitutes offered either online or offline. If Internet purchases of each service

were subjected to sales taxes, who do you predict (based on your elasticity estimations) would bear most of the burden of taxation: Internet sellers or Internet consumers?

8) Traditional firms argue that the fact that imposing taxes on e-commerce firms might cause some of them to discontinue operations is evidence that the current tax exemption that many e-commerce firms experience gives these firms an unfair advantage in the marketplace. Whether or not you agree with this view, provide counterarguments in support of the status quo.

9) Many e-commerce firms argue that they are part of infant industries that deserve a chance to grow and develop before being subjected to various forms of taxation and tax collection costs they currently avoid. Whether or not you agree with this view, provide counterarguments favoring subjecting e-commerce firms to the same taxes imposed on firms in the physical marketplace.

10) Make lists of features of the Internet that argue for categorizing it as either a private or a public good. How do you believe it should be categorized? Why?

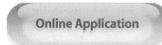

Online Application

Internet URL: http://www.ecommercecommission.org/report.htm

Title: **Advisory Commission on Electronic Commerce, Report to Congress**

Navigation: Go directly to the above URL and then download the PDF file containing the report (you will have to download the free version of Adobe Acrobat Reader first if you do not have it installed on your computer).

Application: Perform the following operations, and answer the following questions.

1) In the Table of Contents, click on "Sales and Use Taxes" in Section II, and read this section. Why do you think the Advisory Commission recommended that states try to develop a common framework for imposing and collecting sales and use taxes?

2) Back up to the Table of Contents and click on "Internet Access Taxes" in section II, and read this short section. What arguments can you offer in support of the Advisory Commission's recommendation to permanently ban taxes on Internet access? Are there any arguments that might be offered against this recommendation?

For Group Study and Analysis: Divide the class into two groups to debate the statement, "Internet sales taxes should be permanently banned."

Selected References and Further Readings

Advisory Commission on Electronic Commerce. *Report to Congress,* April 2000.

Bruce, Donald, and William Fox. "E-Commerce in the Context of Declining State Sales Tax Bases," Center for Business and Economic Research, University of Tennessee, April 2000.

Goolsbee, Austan. "In a World without Borders: The Impact of Taxes on Internet Commerce," *Quarterly Journal of Economics* 115 (2, May 2000), pp. 561–576.

Goolsbee, Austan, and Jonathan Zittrain. "Evaluating the Costs and Benefits of Taxing Internet Commerce," *National Tax Journal* 52 (3, September 1999), pp. 413–428.

Kaul, Inge, Isabelle Grunberg, and Marc Stern, eds. *Global Public Goods.* New York: Oxford University Press, 1999.

McClure, Charles, Jr. "The Taxation of Electronic Commerce: Background and Proposal." In *Public Policy and the Internet: Privacy, Taxes, and Contract,* ed. Nicholas Imparato. Stanford, Ca.: Hoover Institution Press, 2000.

Organization for Economic Cooperation and Development. Committee on Fiscal Affairs. "Implementing the Ottawa Taxation Framework Conditions," June 2000.

Rosen, Harvey. *Public Finance.* 5th ed. New York: McGraw-Hill, 1999.

U.S. General Accounting Office. "Sales Taxes: Electronic Commerce Growth Presents Challenges; Revenue Losses are Uncertain," Report to Congressional Requesters, June 2000.

Wiseman, Alan. *The Internet Economy: Access, Taxes, and Market Structure.* Washington, D.C.: Brookings Institution, 2000.

Chapter 13

Electronic Commerce and the World Trading System

FUNDAMENTAL ISSUES ▼

1. What are a nation's production possibilities, and what do they tell us about the costs of producing goods and services within that nation? ▶
2. What is absolute advantage, and how can it help explain why nations engage in international trade? ▶
3. Why is absolute advantage alone insufficient to account for trade among nations? ▶
4. What is comparative advantage, and how does it allow countries to experience gains from trade? ▶
5. How can economies of scale and imperfect competition help to explain intra-industry trade via electronic commerce? ▶
6. Why and how do nations seek to restrain offline and online foreign competition, and what aspects of the electronic marketplace and the world trading system hinder their efforts? ▶

<E-Commerce Today>

The U.S. Textile Industry Finds Its Salvation on the Web

For more than a quarter of a century, the U.S. textile industry has benefited from the actions of a little known group called the Committee for the Implementation of Textile Agreements (CITA). This committee is composed of appointees from the U.S. Departments of Commerce, Labor, State, and Treasury, along with the chief textile negotiator of the Office of the President. Throughout the 1980s and 1990s, CITA reduced or threatened to reduce quota limitations on a number of textile imports. Economists have estimated that the annual benefit of CITA quotas for U.S. textile firms has been as high as $12 billion in additional profits.

A gradual phase-out of U.S. textile quotas is under way, however. The United States has pledged to be in full compliance with treaties ending protection of domestic textile industries by 2005. When the U.S. government made this commitment in the mid-1990s, some observers went so far as predict the ultimate demise of the U.S. textile industry. In fact, U.S. textile imports continued to rise in the early 2000s. Textile employment dropped by a lower-than-expected 7 percent before stabilizing and even showing signs of recovery in 2000 and 2001. U.S. textile producers' share of the global market dipped slightly before leveling off at about 25 percent of world textile sales, and some textile experts even predicted the U.S. share might begin to grow once again.

A key factor helping to contribute to continuing strength of U.S. textile exports has been that many U.S. textile manufacturers have taken advantage of the lead the United States enjoys in business-to-business commerce on the Internet. By cutting distribution costs and speeding up deliveries, they have been able to retain, and in some cases, enhance their shares in the global textile marketplace. Today, many Latin American and Asian textile manufacturers are complaining that U.S. firms' ready access to business-to-business e-commerce constitutes a type of barrier to free and open international trade.

Developments in electronic commerce promise to revolutionize many aspects of trade among the world's nations. In this chapter, you will learn why international trade takes place and why it is spreading through the electronic marketplace. You will also learn why some countries try to restrain e-commerce activities across their borders, how they might attempt to implement such restrictions, and what aspects of electronic commerce and the international trading environment could hinder their efforts.

Absolute Advantage and International Trade

Residents of different nations have various reasons for wishing to engage in cross-border trade. Traditional explanations for international trade focus on advantages that some countries may have, compared with others, in producing the goods and services they export abroad.

PRODUCTION AND CONSUMPTION POSSIBILITIES

The residents of any nation normally produce and consume many different goods and services. For simplicity, however, let's imagine a situation in which a country produces only two items. This will assist in developing understanding the fundamental rationales for international trade.

A Nation's Production Possibilities

In particular, let's consider a particular nation called Rustbelt. This nation's residents, which currently engage in no international trade, produce and consume steel and e-commerce services, such as Web-based processing of business records and Internet selling services. Given current technology and resources—people, machines, and raw materials—Rustbelt has fixed capabilities to produce steel and e-commerce services within a given year. Economists call these capabilities its **production possibilities,** which are displayed in Table 13-1.

> **Production Possibilities**
> *All possible combinations of total output of goods and services that residents of a nation can produce given currently available technology and resources.*

The maximum amount of steel the people of Rustbelt can produce within a year is 1.4 million units. To produce this amount of steel, Rustbelt's residents must devote all of their resources to producing steel. This means that the nation cannot produce any units of e-commerce services during that year. By way of contrast, if Rustbelt's residents are willing to forgo all steel production during the year, they can produce 2 million units of e-commerce services. Producing this quantity of e-commerce services, however, entails devoting all of the nation's resources to production of Web-based services. Thus, this is the maximum number of units of e-commerce services that Rustbelt can produce, given its current technology and resources.

Table 13-1 shows that given a fixed technology and fixed resources, producing more of one item requires producing less of another item. Hence, a nation faces a *production possibilities trade-off.* In the case of Rustbelt, Table 13-1 indicates that if its residents initially were producing nothing but 1.4 million units of steel but decided to develop a completely "high-tech" economy producing nothing but 2 million units of e-commerce services per year, they would have to halt steel production.

Production Possibilities and Opportunity Cost

Rustbelt's residents must give up producing 1.4 million units of steel to produce 2 million units of e-commerce services instead. Thus, the *opportunity cost* of pro-

Table 13-1: Rustbelt's Production Possibilities.

Millions of Units of E-Commerce Services	Millions of Units of Steel
0	1.40
0.80	1.20
1.00	1.10
1.20	0.98
1.40	0.82
1.60	0.62
1.80	0.38
2.00	0

ducing 2 million units of e-commerce services is the 1.4 million units of steel they could have otherwise produced.

Now suppose that Rustbelt has chosen not to be purely a steel producer or a producer of Web-based services. If its residents currently produce 0.8 million units of e-commerce services, then Table 13-1 indicates that, given current production possibilities, 1.2 million units of steel can be produced as well. If Rustbelt's residents choose to produce 0.2 million more units of e-commerce services, thereby yielding a total of 1 million new units of e-commerce services this year, they must reallocate to the provision of e-commerce services some of the resources they previously allocated to producing steel. Consequently, they must cut back on steel production. As Table 13-1 shows, Rustbelt's residents can increase their production of Web-based services from 0.8 million to 1 million only if they reduce steel production from 1.2 million to 1.1 million units. Thus, producing 0.2 million more units of e-commerce services entails incurring an opportunity cost equal to 0.1 million units of steel.

Suppose that Rustbelt's residents aim for an even more high-tech production mix by raising their provision of e-commerce services by 0.2 million more units, to 1.2 million units of e-commerce services. To do this, they must cut steel production from 1.1 million units to 0.98 million units. Producing another 0.2 million units of e-commerce services, therefore, requires Rustbelt's residents to incur an opportunity cost equal to 0.12 million units of steel.

If Rustbelt's residents increase provision of e-commerce services by yet another 0.2 million-unit increment, from 1.2 million units of e-commerce services to 1.4 million units of e-commerce services, then Table 13-1 indicates that steel production must decline from 0.98 million units to 0.82 million unit. The opportunity cost of producing the next 0.2 million units of e-commerce services, therefore, is 0.16 million units of steel.

Note how each 0.2 million-unit increase in production of e-commerce services requires a successively larger—0.1 million, then 0.12 million, and then 1.6 million—reduction in the number of units of steel that Rustbelt can produce. This illustrates a fundamental characteristic of the production possibilities trade-off: The opportunity cost of producing additional units of a particular item increases as more of that item is produced.

Imperfectly Shiftable Resources and Higher Opportunity Cost

Let's consider why opportunity cost increases by thinking about an initial situation in which Rustbelt's residents produce only steel. If the residents of Rustbelt start transferring resources from steel production to production of Web-based services, at first they will transfer over those people who are best at designing and manufacturing computers, Internet connections, Web servers, and Web pages. They will also shift resources that are best suited to production of e-commerce services—silicon, precious metals, and fiber optic cable.

As they continue to increase their production of e-commerce services, however, Rustbelt's residents will discover that fewer resources readily lend themselves to producing Web-based services. Some people transferred from steel production to provision of e-commerce services may know a lot about steel production but relatively little about programming computers or designing Web pages. Iron and other resources that are useful for producing steel will also be less readily applied to providing e-commerce services. Thus, each successive 0.2 million-unit increase in production of e-commerce services requires transferring successively larger numbers of resources away from steel production. The result is a successively larger reduction in steel production due to each incremental increase in the provision of e-commerce services, and hence a higher opportunity cost of producing e-commerce services.

The Production Possibilities Frontier

The production possibilities for Rustbelt are displayed in Figure 13-1. This figure plots the combinations of steel and e-commerce service production from Table 13-1 on page 413, with the amount of steel measured along the vertical axis and units of e-commerce services measured along the horizontal axis. These production combinations, plus all other feasible combinations of production of goods and services given technology and available resources, lie along a curve called the **production possibilities frontier.** Rustbelt's residents can produce combinations of steel and units of e-commerce services on or inside the frontier, but they cannot produce combinations that lie beyond the frontier.

Point A in Figure 13-1 corresponds to the second line of Table 13-1. At this point, Rustbelt's residents can produce 0.8 million units of e-commerce services and 1.2 million units of steel in a year's time. Point B corresponds to the fifth line of Table 13-1, which indicates that Rustbelt's residents are able to raise their production of e-commerce services to 1.4 million if they reduce their production of steel to 0.82 million units.

Production Possibilities Frontier

A diagram showing all feasible combinations of goods and services that may be produced in a nation, given its technology and available resources.

Figure 13-1:
The Production Possibilities Frontier for Rustbelt.

This curve, which depicts the production possibilities for Rustbelt given in Table 13-1 on page 413, is the nation's production possibilities frontier. Residents of Rustbelt can produce combinations of steel and e-commerce services along or within the region bounded by the production possibilities frontier, but they cannot produce combinations outside the frontier. By shifting production from point A to point B, Rustbelt's residents can expand their production of e-commerce services by 0.6 million units, from 0.8 million units to 1.4 million units, but only at an opportunity cost of 0.38 million units of steel, from 1.2 million units to 0.82 million units. The opportunity cost of a single unit of e-commerce services at point A is the slope of the line tangent to the production possibilities curve at that point. Likewise, the opportunity cost of one unit of e-commerce services at point B is the slope of the tangent line at that point.

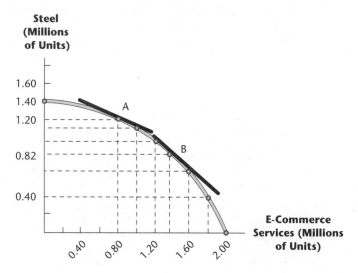

Considering the opportunity cost of increasing production of e-commerce services by *one single unit* if Rustbelt's residents currently are producing at point *A* requires examining the *slope* of a line tangent to the production possibilities frontier at point *A*. The slope of a line is the "rise" divided by the "run." Thus, a 1-unit increase in the provision of e-commerce services is a 1-unit horizontal movement, or run, along the line. The accompanying vertical movement down along the line is the rise. This is negative because it tells us the opportunity cost of the 1-unit increase in production of e-commerce services, measured in units of steel.

Likewise, the opportunity cost of a 1-unit increase in production of e-commerce services at point *B* is the slope of the line tangent to the production possibilities frontier at that point. The rise accompanying a 1-unit run along this tangent line is a larger negative amount, which means that the opportunity cost of providing e-commerce services is higher at point *B* as compared with point *A*. The reason is that when more resources are already devoted to production of e-commerce services, moving sufficient resources from steel production to the provision of e-commerce services to achieve a 1-unit increase in production of e-commerce services entails a higher opportunity cost measured in units of steel.

Consumption Possibilities and Choices

By assumption, residents of Rustbelt engage in no international trade, so steel and e-commerce services that Rustbelt's residents produce stay within the nation's borders for domestic consumption. Hence, Rustbelt's **consumption possibilities,** or the amounts of goods and services that its residents are able to consume, are exactly the same as its production possibilities. The production possibilities depicted in Table 13-1 on page 413, therefore, are also Rustbelt's consumption possibilities.

How much will the residents of Rustbelt choose to produce and consume? This will depend on their preferences. If they have a taste for units of steel prepared in a variety of different ways, they will choose a combination toward the upper part of Table 13-1. By way of contrast, if they enjoy playing computer games and surfing the Internet, they will choose a production mix toward the lower part of Table 13-1.

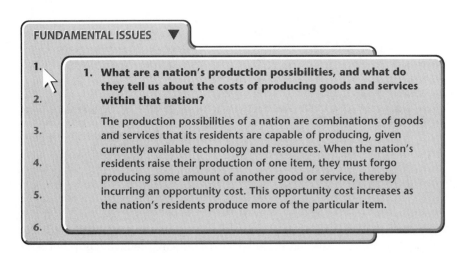

FUNDAMENTAL ISSUES ▼

1.
2.
3.
4.
5.
6.

1. **What are a nation's production possibilities, and what do they tell us about the costs of producing goods and services within that nation?**

   The production possibilities of a nation are combinations of goods and services that its residents are capable of producing, given currently available technology and resources. When the nation's residents raise their production of one item, they must forgo producing some amount of another good or service, thereby incurring an opportunity cost. This opportunity cost increases as the nation's residents produce more of the particular item.

ABSOLUTE ADVANTAGE, SPECIALIZATION, AND TRADE

A number of factors, such as differing terrains, climates, and technologies, result in differing abilities of countries to produce various goods and services. This means that some countries can produce goods or services at a lower cost, as compared with other nations. This is one possible reason for international trade.

Absolute Advantage

If a country is able produce more of a good or service from given inputs of resources, as compared with other nations, then it has an **absolute advantage** in

Table 13-2: Weekly Production in Rustbelt and Tech Kingdom without Specialization.

| Product | Rustbelt | | Tech Kingdom | | Combined |
	Workers	Weekly Output	Workers	Weekly Output	Weekly Output
E-Commerce Services	100	30	100	40	70
Steel	100	50	100	25	75

producing that item. Table 13-2 illustrates this concept. If a representative set of 100 workers from Rustbelt is assigned to provide e-commerce services using a fixed set of additional productive resources, then in a week's time they can produce 30 units of e-commerce services. Alternatively, if another set of 100 Rustbelt residents is put to work producing steel, the result is 50 units of output in a week's time. In a neighboring country called Tech Kingdom, during a given week one set of 100 workers can, using an identical set of additional resources, provide 40 units of e-commerce services, while another group of 100 workers can manufacture 25 units of steel. Thus, if the two countries do not engage in trade, the combined weekly output by the 200 workers is 70 units of e-commerce services and 75 units of steel.

Because 100 workers in Rustbelt can produce more units of steel than the same number of workers can produce each week in Tech Kingdom, Rustbelt has an absolute advantage in producing steel. By the same token, Tech Kingdom has an absolute advantage in providing e-commerce services, however, because 100 workers in that nation can provide more units of e-commerce services than the same number of workers in Rustbelt are able to produce during a given week. (There is general agreement that the United States has an advantage in offering services on the Internet, although the full extent of this advantage may be understated by official trade statistics; see on the next page *Management Online: Will Trading Services on the Internet Bolster the U.S. Trade Balance?*)

Absolute Advantage as a Basis for Trade

Absolute advantage can provide a rationale for cross-border trade between Rustbelt and Tech Kingdom. The reason is that, in principle, both countries can gain from specializing in producing the items for which they have an absolute advantage. To see why this is so, take a look at Table 13-3. Rustbelt has an absolute advantage in producing steel, and if both groups of workers in Rustbelt produce steel, the 200 workers together can produce 100 units of steel each week. At the same time, if the 200 workers in Tech Kingdom provide e-commerce services, the item that Tech Kingdom has an absolute advantage in producing, their weekly output is 80 units of e-commerce services.

If you look above at Table 13-2, you will see that specialization increases the total output of both nations. The 100 units of steel the 200 workers in Rustbelt

MANAGEMENT *Online*

Will Trading Services on the Internet Bolster the U.S. Trade Balance?

Politicians and media pundits have worried about the ballooning U.S. *merchandise trade deficit*—the gap between exports and imports of physical goods—which nearly reached $450 billion in 2000. Although a number of economists have also expressed concerns about this growing deficit in trades of goods, they also point out that the United States consistently experiences a *surplus* of exports of services relative to imports of services. In 2000, for example, this surplus was about $80 billion. Furthermore, the U.S. surplus in service trade has been expanding in recent years, and electronic commerce is adding to this growth.

Providing Virtual Services to the World

Consider, for instance, Netlink Transportation Services LLC, which is based in Rochester, New York. Netlink is a "virtual banking-services provider" that, among other things, maintains payroll records for Mexican factory workers. Using its advantage in processing data electronically, Netlink essentially exports its ability to monitor payrolls of workers around the globe.

Netlink is just the tip of the iceberg in the booming Web-service-exporting sector of the U.S. economy. Such activities contribute to the more than approximately $300 billion in total service exports by U.S. firms each year, which help cut into the nation's large combined trade deficit in goods and services.

continued

can produce each week is greater than the 75 units the same number of workers in both nations can produce when the countries do not specialize. Likewise, the 80 units of e-commerce services that the 200 workers in Tech Kingdom are able to provide in a week's time is greater than the 70 units of e-commerce services that a total of 200 laborers in both countries can make without specialization.

This means that both countries have an incentive to specialize in production and engage in trade. To see why, suppose that the countries' residents agree to trade 1 unit of steel for 1 unit of e-commerce services, and assume that the act of making a trade consumes no resources. Of course, individuals and companies must use resources when they make cross-border exchanges, so in reality there are various costs of trade. (Some of these costs are imposed by policymakers, but using the Internet has helped reduce these expenses in some nations; see on page 420 *Policymaking Online: Using the Internet to Cut the Bureaucratic Costs of Trade in Singapore and Elsewhere.*) Suppose further that the residents of Rustbelt exchange 35 units of steel for 35 units of Tech Kingdom's e-commerce services each week. From

The Big Undercounting Problem

There are good reasons to expect that not all U.S. Web-based service trade with other nations will show up in its export column, however. Consider the example of Electronic Data Systems (EDS). More than 40 percent of its total revenues are derived from services it provides to companies abroad. Nevertheless, only 2 percent of its sales are recorded as exports. The reason is that EDS has branch offices abroad, and workers located in Texas transmit services electronically to these offices, often using the Internet. These overseas offices, in turn, conduct final exchanges with the company's overseas clients. Because only final exchanges are recorded as transactions that occur abroad between the EDS overseas office and the foreign client, they are not officially recorded as service exports, even though EDS actually processes the services in the United States. All told, economists estimate that at least $300 billion of such intracompany service exports went unreported, which exceeds the total U.S. service surplus.

Another problem arises with the measurement of sales of downloadable services. Back in 1995, total overseas software sales by U.S. firms totaled $13 billion. In the most recent years, however, officially recorded software exports typically amount to only about $3 billion per year. Most economists do not really think that U.S. software manufacturers are losing out in foreign markets. What has changed is that people and companies located abroad can now download most software and charge the transaction to credit cards for immediate payment in dollars. This makes it difficult to separate out foreign software purchases from domestic software purchases. Hence, data on U.S. software service exports are probably greatly understated.

For Critical Analysis:

What can the U.S. government do to improve its trade statistics as more cross-border commerce moves to the Internet?

Table 13-3: Weekly Production in Rustbelt and Tech Kingdom with Specialization.

| Product | Rustbelt | | Tech Kingdom | | Combined |
	Workers	Weekly Output	Workers	Weekly Output	Weekly Output
E-Commerce Services	0	0	200	80	80
Steel	200	100	0	0	100

Table 13-3, you can see that Rustbelt's residents will still have 65 units of steel available for domestic consumption each week, which is greater than the 50 units that Table 13-2 indicates they would have been able to consume without specialization and trade.

POLICYMAKING *Online*

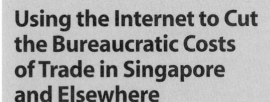

Using the Internet to Cut the Bureaucratic Costs of Trade in Singapore and Elsewhere

For decades, a number of intergovernmental and private organizations, such as the World Customs Organization and the International Chamber of Commerce, have sought to reduce the paperwork burdens that companies face when they move goods across national borders. Until recently, progress had been meager. In some nations companies still must fill out stacks of paperwork and wait for days for government approvals before they can move cargoes from one nation to another. Online processing of trade documents promises to eliminate most of the paper and to sharply cut approval times, however.

Online Trade Documentation in Singapore

In 1989, Singapore became the first nation to develop an electronic data interchange system, called TradeNet, to process documents relating to processing international trade transactions. TradeNet links importers, exporters, freight forwarders, and cargo and shipping agents to more than twenty government trade agencies. In the past, companies importing or exporting goods submitted paper applications for trade permits to each applicable government agency. Now they use TradeNet to file a single electronic document. The system automatically routs the document to the agencies that must give approval.

Before TradeNet was established, importers and exporters typically had to wait two to three days for the Singapore government to approve trade permits. TradeNet usually processes approvals within 15 to 30 minutes. Many companies found that TradeNet reduced their trade-processing costs by as much as 50 percent. Not surprisingly, virtually all trade declarations in Singapore are now processed using TradeNet.

Making Trade Paperwork Virtual

Other industrialized countries have sought to follow Singapore's example. Today, more than 90 percent of customs declarations in the United States, Canada, and nations in the European Union are submitted electronically.

G7 nations and the Asia-Pacific Economic Council currently are developing common data standards for electronic trade documentation. Furthermore, the Kyoto Convention calls on nations engaged in world trade to streamline their customs procedures by making electronic document submission available to all importers and exporters.

For Critical Analysis:

Why might the governments of some nations object to international standards requiring global adoption of electronic customs procedures?

The 35 units of steel that Tech Kingdom's residents are able to obtain through specialization and trade exceed the 25 units they could consume in the absence of trade. Furthermore, the 35 units of e-commerce services that residents of Rustbelt can obtain via trade exceeds the 30 units that Table 13-2 indicates they could have produced on their own. At the same time, the 45 units of e-commerce services that Tech Kingdom can retain after trading away 35 units each week to Rustbelt exceeds the 40 units they would have available for domestic use in the absence of specialization and trade.

FUNDAMENTAL ISSUES ▼

1.

2.

3.

4.

5.

6.

2. What is absolute advantage, and how can it help explain why nations engage in international trade?

A nation has an absolute advantage in producing an item if its residents can produce more of that good or service with a given amount of resources, as compared with other nations. This can give the nation's residents an incentive to specialize in producing goods and services for which their nation has an absolute advantage and to trade those goods and services for items produced in nations that have an absolute advantage in producing those items. Nevertheless, absolute advantage alone cannot fully explain why countries trade, because it is possible for residents of a nation to benefit from trade with another nation even when it has an absolute advantage in producing all goods and services.

Comparative Advantage, International Trade, and Electronic Commerce

You have seen that absolute advantage can provide a rationale for trade among nations. By specializing in producing goods or services for which they have an absolute advantage in production and trading these goods and services, countries potentially can consume more goods and services than they could otherwise. Absolute advantage alone cannot explain international trade, however, because countries with similar amounts of identical resources often trade with one another. This recognition long ago led economists to explore an alternative motivation for international trade, known as *comparative advantage*.

WHY ABSOLUTE ADVANTAGE CANNOT FULLY EXPLAIN INTERNATIONAL TRADE

Another way to illustrate how countries can gain from specialization and trade is by examining their overall production possibilities. Take a look at Table 13-4 on page 422, which displays Rustbelt's production possibilities from Table 13-1 alongside the overall production possibilities available to Tech Kingdom.

Absolute Advantage Cannot Always Motivate Trade

Table 13-4 indicates that Rustbelt has an absolute advantage over Tech Kingdom in producing steel. If the residents of both countries produce nothing but steel, Rustbelt can produce 1.4 million units, whereas Tech Kingdom can produce only 1.2 million units. Tech Kingdom has an absolute advantage in producing e-commerce services, because if residents of both Rustbelt and Tech Kingdom

Table 13-4: Production Possibilities in Rustbelt and Tech Kingdom.

Rustbelt Millions of Units of E-Commerce Services	Millions of Units of Steel	Tech Kingdom Millions of Units of E-Commerce Services	Millions of Units of Steel
0	1.40	0	1.20
0.80	1.20	0.70	1.17
1.00	1.10	1.00	1.10
1.20	0.98	1.30	0.99
1.40	0.82	1.60	0.85
1.60	0.62	1.90	0.67
1.80	0.38	2.20	0.24
2.00	0	2.50	0

produce only e-commerce services, those in Tech Kingdom can produce 2.5 million units of e-commerce services, as compared with the 2 million units of e-commerce services that residents of Rustbelt can provide.

It is not obvious from the table, however, that this absolute advantage will necessarily induce the two countries to trade. For instance, each country might happen to produce 1 million units of e-commerce services and 1.1 million units of steel (see the third line of Table 13-4). If both countries choose this identical production mix, it is unclear why they might want to trade—at least from the standpoint of any argument based on the idea of absolute advantage.

Thus, absolute advantage has limited usefulness in helping us to understand why many countries trade. Consider, for instance, the weekly production capabilities of two groups of 100 residents in Rustbelt versus two other groups of 100 residents in Silicon Island, an island country, given in Table 13-5. As you can see, Rustbelt has an absolute advantage over Silicon Island in producing *both* steel *and* e-commerce services. From the perspective of absolute advantage, therefore, Rustbelt has no incentive to specialize and engage in trade with Silicon Island.

Opportunity Cost and Trade

Nevertheless, there are good reasons to think that both Rustbelt and Silicon Island would gain from trading. Table 13-5 indicates that to provide 30 more units of e-commerce services in a given day, Rustbelt must reallocate 100 workers from steel production and give up 50 units of steel. Thus, the opportunity cost of a unit of e-commerce services in Rustbelt is 50 units of steel divided by 30 units of

Table 13-5: Weekly Production in Rustbelt and Silicon Island without Specialization.

▼

Product	Rustbelt Workers	Rustbelt Weekly Output	Silicon Island Workers	Silicon Island Weekly Output	Combined Weekly Output
E-Commerce Services	100	30	100	15	45
Steel	100	50	100	10	60

e-commerce services, or $5/3$ units of steel per unit of Web-based services. In Silicon Island, producing 15 more units of e-commerce services would require giving up only 10 units of steel, so the opportunity cost of 1 unit of e-commerce services in Silicon Island is 10 units of steel divided by 15 units of e-commerce services, or 2/3 unit of steel per unit of e-commerce services. Even though Rustbelt has an absolute advantage in producing e-commerce services, the *opportunity cost* of producing e-commerce services is lower in Silicon Island.

Table 13-5 also indicates that to produce 50 more units of steel on a given day, Rustbelt's residents must give up 30 units of e-commerce services, so that the opportunity cost of producing steel in Rustbelt is 30 units of e-commerce services divided by 50 units of steel, or $3/5$ unit of e-commerce services per unit of steel. In Silicon Island, producing 10 more units of steel on a given day requires forgoing the production of 15 units of e-commerce services. Consequently, the opportunity cost of producing a unit of steel in Silicon Island is 15 units of e-commerce services divided by 10 units of steel, or 1.5 units of e-commerce services per unit of steel. Hence, the opportunity cost of producing a unit of steel is lower in Rustbelt than in Silicon Island.

Now, for the sake of argument, let's suppose that residents of Rustbelt and Silicon Island are willing to exchange 1 unit of steel for 1 unit of Web-based services, and *vice versa*. Trading items at this rate of exchange is beneficial for the residents of Rustbelt, because giving up 1 unit of steel to Silicon Island residents in exchange for a unit of e-commerce services is a better deal than sacrificing 5/3 units of steel to obtain a unit of e-commerce services within its own borders. Likewise, giving 1 unit of e-commerce services for 1 unit of steel from Rustbelt is more advantageous for residents of Silicon Island, because this is a better deal than giving up 1.5 units of e-commerce services to obtain a unit of steel within its own borders.

Clearly, absolute advantage alone cannot fully explain why many countries engage in international trade. Differences in internal opportunity costs are likely to be fundamental determinants of whether countries can gain from trading goods and services with other nations.

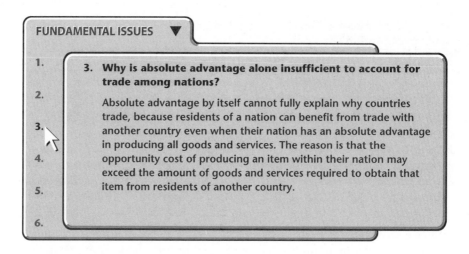

FUNDAMENTAL ISSUES ▼

1.

2.

3.

4.

5.

6.

3. Why is absolute advantage alone insufficient to account for trade among nations?

Absolute advantage by itself cannot fully explain why countries trade, because residents of a nation can benefit from trade with another country even when their nation has an absolute advantage in producing all goods and services. The reason is that the opportunity cost of producing an item within their nation may exceed the amount of goods and services required to obtain that item from residents of another country.

COMPARATIVE ADVANTAGE AND GAINS FROM TRADE

As the previous example indicates, residents of two countries may have an incentive to trade goods or services even if one nation has an absolute advantage over the other in producing the goods or services. The reason is that opportunity costs of producing goods and services vary from country to country. If the opportunity cost of producing a good or service in even a very small country with meager production of goods and services is low relative to the opportunity cost of producing the same good or service in a large nation capable of producing massive quantities of output, trade may still take place.

Comparative Advantage

When residents of a country are able to produce a good or service at a lower opportunity cost compared with other nations, then that country is said to have a **comparative advantage.** Even if a country is at an absolute disadvantage in producing goods or services, that country may still have a comparative advantage, which can induce other nations to engage in trade with that country.

To see why comparative advantage is such a crucial factor influencing international trade, consider Table 13-6, which gives overall production possibilities for Rustbelt and Silicon Island. The feasible combinations of steel and e-commerce service production for Rustbelt are again the same as in Table 13-1 on page 413. Note that Silicon Island is capable of producing both fewer units of e-commerce services and fewer units of steel than Rustbelt. Thus, Rustbelt has an *absolute advantage* in producing both items.

Nevertheless, Rustbelt does not necessarily have a comparative advantage in producing both items. Suppose, for example, that in the absence of trade both nations choose to produce combinations of units of e-commerce services and

Comparative Advantage
The ability of a nation's residents to produce an additional unit of a good or service at a lower opportunity cost relative to other nations.

Table 13-6: Production Possibilities in Rustbelt and Silicon Island.

Rustbelt Millions of Units of E-Commerce Services	Millions of Units of Steel	Silicon Island Millions of Units of E-Commerce Services	Millions of Units of Steel
0	1.40	0	0.60
0.80	1.20	0.20	0.59
1.00	1.10	0.30	0.57
1.20	0.98	0.40	0.54
1.40	0.82	0.50	0.48
1.60	0.62	0.60	0.40
1.80	0.38	0.70	0.30
2.00	0	0.80	0

steel listed in the fifth row of Table 13-6. Hence, Rustbelt currently produces 1.4 million units of e-commerce services and 0.82 million units of steel during the year, while Silicon Island produces 0.5 million units of e-commerce services and 0.48 million units of steel. Table 13-6 indicates that if Rustbelt were to increase its provision of e-commerce services by 0.2 million, to 1.6 million, it would have to give up 0.2 million units of steel, which implies an *average* opportunity cost of 1 unit of steel per unit of e-commerce services. In Silicon Island, however, increasing provision of Web-based services by 0.2 million units, to 0.7 million units, would entail reducing the amount of steel production to 0.3 million, or by 0.18 million units. This means that the *average* opportunity cost of increasing production of e-commerce services by 1 unit in Silicon Island is 0.09 unit of steel. Over these ranges of production possibilities, therefore, Silicon Island has a comparative advantage in providing e-commerce services.

Over the same ranges, Rustbelt has a comparative advantage in producing steel. Increasing steel production from 0.62 million units to 0.82 million units in Rustbelt requires giving up producing 0.2 million units of e-commerce services, or an *average* opportunity cost of 1 unit of e-commerce services per unit of steel. In Silicon Island, however, raising steel production from 0.3 million units to 0.48 million units, or by 0.18 million units, entails forgoing the production of 0.2 million units of e-commerce services, which implies an *average* opportunity cost of approximately 1.11 units of e-commerce services per unit of steel (0.2 million units of e-commerce services divided by 0.18 million units of steel). Thus, the opportunity cost of producing steel over these ranges of production possibilities is lower in Rustbelt. It has a comparative advantage over Silicon Island in steel production.

Production Possibilities and Trade

These calculations indicate that Rustbelt has a comparative advantage in steel production while producing 1.4 million units of e-commerce services and 0.82 million units of steel and that Silicon Island has a comparative advantage in providing e-commerce services while producing 0.5 million units of e-commerce services and 0.48 million units of steel. Does this mean there may be incentive for Rustbelt's residents to specialize in producing steel to trade e-commerce services that Silicon Island's residents specialize in providing?

To answer this question, note that, based on the above calculations, if Rustbelt's residents wish to obtain more e-commerce services than the 1.4 million they currently produce, on average it would cost 1 unit of steel to obtain each unit of e-commerce services. This means that Rustbelt's residents will be willing to obtain more units of e-commerce services through trade with Silicon Island's residents if Silicon Island's residents will be willing to accept less than 1 unit of steel in exchange.

At the same time, if Silicon Island's residents desire to consume more than the 0.48 million units of steel they currently produce, then on average it would cost 1.1 units of e-commerce services to obtain each unit of steel. Silicon Island's residents will be willing to offer to trade their e-commerce services for steel produced in Rustbelt as long as they can trade less than 1.1 units of e-commerce services for each unit of Rustbelt's steel. A rate of exchange of 1.1 units of e-commerce services per unit of steel is approximately the same as a rate of exchange of 0.9 unit of steel per unit of e-commerce services. Thus, as long as the rate of exchange of steel for units of e-commerce services is higher than 0.9 unit of steel per unit of e-commerce services, Silicon Island residents will be willing to trade e-commerce services for steel produced in Rustbelt.

We can conclude that in this example, as long as the rate of exchange of steel for e-commerce services is *between* 0.9 unit of steel per unit of e-commerce services and 1 unit of steel per unit of e-commerce services, Rustbelt's residents are willing to consider trading some of their steel for Silicon Island's e-commerce services, and Silicon Island's residents are willing to consider trading some of their e-commerce services for Rustbelt's steel. As long as the exchange rate of steel for e-commerce services is within this range, both can come out ahead if they can agree about how many units of steel and e-commerce services to trade.

Figure 13-2 illustrates this point. The figure depicts the production possibilities frontiers for Rustbelt and Silicon Island, based on the information in Table 13-6 on page 425. The production possibilities frontier for Silicon Island lies completely inside Rustbelt's production possibilities frontier, so Rustbelt has an absolute advantage in producing both steel and e-commerce services. Absolute advantage cannot explain trade between Rustbelt and Silicon Island.

In our example, we examined *average* opportunity costs for Rustbelt and Silicon Island in a range containing the fifth row of Table 13-6, where initially Rustbelt produces 1.4 million units of e-commerce services and 0.82 million units of steel and Silicon Island produces 0.5 million units of e-commerce services and 0.48 million units of steel. These are denoted as points *R* and *S* in the figure.

Figure 13-2:
The Production Possibilities Frontiers for Rustbelt and Silicon Island.

These curves show the production possibilities frontiers for Rustbelt and Silicon Island based on Table 13-6 on page 425. Points R and S correspond to the points contained in the range containing the fifth row of Table 13-6, where initially Rustbelt produces 1.4 million units of e-commerce services and 0.82 million units of steel and Silicon Island produces 0.5 million units of e-commerce services and 0.48 million units of steel. The exact opportunity cost of higher production of e-commerce services in Rustbelt equals the slope of the line tangent to point R, and exact opportunity cost of higher production of e-commerce services in Silicon Island equals the slope of the line tangent to point S. Because the line tangent to point S is slightly less steeply sloped than the line tangent to point R, at point S Silicon Island can produce an additional unit of e-commerce services at lower opportunity cost than Rustbelt can produce at point R. If the two nations can agree to a rate of exchange of steel for e-commerce services between the values of these two slopes, there is an incentive for both nations to trade.

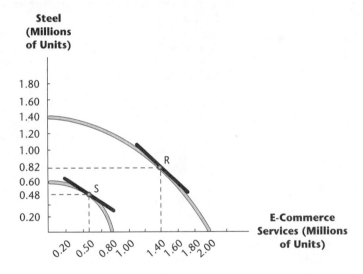

Recall that the opportunity cost of increasing the provision of e-commerce services by a *single* unit is equal to the slope of the production possibilities frontier at the current production combination. Consequently, the *exact* opportunity cost of higher production of e-commerce services in Rustbelt equals the slope of the line tangent to point *R*. Likewise, the *exact* opportunity cost of higher production of e-commerce services in Silicon Island equals the slope of the line tangent to point *S*. The line tangent to point *S* is slightly less steeply sloped than the line tangent to point *R*. At point *S*, therefore, Silicon Island can produce an additional unit of e-commerce services at less cost than Rustbelt can produce at point *R*. As long as the rate of exchange of steel for e-commerce services is between the values of these two slopes, there is an incentive for both nations to consider engaging in trade.

GLOBALIZATION *Online*

POLICY MAKING   **GLOBALIZATION**   MANAGEMENT

The Current U.S. Advantage in Electronic Commerce— Comparative or Absolute?

As noted in Chapter 2, Web sellers such as Amazon.com, and eBay.com have benefited from the so-called *first-mover advantage.* They jumped into the electronic marketplace ahead of the pack, carved out big market shares, and held onto customer loyalty by finding places among the bookmarks on consumers' Internet browsers, keeping customers abreast of new products that past purchases have revealed they might like to buy, and taking advantage of patented one-click shopping technologies. According to some commentators, the United States exults in a dominance of the electronic marketplace. Being first in embracing the Internet has made the United States such a global leader in electronic commerce, they say, that the American lead will do nothing but grow, with the United States benefiting from a long-term trade surplus from sales of information technology hardware, computer data processing, and software design.

The principle of comparative advantage make clears that being first and biggest will not necessarily translate into a trade advantage for the United States. Decades ago, any eco-

nomic pundit would have assured you that the U.S. dominance of a number of manufacturing industries, such as the oil and steel industries in which top U.S. producers had a first-mover advantage, was also unassailable. It took decades, but ultimately other countries caught up. Now the United States imports much of its oil, and its steel industry is a shadow of its former self.

Beyond a doubt, the United States currently has an absolute advantage in information technology products and services. In many areas, it also has a comparative advantage. Nevertheless, within just a few years Ireland has developed into a European center for processing information for firms throughout Europe and even for some firms based in the United States. India and Russia have already become net exporters of software code, and U.S. firms are their primary customers. Comparative advantage ultimately will play a fundamental role in determining which countries are net exporters or net importers in the virtual marketplace, just as it has in the physical markets for goods such as oil and steel.

For Critical Analysis:
What factors are likely to determine whether the United States achieves a long-lasting comparative advantage in information technology products and services?

Gains from Trade

Gains from Trade
Additional goods and services that a nation's residents can consume, over and above the amounts that they could have produced within their own borders, as a consequence of trade with residents of other nations.

Let's suppose that residents of Rustbelt and Silicon Island agree to exchange steel and e-commerce services at a rate of exchange of 0.95 unit of steel per unit of e-commerce services (which is approximately the same as 1.053 unit of e-commerce services per unit of steel). Let's further suppose that at this exchange rate Rustbelt trades 0.2 million of steel to Silicon Island in exchange for 0.2106 million units of e-commerce services (0.2 million × 1.053 = 0.2106 million).

We can use Table 13-6 to determine that as a result of this exchange, each country will experience **gains from trade,** or the ability to consume goods and services in excess of the amounts it could have produced on its own. In Table 13-6, if Rustbelt's residents had given up 0.2 million units of steel from 0.82 million units to 0.62 million units, they could have increased their own provision of e-commerce services by 0.2 million from 1.40 million units to 1.60 million units. Hence, the trade with Silicon Island entails a gain from trade equal to 0.0106 million (i.e., 10,600) units of e-commerce services for Rustbelt.

For Silicon Island, recall that the average opportunity cost of steel was equal to 1.11 units of e-commerce services per unit of steel. Hence, obtaining 0.2 million units of steel (in the production possibilities range that we considered) would cost Silicon Island residents about 0.22 million units of e-commerce services if they had produced them. Because they are able to trade only 0.2106 million units of e-commerce services for 0.2 million units of Rustbelt's steel production, however, Silicon Island's residents experience a gain from trade equal to 0.0094 million (that is, 9,400) units of e-commerce services. (For the United States, providing e-commerce services has become a source of gains from trade, but it remains to be seen if the United States will maintain a comparative advantage; see *Globalization Online: The Current U.S. Advantage in Electronic Commerce—Comparative or Absolute?*)

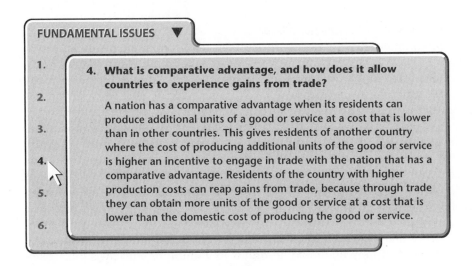

FUNDAMENTAL ISSUES ▼

1.

2.

3.

4.

5.

6.

4. What is comparative advantage, and how does it allow countries to experience gains from trade?

A nation has a comparative advantage when its residents can produce additional units of a good or service at a cost that is lower than in other countries. This gives residents of another country where the cost of producing additional units of the good or service is higher an incentive to engage in trade with the nation that has a comparative advantage. Residents of the country with higher production costs can reap gains from trade, because through trade they can obtain more units of the good or service at a cost that is lower than the domestic cost of producing the good or service.

Intra-Industry Trade and the Globalization of Electronic Commerce

Together, absolute and comparative advantage can explain why countries tend to specialize in producing and trading various goods and services. These concepts cannot, however, explain why a U.S. resident might purchase DVDs at the site of the Brazilian Web firm Submarino.com when plenty of U.S.-based Internet retailers stand willing to sell these items. Nor can they explain why residents of the United Kingdom might place an order for books at the Web site of Amazon.com when they can buy them on the Internet at British-based Waterstones.co.uk or Bookshop.co.uk. Nevertheless, cross-border trade of similar goods and services is increasingly common in both the electronic marketplace *and* the physical marketplace.

INTRA-INDUSTRY TRADE

Intra-Industry Trade
International trade of goods or services that are close substitutes.

International trade in similar goods or services that are close substitutes is called **intra-industry trade.** Examples in the physical marketplace include automobiles, computers, beer, and other goods that flow across a nation's borders as both exports *and* imports. In the electronic marketplace, intra-industry trade in computer software, financial services, and auction services is increasingly commonplace. Another aspect of intra-industry trade is the cross-border exchange of component parts or services at various stages of production prior to completion of a final product, such as when a U.S.-based data-processing firm transmits billing reports over the Internet to its Montreal office for translation into French before final transmission to a Canadian client.

Economies of Scale and International Trade

Explaining intra-industry trade flows and their implications often requires examining situations in which economies of scale are important and in which companies have some ability to determine the prices of their products independently from the actions of other producers. Recall from Chapter 2 that *economies of scale* exist when a firm's long-run average cost—the ratio of its total production cost to its output when it is able to adjust quantities of all factors of production—declines as its production expands. At most firms, continued increases in production ultimately result in *diseconomies of scale,* or increases in long-run average cost. At the scale of operations where the company minimizes its long-run average cost, it has achieved its *minimum efficient scale.* When all firms in a given industry have achieved their minimum efficient scale, then the industry itself operates at its minimum efficient scale.

It is possible that an industry limited to producing and selling only within one nation's borders may be unable to attain its minimum efficient scale. Taken alone, this reinforces why a nation might gain a comparative advantage in producing a particular good or service. It is conceivable, for instance, that several U.S. e-commerce industries might achieve their minimum efficient scale at lower longer-run average cost, as compared with e-commerce industries based in many other countries. Thus, some U.S. e-commerce industries may have the capability to expand their output beyond quantities that U.S. residents wish to consume. This could allow some U.S. Internet sellers to export their products to other countries at a lower per-unit cost.

To see why this could be so, take a look at Figure 13-3. This figure depicts a possible long-run average total cost (*LRATC*) curve for any given national e-commerce industry, under the assumption that all countries have access to the same e-commerce technologies. Suppose that in the absence of trade, two countries, the

Figure 13-3:
A Hypothetical Long-Run Average Cost Curve for an E-Commerce Industry.

Groups of e-commerce firms located in the United States and the United Kingdom produce essentially the same products using the same technology. Hence, they face the same long-run average total cost (LRATC) curve. Because the demand for the products of firms in the U.S.-based e-commerce industry is greater relative to the demand for products of firms in the U.K.-based e-commerce industry, however, U.S. output is higher, at point US, than U.K. output, at point UK. In the absence of trade, therefore, British e-commerce firms operate at a cost disadvantage relative to U.S. firms. Hence, U.S. firms have a cost advantage over U.K. firms if international e-commerce trade takes place, and U.S. firms are better positioned to expand toward the minimum efficient scale (MES).

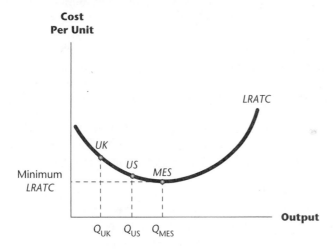

United States and the United Kingdom, have e-commerce industries that sell goods and services for domestic consumption. The demand for products of the U.S.-based e-commerce industry, however, is much larger as compared with the British market. Hence, in the absence of trade, U.S. e-commerce production initially is Q_{US} at point *US* along the long-run average cost curve. British e-commerce production is Q_{UK} at point *UK*. In the absence of trade, British e-commerce firms operate at a cost disadvantage relative to U.S. companies, simply because their scale of operations is lower.

Now suppose that consumers in the two countries begin visiting the Web sites of both nations' e-commerce industries. Even though British e-commerce firms have access to the same technology, U.S. firms immediately operate with a cost advantage over British firms. Furthermore, by expanding their operations, U.S. companies can reach the minimum efficient scale at point *MES*. U.S. e-commerce firms then could achieve a scale of operations at Q_{MES} units. The bulk of U.S. firms' sales might still be to domestic consumers, but they could export to other nations such as the United Kingdom. In the end, the United States would develop a specialization in this niche of the electronic marketplace, and British residents might do the bulk of their Internet shopping for this industry's products at the Web sites of U.S. firms.

Monopolistic Competition and Cross-Border Internet Trade

It turns out that economies of scale can also help to explain why nations with industries producing *similar* but slightly differentiated goods and services may experience international trade involving the products of those industries. This explanation relies on combining the idea of economies of scale with the possibility that competition might exist among firms in different countries that sell closely related, yet slightly different, products. It focuses on how gains from intra-industry trade may arise from cost efficiencies that producers experience and how intra-industry trade offers benefits to consumers in the form of an expanded product variety.

As you learned in Chapter 3, the theory of monopolistic competition applies to a situation in which there are many firms that sell differentiated products. A monopolistically competitive firm can earn positive economic profits in the short run, so that total revenues can exceed the opportunity cost of being part of that industry instead of another industry. Positive economic profits, however, encourage other firms to enter the industry. As they enter and capture some of the existing firm's customers, the demand for its product declines, and its economic profit declines toward zero. In the long run, the total revenue earned by a firm in a monopolistically competitive industry just covers the opportunity cost of remaining in the industry.

To see how intra-industry trade tends to affect production and pricing decisions at monopolistically competitive firms in the electronic marketplace, take a look at Figure 13-4. The figure depicts an initial long-run situation, at point N, for a domestic company in the absence of any intra-industry trade. To maximize its profit, the firm produces to the point at which marginal revenue cost equals marginal revenue. In this "no-trade" situation, the firm produces Q_N units, charges the price P_N, and earns an economic profit equal to zero. Thus, its total revenue is just sufficient to cover the opportunity cost of being in this industry.

Now think about what happens when intra-industry international trade takes place, so the firm is able to export some of its output for sale to residents of other nations. The firm experiences an increase in demand for its product, because foreign residents can now purchase it. By itself, this encourages the firm to expand its output. At the same time, companies in other countries are able to sell competing products domestically. This tends to reduce the demand for the domestic firm's product, thereby countering somewhat the initial expansion of overall demand.

Simultaneously, the availability of substitute products from abroad causes the demand for the domestic firm's product to become more elastic. As a result, after trade takes place the domestic firm ends up in a new long-run situation such as the one shown by point T. It produces and sells more output, Q_T. In addition, there is a downward movement along the firm's long-run average cost curve, so the firm experiences economies of scale. The firm operates more efficiently and on net produces more output to sell at a lower per-unit price, P_T. Consequently, the firm's domestic *and* foreign customers gain from intra-industry trade.

In fact, in the long run the domestic firm responds to open trade by cutting the price of its product. The reason is that expanding its output allows the domes-

Figure 13-4:
Rivalry and Long-Run Equilibrium with Trade in a Monopolistically Competitive Electronic Marketplace.

The initial long-run equilibrium for this domestic e-commerce firm in the absence of international trade is at point N, where the firm earns zero economic profits producing Q_N units that it sells at a price of P_N. When intra-industry international trade takes place, the firm experiences an increase in the demand for its product from foreign residents. At the same time, however, companies located abroad are able to sell their products domestically, which tends to reduce demand somewhat. The availability of more substitute products from abroad also makes the demand for the domestic firm's product more elastic. This results in a new long-run equilibrium with intra-industry trade at point T, at which the firm produces more output, Q_T, at a lower long-run average total cost which it sells at a lower price, P_T.

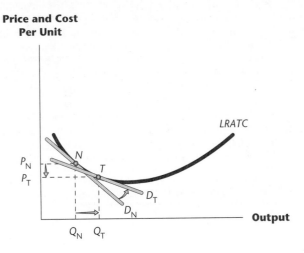

tic firm to experience economies of scale. Its average production cost falls as it increases its output. Because the firm produces more efficiently, keeping its price low to retain its customers in the face of greater competition from abroad is also consistent with its efforts to maximize profit. Nevertheless, in the long run the maximum economic profit that each domestic firm earns remains equal to zero.

In this way, intra-industry trade broadens the range of products from which consumers can choose. The opportunity to export their products encourages domestic firms to increase their production. They experience economies of scale as they push up their output, which enables them to reduce their prices in the face of competition from foreign imports. On net, domestic residents are able to consume more industry output at lower prices. So can foreign residents, where these effects are identical. Thus, both domestic and foreign residents experience gains from intra-industry trade.

FUNDAMENTAL ISSUES ▼

1.

2.

3.

4.

5.

6.

5. How can economies of scale and imperfect competition help to explain intra-industry trade via electronic commerce?

A firm or an industry experiences economies of scale when long-run average cost declines as total output expands with greater usage of all factors of production. At the minimum efficient scale of a firm or industry, long-run average cost is minimized. Any further increase in output would push up long-run average cost and result in diseconomies of scale. Opening national borders to international trade, including cross-border marketing and distribution by Internet sellers, gives a cost advantage to countries with firms that already have experienced economies of scale. The industry in this nation can more speedily use this opportunity to expand to the minimum efficient scale for output of the good or service produced by that industry. When consumers can readily distinguish among the products of different firms and firms in the industry can easily enter or leave the industry, then monopolistic competition prevails. In the long run, firms enter or leave the industry until revenue just covers the opportunity cost of being in that industry instead of some other industry. In the presence of international trade, each firm tends to expand its output to reduce its long-run average cost, which permits charging a lower price to help retain customers in the face of greater intra-industry competition from firms in other countries.

Regulating International Trade in the Electronic Marketplace

Given that consumers and many producers benefit from international trade, you might conclude that the world's nations would agree to open their borders to both offline and online sources of foreign competition. In fact, all the world's nations enforce at least some types of restraints on cross-border flows of physical goods, services, and financial assets. Undoubtedly, a number of countries will attempt to extend similar competitive restraints to the electronic marketplace.

PROTECTING E-COMMERCE INDUSTRIES FROM CROSS-BORDER COMPETITION

Rules and laws designed to insulate domestic producers from foreign competition are called *protectionist policies*. There are several arguments supporting such policies, and there are also a variety of ways of enforcing them. In some respects, such policies are easier to implement in the electronic marketplace, but in others enforcement of protectionist restraints could prove more difficult.

Arguments Against Free Trade, Offline or Online

There are seven common arguments against free trade. Residents around the world are marshaling these arguments in asking their home nations to apply protectionist policies to e-commerce industries.

1) **The infant industry argument**—As you learned in Chapter 12, the *infant industry argument* is based on the premise that industries in their earliest stages of development should be nurtured and treated differently, at least for a time, from other industries. Just as this argument is commonly advanced to justify exempting youthful industries from some forms of taxation, it is often offered as a rationale for protecting such industries from foreign competition. A nation might feel that if a particular industry, such as a budding e-commerce industry, were permitted to develop domestically, it might eventually become efficient enough to compete effectively at a global level. If some restrictions were placed on the ability of domestic consumers to import goods and services from companies located abroad, domestic firms might have time to develop into globally viable producers. For instance, a new domestic e-commerce industry that has not had sufficient time to take advantage of economies of scale experienced by foreign producers might be able to expand its scale of operations to a more cost-efficient level while it is protected from rivalry from foreign firms.

2) **Protecting domestic jobs**—A standard rationale for protectionist policies is that they help prevent the erosion of domestic job opportunities. During the late 1990s and early 2000s, many nations envied the boom in the U.S. job market fueled in part by the rapid growth of employment at Internet sellers. It was not long until the view took hold in some countries that their residents might have experienced a similar boost in employment opportunities if their electronic marketplace had been able to blossom without competition from abroad.

3) **Countering foreign export-promotion policies**—Traditionally, another important rationale for enacting protectionist restraints against foreign competition has been a perceived need to counter other nation's actions to promote the capability of their own producers to export goods and services. A number of countries offer **subsidies,** which essentially are negative taxes such as grants or special tax exemptions, to companies to encourage them to increase their export volumes. In the face of such efforts by other nations, many countries seek to defend their home industries by implementing protectionist policies.

4) **Combating dumping by foreign producers**—In recent years, a key argument in favor of protectionist policies has been the alleged phenomenon called **dumping.** This is occurs when a foreign producer sells its goods at a

Subsidy
A negative tax, such as a payment or tax exemption giving domestic firms a greater incentive to export goods and services.

Dumping
Sale of goods or services in another country at a lower price than the domestic price, or at a price less than average total cost.

price below the cost of producing the product or at a price below the domestic market price. Few exporting firms are likely to engage in dumping at prices below average production costs for very long, but it is not uncommon for companies to sell some of their items abroad at prices lower than the prices in their home markets, simply because market conditions sometimes temporarily produce such price discrepancies. Nevertheless, this does little to diminish the outcry from producers confronted with competition from cheaper imported goods that foreign producers sell at higher prices in their home countries. Already there have been claims in countries such as France that U.S.-based Internet sellers such as Amazon have "dumped" some of their products at prices lower than prevailing U.S. prices at the Web sites they operate for marketing those products abroad.

5) **Protecting domestic national security**—Even before the advent of the Internet, there had been growing concern within the U.S. government about the potential for foreign nations to co-opt U.S. information technologies for use against the United States in some future armed conflict. When a U.S. consumer calls for technical support with a problem with a personal computer, two questions that he sometimes has to answer are whether he uses the computer outside the United States and what use he makes of the computer. Never mind that if his intent is to use the computer in a planned cyberattack on U.S. interests, the last thing he will do is answer the questions honestly. The fact is that laws have required computer manufacturers to ask these questions to help gather data about international use of domestic consumers. Data indicating increasing applications of U.S. computer technology abroad have induced some members of Congress to push for toughening existing legal limitations on U.S. exports of "high-tech" hardware and software.

6) **Protecting the environment**—A number of environmental groups have traditionally opposed international trade. They worry that by increasing the breadth of the world marketplace, international trade worsens the scope for global market failures that harm the environment. In addition, environmentalists have a concern that greater international trade erodes regulatory standards as governments help domestic industries respond to heightened international competition. More broadly, a number of environmental groups contend that increased economic growth ultimately is unsustainable, and growth-enhancing international trade only speeds the pace at which the world's resources will be exhausted. Those who view international trade as an environmental menace perceive the resulting market failures to be insurmountable and the economic growth that trade promotes to be counterproductive. Consequently, these groups often lobby and protest against further efforts to expand global trade, and increasing some environmentalists openly speak of the growth of cross-border electronic commerce as just another "threat" to the world environment.

7) **Protecting domestic residents from sub-standard or harmful products**—Many nations restrict imports of goods or services because of fears that items produced abroad may be of low quality or even hazardous. Some countries require Internet service providers to block access to certain Web sites that they believe would be morally corrupting. In the United States, people who purchase pharmaceuticals online cannot buy a number of foreign-produced drugs that are disallowed from distribution by U.S. retailers. In addition, they can purchase only medications that have been prescribed by approved, usually domestically located, health-care providers. (Some enterprising companies try to use the Internet as a means of getting around such legal limitations, however; see on the next page *Globalization Online: Dodging Regulations by Making a Mouse Click Reverberate Around the Globe.*)

Ways to Protect Budding E-Commerce Firms from Foreign Competition

There are two fundamental ways that nations convinced of the merit of one or more of the above arguments can implement protectionist restrictions. They can, for instance, establish systems of **quotas,** or quantity restrictions on imported goods and services. Traditionally, it has been straightforward to impose quotas by blocking physical goods or providers of services at border checkpoints. In some respects, applying quotas may be simplified in the domain of electronic commerce, because governments could bar access to foreign Internet sellers by requiring Internet service providers to block foreign Web sites or to monitor and report domestic activity at such sites. In other ways, however, enforcing quotas in the electronic marketplace could prove more difficult. This is particularly true with regard to services that domestic residents can access or download from foreign Web sites. (Policies intended to protect national industries from "unfair competition" by restraining domestic purchases of foreign products are creating controversy in the developing European electronic marketplace; see on page 440, *Policymaking Online: That Price Is Too Low!—German Booksellers Try to Short-Circuit Belgian E-Commerce Competition.*)

> **Quota**
> *A quantitative limit on imports of goods or services.*

Alternatively, countries can discourage purchases of foreign goods and services by imposing special taxes called **tariffs.** For instance, if a country's government desired to protect domestic providers of e-commerce services from competition from foreign rivals, it could establish a tariff on purchases of products from foreign Web sites.

> **Tariff**
> *Tax on imported goods.*

Because cross-border Internet sales might be hard for governments imposing tariffs to monitor directly, it is likely they would find ways to identify these sales by tracking flows of funds. Countries imposing quotas on Internet purchases might even use financial policies to aid in enforcement. To make it harder for domestic residents to make offline or online purchases of foreign products, national governments might establish **capital controls,** which are restrictions on cross-border flows of funds or buying or selling foreign currencies. After all, if people cannot pay for imported items, it is next to impossible to obtain them.

> **Capital Controls**
> *Legal restrictions on the ability of a nation's residents to hold and exchange assets denominated in foreign currencies.*

GLOBALIZATION *Online*

Dodging Regulations by Making a Mouse Click Reverberate around the Globe

Clanton, Alabama, is located in a region of the state that is best known for the peaches grown in dozens of groves and sold in local grocery stores and fruit stands. Recently the town was the center of a high-profile investigation by the U.S. Food and Drug Administration (FDA) of alleged Internet fraud and violations of rules governing the dispensing of medications.

A Complicated Web of Web Transactions

FDA investigators had learned that a "men's clinic" in Clanton was a center for Web-based marketing and distribution of the anti-impotence drug, Viagra. Internet consumers who wished to order the medication were linked to a Web site hosted by a computer in Australia. There, customers filled out virtual forms detailing their medical history, providing legal consent, and authorizing payment. These forms were then transmitted to an office at the Clanton clinic. Clerks forwarded the medical information to a computer network operated by a group of doctors in Romania. The Romanian doctors issued electronic prescriptions to a pharmacy in West Virginia, a state that recognizes foreign prescriptions. The men's clinic then handled deliveries of the pills to U.S. residents who placed orders.

The owners of the Clanton clinic insisted this arrangement was legal. The FDA disagreed. It filed suit and convinced a court to shut down the clinic. The clinic's owners were charged with violating several federal laws, including unlawfully ordering prescriptions and dispensing medications.

continued

THE WORLD TRADING SYSTEM AND THE INTERNET: GATT, GATS, AND THE WTO

Generally speaking, economists who favor free and open international trade and the gains it offers oppose protectionist policies. They tend to promote a more broadly based global approach to international trade governance called *multilateralism*. This approach emphasizes free interaction among nations, with each country treating others equally to the greatest possible extent.

Most Favored Nation Status

Many countries, including the United States, have attempted to promote multilateralism by abiding by a rule known as the *Unconditional Most Favored Nation Principle*. Under this rule, reductions in trade barriers to a country classified as a *most favored nation (MFN)* are automatically extended to other trading partners with MFN status. The motivation behind the MFN principle is that if a number of countries follow the principle, discrimination in international trade arrangements will become less common.

Protecting Consumers or Producers?

This kind of circuitous global procedure for obtaining a good or service via the Internet is becoming increasing common as companies worldwide are testing the limits of their ability to use the Internet to circumvent national and international regulations. To those who favor regulations, many if not most of these activities constitute blatant attempts to violate laws designed to safeguard consumers.

Some economists, however, question the true intent of some regulations. They argue that many companies are simply harnessing borderless Internet connections to bypass intrusive and unnecessary restrictions. A number of these laws, they argue, are really intended to protect producers

from competition. From this perspective, all the Clanton men's clinic was doing was allowing Romanian doctors to compete with U.S. physicians, and the legal restraints on this activity really were designed to protect U.S. health-care providers from foreign competition rather than to protect U.S. consumers.

For Critical Analysis:

What consumer-protection rationales might be offered favoring laws prohibiting the activities of the Clanton men's clinic? How might such laws protect U.S. health-care providers from foreign competition?

To become a most favored nation, a country must demonstrate that it can credibly commit to conduct in international trade that other nations have also adopted. This raises an important question, however: Who is to decide whether a country has established a credible commitment to "acceptable" conduct? The answer most of the world's nations have developed is to establish global trade agreements. More recently, nations have agreed to have their trade conduct monitored by international organizations.

Multilateral Trade Regulation and Electronic Commerce

From 1947 until 1993, nations accounting for more than 85 percent of global international trade flows signed the *General Agreement on Tariffs and Trade (GATT)*. Under terms of this agreement, participating nations meet periodically to iron out disagreements about trade policies.

"Rounds" of GATT negotiations were named according to the location where they took place. The 1993 Uruguay Round of GATT, which 117 nations ratified,

POLICYMAKING *Online*

That Price Is Too Low!— German Booksellers Try to Short-Circuit Belgian E-Commerce Competition

In 2000, a Belgian bookseller, Proxis, launched a German Web site where it offered books at discount prices. The companies supplying the Belgian company's German-language books were major German book wholesalers. When the German companies learned of plans for the Web site, they refused to continue selling books to the company. Although the German book wholesalers contended that they just did not want Proxis as a client, Proxis contended the real problem was that it planned to sell the books at prices that German booksellers regarded as "too low."

To protect small German bookshops specializing in offering titles unavailable in traditional bookstore chains, German publishers and retailers have longstanding price-fixing agreements. Many such agreements exist in Germany. In fact, some of these are enforced by antitrust authorities, which the nation's laws charge with ensuring that companies' pricing policies do not cause undue harm to smaller German firms even if the result is lower prices that benefit consumers.

Proxis filed a complaint with the European Commission's antitrust department, arguing that the German wholesalers' action illegally restrained trade. It remains to be seen, however, whether European Union and German antitrust rules will be reconciled.

For Critical Analysis:

German law presumes that in the long run consumers will be hurt if lower prices available from companies such as Proxis drive rival firms from the marketplace. Evaluate this reasoning.

established the *World Trade Organization (WTO)*. The WTO commenced formal operations on January 1, 1995, and today it encompasses 136 member nations.

The WTO has several basic functions. It oversees rounds of trade negotiations and monitors compliance with trade agreements. In addition, it conducts periodic assessment of national trade policies and assists countries in developing these policies. Furthermore, it settles and adjudicates trade disputes.

The WTO also administers the *General Agreement on Trade in Services (GATS)*, another agreement reached at the Uruguay Round. This agreement covers all international service transactions except those exercised by governmental authorities. It generally requires MFN treatment for services on the same terms as trade in goods. Nevertheless, services receive somewhat different treatment under the GATS than goods do under the GATT. (The growth of electronic commerce is complicating the WTO's task in distinguishing goods from services, however; see *Globalization Online: The WTO Tries to Become a "Wired Trade Organization."*)

GLOBALIZATION *Online*

The WTO Tries to Become a "Wired Trade Organization"

Over the years, technological change in transport and distribution has contributed to international trade. Faster transoceanic transport fed the growth of cross-border trade in the eighteenth and nineteenth centuries. Air transport played an important part in spurring trade among nations in the twentieth century.

The globalization of electronic commerce promises to similarly advance international trade in this century. Growth of cross-border trade in a number of physical goods, such as books and compact disks, has proceeded apace as consumers have discovered the ease with which they can evaluate, order, and receive such products from afar on the Web. Of course, the Internet has become a channel for increased trade in *services,* because anything that can be stored as digital information can be transmitted over the Internet irrespective of national borders. Examples include architectural designs, information about new medical treatments and surgical techniques, and banking, insurance, and brokerage services.

Electronic commerce is emerging as a big problem for the WTO, because WTO rules work differently for tariffs versus quotas. Most nations apply tariffs to goods but subject services to quotas by placing restrictions on access to national markets. E-mail and Web transmissions of digital data are blurring the distinction between traded goods and traded services, however.

Currently, a commercial software package that crosses a national border on a CD is a good subject to tariffs. Is a digital download of the same software from the Internet a service under WTO rules? Or is it no different from a CD and thus a good subject to the WTO's tariff guidelines? Likewise, if an architectural firm ships drawings to a customer in another country, the drawings are treated as goods, and tariffs apply. But what if the firm sends the drawings to its client in the form of an e-mail attachment?

WTO rules concerning how to define goods and services are likely to influence choices between physical and digital methods of trade. National authorities already are having trouble keeping track of the proliferation of Internet-based service offerings. If quotas on cross-border Internet services are difficult for national authorities to enforce, then people will have a strong incentive to shift even more trade to the Internet.

For Critical Analysis:
How might governments try to enforce quotas on imported e-commerce services?

Currently the WTO settles and adjudicates disputes concerning the jurisdiction of regulations and tax policies pertaining to electronic commerce. It also enforces international standards for intellectual property rights established by the *Agreement on Trade-Related Aspects of Intellectual Property Rights,* or *TRIPS.* Undoubtedly future trade disputes arising in the electronic marketplace will find their way to the WTO for settlement and adjudication. This organization promises to be a center of policymaking activities with respect to international trade issues confronting the world's developing e-commerce industries.

FUNDAMENTAL ISSUES ▼

1.
2.
3.
4.
5.
6.

6. **Why and how do nations seek to restrain offline and online foreign competition, and what aspects of the electronic marketplace and the world trading system hinder their efforts?**

Standard reasons for protecting domestic industries from foreign competition include a desire to nurture emerging domestic industries, to preserve jobs of domestic residents, to counter export-promoting policies of other nations and alleged dumping activities by foreign producers, to promote national security, to limit alleged antienvironmental effects of international trade, and to protect domestic consumers from low-quality or dangerous products. Countries typically engage in protectionist policies via systems of quotas or tariffs. The ability to block access to foreign Web sites could help enhance protectionist efforts in some nations. Nevertheless, the increasing trade of services is hard to stop or to subject to tariffs when access to foreign sites is not blocked. In addition, multilateral efforts to regulate national trade policies under the auspices of the World Trade Organization can hinder nations' protectionist tendencies.

Chapter Summary

1) **Production Possibilities and What They Indicate about a Nation's Costs of Producing Goods and Services:** A nation's production possibilities are combinations of goods and services its residents can produce using currently available technology and a fixed amount of productive resources. Increasing production of one item entails reducing production of some amount of another good or service, which implies the nation's residents incur an opportunity cost. The opportunity cost of producing an item rises as the nation's residents produce more of that item.

2) **Absolute Advantage and How It Can Help Explain Why Nations Engage in International Trade:** A country has an absolute advantage in producing a good or service if those residing in that country can produce more of the item than residents of another nation. This can give the nation's residents an incentive to specialize in producing goods and services for which their nation has an absolute advantage. They can trade these items for goods and services produced in other countries with an absolute advantage in producing other items.

3) **Why Absolute Advantage Alone Is Insufficient to Account for Trade Among Nations:** By itself, absolute advantage is unable to completely explain why countries trade. Residents of a country can benefit from trading with another nation even though their nation may have an absolute advantage, because the opportunity cost of producing an item within their country may exceed the amount of goods and services required to obtain that item from residents of another nation.

4) **Comparative Advantage and How It Enables Countries to Experience Gains from Trade:** A country has a comparative advantage when residents of that country can produce additional units of an item at a lower cost compared with other nations. Residents of another nation with a higher cost of producing that item thereby have an incentive to engage in trade with the nation that has a comparative advantage. Residents of the country with higher costs of producing the item can reap gains from trade. By trading they can obtain more units of the item a lower cost relative to cost of producing the item domestically.

5) **How Economies of Scale and Imperfect Competition Can Help to Explain Intra-Industry Trade via Electronic Commerce:** Countries containing firms that have already experienced economies of scale will have lower average production costs than firms in other countries when international trade is permitted. These countries are more readily able to specialize in producing the good or service of that particular industry, such as an industry in the electronic marketplace. Under conditions of monopolistic competition, opening borders to international trade, including cross-border sales by an Internet seller, induces a firm to raise its output. The firm experiences economies of scale, so it reduces the price of its product to attract customers in the face of increased intra-industry competition from firms abroad.

6) **Why and How Nations Seek to Restrain Offline and Online Foreign Competition, and Aspects of the Electronic Marketplace and the World Trading System That Hinder Their Efforts:** Countries often attempt to restrict foreign firms from competing with domestic producers because they wish to foster new domestic industries, to promote job creation at home, to combat the effects of other nations' export policies and potential dumping by foreign firms, to promote national security, to curb possible anti-environmental impacts of international trade, and to protect domestic consumers from low-quality or hazardous products. To restrain cross-border trade, nations usually rely on systems of quotas or tariffs. One aspect that potentially enhances the ability to engage in protectionist policies is the capability to block access to foreign Web sites. International trade of Web-based services from unblocked sites, however, is hard to limit or to subject to tariffs. Furthermore, multilateral rules concerning national trade policies and World Trade Organization enforcement efforts may hamper efforts to extend protectionist policies to electronic commerce.

Questions and Problems

1) The United States is a major exporter of personal computers. In recent years, people have begun using other types of devices to connect to the Internet. Many of these devices are manufactured outside the United States, often in much smaller countries with relatively tiny information-technology industries. What explanation for the existence of international trade appears to best fit this situation? Explain.

2) In the city of Lulea, in Sweden, traditional industries such as mining, forestry, and steel have declined in recent decades. Recently, companies based in the area have begun competing with e-commerce firms inside and outside Europe, and Lulea has become an emerging center of the European electronic marketplace. What explanation for the existence of international trade appears to best fit this situation? Explain.

3) Some observers of the U.S. dominance of the global electronic marketplace believe that the U.S. position is insurmountable. Provide at least two reasons to question this assessment.

4) A source of conflict in international trade in the electronic marketplace is a potential trade-off between free trade and a desire to protect domestic residents from potentially harmful products, such as substandard drugs. Briefly outline one way that nations might cooperatively deal with this problem within the context of online trade in pharmaceuticals.

5) Recently Ministers of Justice of nations of the European Union approved a law that subjects anyone selling goods or services on the Internet to the rules of each of the fifteen EU member nations. How might this law discourage foreign competition even if it was not intended to be protectionist legislation?

6) Discuss why services sold on the Web are more difficult to subject to quotas and tariffs than physical goods.

7) In 2000, Congress considered legislation to make it illegal for U.S. residents to import a number of goods, such as perfumes, shampoos, and wristwatches, unless the products had appropriate safety labels. The proposed law immediately drew harsh reaction from online discount retailers, which charged that this law was a quota in disguise that would damage their businesses. In what way might this law have the same effect as an explicit quota on international trade?

8) As you learned in Chapter 12 (pp. 398–399), a few years ago the European Union attempted to require U.S.-based firms making Internet sales to EU residents to collect value-added taxes that would have applied if the EU residents had purchased the goods or services from companies based in their countries. Some economists argued that the EU was really trying to impose tariffs on U.S. exports of e-commerce products. Do you agree with this view? Why or why not?

9) A couple of years ago, the Chinese government issued rules barring foreign-owned firms from selling audio and video products on the Internet, arguing that the rules were required, in part, to "develop a healthy market" in China. What protectionist rationale does it appear motivated this policy action?

10) In question 9, what type of protectionist policy did the Chinese government implement? What possible problems might it face in trying to enforce the policy?

Online Application

Internet URL: http://www.american.edu/TED/class/karin/karin1.htm

Title: **The Growth of E-Commerce in International Trade and Its Possible Effects on the Environment, by Eric Letvin**

Navigation: Go directly to the above URL.

Application: Read the article, and answer the following questions.

1) According to the article, in what ways might international trade via electronic commerce enhance efforts to protect the environment?

2) How does the author perceive that cross-border e-commerce trade might contribute to environmental endangerment?

For Group Study and Analysis: Divide the class into two groups. Assign one group to develop a list of ways that international e-commerce trade might impinge on the environment, either directly or indirectly. Assign the other group to list ways that growing cross-border trade in the electronic marketplace might be beneficial for the environment. Reconvene the class and discuss the likely net impact of international e-commerce trade on the global environment.

Selected References and Further Readings

Mann, Catherine, Sue Eckert, and Sarah Cleeland Knight. *Global Electronic Commerce.* Washington, D.C.: Institute for International Economics, 2000.

Micklethwait, John, and Adrian Wooldridge. *A Future Perfect: The Challenges and Hidden Promise of Globalization.* Time Books: New York, 2000.

OECD Information Technology Outlook. Washington, D.C.: Organization for Economic Cooperation and Development, 2000.

Ruffin, Roy. "The Nature and Significance of Intra-Industry Trade," Federal Reserve Bank of Dallas *Economic and Financial Review* (4th quarter 1999), pp. 2–9.

Chapter 14

The Electronic Marketplace and Aggregate Economic Activity

FUNDAMENTAL ISSUES ▼

1. What is the traditional explanation of how a change in total depository institution reserves exerts a multiple-expansion effect on these institutions' deposit liabilities? ▶

2. What is the money multiplier, and why is it important? ▶

3. How might widespread adoption of digital cash affect the money supply process? ▶

4. How do economists measure a nation's aggregate output and price level, and how does electronic commerce factor into their output measurements? ▶

5. How are the equilibrium levels of aggregate output and prices determined, and how does electronic commerce potentially influence equilibrium real output and the price level? ▶

6. What are the likely effects of electronic commerce on the U.S. inflation rate? ▶

<E-Commerce Today>

In Europe, Electronic Money Is Okay, But . . .

The U.S. central banking institution, which determines the quantity of money in circulation and thereby influences market interest rates, economic activity, and the level of prices of goods and services, is the Federal Reserve System. The institution with these powers for the eleven out of fifteen members of the European Union that belong to the European Monetary Union is the European Central Bank. Well before the European monetary unit called the euro came into being, the European Central Bank made one thing perfectly clear: Electronic money should be issued primarily through regulated financial institutions.

The European Central Bank indicated that "electronic money is not widespread at present [but has] significant implications for monetary policy in the future. In this regard, it must be ensured that, in particular, price stability and the unit-of-account function of money are not put at risk."

Why was the European Central Bank so worried about the monetary policy ramifications of electronic money? Were its apprehensions justified? Given that the United States is in the lead in developing an electronic marketplace, should the Federal Reserve have similar concerns? The objectives of this chapter are to evaluate how the growing use of digital cash is likely to affect the Federal Reserve's ability to conduct monetary policy and the ways in which electronic commerce will have broader ramifications for overall economic activity.

 ## Monetary Policy with Bank-Issued E-Money

The amount of money in circulation influences the overall purchasing power available to individuals and businesses. For this reason, economists who specialize in **macroeconomics,** the study of a nation's total economic activity, focus considerable attention on how central bank policies affect the quantity of money.

Macroeconomics
The study of a country's aggregate economic activity.

MONEY, RESERVE REQUIREMENTS, AND DEPOSIT EXPANSION

In Chapter 9, you learned about depository financial institutions—commercial banks, savings banks and savings and loan associations, and credit unions. These institutions are "special" in a very important respect. They issue **transactions deposits:** *demand deposits* and *other checkable deposits,* which include *negotiable-order-of-withdrawal (NOW) accounts* and *automatic-transfer-system (ATS) accounts.*

Transactions Deposits
Checking deposits at depository institutions.

How have depository institution reserves changed in recent months? Find out by viewing the Federal Reserve's H.3 Statistical Release at http://www.federalreserve.gov/releases.

Monetary Aggregates
Sums of various groupings of financial assets reported by the Fed.

Monetary Base
Government-supplied currency and reserves that serve as a foundation for a nation's monetary system.

Currency
Coins and paper money.

Total Reserves
The total balances that depository institutions hold on deposit with Federal Reserve banks or as vault cash.

M1
Currency and travelers' checks plus transactions deposits.

M2
M1 *plus savings and small time deposits, overnight Euro dollars and repurchase agreements, and balances of individual and broker-dealer-money market mutual funds.*

Demand deposits are non–interest-bearing checking accounts, while NOW accounts are interest-bearing checking accounts. ATS accounts are combinations of interest-bearing savings accounts and non–interest-bearing demand deposits. Typically, holders of ATS accounts maintain small demand-deposit balances. Yet they may write sizable checks payable from their demand-deposit accounts, because funds are transferred automatically from their savings accounts to cover shortfalls.

Transactions deposits are fundamental components of the most common measures of the quantity of money in the economy. Hence, depository institutions traditionally represent the crucial link between policies to influence the quantity of money and the effects that these policies have on that quantity. The advent of Internet banking and electronic money offers the potential for changes in this state of affairs in future years.

Traditional Measures of Money: Monetary Aggregates

The measures of money that the Federal Reserve (the "Fed") reports are sums of various groupings of financial assets. For this reason, the Fed calls them **monetary aggregates.** Each of these monetary aggregates differs according to the liquidity of the assets included or excluded.

The narrowest measure of money is the **monetary base,** which economists sometimes call "high-powered money." It is the amount of money produced directly by actions of the government or a central bank that acts on its behalf. The U.S. monetary base is the sum of *currency* outside the government, the Fed, and depository institutions plus *total reserves* of depository institutions. **Currency** is the dollar value of coins (mainly pennies, nickels, dimes, and quarters) minted by the U.S. Treasury and held *outside* the Treasury, the Federal Reserve banks, and depository institutions plus the dollar value of Federal Reserve notes issued by twelve Federal Reserve banks. Depository institutions' **total reserves** are funds that these institutions hold either as deposits with Federal Reserve banks or as cash in their vaults. The source of these funds is the Fed itself.

A broader definition of money, a monetary aggregate called **M1,** has three components: currency, traveler's checks issued by institutions other than depository institutions, and *transactions deposits* held at depository institutions. The currency component of *M1* is the same as that used to compute the monetary base. Only traveler's checks issued by nondepository institutions such as American Express, Citibank, Thomas Cook, and other such firms are included as part of *M1*.

Another important aggregate is **M2.** Table 14-1 shows how to tabulate this even broader measure of the quantity of money in circulation. As you can see, *M2* is equal to *M1 plus* several other assets that people cannot directly spend but that are easily convertible to cash.

Panel *(a)* of Figure 14-1 compares the magnitudes of these three key monetary aggregates. Panel *(b)* shows annual percentage growth rates in *M1* and *M2*, the aggregates the Fed uses most often to track the total quantity of money in circulation. As the figure indicates, these two monetary aggregates have grown at different rates. Sometimes growth of one has declined while the other is growing more quickly. This has complicated the Fed's efforts to decide which of these aggregates

Table 14-1: Components of *M2.*

1. *M1:* Currency, transactions deposits, and travelers' checks.

2. *Savings deposits and money market deposit accounts at depository institutions.* Savings deposits are interest-bearing deposits without set maturities, and money market deposit accounts are savings accounts that permit limited checking privileges.

3. *Small-denomination time deposits at depository institutions.* Time deposits have set maturities, meaning that the holder must keep the funds on deposit for a fixed length of time to be guaranteed a negotiated interest return. Small-denomination time deposits have denominations less than $100,000.

4. Funds held by individuals, brokers, and dealers in *money market mutual funds,* which are mutual funds that specialize in holding money market securities.

5. *Overnight repurchase agreements* at depository institutions and *overnight Eurodollar deposits* held by U.S. residents (other than depository institutions) at foreign branches of U.S. depository institutions. A repurchase agreement is a contract to sell financial assets, such as U.S. Treasury bonds, with a promise to repurchase them at a later time, typically at a slightly higher price. An *overnight* repurchase agreement permits the original holder to get access to funds for one day. Overnight Eurodollar deposits are one-day, dollar-denominated deposits in foreign depository institutions and in foreign branches of U.S. depository institutions. Despite the name Eurodollar, such deposits might, for instance, be in Japanese or Australian branches of U.S. banks.

What are the latest trends in the monetary aggregates? To find out, go to the Federal Reserve's H.6 Statistical Release at http://www. federalreserve.gov/ releases/.

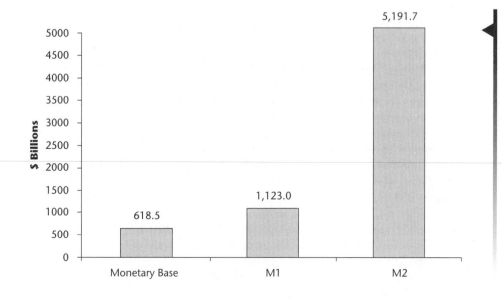

Figure 14-1: Comparing the Monetary Base, *M1,* and *M2.* ($ Billions)

Sources: Board of Governors of the Federal Reserve System, H.6(508) *Statistical Release* and H.3(502) *Statistical Release,* July 26, 2001.

is the more useful measure of money. The use of digital cash promises to add to complications that the Fed faces.

Required Reserves and Depository Institution Balance Sheets

A key reason that depository institutions hold cash in their vaults or on deposit at the Fed is that they are *required* to do so. The Federal Reserve establishes its reserve requirements using **required reserve ratios.** These are fractions of transactions deposit balances that depository institutions legally must maintain either as deposits with Federal Reserve banks or as vault cash. Currently, the Federal Reserve subjects most transactions deposits to a required reserve ratio of 10 percent. Hence, if the institution issues $1,000 million ($1 billion) in transactions deposits, then the total amount of reserves it would be obliged to hold would be $100 million. This total amount of legally mandated cash reserve holdings would be its **required reserves.**

The existence of this reserve requirement implies that a single depository institution can use any new transactions-deposit funds to make new loans or buy new securities only to the extent that it has cash reserves above the required level. That is, the depository institution can lend or purchase securities only if it possesses **excess reserves,** or reserves in excess of the reserves that it must hold to meet the Fed's reserve requirement.

Consider a depository institution with $1,000 million in transactions-deposit liabilities. To make the example more concrete, let's assume this depository institution is based in New York. To simplify, let's also assume the institution has no other liabilities and a net worth equal to zero. If it were to hold all these funds as cash assets, then it has total reserves of $1,000 million. Figure 14-2 displays the assets and liabilities for this depository institution, which are placed inside a **T-account,** which is a listing of the assets of the depository institution alongside its liabilities. Depository institutions' assets must be matched exactly by the sum of its liabilities and net worth. Consequently, this depository institution's total reserves of $1,000 million exactly balance with its transactions-deposit liabilities of $1,000 billion. Because T-accounts display such a balancing of assets and liabilities, they are often called *balance sheets.*

As Figure 14-2 indicates, this depository institution's required reserves are $100 million, or 10 percent of its transactions deposits of $1,000 million. Thus, its excess reserves are $900 million, or the amount by which its total reserves of $1,000 million exceed the institution's legal reserve requirement of $100 million. Excess reserves earn no interest income for the depository institution, so the New York institution's managers will allocate its $900 million in excess reserves to alternative uses, such as holdings of loans and securities.

Figure 14-3 shows the result of such a managerial reallocation of the depository institution's assets. Once the institution's managers have used all available excess reserves to make loans or to buy securities, then the institution is said to be fully "loaned up," meaning it has expanded its loans and other interest-bearing assets as fully as possible in the face of its required reserve ratio. For a fully loaned-up institution, excess reserves are equal to zero, and total reserves equal

Required Reserve Ratios
Fractions of transactions deposit balances that the Federal Reserve mandates depository institutions to maintain either as deposits with Federal Reserve banks or as vault cash.

Required Reserves
Legally mandated reserve holdings at depository institutions, which are proportional to the dollar amounts of transactions accounts.

Excess Reserves
Depository institution cash balances at Federal Reserve banks or in their vaults that exceed the amount that they must hold to meet legal requirements.

T-Account
A side-by-side listing of the assets and liabilities of a business such as a depository institution.

Assets		Liabilities	
Total Reserves	$1,000 million	Transactions Deposits	$1,000 million
Required Reserves			
($100 million)			
Excess Reserves			
($900 million)			
Total Assets	$1,000 million	Total Liabilities	$1,000 million

Figure 14-2:
T-Account for the New York Depository Institution.

Assets		Liabilities	
Total Reserves	$ 100 million	Transactions Deposits	$1,000 million
Required Reserves			
($100 million)			
Excess Reserves			
($0 million)			
Loans & Securities	$ 900 million		
Total Assets	$1,000 million	Total Liabilities	$1,000 million

Figure 14-3:
T-Account for the New York Depository Institution When It Is Fully Loaned Up.

required reserves, as in Figure 14-3. Once this depository institution's managers have allocated all excess reserves to loans and securities, the institution's excess reserves fall to zero, and its total reserves decline to the level of its required reserves, or $100 million.

THE TRADITIONAL DEPOSIT EXPANSION PROCESS

The New York–based depository institution in the example would be one among thousands of such institutions throughout the United States. To understand how its indirect interactions with these other institutions in the face of transactions by the Federal Reserve have traditionally influenced the total quantity of deposits in *all* institutions combined, let's expand the example.

How a Reserve Increase Affects a Single Depository Institution

Suppose that a New York securities dealer has a transactions deposit account at the New York–based depository institution we have been considering. Let's suppose that the Federal Reserve Bank of New York buys $100 million in U.S. government securities from the securities dealer. The dealer receives $100 million from that Federal Reserve bank, which the dealer places in its transactions account at the depository institution with the T-accounts shown in Figures 14-2 and 14-3.

As shown in Figure 14-3, before the dealer's transaction with the New York Federal Reserve bank, the New York institution had $1,000 million in transactions-deposit liabilities, $100 million in total reserves, and $900 million in loans and securities. Figure 14-4 on page 452 displays the situation faced by this depository institution after the dealer's transaction with the Fed. Because $100 million in

Figure 14-4:
New York Institution's
T-Account after New
York Securities Dealer's
Transaction.

Assets		Liabilities	
Total Reserves	$ 200 million	Transactions Deposits	$1,100 million
Required Reserves			
($110 million)			
Excess Reserves			
($90 million)			
Loans & Securities	$ 900 million		
Total Assets	$1,100 million	Total Liabilities	$1,100 million

Figure 14-5:
New York Depository
Institution's T-Account
Once It Again Is Fully
Loaned Up.

Assets		Liabilities	
Total Reserves	$ 110 million	Transactions Deposits	$1,100 million
Required Reserves			
($110 million)			
Excess Reserves			
($0 million)			
Loans & Securities	$ 990 million		
Total Assets	$1,100 million	Total Liabilities	$1,100 million

new funds have flowed into the dealer's transactions-deposit account with the depository institution, the depository institution now has $100 million in new cash reserves, or total reserves of $200 million. But the depository institution also has $1,100 million in transactions-deposit liabilities, so its required reserves have risen from $100 million to $110 million (10 percent of the $1,100 million in total transactions deposits). Because the institution has $200 million in total reserves but faces a reserve requirement of $110 million, it has $90 million in excess reserves. As a result of its customer's transaction with the New York Federal Reserve bank, the New York depository institution is no longer fully loaned up.

The managers of this depository institution have an additional $90 million in excess reserves that they either may lend or may use to buy securities. Figure 14-5 shows the T-account for the New York institution once its managers have reallocated its assets so that the depository institution once again is fully loaned up. When this position is reattained, the institution's excess reserves again equal zero, and its total reserves equal its required reserves, which now are equal to $110 million. The amount of loans and securities of the institution have expanded to $990 million, so the institution's total assets remain equal to $1,100, which is the same as the amount of its total transactions-deposit liabilities.

Assets		Liabilities	
Total Reserves	+$90 million	Transactions Deposits	+$90 million
Required Reserves			
(+$9 million)			
Excess Reserves			
(+$81 million)			
Total Assets	+$90 million	Total Liabilities	+$90 million

Figure 14-6:
Chicago Depository Institution's T-Account Changes After Second Security Purchase.

Assets		Liabilities	
Total Reserves	$ 9 million	Transactions Deposits	+$90 million
Required Reserves			
(+$9 million)			
Excess Reserves			
($0 million)			
Loans & Securities	$ 81 million		
Total Assets	+$90 million	Total Liabilities	+$90 million

Figure 14-7:
Chicago Depository Institution's T-Account Changes Once It Is Again Fully Loaned Up.

How a Reserve Increase Spills From One Institution to Others

For the New York institution, note in Figure 14-5 that the $100 million transaction between the securities dealer and the Federal Reserve Bank of New York has led to a $10 million expansion of total reserves, from $100 million to $110 million, and a $90 million expansion of loans and securities, from $900 million to $990 million. Yet this is not the conclusion of the story for *all* depository institutions. When the New York institution extends more loans and buys more securities, the recipients of the $90 million in new loans and funds that it pays for securities now have $90 million in funds *they* may deposit in transactions-deposit accounts at the depository institutions at which they maintain such accounts.

To make this point more concrete, let's suppose that the way the New York–based depository institution expanded its combined loan and security assets was by buying $90 million in government securities from a securities dealer based in Chicago. Furthermore let's assume that the New York depository institution makes payment by transferring the $90 million directly into the Chicago securities dealer's transactions-deposit account in a Chicago–based depository institution. Figure 14-6 shows only the changes faced by the Chicago institution after this second transaction occurs. Its transactions-deposit liabilities have *increased* by $90 million, and its required reserves have *risen* by $9 million (10 percent of the $90 million in new deposits). Hence, the Chicago depository institution now has $81 million in new excess reserves that *its* managers may use to make new loans or to buy new securities.

Table 14-2: The Ultimate Effects Stemming from the Federal Reserve Bank of New York's $100 Million Security Transaction.

Depository Institution	Increase in Required Reserves	Increase in Loans and Securities	Increase in Transactions Deposits
New York	$ 10.0 million	$ 90.0 million	$100.0 million
Chicago	9.0 million	81.0 million	90.0 million
San Francisco	8.1 million	72.9 million	81.0 million
All Other	72.9 million	656.1 million	729.0 million
All Depository Institutions Combined	$100.0 million	$900.0 million	$1,000.0 million

Suppose that the Chicago–based depository institution makes a loan of $81 million to a San Francisco–based company. Then, as shown in Figure 14-7 on page 453, this means that the Chicago bank's total reserves expand by only the required amount, or by $9 million. Its total assets rise by $90 million, or by the amount of the increase in deposits caused by the security transaction between the New York–based depository institution and the Chicago securities dealer.

The Ultimate Chain Reaction: Aggregate Deposit Expansion

This story *still* is unfinished. When a San Francisco company spends the $81 million that it borrows to purchase a needed piece of equipment, then its payment for this equipment will show up in the account the equipment manufacturer has at some other depository institution, perhaps in Dallas. This causes the reserve requirement at this new institution to rise by 10 percent of $81 million, or $8.1 million, leaving it with $72.9 million in new excess reserves that it can use to make new loans or to purchase new securities.

Indeed, this process of redepositing followed by further lending and security purchases by institutions continues through a long line of institutions and customers. Table 14-2, shows how the story plays out to its ultimate conclusion. Eventually, required reserves at *all* depository institutions will rise by $100 million. Loans and securities at *all* institutions will rise by $900 million. Total transactions deposits at *all* institutions ultimately will increase by $1,000 million, or $1 billion. (An explanation for how to obtain the total change follows shortly.)

This example illustrates how a Federal Reserve Bank of New York transaction with a single securities dealer can cause transactions deposits across many depository institutions across the nation to expand by *more* than the amount of the transaction. In the example, a $100 million reserve injection via the purchase of securities by the New York Federal Reserve bank has resulted in a tenfold increase in total transactions deposits, to $1,000 million.

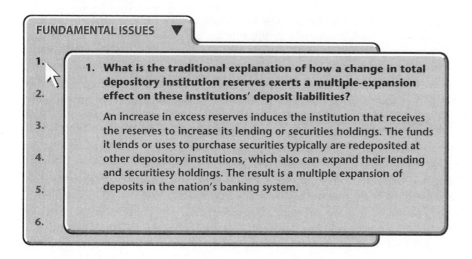

FUNDAMENTAL ISSUES ▼

1.
2.
3.
4.
5.
6.

1. **What is the traditional explanation of how a change in total depository institution reserves exerts a multiple-expansion effect on these institutions' deposit liabilities?**

   An increase in excess reserves induces the institution that receives the reserves to increase its lending or securities holdings. The funds it lends or uses to purchase securities typically are redeposited at other depository institutions, which also can expand their lending and securitiesy holdings. The result is a multiple expansion of deposits in the nation's banking system.

THE FED, ELECTRONIC IMPULSES, AND DEPOSIT EXPANSION

Why does the Federal Reserve's involvement in a transaction make such a difference in the overall quantity of money in circulation? The reason is that the Federal Reserve is the single institution empowered to create depository institution reserves. When the Federal Reserve Bank of New York buys a security from a dealer, it produces reserves that previously had not existed in the banking system. This ultimately leads to the expansion of deposits summarized in Table 14-1.

Federal Reserve Open Market Operations

When the Federal Reserve buys or sells securities in the money or capital markets, it engages in **open-market operations.** In the previous example, in which the New York Federal Reserve bank purchased $100 million in securities from a New York securities dealer, there was an **open-market purchase,** which increases bank reserves and thereby boosts the monetary base. In contrast, the Federal Reserve Bank of New York would have engaged in an **open-market sale** if it had sold U.S. government securities to the dealer. This would have reduced bank reserves and the monetary base.

To better understand the mechanics of a Federal Reserve open-market purchase, let's consider what must have occurred to initiate the first step of the previous example. Figure 14-8 displays T-accounts both for the Federal Reserve and for the New York–based depository institution. When the New York Federal Reserve

Open-Market Operations
Federal Reserve purchases or sales of securities.

Open-Market Purchase
A Federal Reserve purchase of a security, which increases total reserves at depository institutions and raises the size of the monetary base.

Open-Market Sale
A Federal Reserve sale of a security, which reduces total reserves of depository institutions and reduces the magnitude of the monetary base.

Federal Reserve		New York Depository Institution	
Assets	Liabilities	Assets	Liabilities
Securities +$100 million	Reserve Deposits +$100 million	Reserve Deposits +$100 million	Transactions Deposits +$100 million

◀ **Figure 14-8:**
T-Accounts for a Federal Reserve Open-Market Purchase.

What open-market operations has the Federal Reserve undertaken today? Find out by reading the Federal Reserve Bank of New York's summary at http://www.ny.frb.org/pihome/statistics/dmm.html.

bank purchases securities from a New York dealer with a transactions-deposit account at the New York institution, it typically makes a *wire transfer.* As you learned in Chapter 10, this is a transfer of funds—via computer—from the Fed directly to the New York bank account of the dealer receiving the funds. The wire transfer, which in this case is known as a *book-entry security* transaction, digitally transfers ownership of the securities from the dealer to the Federal Reserve. Consequently, the New York–based depository institution gains $100 million in reserve assets, while the Federal Reserve increases its reserve deposit liabilities by $100 million. But the Federal Reserve gains a matching $100 million in new assets—the securities it has purchased from the New York dealer.

Thus, a Fed wire transfer of funds used to purchase securities is the action that causes the New York institution's transactions deposits to rise by $100 million in the first place. Where do these funds come from? The answer is that the Fed creates them. Note that in an electronic environment, the Fed does not have to start a printing press to create the funds. It simply enters numbers into data files and then transmits the data to a receiving bank. The Fed effectively alters the quantity of money in circulation by transmitting *electronic impulses.*

The Fed and the Deposit Expansion Multiplier

You now have encountered the key concepts required to understand how the Federal Reserve influences the total quantity of deposits in the nation's banking system. Now let's see how to determine the *amounts* by which actions of the Federal Reserve potentially can expand, or contract, the total quantity of deposits at the country's depository institutions.

Consider once again the example of an open-market purchase of $100 million by the Federal Reserve Bank of New York. The immediate effect of this purchase is an increase in total reserves in the banking system—specifically, at the New York institution—of $100 million. Let's call a change in total reserves ΔTR, where the Greek letter delta (Δ) indicates a change in a variable. Then the direct effect of the open-market purchase is a reserve increase equal to $\Delta TR = +\$100$ million.

Recall that a key assumption for the example has been that the legal required reserve ratio is equal to 10 percent, or 0.10. Let's denote this reserve ratio as $rr_D = 0.10$. In addition, let's denote the change in deposits in the banking system by ΔD. This means that any change in required reserves (RR) in the banking system, ΔRR, is equal to $rr_D \times \Delta D$, because the level of required reserves equals $rr_D \times D$, where rr_D is the constant required reserve ratio. Also remember another assumption, which is that the New York–based depository institution and all other depository institutions desire to be fully loaned up, meaning that they prefer to hold no excess reserves. That means that the amount by which required reserves change matches the change in total reserves, or $\Delta RR = \Delta TR$.

Putting all this together implies that $rr_D \times \Delta D = \Delta TR$, so that the required reserve ratio times an expansion in total deposits yields an increase in total reserves in the banking system. Now let's divide both sides of this equation by rr_D to get an expression for the change in deposits: $\Delta D = (1/rr_D) \times \Delta TR$. This final expression indicates that the change in deposits equals a factor $1/rr_D$ times a change in total reserves. In the example, $rr_D = 0.10$, and so $1/rr_D = 10$. Hence, a change in reserves causes a tenfold increase in deposits. This explains the claim in Table 14-1 that a $100 million increase in total reserves caused by an open-market purchase ultimately causes deposits at all depository institutions to expand by $1,000 million, or by ten times the amount of the reserve increase. To determine this amount, let's use the expression just developed:

$$\Delta D = (1/rr_D) \times \Delta TR = (10) \times (+\$100 \text{ million}) = +\$1,000 \text{ million}.$$

The factor $1/rr_D$ is called the **deposit expansion multiplier,** because it indicates how much deposits in the banking system can rise or fall as a result of an increase or decrease in reserves by the Federal Reserve. In the example, the value of the deposit expansion multiplier is $1/r = 1/(0.10) = 10$.

Deposit Expansion Multiplier
A number that tells how much aggregate transactions deposits at all depository institutions will change in response to a change in total reserves of these institutions.

DEPOSIT EXPANSION AND THE MONEY MULTIPLIER

Of course, real-world monetary aggregates the Fed cares about include currency as well as transactions deposits. To see how monetary policy affects a monetary aggregate such as *M1*, this must be taken into account.

Relating the Monetary Base and *M1*

Let's define one of these, the monetary base, *MB*, to be the amount of currency, *C*, plus the total quantity of reserves in the banking system, *TR*, or $MB = C + TR$. If depository institutions hold no excess reserves, then $TR = RR = rr_D \times D$. Let's also assume that consumers and businesses desire to hold a fraction *c* of transactions deposits as currency. It follows that $C = c \times D$, so the expression for the monetary base, after making these substitutions, can be written as $MB = (c \times D) + (rr_D \times D) = (c + rr_D) \times D$. Hence, it is possible to express the monetary base as the sum of the desired currency ratio and required reserve ratio multiplied by the amount of transactions deposits in the banking system.

Let's define *M1* to be equal to the sum of currency and transactions deposits, or $M1 = C + D$. Because $C = c \times D$, *M1* can be expressed as $M1 = (c \times D) + D = (c + 1) \times D$. Now dividing by *MB* yields the following expression:

$$\frac{M1}{MB} = \frac{(c + 1) \times D}{MB} = \frac{(c + 1) \times D}{(c + rr_D) \times D} = \frac{c + 1}{c + rr_D}.$$

Multiplying both sides of this equation by *MB* then implies that

$$M1 = \frac{c + 1}{c + rr_D} \times MB,$$

which is an expression for the quantity of money given the value of the monetary base and the ratios *c* and rr_D. This expression indicates that once the Federal Reserve determines the size of the monetary base, the amount of the monetary aggregate *M1* depends on the required reserve ratio rr_D and the desired ratio of currency to transactions deposits for consumers and businesses given by *c*.

The Money Multiplier

Now let's consider how this algebra relates back to the basic deposit expansion process. First, note that if *c* and rr_D are unchanged, the above expression for the value of the *M1* measure of money indicates that a change in the money stock is induced by a change in the monetary base, or

$$\Delta M1 = \frac{c+1}{c+rr_D} \times \Delta MB.$$

Because rr_D is less than 1, the factor multiplied by *ΔMB* in this new expression is greater than 1. This means that a change in the monetary base has a *multiple* effect on the quantity of money. In fact, let's define a "money multiplier" m_M to be equal to the factor $(c + 1) / (c + rr_D)$, so that the final expression relating a change in the monetary base to a resulting change in the quantity of money is $\Delta M1 = m_M \times \Delta MB$.

Money Multiplier
A number that tells how much the quantity of money responds to a change in the monetary base.

The **money multiplier,** m_M, is the number that gives the size of the effect of a change in the monetary base on the quantity of money. To get an idea of roughly how large this multiplier might be, let's suppose that the desired ratio of currency holdings relative to deposits, *c*, equals 0.25. The value of the money multiplier would be $m_M = (c + 1) / (c + rr_D) = (0.25 + 1) / (0.25 + 0.10) = 1.25 / 0.35$, which is approximately equal to 3.6. Consequently, an increase in the monetary base would raise the total quantity of money by just over 3.5 times.

Recall that the earlier example implied a deposit expansion multiplier that was equal to ten. Why is the money multiplier in this example nearly a third of that size? The earlier example ignored the existence of currency. If securities dealers, businesses, and consumers desire to hold some cash in the form of currency, then each time a depository institution purchases new securities from dealers or makes new loans to businesses or consumers, some funds must leave the banking system in the form of currency holdings. At every step of the deposit expansion process, fewer funds are redeposited in depository institutions, leaving fewer funds for the institutions to use for security purchases or loans. As a result, the multiplier's value must be smaller when currency accounts for part of the quantity of money. (A regulatory loophole and information technology together have further complicated the relationship between the monetary base and the *M1* aggregate; see *Policymaking Online: Are Sweep Accounts Making* M1 *Irrelevant?*)

How much are balances in sweep accounts growing? Track sweep accounts balances at http://www.stls.frb.org/research/swdata.html.

POLICYMAKING *Online*

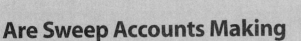

POLICY MAKING   GLOBALIZATION   MANAGEMENT

Are Sweep Accounts Making *M1* Irrelevant?

Bankers have long regarded reserve requirements as a type of tax. After all, required reserves do not bear interest, so the billions of dollars in required reserves that depository institutions hold amount to an interest-free deposit with the Federal Reserve. The Fed then allocates those funds to holdings of Treasury securities that pay a market interest rate. The Fed uses a portion of its interest earnings to fund its operations and turns the rest over to the U.S. Treasury. Hence, reserve requirements are a source of revenues to the federal government.

As shown in Table 14-3 on page 460, the official 10 percent ratio for transactions deposits in the United States is much higher than the required reserve ratios of other nations. The *effective* U.S. required reserve ratio is much lower than 10 percent, however. The reason is that a steadily increasing number of U.S. banks evade the bulk of reserve requirements they otherwise would face via *sweep accounts*.

These accounts, which appeared in the United States beginning in early 1993, shift funds from transactions deposits subject to reserve requirements to interest- or non–interest-bearing savings deposits that are exempt from reserve requirements. As panel *(a)* of Figure 14-9 on page 461 shows, total funds in U.S. sweep accounts (and, thus, total funds exempt from the 10 percent required reserve ratio) have increased dramatically since 1995. Panel *(b)* indicates that the result was a significant decline in the actual reserves that U.S. banks held at Federal Reserve banks.

By definition, funds electronically "swept" from transactions deposits subject to reserve requirements to savings deposits are transferred out of *M1*. Thus, sweep accounts tend to depress the size of *M1*. They leave *M2* unaffected, because both transactions and savings deposits are contained within this broader monetary aggregate. This helps explain why, as shown in Figure 14-10 on page 462, *M1* has recently leveled off even as the economy has grown. By way of contrast, *M2* has continued to increase steadily over time.

For Critical Analysis:
Why do bank customers as well as banks incur a tax from the imposition of reserve requirements?

continued

FUNDAMENTAL ISSUES ▼

1.

2.

3.

4.

5.

6.

2. What is the money multiplier, and why is it important?

The money multiplier is a number that determines the size of the effect on the quantity of money caused by a change in the monetary base. The reason that the money multiplier is important is that the Federal Reserve can only influence the quantity of money by varying the size of the monetary base. Consequently, the money multiplier determines how Federal Reserve policy actions will affect the money stock.

continued from page 459

Table 14-3: Required Reserve Ratios in Selected Nations.

Required Reserve Ratio for Transactions Deposits	1989	2002
Canada	10.0 %	0.0 %
France*	5.5 %	2.0 %
Germany*	12.1 %	2.0 %
Japan	1.75%	1.2 %
New Zealand	0.0 %	0.0 %
United Kingdom	0.45%	0.35%
United States	12.0 %	10.0 %
Required Reserve Ratio for Nontransactions Deposits	**1989**	**2002**
Canada	3.0 %	0.0 %
France*	3.0 %	2.0 %
Germany*	4.95%	2.0 %
Japan	2.5 %	1.3 %
New Zealand	0.0 %	0.0 %
United Kingdom	0.45%	0.35%
United States	3.0 %	0.0 %

*Required reserve ratios have been established by European Central Bank since 1999.
Source: Gordon Sellon, Jr. and Stuart Weiner, "Monetary Policy without Reserve Requirements: Analytical Issues," Federal Reserve Bank of Kansas City *Economic Review* 81 (Fourth Quarter 1996), pp. 5–24, and Bank for International Settlements.

continued

Figure 14-9:
Sweep Accounts and Reserves of U.S. Depository Institutions at Federal Reserve Banks.

Panel (a) depicts the growth of sweep accounts, or shifts of funds from transactions deposits subject to reserve requirements to nontransactions deposits with no legal required reserve ratios. Panel (b) shows that the effect of these sweep accounts has been a steady decline in reserve balances that depository institutions hold with Federal Reserve banks.

Source: OCD Sweep Account Data, Federal Reserve Bank of St. Louis, and H.Y. Statistical Release.

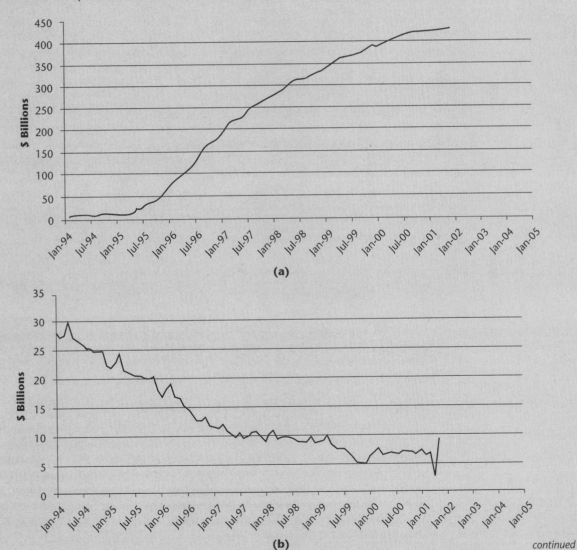

(a)

(b)

continued

continued from page 461
Figure 14-10:
M1 **and** *M2* **Since 1959.**

Both M1 *and* M2 *grew steadily until sweep accounts were established beginning in1993. Since that time,* M2 *has continued to trend upward, but* M1 *has remained level.*

Source: *Economic Report of the President, 2001, and Federal Reserve's H.6(508) Statistical Release.*

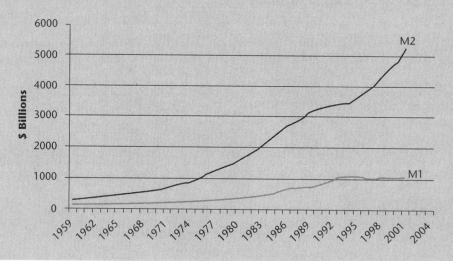

Public versus Private Money—Could E-Money Make the Federal Reserve Obsolete?

As you learned in Chapter 10, there are several electronic-money, or *e-money*, mechanisms in use or under consideration. The use of stored-value cards is already widespread in several regions of the world. Furthermore, smart cards and online banking and payments techniques may engender growing use of *digital cash*, or funds contained in security-encrypted programs contained on microchips or on hard drives.

How is digital cash likely to affect the process by which the quantity of money in circulation is determined? It turns out that there are two dimensions along which this question can be answered. The first focuses on the most immediate and straightforward effects of widespread adoption of digital cash, which are easiest to assess. The second dimension, however, leads to less clear-cut conclusions, because it takes into account a number of indirect effects the use of digital cash may have on the money supply process.

THE DIRECT EFFECTS OF DIGITAL CASH ON THE MONEY SUPPLY PROCESS

When assessing the implications of digital cash for the quantity of money in circulation, the first thing to recognize is that the broad adoption of smart cards and other mechanisms for using digital cash undoubtedly will require redefining monetary aggregates. Because digital cash will function as a medium of exchange, it ultimately will be included in the *M1* definition of money. In turn, *M1* is included within broader monetary aggregates, so *M2* also will include digital cash.

The Revised Money Multiplier with Digital Cash

Let's denote digital cash as *DC*. In a future environment with widespread use of digital cash, the *M1* definition of money will be the sum of government-issued currency, *C*, privately issued digital cash, *DC*, and transactions deposits, *D*. Thus, the expression for *M1* will be $M1 = C + DC + D$.

Let's denote the public's desired holdings of digital cash relative to transactions deposits as *dc*, so that $DC = dc \times D$. Recognizing again that $C = c \times D$, in an environment with a significant volume of digital cash in circulation, the expression for the *M1* definition of money would be $M1 = (c + dc + 1) \times D$.

To determine an expression for the *M1* money multiplier, let's first recall that this multiplier is equal to *M1/MB*, where *MB* is the monetary base, or the amount of money issued directly by the government, which does not include privately issued digital cash. Hence, the monetary base can be expressed as $MB = RR + C = (rr_D + c) \times D$. Thus, in the presence of digital cash, the money multiplier is equal to

$$\frac{M1}{MB} = \frac{(c + dc + 1) \times D}{(rr_D + c) \times D}$$

$$= \frac{c + dc + 1}{rr_D + c}.$$

This expression indicates that, other things being equal, the widespread use of digital cash—the addition of the factor *dc*, and an increase in its value as more and more people adopt digital cash—increases the money multiplier. The inclusion of *dc* in the money multiplier raises the value of the numerator, thereby pushing up the multiplier's value. If people hold digital cash on smart cards, their personal computers, or other devices, then an increase in reserves in the banking system induces an expansion effect on the volume of transactions deposits, as well as on the volume of *digital cash*.

Digital Cash in the Deposit-Expansion Process

To see why this is so, imagine that the Fed in a "cybereconomy" of the not-so-distant future buys $1 million in government securities. Transactions deposits initially increase by $1 million, but the initial recipient of these funds allocates a portion of this amount to both government-issued currency *and* digital cash. The depository institution of the recipient can lend out the remaining deposits, less an amount it must hold to meet its reserve requirement. There is a corresponding deposit at another institution, and the depositor will allocate some of these funds to government currency *and* to digital cash. This generates an initial "leakage" of digital cash from transactions deposits at each stage of the deposit-expansion process, which by itself tends to push down the money multiplier. But funds held as digital cash are included in the revised definition of the quantity of money. Therefore, at every stage of the deposit-expansion process, new digital cash is "created" as e-money included in *M1*. On net, the overall quantity of money increases with the addition of digital cash—again, under the assumption that all other things are equal—and the multiplier linking this measure of money to the monetary base also must rise in value.

It is important to recognize that the expansion of digital cash occurs via the deposit-expansion process generated by an increase in bank reserves. If the Fed injects more reserves into the banking system, then this generates a multiple increase in deposits, which, in turn, implies an increase in digital-cash holdings as individuals shift a desired portion of funds from deposit accounts to smart cards and other digital-cash storage devices. Unlike currency holdings, which together with reserves are constrained by the size of the monetary base created by the government, privately issued digital cash varies directly with extent of transactions-deposit expansion.

THE INDIRECT EFFECTS OF DIGITAL CASH ON THE MONEY SUPPLY PROCESS

This discussion indicates that, *other things being equal,* the *immediate* effect of the broad adoption of digital cash will be an increase in the quantity of money and a rise in the value of the money multiplier. Over time, however, other things will not necessarily *remain* equal. Consequently, in the long run it is unlikely that the money-multiplier implications of digital cash will be so clear-cut.

Digital Cash as a Substitute for Government Currrency

In Chapter 10, you learned about the various characteristics of checks, government-issued currency, debit cards, and digital cash. Take a look back at Table 10-3 on page 322, which compares characteristics of these payment media. Recall that if people can use digital cash, then they will compare the features that digital cash offers with the features currently offered by government-provided currency and checking accounts offered by depository institutions. This comparison will allow them to determine which alternative means of payment they will tend to replace by holding digital cash instead.

In most respects, digital cash appears to be best used as a substitute for government-provided currency. Digital cash stored on smart cards without special security features will be as open to theft as government currency, but people will protect much of their digital cash stored on other devices by using passwords and other methods that limit access. In addition, transactions involving digital cash are likely to be less costly as compared with using government currency. People will not have to go to bank branches or automated teller machines to obtain digital cash, which they will be able to download from their accounts on the Internet. Like transactions with currency, digital-cash transactions are final at the moment they are transmitted, and they are anonymous. Unlike currency exchanges, digital-cash transactions need not be conducted on a face-to-face basis.

In most respects, therefore, digital cash looks like a "better" means of payment than government-provided currency. From the perspective of the money-multiplier model of the money supply process, the ultimate displacement of a large portion of government-provided currency with digital cash will reduce the value of the desired ratio of government-provided currency to transactions deposits, thereby reducing the value of c in the money multiplier expression derived on page 463. Although this would reduce the denominator of the money multiplier, it also would reduce the numerator, and the latter effect would dominate. Therefore, a declining use of government-provided currency as people switch to increased use of digital cash should *reduce* the money multiplier somewhat.

Other Effects of Digital Cash on the Money Supply Process

In considering Table 10-2 on page 322, it appears digital cash has some features that recommend its use relative to checks. For instance, making a digital-cash transaction over the Internet is likely to prove more convenient and less costly than sending a check. Consequently, it is possible that digital cash may be a substitute for some portion of transactions deposits. Any direct substitution of digital cash for transactions deposits will not directly influence the quantity of money, however. This would entail only a change in the composition of the quantity of money in circulation.

In evaluating the effect of digital cash on the money supply process, the monetary base has historically included only government-issued money. Some economists argue that in the future it may be more appropriate to include digital cash in the monetary base. Viewed from this perspective, the monetary base would include both government-issued and privately issued forms of money. The discussion to this point has followed the traditional approach to defining the monetary base.

Online Banking and the Money Supply Process

What if online banking permits people to make payments directly from their checking accounts without the need to write checks? Will this affect the money supply process?

By transferring transactions-deposit funds electronically from their accounts via automated bill payment and other Internet-based online payment mechanisms, people will simply avoid writing paper checks. The economic implications of the transactions are identical, aside from possible resource-cost savings, to those that arise if paper checks change hands, provided the funds are redeposited in another depository institution. If normal redepositing occurs, then all that changes is the nature of the transactions that lie behind the normal deposit-expansion process. Many of these are electronic in nature, but the effects on balance sheets are unchanged. Thus, online transmission of checking funds has no fundamental effect on the money supply process.

This is true, however, only if all transactions deposits from which people can transmit funds online are maintained at depository institutions. If other, nondepository institutions find ways to issue transactions deposits via online mechanisms such as the Internet, then these deposits will also function as money that is not subject to reserve requirements. In this event, the money multiplier effectively will rise, potentially by a sizable amount. Any such activities are illegal. Only traditional depository institutions have the power to issue transactions deposits accessible either by check or via the Internet.

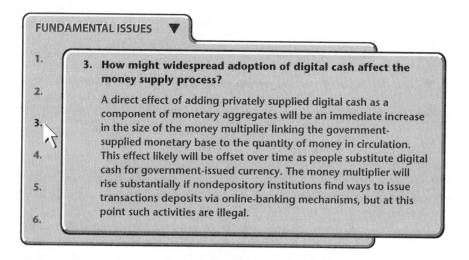

FUNDAMENTAL ISSUES ▼

1.

2.

3.

4.

5.

6.

3. How might widespread adoption of digital cash affect the money supply process?

A direct effect of adding privately supplied digital cash as a component of monetary aggregates will be an immediate increase in the size of the money multiplier linking the government-supplied monetary base to the quantity of money in circulation. This effect likely will be offset over time as people substitute digital cash for government-issued currency. The money multiplier will rise substantially if nondepository institutions find ways to issue transactions deposits via online-banking mechanisms, but at this point such activities are illegal.

Electronic Commerce, Real Output, and the Price Level

Economists have long sought to understand how the changes in the quantity of money in circulation, as well as variations in other factors such as government spending, taxes, exchange rates, labor productivity, and aggregate wages may influence economic activity and the overall level of prices of goods and services.

More recently, they are seeking to determine whether electronic commerce and related applications of new information technologies have fundamentally altered how these factors affect overall economic activity and the price level. Some economists have proposed that a "new economy" has emerged as a result of widespread adoption of these information technologies.

ELECTRONIC COMMERCE, NATIONAL INCOME, AND PRICE DEFLATORS

To determine how various factors relate to the economy's overall performance, economists must first have reliable measures of economic activity. The most important of these is *gross domestic product.*

Measuring Economic Activity: National Income and Product

The primary measure of economic activity during a given interval is the total value, computed using current market prices, of the output of *final* goods and services produced by businesses during that period. This is called the economy's **gross domestic product (GDP).**

    Because it measures only the value of final goods and services, GDP does not include all economic transactions, such as the internal e-business operations within corporations, which take place during a given period. A large portion of B2B commerce is not included in GDP, because many B2B transactions entail exchanges of intermediate inputs that are included in final goods and services. Nearly all C2C transactions, such as those conducted at Web auction sites, are excluded from GDP because they are exchanges of second-hand goods produced in an earlier period. The services that B2B and C2C sites provide to businesses and consumers that wish to exchange goods and services on the Internet are part of GDP, however. Likewise the bulk of B2C e-commerce retail transactions are part of GDP, because they typically entail purchases of final goods and services. Fees that all e-commerce firms, including financial sites and Internet banks, earn from providing services are also included in GDP. (An important component of GDP is business investment, but economists continue to struggle with how to measure investment in today's information-intensive economy; see on the next page *Management Online: New Math for the New Economy.*)

    Businesses earn revenues on the output they sell to consumers, other businesses, and the government. These revenues flow to the individuals who provide *factors of production* to businesses, which the businesses use to produce the goods and services they sell. Factors of production include labor, land, capital, and entrepreneurship. The earnings of the individuals who supply these factors of production are wages and salaries, rents, interest and dividends, and profits. Adding together all these receipts for all individuals in the economy yields the total income earnings of all individuals, or *national income.*

    This means that the total value of output that businesses produced becomes the combined income of all individuals. Consequently, abstracting from minor accounting details distinguishing the government's two measures in the U.S. income

Gross Domestic Product (GDP)
The value, tabulated using market prices, of all final goods and services produced during a given period.

How much is electronic commerce contributing to U.S. national income? Find out by signing up for e-mail updates at http://www.census.gov/ mrts/www/ecom.html.

MANAGEMENT *Online*

New Math for the New Economy

Before 1999, the Bureau of Economic Analysis (BEA), a unit of the Department of Commerce that tabulates GDP statistics, treated business expenses on computer software as "purchased inputs." This meant software was simply an expense item, much like newsprint is an expense for newspaper publishers.

Businesspeople had argued for years that software is a type of capital—a good that depreciates but nonetheless can be used for years and that businesses use to produce other goods. The rapid development of electronic commerce in the 1990s finally convinced the BEA to listen to what businesspeople had been saying. Since 1999, the BEA has included all business software purchases as a category within business investment expenditures. Today business spending on software is treated as a final purchase and is included in GDP.

When the BEA made this change, it also revised prior data for the 1980s and 1990s. One result was a noticeably higher rate of growth of *business productivity*—the additional output of goods and services that businesses can produce from employing additional inputs—for the 1990s, from 1.4 percent per year to an annual growth rate of very nearly 2 percent. For the period 1997–1999, the annual business productivity growth rate was revised upward even more dramatically, from 1.9 percent to 2.6 percent.

For Critical Analysis:

Why do you suppose that the BEA originally hesitated to count spending on software as business investment?

---

and product accounting procedures, *national income and GDP must be identical.* This means that for all intents and purposes, GDP also is a good measure of the total income receipts of all individuals.

Real versus Nominal National Income

As shown in Figure 14-11, U.S. GDP has persistently increased over time. It has done so for two reasons. One reason is that the economy has grown, meaning that businesses have expanded their resources and found ways to increase their production of goods and services. Another reason is that prices have risen over time. Such overall price increases, or inflation, have increased the *measured value* of income and output in the economy. This means that you cannot necessarily look at Figure 14-11 and conclude that the actual production of goods and services consistently has increased in the United States. Some portion of the general rise in GDP shown in the figure occurred simply because prices rose over time as well. Using GDP as a measure of actual productive activity in the economy would lead to an overstatement of the true volume of such activity when inflation occurs.

To see why the distinction must be made, think about a situation in which an employer were to double the wages you receive for providing labor services. This would increase your measured income, but if the overall prices that you have to

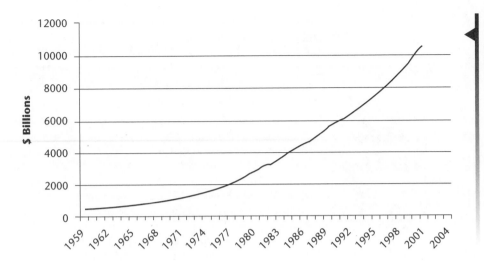

**Figure 14-11:
U.S. Gross Domestic
Product.**

*The dollar value of newly
produced goods and services
within U.S. borders has
increased each year because
actual production has risen
and because the price level has
increased.*

Sources: *Economic Report of
the President,* 2001, and
Economic Indicators, various
issues.

pay to purchase goods and services also were to double, you would be no better
off. Likewise, if total national income as measured by GDP were to double simply
because prices increased by a factor of two, the total volume of economic activity
really would not have changed.

To avoid this problem, economists use an adjusted measure of GDP, called
real gross domestic product. This measure of the total production of final output accounts for the effects of price changes and reflects more accurately the economy's true volume of productive activity. Because the flow of final product makes
its way to individuals as a flow of total national income, real GDP is a measure of
real national income, or the amount of total income that individuals receive net of
artificial increases resulting from inflation.

To distinguish real GDP from the unadjusted GDP measure, economists refer
to unadjusted GDP as **nominal gross domestic product,** or GDP "in name
only" because it has been measured in current dollar terms with no adjustment
for the effects of price changes. Likewise, they refer to unadjusted national income
as *nominal national income,* or simply *nominal income.* (The weight of the real goods
and services produced and traded has declined in recent years, with interesting
implications; see on the next page *Policymaking Online: Electronic Commerce Makes
U.S. Output Weigh a Lot Less.*)

**Real Gross Domestic
Product (real GDP):**
*A price-adjusted measure of
aggregate output, or nominal
GDP divided by the GDP price
deflator.*

**Nominal Gross Domestic
Product (nominal GDP)**
*The value of final production of
goods and services calculated
in current dollar terms with no
adjustment for effects of price
changes.*

The Price Level

Real income measures the economy's true volume of production, so multiplying
real income by a measure of the overall level of prices yields the value of real income measured in current prices, which is nominal income. That is, if y denotes
real income and P is a measure of the overall price level, then total nominal income, denoted Y, is equal to $Y = y \times P$.

POLICYMAKING *Online*

POLICY MAKING   GLOBALIZATION   MANAGEMENT

Electronic Commerce Makes U.S. Output Weigh a Lot Less

According to the Federal Reserve, the U.S. economy has been "downsizing" in an important sense. It is literally getting lighter. This, Fed officials argue, has important implications.

Reducing the Average Weight of a Unit of Real GDP

What Fed policymakers have in mind is that a dollar's worth of the goods and services produced in the U.S. economy weighs much less than it used to, even after adjusting for inflation. For instance, the materials used to build a new bridge over a river today weigh much less than a bridge over the same river erected in the late nineteenth century. With modern synthetic fibers, clothes weigh less than they once did. In addition, telephones and televisions weigh a fraction of what they did decades ago. Furthermore, an ever-increasing proportion of U.S. production includes items that don't weigh anything at all, such as consulting services, psychotherapy, e-mail, and online information and services provided in the electronic marketplace.

The total output of goods and services is about five times as great as it was 50 years ago. But Fed officials note the physical weight of U.S. gross domestic product is only slightly higher today than it was 50 or even 100 years ago, because only a small portion represents growth in the tonnage of physical materials such as oil, coal, ores, wood, and raw chemicals.

The remainder represents new insights into how to rearrange those physical materials into new forms, many of which are virtual goods and services exchanged on the Internet.

The "Weightiness" of Traded Output

Fed policymakers have used a statistic tabulated by the U.S. Commerce Department to document the reduced average weight of goods and services. This statistic is the weight of imports and exports moving across U.S. borders by ship or air. It turns out that the value of a pound of U.S. imports and exports has risen 4 percent per year over the past 30 years, after adjusting for inflation. In other words, a dollar's worth of today's imports and exports weighs about 30 percent of what a dollar's worth of imports and exports weighed in 1969.

The lighter a nation's output is, the easier it is to move. A typical newspaper weighs 8 to 15 ounces, and each copy has to be moved from a printing plant to the doorstep of a subscriber's home. Many newspaper publishers now sell the same information online in a form that does not weigh anything and costs next to nothing to move via the Internet. E-commerce firms that sell downloadable products provide truly weightless output. The overall contribution of the electronic marketplace to the ever-lighter output of U.S. industry, Fed officials observe, may help explain why there is so much more international trade today as compared with years past.

For Critical Analysis:

How could a reduction in the weight of a nation's output help contribute to an increase in the nation's total production?

GDP Price Deflator

A measure of the overall price level; equal to nominal GDP divided by real GDP.

Because economists measure real income using real GDP and nominal income using nominal GDP, the factor P is called the **GDP price deflator,** or simply the *GDP deflator*. It is called a deflator because the expression for nominal income, $Y = y \times P$, can be rearranged to obtain $y = Y/P$. That is, real income y is equal to nominal income Y adjusted by dividing by, or "deflating" by the factor P. For instance, suppose that nominal GDP, Y, is equal to $10 trillion but that the value of the GDP deflator, P, is equal to 2. Then computing real GDP would entail deflating the $10 trillion figure for nominal GDP by a factor of one-half. Dividing $10 trillion by 2 yields a $5 trillion figure for real GDP.

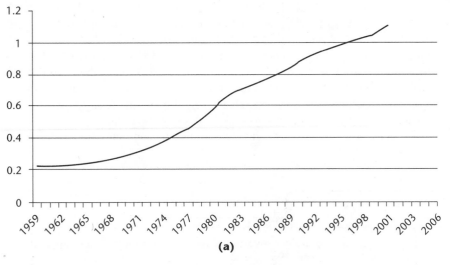

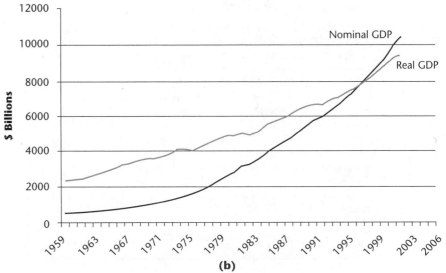

**Figure 14-12:
The GDP Deflator and
Real and Nominal GDP.**

*Panel (a) shows annual
values of the GDP deflator.
Panel (b) displays nominal
GDP (the same chart as
Figure 14-11 on page 469)
and real GDP. As panel (b)
indicates, because real GDP
accounts for the effects of
price changes, it exhibits
less growth from year to
year.*

Sources: Economic
Report of the President,
2001, and *Economic
Indicators,* various issues.

Denoting a Base Year

A value of 2 for *P* means little unless there is a reference point for interpreting
what this value means. Economists do this by defining a **base year** for the GDP
deflator, which is a year in which nominal income is equal to real income ($Y = y$),
so the GDP deflator's value is one ($P = 1$). Consequently, if the base year were, say,
1973, and the value of *P* in 2003 were equal to 2, then this indicates that between
1973 and 2003 the overall level of prices would have doubled.

Currently, the U.S. government uses 1996 as the base year for the GDP deflator. Panel *(a)* of Figure 14-12 shows the values of the GDP deflator since 1959. As
you can see, the overall level of prices increased by almost a factor of 5, from 0.22
to more than 1.1, between 1959 and 2001. This means that an item that required

Base Year

*A reference year for price-level
comparisons, which is a year in
which nominal GDP is equal to
real GDP, so that the GDP
deflator's value is equal to one.*

$1 to purchase in 1959 would have required more than $5 to purchase in 2001. Alternatively stated, $5 in 2001 would have purchased less than the equivalent amount of goods and services that $1 would have purchased in 1959.

Panel *(b)* of Figure 14-12 plots real and nominal GDP figures since 1959. Note that in 1996 nominal and real GDP are equal because 1996 is the base year in which $P = 1$ so that $Y = y$. Clearly, adjusting for price changes has a significant effect on how to interpret GDP numbers. This is why it is so important to use the GDP deflator to convert nominal GDP into real GDP. Only the latter measure can provide meaningful comparisons of the actual volumes of economic activity over time.

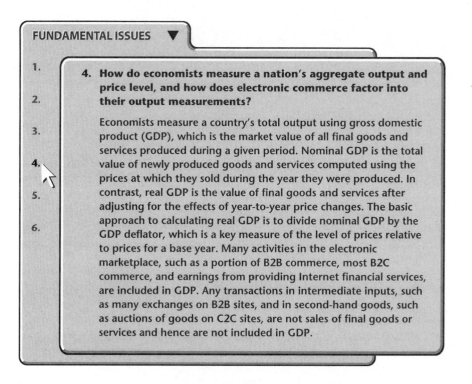

FUNDAMENTAL ISSUES ▼

1.

2.

3.

4.

5.

6.

4. How do economists measure a nation's aggregate output and price level, and how does electronic commerce factor into their output measurements?

Economists measure a country's total output using gross domestic product (GDP), which is the market value of all final goods and services produced during a given period. Nominal GDP is the total value of newly produced goods and services computed using the prices at which they sold during the year they were produced. In contrast, real GDP is the value of final goods and services after adjusting for the effects of year-to-year price changes. The basic approach to calculating real GDP is to divide nominal GDP by the GDP deflator, which is a key measure of the level of prices relative to prices for a base year. Many activities in the electronic marketplace, such as a portion of B2B commerce, most B2C commerce, and earnings from providing Internet financial services, are included in GDP. Any transactions in intermediate inputs, such as many exchanges on B2B sites, and in second-hand goods, such as auctions of goods on C2C sites, are not sales of final goods or services and hence are not included in GDP.

AGGREGATE DEMAND, AGGREGATE SUPPLY, AND WHERE ELECTRONIC COMMERCE FITS IN

How might electronic commerce affect a nation's income and prices? To move toward answering this question, let's first consider how a nation's total output of goods and services and its price level are determined.

Aggregate Demand

One of the curves shown in Figure 14-13 is a downward-sloping relationship between the price level P and the amount of real output y that consumers and busi-

Figure 14-13:
Aggregate Demand, Aggregate Supply, and the Equilibrium Price Level.

When the price level rises, the real purchasing power of the quantity of money in circulation rises, there is upward pressure on interest rates, and the prices of domestic goods and services rise relative to the prices of foreign goods and services. These three factors tend to reduce total desired spending on real output, so the aggregate demand (AD) curve slopes downward. Changes in the quantity of money, government spending, taxes, and the value of the dollar can shift the aggregate demand curve. In the long run, all input and output prices adjust equiproportionately, so that a change in the price level brings about no net change in real output, which implies that the long-run aggregate supply (LRAS) curve is vertical. In the short run, however, wages and other input prices do not necessarily rapidly adjust to changes in output prices, so that real output increases following a rise in the price level and the short-run aggregate supply (SRAS) curve slopes upward. At the equilibrium price level P_1, the total quantity of real output produced by firms equals the total quantity of desired spending, y_1.

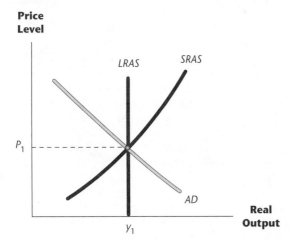

nesses desire to purchase. This relationship is the economy's **aggregate demand (AD) curve,** which depicts the various combinations of price levels, P, and corresponding levels of real output of goods and services, y, which people are willing to purchase. The amount of real output demanded declines as the price level rises, so the aggregate demand curve slopes downward, as shown in the figure.

There are three reasons the aggregate demand curve slopes downward. First, a rise in the price level reduces the real quantity of money in circulation, thereby inducing individuals and businesses to cut back on their purchases of real output. Second, there is a fall in real liquidity in the economy caused by a price-level increase. As a result, there is an excess quantity of real liquidity demanded, and market interest rates tend to rise, which gives households and firms an incentive to reduce expenditures financed by borrowing. Third, an increase in the prices of domestically produced goods and services makes them more expensive to residents of other nations. Hence, foreign purchases of exports decline, which contributes to an overall reduction in spending on domestically produced output.

Aggregate Demand (AD) Curve
Total levels of desired spending on real output at all possible price levels for the economy.

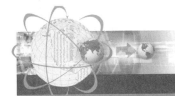

POLICYMAKING *Online*

Will the Fed Lose Its Ability to Affect Aggregate Demand in a Digital Economy?

A key channel through which monetary policy actions affect aggregate demand is by altering market interest rates and thereby influencing the willingness of individuals and firms to borrow and spend at any given price level. Thus, a significant policy issue is whether the advent of digital cash will make it impossible for the Fed to continue to influence market interest rates.

Interest Rate Determination

The Fed currently establishes an *interest rate target* and varies the quantity of money in circulation as required to achieve its target for the general level of interest rates. Figure 14-14 shows how the Fed does this. The downward-sloping curve depicts the total *demand for money* in the economy. People hold money to engage in transactions, but they also hold money as an alternative to holding other financial assets. There is a relatively low risk to holding money, but most forms of money pay zero or very low interest rates. By holding money people incur an opportunity cost equal to the market interest rate that they could have earned by holding a financial asset such as a Treasury security.

The vertical curve is the economy's *supply of money*. As you learned earlier in this chapter, the Fed influences the

quantity of money supplied, which initially equals the money multiplier m_M^1 times the monetary base MB_1, by varying the monetary base using open-market operations. The interest rate adjusts to ensure that individuals and firms are willing to hold this quantity of money. Hence, at the initial equilibrium point A in Figure 14-14, people are willing to hold the quantity of money $M_1 = m_M^1 \times MB_1$ as long as the interest rate equals r_1.

Targeting the Interest Rate with an Unstable Money Multiplier

As discussed earlier, the widespread adoption of digital cash is likely to have both direct and indirect effects on the money supply process. The net result is likely to be a net increase in the size of the money multiplier, such as the increase to m_M^2 shown in the figure, which causes the total quantity of money to rise to $M_2 = m_M^2 \times MB_1$. If this were to occur, there would be an excess quantity of money supplied at the interest rate r_1, so the interest rate would tend to fall toward a new equilibrium value r_2.

In principle, all the Fed would have to do to keep the interest rate at its original level would be to reduce the monetary base to MB_2 and shift the money supply curve back to its original position, at the initial quantity of money $M_1 = m_M^2 \times MB_2$. There are two problems, however. First, there are likely to be a series of changes in the money multiplier caused by greater adoption of digital cash, and these changes are likely to be hard to predict. Second, if the money multiplier rises by a sizable amount, the Fed may have to shrink the monetary

continued

An increase in aggregate demand, which corresponds to a rightward shift in the aggregate demand curve, results from any factor contributing to higher total expenditures on goods and services. Examples include an increase in government spending or a fall in the value of the dollar that makes U.S. goods and services less expensive to foreign residents and thereby boosts their spending on export goods. A rise in the quantity of money can exert a particularly strong effect on aggregate

Figure 14-14:
Targeting the Interest Rate.

The demand-for-money curve slopes downward, because as the interest rate increases, the opportunity cost of holding money instead of interest-bearing assets rises, inducing people to cut back on their money holdings. The position of the vertical money supply curve is determined by the quantity of money supplied by the Federal Reserve, which equals the money multiplier times the monetary base. A widespread increase in the use of digital cash will tend to cause the money multiplier to increase, from m_M^1 to m_M^2. Other things equal, this would push the interest rate downward, from r_1 toward r_2. To keep the interest rate at a target level equal to r_1, the Federal Reserve would need to reduce the monetary base, from MB_1 to MB_2, and thereby reverse the initial rightward shift of the money supply curve.

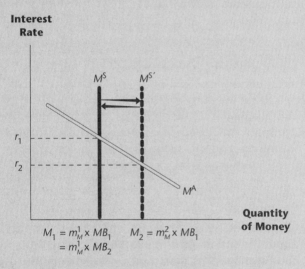

base considerably to maintain its interest rate target. A smaller and smaller quantity of currency and total reserves may become associated with an ever-larger quantity of currency, checking- and debit-account deposits, and digital cash.

For Critical Analysis:
What would be the pros and cons of targeting the quantity of money instead of interest rates as digital cash becomes more widespread?

demand, which is why the Federal Reserve is so concerned about the ramifications of digital cash with respect to its efforts to influence the amount of money in circulation. (A fundamental concern for monetary policy is whether the Fed can continue to have leverage over interest rates; see *Policymaking Online: Will the Fed Lose Its Ability to Affect Aggregate Demand in a Digital Economy?*)

Aggregate Supply

Consider an environment in which wages and prices are completely flexible, in which the quantities of available factors of production are fixed, and in which the technology for using these factors to produce goods and services is not undergoing rapid changes. In such a setting, if some business firms were to attempt to expand their production of goods and services by bidding factors of production such as labor away from other firms, then they could do so only by offering higher wages. This would enable these business firms to produce more goods and services, but the remaining firms that lost some of their labor resources would produce fewer goods and services and would have to pay higher wages to retain many of their workers. In addition, because labor costs would increase at all firms, the prices of their products would increase.

The result of this process would be that wages and prices would increase while output of goods and services would rise at some businesses and decline at others. On net, total real output would be unchanged, even though the level of prices would have increased. Figure 14-13 on page 473, displays the resulting vertical **aggregate supply curve,** which depicts the levels of aggregate real output that all businesses are willing and able to produce, y, at various levels of prices, P, the amount of real output that can be produced using all available factors of production and given time for the prices of all inputs and outputs to adjust. The vertical aggregate supply curve is the economy's *long-run aggregate supply (LRAS) curve,* which shows that given the economy's productive capabilities and complete flexibility of all wages and prices, firms produce a fixed quantity of real output irrespective of the price level.

Aggregate Supply Curve
Total real output of goods and services produced by all firms in the economy at all possible levels of prices.

The aggregate supply curve is vertical only when the prices of all factors of production and goods and services are fully adjustable. This is likely to be true over a long-run horizon. In the short run, however, many prices are "sticky," meaning they do not change much or quickly in response to changes in demand conditions.

One key source of price stickiness is inflexibility of wages, which compose about three-fourths of the production costs for a typical business. If wages are not very flexible, perhaps because of minimum wage laws or labor contracts, when the price level increases wages and other input prices do not necessarily adjust in equal proportion. As a result, the prices that firms receive for the output they sell increase at a faster pace than do wages and other input prices. Hence, firms' revenues from increasing output outstrip their costs, which gives them an incentive to expand output.

In the short run, therefore, an increase in the price level causes a rise in total real output. Consequently, the *short-run aggregate supply (SRAS) curve* slopes upward, as shown in Figure 14-13. In addition, the aggregate supply curve has a convex shape, because there is a capacity limit on how much any nation can boost its output beyond the long-run level determined by the *LRAS* curve.

The Equilibrium Price Level

Figure 14-13 on page 473 also displays the determination of the equilibrium price level, denoted P_1. Because the *SRAS* and *LRAS* curves cross the aggregate demand curve at this price level, it is both the short-run and long-run equilibrium price level. At this level of prices, all individuals and businesses are satisfied purchasing the total amount of real final output businesses produce given the available quantities of factors of production. If the price level were greater than P_1, then consumers and businesses would be unwilling to buy all the output produced with available resources. Thus, the price level would fall back toward P_1.

In contrast, if the price level were below P_1, then consumers and businesses would desire to purchase a greater volume of aggregate output than businesses could produce given the available amounts of factors of production. They would bid against each other to try to purchase desired quantities of goods and services, and the general level of prices would rise toward P_1.

How the Electronic Marketplace Fits into the Aggregate Demand–Aggregate Supply Model

There are two ways that e-business and e-commerce applications of information technologies might directly influence the price level and real output of goods and services. First, the availability of a broader range of shopping choices in the electronic marketplace could affect the tastes and preferences of consumers. As a result, they might increase their total spending at any given price level, causing the aggregate demand curve to shift rightward, as shown in panel *(a)* of Figure 14-15 on page 478, as the shift from AD_1 to AD_2.

In addition, the application of e-business methods, the use of B2B exchanges to reduce expenses on input purchases, and the like undoubtedly enhance business productivity. (For several years, however, there was considerable doubt about whether e-business and e-commerce applications would actually raise business productivity; see on page 479 *Management Online: Was There a Productivity Paradox?*) Panel *(b)* shows an apparent relationship between the extent of computer use and productivity growth, which increases the capability of businesses to produce more goods and services at any given price level, thereby shifting both the short-run and long-run aggregate supply curves rightward by the same distance, from $SRAS_1$ to $SRAS_2$ and from $LRAS_1$ to $LRAS_2$.

Figure 14-15 shows a fundamental prediction economists can make using the aggregate demand–aggregate supply framework. The development of the electronic marketplace should lead to both a short-run and long-run increase in real output of goods and services. The implications for the equilibrium price level, however, are not clear-cut. Let's next turn our attention to how the growth of electronic commerce is likely to influence year-to-year changes in the price level, or inflation.

Figure 14-15:
**Possible Aggregate Demand and Aggregate Supply Implications of Growth
in the Electronic Marketplace.**

*E-commerce and e-business applications throughout the economy can have two possible effects.
First, the wider availability of more products online as well as offline could induce consumers to
raise their desired spending at any given price level, causing the aggregate demand curve to shift
to the right, from AD₁ to AD₂ in panel (a). Second, business productivity could increase. As panel
(b) shows, countries with greater per capita computer use have experienced larger boosts in
productivity. This enables firms to produce more real output at any given price level, resulting in
rightward shifts of both the short-run and long-run aggregate supply curves as shown in panel
(a). On net, the equilibrium level of real output should unambiguously increase. The net effect on
the equilibrium price level is uncertain. In this example it remains unchanged.*

Source: Casey Cornwell and Bharat Trehan, "Information Technology and Productivity,"
FRSB Economic Letter, Federal Resource Bank of San Francisco, No. 2000–34, November 10,
2000.

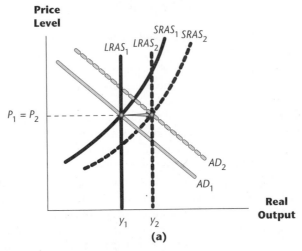

(a)

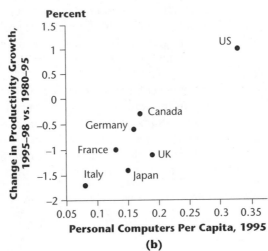

(b)

MANAGEMENT *Online*

POLICY MAKING   GLOBALIZATION   **MANAGEMENT**

Was There a Productivity Paradox?

In a 1987 book review, Nobel economist Robert Solow offered the aside, "You can see the computer age everywhere but in the productivity statistics."

The Productivity Paradox

Solow's comment summarized what economists called the "productivity paradox": the apparent failure of many indus-

tries to achieve significant productivity enhancements from information technologies.

The service-sector productivity trend shown in panel (a) of Figure 14-16 on page 480 illustrates the paradox. Manufacturing productivity has advanced at a steady pace. It was service industries, however, which were expected to gain the most from adopting information technologies. For instance, electronic data interchange was supposed to provide sizable productivity enhancements for bankers and other financial-service workers. More broadly, economists had anticipated

continued

FUNDAMENTAL ISSUES ▼

1.

2.

3.

4.

5.

6.

5. How are the equilibrium levels of aggregate output and prices determined, and how does electronic commerce potentially influence equilibrium real output and the price level?

The aggregate demand curve displays total desired spending on real output at each possible price level, and the equilibrium price level is determined where the aggregate demand curve crosses the aggregate supply curve. In the long run, prices of both outputs and inputs change in equal proportions, so the long-run aggregate supply curve is vertical. In the short run, wages and other input prices fail to adjust in equal proportion to a rise in the price level, so the short-run aggregate supply curve is upward sloping. To the extent that the availability of new goods and services in the electronic marketplace encourages consumers to increase their spending at any given price level, the growth of electronic commerce could induce a rise in aggregate demand. At the same time, the application of information technologies is likely to increase business productivity, thereby resulting in increased aggregate supply. Thus, the development of the electronic marketplace tends to push up equilibrium real output but has less certain effects on the equilibrium price level.

continued from page 479
Figure 14-16:
Productivity Growth and Service-Industry Employment.

Panel (a) shows that nonfarm productivity growth in service industries has been outpaced by growth of manufacturing productivity, even though service industries are heavy users of information technologies. As shown in panel (b), employment in service industries as a share of total employment has grown considerably, indicative of the sizable relative growth of these industries within the U.S. economy. Thus, as shown in panel (a), the slow growth of service-industry productivity has tended to drag down overall productivity.

Sources: U.S. Department of Commerce, U.S Department of Labor, Bureau of Labor Statistics.

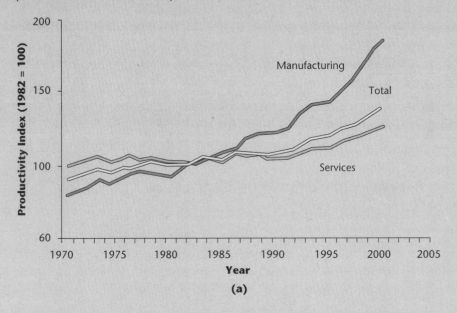

(a)

that e-business and e-commerce applications, such as Internet software downloads and Web-based customer-service interfaces, would greatly increase the efficiency of providing services.

Resolving the Paradox
What happened to the big productivity enhancements the information-technology revolution was supposed to engender?

One possibility is that they have been slow to materialize because the use of computers has failed to provide the benefits that nearly everyone had expected. Some economists contend that despite the considerable investment in computers, these devices make up such a small fraction of the total capital stock

continued

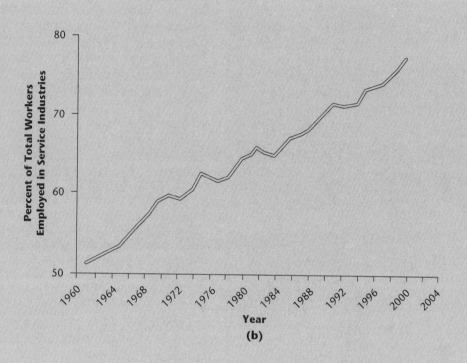

Year

(b)

that they are unlikely ever to be an important source of economic growth.

Another possibility is that other factors, such as a diminished worker education and training, reduced productivity even as computers have added to it. As a result, net productivity grew more slowly.

A third possibility is that measures of overall productivity are outdated. Many economists have argued that current measures of the output of service industries understate the actual output rates of these industries, which include banks, insurance companies, brokerage firms, and other heavy users of new computer technologies. In spite of efforts to better measure productivity that the government implemented in 1999, economists find that the U.S. banking industry is roughly half as productive as it was in the 1970s. No economist, however, believes this is really so. As you can see in panel *(b)* of Figure 14-16, the

relative importance of service industries as employers has increased steadily since the 1960s. This means that difficulties in measuring productivity in service industries are increasingly affecting aggregate productivity statistics.

There is a fourth possibility. Overall productivity in the U.S. economy remained relatively flat for some time after telephones, typewriters, electric lights, and automobiles came into use. The economy may have experienced a similar lag in the response of productivity to the inventions and innovations we are experiencing today. If so, then an upsurge in U.S. productivity growth that took place in the late 1990s and early 2000s may re-emerge and continue for a number of years into the future.

For Critical Analysis:

What might account for a lagged response of productivity growth to information-technology innovations?

Can Electronic Commerce Help Restrain Inflation?

Five decades ago, A. W. Phillips found strong evidence for an inverse relationship between nominal wages and unemployment rates in the United Kingdom. It appeared that nominal wages typically moved the same direction as the inflation rate. This led to the idea of plotting the inflation rate and the unemployment rate on the same diagram. The result was the **Phillips curve,** which was a plot of a hypothesized short-run inverse relationship between unemployment and inflation rates for a given period.

Phillips Curve

A plot of inflation rates and corresponding rates of unemployment, which the basic aggregate demand–aggregate supply framework indicates should slope downward in the short run but should be vertical at the natural unemployment rate in the long run.

THE PHILLIPS CURVE

To understand why there might be a short-run inverse relationship between the inflation rate and the unemployment rate, take a look back at the short-run aggregate supply curve shown in Figure 14-13 on page 473. Note that because the *SRAS* curve is convex, at relatively low output levels where the unemployment rate would be relatively high, increases in output lead to relatively small proportionate increases in the price level, or relatively low inflation. By way of contrast, at relatively high output levels where the unemployment rate would correspondingly be relatively low, increases in output lead to relatively large proportionate increases in the price level as the economy approaches a full-capacity production level. Hence, there would be relatively high inflation.

Panel *(a)* of Figure 14-17 shows there was indeed a downward-sloping Phillips curve during the 1960s. As economists quickly recognized in the 1970s, the Phillips curve is a short-run relationship that changes whenever there is an altered shape or position of the economy's *SRAS* curve. Variations in the position of the *SRAS* curve during the 1970s and 1980s caused by factors such as fluctuating energy prices caused the Phillips curve relationship to break down, as depicted in panel *(b)* of the figure.

Most economists interpret the scattershot pattern of inflation–unemployment combinations in panel *(b)* as consistent with short-term variations of the unemployment rate around a **natural rate of unemployment.** This is an unemployment rate consistent with production of a level of real output along the nation's long-run aggregate supply curve in Figure 14-13. In the long run, many economists conclude that the Phillips curve should be vertical at the natural unemployment rate. Along a *long-run Phillips curve,* the unemployment rate does not vary with the inflation rate.

Natural Rate of Unemployment

The unemployment rate that arises when firms produce levels of real output consistent with the position of the long-run aggregate supply curve.

Since the early 1990s, however, another unusual pattern of inflation–unemployment combinations has emerged, as panel *(c)* shows. If anything, there appears to have been a *direct relationship* between inflation and unemployment in the United States. As the inflation rate has fallen, so has the rate of unemployment. One factor that may have helped contribute to this pattern is development of the electronic marketplace.

Figure 14-17:
Inflation and Unemployment in the United States.

▼

Panel (a) shows that there was an apparent inverse relationship between the inflation rate and unemployment rate during the 1960s, as predicted by the shape of the short-run aggregate supply curve. During the 1970s and 1980s, however, the position of the short-run aggregate supply curve varied because of energy price fluctuations and variations in inflation expectations. This helps explain the breakdown in the Phillips curve during these two decades. As panel (c) indicates, since the early 1990s there has been an apparent upward-sloping relationship between the inflation rate and the unemployment rate.

Sources: Economic Report of the President, 2001, *Economic Indicators* (various issues), and author's estimates.

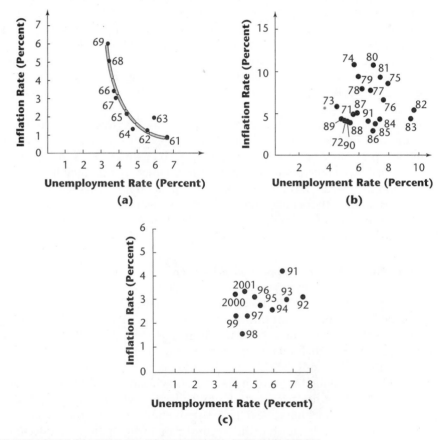

ELECTRONIC COMMERCE, COMPETITION, AND INFLATION

A number of factors should have contributed to a significant increase in the over-all extent of competition in U.S. industries. Beginning in the late 1970s, the U.S. government launched a major effort to deregulate many major industries that previously had been subject to a number of restrictions on the entry and exit of firms and regulation of prices or quantities. As deregulation continued into the

1980s and 1990s, many barriers to international trade also fell by the wayside. As the scope of the electronic marketplace began to broaden during the 1990s, the range of products available to consumers increased considerably. This increased range of substitute products has tended to reduce inflation in the United States even as e-business and e-commerce applications of information technologies have stimulated greater output growth and lower unemployment.

Increased Competition and the Phillips Curve

Some economists argue that the inflation–unemployment trade-off is affected by overall competition in markets for goods and services. The basis of this argument hinges on the effects of an increased range of substitute goods on the price elasticity of demand. Because there are more product choices available in many industries, firms in these industries have found demand for their products to be more price-elastic than it had been previously. This has left less range for price changes, which automatically tended to restrain price increases in the face of rising demand.

At any given unemployment rate, therefore, increased competition across the economy tends to restrain inflation even as the unemployment rate falls. Thus, greater economywide competition probably has made the short-run Phillips curve *more shallow.*

In addition, intensified competition for goods and services theoretically can reduce the natural rate of unemployment. To the extent any markets for goods and services previously have been less than fully competitive, firms in such markets have used monopoly power to restrain their output. Hence, they hired fewer workers than they would have otherwise. As competition has increased, basic economic theory implies that employment should have tended to rise. Consequently, the natural unemployment rate likely has declined as overall competition has increased in the U.S. economy.

Gauging the Effects of Greater Competition on Inflation

Panel *(a)* of Figure 14-18 displays estimates of an index measure of the overall degree of competition in the United States. These estimates indicate that there has been a period of steady increases in competition in U.S. product markets, arising both from greater competition among U.S. firms and from increased competition from foreign sources. Panels *(b)* and *(c)* show estimated Phillips-curve relationships for the late 1970s and early 2000s that take into account the changing degree of economywide competition. As you can see, there is evidence that rising competition since the late 1970s has had two effects: It has tended to make the short-run Phillips curve more shallow, and it has shifted the long-run Phillips curve to the left.

These estimates indicate that the natural rate of unemployment declined from about 6.5 percent in 1979 to about 5.5 percent in 2001. The study from which these estimates are taken, by John Duca of the Federal Reserve Bank of Dallas and this author, indicates that more than a third of the estimated drop in the natural unemployment rate has resulted from greater competition in U.S. markets for goods and services. In this sense, part of the drop in unemployment that took place during the 1990s may have resulted from heightened competition in a truly "new economy" that now includes an electronic marketplace.

Figure 14-18:
Increased U.S. Product-Market Competition and Implications for Short- and Long-Run Phillips Curves.

Panel (a) shows that an index of aggregate competition in U.S. markets for goods and services has increased since the early 1970s. Panels (b) and (c) provide estimates of the position of the short- and long-run Phillips curves indicate that between 1979 and 2001. They indicate that the short-run Phillips curve became more shallow and the long-run Phillips curve shifted leftward. One possible factor accounting for these changes was greater competition in U.S. markets for goods and services.

Source: John Duca and David VanHoose, "Has Greater Competition Restrained U.S. Inflation?" *Southern Economic Journal* 67 (2000) and author's estimates.

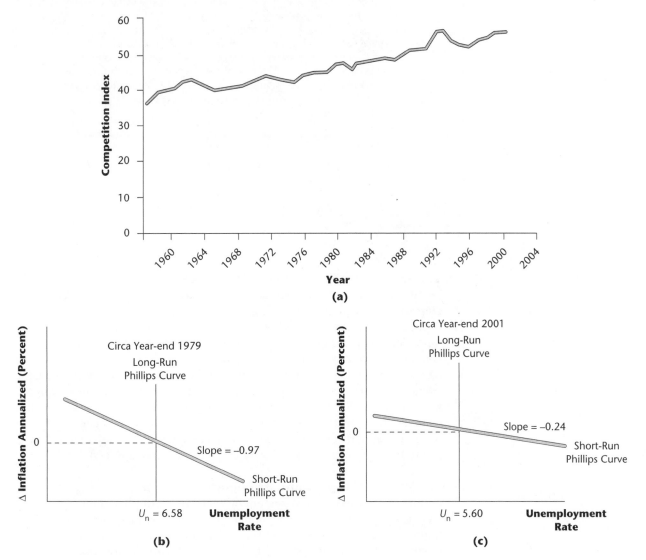

FUNDAMENTAL ISSUES ▼

1.

2.

3.

4.

5.

6.

6. **What are the likely effects of electronic commerce on the U.S. inflation rate?**

The basic aggregate demand–aggregate supply framework implies an inverse, short-run Phillips curve relationship between the inflation rate and the unemployment rate. Another implication, however, is that the long-run Phillips curve should be vertical at a natural rate of unemployment consistent with the position of the economy's long-run aggregate supply curve. Nevertheless, since the early 1990s there has been an apparently *direct* relationship between U.S. inflation and unemployment. One factor that helps explain this observation is greater overall competition in the United States. To the extent that the development of the electronic marketplace has contributed to this rise in U.S. competition, it has helped to reduce the natural unemployment rate and to restrain the inflation rate.

Chapter Summary

1) **The Traditional Explanation of How a Change in Total Depository Institution Reserves Causes a Multiple-Expansion Effect on Their Deposits:** An increase in total reserves at one depository institution induces it to expand its lending and its holdings of securities. The recipients of these funds deposit some or all of the funds in their transactions accounts at other depository institutions, which enables those institutions to increase their loans and security holdings. Hence, the initial increase in reserves causes a multiple expansion of transactions deposits throughout the banking system. The main way the Federal Reserve alters reserves in the banking system is by conducting open-market operations, which are Fed purchases or sales of securities. An open-market purchase by the Fed increases total reserves of depository institutions. An open-market sale by the Fed reduces total reserves of these institutions.

2) **The Money Multiplier and Its Importance:** The money multiplier is a number that sums the total amount by which the quantity of money will change in response to a change in the monetary base. This number is important because Federal Reserve policies that alter the amount of total reserves in the banking system affect the size of the monetary base. Consequently, to know how much it should change total reserves to induce a

given change in the quantity of money, the Federal Reserve needs to know the size of the money multiplier. Any factor that affects the extent of the deposit expansion process influences the size of the money multiplier. One important factor is the amount of currency consumers and businesses wish to hold in relation to their holdings of transactions deposits. Another is depository institutions' desired holdings of currency relative to transactions deposits. A third key factor is the required reserve ratio for transactions deposits that the Federal Reserve establishes. Finally, changes in banks' desired holdings of excess reserves influence the portion of new reserves banks that lend, thereby affecting the money multiplier.

3) **Electronic Money and the Money Supply Process:** Including privately supplied digital cash as a component of monetary aggregates will have the direct effect of increasing the money multiplier relating the government-issued monetary base to the quantity of money in circulation. If people substitute digital cash for government-issued currency, then this effect will tend to dissipate over time. The money multiplier will rise considerably if nondepository institutions circumvent current legal restrictions on their ability to issue transactions deposits using online-banking mechanisms.

4) **How Economists Measure a Nation's Aggregate Output and Price Level, and How Electronic Commerce Factors into Their Output Measurements:** Gross domestic product (GDP), which is the market value of all final goods and services produced during a given period, is the primary measure of a nation's total output. Nominal GDP is the total value of newly produced goods and services computed using the prices at which they sold during the year they were produced, while real GDP is the value of final goods and services after adjusting for the effects of year-to-year price changes. Real GDP equals nominal GDP divided by the GDP deflator, which is a fundamental measure of the current price level relative to the price level in a base year. A large number of e-commerce transactions, such as a fraction of B2B exchanges, the bulk of B2C commerce, are included in GDP. So are fees that e-commerce firms and Web-based financial institutions earn from providing Internet services. All Web exchanges of intermediate inputs, such as many B2B transactions, and trades of second-hand goods, such as auctions of goods on C2C sites, do not entail sale of final goods or services. These transactions are excluded from GDP.

5) **How the Equilibrium Levels of Aggregate Output and Prices Are Determined, and How Electronic Commerce Potentially Influences Equilibrium Real Output and the Price Level:** The equilibrium price level is determined by the point where the aggregate demand curve, which shows total desired spending on real output at each possible price level, crosses the aggregate supply curve. In the long run, prices of both outputs and inputs adjust equiproportionately, which yields a vertical long-run aggregate supply curve. Wages and other input prices typically do not adjust immediately following a rise in the price level. Thus, the short-run aggregate supply curve slopes upward. If consumers respond to the growth of the

electronic marketplace by raising their spending at any given price level, the result would be an increase in aggregate demand. Nevertheless, applying e-business and e-commerce techniques is likely to increase business productivity, causing an increase in aggregate supply. On net, therefore, growth of the electronic marketplace tends to push up equilibrium real output. Its effects on the price level are less clear-cut.

6) **The Likely Effects of Electronic Commerce on the U.S. Inflation Rate:** An inverse, short-run relationship between the inflation rate and the unemployment rate called the Phillips curve is an implication of the basic aggregate demand–aggregate supply framework. In addition, there should be a vertical long-run Phillips curve at a natural unemployment rate consistent with the position of the economy's long-run aggregate supply curve. Since the early 1990s, however, there has been an apparently *direct* relationship between the inflation rate and the unemployment rate. Increased overall competition in U.S. markets for goods and services is one factor that helps to explain this observation. To the extent that the development of the electronic marketplace has contributed to this rise in U.S. competition, the advent of electronic commerce has pushed down the natural unemployment rate and helped to restrain inflation.

Questions and Problems

1) Briefly review the ways in which increased use of smart cards and online accounts at financial institutions may affect the money supply process. Economists continue to evaluate whether digital cash is more likely to displace government-issued currency or bank-issued checking accounts. From the standpoint of controlling the total quantity of money in circulation, does it matter? Explain your reasoning.

2) Suppose that the required reserve ratio for transactions deposits is equal to 0.05. The public's desired ratio of government-issued currency to transactions deposits is equal to 0.4, and the public's desired ratio of digital cash to transactions deposits is equal to 0.1. The *M1* definition of money includes digital cash. Depository institutions desire to hold no excess reserves. The Federal Reserve engages in a $2 million open-market purchase of government securities from a dealer who has an account with a New York bank. Trace through the first three steps of the deposit expansion process that results, showing what happens to depository institution holdings of reserves and to the public's holdings of transactions deposits, government currency, and digital cash at each step. Based on your work, why does it make sense that the inclusion of digital cash increases the *M1* money multiplier on net, even though at each stage of the deposit-expansion process the public converts a

portion of transactions deposits to digital cash outside the banking system? Explain your reasoning.

3) Suppose that at some future time, nondepository institutions that do not hold reserves with Federal Reserve banks begin issuing digital cash that people can use to purchase goods and services at nearly any Web-based retailer. In your view (which you should support with one or two sentences of explanation), should the total amount of digital cash that they issue be included in
   (a) the monetary base?
   (b) *M1?*
   (c) *M2?*

4) In the situation described in question 3, would digital cash issued outside the traditional banking system affect the money multiplier? Explain.

5) Would it really make a difference for the Federal Reserve's ability to conduct monetary policy if nondepository institutions and commercial firms began issuing digital cash? Would it matter depending on whether the Fed attempted to target monetary aggregates or interest rates? Take a stand, and support your answer.

6) In what circumstances would transactions via B2B exchanges be recorded in GDP? When would such transactions not be tabulated as part of GDP? Try to provide concrete examples to help illustrate your answers to both questions.

7) Why are nearly all transactions conducted through C2C auction sites unlikely to be eligible for inclusion in GDP?

8) If the future adoption of additional e-business and e-commerce technologies failed to have any effects on business productivity but induced an increase in aggregate demand, what would happen to equilibrium real output and the price level in the short run? In the long run? Use appropriate diagrams to assist in explaining your answers.

9) Many economists believe that the effects of electronic commerce on aggregate demand in the U.S. economy are likely to be relatively small. Propose at least one reason why they might reach this conclusion.

10) Suppose that the government adopts new regulations that hinder online and offline competition. How might this affect the unemployment and inflation rates? Use an appropriate diagram (or diagrams) to assist in explaining your answer.

Online Application

Internet URL: http://www.census.gov/econ/www/ebusiness614.htm

Title: **Measuring the Electronic Economy**

Navigation: Go directly to the above URL; or start at (http://www.census.gov), and then click on "More," under the "Business" heading. Then click on "E-Statistics" followed by the "Measuring Electronic Economy: Definitions, Underlying Concepts, and Measurement Plans."

Application: Read the article, and then answer the following questions.

1) Based on this article, how frequently will the Bureau of the Census be able to estimate the total value of goods and services traded on the Internet?

2) What types of activities in the electronic marketplace will be included in gross domestic product? What types of activities will be excluded?

For Group Study and Analysis: Divide the class into groups, and have each group develop a list of ways in which electronic commerce complicates the task of measuring GDP in the United States. Put the groups back together, and combine the lists. Then determine which single complication is most likely to pose the greatest problem for compiling GDP.

Selected References and Further Readings

Berentsen, Aleksander. "Monetary Policy Implications of Digital Money," *Kyklos* 51 (1, 1998), pp. 89–117.

Bernkopf, Mark. "Electronic Cash and Monetary Policy," *FirstMonday* (Internet Journal at http://www.firstmonday.dk), 1996.

Cornwell, Casey, and Bharat Trehan. "Information Technology and Productivity," *FRSB Economic Letter,* Federal Reserve Bank of San Francisco, No. 2000–34, November 10, 2000.

Duca, John, and David VanHoose. "Has Greater Competition Restrained Inflation?" *Southern Economic Journal* 66 (January 2000), pp. 479–491.

European Central Bank. *Report on Electronic Money.* Frankfurt, Germany, August 1998.

Freedman, Charles. "Monetary Policy Implementation: Past, Present, and Future—Will the Advent of Electronic Money Lead to the Demise of Central Banking?" *International Finance* (Forthcoming 2001).

Friedman, Benjamin. "The Future of Monetary Policy: The Central Bank as an Army with Only a Signal Corps," *International Finance* 2 (November 1999), pp. 321–338.

Goodhart, Charles. "Can Central Banking Survive the IT Revolution?" *International Finance* (Forthcoming 2001).

Tanaka, Tatsuo. "Possible Economic Consequences of Digital Cash," *FirstMonday* (Internet Journal at http://www.firstmonday.dk), 1996.

Glossary

ab red with other nations.

absolute advantage the ability of a nation's residents to produce a good or service at lower cost, measured in resources required to produce the good or service, or, alternatively, the ability to produce more output from given inputs of resources, as compared with other nations.

adverse selection a situation in which a number of the products offered for sale in a market are those with the worst quality or in which many of those who offer to purchase a product have bad characteristics.

advertising the act of distributing information intended to promote a consumer's purchase of a product.

aggregate demand curve total levels of desired spending on real output at all possible price levels for the economy.

aggregate supply curve total real output of goods and services produced by all firms in the economy at all possible levels of prices.

aggregators also known as "screen scrapers," these companies give their customers the capability to download all online financial information from Web sites operated by institutions such as banks, insurance companies, and stockbrokers for access at a single Web site.

allocative efficiency charging a price equal to the cost of producing the last unit of output sold; marginal cost pricing.

antitrust laws statutes designed to achieve benefits of competition for consumers and producers.

asymmetric information information possessed by one party in a transaction but unavailable to another party.

automated clearing house (ACH) a computer-based facility for clearing and settlement facility that replaces check transactions by interchanging credits and debits electronically.

average cost pricing setting the price of an item equal to the average total cost of producing and selling the item.

average fixed cost (AFC) a firm's fixed costs divided by its output.

average total cost (ATC) a firm's total costs divided by its output; the sum of the firm's average variable cost and its average fixed cost at that rate of output.

average variable cost (AVC) a firm's variable costs divided by its output.

banknotes privately issued paper currency.

banner ad an Internet advertisement that appears as a graphic display on a Web page and that is linked to the advertiser's home page.

barriers to entry factors hindering entrepreneurs from opening a new firm within an industry.

base year a reference year for price-level comparisons, which is a year in which nominal GDP is equal to real GDP, so that the GDP deflator's value is equal to one.

best price the lowest price available for a good or service that is consistent with a consumer's preferences regarding product quality.

broker a financial institution that specializes in matching buyers and sellers of securities in secondary markets.

bundling offering two or more products for sale as a set.

business method patents patents for process innovations that involve the use of computer software and methods of organizing business operations.

business-to-business (B2B) e-commerce online purchases and sales that involve business firms on both sides of the transactions.

business-to-consumer (B2C) e-commerce exchanges of goods and services that are transacted via computer networks and involve sales by businesses to individual consumers.

capital controls legal restrictions on the ability of a nation's residents to hold and exchange assets denominated in foreign currencies.

capital market market for a security with a maturity of one year or more.

certificate authority a group charged with supervising the terms governing how buyers and sellers can legitimately make digital-cash transfers.

certification a verification process for determining if a product's quality meets industry standards.

charter a license to operate a depository financial institution such as a commercial bank.

clearing house interbank payment system (CHIPS) a large-value wire transfer system linking about 90 depository institutions and permitting them to exchange large dollar sums electronically.

closed stored-value system an e-money system in which consumers use cards containing pre-stored funds to buy specific goods and services offered by a single issuer of the cards.

commercial paper a short-term debt security issued by businesses in lieu of borrowing from banks.

comparative advantage the ability of a nation's residents to produce an additional unit of a good or service at a lower opportunity cost relative to other nations.

compatibility the ability to use one product in combination with another.

complements items that are commonly consumed simultaneously.

concentration ratio the share of total industry sales by the top few firms.

constant-cost industry an industry in which a long-run expansion of industry output caused by entry of new firms leaves the market price unchanged.

consumer lock-in a situation in which switching costs are always higher than the perceived benefit from using an alternate product.

consumer surplus the amount consumers would have been willing to pay for a good or service over and above the price they actually pay in the marketplace.

consumer-to-consumer (C2C) e-commerce the sale of an item by one individual to another individual, sometimes with the assistance of an e-commerce intermediary.

consumption possibilities all possible combinations of goods and services that a nation's residents can consume.

cookie a small text file that an Internet seller's Web server may download onto the hard drive of the computer of the visitor to the seller's site; this text file can store information about Web transactions by the visitor that the Web server can use to recognize the visitor as the visitor navigates the seller's Web pages or when the visitor reestablishes connection with the site at a later date.

copyright an author's legal title to the sole right to reproduce, distribute, perform, or display creative works, including articles, books, software, and audio and video recordings.

corporate bonds long-term debt securities of corporations.

cross-certification a process by which digital-cash algorithms used on one e-money system may be recognized and verified as authentic digital cash by another e-money system.

cross price elasticity of demand the percentage change in the quantity of an item demanded resulting from the percentage change in the price of a related item.

cross selling marketing financial products in bundles, thereby engaging in price discrimination in an effort to enhance an institution's revenues and profits.

cultural affinity hypothesis a theory that sellers experience lower costs in interacting with buyers who share their characteristics.

currency coins and paper money.

data mining the process of searching for patterns in large masses of information.

day trader a person who conducts many securities transactions each day, with the goal of earning a living from trading profits.

dealer a financial institution that specializes in selling securities from its own portfolio and earning profits from this activity.

debit card a plastic card that allows the bearer to transfer funds to a merchant's account if the bearer authorizes the transfer by providing personal identification.

decreasing-cost industry an industry in which a long-run expansion of industry output caused by entry of new firms causes a fall in the market price.

demand-pull hypothesis a theory of innovation in which managers and employees initiate process and product innovations based on observations of factors influencing customer demand in the marketplace.

deposit expansion multiplier a number that tells how much aggregate transactions deposits at all depository institutions will change in response to a change in total reserves of these institutions.

derivative security a security with a return that depends on the return of another security.

digital cash funds contained on computer software, in the form of secure algorithms, which is stored on microchips and other computer devices.

digital divide the observed propensity for some groups of people to have greater Internet access than others; the most important source of digital divides is income differences across groups.

digital signature software algorithms that guarantee the authenticity of the digital cash held on a smart card or other digital-cash storage and communications device.

direct marketing advertising targeted at specific consumers, typically in the form of postal mailings, telephone calls, or e-mail messages.

diseconomies of scale an increase in long-run average cost that accompanies an increase in output.

distributed denial-of-service attacks efforts by individuals or groups attempt to overload companies' servers and shut down access to their Web sites.

domain name an electronic network address recognizable by browser programs, which includes a top-level domain such as "com" and a subdomain indicating the specific location of the host, such as "Lands' End."

dominant firm a firm that sells the bulk of industry output and has the ability to set the market price in the face of entry by other price-taking firms.

dumping sale of goods or services in another country at a lower price than the domestic price, or at a price less than average total cost.

economic incidence the determination of the relative burden of a tax that is borne by parties to market transactions.

economic profit total revenue minus total expenses, including the opportunity cost of being in the current industry instead of an alternative industry.

economies of scale a reduction in long-run average cost that accompanies an increase in output.

economies of scope the cost of producing two or more goods or services within one firm is lower than the combined costs at separate firms if they were to individually produce each good or service.

efficient market a market in which consumers are very sensitive to price changes, firms' prices respond quickly to changes in consumer demand and firm operating costs, and prices equal both marginal production costs and average production costs.

electronic business (e-business) any internal decision-making or implementation processes that organizations such as commercial firms, nonprofit organizations, or government agencies conduct using computer-mediated electronic networks.

electronic commerce (e-commerce) using a computer-mediated electronic network such as the Internet as a mechanism for transferring ownership of or rights to use goods and services.

electronic communications networks (ECNs) internet-based networks that use computer software to match buyers and sellers of shares of stock.

electronic marketplace a virtual location for prospective sellers and buyers to electronically meet through network-communications links.

excess reserves depository institution cash balances at Federal Reserve banks or in their vaults that ex-

ceed the amount that they must hold to meet legal requirements.

exclusion principle the principle that no one, including someone who has failed to pay for an item's provision, can be excluded from the benefits of the item if that item is a public good.

experience good a product that an individual must consume before the product's quality can be established.

Fedwire a large-value wire transfer system operated by the Federal Reserve that is open to all depository institutions that legally must hold reserves with the Federal Reserve.

financial intermediary an institution that serves as the "middleman" in channeling funds from savers to borrowers.

first-best optimum a market outcome in which the price of a good or service equals its marginal production cost, so that allocative efficiency is achieved by society as a whole.

first-mover advantage a competitive advantage that the first firm in an industry obtains because it initially faces no rivals and that it may be able to maintain if it can operate at a lower cost than potential rivals or develop good will with customers that rivals cannot readily duplicate.

foreign exchange market a system of private banks, foreign exchange brokers and dealers, and central banks through which households, businesses, and governments purchase and sell currencies of various nations.

forward market a market for the exchange of a financial asset at a future date.

framing including a company's Web site within a Web site operated by another individual or company.

free banking laws state laws in force in many U.S. states between 1837 and 1861 that allowed anyone to obtain a charter authorizing banking operations.

free-rider problem failure of an agent that benefits from the provision of a product to contribute to the provision of the product.

gains from trade additional goods and services that a nation's residents can consume, over and above the amounts that they could have produced within their own borders, as a consequence of trade with residents of other nations.

GDP price deflator a measure of the overall price level; equal to nominal GDP divided by real GDP.

global public good a good or service that yields benefits to the world's people simultaneously, cannot provide benefits to one person without others around the world deriving benefits at no additional cost, and cannot be withheld from a person who has failed to contribute to its provision.

gross domestic product (GDP) the value, tabulated using market prices, of all final goods and services produced during a given period.

Herfindahl–Hirschman Index the sum of the squares of the market shares of each firm in an industry.

hypertext transfer protocol (HTTP) a stateless communications procedure by which individual computers communicate with server devices operated by Internet service providers.

illiquidity a situation in which a banking institution lacks the cash assets required to meet requests for depositor withdrawals.

imperfect price discrimination charging different prices to distinct groups of consumers or charging a different price to a consumer depending on whether the consumer is classified within a group that buys relatively small or large quantities.

increasing-cost industry an industry in which a long-run expansion of industry output caused by entry of new firms results in an increase in the market price.

indifference curve a curve displaying combinations of choices among which a consumer is indifferent, because each choice yields the same satisfaction.

industrial policy a government policy designed to assist the development of specific national industries.

industry standards measurable or identifiable criteria that a group of firms in an industry indicate their products should satisfy to merit purchase.

industry structure the number of and size distribution of firms within an industry.

infant industry argument the contention that an industry in its earliest stages of development should be exempted from taxation.

information intermediaries companies or organizations that specialize in evaluating the quality of goods and services produced by firms in various industries.

informational advertising advertising that emphasizes the transmission of knowledge about the features of a product.

information-intensive product a good or service for which a fundamental productive input is a swiftly developing foundation of knowledge.

innovation transforming an invention into something that lowers costs of production, reduces the costs of operating a business, or provides concrete benefits inducing consumers to buy a product.

insolvency a situation in which the value of a bank's assets falls below the value of its liabilities.

intellectual property rights laws regulating ownership of creative ideas that is typically granted in the form of a copyright, trademark, or patent.

interactive marketing advertising that permits a consumer to follow up directly by searching for more information and placing direct product orders.

Internet bank a bank that operates exclusively on the Internet, without physical branch offices.

Internet service providers (ISPs) companies that provide individuals and businesses with access to the Internet via server devices linked to network services providers.

intra-industry trade international trade of goods or services that are close substitutes.

invention creation of a new process for producing a good or service, a novel business organization method, or a unique product.

investment spending expenditures by businesses on capital goods that they use to produce more goods and services.

large-value wire transfer systems payment systems such as Fedwire and CHIPS that permit the electronic transmission of large dollar sums.

law of diminishing returns an economic law that states that at some point the continued use of additional amounts of a variable factor together with fixed factors eventually results in progressively smaller increases in output.

law of one price an economic law that in a perfectly competitive market, all firms should sell their products at the same price.

lemons problem the possibility that adverse selection leads to a general reduction in product quality in a marketplace.

limit pricing discouraging entry of potential rivals by setting a price below their average production cost.

liquidity the ease with which a person can sell or redeem an asset for a known amount of cash at short notice and at low risk of loss of nominal value.

long-run average cost a firm's total cost divided by its output when the firm has sufficient time to alter its utilization of all factors of production.

long-run industry supply the relationship between market prices and quantities in a perfectly competitive industry after firms have had time to enter or exit the industry.

M1 currency and travelers' checks plus transactions deposits.

M2 M1 plus savings and small time deposits, overnight Euro dollars and repurchase agreements, and balances of individual and broker-dealer-money market mutual funds.

macroeconomics the study of a country's aggregate economic activity.

major innovation a process or product innovation that brings about a significant change in an existing market or the creation of a new market.

marginal benefit an additional benefit, perhaps in the form of higher firm profitability or increased consumer satisfaction, from an activity such as distributing product information or searching for product price and quality information.

marginal cost (MC) the additional cost that a firm incurs by producing one more unit of output; the slope of the firm's total cost curve.

marginal factor cost the additional cost that a firm incurs from employing an additional unit of a factor of production.

marginal product an addition to a firm's output stemming from using an additional unit of an input; the slope of the firm's production function.

marginal revenue the additional revenue that a firm receives from selling one more unit of its product.

marginal revenue product marginal revenue times marginal product of a factor of production, which is the contribution to a firm's total revenue of an additional unit of that input.

marginal-willingness-to-pay condition a condition that some economists promote as a criterion for evaluating allocative efficiency in an industry with relatively high entry barriers such as large fixed costs or significant economies of scale.

market an arrangement that people have for trading goods and services.

market externality a spillover effect influencing the welfare of third parties not involved in transactions within a marketplace.

market failure inability of unhindered private market processes to produce outcomes that are consistent with economic efficiency, individual freedom, of other broader social goals.

market feedback a tendency for a good or service to fall in or out of favor as a result of network externalities.

market transparency the availability of detailed information about the various risk characteristics of securities.

mass marketing advertising intended to reach as many consumers as possible, typically through television, newspaper, radio, or magazine ads.

menu costs fixed costs of adjusting prices.

merit good a good or service that residents of a nation determine, typically through a political process, to be socially desirable.

meta tag an HTML software code that provides an Internet search engine with information that will link a Web site to a Web search request.

minimum efficient scale the output rate at which a firm minimizes its long-run average cost.

minor innovation a process or process innovation that results in relatively small cost reductions or revenue enhancements or that primarily allow firms to differentiate their products.

monetary aggregates sums of various groupings of financial assets reported by the Fed.

monetary base government-supplied currency and reserves that serve as a foundation for a nation's monetary system.

money market market for a security with a maturity of less than one year.

money multiplier a number that tells how much the quantity of money responds to a change in the monetary base.

monopolistic competition an industry structure in which there are many consumers and many firms, each of which sells a miniscule fraction of total industry output and can easily enter or leave the industry, but which produces a good or service that consumers can readily distinguish.

monopoly a single producer in a marketplace.

monopsony a single buyer in a market.

moral hazard the potential for either the buyer or seller of a product to exhibit undesirable behavior after arranging or completing an exchange.

natural rate of unemployment the unemployment rate that arises when firms produce levels of real output consistent with the position of the long-run aggregate supply curve.

negative market externality a situation in which accounting for all social costs associated with production of a good or provision of a service would reduce the quantity forthcoming in the marketplace.

network externality a situation that arises when the benefit that a consumer perceives to be available from using an item depends on how many others use it.

network industry an industry in which the value that consumers place on the industry's product depends in part on how many other people consume the product.

network service providers companies operating systems that support electronic networks by handling large volumes of data flow at high speeds.

nexus a geographic overlap between a company's physical location and the location of its customers.

nominal gross domestic product (nominal GDP) the value of final production of goods and services calculated in current dollar terms with no adjustment for effects of price changes.

oligopoly an industry structure in which only a few firms are insulated by barriers to entry from any immediate threat of additional competition.

online banking providing financial intermediation services on the Internet.

open-market operations Federal Reserve purchases or sales of securities.

open-market purchase a Federal Reserve purchase of a security, which increases total reserves at depository institutions and raises the size of the monetary base.

open-market sale a Federal Reserve sale of a security, which reduces total reserves of depository institutions and reduces the magnitude of the monetary base.

open smart-card system an electronic system in which consumers use smart cards with embedded microprocessors, which may be issued by a number of institutions, to purchase goods and services offered by multiple retailers.

open stored-value system a system in which consumers buy goods and services using cards containing pre-stored funds offered by multiple card issuers and accepted by multiple retailers.

opportunity cost the value of the next best alternative.

over-the-counter (OTC) stocks equity shares offered by companies that do not meet listing requirements for major stock exchanges but instead are traded in decentralized markets.

patent an inventor's legal title to the sole right to manufacture, utilize, and market an invention for a specific period.

ment intermediary an institution that facili-
s the transfer of funds between buyer and seller during the course of any purchase of goods, services, or financial assets.

payment system a term that broadly refers to the set of mechanisms by which consumers, businesses, governments, and financial institutions exchange payments.

perfect competition an industry structure in which there are many consumers and many firms, each of which produces indistinguishable products, sells a miniscule fraction of total industry output, and can easily enter or leave the industry.

perfect price discrimination charging each consumer the maximum price that the consumer is willing to pay for each unit consumed, thereby capturing the entire amount of consumer surplus; also known as first-degree price discrimination

persuasive advertising advertising that is intended to alter a consumer's tastes and preferences and induce the consumer to purchase a particular product.

Phillips curve a plot of inflation rates and corresponding rates of unemployment, which the basic aggregate demand–aggregate supply framework indicates should slope downward in the short run but should be vertical at the natural unemployment rate in the long run.

point-of-sale (POS) networks systems in which consumer payments for retail purchases occur through direct deductions from their deposit accounts at depository institutions.

positive market externality a situation in which accounting for all social benefits associated with production of a good or provision of a service would increase the quantity forthcoming in the marketplace.

predatory pricing a situation in which a firm sets artificially low prices intended to induce competitors to leave the industry and to dissuade potential rivals from entering the industry.

price discrimination charging different consumers different prices for the same product or charging the same consumer different prices for different quantities of the same product.

price elasticity of demand the absolute value of the percentage change in quantity demanded associated with a given percentage change in the price of a product.

price–quality trade-off implied relationship between price and quality in a monopolistically competitive market.

primary market a market for the exchange of newly issued securities.

principle of rival consumption the principle that individuals are rivals in consuming private goods, because consumption of such items by one person reduces the ability of another person to consume those items.

private good an item that can only be consumed by one person at a time.

process innovation development and market introduction of a new technology for producing existing goods or services or a new method of organizing businesses.

product innovation the creation, production, marketing, and distribution of an entirely new good or service.

production the act of applying a technological process to inputs to manufacture a good or provide a service.

production function the relationship between the maximum output of a firm and the quantity of inputs utilized by the firm.

production possibilities all possible combinations of total output of goods and services that residents of a nation can produce given currently available technology and resources.

production possibilities frontier a diagram showing all feasible combinations of goods and services that may be produced in a nation, given its technology and available resources.

progressive tax a system of taxation in which a higher percentage of income is taxed as income increases.

public good any good or service that can be consumed by many people at the same time, cannot be consumed by one individual without others also consuming it at no extra cost, and cannot be with-held from a person who has not contributed to funding its production.

quota a quantitative limit on imports of goods or services.

real gross domestic product (real GDP) a price-adjusted measure of aggregate output, or nominal GDP divided by the GDP price deflator.

regressive tax a system of taxation in which a lower percentage of income is taxed as income increases.

relevant market the extent of the marketplace containing all available products that directly impinge on the prices charged by individual firms.

required reserve ratios fractions of transactions deposit balances that the Federal Reserve mandates depository institutions to maintain either as deposits with Federal Reserve banks or as vault cash.

required reserves legally mandated reserve holdings at depository institutions, which are proportional to the dollar amounts of transactions accounts.

resale price maintenance setting a minimum price that retailers are permitted to charge for a product.

retail payments transfers of funds amounting to tens of thousands of dollars or less.

sales taxes taxes assessed on the value of purchases of goods and services from firms located within the nexus that applies for sales taxes.

satiation consumption level the maximum feasible quantity of a good or service that consumers desire to purchase at an explicit price of zero.

search engines software programs that Internet users can access via Web sites to search other Web sites for key words, names, or phrases.

search good a product with characteristics that enable an individual to evaluate the product's quality in advance of a purchase.

secondary market a market for the exchange of previously issued securities.

second-best optimum the market outcome in which the price of a good or service equals its average cost of production. Consumers pay the lowest price necessary to induce sellers to provide the item.

security a financial claim requiring a borrower to make future payments to those who have provided funds used by the borrower to finance its activities.

self selection consumers voluntarily sort into identifiable groups by choosing among alternative pricing schemes offered by a firm.

shopbot a software program that searches large volumes of information contained in networks for answers to questions posed by a potential consumer of a product; also known as an intelligent agent.

short run an interval sufficiently brief that a firm cannot change the quantity of at least one of its factors of production.

smart card a card containing a microprocessor that permits storage of funds via security programming, that can communicate with other computers, and that does not require online authorization for funds transfers to occur.

spam mass marketing via unsolicited e-mail messages to numerous recipients.

spot market market for immediate exchange of financial assets.

standard product an item that producers of complementary goods strive to ensure will be compatible with their products.

statutory incidence the determination of the party that is legally responsible for transmitting a tax payment to the government.

statutory penalties pecuniary penalties authorized by laws, which may or may not reflect actual losses caused by intellectual property violations in the marketplace.

stock exchanges organized marketplaces for corporate equities and bonds.

subsidy a negative tax, such as a payment or tax exemption giving domestic firms a greater incentive to export goods and services.

switching cost the combined explicit and implicit opportunity cost of using one product as an alternate to another.

T-account a side-by-side listing of the assets and liabilities of a business such as a depository institution.

tariff tax on imported goods.

tax base the value of goods, services, incomes, or wealth subject to taxation.

tax incidence the effect of a tax on the distribution of income or wealth, or the burden created by a tax.

tax rate the fraction of a tax base an individual or company is legally required to transmit to the government.

technical efficiency production of an output rate at the minimum feasible average total cost.

technology-push hypothesis a theory of innovation that emphasizes the potential role of companies' research staffs in initiating process or product innovations.

tie-in sales purchases of a particular product that are permitted only if a consumer buys another good or service from the same firm.

total reserves the total balances that depository institutions hold on deposit with Federal Reserve banks or as vault cash.

trademark a company's legal title to a word or symbol that identifies its product and distinguishes it from the products of other firms.

transaction costs all the costs associated with economic exchanges, including the costs of acquiring and disseminating information, plus the costs of negotiating and enforcing contracts.

transactions deposits checking deposits at depository institutions.

two-part tariff charging a lump-sum fee to consume a product and a per-unit charge based on the quantity consumed.

universal resource locator (URL) the address scheme that a browser program uses to connect to sites using domain names.

use taxes taxes assessed on the value of purchases of goods and services from firms located outside the nexus that applies for sales taxes.

versioning selling essentially the same product in slightly different forms to different groups of consumers.

vertical integration incorporating two or more successive stages of production and distribution of a product within the same firm.

vertical restraint a legally binding limitation that a nonintegrated firm places on another firm from which it buys or to which it sells.

virtual product a digital product that is typically produced at a relatively high fixed cost but distributed for sale at a relatively low marginal cost.

web server a software program residing on an Internet seller's server that controls access to the seller's Web site, enables the seller to easily update the site as needed, compiles logs of transactions with those who visit the site, and operates external programs that assist the buyer in engaging in transactions with the seller.

wholesale payments transfers of funds amount to hundreds of thousands of dollars or more.

Index